Peter Neville-Hadley

China
the Silk Routes

i

Cadogan Books plc
27–29 Berwick Street, London W1V 3RF, UK
e-mail:guides@cadogan.demon.co.uk

The Globe Pequot Press
6 Business Park Road, PO Box 833, Old Saybrook, Connecticut 06475–0833

Book and cover design by Animage
Maps © Cadogan Guides, drawn by Map Creation Ltd

Cover photographs © Peter Neville-Hadley

Editor: Dominique Shead

DTP: Adrian McLaughlin
Proof-reading: Lorna Horsfield
Indexing: Isobel McLean
Production: Book Production Services

Series Editor: Rachel Fielding

A catalogue record for this book is available from the British Library
ISBN 1-86011-052-5

Printed in Great Britain by Redwood Books Ltd.

Acknowledgements

Thanks in Kazakstan and Kyrgyzstan to many ex-pats for their assistance, advice, hospitality, and last minute rechecking of details, particularly to Tracey Chambers in Almaty and Richard Stoddard in Bishkek. Thanks, too, for help with officialdom and providing in-depth local knowledge to Dauren Valiev of Kan Tengri and to the indefatigable Karlygash Makatova. Thanks to Ted, Beth, and Peter of Dūnhuáng's Manhattan Café for exceptional hospitality and local introductions, and to Kashgar's John Hu for helping with yet another version of the rules on the Torugart Pass. Dr. Suni Boraston, M.D., M.H.Sc., of the Vancouver/Richmond Health Board Travel Clinic kindly gave up time to look over the medical information, and the 'How Chinese Works' and 'Language' sections were checked by Zhào Yù, but any remaining errors are mine not theirs. Thanks to those Mandarin teachers who put up with my inattention for so many years, and especially to Zhāng Hóng, who suffered the longest. For their company and in some cases for test-driving early versions of parts of this text, thanks to Alastair Bishop, Bridget MacDonald, Vincent Dachy, Gerald Fimberger, Maartje Schneemann, Leon Batta, Euan Taylor, Bradley Rowe, Arno Hofste, Thomas Woidemann, Gary Russell, Akamatsu Nobuya, Jennifer Friedenrich, Sasha Atepolikhin, Jos Van Herreweghe, Christel Arts, Gilbert Yahia Bel-Bachir and unknown Dutch friend, Eric Mohl, Karen Catchpole and Iwata Junjiro. Thanks for many kindnesses small and large to innumerable residents of China unlikely ever to see this paragraph, and best not named. Thanks to Horacio Monteverde for overcoming my reluctance even to consider this project, to Jacqueline Lewin for helping to shape its conception, and to editor Dominique Shead for encouragement even as the book swelled to twice its original planned size. Thanks to Diane (Měijuān) for putting up with the long absences, physical and mental, needed to produce it, and without whose support it could never have been completed. It was written, designed, illustrated, and published entirely on Apple Macintosh computers, and the author was fuelled by coffee and scones from Delany's on Denman. For effortless transport between North America, Germany, France, England, and Kazakstan, thanks to KLM, Lufthansa, and Eurostar, and thanks to Steppes East for invaluable advice.

About the Author

Peter Neville-Hadley first visited China in 1986, returning repeatedly to visit new areas while improving his Mandarin. Abandoning a London-based career in theatre marketing, he contributed to the 2nd edition of Cadogan's Central Asia guide, and spent two years travelling and researching this book. He crossed and recrossed China several times, revisiting some cities on as many as four occasions to try and keep the guide as up-to-date as possible. He now lives in Vancouver with Chinese-Canadian Diane (Lín Měijuān).

Please help us to keep this guide up to date

China and the countries of Central Asia are undergoing constant change, altering regulations for travellers, suffering from inflation and fluctuating exchange rates, privatising organisations, arbitrarily revising prices, building new facilities, and altering everything from place names to dialling codes. We've done our best to ensure that information is accurate at the time of going to press, but we would be delighted to hear from travellers about changes or suggested improvements to the guide. All contributors will be acknowledged in the next edition and authors of the best letters will receive a copy of the Cadogan Guide of their choice. Please write to Cadogan Books, 27–29 Berwick Street, London W1V 3RF, England, or e-mail us on guides@cadogan.demon.co.uk.

Contents

The publishers would like to thank the following copyright holders for permission to quote extracts: Jonathan Cape/Random House (UK rights) and Mrs Kate Grimond (US rights) for *News from Tartary* by Peter Fleming; Methuen/Routledge for *Turkistan Tumult* by Aitchen K. Wu; Lady Teichman for *Journey to Turkistan* by Eric Teichman; Dover Publications for *The Travels of Marco Polo* by Marco Polo; Hodder Headline for *The Gobi Desert* by Mildred Cable with Francesca French; HarperCollins/OUP for *Buried Treasures of Chinese Turkestan* by Albert von Le Coq; Little, Brown/Kodansha for *The Desert Road to Turkestan* by Owen Lattimore.

For most of recorded time the Silk Routes of Central Asia and China have been closed to foreigners, unless they arrived with thousands of mounted bowmen and turned the sky dark with clouds of arrows. While until recently modern-day travellers felt that a similar level of force would be useful to get through the barriers of bureaucracy, it is now possible to travel freely through most of the region, and the only bandits left haunting the old trade routes are taxi drivers. Buses ply between oases, and the fall of the Soviet Union has opened routes to Kyrgyzstan and Kazakstan. The completion of the railway connection

Introduction

from China's northwest to Almaty offers a way from Moscow to Běijīng to rival the Trans-Siberian, but with more to see. Once a closed-border cul-de-sac, the region has once again become the meeting point of routes to the Indian sub-continent, the countries of the Commonwealth of Independent States, Tibet, and the heart of China itself.

The journey begins (or ends) at the walled city of Xī'ān, the capital of China when the Silk Routes were at their peak, with its vast army of buried warrior figures, still eerily defending the grave of Qín Shǐ Huángdì, the first unifier of China, 14 centuries after his death. However much you have antici-pated the sight of these ranks of hundreds of individual soldier statues, nothing can prevent the hair from rising on the back of your neck. From Xī'ān the routes swing northwest through Gānsù and Níngxià provinces, where the yellow earth colours the Yellow River, and thou-sands still live in caves.

Travelling between market towns like the merchants of the Silk Routes' heyday, it's easy to spot abandoned fortifications, beacon towers, and the last mud sputterings of a Great Wall that began thousands of miles to the east, on the shores of the Yellow Sea. At the edge of the Taklamakan Desert is the great fort at Jiāyùguān, marking the end of familiar China, and a reminder of both Xī'ān's great fortifications and Běijīng's Forbidden City. For banished Chinese it marked the end of the world, and passing beneath its painted towers they wrote laments on its walls.

Beyond, the roads from China proper to modern-day Pakistan, Kyrgyzstan and Kazakstan cross a region of fearsome beauty. Though surrounded on three sides by some of the world's highest mountains, several over 6000m, it also features immense inland depressions—including the Turpan Basin, a furnace more than 100m below sea level with summer temperatures capable of reaching 48°C. Near its heart is an unlikely splash of brilliant green—the restful oasis town of Turpan. A small miracle, it's irrigated by mountain streams brought through miles of underground channels, and its pavements are shaded by trellised vines of grapes plump enough to grace Renaissance statues.

The region is further from the sea than any place on earth, and boasts one of the planet's more extreme deserts, the infamous Taklamakan, its name in the local Uighur language translating enticingly as, 'If you go in, you won't come out'. Strings of oases lie along its northern and southern edges like beads on a necklace, kept alive by streams and seasonal meltwaters from its mountainous borders. These were the motorway service stations of their day, giving travellers the opportunity to rest and refuel before tackling the next stretch of desert. The routes to Kashgar from the east hop around the desert's rim from oasis to oasis, one town famous for raisins, one for melons, another for jade, and yet another for its hospitable people and their musical traditions, praised by travellers since the 5th century.

The region was once a thriving centre for Buddhism, and if the idea of reincarnation lives on in what is now a Muslim stronghold, it is in the previous incarnations of the oasis towns themselves. Each has its predecessors; abandoned, half buried in sand, ten or a hundred kilometres out of town, their fates sealed by the capricious change of direction of some vital watercourse, or the gradual drying of the whole region. Visitors can explore immense cave-temple complexes in the cliffs formed by long-dried rivers, and wander amongst vast ruins of abandoned metropolises.

Some routes begin at Běijīng, almost continuously the seat of power in China since the 13th century, with its great imperial palaces, tombs and temples, and its shoals of bicycles. Constantly transforming itself, Běijīng offers curly-eaved China as the West wants to find it, alongside ugly utilitarian buildings indistinguishable from anything in Russia or Eastern Europe, and the latest extravagant efforts of fashionable international architects. Routes follow the immense loop of the Yellow River west, or set out across seas of grass in the vast open pasturelands of Inner Mongolia, then seas of sand in the Gobi. Here the mausoleum said to contain the ashes of the master of mounted blitzkrieg, Genghis Khan, who emerged from the grasslands to conquer the cities, stands in the middle of nowhere. After 750 years he's still a hero to Mongolians, and visitors can pay their respects to his memory. Sections of the Great Wall which failed to keep him out of China wind through the region, abandoned and melancholy.

From seething Rawalpindi in Pakistan the recently opened Karakoram Highway crosses immense mountain ranges: a metalled road laid onto a 2000-year-old trade route previously barely fit for horse or human, including an often avalanche-interrupted, 15,000ft pass on the highest paved road in the world. It tumbles down to meet another mountainous route from Kyrgyzstan and the roads from China proper at Kashgar, home to one of the most colourful markets in the whole of Asia. Here crowds of Turki and Indo-European descent bargain with visiting Pakistanis, Russians, Tajiks, Kyrgyz, Kazaks and Uzbeks for ceramics, clothes, door frames, knives, wood, baskets, and anything with four legs from billiard tables to camels. This is the most remote territory under Běijīng's control, and there's scarcely a Chinese in sight.

Central Asia has never been so open, and though there are just the beginnings of organized travel the Silk Routes remain largely undiscovered. In the newly independent CIS countries, the valleys of northeast Pakistan, and the remoter corners of China, travellers are still greeted with a mixture of curiosity and courtesy that puts the big tourist destinations to shame.

Now is the time to go. Rapid change has become the norm in China. Ürümqi already has a Holiday Inn, and it's best to see Turpan before it gets a McDonald's.

Guide to the Guide

All roads lead to the Taklamakan Desert, the most fearsome challenge travellers faced before the arrival of surfaced roads, and still not to be toyed with. It is the heart of China's largest and most remote administrative region, Xīnjiāng.

The book begins with Xī'ān, China's capital at the height of Silk Route trade, and then follows the old cart track, now with modern road and rail lines, west up Gānsù Province through Lánzhōu to Dūnhuáng, where this route anciently split into two around the north and south sides of the Taklamakan Desert. This guide first takes the north side, deviating over the Tiān Shān to cover the regional capital of Ürümqi, then back around the top of the desert to the ancient market town of Kashgar, the last major town before the Pakistani border. It then follows the more difficult southern route back around the desert either to Korla (which completes the desert circuit) or in a near-parallel to the original way, now closed, over a difficult mountain route back to Dūnhuáng.

The remainder of the book deals with routes that feed into this main route and the loop around the Taklamakan Desert. It first deals with Běijīng and follows the old camel trails through Shānxī, Inner Mongolia and Níngxià around the Yellow River to join the main route at Lánzhōu. Not long before Lánzhōu, the slightly more intrepid traveller can turn on to an old back route down Níngxià's spine, becoming from the Chinese point of view an inbound traveller again, crossing a spur of Gānsù and arriving at Xī'ān. These two sections together make a fascinating, if slow alternative to the overnight train from Běijīng to Xī'ān.

The book closes with the routes in from China's western neighbours, first Almaty in Kazakstan and the still little travelled route from there to Ūrūmqi, then Bishkek in Kyrgyzstan and the even less travelled road over the Tiān Shān from there to Kashgar, and finally Islamabad and the spectacular Karakoram Highway from Pakistan.

Itineraries

Depending on your degree of adventurousness and self-reliance, the routes divide into two kinds. The main roads are familiar with foreign travellers, and are those taken by the still relatively few travel companies that venture into the area. These have fairly comfortable if not luxurious hotels, the more famous sights, and a degree of made-for-tourist entertainment for those who want it. The biggest stops on the busiest highway are Xī'ān, Lánzhōu, Jiāyùguān, Dūnhuáng, Turpan, Ürümqi and Kashgar, although of these only Xī'ān is in the top few cities for numbers of foreign visitors. In between these lie smaller backwaters, such as Gāngǔ, with its giant cliff-carved Buddha and ridge-top temples, Lèdū with its secluded Lamaist temple complex, and the village of Mǎtí Sì, with its honeycomb of miniature cave temples. Foreign visitors to these towns are few, accommodation is often rudimentary, and public transport infrequent. Somewhere in between in scale lie sites which, while rarely included on organized tours, still attract large numbers of independent travellers, such as the Labrang Monastery at Xiàhé, which have developed hotels and restaurants to cater for them.

Then there are backroads which are more of a struggle. Beyond Dàtóng the route around the Yellow River sees few visitors, despite passing through two regional capitals full of attractions, with plentiful public transport, and accommodation of all types. Very few indeed are those who take the route through Níngxià between Zhōngwèi and Xī'ān, despite its offering of Muslim, Daoist and Buddhist marvels, and scenery ranging from the semi-desert to the spectacularly lush. Accommodation is simple but cheap, and buses are frequent if not the most modern. The toughest route of all is the Southern Taklamakan, with basic accommodation, unreliable buses often delayed by drifts of sand—especially the connection through Qīnghǎi to Dūnhuáng where some accommodation defies description and transport cannot be guaranteed at all. There's little to see, but bags of 'real life', from towns of mud-walled compounds where the donkey is still the main form of motive power, to the grim apartment blocks of desolate oil and mining towns where the word 'remote' seems too domestic and familiar to apply. The hardened backpacker will breeze through it in the knowledge that he'll have good stories to tell in the cafés of Dūnhuáng to the softies who've arrived by sleeper from Xī'ān. The man who makes the month-long illegal hitchhike from Kashgar to Lhasa (not covered in this book) will snigger at both. Your aim must be to read this book carefully, choose your level of difficulty, and enjoy yourself. No one else's opinion matters.

A Note on Names

Chinese place names are spelt in the PRC official Romanization system called *pīnyīn*. You will not find Peking in this book, but Běijīng. Every Mandarin word is marked with the tones necessary to make your meaning clear, and to help you communicate your needs to ticket sellers and others. An explanation of tones and of how to pronounce the letters and sounds is given in **Language**, p.513. Those doing background reading of histories and memoirs can expect to find a startling range of alternative spellings, and these have been left intact where other authors have been quoted.

Place names in Uighur, Mongol and Tibetan minority areas have been left in the spellings of those names most commonly found in English, and are usually given priority over the Mandarin adaptations. But the Mongol Hohhot, for example, is followed by the Mandarin Hūhéhàotè, and in all cases the Chinese characters are given. If all else fails, point to these.

In Kazakstan and Kyrgyzstan, street names are changing faster than even the residents can keep up, and in the process moving from Russian to the local language, from the Cyrillic to the Latin alphabet, and from one transliteration system to another. You may encounter Kazak as Qazaq, where the principle interests of a writer is Turki rather than Chinese; variant spellings are spreading to the names of Xīnjiāng towns, too. But to begin Kashgar with a 'Q' is to confuse matters unnecessarily (especially since the *pīnyīn* value of 'q' is a hard 'tch'). Kazakstan remains just that, as requested by the Kazak government.

Travel

The trade routes that ended and began in the heart of China had their other ends at the Mediterranean, and in India. The starting points for the routes covered in this book are Běijīng and Xī'ān in China, Bishkek in Kyrgyzstan, Almaty in Kazakstan, and Islamabad in Pakistan.

By Air to Běijīng
from or via Europe

Most major European airlines fly to Běijīng and/or Hong Kong, China's two main gateways.

Air China often has the cheapest direct flights, and flies to Běijīng from Berlin, Copenhagen, Frankfurt, London, Madrid, Moscow, Paris, Rome, Stockholm, Vienna and Zürich. London ✆ (0171) 630 0919, Frankfurt ✆ (069) 233038, Berlin ✆ (030) 242 3460, Paris ✆ (01) 4266 1658, website *http://www.airchina.com/*. **China Eastern Airlines**, a product of the creation of separate airlines from the original CAAC, flies to Brussels, Milan and Munich. Similarly, **China Southern Airlines** flies from Amsterdam.

British Airways has direct flights from London. UK ✆ (0345) 222111, US and Canada ✆ toll-free 1-800 247 9297, website *http://www.british-airways.com/*.

Cathay Pacific flies to Hong Kong from London, Glasgow, Manchester, Paris, Amsterdam, Frankfurt, Zürich and Rome, with connections to Běijīng on Dragonair. London ✆ (0171) 747 8888, website *http://www.cathaypacific-air.com/*.

KLM flies twice weekly from Amsterdam and **Lufthansa** from Frankfurt daily. For both *see* 'By Air to Bishkek and Almaty', below.

Air France flies from Paris. London ✆ (0181) 742 6600, Paris (01) 44 08 22 22, US ✆ toll-free 1-800 237 2747, Canada ✆ toll-free 1-800 667 2747.

Finnair often offers good fares for those prepared to go via Helsinki. London ✆ (0171) 408 1222, US and Canada ✆ toll-free 1-800 950 5000.

Alitalia flies twice weekly from Rome, **SAS** flies four times weekly from Copenhagen.

Budget travel. Some of the major European airlines have made it big business to use their home airports as hubs, offering travellers willing to change planes a substantial discount over those taking direct flights with other airlines. However, for the biggest discounts, travellers need to look further east, preferably to countries with relatively weak economies, or those well out of the way. Lot Polish Airlines via Warsaw (UK ✆ (0171) 580 5037, US ✆ toll-free 1-800 223 0593, Ontario and Québec ✆ toll-free 1-800 668 5928, rest of Canada ✆ (416) 236 4242, Sydney ✆ (02) 9299 5900, website *http://www.lot.com/*), Malaysian Airlines via Kuala Lumpur, Aeroflot via Moscow, Uzbekistan Airways via Tashkent, and PIA via Karachi or Islamabad all offer cheaper routes to Běijīng than the majors (*see* below for contact details). Further east, consider Thai Airways via Bangkok, Garuda Indonesia via Jakarta, and Philippines Airlines via Manila. You might even look at Ethiopia Airlines and Iran Air.

The cheapest fares on the major airlines and on alternative routes are usually obtained from discounters, consolidators, and 'bucket shops' with good reputations, such as Flight Centre or STA Travel, and others to be found in the pages of *Time Out*, *Village Voice*, *The Georgia Straight* or equivalent local listings magazines, and in the travel sections of Sunday newspapers.

There are as yet surprisingly few direct flights between North America and China, but a recently signed agreement will no doubt change that. Cheaper routes involve stopovers in Seoul or Tokyo, the Philippines or Indonesia.

Canadian Airlines flies from Vancouver four times weekly. Canada ✆ toll-free 1-800 665 1177, US ✆ toll-free 1-800 426 7000, website *http://www.cdnair.ca/*.

Northwest Airlines flies nonstop from Detroit, also from LA and via Tokyo. US and Canada ✆ toll-free 1-800 225 2525, website *http://www.nwa.com/*.

United Airlines flies from major US cities via Tokyo. US and Canada ✆ toll-free 1-800 241 6522, website *http://www.ual.com/*.

Air China is usually one of the cheaper airlines, although not by much, and flies to Běijīng from Vancouver, Seattle, San Francisco, Los Angeles, Chicago and New York. Toronto ✆ (416) 581 8833, Vancouver ✆ (604) 685 0921, New York ✆ (212) 371 9898, San Francisco ✆ (415) 392 2612, website *http://www.airchina.com/*.

Cathay Pacific flies to Hong Kong from Toronto, Vancouver, New York and Los Angeles. Connections to Běijīng are with Dragonair. US ✆ toll-free 1-800 233 2742, Canada ✆ toll-free 1-800 268 6868, website *http://www.cathaypacific-air.com/*.

Asiana flies from five US cities via Seoul. US toll-free ✆ 1-800 227 4262, website *http://www.asiana.co.kr/*. **Korean Airlines** also flies via Seoul. US ✆ toll-free 1-800 438 5000, Vancouver ✆ (604) 689 2000.

Japan Airlines has flights via Tokyo. US and Canada ✆ toll-free 1-800 525 3663, website *http://www.jal.co.jp/*. **ANA** also flies via Tokyo.

Air New Zealand flies to Hong Kong three times weekly from Auckland, with organized connections to Běijīng. Auckland ✆ (09) 357 3000, Australia ✆ 13 2476, ✆ HK (852) 2524 8606, website *http://www.airnz.co.nz/*.

Quantas flies twice weekly to Běijīng from Sydney via Shànghǎi, Australia ✆13 1211, website *http://www. qantas.com.au/*.

Air China flies from Sydney ✆ (02) 232 7277, and Melbourne ✆ (03) 642 1555.

Cathay Pacific flies to Hong Kong from Auckland, Cairns, Brisbane, Sydney, Melbourne, Adelaide and Perth. Australia ✆ toll-free 131747, Auckland ✆ (9) 379 0861, website *http://www.cathaypacific-air.com/*.

Other carriers with reasonable connections via a variety of Asian cities include **Singapore Airlines, ANA, JAL, Asiana** and **Korean**.

By Air to Bishkek and Almaty

While there are direct flights to Central Asia from Europe, there are none from North America. North Americans should consider travelling via Amsterdam, Frankfurt or Istanbul, via Běijīng and Ürümqi, or via Moscow.

Lufthansa has the most extensive Central Asian network of Western airlines, and flies from Frankfurt to Almaty five times a week with worldwide connections to Frankfurt. It also flies six times weekly to Běijīng. UK ☎ (0345) 737747, US ☎ toll-free 1-800 645 3880, Canada ☎ toll-free 1-800 563 5954, website *http://www.lufthansa.com/*.

KLM flies from Amsterdam to Almaty on Tuesdays and Saturdays, also with an extensive network of connections and smooth interchanges at Amsterdam's Schipol airport. UK ☎ (0181) 750 9000, US ☎ toll-free 1-800 374 7747, Canada ☎ toll-free 1-800 361 1887, Australia ☎ toll-free 008 222 747, website *http://www.klm.nl/*.

British Airways is planning flights to Almaty and on to Bangkok beginning in late 1997 (*see* above for contact information).

British Mediterranean flies to Bishkek from London Heathrow every other Wednesday on charter to the Canadian mining company, Kumtor, but with some spare seats to sell. For information call British Airways.

Turkish Airlines flies to Almaty four times a week from Istanbul to Almaty, and offers some of the cheapest connections from New York, several European capitals, and other German cities. It also has flights to Bishkek. London ☎ (0171) 499 4499, New York ☎ (212) 339 9650, LA ☎ (310) 646 5214, Sydney ☎ (2) 9221 1717, website *http://www.turkishairlines.com*.

Aeroflot flies to Almaty and Bishkek from Moscow (connected to North America's east and west coasts). UK ☎ (0171) 355 2233, US ☎ NY (212) 332 1050, LA ☎ (310) 281 5300 (also in Chicago, SF, Miami, Seattle, Washington and Anchorage), Australia ☎ Sydney (2) 233 7911.

MIAT Mongolian Airlines flies on Wednesdays from Ulan Batar to Almaty, and also has connections to Běijīng, Berlin and Moscow. Puzzle your local travel agent by asking. *http://www.arpnet.it/~mongolia/* is the web page of an Italian agent for MIAT.

Transaero has flights to Almaty from London, Paris, Berlin, Frankfurt and, bizarrely, Orlando, and has codeshare flights from other European and North American cities, all via Moscow. Chicago ☎ (312) 937 3100, NY ☎ (212) 582 0505, Frankfurt ☎ (4969) 921 8710. For other contacts try *http://www.transaero.com/*.

Cheaper airlines include **Uzbekistan Airways** which flies to Almaty via Tashkent, from London, Manchester, Amsterdam, Frankfurt, Athens and Istanbul, and from New York via Amsterdam and Tashkent. London ☎ (0171) 935 1899, New York ☎ (212) 489 3954. Minsk-based **Belavia** flies from Shannon and London via Minsk. London ☎ (0171) 393 1201, Shannon ☎ (61) 472921. **Kazak Airlines** is widely believed to have maintenance routines well below international standards and may not be flying at all. At times it is alleged to have been barred from some Western airports for nonpayment of landing fees. When in the air it flies to Almaty from Vienna, Hannover, Frankfurt, Budapest, Běijīng, Delhi, Moscow (cheaper than Aeroflot or Transaero) and other Russian and former Soviet destinations. **Kyrgyzstan Airlines** (Kyrgyzstan Aba Joldoru) flies to Bishkek from Istanbul, Frankfurt, Moscow and St Petersburg. A private Pakistani airline called **Aero Asia** flies from Karachi to Bishkek.

Austrian Airlines flies to Almaty from Vienna, codesharing **Swissair** connections from Geneva and Zürich, and **PIA** flies from Islamabad and Karachi.

Flights from the US west coast still head east to Central Asia via Europe. You can change at Běijīng or Hong Kong and fly to Ürümqi, then take Kazak Airlines or China Xīnjiāng Airlines from there to Almaty. Coming via Japan you can fly into Xī'ān from Nagoya and on to Ürümqi from there, too.

By Air to Islamabad

The main international entry point to Pakistan is Karachi, although some airlines supply links to Islamabad using small domestic carriers.

PIA is the obvious choice (at least until you fly with them once), with departures from several British cities and European capitals, and connections from North America. London ✆ (0181) 759 2544, Birmingham ✆ (0121) 643 7850, Bradford ✆ (01274) 731 705, Manchester ✆ (0161) 839 7506, Glasgow ✆ (0141) 221 9936, Amsterdam ✆ (20) 626 4710, Frankfurt ✆ (069) 690 24281, US ✆ toll-free 1-800 221 2552, Canada ✆ toll-free 1-800 387 1355, website *http://www.piac.com/*.

British Airways flies to Islamabad direct. For contact information *see* 'By Air to Běijīng', p.2

By Train

Travelling by train is the best way to get a feeling for the immense distances across Europe and Asia while retaining a high level of comfort.

The 'Euro-Asia Continental Bridge' is the name given to the more than 10,000km-long line connecting the Yellow Sea to the North Sea, and made possible by the completion of the link from Ürümqi to Almaty. It cuts off about 1200km from the shortest Trans-Siberian route and perhaps constitutes the newest Silk Route, although the Russians and other Europeans shopping in Běijīng's silk markets still seem to prefer the Trans-Siberian. With the opening of the Eurostar London to Paris services it's now possible to go all the way to China and Central Asia by rail with minimal changes. One of these will probably be Moscow, from where trains to Běijīng run via Ulan Batar (Trans-Mongolian) or Harbin (Trans-Manchurian), or south to Almaty and Bishkek. For the truly adventurous, the new line linking Iran with Turkmenistan might provide an alternative route via southern Europe and Turkey. Some have succeeded in travelling from Turkey via Tblisi in Georgia and Baku in Azerbaijan across the Caspian Sea to Turkmenistan.

Caution is needed on trains in the former Soviet Union, where robbery is becoming common. Take wire to wrap around the latch of your compartment door to prevent unauthorized entry at night.

By Road

Adventurous people are now buying vehicles in Europe and driving them to Central Asia for sale, typically via Poland and Ukraine, which defrays all or part of the cost of getting there. The Peugeot 405 is the vehicle of choice, and some have even been sold for a profit.

Another popular land route is from Turkey across Iran to Pakistan (which can also be done by a series of buses, although crossing the Iran-Pakistan border takes some haggling with private transport). Rather hairier would be to go northeast from Tehran through Turkmenistan and

Uzbekistan, although this route is offered by at least one tour operator—Hinterland Travel, *see* below. Take careful advice: the civil war in Turkmenistan and potential overspill from that in Afghanistan is likely to continue to make this a hazardous if not impossible trip. A conservative viewpoint is always available from your Foreign Office or equivalent.

Specialist Holidays

Those with only two or three weeks to spend should either limit their itineraries to a very few places with plenty of alternative routes, or take an organized tour. All of the countries in this book have poor infrastructures and unreliable political situations leading to unexpected changes of regulations and of state-operated services. Landslides, rainfall, conferences, elections and demonstrations suddenly create blockages, siphon up tickets, close borders, and destroy carefully planned itineraries. The companies below organize small group tours and specialist holidays, such as climbing, cycling, trekking and riding, and are used to dealing with sudden changes of plan. They range in size from the big companies like Exodus and Explore, with worldwide representation, to smaller organizations such as Steppes East, often the first tour company over the passes and into the remoter corners of China and Central Asia. They are also often willing to tailor-make itineraries.

You can also contact local agents directly (although this is not recommended for China), and details of reliable companies are given in the relevant city pages.

Boojum Expeditions (horseback treks in northern Xīnjiāng), 14543 Kelly Canyon Road, Bozeman, MT 59715, USA, ✆ (406) 587 0125, ✆ (406) 585 3474, email *boojum@mcn.net*, website *http://www.boojumx.com/*.

Exodus Expeditions (trekking, cycling and travel by specially built vehicle; KKH, Central Asia and China), 9 Weir Road, London SW12 OLT, ✆ (0181) 675 5550, email *sales@exodus-travels.co.uk*. Canada and the US: G.A.P. Adventures, 266 Dupont St, Toronto, Ont. M5R 1V7, ✆ toll-free 1-800 465 5600, email *adventure@gap.ca*. Australia: Top Deck Adventure, 8th Floor, 350 Kent St, Sydney NSW 2000, ✆ (02) 9299 8844, email *topdeck @s054.aone.net.au*. New Zealand: Eurolynx Tours Ltd., 3rd Floor, 20 Fort St, Auckland 1, ✆ (09) 379 9716, email *a11nz236@gncomtect.com*, website *http://www.exodustravels. co.uk/*.

Explore Worldwide (overland by coach, including Karakoram Highway, China, Central Asia), 1 Frederick Street, Aldershot, Hampshire GU11 1LQ, ✆ (01252) 319448, email *info@ explore.co.uk*. US: Adventure Centre, ✆ toll-free 1-800 227 8747, email *ex@adventure-center.com*. Canada: WestCan Treks, ✆ toll-free 1-800 690 4859, email *westcan@huey. cadvision.com*, website *http://www.explore.co.uk/*.

Geographic Expeditions (a variety of more luxurious tours across China, Central Asia and Pakistan), 2627 Lombard St, San Francisco, CA 94123, ✆ (415) 922 0448, ✆ (415) 346 5535, email *info@geoex.com*.

Hinterland Travel (economical overland trips across Central Asia, up the KKH, and across China), 2 Ivy Mill Lane, Godstone, Surrey RH9 8NH, ✆ (01883) 743584, ✆ (01883) 743912.

Mountain Travel Sobek (from Xī'ān to Islamabad, and Central Asian tours), 6420 Fairmount Ave, El Cerrito, CA 94530, ✆ toll-free 1-800 227 2384, ✆ (510) 525 7710, email *info@ MTSobek.com*, website *http://www.MTSobek.com/*.

O.T.T. Expeditions (serious mountain climbing in the Pamirs), 62 Nettleham Road, Sheffield S8 8SX, ☎ (0114) 258 8508, 📠 (0114) 255 1603, email *andy@ottexpd.demon.co.uk*.

Regent Holidays (tailor-made holidays throughout China and Central Asia), 15 John Street, Bristol BS1 2HR, ☎ (0117) 921 1711, 📠 (0117) 925 4866.

Steppes East (in the forefront of Central Asia travel with a wide variety of itineraries and transport options, several of which follow this book into, out of, and across China), Castle Eaton, Swindon, Wiltshire SN6 6JU, ☎ (01285) 810267, 📠 810693, email *sales@steppeseast. co.uk*, website *http://www.steppeseast.co.uk/*.

Voyages Jules Verne (upmarket, comfortable Silk Route sightseeing), 21 Dorset Square, London NW1 6QG, ☎ (0171) 616 1000, email *sales@vjv.co.uk*, website *http://www.vjv.co.uk/*.

Entry Formalities

China

> *In Lanchow the authorities, when they gave us back our papers, had assured us that they were in order for Chinghai. But they were not; before sending us on to Sining, Lanchow should have provided us with a special passport. By failing to do so Lanchow had neatly delegated the responsibility for stopping us to her neighbours, while at the same time increasing both the likelihood and the legality of such action on their part; it was a beautifully Chinese gambit, in the best tradition of passive resistance. It looked as if we were done for.*
>
> Peter Fleming, *News from Tartary,* 1936

Under ordinary circumstances you can easily obtain a visa at an embassy in any major capital, or from a consulate if you live near it. These are usually valid for one month, but two or three months may be given if requested at some embassies, beginning within 60 days from the date of issue. However, at times of political unrest, or if a politically sensitive event is taking place, new regulations may temporarily be introduced without notice. The authorities do not care if this disrupts your plans or causes you to lose money on services already booked and paid for. Visas usually take five days to obtain, but the process can be speeded up by the payment of extra fees. Visa fees vary according to your country of origin. Double-entry visas are available for tourists, but multiple-entry are only for businessmen.

When completing the application form, be sure only to list anodyne cities such as Běijīng, Shànghǎi and Xī'ān as your destinations. The visa is valid for the whole of China whatever you write, but you may be turned down if you mention Xīnjiāng (unless you are applying in Islamabad, Bishkek or Almaty) or Tibet.

Visas can usually be extended without difficulty within China. Each extension is for one month, and up to three are allowed, although the third one is sometimes given with reluctance. Extensions are usually given by the Aliens Entry-Exit Department of the local Public Security Bureau (police) in larger cities, up to four days before your current visa or extension expires. In some towns this is a swift, polite and efficient process, run by fluent English speakers. In others the relevant officer may be off doing something else, and no-one else will take responsibility. *These offices are closed on Saturday and Sunday, and do not always keep to their published opening hours. Never leave it until the last moment to apply for an extension. If you overrun, the PSB will delight in inventing a fine for you to pay.* Extensions for most nationals are ¥25 ($3), with the following exceptions: UK ¥65 ($8), Canada ¥110 ($13.50), Japan ¥120 ($15.50), Australia ¥65 ($8), Italy ¥45 ($5.50). Countries are added to or subtracted from this list according to the latest state of their relations with China. Nothing in China is ever consistent (except inconsistency), and in some less-visited cities nationals of all countries pay only ¥25. Expect these prices to have changed. Double-entry visas cannot be extended.

For those hoping to pick up visas en route, note that the embassy in Bishkek will not issue visas without a confirmation fax or telex from a state-approved travel agent that you have purchased services. Otherwise they *may* be persuaded to issue a visa marked 'not good for the Torugart Pass'. The Almaty embassy is inconsistent but now usually provides tourist visas without difficulty. At worst you may only be given a transit visa to get you to Pakistan, and only if you go and buy a Pakistani visa first. The Chinese embassy in Islamabad issues visas reliably. In all cases visas are issued in five working days, which can be speeded up by the payment of extra fees.

Chinese customs make little fuss over tourists. A customs declaration form must sometimes be filled in, and currency amounting to more than $5000 must be declared. You must also list electronics, jewellery and other valuables. One copy of the form must be kept for when you leave China, and the only difficulties that you are likely to encounter are if you lose it. Otherwise the declaration is little more than a formality. If you do acquire an antique you must get clearance to export it, or it may be confiscated at the border until such clearance is obtained. You may export up to ¥5000RMB, but there's little point, as no-one else will want it. If you have kept receipts proving that you have exchanged more than you want to reconvert, then any excess can be converted to hard currency (usually US$) at the Bank of China before you leave.

Kazakstan and Kyrgyzstan

Both countries now have several embassies overseas. In general the Kazaks do not answer the phone, and if they reply to your letter they may take up to three months to do so. They refuse to issue a tourist visa unless you have an invitation, otherwise known as visa support. The Kyrgyz Washington embassy, however, will fax you full information within minutes of your call, together with an application form. You are also required to write a polite letter with details of your reasons for visiting the country and what you plan to do, which is a formality. Where no Kazak or Kyrgyz embassy exists, you must apply at a Russian embassy. Sometimes the Kazaks issue Kyrgyz visas, too. As new embassies open the situation will certainly change.

If you are on an organized tour, let the travel agent deal with your Kazak and Kyrgyz visas. As an independent traveller to Kazakstan you'll have to buy your invitation from agencies in Almaty, although it's not necessary to purchase further services (*see* p.429). If you are applying for a Kyrgyz visa from home, an invitation is not usually necessary, unless you have to apply through a Russian or Kazak embassy, when it may be. Invitations can be purchased from agencies in Bishkek (*see* p.452). Kyrgyz tourist visas are valid for up to two months if you ask, but Kazak ones not usually for more than two weeks. Extensions *may* be possible, but only with considerable chasing around various ministries, and the payment of high fees. Transit visas are valid for three days, and can be obtained without an invitation if you have a visa for a neighbouring country or a valid air ticket out of Almaty or Bishkek. Visas could once be obtained at Almaty airport, but no more. On the other hand, it is said that it may soon be possible to acquire Kyrgyz visas at Bishkek airport. It's always better to get them before you arrive.

Tourist visas for the southern republics are valid for three days' transit through each of the others (with the exception of Turkmenistan), but transit visas can help to smooth problems at the borders with China. The easier-to-obtain Kyrgyz visa will allow you to pass through Kazakstan for three days on your way to or from China, for instance, and the Kazak visa works the other way. Passports are almost never checked at internal CIS borders, but when leaving Kazakstan for China, or when going to register your presence in Bishkek, you may encounter problems with corrupt officials who demand proof that you have *not* been in the country more than three days, or payment of a 'fine'. For details of how to come through such problems unscathed *see* 'To China by rail and road', p.444. The conversion of a transit visa to a tourist one can only be achieved with much kneeling and large amounts of cash, and should only be attempted in an emergency, and with the help of a local agency.

When staying more than three days in either country on a tourist visa, you must **register** your presence with the relevant ministry in Bishkek or Almaty, within three days, or on a Monday if you arrived on Friday or Saturday. Details of how to register are given in the relevant city sections.

You can pick up Kazak transit and tourist visas en route at the embassies in Islamabad, Běijīng and Bishkek, and the consulate in Ürümqi, under the conditions set out above. Kyrgyz visas can be obtained in Almaty and Běijīng, and from the Russian embassy in Islamabad (but only with an invitation).

When entering the CIS you must complete a *deklaratsy* or declaration form, setting out in detail your holdings of all currencies, negotiable instruments, and other valuables. Although the form is usually in Russian and the local language only, complete *two copies* with great care. There's a detailed description of how to do this in 'To Kyrgyzstan via the Torugart Pass', pp.289–90. Inconsistencies in your form, or the lack of one, will leave you open to 'fines' when you leave the country. For a full discussion of these problems, *see* 'To China by rail and road', p.444.

Pakistan

Pakistan has standard single and multiple-entry visas, which are easily obtainable. An extra fee is sometimes payable if you are applying in a country other than your country of residence, and fees vary according to nationality. You can pick up visas in Běijīng and Almaty, and there are plans to begin issuing them in Bishkek. It is also possible to get transit visas on arrival in Pakistan, although this is not recommended. Originally they were valid for 72 hours only, which meant that those entering Pakistan via the KKH were obliged to travel almost nonstop to Islamabad, the only place where the transit could be converted into a tourist visa. Recently visas valid for two weeks and longer have been issued at the China-Pakistan border, but the situation could change at any time. It is no longer necessary to get the Temporary Certificate of Registration upon arrival in Pakistan, but if you are staying for more than a month, you must register before the month is up. This can be done at Islamabad, Rawalpindi and Gilgit. Details are given in the relevant city sections.

Ascertain the date of Chinese New Year, usually early February, and occasionally late January. Do not attempt to travel in China for a week or so either side unless you are on an organized tour. If you are in China at that time, plan to reach a destination worth spending a week to ten days in well before the holiday season begins. In 1997 about 133 million railway journeys and 1.53 billion bus and boat trips were made during the holiday period, swamping even the nearly 40,000 extra services provided.

By Air

Travelling by air must be the least authentic way of all to follow the Silk Routes, and is only recommended for those in a hurry. Air travel did arrive in Central Asia fairly early in its history, however, beginning with the services of the Eurasia Air Line:

> *This enterprising Sino-German concern intended originally to open an air service from Peking, across Mongolia, Siberia and Russia to Berlin. Trouble with the Outer Mongols, who shot down one of the machines , put a stop to this plan, and the Eurasia Company sought an alternative route to Europe across Sinkiang and Central Asia. They made several successful flights to Urumchi, but the Mohammedan rebellion intervened and the political difficulties soon became aggravated to the point of compelling the abandonment of the enterprise. In 1935 the Eurasia machines were flying regularly to Ninghsia and Lanchow in Kansu, but not beyond.*

Eric Teichman, *Journey to Turkistan*, 1937

in China

Aviation in China until 1988 took place under the name of the Civil Aviation Administration of China (CAAC). Now a central authority and co-ordinating body (it also produces a combined timetable and runs most ticket offices), its six divisions have broken up into 30 airlines with their own identities, although competition on individual routes is limited. Air China, China Eastern, China Southern, and Shànghǎi Airlines all have IATA affiliation and are thought to be the only airlines carrying out internationally recognized standards of maintenance. Air China's fleet is modern, it claims a 100% safety record dating back to its beginnings as CAAC Běijīng in 1954, and it is working hard to throw off the reputation for poor service connected with the name CAAC (*Cancel At All Costs*).

Within China, safety records are generally poor, but flying is still safer than travelling by road. Aircraft used vary between vintage Soviet twin-props and jets, to new Airbuses and Boeings. Recently the government removed a 30% import tax on foreign-made aircraft, which is leading to a more rapid modernization of the fleet. Pilots are rumoured to be mostly ex-military, and to need special training not to throw their civilian planes around the sky as if in combat. If this story is true, it is not always clear that the training has been effective.

Internal airfares, once more expensive for foreigners than for local people (who were given a 'discount' according to Chinese airlines), were brought into harmony in July 1997. Chinese prices went up most, and foreigners' came down to meet them, so expect to find tickets selling for less than the prices quoted in the main text.

Many air ticketing offices have difficult and surly staff, and feature nearly the same juvenile scrums at ticket windows as bus stations and railway stations. Your first task is to obtain and complete a reservation form, which at bigger offices is available from a separate counter or table near the door. Local travel agents with terminals on the system should sell you a ticket commission-free, others charging between ¥30 ($4) and ¥50 ($6) to make your booking and collect the ticket. They may also have the *guānxi* (connections) to get you a ticket when the airline staff tell you the planes are full.

Watch out for departure taxes (CAAC Airport Management and Construction Fee): ¥50 ($6) for domestic flights, ¥90 ($11) for international ones (some offices wrongly interpret this as ¥50 for Chinese and ¥90 for foreigners—resist).

Potentially useful Silk Route flights within China include connections to Lánzhōu and Ürümqi from most major cities, and from Ürümqi to Kashgar, Korla, Khotan and Charchan. Never absolutely depend on a flight's departure, especially if you have to make an international connection, for instance.

in Kazakstan and Kyrgyzstan

There are flights from Almaty to Ürümqi with Kazak Airlines (one a week) and China Xīnjiāng Airlines (two a week).

in Pakistan

Most PIA staff seem to have no idea what is happening at all. However, PIA has flights two to three times daily between Islamabad and Gilgit, which weave through spectacular mountain scenery, and save those in a hurry from a 17-hour bus trip. *See* Islamabad and Gilgit sections for full details.

By Train

in China

This is by far the best way to tackle the vast distances across China. Buses may now sometimes be faster, but the trains give you more space, the chance to move around, to meet Chinese and attempt conversation, and to concentrate on the scenery rather than the driver's near misses. Trains are usually both reliable and punctual. The signalling system is modern, and accidents are rare.

Railway tickets are the same price for foreigners and Chinese and, at 5.861 *fēn* per kilometre ($0.007), represent one of China's best bargains. Even supplements for sleeping accommodation and speed leave the trains absurdly good value. Price increases seem to be less related to inflation than to increases in disposable income. When demand for unreserved hard-seat carriages is at several times their capacity, the government raises the prices, which reduces the pressure. Following a rise at the end of 1995, passenger traffic dropped off by 12½% in 1996, but still amounted to *942 million* passenger-journeys.

Everything in Chinese railways is done on a grand scale. In 1996 1500 stations were closed to passenger traffic as being uneconomic, while more than 10,000km of new track was planned for completion by the end of the year 2000. New air-conditioned rolling stock has begun appearing on the lines mentioned in the book, and elsewhere in China 160kph trains are running, and 200kph ones will begin service in 1998. An increase in cross-border services is also expected, including those between China and Kazakstan.

Ordinary trains are not fast, but during the life of this book will increase speed between major cities by about one third (to around 106kph for the best of them). Timetables in Chinese are on sale at stations and elsewhere if you feel like tackling them, using the train numbers given and comparing place name characters, but note that the authorities will frequently change the train times and not reprint tables until the current ones have sold out, leaving the inaccurate ones on sale. Like the times quoted in this book, they should only be regarded as a general guide.

The problem with Chinese trains is in **buying tickets**. Larger cities such as Běijīng and Xī'ān have special ticket windows for foreigners. Elsewhere you fight it out with everybody else, or use a travel agent to do the fighting for you. In some towns there is a separate window for sleeping accommodation, or it may be sold along with ordinary seats at the window dealing with each destination. If you can identify the right window using the characters given for each place name, you may be able to walk straight up and buy your ticket. More likely you will just be one member of a long queue, and you may seem to get further away from your window rather than nearer it as people push in, or bribe those nearer the front to buy their tickets for them.

While some stations are well regulated with officials keeping the lines in order, if you see people sitting up on the counter next to the ticket window, leering vulture-like down at the queue, you are probably at a station where large numbers of tickets have been sold through the back door, and where demand exceeds supply. These people are touts (scalpers) and you should not believe anything they tell you about ticket availability, and still try for yourself. Buying tickets from these sources is an extreme measure, and should only be considered if you have someone to hand who can read them, or you may pay soft sleeper prices for a hard seat (*see* the characters given in the Language section). Even then, there are fake tickets in abundance. When you reach the ticket window, and have physically removed those who tried to thrust in front of you at the last moment, be prepared with several different options, and not just with a request for tickets for one designated train. Tickets go on sale no earlier than four days in advance, including the day of purchase and the day of travel, and often later than that, depending on local policy.

The majority of the tickets for a train are sold in the town where it starts, and to increase your chances of getting a ticket you should always look first for trains which start from where you are. Small intermediate stations have tiny allocations for trains that stop there, or none at all. Your only hope is to buy an unreserved hard class seat, and to **upgrade** on the train. Your chances of actually sitting down with an unreserved ticket are slim, and are subject to the ends and beginnings of university terms, migrations of seasonal labourers and Communist Party official junkets, rather than any idea of a 'tourist season'. Even at peak times, foreign tourists are mere droplets in an ocean of Chinese. Your chances of upgrading also depend upon the attitude of the staff on board. Some go out of their way to help a lost-looking foreigner, and others will reserve any places that come free for Chinese prepared to bribe them. The on-board office will usually be at the end of one of the hard seat carriages in the middle of the train, often nos.11 or 12. In some cases soft sleeper upgrades are handled by the staff in those carriages, so if a soft sleeper is what you are after, it may be best to ask there first. Note that the train is usually so packed with humanity that walking up and down it with luggage is either very trying or impossible. Try to get on the train at the door nearest to the office.

Seating comes in four classes: hard seat, soft seat, hard sleeper, and soft sleeper.

Hard seat (*yìng zuò*) is usually wooden benches, and a mixture of reserved and unreserved tickets, except on air-conditioned trains, where all seats are reservable and no-one else is allowed on board. At its worst it is ankle deep in peanut shells, fruit peel, sunflower seed husks and mucus, dimly perceivable through choking clouds of cigarette smoke. People with unreserved seats will be asleep on the tables, and, unbelievably, on the floor. In the better trains the attendants regularly empty the bins and mop the floors, stridently admonishing those throwing things on the floor. Since most like to smoke themselves, the no-smoking rule is almost never enforced.

Soft seat (*ruǎn zuò*) is relatively rare, and usually found on short daylight trips such as that between Xīníng and Lánzhōu. It features comfortable seats, all reservable, and is sometimes merely soft sleeper accommodation where everybody sits on the lower beds.

Hard sleeper (*yìng wò*) has firm couchettes in piles of three, separated by partitions into groups of six altogether, with a passageway along the side of the carriage. There is no privacy or screening of any kind. The price for hard sleeper tickets decreases the further you get away from the ground, but the differences are minimal. The upper berth is often favoured by foreigners as it gets them up and away from the mêlée, and can spare them from excessive curiosity (the only kind available). Everyone sits on the bottom berths during the day, so there's little sense of control over your environment if that's the berth you have. Speakers set in the ceiling play saccharine music and broadcast announcements, including the dining-car menu and extremely rosy descriptions of the next town and its happy inhabitants. In the top berth you may find one over your head. It cannot be turned off, and nor can the lights, which come on early in the morning and go off altogether at night. Each group of six berths has two thermoses of boiled water, but often someone has to volunteer to trek down to wherever the boiler is in order to refill them.

Soft sleeper (*ruǎn wò*), has four comfortable beds in a compartment with a lockable door, plastic flowers on the table, carpeting, twin thermoses of boiled water which the attendants usually top up for you, and a volume control beneath the table for the speaker. Windows both in the compartment and the corridor have net curtains. Soft sleepers are the haunt of the party official, the self-made entrepreneur, and the employee of the multinational. Only in sleeper buses and trains will you sleep in the same room as Chinese. Upper and lower berths cost the same price, but again the upper berth offers a little more control over when you can go to sleep at night or take an afternoon nap.

If you end up with a compartment all to yourself, you may get moved in with other people so as to give the attendants less cleaning to do, or leave them space to spend the night drinking, smoking and gambling. Bed linen is provided and usually clean, although it may be collected well before you arrive at your destination if it pleases the attendant to do so. In all classes of train, the small, garishly coloured towel provided is intended to function as a pillow-slip. Standards of cleanliness vary from crisp and spotless on the newest trains, to rotting and dingy on older ones.

Rail ticket **prices** are calculated according to the number of kilometres travelled, with supplements added according to the speed of the train, the class of berth, and whether there's air conditioning. (The new a/c trains also have a video monitor in each group of berths in hard sleeper, but not soft.) All tickets are one way, except for Chinese students travelling between

Railway tickets

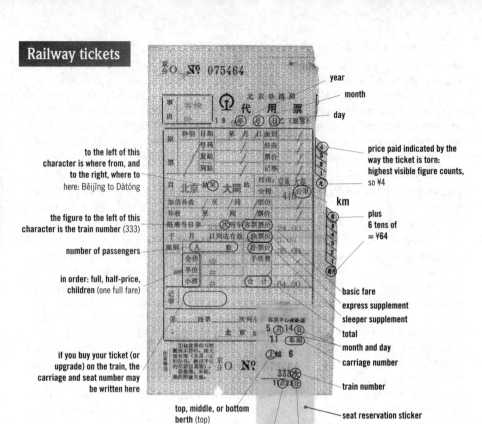

to the left of this character is where from, and to the right, where to — here: Běijīng to Dàtóng

the figure to the left of this character is the train number (333)

number of passengers

in order: full, half-price, children (one full fare)

if you buy your ticket (or upgrade) on the train, the carriage and seat number may be written here

year

month

day

price paid indicated by the way the ticket is torn: highest visible figure counts, so ¥4

km

plus 6 tens of = ¥64

basic fare

express supplement

sleeper supplement

total

month and day

carriage number

train number

seat reservation sticker

top, middle, or bottom berth (top)

北京站上车

minutes   hours

departure time

front   **reverse**

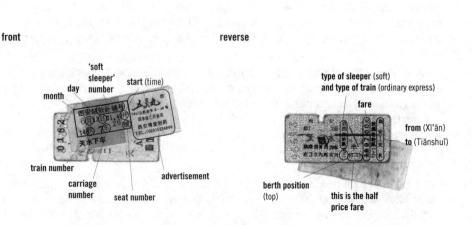

'soft sleeper' number

start (time)

day

month

train number

carriage number

seat number

advertisement

type of sleeper (soft) and type of train (ordinary express)

fare

from (Xī'ān)

to (Tiānshuǐ)

berth position (top)

this is the half price fare

40 designated cities. Children under 1m travel free, and under 1.3m pay 25%. There are marks on the wall near the ticket windows by which children are measured. Ticket offices are almost always entered by a different door than the one that leads to the platforms, and may be in a separate building altogether. Important exceptions in this book are Běijīng Zhàn (the main railway station) and the new Běijīng Xī Zhàn (Běijīng West Station), which have special foreigners' ticket windows inside the main station building. Your ticket is checked on the way to the platform. When you board the train for a sleeper, your ticket is taken away and you are given a plastic or metal token with the number of your berth on it. *Do not lose this.* When it is nearly time to get off (any time between 5 and 30 minutes beforehand) the attendant will come and return your ticket and retrieve the token. The ticket is checked again as you leave the station, so keep it ready.

Note that at major railway stations all baggage is **X-rayed** upon entering the station. Despite the fact that the main occupation of people on trains is staring at other people on trains, **theft** is increasing, including opportunistic snatching of valuables through train windows. Even some Chinese now tie their luggage to the racks, and it's important to have your compartment locked if it will be unattended while you visit the dining car or go for a walk on the platform.

Dining cars on trains serve poor but usually tolerable food, with a choice of six or eight dishes at slightly higher prices than you would find for the same meal in an ordinary restaurant. It's mostly soft-sleeper Chinese who use the dining car, and it's not usually full. Find the attendant at one end with a pile of coloured tickets, and a handwritten menu with prices. Opportunists may occasionally attempt to charge the foreigner more than the prices written there, but they have no right to do so. Beer is always available, and sometimes soft drinks, but never chilled. Breakfast is normally steamed bread. Attendants usually bring round trolleys laden with snacks and some prepared meals in styrofoam boxes. Most Chinese bring their own food (to see what's popular examine the floor), and buy from vendors on platforms when the train stops. Bring some snacks of your own, in case the train food turns out to be particularly awful, and bring some extra to share, as the Chinese in your compartment or carriage will almost certainly offer you something of theirs.

Be prepared for revolting lavatories, no running hot water for washing, even no cold water, and floods in the washroom, probably all at the same time. Take toilet paper, handwipes if you wish (available in China), and a mug for making tea and for cooling down boiled water to use for brushing your teeth.

in Kazakstan and Kyrgyzstan

Although there is a rail connection between Almaty and Bishkek it's considerably quicker and safer to take the bus. Buying tickets for the Almaty to Ürümqi train is easy. For a full account see 'To China by Rail and Road', p.444.

in Pakistan

The only relevant section of the decaying Pakistani rail system is that from Rawalpindi to Taxila, where it makes a pleasant alternative to road transport. Lower and upper a/c classes offer respite from the summer heat for those that need it, although a breeze from the open windows of more proletarian classes is just as good.

Cart transport is the most practical way of conveying a traveller and his goods over the main trade-routes of the Gobi, but unfortunately it necessitates the use of a carter and, as the Chinese proverb has it, 'As to carters, there's ne'er a good one.'

Mildred Cable with Francesca French, *The Gobi Desert*, 1942

The role of the carter is now taken by the bus driver, minibus driver and taxi driver. All like foreigners, but for the wrong reasons.

According to government figures there were 73,655 deaths in road accidents in 1996 with 788 accidents per day. 174,447 people were injured. The cause of most accidents was put down to 'driver negligence'.

Most buses in China are robust to cope with the rigours of Chinese roads, rather than comfortable, most still having wooden seats with little or no padding, and not designed for foreign width or thigh length. Bruised knees are always a possibility, although private lines now run a variety of smaller, more comfortable buses with large windows, and new sleeper buses are challenging the railways. The roads are also rapidly increasing in quality, although few have more than one lane in each direction. Traffic carries on while repairs are under way, or is simply sent across stretches of desert. In China, all vehicles are 'off-road'.

Luggage is usually piled high on the roof, and not accessible until you arrive at your destination. It's up to you to put it there yourself, although the conductor will usually make sure that everything is secure under rope netting. Smaller items can sometimes be piled on the cowling covering the engine next to the driver. In all buses, big or small, access to the engine is gained from the interior of the bus by lifting this cowling. In older buses a pipe fed by the exhaust gases runs from here along the centre of the bus to provide primitive heating. Do not rest your feet on this or your soles will melt. Breakdowns, and in particular punctures, are frequent, but there is a can-do mentality which gets even the most major problem dealt with by the roadside. Important gasket blown? A temporary replacement is quickly cut from a cigarette sleeve.

Sit as near the front of the bus as possible, not only to get a better view, but because sitting at the back over an unyielding suspension is something your spine will long remember, and will introduce moments of air travel to your terrestrial progress. At the front, however, you may have to cope with frequent use of piercing air horns and deafening engine noise. Latecomers are placed on wooden stools down the aisle, produced from under the main seating, and after those are taken people stand in whatever space remains. The 'maximum capacity' of a Chinese bus is a purely theoretical quantity. Sometimes windows pop out and have to be replaced. Occasionally they are just missing, and in all cases they rattle and the latches don't work so that they must continually be reshut. Sturdy rubber bands are a useful solution, especially in sleeper buses or during sandstorms.

Most travellers first encounter **sleeper buses** on the northern Taklamakan route from Ürümqi to Kashgar. Bunks on two levels run in three rows down the centre of the bus, and can be adjusted between a near horizontal and a more upright reclining position. They are

Bus ticket

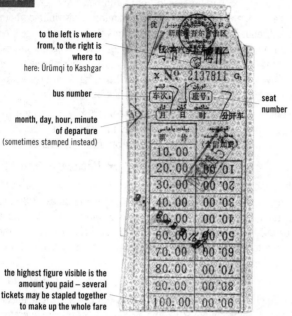

to the left is where from, to the right is where to
here: Ürümqi to Kashgar

bus number

month, day, hour, minute of departure
(sometimes stamped instead)

seat number

the highest figure visible is the amount you paid – several tickets may be stapled together to make up the whole fare

narrow and short. For the minimal disturbance and a maximum control over your environment, try to get an upper berth next to a window. All the men smoke, at least one person is sick, piles of food remains grow on the floor, where babies are also allowed to urinate. Sleeper buses are swift, but pungent.

Ticket offices in bus stations are open all day. Prices are the same for foreigners and Chinese in most parts of China, but in recent years double pricing has appeared in parts of Gānsù and Xīnjiāng. It's not clear whether this is the result of bus company, bus station, or local government initiative, or just spite on the part of the ticket sellers. The situation varies from station to station, type of bus chosen, and route taken. Private operators competing on the same routes will frequently take the initiative to try to charge the ignorant foreigner more. With the exception of certain special services, such as those to airports and railway stations, ticket prices are calculated according to the distance to be travelled. The price per km varies slightly from region to region, but is usually less than one cent. Sleeper buses cost more, and have slightly different pricing according to berth chosen. Advance booking rules vary greatly, but in general tickets are bought the day before travel, and not more than three days before. There are no charges for ordinary quantities of baggage.

On many routes you can just board the bus and buy there, but you will almost certainly end up at the back of the bus. **Ticket numbering** is designed to be as confusing as possible. Sometimes the use of numbers is observed, sometimes not; and when the bus is part full a debate will break out between those at the front who insist that ticket numbers don't matter, and those who have low ticket numbers but who find themselves at the rear and so insist that they do. To confuse matters further, there is disagreement as to whether the number of the seat is written on its back, or the back of the one in front. Numbers are often written in chalk, and partly or completely erased, and sometimes they are randomly distributed about the bus, so separated families and friends may start long negotiations for seat exchanges. Add to this that it may be a pre-dawn winter morning with no lights on the bus so no-one can see the numbers properly, and that if a conductor enforces the seat numbering *everybody tries to move at once*, and you have a bus of Babel. Allowing for dithering, food breaks, road works, and breakdowns, the average speed of a long-distance bus is 43km per hour.

There is an extra problem in western Gānsù, which has compulsory bus **travel insurance**, without which you will not be allowed to buy a ticket. You must buy the People's Insurance Company of China policy—no other is valid. Details are given in the relevant cities.

in Kazakstan and Kyrgyzstan

The bus between Bishkek and Almaty is usually a comfortable Hungarian or tolerable Russian one, as is the bus between Almaty and Ürümqi. It's possible to get as far as At-Bashi by bus on the way from Bishkek to Kashgar, but after that you're on your own. Minibuses on the Chinese side can only be used to leave China, not to enter it. Details are given in the relevant city sections, and 'The road to the Torugart Pass', p.462, 'To China by Rail and Road, p.444, and 'To Kyrgyzstan via the Torugart Pass', p.289.

in Pakistan

The KKH route between Islamabad and Sost is served by trundling psychedelic masterpieces of various sizes, run by the state company NATCO, and a collection of private operators. Smaller vehicles oscillate between neighbouring towns, and between any two points there are numerous options. Every town has a stand where private transport gathers and leaves when all seats have been sold. Keep your passport secure, but to hand. There are frequent checkpoints where foreigners have to record their details in ledgers. Occasionally the guards can be persuaded to pass the book through the window, but usually they insist that foreigners step off the bus to make their entries. Revenge has been taken by many: Mickey Mouse and Donald Duck have apparently been frequent travellers up and down the KKH, as have people with the most bizarre occupations. Details of buses on the highway and between Pakistan and China are given in **The Karakoram Highway**, p.465, and Kashgar sections.

Hitching

There are public buses or various kinds of organized transport (a seat in a trailer behind a tractor, for instance) to even the remotest corners of China. If a travel agent tells you that their vehicles are the only way that you can visit a place, that is almost a guarantee that there's some alternative. Hitching, however, isn't usually it. If you do end up hitching because you simply can't find any other form of transport, be sure that you'll have to pay, and negotiate the price first. There is no casual private motoring of long distances in China (and still precious little in cities). Imported limousines and off-road vehicles contain officials, or belong to travel companies, so if you do succeed in hitching you'll be in a truck, usually perched amongst the goods it's carrying.

In Pakistan you can attempt to flag down any vehicle on the KKH, but expect to pay for the pleasure of a ride. In Kazakhstan and Kyrgyzstan, hitching is the only way to get to some remote places, but there is always payment to be made.

With the exception of foreign residents in major cities in China who may hire self-drive vehicles, all car hire is with driver only. Driving yourself into or around China is not an option, unless you are willing to spend around 18 months in the planning, and have the status of an expedition with letters from your Head of State. Even then your route must be planned in detail, and you will be assigned a guide, who will carry vast amounts of paperwork to placate all the officials whose paths you cross. The cost may run to several thousand dollars.

The China Xīnjiāng Mountaineering Association in Kashgar can arrange for you to travel from Kyrgyzstan to Pakistan through Xīnjiāng, taking about one month to make the arrangements. The fee, of approaching $2000, will include an accompanying jeep, tours of Kashgar, and so on. It is possible to haggle in slow motion by fax or telex to reduce the fee. Motorbikes can be put on the back of a truck, for instance, which shortens the time taken for permits to around 10 days, and you can ride in the truck instead of in the jeep, and discard the guide on the grounds that the truck driver knows where he is going and can keep an eye on you. Result: perhaps $1200. Driving through Turkey, Iran, Pakistan and up the Karakoram Highway is also popular, but few go further unless on bicycles.

A pushbike is the fastest form of independent travel permitted to visitors. Travelling across China by bicycle is now fairly common, and travellers encounter relatively few problems. Although some have had their bikes impounded by officials claiming that they travelled through closed areas, mostly the police just indicate that until the town they name, the bike must go on a bus. Then they find the right bus and put you on it. Cycling in and out over the Khunjerab Pass seems to present no problems at all, not even a permit being required. Those entering or leaving China via the Torugart Pass to Kyrgyzstan must still put their bicycles on the roof of the jeep or minibus, between the new border post not far from Kashgar and the old one just short of the pass itself. There is at least no extra charge for this.Cyclists entering China by road from Almaty have also been told to take buses as far as Ürümqi.

City Transport

City bus routes in many towns have signs with a black number which is the *route* number, and a red number which is the *stop* number. Don't get confused.

City **buses and trolleybuses** often resemble overgrown '60s enamel bread bins, and travel about as quickly. Allowed to stall at every stop, some of them find they can't start again. That's when Chinese public-spiritedness comes to the fore, as perhaps only a third of the passengers get off, and three-quarters of those only do so to enjoy the spectacle of the few others pushing the bus.

Boarding buses is a full contact sport. Either join in or choose an alternative form of transport. Most buses have conductors at the front and rear, and at the middle if this is a concertina-style vehicle with a middle door. Distorted announcements usually consist of little more than 'Hurry up hurry up hurry up' at every stop, addressed to those fighting to get off against the stream of those fighting to get on. In between stops it's 'Buy a ticket buy a ticket buy a ticket'. Most buses have a basic fare that covers most journeys, with additions for longer distances. If you hold out money worth more than the price of one ticket you will be asked '*Jǐ ge*', 'How many', and '*Dào nǎr*', 'Where to?', so either show some fingers or say the number (plus '*ge*') and your destination. Details of the local fares are given in the 'getting around' sections, but be prepared for changes (ask the English speaker in your hotel).

A few buses have a flat-fare slot as you board by a door marked *shàng*. No change is given. In many towns smaller private minibuses (*miànbāochē*) follow the same routes, sometimes for the same fare, sometimes for double.

Buses are run similarly in Bishkek and Almaty, with a flat fare payable to driver or conductor. *Marshrutnoe* minibuses (like ancient school buses) also run set routes for similar fares, but can often be flagged down between stops. Pay the driver. In Pakistani cities elaborately decorated buses race minivans and Suzuki pick-ups for the same business, and can be flagged down anywhere. Pay the conductor according to distance travelled.

Taxis in China are now fairly well regulated in most cities, most of them running meters (although speeds may not always be consistent). In most cities the cheapest taxis are the minivans (*miàndī*), followed by small red cars (*xiàlì*). Flag fall varies from city to city, but the basic rate per kilometre is written clearly on the side windows. Taxi ranks are no more havens of honesty than they are anywhere else in the world, and the foreigner should go armed with a map, and preferably the destination written down in characters. Never take a taxi from outside a hotel frequented by foreigners, major tourist sites or railway stations. Be prepared for problems ('broken' meters, poor navigation, and so on) with those from airports. Taxi drivers never have change, except that the glove compartment is usually stuffed with it. Pay the exact meter fare, and not a *fēn* more. Do not tip.

Below official taxi level there are motorcyclists who will offer to take you pillion (definitely not recommended), and motorbikes with side cars (safer, but uncomfortable). There are also increasing numbers of motorized three-wheelers. Agree the fare first.

When getting out of towns to nearby sites, beware CITS or anyone else telling you that you must have a jeep, which usually means that an ordinary *miàndī* (minivan) driver will be happy to take you. If *he* says no, then you do need a jeep.

Bishkek and Almaty both have official taxis, but any private car is willing to work as a taxi if going your way. Just stand at the road side and hold out your hand. There's a generally agreed flat rate for most distances in town, but increasingly foreigners are thought of as automatic overpayers, so agree the price first. In Islamabad, the taximeters are always broken, so here, too, fix a price first, and allow no deviations from the agreement.

Practical A–Z

Books and Maps

For art books, antiquarian books, and out-of-print accounts of Silk Route travel, try Han-Shan Tang Books, 42 Westleigh Avenue, **London** SW15 6RL, ✆ 0181 788 4464, ✆ 0181 780 1565, hst@eastbook.demon.co.uk, website *http://www.demon.co.uk/eastfield/ hstbooks/*. Their site has an efficiently updated searchable catalogue of their stock, which includes books in a wide variety of languages.

If in **Paris** for the Musée Guimet or other reasons, you'll find a number of useful bookshops specializing in oriental material including: Paul Geuthner, 12 rue Vavin, 6è, ✆ 46 34 71 30; Samuelin, rue Monsieur Le Prince, 5è, ✆ 43 26 88 65; Youfeng, in the same street at No.45, ✆ 43 25 89 98. The bookshop in the annexe to the Musée keeps a list of around 20 others.

In the US try Asia Rare Books, 175 W. 93rd Street (Suite 16-D), **New York**, NY 10025, ✆ 1-800 (212) 3408, ARB@maestro.com, website *www.columbia.edu/cu/ccs/cuwl/clients/ arb/*. Also try Paragon Books in **Chicago**, 1507 South Michigan Avenue, Chicago, IL 60605, ✆ 1-800 552 6657, (312) 663 5155, ✆ (312) 6635177, paragon@paragonbook.com, website *http://webart.com/paragonbook/index.shtml/*.

Various **guide books** on individual towns and provinces are published in English in China. Kuqa is a good example, offering you an entirely revised history written in terms of the spread of Marxism-Leninism and Máo Zédōng thought ('The Kuqa people of all nationalities have a fine tradition of revolutionary struggle'), and endless statistics ('The annual total output of cooking oil seeds was 818 tons in 1949, and it was 1735 tons in 1991, increasing 2.1 times.').

The Chinese were amongst the earliest known map-makers, and by the 2nd century AD **maps** of most major settlements had been produced using principles set down four centuries earlier. 1900 years later this process seems to have run out of steam, and there is little attention paid to accuracy. Most cities that have maps (and not all do) only have them in Chinese characters. Pocket-size and larger-format **road atlases** are available in Xīnhuá Shūdiàn (the state-run bookshop with at least one branch in almost every city), but any English rarely runs beyond the table of contents and the title of each map. Look for the *New Traffic and Tourist Atlas of China*, and the larger-format *Zhōngguó Fēnshěngqìchésījī Dìtúcè*, around ¥14 ($2). Forget about finding detailed relief or trekking maps in China.

Large-scale US charts are available for the entire globe, although some are way behind China's rapid construction of new roads and railway lines, and the growth of the cities, let alone the creation of the new countries of the CIS. An archaic transliteration system is used to name Chinese towns. The scale is 1:500,000, or there's another series at 1:1,000,000, both priced at £7.50 per sheet from Stanfords, 12–14 Long Acre, London WC2E 9LP, ✆ (0171) 836 1327.

A pocket-size Russian-made *Kazakhstan & Central Asia Road Atlas* is now available overseas, dating from 1987, as well as Russian-made large-scale survey maps of Central Asia and Western China. These are stocked by The Four One Co Ltd, 523 Hamilton Road, London, Ontario, N5Z 1S3, Canada, ✆ (519) 433 1315, ✆ (519) 433 5903, and can be viewed and ordered at *http://www.icis.net/fourone/*, four.one@icis.on.ca.

The State Geodetic and Cartographic Agency in Bishkek is a good source for detailed relief maps of the Tiān Shān and other maps of Kyrgyzstan.

See also **Further Reading**, p.531.

Climate and When to Go

In April Kashgar will have pleasantly warm days but cold nights. Almaty, Bishkek and perhaps Ürümqi may still have snow. Xī'ān will be humid and cool, and Běijīng just right. Islamabad will be warm and comfortable. In such a vast area there's no one good time to travel, but in general April, May and early June, and September and early October avoid the worst of the pollution from winter heating in China, and the worst of both summer sun and winter freezes in the deserts and over the high passes. For trekking and climbing expeditions in Central Asia and Pakistan, the midsummer is the best time. Note that although there's traffic over the Khunjerab Pass all year round, regular tourist buses don't start until April, and finish in November. It's best to travel into China this way in May, or into Pakistan in September. The Torugart Pass would be very uncomfortable to cross in winter unless organized transport had been arranged.

In most of the Chinese towns mentioned in this book, average winter temperatures fall to −8°C, less at higher altitudes and in Ürümqi where −12°C is possible, dropping further as you go west into Kazakstan and Kyrgyzstan (−16°C or less). In the Taklamakan and Gobi deserts July averages of 24°C are normal, with very little precipitation at any time of the year. Běijīng can also reach averages of 24°C, but most of the routes west from Xī'ān and through Inner Mongolia and Níngxià have a slightly more comfortable average of 20°C. The cities in Inner Mongolia, Gānsù and Xīnjiāng tend to be more comfortable due to low humidity than the more sticky Xī'ān, for instance. Běijīng and the cities through Inner Mongolia have pleasant spring and early summer breezes, but these can sometimes bring with them scouring clouds of Gobi sand. Summer rains can leave a yellow coating on everything. Most of north and north-western China is fairly dry, and what rainfall there is occurs in the summer.

Almaty and Bishkek get most of their rain in April and May, but Almaty is wetter year round than Bishkek, and slightly cooler during June to August, when Bishkek can get as hot as Kashgar, with peaks over 30°C.

Lying within range of the monsoons, by early summer Islamabad is humid and uncomfortable, and there's frequent heavy rain from July to September. Travelling only a short distance up the KKH will put you into a drier, cooler climate. Spring and autumn nights are cool, becoming chilly as you head up the highway, and winters in the mountains are very cold.

Contraception

Condoms are available in all the countries covered in this book, but supplies are patchy and local brands not necessarily of high quality. Bring ample supplies if you think you might need them. In China stock up in Běijīng, where some Western brands are available, but note that manufacturers do make a smaller size for the Asian market. Look for instance in the small groceries (convenience stores) on Dàzhàlán Jiē. In Bishkek and Almaty the roadside kiosks often stock condoms along with Mars bars and telephone tokens.

Crime

The main worry for visitors to China, Pakistan, Kazakstan and Kyrgyzstan is theft, carried out in the overwhelming number of cases by stealth rather than by violence or threat of it, although in China all crime is on the rise. The government's response is a 'Strike Hard' policy, which leads to the execution of thousands every year, some for minor offences. If you do catch a thief in the act, think twice before handing him over to the authorities. In general Chinese cities remain safer for foreigners than most major cities in the West, but some circumspection is needed at night in Almaty and Bishkek.

Wearing a money belt beneath your clothes is advisable, containing all important documents and money that you are unlikely to need during the day. Particular care against pickpockets should be taken in crowded bus and railway stations, when boarding or alighting from buses, and on the buses themselves. Despite the vast numbers of observers, theft on trains is on the increase. Ask the *fúwùyuán* (attendant) to lock your compartment if you are going for a platform stroll during a long stop or to the dining car if the compartment is otherwise going to be empty. Keep valuables away from the windows of the train as snatching from platforms is not unknown. Some travellers have taken to chaining their bags to the racks. Hotels are generally safe and staff trustworthy. Greater caution is obviously needed when staying in a dormitory.

Keep your perception of other risks in perspective. There are a few stories of visitors disappearing in some remote parts of China, but not those dealt with in this book. Occasional bomb blasts, earthquakes, and rioting are considerably less likely to injure you than crossing the street (or even crossing the street in your home town). Nevertheless in 1996 the British Foreign Office was advising British independent travellers to register with them in Běijīng (✆ 6532 1961) or Shànghǎi (✆ 6279 7650). Governments always err on the side of caution when issuing travel advice, but you may wish to check with the relevant department before leaving home.

Electricity

220 volts, 50 cycles AC. In **Kazakstan** and **Kyrgyzstan** the plugs are the European two round pin type. These can also be found in **China**, along with North American-style two flat pins, and sometimes a three flat pin arrangement with two at an angle. In all but the very oldest buildings there is more than one alternative socket at each point. If you get stuck, adaptors can easily be bought in department stores. In **Pakistan** the plugs are ancient two and three fat round pins, and the modern European type. Adaptors from one type to the other are widely available. Shaver sockets will only be found in the more modern and expensive hotels. Bring a battery-powered shaver or use more traditional techniques.

Many Chinese cities suffer from power shortages, especially in the winter, when cuts are rotated around different parts of town on different days of the week. Almaty seems to suffer from voltage fluctuations sufficient to fry some transformers. Those with laptops would be wise to ensure that their voltage converters are robust.

Embassies and Consulates

China and Pakistan have embassies in all major capitals and many consulates, too. There are already Kazakstani and Kyrgyzstani embassies in Europe and the US, as well as in most neighbouring countries in Central Asia. If there is no Kazak or Kyrgyz embassy in your country apply to the Russian embassy, except in Canada where Kyrgyz enquiries have to be referred to the Kyrgyz embassy in Washington. In general, unless you live in a city with a consulate, always apply to the embassy in your capital.

in Australia

Embassy of the People's Republic of China: 247 Federal Highway, Watson, Canberra ACT 2602, ✆ (6) 273 4780.

Chinese consulate: 539 Elizabeth St, Surry Hills, Sydney, NSW 2010, ✆ (2) 698 7373, 698 7838.

Embassy of Pakistan: 59 Franklin St, PO Box 198, Manuka, Canberra ACT 2603, ✆ (6) 290 1676.

Russian Embassy: 78 Canberra Avenue, Griffith, Canberra ACT 2603, ✆ (6) 295 9033.

in Belgium

Embassy of Kyrgystan: 133 Rue de Tennbosch, 1050 Brussels, ✆ (2) 534 6399.

Embassy of Kazakstan: 30 Avenue Vanbever, 1180 Brussels, ✆ (2) 374 9562.

in Canada

Embassy of the People's Republic of China: 511 St Patrick Street, Ottawa K1N 5H3, ✆ (613) 234 2706, 789 9608.

Chinese consulates: 3380 Granville Street, Vancouver BC, V6H 3K3, ✆ (604) 736 3910; 240 St. George St, Toronto, ON M5R 2P4, ✆ (416) 324 6455.

Embassy of Pakistan: Suite 608, 151 Slater Street, Ottawa K1P 5H3, ✆ (613) 238 7881.

Russian Embassy: 52 Range Road, Ottawa, Ontario K1N 8J5, ✆ (613) 236 7220 (also handles Kazak visas, but Kyrgyz are handled in Washington).

Russian consulate: 3655 Ave du Musée, Montréal, Québec H3G 2E1, ✆ (514) 843 5901.

in Germany

Embassy of the People's Republic of China: Kurfurstenallee 12, 5300 Bonn 2, ✆ (228) 361095.

Embassy of Kazakstan: 5 Botschaft der Republik Kazakstan, Schloss Marienfels, 53424 Remagen (Bonn), ✆ (2642) 93830.

Embassy of Kyrgyzstan: 62 Koblenzstrasse, 51173 Bonn, ✆ (228) 365230.

in Holland

Embassy of the People's Republic of China: Adriaan Goekooplaan 7, The Hague, ✆ (70) 3551515.

in New Zealand

Embassy of the People's Republic of China: 2–6 Glenmore St, Wellington, ✆ (4) 472 13823.

Russian Embassy: 57 Messines Road, Karori, Wellington, ✆ (4) 766742.

in the UK

Embassy of the People's Republic of China: 49 Portland Place, London W1N 3AH, ✆ (0171) 636 8845. Consular/Visa Section: 31 Portland Place W1N 3AG, ✆ (0171) 636 1835, 631 1430. 24-hour visa information (premium rate call), ✆ (0891) 880808.

Chinese consulate: Denison House, Denison Road, Victoria Park, Manchester M14 5RX, ✆ (0161) 224 7443.

Embassy of Kazakstan: 33 Thurloe Square, London SW7 2SD, ✆ (0171) 581 4646. Also acts for Kyrgyzstan.

Embassy of Pakistan: 35 Lowndes Square, London SW1X 9JN, ✆ (0171) 235 2044.

Russian Embassy: 10 Kensington Palace Gardens, London W8 4QJ, ✆ (0171) 229 2666, consular section (0171) 229 8027.

in the USA

Embassy of the People's Republic of China: 2300 Connecticut Avenue NW, Washington, DC 20008, ✆ (202) 328 2500.

Chinese consulates: 520 12th Avenue, New York 10036, ✆ (212) 279 4275, 330 7409; 104 Sth. Michigan Av., Suite 900, Chicago 60603, ✆ (312) 380 2507; 3417 Montrose Blvd., 1450 Laguna St., San Francisco 94115, ✆ (415) 563 4885; 502 Shto Place, Suite 300, Los Angeles 90020, ✆ (213) 380 2507.

Embassy of Kazakstan: 3421 Massachusetts Ave NW, Washington DC 20007, ✆ (202) 333 4507, ✉ (202) 333 4509.

Embassy of Kyrgyzstan: 1732 Wisconsin Ave NW, Washington DC 20007, ✆ 202 338 5143, ✉ 202 338 5139. Also handles visas for Canadians.

Embassy of Pakistan: 2315 Massachusetts Ave NW, Washington, DC 20008, ✆ (202) 939 6200.

Pakistan consulate: 12 East 65th Street, New York, NY, ✆ (212) 879 5800.

Russian Embassy: 1825 Phelps Place NW, Washington, DC 20008, ✆ (202) 332 1483.

Russian consulates: 9 East 91st St, New York, NY 010128, ✆ (212) 348 0926; 2790 Green Street, San Francisco, CA 94123, ✆ (415) 922 6642.

in China, Pakistan, and Central Asia

There are Chinese embassies in Islamabad, Almaty and Bishkek, Kazak embassies and consulates in Běijīng, Ürümqi, Islamabad and Bishkek, Kyrgyz embassies in Běijīng and Almaty (and Kyrgyz visas are available from the Russian embassy in Islamabad), and Pakistani embassies in Běijīng, Almaty and Bishkek. Not all of them welcome independent travellers, so read the details given in the 'Onward visas' sections of the relevant cities carefully.

Entertainment

In China karaoke is king, in some cases spilling out of bars and restaurants onto the pavements, and not just the sound, but the equipment and the 'singers' too. There are increasing numbers of nightclubs which alternate karaoke and dancing through the evening. In all these places drink prices tend to be high, sometimes astronomical. If male, beware the pretty girl who comes over to talk to you. Conversing with her is adding between ¥50 ($6) and ¥200 ($24) to the bill, even if you don't speak Mandarin.

Traditional Chinese entertainments such as Chinese opera and acrobatics are available in bigger cities or wherever visitors gather in sufficient numbers, but usually in edited-for-tourists versions where there will be few Chinese in the audience. Much more interesting backstreet low-budget versions can be found, where the older generation will talk, eat and drink their way through the performance, leaving behind mounds of melon seed husks and peanut shells. Younger people are in the video salons watching pirated versions of Western and Hong Kong films. The older hotels often have their own theatres and rustle up quick shows for tour groups. In minority areas this will include performances of minority dances and music.

In Bishkek and Almaty familiar operas, ballets and concerts are available, but the institutions that offer them are facing major financial problems. Traditional Kazak and Kyrgyz folk music is on the rise, sometimes performed in the formal setting of a theatre. The circus remains popular, and both Almaty and Bishkek have permanent concrete 'tents'.

The fortunate may stumble across a game of *ulak-tartysh*, a kind of mounted rugby with a goat carcass for a ball, in Kazakstan, Kyrgyzstan or Xīnjiāng. Kazak and Kyrgyz people throughout Central Asia also play a mounted form of kiss-chase (*kiss-ku* or *kesh-kumai*). In Pakistan, the April and November polo tournaments in Gilgit are further examples of mounted mayhem.

Festivals and Public Holidays

Chinese public holidays: 1 January, Chinese New Year (Spring Festival—a lunar holiday around the beginning of February), 1 May (Labour Day), 1 and 2 Oct and (National Day—founding of the PRC). Offices and businesses will be closed on these days. Chinese New Year officially lasts for three days, but its impact is much greater as all public transport is booked for days either side by everybody heading home for family reunions and feasting. Unless you're on an organized tour, being in China at that time means staying put in one place. In an unusual display of civil disobedience, regulations prohibiting fireworks are ignored by almost everybody.

Other holidays which receive observance by parts of society include 8 March (International Women's Day), 4 May (Youth Day), 1 June (Children's Day), 1 July (Anniversary of the founding of the Chinese Communist Party), and 1 August (Anniversary of the Founding of the PLA—expect the Torugart Pass to be shut).

Important traditional festivals with no official day off, all lunar, include the Lantern Festival sometime between mid-February to mid-March (lantern hanging and riddle posing), the early April Tomb Sweeping Day (visiting and tidying grave sites, paying respect to ancestors), the Dragon Boat Festival in mid-June (boat races, special snacks), and the Mid-Autumn Festival in late September or early October (moon watching and 'moon cakes').

Kazak public holidays: 1 January and often 2 (New Year), 28 January (Constitution Day), 8 March (International Women's Day), 22 March (Nauryz—*see* Islamic holidays below), 1 May Labour Day ('International Day of Workers' Solidarity'), 9 May (Victory Day), 30 August (Independence Day), 25 October (Republic Day). All state and commercial organizations including shops and the international border are shut. Some of these holidays are leftovers from the Soviet period and may gradually be abandoned, although people are reluctant to give up their holidays just for politics.

Kyrgyz public holidays: 1 January and 2, 8 March, 5 May (Constitution Day), 9 May, 13 June (Commemoration Day), 31 August (Independence Day).

Pakistan public holidays: 23 March (Pakistan Day), 1 May (Labour Day), 14 August (Independence Day), 6 September (Defence of Pakistan Day), plus most of the Islamic holidays.

Some Islamic Holidays: The first day of Ramadan (Ramazan, Ruza), a month-long period of fasting during daylight hours observed in Pakistan and patchily amongst Muslims in Central Asia and China. Like most Muslim holidays it is not only lunar but advances every year. From 1997's 31 December (1 Ramadan 1418 by the Muslim calendar) subtract 11 days each year to find the date for 1998 and beyond. Tempers can be a little shorter than usual during this period.

Nauryz (Nawiriz, Navruz, Noruz) is another lunar festival (which actually pre-dates Islam) celebrated around mid-March, when Kazaks, Kyrgyz and Uighurs commemorate their ancestors with feasting, picnicking, horse-racing, *ulak-tartysh* (horseback goat-carcass rugby), tug-of-war, wrestling, etc. There's also a special meal involving mare's intestines with fillings. It was officially reinstated for Soviet Muslims in 1989, but its exact date varies between countries.

Corban (Korban Bairam, Qurban Bayram) is a three-day holiday in early April, when a feast commemorates Abraham's agreement in principle to sacrifice his son. Kashgar is probably the best place to be: thousands throng Idkah Sq for dancing, high-wire walking and other festivities.

Islamic New Year will be in late April in 1998.

Other Islamic holidays with partial observance (1997 dates): 27 January, 6 February, 9-10 February, 17 May, 17 July, 28 November, 15 December. Ismailis such as the Tajik minority in Xīnjiāng and the people of Hunza and Gojal in northern Pakistan have two extra feasts: the anniversary of the accession of the current Imam (11 July) and that of his birthday (13 December), for once not lunar.

Christian holidays: These may be observed by the Russian populations of Bishkek and Almaty, but are Russian Orthodox and often different from those familiar in the West. Some will involve sumptuous religious ceremonies and processions with icons. These are 1997 dates, so expect changes when the feasts are movable (Good Friday, Easter, Ascension): 6 Jan uary (Christmas Eve), 7 January (Christmas Day), 19 January (Epiphany), 15 February (Presentation of Christ in the Temple), 10 March (Start of Lent), 7 April (Annunciation), 20 April (Palm Sunday), 25 April (Good Friday), 27 April (Orthodox Easter), 5 June (Ascension), 15 June (Pentecost), 19 August (Transfiguration), 28 August (Assumption of the Virgin Mary), 21 September (Nativity of the Virgin Mary), 27 September (Elevation of the Life-Giving Cross), 14 November (All Saints' Day), 15 November (All Souls' Day).

Lamaist/Buddhist festivals: These are all lunar and seem to vary from temple to temple, and often attract large numbers of Tibetans and Mongolians. If you can establish when these dates are by the solar calendar you are likely to see 'sunning the Buddha', elaborate religious dances, and mass chanting, accompanied by colourful fairs. For instance, at **Kumbum** the key festivals are 8–15 of the 1st and 4th lunar months, 3–8 of the 6th, and 20–26 of the 9th. At **Labrang** the great Monlam religious meeting takes place annually 4–16 of the 1st lunar month, and there are festivals on the 8th day of the 2nd lunar month, during the 6th, 1–15 of the 7th, and the 29th of the 9th. At **Wǔdāng Zhào** the Mani Fair from the 24th day of the 7th lunar month to the 1st day of the 8th lunar.

Other festivals: In early spring Tajiks in the Pamirs have **Sowing Day** (Tehmozwat), which includes prayers for a good harvest and the splashing of water on guests.

At the festival known as **18 April**, the Sibo (Xībó) people celebrate the anniversary of the 1764 setting out of 1018 officers and soldiers from the northeast to strengthen the border defences in the northwest. There's feasting, music and dancing, wrestling, horse-racing, and archery (at which the Sibo are particularly skilled—some are members of China's Olympic team). Despite its name this festival can occur as early as 5 April, being another lunar holiday, and is celebrated in the Sibo Autonomous County near Yīníng.

The annual **Gilgit Festival** is at the beginning of November, and includes a week-long polo tournament and commemorates the Gilgit rising against the Maharajah of Kashmir in 1947.

*The Chinese are remarkably good cooks, and, though the dishes are
often served in a way which is not very palatable to Europeans, there is
no doubt that the actual cooking is excellent.*

Captain Frank E. Younghusband, *The Heart of a Continent,* 1896

Clearly confused, Younghusband was writing before the Chinese invasion of high street and main street made sweet and sour pork a commonplace of the Western diet. But the Chinese who opened restaurants overseas have all adapted their cuisine to local taste, and it's often sweeter, fattier, and generally less palatable than the real thing. Food in China is cheap, plentiful and delicious, and even without including local and minority specialities offers far more choice than most Chinese restaurants overseas. Xīnjiāng and Central Asia offer simple lamb and rice dishes, filling rope-like noodles, and a variety of disc-like loaves that can make a welcome change from rice after lengthy travel in China. Pakistan has familiar cheap and filling curries, including the recently trendy 'Balti' dishes, and very plain beef and chicken dishes.

Eating Out in China

*The famous bird's nest soup, I never tasted. Mr Chu solemnly told us
that it is considered a great luxury and is very expensive. 'But no one
really likes it,' he added.*

Diana Shipton, *The Antique Land,* 1950

In fact the Chinese eat all sorts of things that much of the rest of the world would shy from, but for those who prefer to stick to recognizable parts of the animal and vegetable kingdoms, there's no need to fear. The names of several staple dishes, and the characters for a range of meats and vegetables as well as local specialities described in the text, are given in **Language**, pp.525–9.

Waitresses stand over you from the moment that they give you the menu. Minority and speciality restaurants aside, it rarely contains surprises, usually consisting of a greatest hits list of the main Chinese cooking schools. The Chinese discuss amongst themselves what they want to eat and then look in the menu to see how much it is. Decision making for them thus doesn't take long, and your waitress may either become impatient, or good-naturedly start making recommendations. In heavily touristed areas letting the waitress decide for you will seriously damage your wallet. In mainstream Hàn restaurants if you don't see what you like on the menu, don't worry—just ask and it can always be made, as long as it's Chinese. Don't ask for pork if the restaurant is Huí (or Uighur). While a few dishes have names that don't give much idea of their contents (such as 'Pock-marked Old Woman's Tofu'), many have names that include a cooking verb, and the ingredients. Despite the simplicity of many of the dishes, no two restaurants produce them tasting exactly the same. In general expect food to get spicier as you travel westwards across China. Take with you a photocopy of a local restaurant's bi-lingual menu, and try ordering with that. Note that the characters used will be full form, rather than the simpler modern style, and so won't correspond to what you see in China, but should be understood nevertheless.

Roadside noodle stalls and hole-in-the-wall restaurants don't have much of a menu, and it's usually written up in chalk on the wall. Only restaurants that are used to tourists have an

English menu, and this can often be a bad thing. Outside the joint-venture and top-flight hotels, it will frequently have higher prices than the Chinese-language one for the same dishes. Some restaurants have different menus but both in Chinese. If this turns out to be the case, leave. If there are credit card signs on the door, then prices will be higher, but only the surroundings will improve (and only Chinese credit cards will be acceptable). If your chopsticks are sealed in sellophane or printed paper sleeves, if there's a small packet of tissues next to your plate, or if the tea cup is a small bowl with a lid containing a mixture of tea, herbs and dried berries looking like a handful of builders' rubble, expect a cover charge of ¥5–10 per person. (The tea, known as 'Eight Treasures Tea', also contains a lump of rock sugar, and has a very refreshing fruitiness.) There will usually be no cutlery, only chopsticks, so practise using these at your local Chinese restaurant before you leave home. If there *is* cutlery, you are probably eating in a restaurant inside a Běijīng international standard hotel, and your surroundings will be rather more pleasant than your bill.

Always avoid restaurants near major tourist attractions. Food will be poor, portions half-size, prices mysteriously in the hundreds rather than tens of *yuán* range, whatever the menu said, and you may be prevented from leaving or threatened with violence if you refuse to pay up. Chinese tourists suffer similar humiliations at these places, if not on quite the same scale.

In all restaurants point to the prices of dishes as you order, and keep a total so that the waitress knows that you know. Shenanigans with the bill are commonplace. Don't allow staff to shepherd you into a private room, as prices will immediately begin to rise, and exorbitant demands can be made from you while you are safely out of sight of other customers (although most of them think you should pay more, anyway). There is no tipping, no service charge, and no charge for chopsticks or tea (except as mentioned above). Never let yourself run low on small change, so that when there are attempts to overcharge you, you can leave exactly the right money on the table and walk out.

Breakfast is perhaps the most difficult and unsatisfactory meal for the Western palate, since plain thin rice gruel, plain steamed bread rolls, and pickles are all most restaurants can manage. At street stalls there will be oily deep-fried dough sticks, and small pots of yoghurt in most areas. You may want to skip straight to dishes that would equally do for lunch, such as noodle soups, *jiǎozi* (like ravioli), fried variants (*guōtiē*), or *bāozi* (steamed, stuffed buns).

Single-bowl noodle dishes come in a variety of forms, with finer noodles in Hàn restaurants shading into thicker, rope-like noodles in Huí and Uighur areas. The latter are invariably peppery, and called *làmián*, the Mandarin version of the Central Asian *laghman*. *Là* means spicy, but *lā,* an alternative name, means 'pulled', which reflects how the noodles are made from enormous skipping ropes of dough, repeatedly tossed and twisted in the air. There are noodles in soup (*tāngmián*) and fried ones (*chǎomián*) in Hàn restaurants, and versions where the noodles have been sliced into small pieces and fried in Uighur places. There are also single-portion fried rice dishes, and in Xīnjiāng the equivalent of Central Asian pilau or *plov,* fried rice with strips of turnip and mutton.

In China, people rarely eat alone, and restaurant dining is based around the proposition that a group will order several dishes and share them. Rice is a filler not a constituent part of the meal. If you want the rice for eating *with* your main dishes rather than after them you'll have to ask for it. Where there are two columns of prices, the lower one is for slightly smaller portions—usually the smaller dishes are still 80% of the original and you'll save perhaps ¥2–3 on a ¥18 dish.

Chinese cooking tends to leave the bone in the chopped meat: you separate bone from meat in your mouth and put the rejected bones on the table in a pile at the side of your plate. To avoid this, select dishes with the key characters *sī* (strips), *piàn* (slices), or *dīng* (boneless pieces)—*see* language section. Fish and seafood should generally be avoided, certainly outside of Běijīng, and the further you go west. Fish on sale is often farmed and tasteless, as well as bony, and there is no guarantee that frozen seafood has been properly kept. **Vegetarians** will have no problems in China, except occasionally in making themselves understood. Useful phrases are given in the language section. In addition to vegetables stir-fried in a variety of ways, there are various *dòufu* (tofu) dishes, noodle soups without meat, and other standards such as egg fried with tomato. If in doubt, go to the kitchen (easily achievable with a little mime) and simply point to the vegetables you want cooked together. Occasionally you may meet with incomprehensible protests based on the supposed incompatibility of certain 'sour' with certain 'sweet' vegetables, but in the end what the crazy *lǎo wài* wants will be produced. Vegans, however, will have difficulties.

Pork is the main meat of the Chinese (often called *dà ròu*, 'great meat'), but it won't be found frequently in Muslim minority areas, Kazakstan or Krygyzstan outside the capitals, or at all in Pakistan. Lamb takes over from pork in Central Asia, appearing as *shashlyk* (kebabs), in noodle dishes, and a wide variety of other forms.

One considerable annoyance when eating out in China is a centuries-old game played wherever groups of men are dining together. Two players each simultaneously thrust out one hand with a number of fingers showing and bellow a number which they guess will be equal to the total number of fingers displayed (so between zero and ten). This is rhythmically repeated until someone gets the answer right, when his opponent is required to 'drink a cup.' As the game proceeds and the drunkenness increases, the volume becomes ever louder, and since several games may be progressing at different tables, staying in the restaurant may become intolerable. What puzzles visitors most is that, while shop assistants are universally incapable of adding together two numbers without using an abacus, these men can simultaneously shout one number, show another, and add two numbers together, all while drunk.

Foreign food is widely available in Běijīng and in the big international hotels elsewhere, but at Western prices, and often not quite right. Several fast-food chains can be found in Běijīng and Xī'ān, and bakeries, too, that can provide baked bread for a change from rice and Chinese steamed bread.

Eating Out in Kazakstan and Kyrgyzstan

During the feast they serve the guest the sheep's boiled head on a plate. The guest must eat the brain. Then he must pluck out and eat one of the eyes. The host eats the other eye. In this way the knots of brotherhood are tied. It is an experience one does not quickly forget.

Ryszard Kapuscinski, *Imperium*, 1993

Most visitors will not be subjected to a banquet, but if invited to one may be asked to carve up a sheep's head. Rules vary as to who should be accorded the left and right ears, and so on.

Consult deeply with the nearest English speaker before attending. For visitors to Almaty and Bishkek, the restaurant fundamentals are *laghman* spicy noodles, *manty* which resemble Chinese *jiǎozi* (noodle bags of meat and vegetables), and *plov*, the rice, lamb and turnip stir fry. Street food is juicy *shashlyk*, kebabs of lamb, and *lepeshka* (pronounced *lipioshka*) bread. There's still a heavy Russian presence on menus, with hearty soups, beef stroganoff, *bishteks* (like hamburgers) and *kotlyet* (cutlet—ground meat, covered in breadcrumbs), sour cabbage, and stuffed pancakes with cottage cheese (*blini*). There's also plain, fried chicken.

Almaty and Bishkek also have a wide range of foreign restaurants with excellent menus, but quite highly priced.

Eating Out in Pakistan

Those in search of the familiar will find Pakistan easy. Western foods are widely understood and produced, as well as excellent cheap curries, often eaten with pieces of nan bread rather than knives and forks. Above Gilgit on the KKH, menus tend to be limited and plain, especially in spring.

Drinking

Everywhere mentioned in this book, the best drink, and usually the safest, is **tea**—*chá* in China, and *chai* elsewhere. Tea automatically comes with your meal in China, and is cheap everywhere else. Don't expect milk, except in Pakistan, where it will probably have been boiled together with the tea, water and sugar. If you want to add sugar to Chinese tea you'll need to carry it with you, as most restaurants will (quite rightly) find this incomprehensible. There are thermoses of boiled water in all hotel rooms in China, however primitive, and thermoses or boilers on trains, so carry tea with you. Tea is available at short notice at any Pakistani hotel, and floor ladies in Kyrgyz and Kazak hotels can usually be cajoled into providing hot water (*tipitok*) or tea for nothing or a few tenge or som. Good **coffee** is not easy to find anywhere. Instant coffee sachets from Western manufacturers are available in China's larger towns, and in versions where the coffee has already been mixed with some powdered milk and a little sugar. Beyond the most upmarket hotels, and Western fast-food joints in Běijīng, this is the nearest you will get to real coffee. Real milk is also rare outside these establishments and a few of the glitzier groceries in larger towns.

Locally produced **mineral water** is widely available in China and Pakistan, and imported brands in Bishkek and Almaty. Do not drink unboiled tap water, or in China and Pakistan even brush your teeth with it (use mineral water or boiled water that's been left to cool instead).

There is no escape from the **soft drink** multinationals. Coca-Cola already has 17 plants in China and in 1996 sold six billion bottles, about three times as much as Pepsi. Local competitors tend to be rather ersatz with the exception of the orange and honey flavoured sports drink, Jiànlìbǎo ('build strength treasure'), widely available. Some bottled and canned fruit juices are available at glitzier groceries in bigger Chinese cities and in Almaty and Bishkek. Restaurants in the CIS often offer *kompot*, a diluted mixed-berry juice.

Alcohol is most commonly consumed in China in the form of beer (*píjiǔ*), made in a lager-style inherited from a turn-of-the-century German brewery still in production in Qīngdǎo on the east coast. Qīngdǎo (Tsingtao) is one of the few nationally distributed brands, and there are dozens of local varieties to try as you travel. Chinese wine (*pútaojiǔ*) is execrable. When

German archaeologist Albert von Le Coq discovered the walls of one cave temple to be covered in a layer of white mould, he knew instantly what to do. 'I fetched Chinese brandy—no European can drink it—and washed down all the walls with a sponge.'

'Wine' is commonly used in translation for all kinds of other alcoholic drinks which have nothing to do with grapes, including *bái jiŭ* ('white spirits') made from rice or sorghum, some of which are pleasant and tame to the palate, but can unexpectedly bite you if you over-indulge.

Alcohol is banned in Pakistan, although with a little effort it's available to non-Muslim foreigners in big hotels, or following the purchase of a licence. Bishkek and Almaty have a vast range of familiar imported drinks from US beers to top-of-the-range French brandies, champagnes, and every vodka known to even the most avid researcher. *Koumis*, the centuries-old drink of the Kyrgyz and Kazak nomads, made from fermented mare's milk, should be tried at least once. Try not to refuse at least a taste of any offered to you (most likely on your way from Bishkek to Kashgar).

Food on the Move

In China rather unsatisfying biscuits (cookies) or peanuts (*in* their shells), make the best accompaniments to bus travel, although Chinese buses always have food stops. On trains you can take advantage of the boiled water (*kāi shuĭ*) from thermos or boiler to make the instant noodles available in shops, or at bus and railway stations. Carrying a mug is essential. A wide range of fruits in syrup (*tángshuĭ*) are sold, such as *tángshuĭmíjú* (mandarin orange segments in syrup), which can make a refreshing change in hot weather. The jars these fruits come in you will already have seen being used by all and sundry to carry eternally topped-up brews of swamp-bottom tea. Plastic-wrapped bread rolls are very white, dry and sweet. Easily portable and safe and easy-to-eat fruits include bananas and mandarin oranges (satsumas) in season. Apples and pears *must* be peeled, and with care (*see* **Health** below). Imported biscuits and chocolate are ever more widely available, but watch out for brands that pass themselves off as foreign while not, and for fake packaging.

Good wholesome, heavy, Russian-style bread is available in the markets and shops of Almaty and Bishkek, with a variety of meats and cheeses for sandwich-making, and tinned goods, excellent peaches and other fruit. There's roadside *shashlyk* and other food on the way from Bishkek to the border, but nothing from there to Kashgar. It's essential to have a good stock for the train from Almaty to Ürümqi, as food provision is unreliable. Familiar brands of snacks are widely available in Pakistani shops.

Guides

Guides in China are employees of either one of China's usually rapacious travel agents, or of sites, such as Dūnhuáng's Mògāo Kū, where guided tours are compulsory. Some know their material quite well, but few can produce more than a prepared script, or have any idea of an alternative to the government-approved view. Those employed at sites tend to be better than those belonging to agencies. Only the most major sites have guides who can speak English, and very few indeed who can speak any other language. Be particularly careful if your tour guide takes you shopping. The choice of shop is almost certainly not fortuitous, and the guide is not an independent and trustworthy advisor, but someone who will later be picking up commission from the shop.

In Běijīng you may occasionally be approached by students or young professionals wishing to improve their English, and who offer to show you around. This is a *quid pro quo*, not a paid arrangement, although you should offer to cover entrance fees and transport costs, and it's an excellent opportunity to get a first-hand account of daily life in China. Don't expect detailed historical or cultural information from your 'guide'.

In Kazakstan and Kyrgyzstan, guides are often highly qualified people whose occupations (doctor, physicist, geologist) no longer offer them a living wage, and who are living off their language skills. To find that your interpreter has a PhD is not unknown, and many are extremely conscientious, and pleasant travelling companions. In Pakistan there are experienced trekking guides as well as charlatans. Try to get a recommendation from other travellers before setting off into the wilderness, and define the length of the trek, the services you require, and the fee to be paid when you return with great clarity, and brook no renegotiation.

Health

What follows is a general introduction to the health problems you may encounter and how to avoid or deal with them. But remember that new medicines are constantly being developed, medical opinion about the best method of treatment sometimes changes, and the health problems themselves change. Family doctors are rarely a good source of up-to-date information about travel medicine but should be able to point you to specialist travel clinics and hospital tropical medicine departments. As some vaccinations cannot be taken together or involve multiple injections, make contact at least three months before you plan to travel. In most developed countries these injections are no longer free, if they ever were, and if you need to have several the expense can be considerable.

Before You Leave

Immunization against typhus in 1935 Běijīng:

> They were thin, wrinkled, resigned old men; beggars by profession. They sat on three hard chairs in a small room opening off a laboratory and full of guinea-pigs in cages. Their ragged trousers were rolled up above their knees and to the dwindled calves of each were clamped a number of little shallow boxes. The sides of the boxes which pressed against the flesh were made of gauze, or something like it; and each box contained 500 lice. For two hours every day, and for the wage of twelve Chinese dollars a month, the three old men pastured, between them, some 18,000 lice.

Peter Fleming, *News from Tartary*, 1936

The essence of 30 lice went into each of the three necessary anti-typhus injections.

Begin by making sure that the basic immunizations you should have even at home are up to date, and get boosters if necessary. These include **polio**, **diphtheria** (especially important for the former Soviet republics) and **tetanus**.

In China and Central Asia it is best to carry as much paperwork as possible, including one of the internationally recognized yellow booklets giving a record of vaccinations, the *International Certificate of Vaccination*. Most of the individuals employed at Central Asian borders to enquire into your health recognize these, but cannot make head nor tail of them, and so may let you pass even if you haven't had the inoculation they are looking for. Health checks are rarely made except at land borders, and even there are usually perfunctory for visitors from developed nations.

The need for other inoculations will depend on exactly where you travel in China, Pakistan, Kyrgyzstan and Kazakstan, and the time of year, but may include those for the following diseases:

Typhoid fever, caught from contaminated food and water. The vaccine won't completely protect you, but can be taken as four oral doses over eight days, and lasts for seven years.

Meningococcal meningitis, an infection of the lining of the brain caught from others with it in the same way you catch a cold. A single injection covers you for three years.

Cholera, an infection of the intestine for which a new vaccine has recently been developed in oral form. Despite the World Health Organization's ruling on the matter, there are occasional checks at the Pakistan–China border for cholera vaccination, and PIA staff will not sell you an air ticket to Almaty without sight of a vaccination record.

If you are arriving from a country with **yellow fever**, you may be asked for proof of vaccination. No inoculations are required for former Soviet Central Asia, but both Pakistan and China require proof of immunization.

Hepatitis comes in a form communicated quite easily through shared utensils and low hygiene (hepatitis A), and in more dangerous forms that require the exchange of body fluids (mainly hepatitis B). Immunization against hepatitis A is important because of poor hygiene standards, and many doctors recommend immunization against hepatitis B to avoid further complications should you receive emergency treatment with contaminated blood or equipment. Both diseases attack the liver and cause weakness and lassitude, but hepatitis B can be life-threatening. For hepatitis A, one injection gives one year's protection, and a second a year later will cover you for at least 10 years. For hepatitis B there are two injections given one month apart and a booster six months later, giving 90% protection for a lifetime. (Fans of alternative medicine may like to know that the Chinese Ministry of Health and the State Administration of Traditional Chinese Medicine recently recommended an intravenous drip made from 'sophora-rhubarb' to cure viral hepatitis.)

Japanese B Encephalitis is a severe brain infection carried by mosquitoes to which you may be exposed in rural areas especially during rainy periods. Three injections are needed over a one-month period to give two years of coverage which can be boosted if necessary.

Mosquito-born **malaria** comes in various forms, and you may need to take two different prophylactic drugs, depending upon the time you travel, and whether you venture into rural areas. You must begin to take these drugs *before* you leave home, and *for four weeks after you leave the malarial area.*

Rabies is endemic in Central Asia. Treat all pets with caution, and give a wide berth to any animal exhibiting erratic behaviour. Long-stayers should consider vaccination.

While You Are There

Colds and sore throats are the common lot of those travelling in China for more than the briefest of periods, so if there is a proprietary medicine you usually use for relief, bring a supply with you. The causes are the general lack of hygiene in China (particularly the spitting, which can also transmit diphtheria, meningitis, and other illnesses) and the lack of resistance to unfamiliar versions of these everyday diseases. Spitting has a long history.

> And everyone of the chiefs and nobles carries with him a handsome little vessel to spit in whilst he remain in the Hall of Audience—for no one dares spit on the floor of the hall,—and when he hath spitten he covers it up and puts it aside.

Marco Polo, The Travels, 13th-century Yule-Cordier edition

Some of these problems come in the slightly more serious form of upper respiratory tract infections. Chinese doctors will prescribe mild doses of antibiotics, sometimes with additional Chinese medicines, or you can ask your doctor at home to prescribe a course of broad spectrum antibiotic to take with you. Remember, however, that the level of pollution in China's larger cities, with airborne particulates as high as ten times the internationally recommended maximum, is enough to give many people respiratory problems for a while, which antibiotics won't cure. Westerners have in general taken far too many in the past, and caution should be used. If you do begin, make sure you complete the course.

Diarrhoea, vomiting, and a variety of **bowel problems** are commonplace, and caused by poor toilet hygiene and bad food. Wash your hands as often as you can (usually not possible at public toilets) and make use of the bathroom in your room (if you have one) in preference to other options. If faced with ancient gnawed chopsticks demand disposable ones, universally available (small particles of food embedded in chopsticks can also transmit hepatitis A). Do not drink the water—this is no time to be macho, not even local people do. Drink tea, bottled water, and soft drinks. Everywhere you go there are thermoses of boiled water to hand, even on trains and in the most undistinguished backwater hotel. Boiling won't get rid of the heavy metals and other contaminants in the water, but is fairly successful at killing bacteria.

Remember in China that the waste you deposit in the public toilet today is tomorrow's fertilizer. Do not swim in China's lakes or rivers. Do not eat salads or any fruit that cannot be peeled and, having touched the outside, don't touch the inside before eating. Avoid fruit with damaged and broken skin, and all water melons. Eat only piping hot food that has been freshly cooked for you. If you do get diarrhoea it is essential to replace lost fluids. Drink canned sugary soft drinks and salty water, or take with you a few sachets of electrolyte replacement which can be dissolved in boiled water which has been allowed to cool. This is better than taking tablets.

Cases of **sexually transmitted diseases** are rapidly increasing in China. Visiting students and other long-stayers are asked to provide proof of a recent AIDS test, but not those on tourist visas. The number of HIV-positive individuals in China is vague, but some experts have estimated that there are more than 100,000 carriers in the country, and note that cases of other more easy to detect sexually transmitted diseases are rapidly rising, particularly gonorrhoea and syphilis, both extremely nasty.

Inoculated or not, avoid **mosquitoes** by covering up from dusk to dawn, and using mosquito repellent. The summer **sun** in the deserts and at high altitudes can very quickly damage your skin, and even in China's smoggy cities is potent. Keep yourself well covered with sunscreen, carry the tube with you for topping up, wear sunglasses with proper UV protection, and consider a hat, however 'uncool' this may look.

Altitude sickness only affects some people, but can be dangerous, and usually occurs after a rapid ascent to above 2500m. It's considered best to gain height slowly, and always to sleep at a place lower than the highest you've attained that day. If giddiness, nausea and sleeplessness don't go away, the only treatment is rapid descent. Avoid drugs, alcohol and nicotine.

Smoke cannot be avoided in China, where with rare exceptions no-smoking signs are purely decorative. 350 million active and 460 million passive smokers get through more than 150 *billion* cigarettes a year, nearly a third of the world's total. The Chinese are still used to obeying rules, and pointing to no-smoking signs is often enough to make them guiltily put out their cigarettes or move to where smoking is permitted, such as at the ends of railway carriages.

It is probably not politically correct to attack **Chinese traditional medicine**, but there has been little rigorous testing of the remedies or the simplistic assumptions behind them (for impotence eat tiger penis). While much is herbal, some treatments involve parts of endangered species, and substances such as bear bile, extracted under conditions so inhumane as to defy description. If you wish to experiment with acupuncture, ensure that disposable needles are being used or select a more hygienic country in which to turn yourself into a pin cushion. If you need a **doctor** head for the nearest international hotel, or failing that any other large hotel that accepts foreigners, all of which have clinics, and can usually both prescribe and dispense more familiar remedies. Don't take chances with Chinese or Central Asian **hospitals** unless absolutely necessary. Take out travel insurance which covers you for emergency repatriation and call your embassy or consulate for advice.

Internet and Other Computer Resources

For those without Internet accounts, much of what follows will be incomprehensible. The Internet is simply a system of interconnected computers using a variety of software programs to store and transfer information. Much of this information is unedited drivel, but there is also some that can be of considerable use to the Silk Route traveller, including first-hand accounts of your destination from those who have just returned. Don't go out and buy a modem and an Internet account just to find out about travel, even if you have a computer already. A library and a telephone remain more authoritative and cost-efficient research tools. However, for those with accounts, relevant email and web page addresses are given throughout this book. You can also send email to Cadogan (*guides@cadogan.demon.co.uk*), where your comments will be welcome, and forwarded to the author where appropriate.

Newsgroups

The obvious starting point is *rec.travel.asia*. In amongst peevish complaints about lost credit cards, smutty postings about sex tourism to Bangkok, and the inappropriate commercial material of travel agents (please boycott all agents who post there) can be found useful nuggets of information. To make the best of the group, read this book carefully, then post a *detailed* question. With luck there will be informative postings to the group, and you will receive email responses, too. If you post a vague query ('What are the best cities in China to visit?'), you'll be told to read a guide book, or that 'Běijīng is kinda cool', which is all you'll deserve.

If you are interested in making contact with travel agents and other commercial organizations, post on *rec.travel.marketplace*, which is where this kind of query belongs.

Another obvious news group is *soc.culture.china*, but as only the briefest of readings with tell you, this is the home of people with chips on their shoulders about Taiwanese independence, interracial marriages, the superiority of Chinese people over everybody else, the greatness of the late Dèng Xiǎopíng, and so on. *talk.politics.china* is much the same.

Of the groups that you can only read and not post to, *clari.world.asia.central* and *clari.world.asia.china* are rapidly being replaced by new media such as *Pointcast* which will deliver information to your computer's desktop.

Mailing Lists and News by email

Mailing lists are usually an improvement on news groups because they are often moderated by the list owner, who keeps debate at a level above the infantile norm of much of the Internet, and prohibits commercial postings. In all cases when subscribing leave the subject line blank unless otherwise instructed, and turn off your signature. Read the acknowledgement message you receive carefully, and *keep it* so you have a reference of the list address, its administrator's address, and the address for signing off, often all different.

The Oriental-List is run for the discussion of travel in China. Send a note requesting subscription to *pnh@istar.ca*.

On CENASIA (Central Asia), discussion ranges from etiquette at Kyrgyz banquets, via the etymology of Kazak words, to Uighur independence movements. Members include academics, foreign government aid workers and residents. Send the message 'subscribe CENASIA *Your Name*' to *listserv@mcgill1.bitnet* or *listserv@vm1.mcgill.ca*.

China News Digest is published every other day by a volunteer group of Chinese students in the USA and, set up in the wake of the Tiān'ān Mén events of 1989, contains a summary of news reports about China from various unchecked but usually reliable sources. Despite occasionally succumbing to we-Chinese-versus-the-world rhetoric, it is generally balanced and informative. For further information on the list server nearest you, and how to subscribe, write to *cnd-info@cnd.org*. A Chinese language publication called HXWZ is also available.

The Open Media Research Institute's Daily Digest of news about the former Soviet Union and Eastern Europe is unfortunately now defunct, but a replacement is provided by Radio Free Europe/Radio Liberty, although this organization perhaps has more of an agenda than OMRI. Send the messsage 'subscribe RFERL-L *Your Name*' to *listserv@listserv.buffalo.edu*.

A mixture of reports from Pakistani media and cricket scores is available by sending the message 'SUB PAKISTAN *Your Name*' to *listserv@asuvm.inre.asu.edu*.

The World Wide Web

Using one of the Web's search engines to look for information on one of the countries in this book or on 'silk route' will give you thousands of pages, many of them privately owned and promoting themselves as definitive while containing little more than links to other pages, which contain links back the way you came. Clicking on much of the remainder will produce error messages. Even commercial pages can be years out of date. A few useful leads are given below.

One of the areas in which the Web shows promise is in last-minute air ticket discounting. Most airline's Web pages are called *www.*name-of-airline*.com*, but some are foolish enough to introduce variations and you'll have to resort to a search engine. For an example with cheap fares for US residents flying to Asia, try *http://www.cathay-usa.com/*. These tickets are *only* available to Internet users. A fine personal compilation of Central Asian connections and constantly updated timetables is kept at *http://www.rz.uni-frankfurt.de/~puersuen/*. CND's website *http://www.cnd.org/* has back issues of their publications, pictures and other information, plus a variety of useful software for Macintosh and other platforms, such as that allowing you to see Chinese text in mail and newsgroup postings, and to view and print out their Chinese language HXWZ magazine. In the Internet world there are two main Chinese character formats: *gb* which has the simplified characters of Modern Standard Chinese, and *big5* which has the full form still in use in Tāiwān and Chinese communities overseas. There's even software which will read out Chinese documents to you, if you have a Macintosh or your other computer is suitably equipped.

Inside China Today has a good selection of news about China and links to other professional sites, *http://www.insidechina.com/*. Quite absurdly, *China Daily*, China's English-language propaganda sheet, now charges for access to its web page (*http://www.chinadaily.net/cd.html*), but some of its less misleading stories also appear in *Inside China Today*. The *South China Morning Post* (*http://www.scmp.com/news/*) and the *Hong Kong Standard* (*http://www.hkstandard.com/online/news/*) have free web pages and were often the first to break stories of unrest or other problems in China that might otherwise been suppressed or grossly misrepresented, but have now been tamed.

The *Inner Asia/Silkroad Study Group* runs an incomplete site with details of their activities, news briefs and material on travel at *http://www.silk-road.com*. You can also subscribe to a newsletter. Send the message 'subscribe *your email address*' to *iassg-request@lists.best.com*.

The *Interactive Central Asia Resource Project* has a list of experts on Central Asian matters, mostly serious academics and others with professional expertise in the region, *http://www.rockbridge.net/personal/bichel/experts.htp*.

The *rec.travel Library* at *http://www.solutions.net/rec-travel/asia/* has links to pages on China, Kyrgyzstan and Pakistan, including personal trip accounts, US State Department advisory notices, and the CIA World Factbook (not nearly as exciting as it sounds). For an excellent collection of links to many kinds of high quality resources to do with China try *http://freenet.buffalo.edu/~cb863/china.html*.

The US Dept of Commerce's *BISNIS* site (Business Information Service for the Newly Independent States) at *http://www.iep.doc.gov/* is evidence of the White House's leadership in government use of the Internet. *http://www.whitehouse.gov/* has links for the US government's view on where it's safe to travel and what precautions to take. The British equivalent is the Foreign and Commonwealth Office's pages *http://www.fco.gov.uk/index.html*.

The addresses of Web pages for specialist book suppliers and travel agents are given in the relevant sections. Other on-line services include Xenon Laboratories' automatic currency exchanger at *http://www.xe.net/currency/* where you can discover the latest values of the Chinese ¥RMB and the Pakistani rupee against any hard and many soft currencies. Giant bookshops with searchable indexes include the intelligently organized Amazon Books (*http://www.amazon.com/*), and Internet Bookshop (*http://www.bookshop.co.uk/*). The Internet contains vast quantities of trivia available to the dedicated browser, from information on Chinese opera (*http://www.chinapages.com/culture/jj.html*) to images of the Great Wall and of the area around Khotan taken from the space shuttle (*http://www.jpl.nasa.gov/radar/sircxsar/archaeology.html*).

Internet Access on the Silk Routes

Expect to find public access email in most major cities by the time you reach China. For details of access in Běijīng, *see* p.330. There's little evidence of Chinese activity in public areas yet, except that travel agents have begun to cross-post advertising in annoyingly inappropriate locations, boasting of their low prices (in fact much higher that you'd be able to get on the spot).

Almaty and Bishkek both have publicly accessible services at reasonable fees, and Almaty has just acquired a free service at the Pushkin Library. On-line services in Islamabad are reportedly restricted to universities, but that will change.

That combination of caffeine and connectivity, the cyber-café, has spread to Europe and far beyond. To keep up with access on your planned route look at the cyber-café guide at *http://www.cyberiacafe.net/cyberia/guide/*. A web page which also acts as a bulletin board where you can pick up messages from home and leave others is run at *http://www.weblane.com/experiencia/bb/*.

Other Computer Resources

The CD-ROM seems not yet to know whether it is a book or a game, or has to be something of each. There is already one called *The Silk Road* by DNA Multimedia Corp and DATT Japan Inc, which is a light entertainment of animation, music, photography, games and tests of skill, all with an emphasis on the Xīnjiāng Turki heritage, and some howlers about China.

Numerous programmes exist for helping you to learn Chinese, such as *The Rosetta Stone*, and *HyperChina*. Once you have learned a little, the *Chinese Language Kit* will enable you to write simplified or full-form characters in almost any Macintosh program, or you can buy Chinese versions individually of most popular programs for Windows.

Laundry

Almost all hotels in China have a laundry service, although in cheaper places this may just mean that the staff take it home and charge you what they think you'll pay—don't expect whiter than white results under either circumstances. Familiar Western brands of washing powder, although not in 'green' versions, are available throughout the country, in handily portable sachets, and you are better off doing it yourself. Take a universal bath plug and an elastic washing line.

Lavatories

Bring a roll of toilet paper, and carry a few sheets with you at all times. Buy a fresh roll well before you run out.

In **China** use the lavatories in your hotel whever possible—the alternatives are not pleasant. Even in booming Shànghǎi only 60% of apartments have flushing toilets, and only 43% of city households are connected to modern sewerage. The rest of the populace uses public toilets in the street. There is no guarantee of finding facilities within public buildings either, or in the cheapest hotels, where a trek to a separate outhouse is sometimes necessary. However, there is no problem identifying public lavatories even at some considerable distance, as the language of the nose is international. One entrance is for women and one for men (*see* **Language** section p.519 for the relevant characters). Facilities usually consist of a row of slits in a concrete base, which may or may not be separated by waist-high walls, open to the front. You must squat, attempting neither to step in earlier near-misses, nor slip into the pit below, which will contain a steaming, maggot-ridden heap of earlier deposits awaiting collection and distribution to the fields. In winter a frozen stalagmite of human faeces may poke its tip through the slit. There is almost never anywhere to wash your hands. Occasionally there may be a ¥0.10 or ¥0.20 charge at the entrance, especially if the facilities are near a bus or railway station, or actually do have running water.

On long bus trips around the Taklamakan's perimeter the bus simply stops when there are enough requests, and men go to one side of the road and women to the other.

In **Kazakstan** and **Kyrgyzstan** matters are more Westernized, with conventional urinals and seats as well as squat toilets, all flushable, which can be found in restaurants, and at railway and bus stations. Occasionally a small fee is payable, in exchange for which you will receive a tiny square of rough toilet paper. Ж is for *zhenski*, meaning 'women', and M is for *muzhskoy*, meaning 'men', and the facilities are likely to be cleaner. In rural areas they tend to be in outhouses.

In **Pakistan** squat toilets are slightly more common, although they do flush, and facilities in restaurants are usually tolerable.

Media

In 213 BC the Qín government ordered the destruction of ethical writings which implied criticism of its authoritarianism. In the Hundred Flowers Movement, a liberation of artistic expression begun in 1956, and of political criticism in 1957, the government encouraged intellectuals to speak out. The result was widespread condemnation of the Communist Party's monopoly of power and the absence of human rights. Intellectuals and officials who spoke up were subsequently dismissed from their posts, and exiled or imprisoned. In 1997 the Chinese President Jiāng Zémín made speeches encouraging higher ethical standards amongst writers and journalists. This was ominous, since Jiāng's definition of meeting higher ethical standards, as a *People's Daily* article made clear, was that journalists should write bright and upbeat stories supporting the party line and socialism, rather then revealing the failings of society to foreigners. When Hong Kong's post-reunification administrator Tung Chee-hwa was given the status of 'state leader', one of the perks was that his photograph would be guaranteed to appear larger than those of provincial leaders in Chinese newspapers. In short, there is no free press in China, nor has there ever been one.

The English-language window onto the grey corridors of the political mind is *China Daily*, a dull mix of hypocrisy, cant, propaganda and window dressing, mixed with a few sports results from around the world, which is distributed free to tourist hotels. Production is always up, Western quality standards have always been obtained, and the minorities are always happy. Typical headlines are 'Frozen food consumption up in Liáoníng Province' and 'Ties with Africa to flourish'. *China Daily* will never report '700 dead in floods', but 'Despite floods, output up'. Reading between the lines of newspapers is a national sport in China. There's a nightly English 'news' broadcast in a similar vein at around 11pm on Channel 2. Foreign news magazines are available at the bigger hotels in Běijīng and at some of the international hotels elsewhere, along with BBC World Service, HK Star TV and CNN.

In Bishkek, the *Kyrgyzstan Chronicle* is a weekly paper of news about the country with some thoughtful editorial about the pace of change and progress, and some news from elsewhere in the CIS. It's available free from the foyers of more expensive hotels, where foreign journals can also be purchased. Almaty has two or three similar English-language titles, but in both countries media freedom is fragile. Pakistan has several outspoken English-language papers, and imported papers are widely available in Islamabad and Rawalpindi.

For reliable news take a short-wave radio and tune in to the following frequencies at different times of day:

BBC Central Asia: 15575, 15565, 12095, 11760, 9410, 6090, 5975, 1413.

BBC China: 21660, 15360, 15280, 11955, 11945, 9740, 7180, 6120, 6065, 5990, 5965, 5905.

(For a complete schedule see *http://www.bbc.co.uk/worldservice.*)

Voice of America: MHz 17.73, 15.42, 11.76, 6.110.

Money and Prices

Inflation and monetary instability are problems in all the countries mentioned in this book, and the prices quoted for goods and services will inevitably be wrong. All have been converted to US dollar equivalents in the hope of avoiding distortion caused by continually fluctuating exchange rates and runaway inflation. China's currency is the most stable, but state-run institutions often increase their prices arbitrarily, and as double prices for foreigners are removed in certain sectors, so they arrive in others. The main purpose of quoting prices is for the comparison of competing services, one with another.

In 1995 China's inflation rate had reached 26% before government measures brought it down to 14.8% by the end of the year, mysteriously just inside the target of 15%. Given China's long history of manufacturing such figures, the announcement was greeted with scepticism, especially as the measure used did not include foodstuffs. The real rate of inflation for ordinary consumers was at least 17.1%. According to government figures it fell again to 6% in 1996, with an effect on consumers of 8.3%. The point for the visitor is that the managed exchange rate has seen a gradual strengthening of the *yuán* against foreign currencies since 1994, fuelled by China's massive trade surpluses, and annual GDP growth of over 10%. Thus China, already up to twice as expensive as neighbours such as India, Pakistan and Nepal, is becoming more expensive for visitors all the time.

In the other countries mentioned in this book, rising inflation tends to lead to a weakening of exchange rates, leaving real costs at a similar level, but other local factors also come into play. For instance prices had been tending to rise along the Karakoram Highway due to increasing tourism. By the time more accommodation and other services had opened to meet demand, political instability in Karachi and Kashmir had led to a sharp drop in visitors, keeping prices low. China's partial liberalization of its economy has led to a steep increase in the cost of many goods and services, while domestic demand for tourism has grown so rapidly that it is also putting upward pressure on many prices. Kazakstan and Kyrgyzstan are still floundering their way towards full market economies, with many strange distortions, and Pakistan is the only country where market forces act fairly freely.

China: $1 = ¥8.3RMB.

Chinese currency is known as *rénmínbì*, which means 'people's money', the unit of which is the *yuán* (¥ or ¥RMB). The most useful notes are ¥50 and smaller, and you should make sure that you have plenty of ¥10 notes for everyday use. There are also smaller notes (in size and value) for *jiào*, or one-tenth of a *yuán*, and tiny notes for *fēn*, or 100ths of a *yuán*, which these days are of little use except to make up one *jiào*.

One small problem for the budding Chinese scholar is that in speech *yuán* are usually called *kuài*, and *jiào* are called *máo*. The numbers used on currency and in financial documents are also different and more complicated than those used in everyday writing, although all money except the *fēn* coins and notes carries Arabic numerals, too. The one-*fēn* note has a picture of a lorry (truck), two-*fēn* a picture of a boat, and five-*fēn* a picture of a plane, but these are dying out. Coins for 1 and 5 *máo* and 1 *kuài* are now beginning to come into circulation.

All money exchange is carried out at branches of the Bank of China, or at desks in hotel foyers which are under the Bank's control. All major and minor hard currencies from pounds and US dollars to Malaysian ringgits and Finnmarks are accepted both in cash and traveller's cheques, and the exchange rate is uniform throughout the country, revised on a daily basis. Considerably better prices are given for traveller's cheques than cash. The rate is nevertheless not a true floating one, but promises to become so by the end of the century. A commission of 0.75% is charged. At major branches you can also cash cheques into US dollars, and convert RMB to dollars as long as you can show receipts to prove that you have changed at least the same amount into RMB in the past. In larger towns you can make withdrawals up to the amount of your credit limit from Visa, Mastercard, American Express and JCB cards, with commission of 4% and sometimes a minimum withdrawal of ¥1200 ($145). Allow at least 30 minutes for clearance, and don't leave yourself in the situation where this is your only source of cash, as sometimes the system breaks down, or lazy bank staff may simply refuse to go through the hassle. At certain banks in major cities, American Express cardholders can cash personal cheques guaranteed by their Amex card. This doesn't really seem credible, but contect Amex for a list of participating banks if you're a cardholder.

China is expected to become the biggest payment-card market in the world in the next 7–10 years, but don't be fooled either by the cards you see in people's wallets or the plethora of Visa and Mastercard signs. In most locations only the Chinese versions are accepted, and these cards have 'Only for use in China' printed on them. If foreign cards are accepted then you are going to be paying well over the odds for whatever goods or services you are buying.

You are not allowed to import or export more than ¥5000 in ¥RMB without special arrangements, and indeed you would be unwise to do anything of the kind, as it's impossible to convert to anything else outside China. Foreign currencies in excess of $5000 must be declared on entry, but no-one seems to care very much. You may from time to time see mention of prices in FEC or Foreign Exchange Certificates. The ¥FEC was a parallel currency for foreigners only, theoretically equivalent to the ¥RMB (as a helpful paragraph in English on the back of each note pointed out) but worth nearly twice as much on the black market. The long-forecast death of the FEC finally came to pass in 1995, and with it the constant stream of sidelong stage whispers that accompanied every walk down the street, 'Hello! Change money?'

It is official government policy to charge foreigners 200–300% more for hotels and tours than local Chinese are charged. On 1 October 1995 rail ticket prices were made equal for Chinese and foreigners, and domestic air tickets followed suit in July 1997. New private hotels in some areas charge foreigners and Chinese the same price.

Budget travellers used to regard illegally changing FEC to RMB on the black market as a legitimate response, and now some resort to purchasing fake student, worker or foreign expert identity cards in order to claim entitlement to Chinese prices. Many visitors of Chinese descent get away with paying domestic prices anyway.

Don't accept a crumpled handful of notes, even if the amount looks right: once you straighten and flatten them out, you may find that one of your notes is only a half.

Kazakstan: US$1 = 75 *tenge*, and **Kyrgyzstan:** US$1 = 18 *som*. Both currencies are weakening. Prices may sometimes be listed in US dollars but payment is almost always in local currency.

The Kyrgyz som is the most stable currency in the former Soviet republics, and its 1995 inflation rate was the lowest in Central Asia—31.9%. In the same period Kazakstan's was 60.3%, including a 158% rise in the cost of services. High inflation continues in Kazakstan, and the tenge steadily weakens against the dollar. In Kyrgyzstan a gradual weaking in the som led to a slide from 12 to 18 in early 1997. Costs of imported goods went up in proportion, but locally produced services became cheaper for visitors.

Full details of banking and money exchange facilities are given in the Almaty and Bishkek sections, but note that cash exchange of US$ and DM is possible on almost every street corner seven days a week. Traveller's cheques can be exchanged at only a limited number of banks, and credit card withdrawals are only possible in Almaty. The import and export of all currency is tightly controlled, so read the information at banks and the rail and road crossings to China very carefully to make sure you do not fall foul of greedy customs officials. US$ cash must be in good condition and dated 1990 or later, or it simply will not be accepted for exchange, or even as a gift.

Pakistan: US$1 = Rs41. The currency is the *rupiah*, or rupee, which is divided into 100 *paisa*, but *paisa* amounts are always rounded up to the nearest rupee. Most currency exchange is handled by the National Bank of Pakistan, although in larger towns the Habib Bank also has a foreign exchange counter. There are private money changers in larger towns popular with tourists who usually have longer opening hours and often offer better rates. The most widely accepted traveller's cheques are those in US dollars and sterling. Many hotels accept payments in dollars or sterling, but at poor rates of exchange. Of the towns and cities mentioned in this book, only Islamabad and Rawalpindi offer credit card withdrawal facilities. Note that 1988 $100 bills are almost impossible to exchange because of a forgery scare.

Museums

Entrance fees are always higher for foreigners than they are for Chinese—from an extra 50% to 10 times as high. Despite this few museums have information in any language other than Chinese and perhaps a minority language. Typically, museum collections are also poorly lit, dusty and uncared for, even in Běijīng. Whole sections of the museum may be closed at random because someone hasn't turned up for work, but don't expect a discount or a refund. In museum shops items that you can find much cheaper in local markets are sold for outrageous sums, and books you can find in Xīnhuá for much less have stickers on their prices.

Increasingly sections of museums seem to be turned over to other enterprises, particularly furniture stores, such as in Lánzhōu and Gùyuán.

Most museums follow the same pattern, presenting their collections in date order. Part of the propaganda process, displays are carefully selected and labelled to promote a viewpoint, such as the willing subservience of a minority group to the imperial court, or the early presence of Hàn in the region. Periods when the Hàn withdrew or were repelled, or when the minorities took power over the Hàn, are glossed over. Everywhere there is the sour reek of nationalism. Despite this there are some fine museums in China, such as the Shǎnxī History Museum in Xī'ān, which should not be missed.

Museums in the Central Asian republics are often sumptuous marble palaces which were also organs of Soviet propaganda, and are now being revised to present an idealized view of each country's principal ethnic groups in some mythical golden age.

Opening Hours

Whatever the most important thing you want to do in a day is, do it first. Few premises open on time in China, and most close early, unless they are private businesses. Museum staff frequently stop selling tickets an hour or so before the museum closes so as to make sure everyone's out of their hair in plenty of time for going home, and staff of all government offices right down to postal workers may decide that they are *xiàbàn* (off work) up to 30 minutes before closing time, even though they carry on sitting at their desks. Two-hour lunch breaks (rising to three hours in western China) are also likely to begin early and end late, cutting down the working hours of the officer in charge of issuing visa extensions, for instance, to a very brief period. 'Work', in this and many other cases, means the strenuous labour of reading the newspaper, drinking tea, and discussing the price of things with any fellow officer who may happen to drop in.

Most offices, shops and museums open around 8am and close around 5 or 6pm. Offices and many museums take a break from 12 noon to 2pm. The 1995 introduction of a five-day working week has confused matters. In general you cannot get a visa extension, an English-speaking policeman, or any other government service on Saturday or Sunday. It is also becoming difficult to change money on those days unless you are a resident of a hotel with money exchange facilities. Banks are usually open, but their foreign exchange counters occasionally not. Most museums and tourist sites stay open seven days, but some shut on Saturdays and Sundays, and in Běijīng some for one other day of the week. However, particular services you may require, such as stamps for overseas letters or *poste restante*, may be unavailable if the one person whose job it is to deal with them is not in that day, or has gone off duty.

Never leave anything important until your last opportunity to do it as this will almost certainly guarantee that the electricity will be off, the one person who can help is sick, the office is closed for a meeting, the flight cancelled, the road dug up, or the border closed for an unforeseen holiday. Allow extra time for everything.

Until only a few years ago, most of China had shut down by 6pm and the rest by 8pm, but now private stores stay open into the evening and private restaurants stay open until 10pm or later. In some smaller towns the choice of places to eat will shrink after 7pm or 8pm—most ordinary Chinese will have eaten well before then.

Officialdom in the Central Asian republics and Pakistan has many similarities with that of China. Despite the presence of far too many workers for the job in hand, everything moves at a snail's pace, starts late, finishes early, and takes a long afternoon break. Shops and businesses close through the middle of the afternoon, reopening until mid-evening. This is also true of Xīnjiāng, and parts of Gānsù, Níngxià and Inner Mongolia.

Packing

> There was a crowd perpetually round the tent: all our actions, all our belongings, were closely scrutinised—by the Mongols with vacant gravity, by the Chinese with magpie curiosity. 'How much did this cost, Mr. Fu? How much did this cost?' It was laughable to recall that we had brought with us a tiny portable gramophone (and three records) because it would be so useful to attract the natives; there were times, at this period, when we would gladly have exchanged the gramophone for its weight in tear-gas bombs.
>
> Peter Fleming, *News from Tartary*, 1936

The best policy is to take as little as you can, and restrict it to what cannot be cheaply and easily obtained in China itself.

Clothes: light, loose, natural-fibre, hand-washable clothes are best, plus one heavy jumper, and a light waterproof jacket with a hood. Take stout walking shoes or boots with good support, and a pair of flip-flops for use in hotel bedrooms and showers. Include something with long sleeves and a high collar for visits to mosques, and for covering up against mosquitoes in the evenings. Despite the heat, sturdy jeans are a good choice for long bus journeys, due to the dirt and hard-edged metal surfaces of much public transport. In Pakistan and outside the major cities of the Central Asian republics, women should be particularly conservative in their clothing and in Pakistan cover their hair (*see* **Social Niceties**, below).

Cheap, if aesthetically unappealing, warm clothing is widely available in China, particularly shaggy, sheepskin-lined army greatcoats, which will see you through even a bitter Xīnjiāng winter, or trimmed sheepskin waistcoats favoured by Uighurs.

Toiletries: many popular brands are now available in the bigger cities of China, at kiosks in Almaty and Bishkek, and throughout Pakistan. In China good toothpaste is a little harder to find than familiar brands of soap or shampoo. Bring one toilet roll to start, plenty of good sunblock, and small quantities of whatever up-market moisturizer or other cosmetics you can't live without.

Other items: a Swiss army knife, an unbreakable mug for drinking hot water and making tea on Chinese trains (both mug and tea can be bought there, however), good UV-proof sunglasses, a universal bath plug, an elastic washing line for drying your hand-washing, a North American to European adaptor or vice versa (just in case), a basic first-aid kit, and a paperback or two for exchange with other travellers when read. Streets in all the towns in this book are either unlit or very poorly lit, have uneven pavements, unguarded trenches, and uncovered manholes. A small torch is useful at night, and for those times when the electricity has failed and the hotel staff can't be bothered to bring you a candle. A sheet sleeping bag is useful if you view with distaste sleeping in someone else's sheets—in many downmarket hotels these are only changed once a week, regardless of the turnover of guests. Photocopy the information pages of your passport and those holding the visas for this trip; if you are travelling with a companion, each should carry the other's copies. Also take or copy a bilingual menu from your local Chinese restaurant to help with ordering food. Take a small day pack for holding guide book, sunblock and other daytime necessaries, as well as for use on buses when your main luggage is out of reach on the roof.

Small gifts of obviously Western origin are nice to offer in exchange for personal kindnesses received (not as tips for services rendered professionally).

Photography

Fuji has nearly 2000 outlets in China and holds 56% of the Chinese market with Kodak having another 33%. Fuji film tends to be DX while Kodak does not, but your camera will probably automatically set itself to ASA100. Konica film is also available, but don't expect to find slide film, high-speed film, or the latest formats anywhere outside the major cities. Care of film is not widely understood, and it's often left to bake in the sun at stalls near tourist sites, so buy in dark department stores or specialist shops with fridges (very few).

Security personnel at CIS, Chinese and Pakistani airports (and Chinese railway stations) claim that their X-rays will not fog film, but it is advisable to carry it with you and have it inspected by hand.

Photography is never allowed inside museums and temples, and in some Lamaist monasteries strips of exposed film have been nailed to the wall as a warning. Resist the temptation to photograph bridges on the Karakoram Highway, border posts and territory, the process of changing the bogies at the Kazak-Chinese border, and anything else remotely military that's obviously been photographed in great detail from satellites already.

From mid-morning to mid-afternoon the glare renders all subjects washed out and flat, so choose your time to visit major monuments appropriately. Ask permission before taking photographs of people, but *do not pay them.*

Police

Policemen in China are generally to be avoided, not because they pose as much of a threat to visitors as they do to their own countrymen, but because they tend to be more of a hindrance than a help. Effectively in China the law is what a policeman says it is, and like most other officials policemen are assumed to be corrupt until proven honest. There are honest policemen, but the response of ordinary Chinese is to keep as far away from the police as possible, and to flatter and bribe when necessary. Visitors to China, although they can potentially yield far more cash, cannot so easily be made into victims, and are mostly left alone by police. However, they are also often reluctant to do their jobs, and will frequently refuse to help visitors by investigating frauds or petty assaults, for instance, or registering thefts for the purpose of insurance reports. Some persistence is necessary.

As with other areas of Chinese administration, the left hand is unaware of the right hand's existence. Officials in two neighbouring areas may give completely different answers to a question and one may refuse to honour documents issued by the other. Two different policemen on different days at the same station may also give different answers, but always with the tendency to say 'no', because this involves both less work and less responsibility than saying 'yes'. Policemen generally have a poor understanding of their own rules and regulations, and a low level of education.

There are two main types of policemen in China, those of the Public Security Bureau, and those of the People's Armed Police. Visitors to China usually encounter only the first, known as the PSB (*gōng'ān*), and then only when applying for an extension to their visas. Occasionally it's also necessary to buy a permit to visit certain areas, but this is increasingly rare. In general, the PSB officers have little interest in foreigners, although the police stations in larger towns have at least one person with a theoretical knowledge of English.

When you are inadvertently guilty of a misdemeanour, politely refuse to pay 'fines'. If you become involved in a dispute with a policeman, always leave him room to back down, and search for an excuse that he can use to do so, once he understands that you are not going to pay the sum he mentioned. *Do not offer a bribe.* When you really have been in the wrong, haggle. Even if the policeman can show that you should pay a fine of ¥2000, haggle it down to ¥50 or so, and ask for a receipt.

In Pakistan and China you are unlikely to face problems, but the police in Almaty and Bishkek occasionally stop younger and less respectable-looking visitors hoping to find an excuse to impose a 'fine'. Stand your ground and do not pay. Demand to be taken to a superior officer. Call for help from witnesses. It rarely comes to anything when there are so many natives to hassle instead. The police stations of the four countries have overmanning and lethargy in common. Don't enter any of them looking like you expect instant action, or indeed for anyone even to look up from their newspapers.

Post

The missionaries Cable and French, arriving in a small oasis town, hurried to see the post-master:

> *'Have they brought any letters for us?' I asked. 'Sackloads,' was his reply. 'There are letters from England, America, Norway, and there is a small parcel from Denmark which looks as if it might contain some-thing to eat. Among the mail-matter there are many Chinese magazines, and as books are scarce here, I opened and read them with the greatest interest. I have passed some on to a friend, but now that you have come, I will get them back for you at once.'*

Mildred Cable with Francesca French, *The Gobi Desert*, 1942

Sending letters home from all of the countries mentioned in this book is cheap and reliable, although Pakistan and China are probably preferred, and the Chinese post office is particularly efficient. Letters from Kazakstan and Kyrgyzstan can take several weeks. In all cases glue the stamps on with the adhesive provided in pots, rather then licking them. Take them back to the counter for franking in front of your face: in China this isn't really necessary at post offices, but at postal counters in hotels there are occasionally problems with theft, or just laziness.

Chinese post offices are mostly open seven days a week and for the same hours every day, although some variations are creeping in as China slowly adapts to the introduction of a five-day working week. Individual counters may close unexpectedly, however, while the clerk takes a lunch break, and no-one else will cover his/her job. There's also a tendency for clerks to refuse to serve people up to 30 minutes before closing time. Their jobs are still 'iron rice bowl' (guaranteed for life), and they don't care about service. Watch out for a tendency to round up the prices to avoid having to look for smaller denominations of stamps, or give change. As with ticket buying there's often a bit of a scrum, with everybody talking over the top of everybody else in their attempt to get service from the scowling clerk. Join in, or send your postcards when you get home.

Take parcels unwrapped, so the contents can be checked, and then wrap them in front of the clerk. Some clerks will assume that you want EMS, the equivalent of a courier service, because you are a rich foreigner. There are considerably lower rates for airmail, surface mail, and mail that contains only printed matter. Occasionally post offices may insist that you buy a tailor-made box from them, and very occasionally that you sew up your parcel in white cloth. Registration can be added for a small fee, is computerized and efficient, and requires you to fill out a small form which is in Chinese and French only. The French played a major role in setting up the Chinese post office, which was still mostly run by foreigners in the first part of the 20th century, and it appears that the original forms are still being used with the addition of a bar-coded sticker that matches one that goes on your parcel. Adding the name of the destination country in Chinese characters will speed things up.

Postcards are only found in hotels and at tourist sites.

Poste restante: the system is mostly reliable in Pakistan and China but not in the CIS. In Pakistan stick to Islamabad and Rawalpindi, and in China to major cities where advised in the 'Tourist Information' section that the system works. Using the postcodes quoted and adding the characters for *poste restante* given in **Language** (*see* p.519) will speed things up, but in general anything addressed in a foreign language tends to end up in the *poste restante* box anyway. There is a charge of ¥1.50 for every item picked up in China. Ask for a receipt.

Shopping

During the early days of the Silk Routes, manufactured objects and especially beads of coloured glass were often passed off to the Chinese as gems, until the technology for glass-making also arrived down the trade routes in the 5th century. Perhaps the Chinese are taking some kind of delayed revenge on the modern tourist.

Take the usual common-sense measures of shopping around, bargaining *very* hard (but with a smile), and not buying souvenirs in hotel foyers or souvenir shops. The sign 'authorized tour unit' is only a guarantee that what you are buying will be highly priced, and not that the goods that you are buying are of particularly high quality or even genuine at all. Some visitors are under the illusion that vendors in markets standardly ask double the normal price for their goods, that the correct response is to offer one-third, and finally to pay half the original asking price. In fact first asking prices are not untypically 10 to 15 times the proper price, and there is no shame whatsoever in offering 10% of the first price, however cheap that may appear in developed-country terms. Some vendors will be unwilling to deal with any foreigner who is not prepared to pay vastly too much money (after all, that is what foreigners are *for*, in the opinion of many) and would otherwise rather lose the sale. At that point it is up to you to decide how much you want to compromise. Never accept the advice of a tour guide, however pleasant, as he or she will almost certainly be on commission.

State-run department stores are struggling to compete with the new private enterprises. In the one, customers are served grudgingly if at all, and the stock includes volleyball nets, Bakelite slide projectors, and very low quality exercise books, but little that you might want. In the new stores the idea of customer service is catching on. Staff have been taught to look alert, dress smartly, and smile. Goods are fairly well displayed and lit, and imported snacks, toiletries, batteries, tapes, and other items useful to the traveller are available. Everything should be labelled in price if it is not, shop elsewhere or you will certainly be overcharged. Haggling is for markets, not stores, and what you have found is an indoor market. The 'Friendship Stores', which used to stock the best souvenirs for hard-currency vouchers only, have mostly disappeared, but some have continued to garner the best of local products. Marked prices are for haggling over at all tourist stores, including these. A 10% discount is the minimum, and you should be able to do better than that.

In most cases, having identified what you want to buy, you are given a receipt to take to a cashier nearby, where you pay and have the receipt stamped, returning to exchange it for the goods you selected. When you buy books, these too receive a stamp. The Chinese do produce a number of attractive art books about Silk Route sites, but note that all have their correct price as set by the publisher printed on them, usually not far inside the back cover, and easily identifiable by the Chinese *yuán* character, or the ¥ symbol. Others simply have a string of five digits found in the same place under the publication date and ISBN number, which expresses the price in *fēn*. 01580, for instance, is only ¥15.80. If the price has been obliterated or stickered over you are being cheated, and should shop elsewhere. Publishers also consider foreigners fair game, and the few books made for the tourist market and which have text in English are not priced, to the delight of museum souvenir shops.

No-one without a serious understanding of Chinese art should consider buying antiques. These are being manufactured daily, and the few real pieces may need export licences. If you are considering buying a carpet, gems or jewellery, you should not do so without having thoroughly familiarized yourself with quality and prices back home, to be sure that you are buying a genuine item, and for a considerably reduced price. Even if a store has some kind of authorized or official status, under no circumstances take it for granted that you are being told the truth, or that it is any less likely that you are being sold a fake. If some imperfection is discovered after purchase, or even if the item turns out to be manifestly other than what it was sold as being, don't expect a refund, or sympathy from the police.

Chinese quality control is poor, so stick to buying simple objects with no pretensions to sophistication: chopstick sets, fans, silk (but check carefully), political posters (found in many Xīnhuá book shops), and soapstone seals (jade? ha!). Silk should generally be bought in lengths rather than as made-up goods, Western sizes and styles not usually being available, but Běijīng's silk markets are worth checking. Chinese paintings are light to carry, if fragile, but ignore claims of the fame of the artist and the uniqueness of the work. Anything that tourists will buy is repainted thousands of times, and many paintings on sale are simply copies of famous classical paintings. There's nothing wrong with this, so long as you accept that you're buying a copy because it appeals to you, and not some original masterpiece. Rubbings from the stelae in Xī'ān and elsewhere also make attractive gifts, but buy away from the main tourist sights. Markets catering to tourists in Běijīng and Xī'ān offer Máo watches and clocks, 'little red books' (of his sayings), old photographs, and old *májiàng* (mahjong) sets made from bone and bamboo, but first asking prices are at least five times what you should pay, and often ten times.

Uighurs and other minorities produce attractive hats, ornate daggers, leather coats and boots, etc. Buy in street markets from the minority people themselves, and prepare for a probably good-natured and enjoyable haggle. The Sunday markets at Kashgar and Khotan, the Friday market at Kuqa, and the streets markets of Kashgar's old town are the ultimate sources of Uighur goods, but watch out for the skins of endangered species such as the snow leopard, woefully plentiful, and avoid trading with any who have them for sale. The streets of Xiàhé and the alleys neighbouring other Buddhist monasteries have devotional items of all kinds, including brassware and gaudy Buddha pictures. Wherever there are Tibetans look also for leather boots and tackle of all kinds, and felt hats.

Then there is the extravagantly kitsch, and the outdated but interesting. In department stores look for items such as fluorescent plastic *májiàng* sets, plastic mosques with little lights at the top of their minarets which are actually tape players, and watches which speak the time in Mandarin. Reliable, non-electronic full-plate cameras of ancient design can be bought very cheaply by those who've always wanted to experiment in the medium but been put off by cost. Check aperture, shutter and winder carefully before purchase.

Islamabad has extensive markets for cloth of all kinds (the gaudier the better), and brash jewellery. Those confident that they know what they are doing can purchase precious and semi-precious stones of all qualities in Gilgit and Karimabad. The same stones well-mounted in traditional ornate Russian-style settings and in strikingly modern pieces can be found for marked prices (which the local people pay too) in the shops of Almaty. The main bazaar also has individuals selling striking Soviet memorabilia, such as enamel military badges, and there's a small antiques market at Gorky Park on a Sunday.

Social Niceties

An introduction to a Chinese person or family is a joy to be looked for. Their generosity knows no bounds and can quickly reach embarrassing levels if disposable incomes are compared. If you are invited to stay with someone, still a delicate proposition politically, consider carefully that you will be enveloped in a way which may be a major economic drain on the family, and behave accordingly. If you are taken out for a meal, *insist* on returning the favour. They will say no for at least half an hour, because this is polite. *Insist*. It will be very unlikely that you will be able to get any indication from them what kind of food they would like to eat, although you may be able to get some indication of what they don't like. Use caution, however: if you suggest Běijīng duck, for example, and they say they don't like it, the real reason may be that they think that it's too expensive. Most families eat out rarely. Be as attentive to them as they were to you, insisting they take the best morsels, topping up their tea cups or glasses, and dealing with the bill swiftly and unobtrusively.

If you are invited to eat in someone's home always take something to eat, perhaps fruit, and something to drink, preferably a relatively expensive (but not for you) type of white spirit. Most localities have their own special brand, often made from sorghum, such as Běijīng's *Běijīng Chún*, or Inner Mongolia's *Měnggǔ Wáng* (King of Mongolia) at ¥30 to ¥40 ($4–5) per bottle. If you have anything from your own country, this, too, will be highly appreciated. They may attempt not to accept your gifts (multiple cries of 'not acceptable'—meaning that you shouldn't have bothered, or 'not necessary', or 'no need to be polite'), all of which you should ignore, and gently but firmly insist. Under no circumstances take any part of your gifts away again. You will yourself be given fruit or something else to take away. Politely decline several times, but finally accept, unless there is a genuine reason why you cannot, in which case do your best to explain this, and it will be accepted.

Drinking is usually undertaken collectively, rather than at your own individual pace, and through a succession of toasts. Don't forget to propose your own in praise of the food, your hosts, and the hospitality in general. The local equivalent of 'cheers', frequently heard, is *gān bēi* ('dry cup'—empty your glass). Should you be eating out, or if you are participating in an official banquet, note that there is no dithering at the end of the meal. All participants quickly vanish.

A few other points: remove your shoes when entering someone's house, despite cries of 'no need, no need' unless you can see that everyone else is wearing street shoes, too. (This also applies throughout Central Asia from yurt to shiny new apartment.) You'll be offered slippers probably too small for your feet. Despite the freedom with phlegm in public places, note that it is very bad form to blow your nose at the table. If you feel the need to sneeze, turn completely away or leave the table if you can. Only help yourself to small amounts of food at a time, and don't refill the rice in your bowl until you have eaten completely what you have. Don't wave your chopsticks around, but note that picking up your bowl and cupping it in one hand is perfectly normal, as is noisy eating, particularly of noodles. It is also perfectly acceptable to drink your soup straight from the bowl. Your tea will be topped up by someone (usually the youngest adult) almost as soon as you drink any, so when you've had enough, leave the glass full. Cleaning your bowl is also a direct invitation to refill it, so start protesting about your repletion well in advance ('*Wǒ chībǎo le*'—I've eaten-to-fullness), and leave a little in it.

Losing your temper in China is rarely a good idea, although your patience may frequently be tried to the limit. When dealing with anyone behind a counter, try to avoid getting them into a situation where they give you a flat 'no'. If you get a 'no' straight away, such as 'no discounts at this hotel', you'll need to offer them an excuse to change their minds, otherwise they cannot do so without losing face. The excuse can be entirely spurious, such as offering them some completely irrelevant piece of identification and saying, 'I'm a student,' or 'I plan to stay for three days', which would normally make no difference at all. This is particularly important if the 'no' has been given publicly.

Be unswervingly polite until it is absolutely clear that it will get you nowhere. At times, however, you may need to make a scene just to get service at all, such as when the bank teller simply can't be bothered to fetch the notes you want. Make it clear that you are not going away until you get service, and usually (but not always) you will win. You may also find that all the Chinese on your side of the counter, as sick of bad service as you are, are cheering you on. Beware, however, of causing someone able to have the last laugh to lose face.

Receipts are very important in China. If you spend 30 minutes gradually winning a refund for some non-performance, then are unable to produce your receipt, your cause is lost. It does not matter if it is undeniable that you paid. It does not matter that the clerk is not denying that you paid. It does not matter that you offer to write a receipt for the refund yourself. If you don't have the original, then you can't have a refund. You will quickly accumulate piles of tissue-paper receipts in China. Keep *all* of them until you are well clear of the city in which you got them. You never know.

Tipping does not exist in any country in this book outside of the top-range joint-venture hotels where the importation of foreign management has brought the tradition with it. In China there used to be signs up in hotels informing guests that tipping was unnecessary and even offensive. Bribery exists in China: tipping does not. Neither should be encouraged to spread. The Chinese do not tip each other, and neither do the Kyrgyz, Kazaks or Pakistanis. Foreigners are already overcharged wherever possible, and further donations are unnecessary. Furthermore, the individuals with whom you do business are already some of the better off. If you want to give charity, choose the obviously starving, ill, deformed and injured who really need it. There are unfortunately all too many of these to choose from. Service charges that are occasionally added to the bill in Kazakstan and Kyrgyzstan should be resisted if they are not mentioned on the menu. This is just a foreigner tax.

Islamic traditions of hospitality are justly famous, and are most obvious in Pakistan—perhaps because more people speak English so their offers are both more easily made and more easily understood. There, seats may be given up on buses for you, and you may find that someone has bought your ticket. Don't decline offers of home cooking unless you absolutely must, and it is polite to sample at least a little of whatever you are given. If offered a small gift, reciprocate with some small but obviously imported treat. Note that Russian hospitality is likely to involve staggering quantities of alcohol, and that many Kazaks and Kyrgyz, Muslims or not, have also learned to drink to excess. Pakistan is officially dry, and alcohol has some of the spurious glamour of soft drugs in the West. As a foreigner you can obtain a licence to buy locally produced beer, but you should be discreet in your consumption of it.

Women should exercise considerable restraint in **Pakistan**, covering themselves loosely from neck to wrist and ankle, and covering their hair with a light scarf. For those planning a long stay, the long-tailed shirt and baggy trouser combination known as the *shalwar kamiz* can be run up quickly and cheaply in any bazaar. Women are usually placed together in the front of buses away from the men, and couples are seated in separate 'family' sections at restaurants. However objectionable you may consider this, there is nothing to gain by arguing the point. If you want to visit Pakistan and have an enjoyable trip, conform. If you don't conform you may be made very uncomfortable.

More conservative clothing is also advisable in the smaller towns of Xīnjiāng, and in the Central Asian republics outside their more cosmopolitan capitals, where, as in China proper, anything goes. Men should avoid wearing shorts while in Pakistan or Central Asia, where they are only worn by children.

Telephones

Even the tiniest towns in **China** have post and telephone offices with satellite uplinks, and connections to overseas countries and long-distance calls within China are quick and clear, much better in fact than local calls. Prices vary greatly from place to place and it's worth saving your international calls for smaller towns and those less frequented by foreign visitors.

Entering a numbered booth, you dial for yourself (begin with 00 for international calls) the number is registered and the call timed by a computer which then prints out a receipt. Long-distance calls within China are usually cheaper at weekends. Almost any hotel which gives you a phone in your room has long-distance dialling within China, and most larger hotels have IDD, too. Prices, however, tend to be 50% higher than those at the telephone office. Some hotels have long-distance phone cabins in their foyers, rather than connections in their rooms. Card telephones can now be found in some hotel foyers and elsewhere and are rapidly increasing in numbers. Phone cards for various RMB values can be bought at reception desks.

International call prices dropped 30% as this book went to press. You'll probably find that most charges are cheaper than quoted at the telephone offices but stayed the same at the hotels.

In **Pakistan** long-distance calling is much more primitive even within the country. Timing tends to be by a man with a stop-watch who may take some persuasion to hold it in view. If possible, take your own, and put it where you can both see it. Beyond Islamabad/Rawalpindi long-distance calling is difficult or impossible (although the tiny phone office at Taxila is fine), and particularly troublesome at Gilgit. Look for the signs 'PCO' (phone call office).

In Almaty the satellite phone booths are expensive but reliable, using cards purchasable from kiosks and from the phone offices. The cheaper route in both **Almaty** and **Bishkek** is to use the government telephone offices, but there are often lengthy queues. In the more primitive places you write down the number and eventually are called to a booth. In others you pay a deposit and are given a token corresponding to the number of the booth where you dial for yourself. The Hotel Dostuck in Bishkek has a satellite link, as does the Bishkek Business Centre (another hotel). For local calls in both towns buy a token from a kiosk, but don't rely on pay phones to work. Use a hotel, restaurant, shop or private phone. The charge is the same (*see* the relevant city sections).

country codes

China +86, Kazakstan +7, Kyrgyzstan +996, Pakistan +92.

Time

China: Běijīng time is GMT+8 hours, with no summer time (daylight-saving time), and the whole country is in a single time zone. This leaves Xīnjiāng clocks at least two hours ahead of the sun, and while all official business, all government office opening hours, and all public transport departures run on Běijīng time, local people often work on the highly unofficial Xīnjiāng time, two hours earlier. Although offices and shops run on Běijīng time, they generally open two hours later than they do in the east, at 10am.

Kazakstan has two time zones but Almaty and the routes into China are all on GMT+6, with summer time at GMT+7. To add as much confusion as possible, air and train timetables in the former Soviet republics still use Moscow time.

Kyrgyzstan: GMT+5 hours, with summer time at GMT+6 between late March and October.

Pakistan: GMT+5 hours.

Only in Pakistan is there an agency that exists to hand out free information to tourists. In China and the CIS there are only commercial operations which exist to sell you services.

in China

China's three big state travel agencies are CITS, CTS, and CYTS, originally designed to deal respectively with foreigners, foreigners of Chinese descent, and young people (but without offering any discount). Now to a certain degree deregulated, they compete in offering the same services, but remain bywords for cupidity, insolence and non-performance. Friendly and co-operative travel agency staff are still so unusual that independent travellers hear about them thousands of kilometres away.

All depend on your unwillingness to try to do things for yourself, and on contacts within ticket offices that may grant them access to seats and beds that you can't get. They depend on the language barrier to fix up transport for you that you could fix for yourself for half the price. Some run one-day tours that are worthwhile for their convenience, and many travellers find it's worth paying ¥50 more for a railway ticket to be spared the confusion and crush of railway stations. This, however, should be the limit of your involvement with these organizations. In larger cities, cafés catering specially to independent budget travellers have begun to spring up, and these are usually the most economical sources of railway tickets, even though their relationship with station staff may be unofficial. They are also often the best sources of reliable jeeps, buses and taxis, because they understand that their ability to continue to make money from foreigners for food and drink depends upon their good reputation.

in the CIS

In Bishkek and Almaty there are the leftovers of the Soviet institution *Intourist*, and newer outfits which are usually a better choice. Contact details are given in the relevant city sections.

in Pakistan

The Pakistan Tourism Development Corporation (PTDC) has offices in Islamabad and in larger towns up the Karakoram Highway, generally with well-informed and helpful staff, and free leaflets. Their own hotels and transport services tend to cost more than those of other local operators, however.

PTDC Head Office: House No.2, Street 61, F7/4, P.O. Box 1465, Islamabad-44000, ✆ (51) 811001–4, ✉ (51) 824173 (has a small library).

PTDC Tourist Information Centre: Flashman's Hotel, The Mall, Rawalpindi, ✆ (51) 518480–5, ✉ (51) 565449.

in Canada

PTDC representative: Bestway Tours, 202–2678 West Broadway, Vancouver BC, ✆ (604) 732 4686, ✉ (604) 732 9744.

in the UK

Intourist: 219 Marsh Wall, Isle of Dogs, London E14 9FJ, ✆ (0171) 538 8600, ✉ (071) 538 5967 (phone, fax or write before visiting).

China National Tourist Office: 4 Glentworth Street, London NW1 5PG, ✆ (0171) 935 9427.

China Travel Service Information Centre: 124 Euston Road, London NW1 2AL, ✆ (0171) 388 8838.

PTDC: Suite 433, 52–54 High Holborn, London WC1V 6RL, ✆ (0171) 242 3131.

in the USA

Intourist: Suite 868, 630 5th Avenue, New York, NY 10111, ✆ (212) 757 3884.

China National Tourism Administration: Suite 6413, 534 5th Avenue, New York, NY 10018, ✆ (212) 760 9700 (information), 760 8218 (business).

PTDC: Suite 506, 303 5th Avenue, New York, NY 10016, ✆ (212) 889 5478.

Where to Stay

China

Hotels in China range from the luxury international chains of the bigger eastern cities, and Chinese attempts at the same thing, to the grim transit hotels of small towns on long bus routes in remote areas. In theory only a hotel which is an 'authorized tour unit' or otherwise endorsed by the local tourism administration, usually with a brass sign outside, can accept you; others are for Chinese only. Some of the smaller towns covered in this book have no such places, and you will have to persuade them to take you in. If you meet with real resistance, ask the PSB (Public Security Bureau or police) to help you. The problem may lie in the Chinese system of selling individual beds. In effect all rooms except doubles and quite often those, too, can function as dormitories. The fewer beds there are in a room, the higher the price per bed. Although reception staff may refuse to give rooms to Chinese couples who cannot prove their married state, male and female foreigners who just buy individual beds are often put in the same room. However, mainland Chinese are never put in the same room as foreigners, so if you are the only foreigner in a busy hotel that only has four-bed rooms available, you may occasionally have to pay for all four beds.

The up-market hotels in China which are Chinese enterprises tend to be overpriced. Everything glitters, but the knobs come off in your hand, the service lacks polish, and so does the room. There may be automatic lifts, but someone is employed to work them, and when that person goes to lunch the lifts are switched off. You may discover a dimly lit cocktail bar on the top floor, for instance, with background jazz, smartly uniformed Hong Kong-trained waitresses, and an impressive drinks menu. However, key cocktail ingredients such as gin will be unavailable. If you don't expect too much, stays at these hotels can be highly entertaining. Any hotel with pretensions, including many cheaper ones, will have a row of clocks on the wall, each with the name of a capital city underneath. There will be at least six, and sometimes as many as ten. Only the one for Běijīng will usually be correct. When they are taken down for dusting or redecoration, no-one notes in what order they should go back up, and foreign summer time (daylight-saving time) is not understood, although it was briefly experimented with in China.

China's star rating system is arbitrary and not to be trusted, since hotels begin to deteriorate quickly from the moment they are completed (although stars are never subtracted as they go downhill). For real quality stay at hotels with familiar Western or Japanese names or joint-venture hotels, which are usually no more expensive than the Chinese ones.

In even the meanest guest house, a thermos of boiled water (*kāi shuǐ*) is provided for making tea or drinking straight. This is brought to the room every morning, sometimes very early, and topped up in the evening, or occasionally during the day if requested. Often tea and cups are provided too, but it is wise to carry your own. Hot water for washing will only be available part time in all but the best hotels, especially off the beaten track. In the traffic hotels at the bottom of the scale there may be only shared toilets consisting of little more than a trough, which is flushed out only once or twice a day. You will usually not be given a key to your room. Instead you may be asked to pay a deposit for a little plastic envelope with your room number, which you show to a *fúwùyuán* or 'service person' on your floor. She will then open the door whenever you want to enter your room. If you can't find her, she is sitting, knitting and chatting with the floor lady of the floor below or above, or in the common bathroom doing her washing.

When checking in you are always asked to complete a form with your name, nationality, passport number, visa number, date of validity, occupation, where you've come from, where you're going to, and when. Leave the latter blank if you don't know. The staff will attempt to check that what you have written correlates with what's in your passport. Almost all hotels insist that you pay in advance. It's best to pay day by day as what seems to be a pleasant hotel may turn out to be without functioning plumbing or some other promised service. If you decide to leave town earlier than expected you may have difficulties obtaining a refund. Hotel staff frequently make mistakes in copying payments into their accounts, whether computerized or not, so it is important to retain your receipts, as without these they will never accept that the mistake is theirs and not yours. Your room will usually be carefully inspected to make sure that you haven't stolen a threadbare towel or cracked cup before you leave, so allow time for this when checking out. The inspection will happen at their speed not yours.

Hotel managements never seem to allow funds for maintenance, and the shiny newness of hotels wears off with remarkable speed. Where staff make an effort to keep the rooms clean, it's often with wholly inappropriate methods and materials that leave fabrics faded and surfaces scratched and dull. Carpets, when seen, are almost always red, and these are mopped along with the floor, remaining soggy for much of the day, becoming ever dingier, and rotting. Even in mid-price hotels it is unlikely that all the bathroom fitments will work, and the carpet in the room will usually be marked by ancient cigarette burns and other substances about which it is best not to speculate. Slippers are provided, but it is better to take your own—they should be suitable for wearing in the shower, too. The heating comes on on a specific day of the year, usually in October, and goes off again in March. The dates vary slightly across the country and are respectively rather later and earlier than you would like, but are set by government regulation and ignore the actual weather conditions. Hotel managements adopt the same policy towards air conditioning where this is a central system, and will leave it as late as possible to turn it on.

However, service industries in China are improving rapidly, and the days when requests for a room at a half-empty hotel routinely met with the response, 'All full', are gone. New hotels are going up all the time, and in many cases these do not have the higher tariff for foreigners which has been standard since tourism in China began. Many of these single-tariff hotels, which have a sense of competition with their neighbours and are trying to work out how to please, have been selected for mention in this book. Heading for the newest hotel you can see is often the best policy, since if they have the same prices for foreigners and Chinese they will be cheaper than the long-established official dump. Cheaper promotional rates for the first few months are also not unknown.

In older hotels, and in some areas where the number of hotels open to foreigners is severely restricted, each bed or room has two prices, usually listed clearly on the wall, one for 'inside guests' (*nèi bīn*) and one for 'outside guests' (*wài bīn*). The higher price for outsiders is inevitably yours. Still, dorm beds with shared bath can cost as little as ¥25 ($3), and doubles with bath as little as ¥40 ($5) per bed outside the busiest tourist areas. Double beds are rare, and 'double' almost always means 'twin'.

Camping in China is generally problematic. There are no official camp sites of any kind, and while some officials indicate that camping is freely permitted (the Xīníng PSB says that camping by Qīnghǎi Lake is permitted, for instance, but the local officers might not agree), in general foreigners are supposed to stay in a hotel which will record their passport details and check their visas are valid.

Kazakstan and Kyrgyzstan

The better hotels are a mixture of solid former guesthouses for party officials, semi-functional sputnik-era towers, and modern joint ventures that actually work. All are very expensive, but increasing competition is starting to bring prices down. In the middle-market and lower ranges, staff are sometimes as unfriendly and unwilling as in the Soviet era, and floor staff keep a watchful eye on who comes and goes. Really cheap budget accommodation is rare in Almaty and Bishkek, and staying in private apartments is often a better option. Staying at larger hotels spares you the necessity of registering your arrival if you plan to stay more than three days, but be very clear about whether the hotel is taking care of this in order to avoid laying yourself open to fines. Formal camping sites only exist for use by climbers, and there are none in the cities, where camping would anyway be unsafe. In rural areas it is safe with a little discretion.

Pakistan

Pakistan has everything from the major international chains in Islamabad to small and very hospitable family-run guesthouses. At the most basic level, hot water for washing arrives in buckets rather than through pipes, but all along the Karakoram Highway there is plentiful choice at all price ranges, and ever-improving standards.

History and Culture

Baron Ferdinand von Richthofen was a noted geographer and traveller, but he should have gone into travel marketing instead. In the 1870s he coined the name *Seidenstrasse* for the ancient trading routes that once connected the Mediterranean with various Chinese capitals. Tourism managers of today, the inventors of 'Theatreland', 'Brontë Country', and 'Wild West Days', would love to have invented expressions so snappily resonant and yet with such an instant ring of historical authenticity as his 'Silk Road' or 'Silk Route'. There are now Silk Road coffee-table books and CD-ROMs, Silk Road travel agencies, and Silk Route hotels spread almost as widely across Asia as the routes once spread themselves. Even modern and unglamorous Chinese-made road atlases give space to trails long abandoned and never suitable for motor vehicles.

Despite the hype, the now familiar name 'Silk Road' is misleading. Silk was merely one product of an inventory of goods exchanged along not one road but a vast and varying network of them, none of which could easily be travelled from end to end. Few people tried, and even fewer succeeded.

Unravelling the Silk Routes

The first recorded Silk Route traveller, General Zhāng Qiān, had politics, not silk in mind, and even at the routes' busiest period in the 7–9th century Táng dynasty, silk only formed a part of a trade which included everything from precious stones to rhubarb. More importantly, the trade routes were the information superhighway of their day. Religious ideas such as Buddhism which travelled into China, and technological ideas such as paper making and movable-type printing which travelled out, were to transform the cultures that received them.

There was never just one Silk Route—even General Zhāng took one way out and a different one back—and the routes themselves varied according to changes in politics and water supplies. As Chinese dynasties and their policing abilities came and went, a particular route might come under the threat of bandit attack, and become too dangerous for caravans to use. Control might be regained by local Turki peoples and lost again to the Tibetans. The river supplying a certain oasis town might dry up or change course, causing it to be abandoned within weeks, and gradually reclaimed by the desert. Legends tell of sandstorms so violent that they buried cities in a matter of hours, and far from being as permanent as the word 'road' suggests to modern ears, some Silk Route sections were more directions across trackless steppe or desert than visible paths.

The Silk Routes were not some ancient M1 or Route 66, to be travelled from one end to the other. The majority of states on the Silk Routes traded with their nearer neighbours, and travellers were like participants in a relay race stretching a third of the way around the world. Chinese merchants might venture only as far as the edge of the Taklamakan Desert, where Parthians (from part of present-day Iran), Sogdians (from an ancient Persian province centred on Samarkand, now in Uzbekistan), or whoever was then in power in the nearest oases would take over. Each caravan moved west, trading as it went, before crossing its chosen mountain range and handing over to Persians and Syrians, who themselves dealt with Greeks and Jews, who dealt with the Romans. The number of people who travelled the whole length of any Silk Route was so small that we know the names of many of them, and they knew their experiences to be sufficiently rare that they published accounts of their travels. Several of these are still in print, centuries after first being published.

The peak of Silk Route trade was during the expansionist Táng dynasty (AD 618–907) whose capital was at Cháng'ān, modern-day Xī'ān. From there the route ran west along the Wèi River and then northwest up a narrow green strip between the Nán Shān (Southern Mountains) and the fringes of the Gobi Desert. At the end of this corridor stood the outpost of Dūnhuáng on the edge of the fearsome Taklamakan Desert, where the route split into two. The north route skirted the edge of the desert along the Tiān Shān (Heavenly Mountains), and the south one ran along the edge of the Kūnlún range separating the region from Tibet. Each of these had their variations, but they eventually met up at Kashgar, where fear of death from heat and sandstorm was exchanged for fear of death from cold and snowstorm. Routes onward required the crossing of substantial mountain ranges, with passes of up to 4,600 m, before connecting with what are now Pakistan, India and the countries of the CIS, and beyond to Baghdad, Damascus and Mediterranean ports.

Much of the territory through which they passed was the battleground for the struggle between settlers and nomads; firstly between agriculturists and nomadic pastoralists with their mobile herds and flocks, and later between city dwellers and the highly mobile forces that pillaged them and attacked their trading caravans, and which would eventually swallow up whole nations. At varying times the areas now occupied by Bishkek and Almaty, and even as far as the lower end of Pakistan's Hunza Valley, recognized Chinese sovereignty, and order was maintained with Chinese garrisons. At other times China contracted behind its traditional boundaries, behind the Great Wall and east of Dūnhuáng, and left the occupants of what is now its Xīnjiāng region and beyond to fight it out amongst themselves.

The history of China's Silk Routes is that of the wax and wane of Chinese dynasties from 138 BC to the present day, and of other peoples who took power during times of Chinese weakness, or swept the Chinese away by force, many of whose descendants form the non-Chinese ethnic groups living along much of the modern routes. It's also the story of intrepid travellers both Chinese and from the West, who made it there and back through the turmoil of civil wars and banditry to bring news of far-off places.

The First Silk Route Traveller

Many of those who have covered all or a significant portion of one Silk Route or another have been spies. **General Zhāng Qiān** was sent west from Hàn dynasty China in 138 BC in search of a people called the Yuèzhī. Like the Chinese (who still today call themselves the 'Hàn') the Yuèzhī had suffered frequent attacks by a mounted nomadic people called the Xiōngnú, and had been driven westwards. Zhāng's task was to recruit the Yuèzhī into an alliance, but soon after setting out he was captured by the Xiōngnú, who held him prisoner for ten years. Escaping, he continued westwards to the Ili area (now in northwest Xīnjiāng and eastern Kazakstan), only to find that the Yuèzhī had moved on. With the assistance of the small states he found there, he continued around the north side of the Taklamakan and over the Pamirs to Ferghana and yet further west and south until he finally tracked down the Yuèzhī in northwest Pakistan.

Unfortunately for Zhāng the Yuèzhī saw no reason to disturb themselves from their new home, even for purposes of revenge on those who had driven them there, and declined to ally themselves with the Hàn. After spending a year gathering information, Zhāng prudently took a route back around the southern side of the Taklamakan, in order to avoid being detained again. He was promptly captured by Tibetan allies of the Xiōngnú, but escaped a year later, finally returning to the Chinese court 13 years after he set out. Of the original 100 people in his party, just one returned with him.

Hàn Dynasty Habits

The Hàn dynasty followed the brief Qín dynasty (221–206 BC), the first to unify China, and maintained the martial impetus of its predecessor. Zhāng Qiān lived in the time of the Western or Early Hàn (206 BC to AD 9) during the reign of the practical and expansionist Emperor Wǔdì (140–87 BC). The information on 36 independent kingdoms in Central Asia and beyond which Zhāng brought back led to Wǔdì's despatch of further expeditions. At the same time, several of what would become very familiar themes of Chinese history, foreign policy and attitudes to other ethnic groups made their appearance. Like many modern Americans, the Chinese felt themselves and their country to be the centre of the world. Unlike them, they have consistently held this point of view for more than 2000 years, and regard non-Hàn as inferior and possibly dangerous, a point of view still actively promoted by the government. In the pre-unity Warring States period (475–221 BC) individual kingdoms had built sections of earthworks to help protect themselves from each other and from those highly mobile northern nomads, the Xiōngnú. The first emperor of the Qín dynasty, upon unifying these kingdoms into China, had set about unifying their sections of wall as well. The Hàn extended the wall considerably and carried on the battle with the Xiōngnú, from whom they wanted nothing except peace and quiet, or fealty. Neither Zhāng Qiān's news of other settled and advanced societies nor subsequent bulletins shook their belief in their own superiority, but did produce a more complex foreign policy than simply that of exclusion. Zhāng Qiān also brought news of improved military hardware—horses from the fertile Ferghana valley, which stretches across parts of present-day Tajikistan, Kyrgyzstan and Uzbekistan. These were larger, faster, and stronger than Chinese horses, and could be of considerable help in the fight against the Xiōngnú.

Trade or Tribute?

The obvious way to obtain the horses was by trade, but Chinese arrogance refused to recognize that trade existed. Several more Hàn expeditions were sent, often numbering a few hundred people and bearing gifts including silk, but no horses were forthcoming in return. Envoys from several states were received at the Hàn court, but the things they brought to trade were regarded as tribute from lesser peoples, and the goods they returned with were regarded as magnanimous gifts, and higher in value than those received. This was another attitude maintained down the centuries, and it aided the convenient fiction that China was surrounded by vassal states, still trotted out to justify the occupation of some of them in modern times. Only a few years ago the Chinese government arbitrarily decided that an unidentified state listed in ancient documents as having sent 'tribute' to China was actually part of North America, and thus that the Chinese, not the Vikings, 'discovered' the continent.

An unwillingness to relinquish horses on the part of the rulers of Ferghana, and a lack of sufficient respect for the gifts they received, led to a display of arrogant ill-temper by two Chinese envoys which ended in their deaths, and thus to the first large-scale Chinese military activity in Xīnjiāng.

Long-term Planning

Perhaps Ferghana thought itself safe, due to the vast distances and fearsome deserts that lay between its territory and that of the Hàn. Intermediate small oasis towns had insufficient food and water resources to support sizeable armies. However, the Ferghanans were the first of many to act in anger but with no long-term aims, and to fail to understand either Chinese self-esteem or genius for long-term planning. For their part the Chinese started a tradition of meeting dissent with military retaliation.

The first punitive expedition of 104 BC ended in complete failure. The large force was exhausted by the difficulties of the Lop salt desert long before it got anywhere near Ferghana. A remnant, having been further depleted by the lack of supplies beyond Lop, got through but was routed while besieging a town. When the survivors returned to Dūnhuáng, only one or two in ten of the army was left.

The Chinese did not give up. In 102 BC an army of 60,000 troops set out from Dūnhuáng in batches, so as to reduce the strain on the resources of the lands through which they were to pass. 30,000 eventually reached Ferghana's capital and secured a victory, also frightening neighbouring states into accepting imperial sovereignty. Traffic around the northern rim of the Tarim Basin increased, but so did the need to protect the route from the Xiōngnú, and from the interference of petty states which lay on it.

Although the Xiōngnú had already been driven from the Gānsù corridor in 121 BC, 115 BC saw the establishment of a military colony at Jiŭquán in western Gānsù, followed by others along the route, effectively forming a continuation of the Great Wall, but less defensive and more indicative of an aggressive forward policy. Hàn expeditions pushed ever further west, and may even have reached Persia. During the 1st century BC Chinese goods began to reach the Mediterranean, and the Chinese may have heard their first rumours of the existence of the Roman Empire.

Hāmì and Turpan were taken over, and the northern Tarim route remained under Chinese control for more than a century, until internal disorder brought about the fall of the Western Hàn dynasty in AD 9 and the formation of the short-lived Xīn dynasty (AD 9–23).

Barbarian vs. Barbarian

The Hàn were restored as the **Eastern** or **Later Hàn** from AD 25 to 220. The period of weakness had led to several smaller Tarim states regaining their independence or becoming subject to the Xiōngnú, who came back to fill the power vacuum caused by China's internal problems. A few decades later the Hàn re-expanded, regained control of their Tarim possessions, restored contacts with Central Asia, and took up the fight against the Xiōngnú again.

'Use barbarian to fight barbarian' was a favourite Chinese saying, and they were often happy to encourage the Xiōngnú to fight amongst themselves. These nomads were most dangerous during periods of unity, inflicting considerable damage on Chinese settlements and communications, but the 1st century AD saw a number of Chinese successes. The Hàn continued to expand and took control of Karashar and Yarkand. They also took the head of the chief of the western Xiōngnú, and caused the leader of the eastern tribes to come to court to kowtow (bang his forehead on the floor) at the feet of the emperor. There were also periods of trade with the Xiōngnú, although the Chinese still regarded it as an exchange of tribute and gifts.

The main restorer of Hàn power was the legendary **Bān Chāo**, who first came west to the Tarim in AD 73 bringing a small force, and took the city of Shanshan with a surprise pre-emptive attack. During the following 30 years he took control of most of the remainder of the Tarim Basin, eventually being rewarded with the title of Protector of the Western Territories. Emissaries were sent to investigate the kingdoms further to the west and beyond Chinese control, including the area of modern-day Iran, and the Persian Gulf.

Around this time Buddhism made its first appearance along the Silk Routes, but had yet to develop a large following. The first mention of Buddhism in Hàn records was in AD 65 with the founding of the first Buddhist community in China. By AD 107 Chinese control of much of the Tarim was lost again to a combination of attacks by Tibetans, the Xiōngnú, and the Kushans (from Afghanistan, Bactria and the Punjab). The Kushans had picked up Buddhism from their Indian conquests, and having taken Kashgar, Yarkand and Khotan, stayed in the region for five centuries, providing a strong Buddhist influence.

Defeat by Silk

In 53 BC, at the other end of the Silk Routes, the Romans had what is often claimed to be their first encounter with silk when the legions of Marcus Licinius Crassus fought the Parthians on the fringes of the Roman Empire's eastern borders. Substantial victories in the Middle East had made the Romans overconfident, and they drastically underestimated the abilities of these scruffy little horsemen. The Parthians could fire arrows with deadly power and accuracy, sending shafts through shield and body together, turning to fire over their shoulders while pretending to retreat. Furthermore they astounded and dismayed the Romans by suddenly unfurling enormous and startling brightly coloured silk banners. Roman standards went to decorate the walls of Parthian cities, along with Crassus' head.

The Romans bartered for samples of this wonderful new material, and regular trade began. The plethora of middlemen ensured that the source of silk, which they could sell for a high price, remained vague. The Romans knew that neither the Parthians nor other dealers were sophisticated enough make it themselves, and they believed that it grew on trees in some far- off place inhabited by the *Seres* or 'Silk People'.

But silk was just a part of the trade. Westbound caravans carried many different goods, including furs, ceramics, spices and humble rhubarb. Eastbound ones carried precious metals and gems, ivory, glass, perfumes, dyes and textiles.

A Trade in Ideas

As soon as crossings of the Karakoram range began, word of the Buddhist Gandhara culture (near what is modern-day Peshawar) started to come back. By the 4th and 5th centuries, the religion had travelled from oasis to oasis encouraged first by merchants and then by mission-aries, and had become well established in the Chinese capital. In AD 399 the monk **Fǎxiǎn** travelled around the south of the Taklamakan recording the existence of substantial monas-teries and splendid Buddhist ceremonial in towns such as Khotan, before going on to Central Asia, India, Sri Lanka and Indonesia. He returned to Nánjīng by ship, spending the rest of his life writing the account of his travels, *A Record of Buddhistic Kingdoms*, and translating the texts he brought back.

When the Hàn dynasty finally disintegrated in AD 220, China fragmented into a number of competing states, with the exception of a brief period of unity under the **Western Jīn** from AD 265 to 316, which was broken up again by the renascent Xiōngnú. Various small dynasties had control of the Gānsù corridor and parts of eastern Xīnjiāng. Buddhism continued to spread, and according to some estimates, by the 4th century perhaps 90 per cent of the Chinese were Buddhists. The religion was adopted by a number of ruling houses, most notably the **Northern Wèi**, AD 386–535, a dynasty carved out of northern China by Sinicized Turki peoples. They built Buddhist caves at Yúngǎng near Dàtóng, and started the Lóngmén caves in AD 494. They sent their own Buddhist pilgrim to India in AD 518 to obtain Buddhist texts, who passed through a Turki empire then in Mongolia (another was by then based near Issyk-Kul), and continued to India taking the southern Taklamakan route, returning in AD 521.

Buddhist cave-temple complexes were built into the soft sandstone cliffs carved by rivers, the most substantial being the Mògāo complex near Dūnhuáng, perhaps because it marked the point at which caravans entered the desert on the south and north routes. Making a gift or paying for a wall-painting constituted an early form of travel insurance, winning protection against bandits and sandstorms in this life, but going beyond today's policies by offering benefits in the next life, too.

The **Suí** reunited China in AD 589, but the dynasty only lasted for two emperors, both of whom were Buddhists. The second emperor Yángdì took the Chinese back to the northwest in force, driving out Turkis and others from Gānsù and eastern Turkestan, and once again establishing colonies along the trade routes. Many small states become tributaries and trade developed with Central Asia and the West, although constantly threatened by Turki forces. Fortunately for the Suí, at the time that they were uniting China, the Central Asian Turkis (descendants of the Xiōngnú) were beginning to fight amongst themselves. The western khanate based on Issyk-Kul (now in Kyrgyzstan) splintered away, and there was internal dissension in the eastern khanate, kept going by the Chinese who once again employed their divide and rule techniques. But in AD 615 the Eastern Turki khan Shibi (reigned AD 609–19) surrounded the emperor at a northern fortress, keeping him there for a month before the siege was broken, and the last military fling of the Suí was another failed campaign against Turkis, too. Once again the deserts and the distances wore out the Chinese armies, and the expenditure emptied the dynasty's coffers. The Suí fell in AD 618.

The Silk Routes' Peak

Silk Route trade reached its peak in the 7th century during the confident and expansionist **Táng Dynasty** (AD 618–907). The second Táng emperor, Tàizōng, finally crushed the Turks on the northern frontier in 630. By the reign of Xuánzōng (AD 712–56), China was the richest and most powerful country in the world, and living through a cultural golden age as well.

China once again moved into the Tarim and Junggar Basins, and expansion continued further than ever before, incorporating parts of Mongolia and Manchuria, Ferghana and the Pamirs. Trade flourished, whatever the emperors might choose to call it, bringing many foreigners to the Táng court at Cháng'ān, who influenced Chinese customs. Persians, Arabs, Uighurs and Jews settled in Táng cities, bringing Islam, Judaism, Nestorian Christianity, Zoroastrianism and Manichaeism with them. Up to the 760s most came by land down the Silk Routes, but after then mostly by sea following the disruption of the land routes.

Buddhism was widespread, and until the 8th century constantly renewed by contacts with India. When links were cut it survived and developed native qualities. To the Chinese the most famous Silk Route traveller was **Xuánzàng**, another Buddhist monk, who left the Táng capital in AD 629 on a mission to collect scriptures. Following the northern route around the Tarim, he visited Wŭwēi, Ānxī, Hāmì, and Turpan, where a hunger strike was necessary to persuade the Buddhist king to let him go on. With escorts, introductions and gifts from the king, he continued to Karashar and Kuqa, then crossed the Tiān Shān to the north to visit the Turkish khan near Issyk-Kul, arriving in AD 630. He went on to visit India before returning via Kashgar, Yarkand and Khotan in AD 645. His travels were mythologized in the classic of Chinese literature, *Journey to the West* or *Monkey*, the source of plots for everything from Chinese opera to television cartoon series.

Xuánzàng brought back more than 600 texts to Cháng'ān, a city which was already one of the largest and most cosmopolitan in the world, and had a population of almost two million by AD 742. Despite having travelled against the emperor's wishes, he was welcomed back by Tàizōng as much because he was a source of military intelligence as because he was a pious man.

Islam Arrives in Force

The Táng maintained good security over the routes to their far-flung possessions, but once again Chinese resources were overstretched. The cost of keeping large numbers of troops under the command of powerful viceroys drained finances. From AD 751 things went into reverse, with the Chinese defeated by advancing Muslim Arabs at the battle of the Talas River (now in Kazakstan), and by Khitan Mongols in the north. Various commanders of outlying regions rebelled, and one even dared to attack Cháng'ān and Luòyáng in AD 755. There followed widespread civil war until AD 763 when the Táng dynasty was restored to Cháng'ān with the help of Uighur Turks (originally from Outer Mongolia) who then settled north of Gānsù. They had become Manichaeists, and added Manichaeist temples and frescoes to the Buddhist ones already there. The Arabs went on to take Kashgar, and their allies, the Tibetans, took control of much of the Tarim Basin and Gānsù corridor, including Dūnhuáng, taken in around AD 766, and spread their Lamaist version of Buddhism. Both took up the role of middlemen from their predecessors. The Uighurs moved south and displaced them both in the 840s. Amidst all the chaos trade suffered, and Chinese xenophobia once again came to the fore. Despite the rebellion of their own commanders, the Chinese blamed foreigners for the problems, a practice still popular in Běijīng today, and Buddhism was outlawed between AD 842 and 845. The empire began to fall apart, finally expiring in AD 907.

During the disruption and civil war that followed in the **Five Dynasties** period, the remaining Tarim states once again threw off Chinese control and went their own way. Reunification began under the Sòng Dynasty from AD 960, but by then sea routes to the Middle East were beginning to take the place of land transport. As for the silk trade, the Persians had managed to master the art of sericulture for themselves, and China was no longer the sole source of supply.

Silk Route Empires

Of the multiple mini-empires into which China now disintegrated, the **Xī Xià** (Western Xià) in western Gānsù and Níngxià had the biggest impact on the Silk Routes. These Tangut people, 400,000 of whose descendants still live in modern Gānsù (the Dōngxiāng or Santa minority), ruled from 1038 to 1227. Of Tibetan stock, they were nevertheless much influenced by the Chinese, and they took up the role of middlemen that geography gave them. After the foundation of the Sòng, the Xī Xià remained independent and from 1044 were paid off by the Sòng for peace in silver, silk and tea—valuable for trading westwards. They also came under unsuccessful attack from the Sòng from 1115 to 1119, until all were eventually defeated by the Mongols, who so thoroughly destroyed the Xī Xià's capital of Karakhoto in modern-day Inner Mongolia, that little was left standing.

As with the Xiōngnú centuries earlier, northern nomadic tribes were only a threat when they put their differences behind them and confederated. This was the case with the Khitan Mongol **Liáo** dynasty, 907–1125, which occupied areas of Inner Mongolia and Manchuria, and parts of China proper—humiliating to the self-esteem of the many Chinese forced to live under foreign rulers. The Liáo were also bought off by the Sòng with silver and silk, and were the first to make Běijīng a capital, although a subsidiary one. After their destruction in 1123 by the Tartars, one member of the imperial house fled west and formed a new empire in Central Asia until that was swallowed up by the Mongols, too.

The **Sòng** dynasty, 960–1279, was quite different in character from its predecessors, and alone amongst Chinese dynasties never had an expansionist phase. The policy of buying peace which began in 1005, and the three-way balance of power between the Sòng, Liáo and Xī Xià, kept the peace for nearly a century altogether, although there were frequent breaches of cease-fire agreements, and intense debate within China amongst those for and against accommodating barbarians. During its 300-year rule it never gained control of the whole of China, let alone reached up through Gānsù to the Tarim Basin or beyond. The Sòng first had a northern capital at Kāifēng from 960 to 1126, and then were driven south by Tartars to a southern one at Hángzhōu from 1127 to 1279. The earlier (Northern) Sòng were not militarily minded, and being cut off from Central Asia turned their attention to the sea instead, developing ship design and naval skills. The bribes paid to Xī Xià, Liáo and other border peoples were a contributing factor to severe inflation. The later (Southern) Sòng state, while smaller than its predecessor, was nevertheless exceedingly rich and rather more technically advanced than Europe in the same period.

The disturbance of the balance of power came when the Sòng made an alliance with the short-lived Jurchen Tartar **Jīn** dynasty (1115–1234) to crush the Liáo. The 'use barbarian to fight barbarian' technique was back, and the Jīn received little help from the Sòng in their successful crushing of the Liáo in 1123. The Sòng had hoped by this means to free themselves of their expensive 1005 treaty with the Liáo, and gain back some northern territory, but instead the Jīn took the Liáo's place in both treaty and territory, expecting exactly the same contributions from the Sòng. Their superior horsemanship and military skills were a preview for Mongol terrors to come, and were used to drive the Sòng south in 1127, following which the Jīn made their capital at Běijīng. They captured the last Northern Sòng emperor, who remained in captivity until his death in 1135, and they continued to harry the Sòng until they were bought off in 1141.

The West Hears of the East

Reunification on a grand scale was the result of a meeting in 1206 of the leaders of various nomadic tribes in Mongolia, who decided to unite their forces under a single leader—

Genghis Khan. As Marco Polo put it, 'They made up their minds to conquer the whole world,' and within two generations they had almost succeeded, creating an empire that stretched from the Caspian and Black Seas to the Sea of Japan.

When the Mongols first entered China in 1209 the Sòng were for a while happy to see barbarian once again beating up barbarian. The Jīn were squeezed into being a buffer state between the Mongols and the Sòng, and the Mongols took Běijīng in 1215 forcing them south. In 1227 following the death of Genghis Khan, the ever-flexible Sòng allied themselves with the Mongols and crushed their erstwhile allies the Jīn, whose state became absorbed by the Mongols in 1234.

Genghis (*circa* 1162–1227) had divided the territories he conquered into four khanates, each under a son of his chief wife, of which northern China was the most easterly territory. Genghis' concentration on expansion to the west had slowed further progress into China, and his death had caused a halt in all proceedings while a new Great Khan was chosen. The Sòng still coveted the same parts of traditional China that they had hoped to get back from the Liáo with the help of the Jīn, and from the Jīn with the help of the Mongols. So they turned on their allies in 1234 and attacked them, thereby almost guaranteeing their own destruction, and total foreign control of China.

While many in Europe shook at the thought of further Mongol expansion westwards, others, parallel in their thinking to the Chinese, were satisfied that it was the schismatic Russian Christians and the hated infidel Muslims who had borne the brunt of the Mongols' attacks— 'barbarian fighting barbarian'. Rapid Islamic military expansion had left the Muslims forming a buffer zone between the Mongols and Christian Europe, but it was only the death of Genghis followed not long afterwards by that of his son Ogatai which halted the advances on the West. Eventually grandson Khubilai took overall control, with various areas of the vast empire divided amongst relatives, and in 1271 he founded the **Yuán dynasty**, completing the conquest of China in 1276. He moved the Mongol capital south to Khanbalik, today's Běijīng, with a summer residence at Shàngdū (Coleridge's *Xanadu* and today's Dolon Nor in Inner Mongolia), and reigned until 1294.

The Mongols had reached Poland by the time of Ogatai's death in 1241, which led them to withdraw slightly and pause while the leaders assembled to decide the succession. The Franciscan **John of Plano Carpini** was sent from Europe to the Mongol headquarters at Karakoram (in Outer Mongolia today) following the election of Ogatai's son Kuyuk in 1246, to gain assurances that the Mongols would proceed no further. The Dominican **William of Rubruk** reached Karakoram in 1256 on a similar mission. Each was initially encouraged by the presence of Nestorian Christians at the court, but neither gained anything except further reason to fear the Mongols, and the material for a book each.

The Mongol empire covered almost the whole length of various Silk Routes, and they formed major lines of communication within it. The Mongols were known not to have strong religious feelings, and they had created a borderless unity as tempting in its time as any European Union or North American Free Trade Area today. Once the threat to western Europe had receded, and news of the Mongol empire began to come back, there were those who saw great opportunities for merchant, missionary and diplomat alike. Trade began to flow again.

Marco Polo

The West's most famous Silk Route traveller was **Marco Polo**, who set out from Europe in 1271 with his father and uncle, and arrived at Khubilai's summer capital in 1275. Staying in the service of the Great Khan for 17 years, he travelled widely throughout China, eventually returning by sea to Venice in 1295. Fighting on behalf of the Serene Republic in its war against Genoa, he was taken prisoner in 1298 and found himself sharing a cell with a well-known romance writer, Rustichello of Pisa. It is to this that we owe our knowledge of Polo's travels; had he not whiled away the time recounting what he had done and seen to the writer, there is no particular reason to believe that his story would ever have appeared in print.

A Description of the World or the Travels of Marco Polo was given the Mills and Boon treatment of its day, with an over-magnification of the hero's importance and treatment at the Mongol court. Also included were some episodes from other Rustichello romances and popular Middle Eastern myths, all wrapped up to make a compelling story. Even without the embellishments, many Venetians, as egocentric as the Chinese, thought their Mediterranean lands to be the centre of civilization, and found Polo's account of the Mongol Empire's greatness improbable, as have many scholars since. Much of the book is vague, and much is hearsay, which may or may not account for the difficulties in correlating some of it with contemporary Chinese records, in which Polo himself fails to appear. He spent some 20 years away, but there are not nearly enough events in the book to fill that length of time, although Silk Route towns such as Jiǔquán and Zhāngyè claim to have had him for one year each on some discreet mission for Khubilai.

Polo is often praised for his detailed observations, yet somehow omits the Great Wall altogether, and dismisses many towns in only a paragraph of commercial information that would make an estate agent's version comparatively exciting reading. Perhaps he omits the Wall because it wasn't for sale. He is also hailed as the greatest traveller ever, given the dangers and difficulties of travelling at that time and through such remote regions. Yet he was only accompanying his father and uncle, who had already been there and back once. They had been preceded by missions from Pope Innocent IV and Louis IX of France, and they had a passport from the Great Khan himself which ensured that everything possible was done to help them on their way.

It is perhaps the debates over the fidelity of the book and the puzzles set by some of its vague references that have kept scholars and others amused up to modern times. There are more than 80 contemporary copies in various versions and several languages in libraries around the world, and the book has remained an international bestseller. Copies of *The Travels* were still being carried by Western adventurers and archaeologists in the 19th and 20th centuries as almost the only written references available to parts of the Silk Routes.

The book long outlasted its main subject, the court and empire of the Great Khan. The Mongols were brilliant warriors and military strategists, but hopeless administrators, who as foreigners faced constant uprisings from the Chinese. Their failure to have a coherent succession policy made them waste time and fight amongst themselves every time a khan died. They were ousted by the Chinese Míng in 1368.

Marco Polo, the Silk Route superstar, is now everything from a cocktail to a class of aeroplane seat. Were he alive today the deals his agents would have signed for shoe advertising campaigns would have been worth even more than the fortune he was rumoured to have brought back from China, and which earned him the nickname *Il Milione*—Mr Millions.

The Decline

The rebel general who became the first emperor of the **Míng** (1368–1644) had surprising origins as a Buddhist novice. This was the first time for well over 200 years that a Chinese emperor had ruled over all of China's traditional territory. The Míng were inward-looking, once again conscious of their own superiority, saw no use for trade, and reverted to regarding it as tribute. There was an almost continuous need to deal with the threat of a potentially resurgent Mongol military, especially as Inner Asia had fused into one Mongol group sharing the heritage of Genghis Khan. The Míng substantially rebuilt and reinforced the Great Wall, in some cases rerouting it, and cladding long sections in stone. Most of what is still visible above ground today is Míng. Nevertheless, Mongol incursions still occurred and one emperor was captured in battle in 1450, then ransomed for a huge sum.

Luckily for the Chinese, even under Khubilai the Mongol court had begun to be influenced by Tibetan Lamaist Buddhism, and in the 16th century the Mongols converted *en masse*, the most powerful Mongol ruler of the day being brought to Buddhism by the third Dalai Lama in 1577. Under this pacifying religion they became more sedentary, losing their mobile advantage over the Chinese, and began to lose territory to them.

The Míng dynasty cut itself off from all outside influences, and much of China's borders returned to approximately their previous limits, leaving the Taklamakan oases to their own devices, and sending the Silk Routes into further decline.

The 13th-century conquering of Central Asia by Islamic forces meant the destruction of all Buddhist sites not already lost to the desert. Given the Islamic horror of representations of the human form, the destruction of Buddhist paintings, either wholesale or by picking out the eyes, was guaranteed. Luckily the shifting sands had claimed several sites preventing this destruction, and some had been forgotten as water sources dried up forcing migration, the arid environment leaving documents, wall-paintings, statues and other artefacts almost perfectly preserved after hundreds of years. The only other sites to survive were those such as Dūnhuáng, which was again under the control of the militarily competent and thoroughly Buddhist Tibetans.

The displacement of populations led to a reduction in the continuously necessary business of water management, leaving more towns to be reclaimed by the desert. The constantly changing middlemen, the lack of security, the opening up of longer distance sea routes, and the hostility between Islam and Christianity all contributed to the decline in trade. Islam was left to root itself firmly in the culture of the local Turki peoples, and remains the predominant religion today.

Surrounded by the army of a peasant uprising from China's northwest, the last Míng emperor hanged himself on 25 April 1644 as it overran Běijīng. The main Míng army was away at the Great Wall blocking the advance of the Manchus through a pass near the coast. The commander came to terms with the Manchus, deciding that driving out the rebels was a better option, and the Manchus took Běijīng without much of a fight on 5 June. Mortifying as it was for the Chinese, they were again to be ruled by foreigners, this time for more than 250 years.

The Last Dynasty

In succeeding centuries contact with the West was through the sea routes to China's southern and eastern seaboards, with missionaries taking the lead. The Manchus set themselves up as the **Qīng** dynasty (1644–1911), China's last. The Qīng quickly became Sinicized, were convinced that everything they needed was to be found within their borders, and for the most part strenuously resisted foreign ideas, severely restricting the movements of the few visitors they allowed in. They did, however, take back control of the Tarim Basin, and finally incorporated Xīnjiāng as part of China in 1884.

The Manchurian Qīng were ethnically related to the Tartar Jīn dynasty of the 12th century and before taking over China had their own dynasty in the northeast called the Later Jīn, changing the name to Qīng in 1636. Chinese resistance was only completely suppressed with the annexation of Táiwān in 1683.

The early Qīng had a succession of brilliant emperors who took steps to reduce Chinese resentment to foreign rule by involving them in the government. By the time of the Qiánlóng emperor (1736–95) China was probably the richest and most populous state in the world. Qiánlóng was expansionist and determined to extend the boundaries of China even beyond those of the Táng. By the mid-18th century there was a protectorate in Tibet, and in 1758–9 the conquest of the Ili and Turkestan regions added about 15.5 million sq km to the empire.

Turkestan's history in the 17th and 18th centuries was shaped by the Junggar Mongols. It was inhabited by sedentary Uighurs and nomadic Kyrgyz and Kazaks, all Muslims, but who did not co-operate with each other. In a 17th-century local dispute, two Sufi Muslim religious and political leaders fought each other for greater power, the loser calling on a Mongol leader called Galden for help in 1670. This merely led to Galden annexing Hāmì, Turpan and neighbouring areas for himself in 1679. The Qīng fought to oust the Junggars from Western Mongolia and Turkestan in a long-drawn-out war, the Kāngxī emperor making it his personal mission, and finally defeating Galden in 1696, although the rebel's descendants continued to make difficulties for the Qīng. In 1713 his nephew Tsewang Rabtan recaptured Hāmì, only to be dislodged again. In the 1720s he attacked the Kazaks west of Junggaria, driving them into the arms of the Russians, whose vassals they became.

The Manchus had united themselves with a system in which both civil and military administrations were organized into units called banners, overriding clan loyalties, and making them strong enough as a unity to take China and keep it. In contrast the Mongols failed either to unite with each other or with the Turki peoples of Turkestan, which enabled Qiánlóng's general Zhàohuì to eliminate the Mongols with spectacular brutality in 1754. The Manchus took firm control of the Tarim and Junggar Basins.

Manchu troops were stationed both in Junggaria, mostly occupied by nomadic pastoralists, and in the more settled Tarim oases, collectively known as Eastern Turkestan. The Qīng bothered no-one as long as the region remained peaceful and paid its taxes. However, individual Qīng officials often exploited and oppressed the local Turki peoples—mainly Uighurs, Kazaks and Kyrgyz—sometimes with the co-operation of local rulers and the Manchu banner troops stationed there. An influx of Chinese Muslims (known as Dungans or Huì) and Hàn Chinese grated on the sensitivities of locals, who feared that Qīng encouragement of Chinese settlers would swamp them, still an issue today.

A resurgence of Islamic militarism led to several holy wars including those of 1815, 1820–28 and 1857. These were inspired by the khans of Kokand, who themselves led an attack in 1830 which compelled the Qīng to make special concessions on trade. There were full-scale Muslim rebellions from 1862 to 1878 sparked by Qīng discrimination against Muslim subjects, during which time a Dungan from Kokand called Yakub Beg led an independent Kashgaria. Although Yakub was eventually crushed again by long-term planning (the army from the east paused to grow its own food supplies en route), the Russians took the opportunity to gain more territory and trade concessions, on the grounds of protecting their own newly acquired Central Asia possessions from Islamic militancy. The Chinese were forced into their first proper treaties with foreign powers, those of Tarbatagai in 1864, and St Petersburg in 1881. Russia was given trading rights in return for the partial return of lost territory, but also at the cost of signing away other territory in the process. The Russians were given permission to trade in Ili and Tarbatagai, and later in Turpan and Jiǔquán, and to set up consulates there. Kashgar was also opened to Russian trade, and in 1864 extensive territories north of Issyk-Kul were ceded to Russia. One of the reasons for declaring Xīnjiāng a province in 1884 was to formalize its status as an internal part of China, making further Russian advances the equivalent to a direct attack on China itself, and thus not to be undertaken lightly.

Poison by Sea

European traders had begun direct contact with China by sea, beginning with the Portuguese in 1514, who acquired Macao as a trading base in 1565, and were followed by the Dutch in the 17th century. Europeans developed a taste for Chinese tea and porcelain, and a massive trade deficit developed, alarming the British so much that in 1792 George III sent Lord Macartney with elaborate examples of British products to entice the Chinese to more balanced trade.

Lord Macartney arrived in China in 1793 ostensibly to celebrate the Qiánlóng emperor's 80th birthday, but in fact to negotiate improved trading opportunities. The Chinese refused all his requests and the Qiánlóng emperor wrote to George III in an edict, 'We have never valued ingenious articles nor do we have the slightest need of your country's manufactures. Therefore, O king, as regards your request to send someone to remain at the capital, while it is not in harmony with the regulations of the Celestial Empire we also feel very much that it is of no advantage to your country.'

The Sinicization of the Manchus had included their adoption of Chinese xenophobia and attitudes to trade. Matters were not helped by Macartney's refusal to kowtow, and King George was sent a message warning him not to break Chinese laws. The Chinese were shortly to learn that their insularity had left them unable to compete with foreign technology, and their xenophobia ill-prepared them for international *realpolitik.*

The flow of silver from West to East was stemmed and then reversed by introducing a product from India that ordinary Chinese were soon not only requesting, but craving—opium. Major trading companies from several Western powers became drug dealers, often operating under their governments' control or licence, with appalling consequences for Chinese society and economy. When in 1838 the Qīng belatedly acted to quell the trade, confiscating and destroying Western stocks of opium at Canton, they simply accelerated their own decline with a succession of military defeats. The Self-Strengthening Movement of the early 1860s belatedly recognized that China could after all learn from foreigners, but in language that still stressed the country's racism and insularity. The exhortation to 'learn the superior barbarian techniques to control the barbarian' was anyway both widely rejected and too little, too late. Ever larger chunks of China fell under the control of foreigners far worse than the Sinicized Manchus, and a series of 'unequal treaties' forced on the Qīng give foreign powers a licence to do more or less as they pleased. The Qīng also faced large-scale internal rebellions, and the dynasty finally ended with the abdication of the last emperor on 12 February 1912.

Silk Route Superpowers

It was not until the superpower politics of the 19th century that the Silk Routes once again attracted international attention. The cry 'The Russians are coming!' long predates the Soviet Union, and was used by a variety of British Empire stalwarts to stir up support for their own expansionist plans. In 1807 information reached London that Napoleon, emboldened by his European successes, had proposed to Tsar Alexander I of Russia that they jointly invade India, the source of much of Britain's wealth. This particular plan was soon forgotten with Napoleon's own invasion of Russia and catastrophic defeat. However, the general idea was not forgotten by either British or Russians, as the latter advanced through the Caucasus, and then turned their attentions east, successively capturing the former Silk Route cities of Tashkent, Samarkand, Bokhara and Khiva. By the middle of the century, Central Asia was permanently in the British headlines.

The British for their part gradually advanced north from India, and up what is now the Karakoram Highway, making alliances where they could, and conquering where they could not. At the beginning of the century the Russian and British Empires were more than 2000 miles apart, but by the end of it the distance was reduced to a few hundred and in one area as little as twenty. Kashgar, which along with the rest of Xīnjiāng had revolted against Chinese rule in 1862, was controlled by the Dungans from the north of the region, and both British and Russians were happy to negotiate with their leader, Yakub Beg, while avoiding formal recognition of his new state. Once Chinese rule had been restored in 1877, the Russians were allowed a consul in Kashgar from 1882, and the British a trade representative from 1890.

The Silk Routes were so long forgotten that the British, who had arrived in India by sea, little thought that a land route could exist. The region was mountainous, but unmapped, and opinion was divided on whether there might be passes through which an army of Cossacks could descend on India. In what came to be known as the Great Game, empire loyalists of both sides, with their egos dwarfed only by their moustaches, feinted and parried, mapped and measured, and sometimes resorted to elaborate disguises. In areas deemed particularly dangerous, the British sent Indian hillmen disguised as Muslim pilgrims, their surveying equipment carefully camouflaged as innocuous items of baggage. The Russians used Mongolians for the same purpose. Constant negotiations went on to secure the allegiance and trade of intervening states, and for the right to place political officers and advisors in each city.

Game this may have been, but it was both bizarre and deadly. **Captain Arthur Conolly**, the man who coined the name Great Game, met his end by being beheaded in Bokhara's main square. **Colonel Algernon Durand**, leading an expedition against the unruly tribes of the

Hunza and Nagar valleys, stood up in thick enemy fire and was shot in the groin with a bullet home-made from a garnet encased in lead. **Captain Francis Younghusband** crossed the Muztagh Pass on the edge of K2, deemed impassable even by locals, wearing boots which only had thin leather soles. On another occasion, bumping into a party of Cossacks with no more right to be in the region than he had himself, instead of coming to blows he accepted an invitation to dinner in a tent thousands of feet up and hundreds of miles from anywhere, for which, of course, he dressed.

Eventually it seemed that open war was inevitable, but Russia stepped back from the brink, and in 1907 the Anglo-Russian Convention was signed bringing the Great Game to a close.

It was not, however, the end of *Boys' Own*-style derring-do. The Bolshevik Revolution revived the idea of a Russian invasion, and Lenin declared in 1920, 'England is our greatest enemy. It is in India that we must strike them hardest.' In 1918 **Lieutenant-Colonel Frederick 'Hatter' Bailey** set out from Kashgar across the passes of the Tiān Shān to Tashkent on a fact-finding mission. Unfortunately during his travels there had been a confrontation between British and Bolshevik troops on the borders of Persia, and they were almost at war. Bailey had to flee for his life, adopting a series of disguises—an Austrian cook, a Rumanian officer, a Latvian official and a German prisoner of war. As an Albanian clerk he was recruited by the Bolshevik Secret Service to find out the whereabouts of a British master-spy—himself.

Digging for Victory

Rumours of lost and buried cities abounded amongst the inhabitants of Xīnjiāng and eventually reached the West. The first hard evidence that these stories were more than legend was brought back by one of the Indian secret agents sent during the Great Game to investigate the oases of the Taklamakan. He brought back news in 1855 of sand-buried ruins near Khotan, which were subsequently visited by a British officer. Other foreigners visited the region in the following years on map-making and other political missions, occasionally stumbling across antiquities, but not always understanding the importance of their discoveries. Competitive collecting of Silk Route artefacts began through the medium of paying locals for whatever they brought in, with the British and Russians in particular vying to acquire new items.

One local treasure-seeker, **Islam Akhun,** realized both that there was a lot of money to be made and that the foreigners were not always able to read the ancient scripts of the papers he retrieved from desert sites. Major documentary finds of Akhun's found their way into collections in London, Paris and St Petersburg between 1895 and 1898, inspiring volumes of commentary and scholarship, before being revealed as elaborate forgeries.

From 1895, with China increasingly in disarray and no-one to stop them, foreign expeditions were made to Silk Route sites with the express purpose of bringing back as much treasure as possible. The Qīng dynasty was in decline, and was gradually losing control of areas far more central than Xīnjiāng. Imperial rule came to an end with the formation of the first Republic in 1911, but still warlords thrived, foreign armies annexed land for their own use, and China was unable to help itself on larger issues, let alone give much attention to the preservation of historic sites. The removals began with Sweden's **Sven Hedin,** continued with Britain's **Aurel Stein,** and France's **Paul Pelliot,** all soon joined by Germans, Russians, Americans and Japanese. Guides at cave temple sites today will point out German archaeologist Albert von le Coq's saw marks. A hole in a wall at Dūnhuáng leads to a hidden library, from which Stein removed more than 8000 manuscripts, including the oldest printed book in the world—the *Diamond Sutra* of AD 868, now on display at the British Library.

The expeditions faced dangers from bandits and all that the desert could throw at them, as well as from their own foolishness. One of Sven Hedin's trips ended in disaster, when finding that some water containers had not been filled by his native assistants, he nevertheless continued across the desert. One of them then drank the remaining supplies himself, and narrowly escaped death at the hands of his companions. Out of water and failing to discover more, they resorted to drinking spirits, the blood of a cockerel and a sheep they had brought with them, and their camels' urine. After several days without water Hedin stumbled across a pool in a dried-up river bed, and was able to carry water in his boots back to one of his dying companions. Another was rescued by some passing shepherds. But two men, including the water thief, died, as did seven out of the expedition's eight camels.

Spheres of influence were mapped out and different archaeological parties almost came to blows over what they regarded as trespass on 'their' sites. The Russians once threatened to expel the Germans by force of arms from a site that they thought of as their own. In the eyes of later Chinese governments, their activities made the word 'archaeologist' synonymous with the word 'thief', and it is perhaps a feeling of embarrassment as much as a lack of space for display which has kept many of the treasures of the Silk Route oases as deeply buried in the vaults of museums as they ever were beneath the sands of the Taklamakan.

The expeditions finally ceased in the mid-1920s, when anti-foreign feeling in China was at an all-time high. Germany had occupied a chunk of Manchuria but, following its defeat in the First World War, the West allowed Japan to take control of the territory rather than returning it to China. The last few expeditions had to be heavily armed, and any discoveries were in theory to be handed over to the authorities, even if it wasn't always clear who these were.

20th-century Travellers

The more remote a destination the more the rare visitor feels obliged to rush into print upon his or her return home. If Silk Route travel in the early part of the century was dominated by spies and archaeologists, the few people who came later were either writers or at least became published. If they have anything else in common it is disobedience to authority. The decision of the Chinese authorities to close an area to visitors often seems to produce much pouting, stamping of feet, and wilful cries of 'I will go. I *will*!' Such is the attraction of the ancient Silk Routes and their sites, that at various times travellers braved civil wars, direct government refusal of permission to travel, and repeated arrest. Some passed through the highly sensitive Lop Nor area east of the Taklamakan where the Chinese once carried out nuclear tests, risking possible imprisonment.

When *The Times* correspondent **Peter Fleming** passed through Khotan in 1935 without any proper visa or permission, it was the headquarters of a rebellion which had removed a string of oases on the Southern Route from Chinese control. After months on the road mostly by horse from Xī'ān, he felt he had received his first contact with civilization when a postman from British India arrived carrying three-month-old copies of *The Times*.

The rest of Xīnjiāng was under the nominal government of a warlord in Ürümqi whose survival depended upon the support of his Russian neighbours. Much of his policy was decided far away in Moscow, and Fleming reported that it seemed almost inevitable that all or part of

Xīnjiāng would join the Soviet Union. He passed a pleasant time playing tennis, football and polo with the staff of the British consulate in Kashgar, and attended an alarming dinner at the Russian consulate at which everybody including the waiters seemed to be armed. He finally crossed the Karakorams to India, having completed the 3500-mile journey in seven months.

Eventually the region was reunified and, following the formation of the People's Republic in 1949, the communists took firm control of Xīnjiāng. As with Inner Mongolia and Tibet, they began a policy of settling Hàn Chinese in the region in order to stabilize it. This continues today, with major salary bonuses being the only draw to reluctant Hàn; in most towns they remain a slightly nervous minority.

The Chinese have undertaken major conservation work at various archaeological sites, and many are at least partially open to visitors. Others seem not to have been visited since foreigners such as Stein passed through at the beginning of the century. The Anglo-Chinese expedition to cross the Taklamakan in the footsteps of Stein in 1993 passed through the ruins at Endere, and found jewellery and coins strewn in the streets by the wind. Sites such as these are not open to the casual visitor, not least because some are a few hundred kilometres out into the desert, and await Chinese time and funding for proper archaeological research.

The Great Wall is now used to attract foreigners rather than repel them, and tourism to China has now grown to about 24 million visitors per annum, fifth in the world, according to the World Tourism Organization (or nearly double that if you believe the Chinese figures). Only a tiny proportion of those visitors yet venture far up the old Silk Routes. Although trains and buses have replaced the camel and horse, Silk Route China is still remote, and has not yet given up all its secrets.

Anticipating China

Seen from near, the Oriental is not that picturesque and imaginative being in pointed slippers... There is quite as much poetry in the life of an Englishman as in that of an Asiatic.

Robert Shaw, *Visits to High Tartary, Yarkand and Kashgar*, 1871

China disappoints in not living up to the many expectations of its visitors. Wispy-bearded old gentlemen do not throng streets of curly-eaved mansions, their hands thrust deep into long sleeves, muttering inscrutable quotations from Confucius. China is neither a museum for the entertainment of foreigners, nor a Charlie Chan movie. The Chinese are abandoning their bicycles for cars when they can, their Běijīng opera for kung-fu videos, and their blue cotton jackets for polyester blouses and suits. If this disappoints it is the visitor who is to blame, not the visited.

At its best, China is an epic country of sprawling, breathtaking spectacle with some of the most extravagant and ambitious monuments ever constructed by humankind. At its worst, China is a third-world country in which millions of ill-dressed people push and shove their way down the heavily polluted streets of hideous, ramshackle cities, thinking of little else beyond how to survive in the continuing and unpredictable social experiment that is Chinese life. It has much in common with other impoverished, over-crowded nations, plus a few quirks of its own.

The key to enjoying a trip to China is to arrive with the right set of expectations, and to anticipate some of the difficulties so that they cause the least annoyance. Absorb the following warnings and advice and be prepared for the most stimulating trip of your life.

Foreigner!

Seeing only the lower classes, the mule-men, the loafers of the streets, and the frequenters of the inns, one is apt to form a very unfavourable impression of the Chinese, and to regard them as a rude, coarse, and unmannerly race, who hate strangers, and take little trouble to disguise their feelings.

Captain Frank E. Younghusband, *The Heart of a Continent*, 1896

There will be days in China when you will think that anyone with the slightest sensitivity, manners, or intelligence was long ago taken out and shot. Neither common sense nor common courtesy seem anything more than rare. The past promotion of earthy worker and peasant values, the periodic destruction of the education system, the continuing political interference with it, and the control maintained over news and information, have produced a nation of people whose ignorance of the outside world and its peoples is as profound as if they had been brought up on Mars. Their world-picture is simple. It contains an 'us', Hàn Chinese—the main ethnic group; and it contains a 'them'—racial also-rans such the despised non-Hàn minorities living within China's borders, and Foreigners (definitely with a capital F), who are both despised and envied at the same time. The lumpen category 'Foreigners' contains everyone else who is not Chinese, in all their infinite variety. People of Hàn descent with foreign passports, however, are a sub-set of the 'us' called *Huáqiáo*—'Overseas Chinese'. Even if they are non-Chinese-speaking first-time visitors to China their treatment will be better than that given to non-Hàn.

Foreigners, initially charmed by the sound of 'Hello' from all sides, quickly learn that rather than being a friendly greeting, these cries have exactly the same function as that of shouting 'Pretty Polly' at a caged parrot until it replies in the same terms. Scarcely one individual from three to senility is capable of seeing a foreigner without saying or shouting 'Foreigner!' (*Wàiguórén* or *Lǎo wài*), often repeatedly, in the same way we would if we saw a camel in the high street (although to see a camel in the high street in some parts of Xīnjiāng is perfectly normal). Ignorance of the outside world and more than 2000 years of self-reassurance have convinced the Chinese of their racial superiority. The foreign visitor feels like the elephant man—a freak wanting to be recognized as a person. (Peter Fleming called it 'playing the two-headed calf'.) In China you're something to laugh at, point at, shout at, and stare at, and you don't know the meaning of the word 'stare' until you've been to China. Cows watching someone cross a corner of their field do not stare so blankly and passively nor with such a long attention span as some Chinese stare at Foreigners.

To perform even the most simple transaction is to become party to something resembling a scene from an opera or Greek tragedy. At a bus station for instance, a large chorus may assemble shouting 'Foreigner, Foreigner' and speculating out loud on what you are. They push close to hear your enquiries at the ticket counter, and the ones at the front report to the ones at the rear what it is that you want, endlessly repeating the same information. They make extended personal comments about your dress and appearance, and ask each other again and again, 'What country is he from?'

> *Of course, in conversation with Europeans they do not excel; they are lamentably ignorant of geography, for instance, and they generally annoy the stranger by asking if his country is tributary to China.*

> Captain Frank E. Younghusband, *The Heart of a Continent*, 1896

The Chinese have unlimited curiosity about foreigners. Unfortunately they all have the same unlimited curiosity, and most conversations are more predictable than liturgical versicle and response. It does not occur to them to question whether it might be interesting or convenient for you to answer their questions at this time, whether you might be falling asleep, trying to read a book, cross the road, or whether you might have just answered the same questions 50 times to everyone passing your compartment in the train. What nationality are you? How old are you? Are you married? Do you have any children? Why not? What work do you do? How much do you earn? How much was your watch? Your coat? Your boots?

> *They asked about these things because they thought that I was a millionaire trader who only knew about the lives of rich and incredible foreigners; but the answers could not hold their interest for long, being too far removed from the world of their own realities.*

> Owen Lattimore, *The Desert Road to Turkestan*, 1929

And so it is now. Your nationality has no meaning for them—they confuse nationality and race and don't know where your country is anyway. *You don't want children?* Incomprehensible.

The information about incomes and prices you might reveal is meaningless without an explanation of income tax, sales tax, and the cost of living which fails to hold their interest, even if your Chinese is up to it. How do you answer questions like, 'How many children are you allowed to have in your country?' Or, 'China and Britain are more or less the same, aren't they?' Or, 'England's that small country that came back to the Motherland in 1997, isn't it?' Although those proposing to visit China often fear the difficulties of being without a common language, sometimes it's easier not to speak Chinese even if you do. The alternative is to spend your days as a kind of multimedia entertainment centre, watched more intensely than a kung-fu video.

> But when one can see the Chinese gentleman at home, one modifies this impression very considerably: and personally, from this and other occasions on which I afterwards had opportunities of meeting Chinese gentlemen, I saw much to admire and even to like in them.

Captain Frank E. Younghusband, *The Heart of a Continent*, 1896

Unfortunately, since few Chinese know English and few Foreigners know Mandarin, opportunities to test out Younghusband's theory are few. Those who have been the guests of ordinary people in their homes know that their generosity can quickly reach embarrassing levels, especially given the disparity of income. But most visitors end up judging China by the behaviour of souvenir sellers and taxi drivers, hardly groups that any country would choose as representative of their cultures.

Even the Chinese recognize that they have problems with their children, although one entirely of their own creation. The one-child policy has left each family pouring rivers of devotion into a single small vessel, and the result in most cases is a *xiǎo huángdì*, or 'little emperor', a miniature tempest of sulks and demands, indulged in everything. 'Look at the *Lǎo wài*,' the parents tell their children tenderly, and in return the children run screaming to tell their parents when they spot you first. This does not bode well for the future. Even the Chinese government says that 80 per cent of the country's 270 million children are 'culturally backward'.

Amidst all the halloo-ing and *lǎo wài*-ing it's easy to forget the acts of kindness you do receive. Rise above the yelling by ignoring it. Whether or not you respond you will be laughed at, but response helps to ensure that the shouting goes on both at you and at others who follow. If you stay in a town for a few days it falls off, at least in the area of your hotel, as it gradually becomes recognized that Pretty Polly doesn't talk. Losing your temper, screaming 'The zoo is *closed*', or staring back goggle-eyed in an impression of your tormentors only serves to draw a bigger crowd.

Remember that you are a multi-millionaire, whatever your faded denim might say. You casually call taxis, you let the drivers keep the change, and you can be asked for 1000 per cent more than the proper price and pay it without even bargaining. This, to the Chinese, who unless they are *nouveaux riches* bent on flaunting their wealth will never pay 1 *fēn* more than they have to, is evidence of insanity or the possession of riches beyond counting. The situation is similar to that of a rich man with a recognizable face, say Bill Gates, strolling through a big city ghetto. Your face may not be individually recognizable, but the shape of your nose or the cut of your clothes, or that camera slung over your shoulder announce you as much as if you had stepped out of a Ferrari.

You don't like being laughed at and pointed at and talked about in a language you don't understand? If yesterday you pointed out to friends a woman riding a bicycle leading a horse or a man riding a tricycle piled high with furniture, it's not obvious that your behaviour is any different. Perhaps you even took a photograph. While some Chinese enjoy the limelight, others don't care for this kind of treatment any more than you do.

Big Nose, Big Price

The source of most discontent is the doubling of prices for *Wàibīn*, 'Foreign Guests', the mealy-mouthed official name for overseas visitors. Even to the most intelligent Chinese, that foreigners should pay more is so self-evidently true that it never occurs to them to question it. The more philosophical amongst visitors to China may care to divert themselves on long train journeys by debating how the Chinese view the statement, 'Foreigners pay more'. Is it an *a priori* truth, innately true without reference to measurement? Or is it simply an analytical truth like 'A batchelor is an unmarried man', true by virtue of the meanings of the words?

Having opened its doors to tourism the Chinese began with an overtly racist pricing system, with three official prices for any tourism services. The lowest price was for ordinary Chinese, few of whom were able to use the services anyway. Somewhere in the middle came 'Overseas Chinese'—foreign nationals of Chinese descent, followed by nationals of the same countries who happened to have bigger noses (*dà bízi*) . Separate hotels were maintained for foreigners (no Chinese allowed in), for Overseas Chinese, and for Chinese (no foreigners allowed in).

These days there are two types of hotels, those foreigners can go into and those they can't (although Overseas Chinese can stay almost anywhere), and two prices: Chinese and non-Chinese, although Overseas Chinese often get away with paying the cheaper price. This double pricing system applies to most hotels, all museums and tourist sights, and in some parts of the country to bus tickets. The mark-up is typically 100 per cent, but in hotels ranges from 20 to 300 per cent, and at sights from 100 to 800 per cent. The government may not be responsible for the relish with which these prices are enforced, even to the defiance of rules giving foreign students in China the local price, but it is hardly surprising that foreigners are looked on by the general populace as walking money-bags to be fleeced as much and as frequently as possible when this is official government policy. Some private restaurants hand foreigners menus with different prices than those they hand to the Chinese, or sometimes double or triple the bill, then bar the door to prevent them from leaving. The police couldn't care less.

> *Now China is seething with the ferment of awakened Asia, and the Chinese Government and people, struggling to assert themselves against the slights and insults, real and imaginary, of Japan, Europe and America, are chauvinistic, suspicious, jealous and ill at ease.*
>
> Eric Teichman, *Journey to Turkistan*, 1937

There has been a tradition since 1949 of blaming foreigners for China's ills, which continues unabated in the government-owned media today. Conveniently for visitors, articles describing the conspiracy amongst foreign powers to restrain China's growing economic power are translated into English and distributed to hotels nationwide through the medium of a propaganda sheet called *China Daily*. Uniting the country against foreigners is the simplest way of taking its attention from the government's own failings. Given that there are no independent sources of information, nothing could be easier. Even the handful of well-educated Chinese are likely to agree, hundreds of millions of dollars in aid annually notwithstanding. You are to blame, Foreigner, and you will pay.

Trying to avoid paying extra is largely pointless, except for those willing to break the law. Foreign student identification is almost never accepted, but you will be approached and offered fake student or worker identification cards for sums which could easily be recouped in a day or two. These work for tickets, but usually not for accommodation. Those who speak Chinese and claim to be students may get the local price anyway, since the Chinese will often flatly refuse to believe that it's possible to learn Chinese anywhere else than China. Haggling with hotels, if done with a smile, often produces results, especially out of season, when a hotel has just opened, or when a lack of business planning has caused several new hotels to open at the same time (not unusual).

To survive all this, don't waste time losing your temper or fighting battles against government overcharging that you can't win, but do refuse to be cheated by private businesses, such as taxi drivers, souvenir sellers or restaurateurs. Anticipating and thwarting their strategies can become an entertaining game, and there's plenty of information on how to do this in **Practical A–Z**. Maintain caution in all transactions, but don't allow one bad experience to affect your entire holiday or to colour your view of China as a whole. Try some of the back roads where both foreign visitors and double pricing are rare, and look out for the new private hotels in almost all towns which charge everyone the same price, and are friendlier and cleaner than those that have been open for longer periods and are entirely state-owned. There's a growing realization amongst hotel staff in general that foreigners are not so bad after all. They leave less of a mess than the new breed of travelling 'big money' private businessmen, treat the staff with greater consideration, and they also remember to say 'thank you'.

Hàn's Inhumanity to Hàn

Foreign visitors, especially those not on organized tours, may feel themselves to be in a hostile environment, but the insolence and discourtesy that some Hàn offer to foreigners is nothing compared to the acts of petty tyranny and considerable cruelty that they can inflict upon each other.

Far from the egalitarianism of their dreams, the communists have created a more selfish society than they could possibly have imagined. The scarcity of good things has led to a state of affairs in which the older and weaker are trampled underfoot in the rush to grab whatever can be grabbed. No one waits for anyone else: the phrase 'it's your turn' might as well not exist in Chinese. If the Japanese have evolved an elaborate (if superficial) courtesy to help them cope with the shortage of space and the shortage of capacity on urban transport, the Chinese solution has been for each individual simply to ignore the existence of the other 1 billion-odd Chinese altogether. The Chinese say '*Xiān lái xiān chī*' ('first come, first eat'), which seems to be taken as an exhortation to push your way to the front regardless of the lame, aged, infirm, juvenile, and healthy alike.

Nowhere else in the world is daily life more accurately called 'the push and shove'. Queues in China are wedge-shaped, and if you join the rear you are likely to end up getting further and further away from your goal, as others push in front or bribe those in front of you to make purchases for them. Pause for a moment to let someone get off the bus and three others will simply push in front of you. Getting on is a matter of pushing as hard as you can, and never mind whether people want to get off or not. Walking along the street is a constant obstacle course as light industry spills onto the pavement and someone always parks their bike exactly across the remaining gap. If you are asking questions at the railway station, post office or hotel, someone will always come and talk over the top of you in mid-sentence.

Should China ever have the opportunity to stage an Olympics and to promote a new Olympic sport, then shouting should be its choice. In every contest from the 3-metre ear drum-piercing yell to the 100-metre window-breaking shriek the Chinese would take gold every time, and with negative drug tests all round. Chinese children begin training early, with shrill efforts that probably interfere with bat navigation. The typical hotel guest sits around in a singlet watching television at volumes beyond the threshold of pain, and with the door wide open, regardless of other guests.

One of the least attractive aspects of daily life is the constant spitting. It's not the brimming spittoons in every corner of every room, or the splatterings of mucus that wait, banana-skin-like on every pavement, so much as the aural qualities of Chinese spitting that most repel. Each morning begins with a chorus of trumpeting, gurgling and retching that is repeated at intervals throughout the day. The spread of infectious diseases is inevitable, and most visitors to China can expect to get a serious head cold sooner or later. Government campaigns to cut down on such anti-social habits are having less and less effect. Smokers (the overwhelming majority of the male population) sit under government no-smoking signs to smoke. When Běijīng recently introduced a smoking ban in public places, its definition of a public place was the street, but not offices, restaurants or shops. Taught for many years to watch each other carefully for deviation from the correct line, it now takes several thousand volunteer busy-bodies to enforce this absurd law with fines. Indoors smoking is still acceptable, but less visible, and many 'laws' in China are of this window-dressing kind.

Looking where you are going is not apparently regarded as a virtue in China, whether walking, cycling or driving (staring at foreigners or pointing them out to friends constitutes one popular distraction). While once this used to lead to multiple bicycle pile-ups with bruises rather than broken bones the result, the large number of vehicles now in the hands of the careless and the certifiable often lead to more bloody results, frequently displayed in gruesome colour on noticeboards in town centres as an awful but ineffectual warning.

Common courtesy is so uncommon that examples of it warrant articles in the national press. The English-language *China Daily* features articles on people who stand up rows of bicycles they have knocked down, rather than just cycling away, such consideration for unknown others being as uncommon as a lunar eclipse. In late 1996 the government introduced a Singapore-style law *requiring* children to look after their ageing parents, a *sine qua non* of the Confucian thinking they successfully destroyed. Many admit that they will ignore it. No-one, not even the elderly themselves, expects it to be enforced.

Only the visitor on the most hermetically sealed of tours can avoid some uncomfortable moments, but coming to China to avoid the Chinese would be regrettable and absurd. There may be not be excuses for selfish behaviour, but there are reasons. There is a rapidly widening gap between China's haves and have-nots, China's history has been one long social experiment since 1949, and the people amongst whom you are travelling and living are the victims and the survivors of the laboratory. Things may be getting better for some, but they could go into reverse at any time, so they'll grab the good times while they can. Remember this: be patient, and don't give up being courteous yourself more than absolutely necessary. Everyone knows that things are not as they should be, and many are just as appalled as you. Give up your seat on a bus to an elderly person and you'll not only receive delighted thanks but stun the rest of the bus into (temporary) silence. If the lack of consideration for others distresses you, use your financial muscle to avoid some of it—use agents to buy your tickets for you, use taxis rather than buses, and so on.

Corruption, Lies, and Laziness

A respected official and Long March veteran was widely quoted in 1996 despising the rampant greed of society. He told of a case the same year in which when a young boy was drowning in a river his sister was unable to get help because no-one would come unless they were paid. Furthermore, the boatman who recovered the child's body wanted the equivalent of $30 or a few weeks' wages before handing it over to the grieving parents. But it is at the top, with the government officials, that the greed in society and the unpredictability which makes everyone so keen to take what they can while they can, begins.

> The whole governmental system is rotten to the core, and every official … lives by systematic fraud. The officials are altogether unpaid otherwise than by plunder, but, since their right to 'Squeeze' is recognised, the amount of their income is limited only by their own discretion and the resources of their districts. Public offices are nearly always sold; justice is sold; the enjoyment of public rights, such as water supply, can be secured only by bribes paid to the official in charge, and there is no immunity whatever from exorbitant taxation, the proceeds of which go mostly to the private pockets of public officials.
>
> Captain H. H. P. Deasy, *In Tibet and Chinese Turkestan*, 1901

Nearly a century later, in 1996, the government ordered officials to declare their incomes. While it presumably knew how much it was paying them, it believed that for some income from other sources would prove to be many times that of their official salaries, so little has changed. Want an official to give you a permit? Begin with gifts and take it from there. Relative going in for surgery? Take the doctors out for a banquet and give money to the nurses so as to get the care needed. Any official from a railway ticket clerk upwards may need bribing to do his or her job.

In general the police in China are lazy and hopeless. Especially if you travel on the relatively quiet routes through minority areas, be prepared for a passport examination in the small hours of the morning. The door of your hotel room will burst open and a group of policemen, hotel employees, and hangers-on, perhaps five or six people altogether, will enter your room, turning on the lights, and shouting *'hùzhào, hùzhào'* ('passport, passport'). Having examined your documents without comprehension (almost none can read anything except Chinese and some not even that) they will exit without saying anything else, probably neither closing the door nor turning off the lights. The real point of this is often to do with making sure that if you are a man you are not sleeping with a Chinese.

As any Chinese will tell you, the police are best avoided since in any dispute they may choose to 'fine' all concerned. Although as a foreigner you are more likely to get their help than local people are if something serious happens to you, they may refuse to deal with relatively trivial matters such as theft reports for insurance use, and have been known arbitrarily to confiscate possessions for imaginary illegality in the hope of a 'fine'. The 'law' of China is what some official decides it is at that particular moment. Běijīng frequently makes what sound like good and long-overdue laws on everything from copyright to prostitution, and a few businesses and brothels are shut down for form's sake. It later turns out that many video pirating operations and hairdressers (sometimes fronts for prostitution) are owned or run by gamekeeper-turned-poacher government officials.

But it's difficult to get even ordinary employees to do their jobs, despite massive overmanning. If you want to buy stamps half an hour before the post office closes, it's often too late—they've started to pack up already. If you want the bank to give you ¥50 notes instead of ¥100s, the teller may tell you to your face that amongst the multi-millions of RMB in his building there are none. What he means is that he will have to get up from his desk to go and get it, and he's not willing to bother. If you want to buy something in a state-run department store, don't expect to get the attention of the people behind the counter very easily. If you do succeed in buying something your goods and change may be thrown at you in an expression of total disgust. You may have booked a guided tour, but don't expect necessarily to get either what you paid for or a refund for non-performance. Want a railway ticket? Sorry, all sold out for bribes through the back door.

Many employees still have what are called *tiěfànwǎn* —'iron rice bowl' jobs. Whether they work or not they get paid, and they will never be sacked (so their rice bowl is unbreakable). Such is the overmanning that many have refined their jobs to turning up, sitting down, knitting, reading the newspaper, and drinking tea. Disturbance of this routine is very unwelcome. The single two most popular words in Chinese are *méi yǒu*, meaning 'not have'. The import is that whatever you want there aren't any left, and the real meaning all too often is, 'I can't be bothered to look for that, I can't be bothered to get up off my seat, it's simpler just to say no, and I don't care.' Many officials will say anything just to get rid of tiresome foreigners who expect them to do something.

You can avoid frustration by allowing plenty of time for whatever you need to do, and never leaving anything until the last moment. Whatever is the most important project for the day, do it first. The government is doing something to tackle poor service, and public institutions often sport signs saying 'Nine characters we often use' (those for 'please', 'thank you', etc.) and 'Fifty expressions we do not use' ('Can't you see I'm busy?'). The arrival of private stores, restaurants and hotels has made things much better than they were, and although the surliness and greed of many who are supposed to provide services makes it difficult to sympathize with them, it's worth remembering that to many their place of work is also their home. Somewhere nearby they probably live in a tiny space in a dormitory provided by their work unit, with very few personal possessions; a little like spending all your life until you marry (and sometimes beyond) at a boarding school. Their jobs are mind-numbingly dull, they lack the *guānxī* (connections) without which nothing in China can be done, and their prospects are nil. Meanwhile the officials, those who do have connections and the criminals (sometimes all the same people) are grabbing the good things in life. Say 'thank you' (*xièxie nǐ*) when picking up your goods or receiving your change, and you'll often startle a smile.

Topics

China has 55 official recognized ethnic minorities totalling around 7 per cent of the population. When that population itself totals more than 1.2 billion, however, 7 per cent means 84 million people. The word *minority* seems inappropriate.

The mainstream Chinese majority call themselves the Hàn, and have a long history of regarding all non-Hàn as inferior and calling them barbarians. Suffering frequent invasions from the north and northwest, their policy towards other ethnic groups both inside and outside their borders was to use military control where possible and to exploit internal divisions, 'using barbarian to fight barbarian'. The creation of the Nationalist government in 1911 brought little change, except that some minorities took the opportunity to fight for independence while central control was weak. At the time of Nationalist leader Sun Yat-sen (Sūn Zhōngshān) only five 'nationalities' were recognized as existing: Manchu (who had taken control of China and ruled it as the Qīng from 1644 to 1911), Mongol, Tartar, Tibetan and Hàn (the main Chinese ethnic group). Sun saw autonomous and semi-autonomous groups coming together to form a greater federal state, and in 1924 the equal status of all ethnic groups and the right of self-determination was adopted as policy at the first National Congress.

After Sun's death in 1925, the approach of successor Chiang Kai-shek (Jiǎng Jièshí) was merely historical Hàn ethnocentricity put into 20th-century language. Ethnic minorities were seen as simply branches of one Chinese tree, which due to having been cut off near border regions and sometimes having little contact with the centre for long periods, had developed some idiosyncrasies—non-Hàn-like behaviour. Rather than being granted independence, everyone should be reassimilated into one great race. The Provisional Constitution of 1931 included Mongolia and Tibet as parts of China although they were *de facto* independent. By 1945, due to Soviet pressure, the independence of Mongolia had to be recognized, but otherwise it was made clear that only the central government could give permission for a minority group to take on self-determination, and that permission would never come from Chiang.

In the 1930s official Chinese Communist Party policy was surprisingly liberal, and spoke of allowing minorities eventual self-determination. This position was weakening by 1945, and when in 1949 the communists took power it proved to be nothing but mere words. Regions, prefectures, and counties with large numbers of minority peoples are now called 'autonomous', but although carefully selected minority representatives are put in place as figurehead leaders, all important political and administrative positions from the post office upwards are held by Hàn Chinese. True power radiates from Běijīng—exactly as under the emperors and with the same results of occasional upheaval.

Much modern Chinese propaganda effort goes into trying to convince the West, the Hàn Chinese, and the minorities themselves that minority people's lives have been greatly improved by the Hàn since the formation of the People's Republic. This used to take the crude form of composing songs insisting that one minority or another loved Chairman Máo 'with a burning love'. These days tame minority members are trotted out for the cameras to say whatever they are told, particularly when protests by other members of the same group are making it clear that the opposite is true. Public relations remains a field in which the Běijīng government is particularly clumsy and unskilled, and so the West remains sceptical, the minorities disaffected, and the ordinary Hàn in the street indifferent or contemptuous. Some Hàn have noticed that being a minority member can have its benefits: two or three children instead of the one that they are restricted to, for instance. To avoid discrimination, Hàn Chinese would once deny any mixed blood. Now some are cynically coming forward to claim their origins in another 'nationality' and the right to that second child. Others are marrying minority people for the same reason.

The government's internal propaganda has at least been successful with the Hàn majority, many of whom are convinced that its policy towards the minorities amounts to extreme positive discrimination which is effectively depriving Hàn of their rights. They simply don't understand what the minorities are complaining about. In 1996 a Hàn general was demoted following accusations that he had tried to force a female Uighur soldier to have sex with him. An inside source was quoted as saying that if the soldier had been Hàn and not Uighur, nothing would have happened: a particularly depressing remark, however it is read.

Turki Peoples

The Hàn Chinese in Xīnjiāng numbered a mere 222,401 in 1946, mostly concentrated in Ürümqi. Many were from Húnán, the home province of the Qīng general who had violently pacified the northwest. A census in 1944–6 listed fourteen groups of which seven were Muslim—Uighur, Kazak, Uzbek, Taranchi, Tartar, Tajik and Kyrgyz. All except the Tajiks spoke related Turkish dialects, and all had fought the Chinese at some time or other. Together they formed 92 per cent of the region's population.

The view of visitors to Xīnjiāng (Eastern or Chinese Turkestan, as it was then known) in the 19th and first half of the 20th century is summed up by Eric Teichman in a rather forthright description of the pecking order:

> ... the Turkis are a patient, contented and submissive people, made to
> be ruled by others. The few that have a knowledge of their rulers'
> tongue talk Chinese in a high-pitched, plaintive, sing-song tone that I
> soon learned to recognize—the voices of a subject race. The Kazak and
> the Kirghiz, on the other hand, descendants of the ancient Huns, have
> a more virile, warlike mien, and are no doubt less easily controlled. But
> of the three races playing the chief rôles in the politics of Chinese
> Central Asia, the Chinese are the rulers born and bred, astute, superior
> beings, the Tungans the fighters, and the Turkis made by Providence to
> be the ruled.

Eric Teichman, *Journey to Turkistan*, 1937

Several of the 'minority nationality' population groups of modern Xīnjiāng are descended from or are namesakes of ancient settlers and nomads. The **Uighurs**, who make up more than half the region's population, had an empire in northern Mongolia in the 7th and 8th centuries. They were driven out by the nomadic Kyrgyz into Xīnjiāng, where they mixed with the local population of Turki and Indo-European origin. Modern Uighurs, Kyrgyz, Kazaks, Uzbeks and Tartars are all of mixed Turkish descent and speak closely related variants of an old form of Turkish. The mixed Turki-Mongol heritage of the Uighurs led to a reintroduction of their 1000-year-old name by a conference held in the USSR in the 1920s, now taken to mean Turki people living in or originally from the Xīnjiāng oases.

Twelve centuries after the arrival of their namesakes they still make up 80 per cent of the population of the Tarim Basin and, at nearly 7.5 million people (or 8.5, or 15, or 22 million, depending on which Chinese or Uighur source you listen to), a little more than half of the population of Xīnjiāng as a whole. Those who pay attention to news reports of occasional Uighur riots and bombings in Xīnjiāng and Běijīng may be surprised to find that they were once widely derided for their passivity. 'The essence of imperturbable mediocrity', said Younghusband, observing them to be content to be ruled by the Chinese and indifferent to the fate of Kashgaria, as long as taxes did not increase too much.

Older male Xīnjiāng Uighurs in their traditional three-quarter-length coats, fur-trimmed hats, and galoshed leather knee boots still look just as they did in 19th-century photographs and probably for hundreds of years before that. Younger men in flat caps, jackets, trousers and work boots are firmly of the 20th century, if not quite of its second half, and discreetly carry small, sharp knives with decorated handles, tucked into leather scabbards. The women wear three-quarter-length skirts with layers of thick, opaque, brown stockings, and the older ones drape their heads in thick, brown, woollen shawls that reach down to their shoulders, and make them look like pieces of furniture put into storage. More emancipated younger women wear varying amounts of make-up, and either leave their heads uncovered or wear the small brightly coloured embroidered caps which were until recently reserved for younger men.

There is no love for the Hàn, who have frequently moved to suppress Islam, the Uighur religion, and today keep it under tight control. In the Great Leap Forward campaign which forced the formation of communes and was disastrous for food production, tens of thousands of Uighurs starved and around 20,000 fled to the Soviet Union, where there are now about 200,000, mostly in Kazakstan and Kyrgyzstan. While these states never had to listen to China when part of the USSR, now independent and desperate to increase trade to shore up collapsing economies, they can scarcely afford to ignore their giant neighbour. Recent intense lobbying by Chinese politicians is paying off with government warnings to Uighur cultural and political groups in the CIS not to support independence movements in Xīnjiāng. Nevertheless, since journalists are never allowed into Xīnjiāng unless under tight control, most accounts of disturbances in Xīnjiāng come from Uighur activists in Kazakstan. There are claims of forced abortions and sterilizations of Uighur women, and pressure on them to marry Chinese. Unfortunately in their efforts to publicize their case, which has a much lower profile overseas than that of the Tibetans, these sources have been caught out in gross exaggeration, reducing the credibility of all of their reports. The government has been successful in flooding Xīnjiāng with reluctant Hàn, who from 3.7 per cent of the population in 1949 are expected to become the majority very soon.

Independence for Xīnjiāng is unlikely ever to happen. Běijīng maintains a large-scale military presence and has demonstrated a willingness to detain thousands, and execute hundreds if need be, at only the slightest provocation. The few uncoordinated assassinations and bomb blasts mounted by independence fighters may make Hàn residents even more uneasy and long for the more familiar east, but will not convince the government to walk away from massive deposits of copper, lead, manganese, nickel and oil. Regardless of the economic impact, the loss of face and the cries for independence that would arise from all sides could not be borne.

The **Kazak** minority in Xīnjiāng, unlike the Uighurs, were recognized by early writers as being doughty and stout-hearted. They still received bad press, with otherwise charitable commentators being moved to bursts of considerable spleen:

As for the Qazaq tribes, it is my opinion that, after all the milling and swirling and campaigning and countermarching in the centuries of the great migrations, God let the whole stew simmer for a while, and when the scum came up he called it Qazaq.

Owen Lattimore, *The Desert Road to Turkestan*, 1929

'Nothing except the strongest measures can make an animal safe against the clever wiles of a Qazaq horse-stealer,' complained Mildred Cable. Although sharing their faith with the Uighurs and Chinese Muslims (Huí), their nomadic way of life, like that of the Kyrgyz, did not make them close to the sedentary groups. Their participation in various uprisings against the Manchus and Hàn tended to be opportunistic—civil war always gave good opportunities for plunder. They counted their wealth in terms of their flocks and herds and missed no opportunity to augment them from those of sedentary peoples, and particularly the Hàn. Although there are perhaps 1.2 million Kazaks in Xīnjiāng, most visitors will first encounter them at Tiān Chí (Heavenly Lake) or outside the hotels in Ürümqi selling accommodation at their yurts near the lake.

The **Kyrgyz** in Xīnjiāng were similar, roaming between the Soviet Union, Afghanistan and China to avoid the rapacity of officials, and having little to do with the settled oases, until the communists on both sides finally slammed the border shut. As *perestroika* began in the Soviet Union, cultural and economic links were re-established between the approximately 170,000 Kyrgyz in Xīnjiāng and those on the Soviet side, spread between modern Kyrgyzstan, Uzbekistan and Kazakstan. No-one quite understands why Běijīng encouraged these contacts, twice sending delegations to Kyrgyzstan in 1989, while simultaneously suppressing contact between the Uighurs on both sides of the same border. The majority of the Kyrgyz in Xīnjiāng live in an 'autonomous prefecture' to the north and west of Kashgar, closed to visitors except those passing through on their way to or from the Torugart Pass. The men can occasionally be identified from amongst the other Turki peoples because, like in Kyrgyzstan itself, they wear the *ak-kalpak*, a tasselled white felt hat. Traditionally the Kyrgyz were pale-skinned, green-eyed and red haired and, despite a thorough mixing with Mongols and the other Turki groups, some still have this stunning combination. On the Chinese side of the border they still use Arabic script.

Xīnjiāng also has about 5000 **Tartars**, mostly in the north including some in Ürümqi, and about 15,000 **Uzbeks** in the same areas and in Kashgar and Kuqa.

The Mongols

The Mongol tribes that united under Genghis Khan in 1206 had conquered part of northern China including Xīnjiāng by 1215, although it was left to Genghis's grandson Khubilai to complete the job. Khubilai's reign as head of the Mongols began in 1260. He adopted the state name of Yuán from 1271, had displaced the Sòng dynasty by 1276 and conquered the last pockets of resistance by 1280. Due to a failure to establish proper principles of succession, which led to most subsequent reigns being short-lived, and due to constant rebellions by the Chinese, Mongol rule was all over by 1368. The last Yuán emperor, who had taken the throne while still a child, fled to Mongolia from where he made abortive attempts to retake China.

The empires of some of the lesser khans survived longer, and after the fall the Yuán dynasty the oasis towns of the Western Regions had a brief period of independence under the more inward-looking Míng dynasty. They were ruled by Turkicized and Islamicized Mongols, and the original Indo-European stock became mixed with Turki and Mongol blood, and thoroughly

Turki in culture. Later, Turkicized and Islamicized Mongols arrived from the khanates in the west, gaining religious and political control of the oasis towns by the end of the 17th century. In the 16th century there were also four nomadic tribes of Mongols roaming the grasslands of northern Xīnjiāng, who, like those in Mongolia proper, had become Lamaist Buddhists. The survivors in modern Xīnjiāng are mostly of the Torgut tribe, part of which migrated to the Volga River area in the 17th century, where some still live. One hundred years later in 1770, the majority decided to return to Xīnjiāng but the Russians tried to stop them, valuing them as cavalry, and in subsequent fighting many died. According to modern Chinese histories, the remainder were welcomed by the Qīng Emperor Qiánlóng, and assigned Xīnjiāng pasture-lands, now named as 'autonomous' counties and prefectures. Another group from the same tribe had left to go on pilgrimage to Tibet but on its return had found its passage blocked by Qīng military activity (or by other Mongol tribes). On appeal to the emperor it was granted grazing grounds in Inner Mongolia in 1705, extended in 1732. Despite being separated for around 300 years, the two groups maintain the same customs and language, although they use different scripts. Despite their adherence to Buddhism, adopted after the fall of the Yuán, the Mongols shared their nomadic life with the Muslim Kazaks, and sometimes intermarried.

Today there are about 5 million Mongolians in Inner Mongolia and the northeast, swamped by Hàn immigration at a rate of six to one, pushed ever further north over the last two centuries, and at times forced into collectives. Any restiveness brought on by the independence of Outer Mongolia to the north is suppressed as necessary.

Huí (Dungans, Tungans)

The Muslims who arrived in the 14th and 15th century were no invading force, but many took Chinese wives, or bought Chinese children in times of famine. They were very successful at converting the Hàn Chinese, and in time they forgot their own languages, adopted Chinese dress, and their descendants became almost indistinguishable from the mainstream Hàn, except in their religion and in retaining somewhat warlike characteristics, fighting both for and against the Chinese government at different times. The Manchu Qīng dynasty deliberately settled them in northern Xīnjiāng to keep control of the other minorities, but had to punish them severely in 1877 after putting down a revolt that they had supported. Viewed as far more rebellious than the other minorities, they went on to lead several bloody uprisings in the 20th century and were claimed by Fleming to be the best fighters in China bar the communists.

Known to the Chinese as Huí, they are counted as a 'nationality', numbering about nine million altogether. Like the other Muslims, they have been largely cut off from the Islamic mainstream since the end of the Mongol Yuán dynasty, but despite there being no others from their ethnic group beyond China's borders, they still seem more international in their outlook and aware of a greater multinational Muslim consciousness. They are now widely distributed across Xīnjiāng, Gānsù, Qīnghǎi and Níngxià, with pockets in several major cities elsewhere. They are most easily identifiable by their white caps, which make them look a little like chefs. The women in some areas, such as Línxià, also wear cowls, sometimes over the top of the caps—green before marriage, black afterwards. Although they have from time to time risen with their co-religionists against the Hàn, they are not greatly liked or trusted by the Turki Muslims.

Despite a long-standing reputation for backsliding, they are reported to be becoming gradually more strict about their Muslim identity, praying more frequently and observing the Ramadan fast. Both Lattimore and Fleming mention a Chinese saying: 'Three Mohammedans are one

Mohammedan; two Mohammedans are half a Mohammedan; one Mohammedan is no Mohammedan', indicating a tendency to ignore their own rules on diet and other matters when not observed. Lattimore also quotes a story he heard from his father, in which a Huí reached a town late at night and found few people around except a food seller with hot meat patties:

> 'What meat have you there?' asked the traveler. 'Pork,' said the Chinese. 'Ah,' said the Mohammedan, 'and what is in these?'— pointing to another row of the same patties on the same tray. 'Pork, of course,' said the Chinese. 'And in these?' the traveller persisted, pointing to a third row. The food seller tumbled to it at last. 'These are mutton,' he said. 'Well, why didn't you say that before!' quoth the Mohammedan, beginning to eat heartily.

Owen Lattimore, The Desert Road to Turkestan, 1929

For a fascinating account of the Huí, see Dru C. Gladney's *Muslim Chinese*, Harvard University Press 1991, which includes detailed sections on the Huí in Běijīng, and at the Nàjiāhù Qīngzhēnsì (mosque) at Yǒngníng, outside Níngxià's capital, Yínchuān.

Manchus

Xīnjiāng's first proper inclusion into China came during the reign of the Manchu Qīng Emperor Qiánlóng (1736–99). Deciding to retake control, he appointed a Manchu bannerman named Zhàohuì, who, after defections, murder of his emissaries, long marches in difficult terrain and shortages that reduced his troop to cannibalism, took Kashgar and Yarkand in 1759, slaughtering Dungan troops with great cruelty. A military governor was then stationed in the Ili region with a second-in-command in Ürümqi.

The Qīng made few changes to Xīnjiāng. While spending vast sums maintaining a military presence (each Manchu garrison had up to 20,000 troops and five times as many dependants), they did not allow fresh Hàn Chinese to settle there. They permitted the local Muslims to carry on unhindered, and while all Hàn were required to shave most of the hair from their heads and leave a long queue or pigtail, the ethnic groups of Xīnjiāng were excused.

Some of the Manchu troops, along with other peoples from China's northeast, were never allowed to return. 3000 Manchu-speaking Sibo were sent with their families in 1764, and eventually settled on the banks of the Ili River, building their own walled villages and preserving their customs. 29,000 still live near Yīníng and have preserved to this day the language and script that had been forgotten by the Manchu emperors long before the end of their dynasty. 1000 Mongol-speaking Daur and their families from the same region were also sent as garrisons, and about 5000 of their descendants now live further north. The Sibo also preserved their military skills and are still the best archers in China, several having places in China's Olympic team. In a festival called 18 April (which almost never takes place exactly on that day because it is a lunar holiday) they commemorate the day more than 250 years ago when their ancestors set off for the long march across China's entire width.

The Manchu Qīng dynasty finally expired in 1911 with the abdication of the last emperor, Pǔyí. Already parts of China were under the control of warlords, and order was breaking down. The arrival of the Nationalist government was an event that took place so far away that there was bewilderment in Xīnjiāng. Some officials were put to the sword, some cut off their queues to show that their allegiance to the Qīng was at an end, others were too afraid to do anything.

Russians

Following the collapse of the Qīng a succession of strong governors took control in Ürümqi. Nominally holding allegiance to the Nationalist government in Nánjīng, they actually did entirely as they pleased. The Nationalists had other problems closer to home, and were often cut off from Xīnjiāng by Huí and Uighur rebellions in Gānsù. As a result, however, the governors could not depend on receiving military support when there were uprisings, which their ineptitude and intolerance frequently stimulated. Russians had first arrived in Xīnjiāng in the 18th century, but the years following the 1911 Russian revolution saw many White Russians (the name given to those who supported the Tsar) arriving in Xīnjiāng as refugees, and many enlisted as mercenaries in the fight against Muslim rebels, creating yet another sizeable Xīnjiāng minority. Some eventually moved on to China's coastal cities, but others stayed in Xīnjiāng, where around 14,000 still live in Yīníng and other towns on the border with Kazakstan.

Tajiks

Beside the Russians, the 35,000 Tajiks are China's only other Indo-European minority, most living in the 'Tajik autonomous county' around Tashkurgan in Xīnjiāng's far west, close to the border with Tajikistan and to similar people living both in Afghanistan's Wakhan Corridor and the Upper Hunza or Gojal region of Pakistan. All speak a variety of Persian. The women can easily be spotted working in the hotels and restaurants of Tashkurgan dressed in bright colours and pillbox hats.

Tibetans

Tibetans are long-time residents not only of Tibet, but of parts of Gānsù and Qīnghǎi. Some argue that in areas such as Gānsù's Xiàhé, away from the struggle for control of Tibet, Tibetan customs have been better preserved than in Tibet itself, or at least better than in its major cities. Monasteries such as Labrang and Kumbum (near Xīníng in Qīnghǎi) were damaged in the Cultural Revolution, but survived the mass destruction that reduced the thousands of monasteries in Tibet to only a handful. Already the most internationally famous of the minorities in China due to the activities of their exiled God-king, the Dalai Lama, their reputation for gentleness like that of their co-religionists the Mongols is belied by a war-like history which sometimes saw them masters of large portions of Gānsù and beyond. Visitors will find them at Labrang, completing the anti-clockwise devotional circuit around the lamasery and topping up the temples' yak-butter lamps. They can also be found pasturing their herds in neighbouring valleys, living in brown and white tents with a traditional geometrical blue pattern. Most retain their traditional costume, the women wearing their hair in long braids, often tucked under a felt cowboy-style hat, with black waistcoats and long skirts trimmed with embroidery. Both sexes wear thick sheepskin coats, usually off the shoulder and tied at the waist, their folds containing recent purchases and other useful items. Their faces, rapidly aged by the bitter winters and the power of the sun at the high altitudes where they live, are nut-brown with deep lines and hectic colour in the cheeks.

Religion

The Chinese have often been accused of having a 'pick and mix' approach to religion, selecting elements that appealed from both native and imported systems, and seeing no conflict in adherence to more than one religion at a time. Those religions discussed below mostly served a literate elite, ordinary people contenting themselves with immensely practical 'folk' religions. Individual deities were connected with hundreds of special topics, different rooms in the house, particular regions of the country, and local landmarks. As with dead forebears, these would be presented with offerings and prayers, but in the expectation of specific requests being fulfilled. Failure to perform could lead to the ancestor's grave being neglected and the idols of the laggardly god smashed, while a substitute object of worship was found.

Most religions produce library-loads of commentaries in addition to their key texts, and split into numbers of sects with conflicting ideas. Few adherents will be satisfied with the summaries below, which are intended to give an introduction to the religions in the Chinese context and their impact on the experience of travelling there today, and not as complete guides to their near-infinite and subtle variety.

Confucianism

Part philosophy, part social theory, and only part religion, Confucianism is based on writings attributed to Confucius (Kǒng Fūzi, 'Venerable Master Kǒng', 551–479 BC), and those of his followers who developed his ideas, such as Mencius (Mèngzi, c. 372–289 BC) and Xúnzi (c. 313–238 BC). The ideas in these writings provided the framework in which the majority of Chinese philosophical thinking took place until modern times. A key text is the Analects (Lúnyǔ), a compilation of Confucius's conversations and pronouncements, made by his followers. This, with the book of Mencius and two other Confucian-interpreted classics, eventually came to be studied in schools, and became the canon upon which candidates for administrative posts were tested. Although Confucianism at times lost its place as the orthodox ideology, it was only at the termination of the imperial examination system in 1905 that its influence on government began to wane. A key idea was that the hierarchy of society reflected a natural moral order — patriarch as head of family, prince as head of state. State ceremonial and more domestic ritual demonstrated the subservience of inferiors to superiors, and observance of these rituals helped to ensure the harmonious operation of society. The prince, so long as he behaved morally, held the 'mandate of heaven', the source of his legitimacy. Like other moral beings, his behaviour would demonstrate rén, a benevolent mixture of filial piety, loyalty, friendship, courtesy, reliability, and a general 'do-as-you-would-be-done-by' reciprocal altruism. In the elaboration of Confucian thought by Mencius, human nature was held to be fundamentally good, but creating the conditions for its nurture was the responsibility of the individual and above all of the ruler. Later interpretations, often known as neo-Confucianism, saw Daoist and Buddhist ideas (such as that of the 'way'—see below) replace some of the original more mechanistic ideas.

In the centuries following Confucius's death, in which states contended for the overall mastery of China, it was argued by Confucians that only a Confucian ruler would succeed in unifying the country, but China's first unification took place under the non-Confucian Qín (221–206 BC). However, Confucianism was adopted as the orthodox state ideology under the following Hàn dynasty. The Táng (AD 618–907) began to build temples to Confucius, which were used to display tablets commemorating the principal men of letters after their deaths.

Confucian sights include Běijīng's Confucius Temple and its stone-carved classic texts, and the Forest of Stelae in Xī'ān with similar carvings and a stone bearing a picture of the sage himself.

Daoism

The *dào*, or 'way', of Daoism is the invisible reality underlying appearances. If Confucianism stresses humanity and rejects mysticism, Daoism sees humanity as getting in the way of perception of the indescribable and imperceptible 'way' with which all Daoists strive to unite. This unity cannot be achieved through the fussy intellectuality of Confucianism, but only by achieving an awareness of inner simplicity and emptiness. The key sage of Daoism was Lǎozi, a contemporary of Confucius sometimes given credit for writing the central Daoist text *Dàodéjīng*, 'The Way and Power Classic', but who probably lived well before that book was written. The complete Daoist canon amounts to around 1400 texts from a variety of sources, many of them 'revealed' to later disciples, together with texts on the alchemical achievement of immortality.

The difficulty in identifying Lǎozi with a concrete historical figure allowed his biography to expand with increasingly superhuman legend as time went by. His reputed disappearance to the West, riding an ox, not long before the arrival of Buddhism, allowed Daoists to claim that the Buddha was either Lǎozi himself in disguise or an Indian disciple who, as a barbarian, had only received a weakened version of Lǎozi's doctrines. The contest between Daoists and Buddhists was only brought to an end by Kubilai Khan who ordered the destruction of all literature containing the story. Despite Daoism's connections with organized rebellion during the Hàn dynasty, it nevertheless received state support, particularly during the Táng dynasty whose emperors considered themselves descended from Lǎozi. There were various other important sages, but no others received his deification. One 2nd-century figure, Zhāng Dàolíng, led a Daoist 'Way of the Celestial Masters' movement which survived conflict with the Hàn emperors to be claimed as an antecedent by every organized Daoist group since, up to and including that of the current Celestial Master, who lives in Táiwān and is the 64th in a line of what Westerners in 19th-century China called the 'Daoist Popes'.

Members of the Daoist pantheon (around 72,000 deities, depending on the school) sometimes share space with Buddhist and Confucian images, such as at Dàtóng's Hanging Monastery, and Zhōngwèi's Gāo Miào. There are several Daoist holy mountains in China, but Píngliáng's Kōngtóng Shān claims to have been amongst the most important ever since the first emperor of China, Qín Shǐ Huángdì, visited it.

Buddhism and Lamaism

Buddhism was an alien import to China which was at times denounced as a barbarian religion and banned. Arriving via the Silk Routes from Gandhara, it gradually spread from oasis to oasis around the Tarim basin, and by AD 166 could count a Hàn emperor amongst its devotees. The religion gained ground in the 4th century when it attracted the attention of the upper strata of Chinese society through the activities of scholar-gentleman monks, familiar with both secular and religious literature, and by the 5th century was widespread. The speculation in China that Daoist founder Lǎozi was the originator of Buddhism partially sprang from the use of existing Daoist vocabulary to translate Buddhist terms which gave a false sense of similarity between the two systems. More rigorous translations were produced and an acceptance of Buddhism on its own terms began towards the end of the 4th century.

The Buddhist begins by recognizing that life is impermanent, without real essence, and characterized by suffering. His concern is to escape from the cycle of successive lives in which the form of each depends upon behaviour in the one before, and to arrive at *nirvana* (literally 'extinction'), a transcendent state without further pain, death or rebirth. This can be achieved by discipline, moral behaviour, wisdom and meditation, leading to the denial of all desires and cravings. The key text of Buddhism is the three-part *Tripitaka* ('Three baskets'), containing accounts of the origins of the Buddhist community and rules for the behaviour of monks and nuns, discourses attributed to the Buddha and his immediate disciples, and various philosophical and psychological texts. Laying stress on individual texts over others and interpreting them in different ways has led to the creation of numerous different schools of Buddhism, some of them native to China.

The historical Buddha ('awakened one') and founder of Buddhism, Shakyamuni, was born the son of a prince in what is now Nepal in 563 BC. In general a Buddha is a being who has achieved full enlightenment, and thus *nirvana*, and during his final passage through life can be identified by numerous signs. According to Buddhist doctrine Shakyamuni had been preceded by numerous Buddhas and will be followed by many others. These are usually symbolized at Chinese Buddhist sites by the statues of the 'Buddhas of the three times'—Dipamkara (past ages), Shakyamuni (present age) and Maitreya (future ages).

The peak of Buddhist strength in China was during the Suí (589–618) and Táng (618–906), when the main Chinese schools were developed and the monasteries became numerous, rich and powerful. Although Buddhism had been persecuted before, in 845 it received a blow from which it never completely recovered as the Chinese state ordered the dismantling of the monasteries and the return of monks and nuns to everyday life. Subsequent centuries saw a fusing of the various schools into one, but the arrival of the Manchu Qīng in 1644 saw the Lamaist version of Buddhism come to the fore.

Lamaism, or Tibetan Buddhism, evolved both from the indigenous shamanism of *Bon*, and a particular Indian form of Buddhism. Khubilai Khan appointed the Tibetan Grand Lama as his religious advisor in the 13th century, and by the 17th it had become the dominant creed of the Mongols. The Manchus had been converted to Lamaism before conquering China in 1644, and supported Lamaism to keep the Dalai Lamas happy and to keep control over Tibet and Mongolia. 'Lama' is a term now often applied indiscriminately to Buddhist monks, but which more exactly is applied only to the most senior and enlightened after rigorous qualification. The key lamas of Tibetan Buddhism are each seen as a reincarnation of their previous selves, and the two most senior, the Dalai Lama and Panchen Lama, have each come to hold political as well as spiritual authority. Following the death of one of them, the other leads a search committee which investigates children with the right physical characteristics and subjects them to tests of recognition of items owned by previous incarnations. The 14th Dalai Lama was born in 1935 and now lives in enforced exile in India, still regarded by Tibetans and Mongolians as their spiritual leader. The late Panchen Lama became a creature of the Běijīng government, and mostly resided in the Chinese capital. Following his death, in a mammoth piece of absurdity, the strictly atheist communist government formed its own search committee and in 1995 nominated a child in opposition to the Dalai Lama's selection, who was whisked away and has not been seen since. Tibetans are quite clear which is the right selection, however.

Buddhists are usually vegetarians, but most Tibetans and Mongols are not. The inappropriateness of both the mountainous regions occupied by the one and the nomadic lifestyle in the grasslands of the other made intensive vegetable farming impractical, and even then unlikely to provide the calorific needs of life in a harsh environment. But the matter of the occupation of the body of an animal by the soul of another being remains a concern:

I learned that by the Mongol way of thinking it is not right to fire at antelope, nor at wild asses, when they are in big herds. It may be that the soul of a saint or a Buddha has passed into the body of a wild animal, whose holiness gathers the others about it in great numbers. A Mongol will spend a great deal of time first breaking up a herd and then going after two or three evidently profane animals which have separated, rather than run the risk of shooting a 'magic' creature.

Owen Lattimore, *The Desert Road to Turkestan*, 1929

Since the communist victory of 1949 a nominal freedom of religious belief has not included the right to believe anything that deviated from the Party line. Land reforms of 1950–2 stripped the monasteries of their lands, and left the monks with no alternative but to return to conventional life. The Cultural Revolution of 1966–76 saw the mass destruction of Buddhist buildings and relics. Since then there has been partial restoration of a few monasteries, and a limited amount of teaching is permitted.

Despite the destruction there are vast numbers of Buddhist temples, pagodas and cave sites to see on the Silk Routes, each richly furnished with statuary and paintings. Constantly repeated images include those of the 'Buddhas of the three times', the four celestial kings (guardian figures), Bodhisattvas (beings on the road to enlightenment willing to share their spiritual credit with others), Arhats (beings about to attain *nirvana*), and the eight auspicious symbols (parasol, two fish, conch shell, lotus blossom, vase of sacred water, wheel of teaching, knot of eternity, banner of victory).

Islam

Conversion of the Uighurs and others to Islam began in the 10th century and by the time of the Mongol invasion of the 13th century was widespread. It had originally arrived at China's southern ports in the 8th century with Arab merchants, but its spread in Xīnjiāng came through land contacts. While the Mongol Yuán dynasty (1276–1368) had no religion (Kubilai Khan asked the Pope for religious teachers who never arrived, and had a Tibetan lama as his main religious adviser), it had Muslim allies who undertook the suppression of parts of China on behalf of the Mongols. The vast borderless area that constituted the Mongol empire allowed Muslims from Central Asia to move more freely into China's north- and southwest. Small Uighur states continued to exist during Mongol rule. Educated Uighurs became influential at the Mongol court and taught the Mongols how to write using the Uighur script, although they eventually abandoned this themselves in favour of the Arabic script of the text of their new religion.

From the beginning of the closed and inward-looking Míng period to modern times, Muslims in China have been cut off from the Islamic mainstream, and become Chinese Muslims. In much of China, Muslim intermarriages with Hàn Chinese and their adoption of Chinese names, customs and language made them almost indistinguishable from other Hàn, and today they are labelled by the government as a separate 'nationality', the Huí. The other Muslim minorities, such as the Uighurs, are mostly of Turki stock, and despite their shared faith do not always have good relations with the Chinese-speaking Huí, who outside their dietary restrictions and prayer habits seem little different from the Hàn. The decline of the Qīng in the 19th century saw a re-emergence of Muslim sensibilities and a number of revolts, mostly in provinces such as Xīnjiāng and Gānsù where Muslims of all kinds were in the majority.

In general Chinese government policy towards Muslims has tended to fluctuate in relation to its sense of threat from the outside, and Muslim occupation of sensitive border areas has informed a history of intolerance by the Hàn. The Muslim response has varied, those Muslims forming visible minorities in the major cities of China proper tending to be quiescent, and those forming majorities in outlying areas whether Huí or Turki periodically rising up against Hàn oppression. Islam draws no distinction between religious and secular behaviour, and thus its adherents are bound to try to obtain Islamic government in order to ensure that the will of Allah is carried out. Muslim minorities therefore suffer strain between loyalty to the countries in which they live and loyalty to Islamic principles. Left to themselves they can submit to the non-Muslim ruler, but when oppression becomes too great, as it periodically has in 19th- and 20th-century China, there is a tendency to rise up. This is a lesson that the Hàn have had to learn again and again.

On the other hand, if given a larger voice, Muslims will tend to speak up for secession (as during the 'Hundred Flowers' campaign, the one time when criticism of the Party was invited). However, much play was made of Muslim protests during the Tiān'ān Mén Square incidents of 1989 which were directed *to* the government rather than *at* it. These were 'good' protesters in contrast to the 'bad' students who had occupied the square. The recent emancipation of Muslim communities in the newly independent states bordering Xīnjiāng has caused the Chinese government some disquiet, fearing that the Uighurs will want to emulate their neighbours. There is plentiful talk of emancipation in Xīnjiāng amongst Uighurs, but except for occasional local outbursts of discontent and isolated acts of terrorism, this is likely to remain just talk. Chinese victories in Central Asia, since shortly after the time of Zhāng Qiān, have always demonstrated superior long-term planning on the part of the Hàn, and little to none on the part of the local Huí, Uighurs and others. Secessionists seem to be emotional and impractical, especially considering the lack of defensible borders to Xīnjiāng's east, and the maintenance by the Chinese of around 3 million men under arms.

All but the Indo-European Tajiks of western Xīnjiāng are considered Sunnis, although their isolation has meant that few understand the differences between Sunni and Shia (a matter of argument about descent from the Prophet, and interpretation of his actions). Several variations of mystical Sufism which arrived in the 17th century, based around charismatic preachers, tended to ignite consciousness of being part of a larger Muslim group rather than just members of a village with a mosque, particularly amongst Huí.

Both Sunnis and Shias can be found in Pakistan as well as Ismailis, a branch of the Shias who differ with them on the descent of authority from the sixth generation after Mohammed. Along with the Tajiks of western Xīnjiāng, they recognize the Geneva-based Aga Khan as their spiritual authority, and his practical assistance to them has included funding schools and infrastructure projects.

Islamic sights include the Great Mosque in Xī'ān and the neighbouring Muslim quarter, the mosque at Tóngxīn, the Tombs of the Muslim Kings at Hāmì, and the mosques and tombs of the towns around the Tarim Basin's perimeter.

Christianity

The Nestorian Christians were the first to reach China. Named after Nestorius, Bishop of Constantinople in the 5th century, their view that Christ had two separate human and divine personalities was banned as heretical. Nevertheless, the church flourished in Persia and spread to India and China from the 6th to the 10th century. Envoys from Europe to the Mongol court such as the Franciscan John of Plano Carpini (1246) and Dominican William of Rubruck (1253) found themselves reliant on the Nestorians, who were already in place, for communication with the Mongol Khans. However, the Franciscan John of Monte Corvino reached Běijīng in 1294 and in 1308 was consecrated first Archbishop of the Catholic Church in China. Catholics came under attack during revolts against Mongol rule and the last Western bishop was expelled in 1369, the year after the restoration of Chinese rule over China by the Míng.

The next major achievement by Christianity was the permission given to the Jesuit Matteo Ricci to live in Běijīng from 1602. Ricci had entered China from Portuguese-controlled Macao, and decided on an approach different from that of his fellow missionaries, dressing as a scholar rather than as a member of the priestly class. He devoted himself to gaining a thorough understanding of the classics needed to pass the imperial examinations, the route to advancement in Chinese society, and taught the sons of the influential not only the content of the classics but memory techniques known to Jesuits and thought of as a branch of ethics. It was thus that he gained the support necessary to reach Běijīng, a move strongly resisted by the inward-looking Míng and the eunuchs who held power at the court. Once there, Ricci won respect by his demonstrations of technical skill with clocks and maps. He adapted Catholic rites to make them more understandable for Chinese converts, and did not forbid the continuance of traditional ancestor-worship and other rites. By 1610 the Chinese claimed 2000 converts, but most of these were sick infants baptized only shortly before they died (a policy continued with sick, unwanted and abandoned infants—usually girls—right up to the time of the Boxers, contributing to Chinese suspicions that the children were used for alchemical and deviant sexual purposes).

Their erudition kept the Jesuits at court through the transfer from the Míng to the Manchu Qīng in 1644, despite the Manchu's adherence to Tibetan Buddhism. The Emperor Kāngxī issued an edict of tolerance to the Christian religion in 1692, but this allowed other missionary sects to join the Jesuits, not all of whom agreed with Ricci's accommodation of ancestor worship, homage to Confucius, and other traditions. While the struggle to 'save souls' took place in China, infighting at the Vatican led to Ricci's position being at first confirmed and then rejected. A legate sent by Pope Clement XI had meetings with Kāngxī in 1705 and 1706, then ordered all missionaries under pain of excommunication to forbid converts to practise these rites. Kāngxī despised this intolerance, and ordered the expulsion from China of all those who failed to sign a certificate accepting his position. Most Jesuits signed, but Franciscans and Dominicans didn't. It was the Christians' own squabbling that lost them their influence in China.

If Matteo Ricci was a marketing expert par excellence, who observed the needs of the powerful and earned their support through assisting them, the Christians who followed down the centuries seemed to have lacked the touch, right up to modern times. The treaties forced on China by foreign powers in the mid-19th century allowed a flood of missionaries from all over the world into the country. In a repeat of 17th-century problems different sects fought amongst themselves and deliberately confused issues by choosing different translations for Christian terms, including 'God'. Many observers commented that Chinese converts were 'rice Christians', whose Christianity lasted only as long as the free hand-outs of food some well-funded missionaries were able to provide. The novelist Pearl S. Buck, daughter of two Presbyterian missionaries to China who lived much of her life there, thought that they had no more effect than 'a finger drawn through water'.

Some ideas did indeed stick, however. The Tàipíng Rebellion, which between 1845 and 1864 gained control of large areas of China including Nánjīng, was led by a man who claimed to be

Jesus Christ's younger brother. Two of his lieutenants claimed to speak with the voices of God and Jesus. Missionaries were excited about this new religious community, at least until some broke through Qīng lines and found the Tàipíng ideas deviant and heretical. Cynical communist historical orthodoxy claims the Tàipíng as revolutionaries.

Following directions to various sights you will pass churches tucked away in back streets (e.g. in Xīníng, Hohhot, Yínchuān) but these are neither ancient nor of architectural merit. Běijīng's Catholic Southern Cathedral, originally built in 1703 although the current building is considerably more modern, is said to be on the site of Matteo Ricci's house. The most ancient Christian artefact is the Nestorian Tablet in Xī'ān's Forest of Stelae, rediscovered by the Jesuits in 1623, and thought (perhaps hoped) to be a fake, until Nestorian documents were found in the Library Cave at Dūnhuáng (along with Daoist, Confucian, Manichaean and Buddhist papers). It records a Nestorian mission to the Táng capital Cháng'ān (Xī'ān) in AD 635.

Manichaeism

Manichaeism arrived in China in AD 694 and, although long forgotten, is thought by some to have had more impact on China than other Persian religions, including both Nestorian Christianity and the fire-worshipping Zoroastrianism (the latter being only for Persians who lived in Cháng'ān during the Táng). Incorporating elements of Christianity and other religions, it viewed Satan as co-eternal with God, and Manichaeans believed in a continuing conflict between the forces of light and dark. Although they were prohibited in AD 732 from making further converts in China, the mass conversion of the militarily powerful Uighurs around 30 years later ensured that Manichaeism made progress amongst the Hàn, too, and by 768 there was a temple in Cháng'ān. The religion declined in China with the Uighurs during the 9th century, and was persecuted along with other imported religions. However, it is mentioned by Polo, but was again suppressed in 1370.

The only known portrait of the religion's founder, Mani (c. AD 216–74), was on a fresco brought back by von Le Coq, but destroyed in the Allied bombing of Berlin in the Second World War.

Collections Overseas

The Chinese complain, and the foreigner cannot well deny it, that caravan-loads of treasures from the temples, tombs and ruins of Chinese Turkestan have been carried off to foreign museums and are for ever lost to China.

Eric Teichman, *Journey to Turkistan*, 1937

China is not currently demanding the return of the Silk Routes treasures. Instead Chinese academics visit institutions overseas to study conservation techniques, and expertise and funds flow into China for the preservation and display of what remains there. The views of Chinese curators are mixed. Nationalism drives a desire to see various treasures returned, but some frankly admit that had the artefacts not been removed, most would probably no longer exist. Left in China they would have disintegrated through neglect, been stolen by treasure-hunters, defaced for religious reasons, or smashed up in some campaign against religion or 'old thinking'.

When there's talk of foreign 'theft' of China's treasures, the voices of the Turki and Indo-European minorities can be heard faintly in the background—'*Whose* treasures?' The great discovery of foreign archaeologists in what was then called Chinese Turkestan was of influences from the west, not east. As Albert von Le Coq put it, 'Instead of a land of the Turks, which the name Turkestan led us to expect, we discovered that, up to the middle of the 8th century, everywhere along the silk-roads there had been nations of Indo-European speech, Iranians, Indian, and even Europeans.' The documents removed from Dūnhuáng and elsewhere contained at least 17 different languages in two dozen scripts.

Few these days would seek to justify the removal of the treasures. Yet China has seen officially sanctioned destruction on a scale scarcely equalled in world history. In recent times even the Chinese government has admitted that some officials entrusted with the preservation of cultural heritage have turned out to be the main dealers in items for illegal export. Pollution, already way beyond levels acceptable in developed countries, is causing damage to frescoes and buildings. New museums in Xī'ān, Shànghǎi, and (soon) Běijīng, as well as a Japanese-built museum in Dūnhuáng, show improvements in presentation and access, but politics still interfere in the labelling and selection of objects for display. The Chinese government stands accused of hiding new finds which, like many of the artefacts in foreign museums, undermine the official history of long-term uninterrupted Hàn hegemony in the northwest.

Whatever the rights or wrongs, several of the great treasure houses of Europe, North America and Japan have displays that provide a better introduction to the art of the Silk Routes than China itself. This is a list of the principal overseas collections to bear in mind when travelling elsewhere than China. The opening of the Channel Tunnel has made Paris and London an easy day-trip from each other by Eurostar train. Consult travel agents, or visit any London or Paris mainline station; UK ✆ (0345) 303030, US ✆ toll-free 1-800 677 8585, Canada ✆ toll-free 1-800 361 7245, website *http://www.eurostar.com/*, *http://www.raileurope.com/* (North American agents, rail passes). Berlin is in reasonable reach of most European capitals, and an easy side-trip if you are on your way to Central Asia via Frankfurt. Those taking the Karakoram Highway route into China could consider a diversion via Delhi, and Tokyo and Seoul are possible stopovers on flights west from North America.

London

British Museum, Great Russell Street, London WC1B 3DG, ⓜHolborn, Tottenham Court Rd, Russell Sq, Goodge St, ✆ (0171) 636 1555, recorded information ✆ (0171) 580 1788, website http://www.british-museum.ac.uk/. Open Mon–Sat, 10–5, Sun 2.30–6.

Aurel Stein's vast hauls from Taklamakan sites were divided between his co-sponsors, the British Museum and the British government in India (now in the Delhi National Museum, *see* below). The most important object on display is the *Diamond Sutra* of AD 868, claimed to be the oldest printed book in the world (actually in the form of a scroll), and taken from the 'library cave' at Dūnhuáng. Neighbouring cabinets often contain fragments of other documents demonstrating the variety of scripts, but the majority of the thousands of documents, wooden plaques and terracottas from near Khotan, and other items remain buried in the vaults either for conservation reasons or lack of space. The ceramics department contains a tombstone from Astana, and there's a 50.4cm-high head of Buddha from Miran. The British Library itself (currently within the British Museum but due to move to a new building next to St Pancras Station) has some of the Islam Akhun forgeries (*see* 'The Book Factory', p.296).

The British Library has a searchable website with information about Stein, other archaeologists, and their finds: *http://portico.bl.uk/*.

Paris

Musée National des Arts Asiatiques Guimet, 6 place d'Iéna (at avenue du Président Wilson), **Ⓜ** *Iéna,* **Ⓒ** *(01) 47 23 61 65. Open Wed–Mon, 9.45–6.*

Originally three floors of oriental antiquities, the museum is being extended downwards into the earth, and may not reopen until 1999. A vast collection includes pieces acquired by Paul Pelliot and others from Xīnjiāng sites. There's an annex at 19 avenue d'Iéna, a few moments' walk away, containing two stories of Buddhist art from China and Japan, mostly statuary and devotional items, some from Xīnjiāng sites.

Berlin

Museum für Indische Kunst, Lansstrasse 8, Dahlem, 14195 Berlin, **Ⓜ** *Dahlem-Dorf,* **Ⓒ** *(030) 830 1361. Open Tues–Fri, 9–5; Sat and Sun 10–5.*

> *Yet it must be recognized that the Berlin collection is the best adapted for the study of the developments shown by Buddhist art on its way through Central Asia to China; for the German expeditions alone took with them a man who thoroughly understood how to accomplish the difficult work of sawing off the mural paintings and packing them in such a way as to reach Berlin uninjured.*
>
> Albert von Le Coq, *Buried Treasures of Chinese Turkestan*, 1928

Gratingly immodest as ever, von Le Coq was nevertheless right that his assistant Herr Bartus's freedom with his foxtail saw has led to a magnificent exhibition filling several rooms of this museum. While there are statues, figurines, and fragments of painted fabric, the highlights are the extensive displays of murals from sites all around the north side of the Taklamakan, especially Bezeklik near Turpan and the sites around Kuqa. Murals are carefully placed in the same positions they would have had relative to each other and to the viewer in their original locations, larger ones being reassembled jigsaw-like from the smaller pieces into which they had been cut. Where von Le Coq's team took away most of the surfaces of smaller cave temples, full scale-replicas of the caves have been built, with the murals in position inside them.

The grandeur of some of the sites apart, visiting this museum is perhaps even superior to visiting the original cave temples.

St Petersburg

Hermitage Museum (Ermitazh), 36 Dvortsovaya Naberezhnaya, St Petersburg, **Ⓒ** *812/311–3420, website http://www.hermitage.ru/ (Russian only) or try http:// www.museum.ru/museums.html. Open Tues–Sun, 10.30–6.*

Several Russian explorers and archaeologists such as Przhevalsky, Koslov and Oldenburg were amongst the first into Central Asian and western China, and it was they who rediscovered the forgotten Xī Xià dynasty and pioneered the field of Tangut studies. Most of their finds eventually disappeared into the vast hoard of the Hermitage that was once the private collection of the Tsars, greatly expanded by confiscations following the revolution and ill-gotten gains during the Second World War. Whether any Silk Route items will be on display is subject to rotation of the collection, but begin looking in the seventh section.

Here, too, are a great number of works not on view to the general public, either for lack of space or funds, or for reasons of preservation. These include 365 scrolls and approximately 18,000 fragments from Dūnhuáng. There are continuing collaborations with the British Library's International Dūnhuáng Project on conservation matters.

Stockholm

Folkens Museum Etnografiska (Ethnographical Museum), Djurgårdsbrunnsvägen 34, S-102 52 Stockholm, © (08) 666 50 00, website http://www.telemuseum.se/ museer/Folkmus/1e.html. Open Tues–Fri 11–4, Wed 11–8, Sat and Sun 12–5; closed Mon.

The museum has a large collection of artefacts brought back by Sven Hedin's expeditions between 1893 and 1935, supplemented by yurts and a selection of his sketches.

There are also Neolithic materials from the Silk Routes at the Östasiatiska Museet (Museum of Far Eastern Antiquities), Tyghusplan, Skeppsholmen, S-103 27 Stockholm, © (08) 666 42 50, website *http://www.telemuseum.se/museer/Ostasiatiska/Home. HTML.*

Delhi

National Museum, Janpath, © 301 9538. Open 10–5; closed Mon.

The museum recently remodelled parts of its upstairs galleries to give better space to its share of Aurel Stein's finds. Somewhat less bashful than the British Museum, it has his portrait hanging at the entrance to the collection, which includes paintings on silk from various sites, and samples of the Ghandaran artefacts whose influence was to spread into the Taklamakan.

Tokyo and Seoul

Tokyo Kokuritsu Hakubutsukan (Tokyo National Museum), 13–9 Ueno Koen, Taito-ku, © (03) 3822 1111. Open 9–4; closed Mon.

The museum has managed to reassemble parts of a private collection belonging to one Count Otani, who sent collecting missions to China from 1902. The collection of items from both north and south Taklamakan sites was later broken up and sold; other pieces ended up in the National Museum, Seoul, currently in the grounds of the Kyôngbokkung Palace, but forecast to move.

Cambridge (USA)

Arthur M. Sackler Museum, Harvard University, 485 Broadway, Cambridge, MA 02138, © (617) 495 9400, website http://www.fas.harvard.edu/~artmuseums/ AsianArt.html. Open Mon–Sat 10–5, Sun 1–5; closed on national holidays.

Langdon Warner was a respected orientalist, but he was a relative latecomer to the Silk Routes, and brought back less than anyone else. Nevertheless the Harvard collection contains a splendid seated Bodhisattva statue, wall paintings and banners from Dūnhuáng, and objects from Warner's work at the Xī Xià city of Karakhoto, northeast of Dūnhuáng near the Outer Mongolia border. The collection is rotated, and many items are too delicate to place on public display more than briefly; but there are usually four or five Silk Route pieces exhibited on the fourth floor, and there's an impressive collection from elsewhere in China.

'I speak Chinese' is a statement that carries less meaning than might at first appear. There are several groups of Chinese dialects so different from each other that they are often spoken of as different languages. The Cantonese speaker at your local Chinese restaurant would not be understood by a speaker of Mandarin for instance, nor vice versa.

Mandarin, also known as Modern Standard Chinese or *Pǔtōnghuà*, 'common speech', is the official language of the People's Republic, and used in all schools. It's commonly assumed by foreigners that Mandarin must be very difficult to learn, but in fact it is in many ways simpler than European languages. The basic sentence structure is subject–verb–object, just as in English. Verbs have a single form for all persons, and there are no tenses. Nouns have no plural forms or genders, and there are no articles, definite or indefinite. The apparent complexity of Chinese lies in the unfamiliar nature of its sounds, and its apparently inscrutable writing system.

Tones

Mandarin, like other forms of Chinese, is a tonal language. Most of its sounds begin with a simple consonant, and end with a vowel, or a vowel with a nasal finish—*n*, or *ng*. Some are just vowel sounds on their own, but there are no combinations of consonants like the *str* in 'straight'. To expand its limited range of noises, it has developed four different ways of pitching them (Cantonese, by the way, has eight).

1st: *Mā*, said with a high, sustained tone ('Mum')

2nd: *Má*, said with a rising tone ('to tingle')

3rd: *Mǎ*, said with a falling and then rising tone ('horse')

4th: *Mà*, said with an abrupt falling tone ('to swear')

Some sounds can also be said neutrally. *Ma* at the end of a sentence indicates it's a question rather than a statement.

If this seems bizarre, consider that many languages use tone or pitch to convey meaning, but in a different way. For instance:

Mm? (Sorry, what was that you said—I wasn't paying attention.)

Mm. (I'm listening to what you're saying and I agree.)

Mmmm. (That was nice. Do it again.)

Unfortunately Mandarin still has too many homophones (words that sound the same but have different meanings). *Mā* can also mean 'to wipe' and *mǎ* can also mean 'yard', but each is *written* differently. Context is usually enough in speech to make it clear what is meant—there aren't many sentences in which you could substitute 'yard' for 'horse' and still make sense. Where there is confusion during a conversation the speaker will describe the component parts of the character he means, sketch it in his palm with a finger, or give another example of its use. Just as the word 'horse' can be combined with others in English to make new ideas (e.g. horseback, horse trough, horse hair) so can *mǎ*, and other Chinese characters. *Mǎ'ān* is 'saddle', and *mǎkù* are jodhpurs or riding breeches ('horse trousers'). Entertainingly *mǎhū* ('horse tiger') is 'careless', *mǎmǎhūhū* ('horse horse tiger tiger') is 'not so bad, so-so', and *mǎshàng* ('on horseback') is 'immediately', which tells you something about how quickly things get done in China.

Characters

Chinese is not written phonetically. If you see an unfamiliar character you can sometimes see a hint as to how it should be pronounced (one character equals one syllable), but only a hint. On closer examination, what at first seems to be an infinite variety of forms turns out to be constructed from a limited number of elements put together in different combinations. All but the simplest characters can be divided into two parts, the *radical* and the *phonetic*. The radical may give some indication of the class of idea that the whole character deals with, while the phonetic part may indicate that the whole character sounds something like the phonetic part would if it stood on its own. Take the five *ma* examples:

马 *Mǎ* (horse) is functioning as the phonetic element in *mā* ('Mum') and *ma* (question particle), standing on the right in each case.

妈 吗

mā *ma*

It's also the bottom half of *mà* (to swear). 骂

The radical element can also be the left, right, top or bottom part of a character, or even something in the middle. In *mā* it's the left half, which is the female radical, and entirely appropriate for 'Mum'. In *ma* it's the 'mouth' radical, appropriate for the question particle (*see* p.109).

烽 The character *fēng* means 'beacon'. The left-hand side of *fēng* is the fire radical *huǒ*, and together with *huǒ* by itself, meaning 'fire', and *tái* meaning 'tower', it makes up the word for the beacon towers that dot the landscape on both sides of the Great Wall, and in some cases replace it (*fēnghuǒ tái*).

烽火台

丰 The lower right-hand side is pronounced *fēng* when standing by itself (meaning 'plentiful'), and is a phonetic element in several other characters.

It shows up in *fēng*, 'bee', where the radical (on the left) is the one for insects. 蜂

蜂蜜 You are most likely to see it on menus—*fēngmì* is 'honey'. Reverse the characters to *mìfēng* and you get 'honey bee'. Note the slightly squashed version of the insect radical at the bottom of the *mì* character.

In the next *fēng* the radical is for mountains, and this character means 'peak' or 'summit'. 峰

锋 Yet another *fēng* has the metal radical, and means 'cutting edge' (of a sword for instance). While you're not likely to see this character often, the metal radical is commonplace for the traveller, appearing in...

钱 *qián* meaning 'money'...

zhōng meaning bell (in bell tower) ... 钟

铁路 and *tiě* meaning 'iron'. *Tiělù*, 'iron road', is railway line.

Using Dictionaries

It's impossible to use a dictionary to look up a character you don't know how to say unless you know how to write Chinese characters. It's only necessary to master a small number of strokes to be able to write Chinese, but everyone is expected to make these strokes in the same way and in the same order when writing a character. In everyday handwriting the pen may not be lifted from the paper between every stroke, and unless everyone used the same order and direction a wide variety of different squiggles would result although the same character was intended. Writing clear characters with individual strokes is like block printing (using capital letters) with the Roman alphabet. The number of strokes is fairly well hidden in most printed forms.

口 *Kǒu*, for instance, takes three strokes to write, not four. The first is the left side of the box, drawn downwards, the second is drawn across the top from left to right and then down the right side in a single stroke. The third closes the box from left to right.

The first task when using a dictionary is to identify the radical of the character you want to interpret. At the front of the Chinese–English section you'll find a table listing all the radicals in order of the number of strokes it takes to write them. To look up *mā*, with experience you'd be confident that the radical was the female part on the left, which takes three strokes. 妈

Turning to the part of the table that lists three-stroke radicals and running your finger down the 39 possibilities until you saw the female character, you'd be referred to another table on the following pages, which would list all the characters which have the female radical, in order of the number of strokes it takes to complete them. In the case of *mā* this would be three more strokes, and it would not be difficult to spot the right character amongst the eleven or so possibilities (depending on the size of your dictionary). You would now be given the number of the page on which to find it in the main body of the dictionary, or the pronunciation, written in the offical Romanized form of Chinese known as *pīnyīn*. The rest of the dictionary is in alphabetical order of *pīnyīn* spelling, and then in order of tone, e.g. *luò, mā, má, mǎ, mà, ma, mai*. (Note in passing that Mandarin hasn't even employed all the possibilities open to it—there is no first tone *māi*, for instance.)

This procedure sounds complex, but a little familiarity with Chinese makes it swift and fairly straightforward, although there are many inconsistencies. *Mà* ('to swear'), for instance, might be expected to have one of the little mouths as its radical, but in dictionaries it's found under the horse radical, although that is also apparently the phonetic element, and the connection between horses and swearing is probably only apparent to jockeys and gamblers. To confuse matters further, dictionaries may differ on which is the radical for a particular character.

Simplification

Originally, although Chinese people spoke several mutually incomprehensible languages (or dialects—the debate is between linguists, and in Běijīng has political overtones to do with the gospel of Hàn unity), they could at least write to each other, since they all wrote the same characters, and employed largely the same grammar. The harmonization of the writing systems of individual kingdoms was enforced following the unification of China under the Qín dynasty (221–207 BC). After the communist victory of AD 1949 this unity began to be dismantled, for the laudable purpose of increasing literacy by reducing the number of characters and making them easier to write. The result is that many of the characters in your local restaurant's menu are often more complicated than the ones that you will see in mainland China, since most expatriate Chinese left long before the simplification began, or came from Hong Kong which escaped it until the Chinese takeover.

 Take the character for 'meal', or 'cooked rice', for example: *fàn*. In Modern Standard Chinese it takes a mere seven strokes to write, but in the original full form it took nine to write the radical alone (the left-hand side).

This still appears in its original form when it stands by itself as *shí*, meaning 'meal' or 'food'.

Full form characters are making a come-back in the giant brass letters on new shop, hotel and restaurant signs. These, incidentally, are usually read from left to right, but some, like many older inscriptions on temples and gates, are read from right to left.

Mandarin in Roman Characters

The modern official Romanization system is *Hànyǔ Pīnyīn*, which means 'Chinese language combine sounds', and has largely replaced a bewildering variety of alternative systems. The most popular of the earlier versions was Wade-Giles, still preferred by those who studied Chinese before the sixties, and still in use in many important text books. It's usually easy to identify because it uses apostrophes to indicate hard frontal sounds by placing them after consonants that would otherwise be relatively soft. For instance, *p* is sounded as *b*, unless it appears as *p'*. It may suddenly seem clear why Běijīng ended up as Peking in English—that's how it was written in Wade-Giles, and only the language student would know to soften the initial *p* to a *b*, and the *k* to a *j*. The French developed the official Post Office Romanization of place names, influenced by the values of Roman characters in the French language, and this, too, contributed to the confusion.

A familiarity with *pīnyīn* is easier to master than written Chinese, and since all important Chinese names and places are given in *pīnyīn* in this book, will be a great aid to communication. Unlike in earlier systems, most letters have values similar to those the English speaker would expect, though Chinese does have some noises not found in English. It's particularly important to grasp, for instance, that the *zh* in Gānsù Province's capital *Lánzhōu* is a soft kind of *j*, and the *ou* is the *ough* of *dough*. Ticket-sellers hearing 'Lan-zoo' or 'Lan-chow', common mispronunciations amongst foreign visitors, are not likely to understand. Something resembling 'Lan-joe' has a chance of success. A guide to *pīnyīn* is given in **Language**, *see* p.514.

Apostrophes also appear in *pīnyīn* but only to make it clear where breaks in sound should come. The ancient name of Xī'ān was Cháng'ān, made from two characters for *cháng* (long) and *ān* (peace), not any form of *chan* and *gan*. Xī'ān needs the apostrophe to show that it's made from two characters and syllables, *xī* (west) and *ān* (peace), not a single *xian* (pronounced differently and meaning 'first'). Although there are rules for the application of the apostrophe, there's little consistency in how they are used in real life. In this book they are added wherever it helps to make the word clearer to those unfamiliar with Mandarin. Oddly, *pīnyīn* is rarely tone-marked except in language texts, rather defeating its object of helping you to say the right sound (although in this book every *pīnyīn* word is tone-marked).

There's a lot of variation, too, as to how *pīnyīn* should represent longer strings of syllables—what should be joined together, and what separated. This book breaks things up whenever it will aid clarity. You'll occasionally see *pīnyīn* on street signs and shop signs, sometimes written as long strings and perhaps broken in the middle of a word to go to the next line.

Pīnyīn has been introduced to primary schools to aid children in producing the same sounds. Mandarin has only been the national language of China since the time of the Republic, although it became the official language of administration under the Manchu Qīng dynasty, and is essentially just the Běijīng dialect of the language. Even today, a mere 100km from the capital, the sounds made when speaking at home may vary quite widely from those of the schoolroom, and the introduction of the foreign alphabet has increased the likelihood of Modern Standard Chinese becoming truly standard. However, only younger adults educated after 1976 are likely to have any grasp of *pīnyīn*, and it plays no significant role in life after school.

Everyday Grammar

Questions

There are three main ways of asking questions in Chinese, and since you'll want to ask quite a few, and will be asked many yourself, it's worth at least learning to recognize a question from a statement. As in English, one way of asking questions is to use question words such as 'who', 'what' and 'where'. You'll frequently hear: *Nǐ shì nǎguó rén?* 'You are which country person?', to which the answer is *Wǒ shì Yīngguó rén*, 'I am Britain person' (a list of other nationalities is given in **Language** p.518). Note that for all persons, singular or plural, the verb to be is *shì*. There's no memorizing the conjugations of regular and irregular verbs in Mandarin: every one is of this one-size-fits-all kind.

Questions are also frequently asked by offering you a choice: *Nǐ shì bú shì Měiguó rén?*, 'You are not are America person?'. If you are, the response is *shì*, 'am', and if you aren't, the response is *bú shì*, 'not am'. You'll also often hear, *Nǐ dǒng bù dǒng?*, 'You understand not understand?'. If you did, say *dǒng*, and if not, *bù dǒng*. Chinese doesn't really have words for 'yes' or 'no'. The tendency is to concentrate on the main verb and affirm or deny it. *Duì*, meaning 'correct', is the nearest thing to 'yes', and *bù* (sometimes *bú*, often toneless) is used in most cases to make verbs negative. The exception is the verb 'to have', *yǒu*, which is negated by *méi*. *Méi yǒu* is the Mandarin expression you will hear more frequently than any other during your trip: 'There aren't any', 'We don't have any', and 'Whatever you want to happen isn't going to come to pass'.

The third main way of asking questions is to use the question particle, *ma*. Add it to the end of any statement and you have a question. *Tā shì Jiānádà rén ma?* 'He is Canada person [question]?' Chinese has several useful particles which go at the ends of sentences, such as *ba*, used for making suggestions or propositions, and *ne*, indicating that there's a continuing subject of conversation. For instance, *Nǐ hǎo ma?*, a standard greeting, 'You well [question]?', is often answered, *Wǒ hěn hǎo. Nǐ ne?*, 'I very well. You [same topic]?'

Time

Particles after verbs and sentences play a role in indicating time, since verbs don't modify to show tense. *Tā qù Zhōngguó*, 'He is going to China', is also 'He will go', 'He went', etc. Extra terms such as 'tomorrow' and 'before' are usually added to give a sense of time: *Zuótiān tā qù Zhōngguó le*, 'Yesterday he went to China'. Suffixes called aspect-particles, such as *le* and *guo*, clarify matters further. Chinese is mostly concerned with putting events in order, and with whether they are over and done with yet, or still continuing: *Tā qùle Zhōngguó*, 'He's gone to China' (at a specific time, but he hasn't come back yet), or *Tā qùguo Zhōngguó*, 'He's been to China' (at some unspecified time and returned). Roughly, *le* at the end of a sentence or after a verb gives a sense of change or completion, and *guo* after a verb indicates that something happened over a period of time but it's now finished. Another particle *zhe* is used to indicate that two actions are happening at the same time. This may sound odd at first, but with a little familiarity it makes English, French and German look unnecessarily complicated.

Quantities

There's no plural form for nouns, so indications of quantity are important, as are expressions such as 'some', 'many' and 'a set of'. *Tā mǎi shū ma?* means 'Is he buying books?' *Tā mǎi yì běn shū ma?* means 'Is he buying a book?' All expressions of quantity require the use of a *measure word*. You can't say 'a fish' or 'two fish' in Chinese; the required structure is number + measure word + noun. This is like saying 'a slice of toast' or 'a round of ammunition' in English, using simple expressions of quantity like 'a cup of', 'a kilo of', and using collective nouns like 'flock' or 'shoal'. There's no real translation of *běn* in the sentence above that works in this context: 'Is he buying one volume book?' is like the pidgin English used in early days of British trade in Canton.

Objects with similar characteristics use the same measure word. Most things that are flat use *zhāng*, for example. Three tickets are *sān zhāng piào*, two tables *liǎng zhāng zhuōzi*. Long and flexible things use *tiáo*. *Sì tiáo yú* are four fish, *yì tiáo lù* is a road. One of the pleasures of learning Mandarin is that since the Chinese have had little contact with the West they do not share the same metaphors or link ideas in the same way. To learn the language is also to learn new and often entertaining ways of looking at the world.

Although there are large numbers of measure words, only a limited number are in everyday use, and some can be replaced by the all-purpose *ge*. Most useful to the traveller are quantitative expressions like *yì bēi chá*, 'a *cup of* tea', *liǎng wǎn bǎifàn*, 'two *bowls of* rice', and *qǐng lái yí fèn huíguō ruò*, 'please bring a *portion of* "return-to-the-pot pork".'

Learning More

A far more erudite and complete introduction to Chinese for both those who intend to study the language and those who are just curious about how it works, can be found in *About Chinese*, by Richard Newnham (Pelican Books, revised edition 1987). Your local China friendship society is usually a good source of information on where to find classes and other information about China. In the UK try the Great Britain–China Centre, 15 Belgrave Sq., London SW1X 8PS, ✆ (0171) 235 6696, ✆ (0171) 245 6885, gbcc@gn.apc.org, which offers classes, lectures, social events, a specialist library and an excellent magazine.

Xī'ān to Lánzhōu

The Imperial Highway

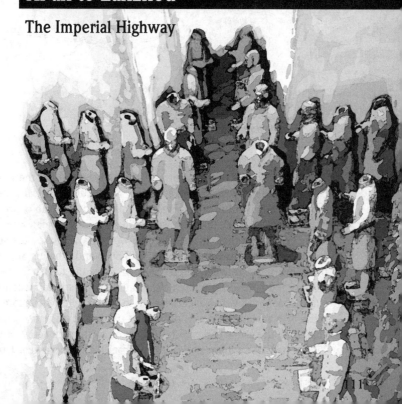

The Terracotta Warriors

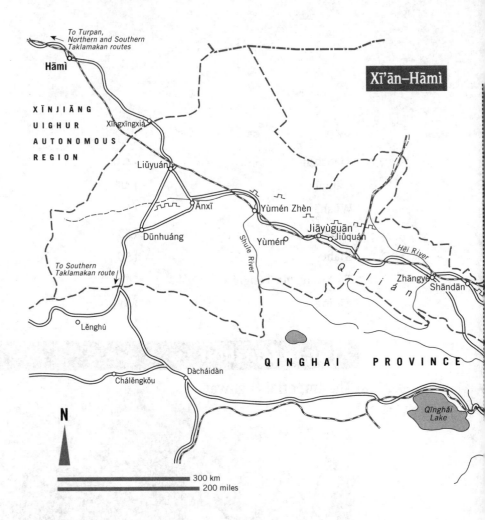

The deep twin ruts of the cart track sometimes known as the Imperial Highway
probably saw more trade than any other Silk Route, especially during the
wealthy and powerful Táng dynasty. Replaced today by an expressway (at least
in part) and a railway line, the route still sees more foreign faces and more
foreign exchange than any other going west, drawn not by the silk trade, but
by the spectacular cave temples of Màijī Shān and Bǐnglíng Sì. Most visitors
travel overnight between the best-known sites, but to either side of the
modern route lie lesser-known caves and temples still to make it into the
glossy brochures, yet easily accessible to the traveller with more time. To visit
these is to avoid the streams of mineral trucks and oil-transporting trains that
constitute the camel caravans of today, and to stumble across Huí mosques and
Tibetan temples a mere stone's throw from the Chinese heartlands.

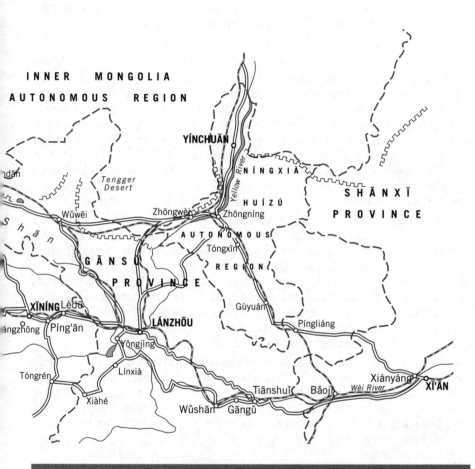

Xī'ān

西安   This is where it all began, or ended. For much of the active life of the Silk Routes Xī'ān was the funnel for intelligence, money, people and goods arriving from and leaving for what the Chinese called the 'Western Regions'. At times it was the world's largest, richest and most cosmopolitan city, and capital of its largest, richest and most powerful nation.

Although later partially rebuilt by the Míng, Xī'ān lost its capital status for good at the end of the Táng dynasty. The American archaeologist Langdon Warner, passing through in 1923, was disappointed.

Instead of imperial banquets we ate grubbily with our thumbs at the
inn. Instead of splendid processions of court nobles and proud ecclesi-
astics, a sinister double line of yellow uniforms shuffled swiftly up the
main paved street with three bound prisoners in their clutches. A
hundred yards or so from where we stood there was a halt of scarce
half a minute and (happily we did not see it) three heads rolled off from
three luckless carcasses and the soldiers shuffled on, leaving the carrion
to be swept up.

Langdon Warner, *The Long Old Road in China*, 1926

The 1974 discovery of the Qín Terracotta Warriors, the opening of China's doors to foreign tourism, and the partial deregulation of the economy changed everything. The warriors were kept secret until they were ready for display, but after that tourists rushed to visit them in numbers rivalling those at the main sights of Běijīng. Meanwhile China's economic boom brought both a forest of shiny new towers and the severe pollution caused by industry, motor vehicles and increasing population that almost hides them from view. The city has re-expanded to cover almost the same area as at its Suí and Táng peak, although the Silk Route is mentioned only to attract tourists. A monument of stone camels has been built near where the Táng city's west gate once stood, and is officially designated the Routes' starting point.

There is enough to see in and around Xī'ān to keep even the most active visitor busy for a week or two. In addition to the official sights, it's easy to discover buildings of considerable antiquity just by wandering around the back alleys, even if they've been changed in use or covered with a patina of modern additions. At the end of the signwriting market, you can find the entrance to a library from the time of the Emperor Qiánlóng (1711–99) and now home to many families. Other back streets have temples functioning as schools or workshops, their high, slooping roofs easily visible but their entrances hard to find. The northwest quarter within the Míng walls is still home to large numbers of Huí, their way of life giving a foretaste of the cultures of Níngxià and much of Gānsù to the west.

No city on the Imperial Highway is more visited than Xī'ān, and this brings its own problems. Emerging from the passage under the Drum Tower you may be accosted by pretty girls with excellent English who say they are art students raising funds for a visit to Germany (or some-times the Edinburgh Festival)—won't you please come and see their 'unique' paintings which you'll later see in every gift shop and at every tourist site. The 'students' have been just about to go to Germany for at least five years, and still are.

History

Traces of activity from as early as 800,000 years ago have been found in this area, the land within the Yellow River's great northern loop being traditionally the cradle of the Chinese race. The earliest known examples of Chinese writing were unearthed nearby at Bànpō on pottery wares from Neolithic times, carbon-dated as belonging to the Yǎngsháo culture, between 5000 and 3000 BC.

Previous versions of Xī'ān have been capitals for far longer than Běijīng and home to kings and emperors under the Western Zhōu, Qín, Western Hàn, Xīn, Suí, Táng, and a host of inter-mediate smaller dynasties. Cháng'ān (eternal peace), the version built under the earlier (Western) Hàn to the northwest of modern Xī'ān, was China's first metropolis. With an area of around 35 sq km, it was probably equalled only by Rome in size. The remains of its walls and the bases of its palaces can still be seen, although the land in between has long been ploughed. At the time of Emperor Wŭdì (reigned 141–87 BC), when Zhāng Qiān went on missions to the Western Regions, the city may have contained as many as 200,000 people—including representatives of foreign powers contacted by Zhāng and his successors, and students from all over China.

The Eastern (Later) Hàn chose Luòyáng as their capital but their eventual successors, the Suí, built a new capital slightly southeast of Cháng'ān on the site of modern Xī'ān. The first Suí emperor moved into the incomplete city, now named Dàxīng Chéng (City of Great Prosperity) in AD 583, six years before the unification was completed. Surrounded by walls of rammed earth nearly 10km by 9km and probably more than 10m high, the city was divided into three areas: the palace, the administrative quarter and the residential area. The latter occupied nearly 90 per cent of the city, and was divided into 108 individually walled compounds of hovels, mansions and temples. Dàxīng Chéng was then the largest city in the world, and the largest in the whole of Chinese imperial history. At times earlier courts had been forced to roam, as the land around Xī'ān was not fertile enough to sustain them, but the Suí solved this by building the Grand Canal system connecting their capitals and the food-poor northern border with the lush rice paddies to the south. The result was almost 2000km of canals 40 paces wide. Other vast earthworks included the construction and repair of a long section of the Great Wall in northern Shānxī, said to have involved more than a million labourers.

Civil war and failed attacks on Korea brought down the Suí, Dàxīng Chéng falling to a rebel who was to become the first Táng emperor in AD 617. The city was renamed Cháng'ān to suggest continuity with the Hàn dynasty and to support the legitimacy of the new one. If under the Suí the city became the largest in the world, under the Táng it became the most cosmopolitan. Persians, Arabs, Jews, Uighurs and other Central Asian traders who arrived by land along the Silk Routes and later by sea were allowed to establish communities in Cháng'ān. They brought their own cultures, technologies, and religions, including Nestorian Christianity, Manichaeism, Zoroastrianism, Islam and Judaism. Profoundly influencing Táng art, cuisine and fashions, they were treated with a liberality unique in Chinese history, and allowed to live by their own laws in communities ruled by their own headmen.

Although re-established, the Táng never really recovered from the weakness caused by the rebellion which captured Cháng'ān in AD 756 (see 'Huáqīng Chí', p.132). Militarily exhausted, they were unable to resist a rebellion by the Uighurs and the Tibetan occupation of Gānsù, which cut the land routes to the west. Cháng'ān was captured again by a confederation of bandit gangs in AD 860 and, although the emperor returned to the city in 883, it had suffered severe destruction. The dynasty finally expired in 907, and with it Cháng'ān's days as the capital of a unified China. The city walls currently visible, impressive as they are, were erected by the Míng (1368–1644) on roughly the site of the Táng *palace* only. The next lengthy imperial stay was not until late 1900, when the Empress Dowager Cíxǐ and Emperor Guāngxù fled to Xī'ān to avoid the foreign armies that had come to relieve the Běijīng legation quarter besieged, with Qīng complicity, by the Boxer rebels.

Occupation by imperial dynasties over the centuries has left the plain around Xī'ān riddled with the tombs of emperors, their families, and privileged ministers. Grave-robbing has always flourished, right up to modern times. Archaeologists' finds, impressive though they frequently are, are others' leftovers. In 1994 the Xī'ān police set up a special bureau to counter the black

books and maps

Map sellers with maps in English and Chinese at ¥2 are difficult to avoid outside the railway station and around the Bell Tower. All travel agents and hotels also have these and Dad's and Mum's restaurants give them free. The Xīnhuà Shūdiàn just east of the Bell Tower and the Wàiwén Shūdiàn immediately east of the Wǔyī Bīnguǎn (May First Hotel) have good selections of novels in English, plus art and history books.

money

Larger hotels in Xī'ān now only change traveller's' cheques for residents, but will exchange cash for others. The branch of the **Bank of China** just east of Hotel Royal Xī'ān on the south side of Dōng Dàjiē (*open 9–5, Sat and Sun 9–3*) has foreign exchange upstairs at counters 6 to 8. There's another branch on the west side of Jiěfàng Lù, a short walk south of the railway station (*open Mon–Fri 9–11.30 and 2–5.30*). Use window no.6. Other branches handle cash exchange only. There's a particularly attractive one on Xī Dàjiē in an old, red-pillared building.

photographic

Film is available from almost all of Xī'ān's myriad department stores, legions of photo shops, and from foyers of larger hotels. Department stores with marked prices are the cheapest. Kodak film is typically ¥20 ($2.50). A wider selection of film including Fujichrome and Ektachrome, and a developing service—about ¥28 ($3.50) for 36 prints, is available from a shop with a big Kodak sign on the north side of Dōng Dàjiē.

---

market in cultural relics, the first such organization in China. In 1995 it nevertheless investigated no fewer than 278 cases of tomb robbing, nabbing 705 suspects, several cars, mobile phones and guns, and retrieving more than 5000 relics.

Official archaeological finds continue. In 1996 the largest Táng dynasty stone coffin yet found was discovered in a secret burial chamber 20km north of Xī'ān. The tomb belonged to a Táng justice minister and had three parts, of which grave robbers had discovered only two. In addition, more than 160 exquisite tri-coloured pottery figurines were recovered. It is said that an archaeologist now accompanies all construction crews at the beginning of their work. More discoveries can be expected, adding yet further to the reasons to visit Xī'ān.

Getting to and from Xī'ān

by air

The CAAC booking office is in Láodòng Nánlù, corner of Xīguān Zhèngjiē (*open 8am–9.30pm*). There is a foreigners' window at the right-hand end where English is spoken. The only international flight is daily with China Northwest to Nagoya, for ¥4100 ($495) one way, ¥7400 ($890) return, sometimes with discounts available due to low numbers. There are direct flights to most major cities in China, including Hong Kong ¥1740 ($210) one way, ¥3280 ($395) return, Běijīng up to seven times daily (1½ hours) ¥980/$120, Lánzhōu ¥560 ($68), Ürümqi ¥2090 ($250), as well as Yínchuān.

post office and telephones

The main **post office** (*open 8.30–8*) is the large building on the northeast side of the Bell Tower. The international mail counter is no.12 on the left; *poste restante* is at counter 22 on the right, ¥1.5 per item received. There is another useful office just west of the Jiěfàng Fàndiàn opposite the railway station (*open 8–8*).

National and **international phone calls** can be made from the Diànxīn Dàlóu on the corner of Xī Xīnjiē up Běi Dàjiē, just north of the Bell Tower (*open 7 days, 24hrs*). Enter from Běi Dàjiē and thrust through the hosts of Chinese buying mobile phones to the cabin marked International Telecommunications to the left. There's a deposit of ¥500 for international or ¥100 ($12) for domestic calls. Prices for each country are listed on a board: ¥26.65 ($3.50) per minute to North America, most European countries around ¥29.95 ($4) and Japan ¥18.55 ($2.50).

Faxes can also be sent, with a minimum three-minute charge. Incoming @ 721 8799; ¥6 per page to receive.

visa extensions

Visa extensions are available without too much fuss at the PSB's Division of Aliens Entry and Exit Administration on the south side of Xī Dàjiē two blocks west of the Bell Tower (*open 8–12 and 2–6; closed Sat and Sun*).

There's a bus every hour from the office to the airport which is near Xiányáng, one hour away, ¥15 ($2). Take the bus at least two hours before your flight. Remember airport taxes: domestic ¥60 ($7.50), international ¥90 ($11).

by train

Xī'ān is well connected by rail, and buying tickets is easy by Chinese standards. The main railway station is just outside the city walls on the northeast side: reached by trolleybus 101 and bus 201 from the Bell Tower, and connected by bus to most hotels. There's a counter for soft and hard sleeper tickets and for all foreigners' purchases upstairs over the main Chinese booking office at the right-hand end as you face the station building (*open 8.30–10.30 and 2.30–4.30; closed Fri and Sat pm and all day Sun*). The counter is on the left. You will be given a slip to take to the window at the other end of the room (probably no.4), where you queue again, pay, and receive your tickets. This is usually time-consuming but straightforward. Avoid Mondays and early mornings, and allow at least one hour.

Hotel travel agencies will get your ticket for you for fees varying between ¥40 ($5) and ¥90 ($11).

There are several trains daily to Běijīng, but the a/c 42 at 18.35 is particularly convenient and faster if slightly more expensive (e.g. hard sleeper ¥180/$22 compared to ¥160/$20), and the night train is the other choice: no.36 at 21.07. Other trains

Xī'ān

HUANCHENG BEILU

BEI MEN
(ANYUAN MEN)

XINGHUO LU

FENGHE LU

H A
R R C
B

6

DAQING LU

LIANHU LU

XIWI

To Airport, Xiányáng,
West Route, Tiānshuī
& Píngliáng

HUANCHENG XILU

BEI DAJIE

8 XI XIN

DAMAI SHI JIE

MIAOHOU JIE

Muslim
Quarter 11

BEIGUANGJI JIE

XIYANG SHICHANG

BEIYUAN
MEN

9

K

XI MEN
(ANDING MEN)

M

10

HUAJUE 12
XIANG

C

14

R

PING'AN
SHICHANG

17

XIGUAN ZHENGJIE

XI DAJIE

N

L 16

13

20

CHENGHUANGMIAO
XIAOSHANGPIN SHICHANG

21

ZHUBA SHI

S H

NAN DAJIE

X R

Y H

HUANCHENG NANLU

LAODONG NANLU

NAN MEN
(MINGDE MEN)

24

TAIBAI BEILU

H AA

NANGUAN ZHENGJIE

YOUYI XILU

LINGYUAN LU

25

CHANG 'AN LU

YOUYI I

NANER HUANLU

N

XIAOZHAI DONGLU

To Xīngjiāo Sì

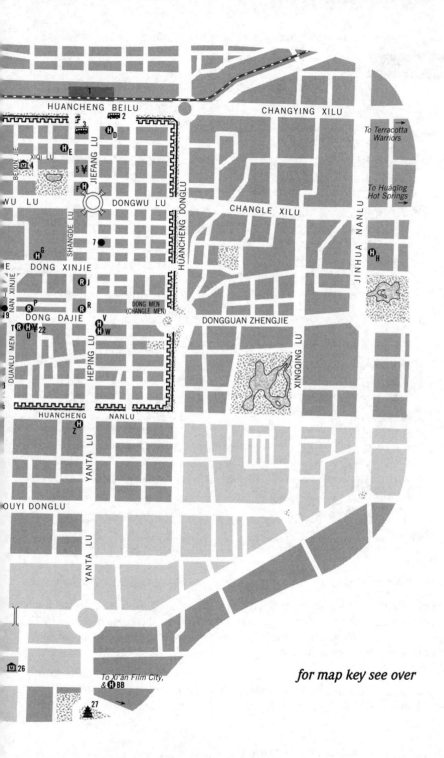

HUANCHENG BEILU

CHANGYING XILU

To Terracotta
Warriors

To Huáqīng
Hot Springs

BEIXIN JIE

XIQI LU

JIEFANG LU

SHANGDE LU

DONGWU LU

CHANGLE XILU

JINHUA NANLU

WU LU

DONG XINJIE

HUANCHENG DONGLU

NAN XINJIE

DONG DAJIE

DONG MEN
(CHANGLE MEN)

DONGGUAN ZHENGJIE

DUANLU MEN

HEPING LU

XINGQING LU

HUANCHENG

NANLU

YANTA LU

OUYI DONGLU

YANTA LU

To Xi'an Film City,
& BB

for map key see over

119

Xī'ān map key

KEY

火车站	1	Railway station
	2	Buses to Museum of Terracotta Warriors, Bànpō Museum, Huáqīng Hot Springs
西安汽车站	3	Xī'ān Qìchēzhàn
八路军西安办事处纪念馆	4	Memorial Museum of Eighth Route Army Xī'ān Off Bālùjūn Xī'ān Bànshìwài Jìniànguǎn
中国银行	5	Bank of China Zhōngguó Yínháng
玉祥门汽车站	6	Yùxiáng Mén Qìchēzhàn
民生百货商店	7	Mínshēng Department Store Mínshēng Bǎihuò Shāngdiàn
电信大楼	8	Telephone office Diànxìn dàlóu
人民剧院	9	People's Theatre Rénmín Jùyuàn
清真大寺	10	Great Mosque Qīngzhēn Dàsì
城隍庙	11	City God's Temple and market Chénghuángmiào
鼓楼	12	Drum Tower Gǔ Lóu
钟楼	13	Bell Tower Zhōng Lóu
邮局	14	Post office Yóujú
华韵苑	15	Huá Yùn Yuàn Theatre
唐城大厦	16	Tángchéng department store Tángchéng Dàshà
新华书店	17	Xīnhuá Shūdiàn
外文书店	18	Wàiwén Shūdiàn
美术音乐书店	19	Měishù Yīnyuè Shūdiàn
中国民航	20	CAAC Zhōngguó Mínháng
公安局	21	PSB Gōng'ānjú
中国银行	22	Bank of China Zhōngguó Yínháng
碑林博物馆	23	'Forest of Stelae' Bēilín Bówùguǎn
	24	Buses to Xīngjiāo Sì
小雁塔	25	Little Goose Pagoda Xiǎoyàn Tǎ
陕西历史博物馆	26	Shǎnxī History Museum Shǎnxī Lìshǐ Bówùguǎn
大雁塔	27	Big Goose Pagoda Dàyàn Tǎ

HOTELS AND RESTAURANTS

人民大厦公寓	A	Rénmín Dàshà Gōngyù 'Flats of Rénmín'
	B	Mum's Home Cooking
	C	Dad's Home Cooking
解放饭店	D	Jiěfàng Fàndiàn
尚德宾馆	E	Shàngdé Bīnguǎn
龙海大酒店	F	Lónghǎi Dàjiǔdiàn
人民大厦	G	Rénmín Dàshà People's Hotel
陕西机械学院招待所	H	Shǎnxī Inst of Mech Eng Zhāodàisuǒ Shǎnxī Jīxiè Xuéyuàn Zhāodàisuǒ
贾三饭馆	I	Jiǎsān Fànguǎn
肯德鸡	J	Kentucky Fried Chicken Kěndé Jī
	K	Dumpling restaurants
德发长酒店	L	Défācháng Jiǔdiàn
白蜗牛餐厅	M	Báiwōniú Cāntīng
西京饭店	N	Xījīng Fàndiàn
五一宾馆	O	Wǔyī Bīnguǎn
	P	Bob and Betty's
	R	Kebab stall
钟楼饭店	S	Bell Tower Hotel Zhōnglóu Fàndiàn
老孙家饭庄	T	Lǎosūnjiā Fànzhuāng
皇城宾馆	U	Hotel Royal Xī'ān Huángchéng Bīnguǎn
凯悦饭店	V	Hyatt Kǎiyuè Fàndiàn
华商酒店	W	Huáshāng Jiǔdiàn China Merchants Hotel
肯德鸡	X	Kentucky Fried Chicken Kěndé Jī
民生大酒店	Y	Mínshēng Dàjiǔdiàn
胜利饭店	Z	Victory Hotel Shènglì Fàndiàn
西北大学宾馆	AA	Northwest University Guesthouse Xīběi Dàxué Bīnguǎn
唐华宾馆	BB	Xī'ān Garden Hotel Tánghuá Bīnguǎn

include the 275 to Xīníng at 16.10, the 143 to Korla/Ürümqi at 21.40 (each destination on alternate days), the 3 to Xiányáng at 05.30, the 176 to Bāotóu at 15.22. Check destination boards, timetables and agents for trains on the newly opened line to Zhōngwèi (two slow trains daily).

by bus

Xī'ān has several bus stations, of which the following two are the most useful. The **Xī'ān Qìchēzhàn** is opposite the railway station with buses to Xiányáng (28km,

北院门	Běiyuàn Mén	劳动南路	Láodòng Nánlù
北大街	Běi Dàjiē	莲湖路	Liánhú Lù
北广济街	Běiguǎngjì Jiē	庙后街	Miàohòu Jiē
北门（安远门）	Běi Mén (Ānyuǎn Mén)	南大街	Nán Dàjiē
北新街	Běixīn Jiē	南二环路	Nánèr Huánlù
长安路	Cháng'ān Lù	南关正街	Nánguān Zhèngjiē
长乐西路	Chánglè Xīlù	南门（明德门）	Nán Mén (Míngdé Mén)
长缨西路	Chángyīng Xīlù	南新街	Nán Xīnjiē
城隍庙小商品市场	Chénghuángmiào Xiǎoshāngpǐn Shìchǎng	平安市场	Píng'ān Shìchǎng
大麦市街	Dàmài Shì Jiē	尚德路	Shàngdé Lù
大庆路	Dàqìng Lù	陵园路	Língyuán Lù
东大街	Dōng Dàjiē	太白北路	Tàibái Běilù
东关正街	Dōngguān Zhèngjiē	小寨东路	Xiǎozhài Dōnglù
东门（长乐门）	Dōng Mén (Chánglè Mén)	西大街	Xī Dàjiē
东五路	Dōngwǔ Lù	西关正街	Xīguān Zhèngjiē
东新街	Dōng Xīnjiē	西门（安定门）	Xī Mén (Āndìng Mén)
端履门	Duānlǚ Mén	兴庆路	Xīngqìng Lù
丰禾路	Fēnghé Lù	西七路	Xīqī Lù
古文化街	Gǔ Wénhuà Jiē	西五路	Xīwǔ Lù
和平路	Hépíng Lù	西新街	Xī Xīnjiē
化觉巷	Huàjué Xiàng	西羊市	Xīyáng Shì
环城东，南，西，北路	Huánchéng Dōng/Nán/Xī/Běilù	西一路	Xīyī Lù
解放路	Jiěfàng Lù	雁塔路	Yàntǎ Lù
金花南路	Jīnhuā Nánlù	友谊东，西路	Yǒuyì Dōng/Xīlù
		竹笆市	Zhúbā Shì

¥2.70), Píngliáng (309km, ¥25.30/$3), to Gùyuán (400km, ¥31.90/$4), and Yínchuān (743km, ¥58/$7 for a seat or ¥164/$20 on a sleeper bus).

The **Yùxiáng Mén Qìchēzhàn** is just outside the Yùxiáng Mén and slightly to the north, reached by trolleybus 103 from the railway station, and buses 10 and 12 along Liánhú Lù. The ticket office is immediately on your right, and a sign on the wall opposite has prices. There are buses to Píngliáng (305km, ¥25.30/$3, 8 deps), Gùyuán (396km, ¥31.90/$4, 10 deps), and an afternoon sleeper bus to Yínchuān (743km, ¥110/$13.50).

Xī'ān's centre is the substantial Bell Tower, marking the crossroads of the principle north–south and east–west avenues, and visible from all four main city gates. The main arteries are Dōng, Nán, Xī and Běi Dàjiē (East, South, West, and North Avenues) running from the Bell Tower to the relevant gates. Many hotels and much of Xī'ān's main shopping areas are along these four streets. The Muslim quarter, the Great Mosque, the Drum Tower and several other sights are all within walking distance of the Bell Tower.

There are five **trolleybus** routes (nos.101–105) with a flat fare of 5 *máo* (no change). All run east–west, the 101 and 103 also turning north to reach the railway station. **Bus** tickets begin at 5 *máo* flat fare for ordinary buses, plus 3 *máo* every few stops on the special, limited stop (*zhuānxiàn*) buses. The **minibuses** run some of the same routes (but sometimes with short cuts) for about double this, but with the proper rates usually posted inside. Some routes are minibus-only: the 501 passes the Rénmín Dàshà Gōngyù (Flats of Rénmín), and weaves through the backstreets of the Muslim quarter, passing close to the Bell Tower and the Shǎnxī History Museum, terminating at the Big Goose Pagoda. **Taxis** have a flagfall of ¥5, ¥6, or ¥8 depending on size, and cost ¥1.20–1.60 per km. Stand for no nonsense (most drivers seem fairly co-operative) and, if in doubt, point significantly at the registration number on the inside of the windscreen or write it down.

Xī'ān ① (029)   *Tourist Information*

Most large hotels and many small ones have their own travel agencies which at least can arrange minibus tours to the Terracotta Warriors. The best sources of friendly information on all topics, plus assistance with ticket buying, are the staffs of Dad's Home Cooking and Mom's Home Cooking, opposite, nearby, or inside the Flats of Renmin Hotel (*see* 'Eating Out', p.143). The best tours are from the Jiěfàng Fàndiàn (*see* p.140).

Xī'ān Chéngqiáng (Xī'ān City Walls)

Open daylight hours; adm ¥10 ($1.25).   西安城墙

Constructed in 1370–8, during the reign of the first Míng emperor on the remains of Suí and Táng palace walls, these are the largest and best preserved in China, running for nearly 14km around the centre. With a core of mud covered by three layers of brick, they undergo almost continuous rebuilding and restoration while being casually breached elsewhere to widen existing roads or add new ones. 15–18m wide at the base, they rise for 12m to a width of 12–14m at the top. There are numerous salients and corner turrets, and four main city gates. A surrounding moat was originally drawbridged.

The gates are all double towers, with a courtyard between. The outer towers have rows of small windows for archers, and the inner ones are the gate towers proper, triple-layered and nearly 35m high. These now all contain shops, some labelled as 'exhibitions'. However, the South Gate (Míngdé Mén) has a fine exhibition of stele rubbings, which is free. The West Gate (Āndìng Mén) has views of a pretty humpbacked bridge over the moat to the south. The East Gate (Chánglè Mén) was almost completely rebuilt in 1996. Lesser towers can be seen to the north repeating themselves until they disappear into the smog. On the corner across the road stand waiting-for-work (government language for 'unemployed') decorators, their long-handled rollers looking faintly martial.

The best section for walking or cycling is the stretch from West to East gates via the South.

Zhōng Lóu (Bell Tower) 钟楼

Open 9–5.30; adm ¥15 ($2).

Foreigners pay a lower, Chinese price of ¥10 ($1.25) off-season. There's also a compulsory bag deposit for ¥1 (although other prices for foreigners are sometimes invented at random). The tower is reached from the pedestrian underpass beneath Běi Dàjiē.

First built in 1384, the 36m-high tower was substantially restored or rebuilt in 1582, 1740 and 1953, but maintains its typical Míng architecture. Of brick and wood, its three layers of eaves contain a two-storeyed interior, the upper storey being double height. Climbing the outer staircase of the brick plinth and entering the tower, you will find the inevitable gift shops enlivened by occasional performances of traditional music by somewhat inexpert music students on a variety of percussive, stringed and wind instruments. Upstairs, a small exhibition of Qīng porcelain, furniture and fine, if somewhat mildewed, Chinese paintings includes items of considerable beauty poorly lit beneath a colourful ceiling of overlapping beams. The balcony gives views along Xī'ān's main arteries, sclerotic with traffic, to the main city gates. With luck, a little wind will bring slightly fresher air than at street level.

Gǔ Lóu (Drum Tower) 鼓楼

Open 9–5.30; adm ¥5.

Enter the Drum Tower from its northwest corner. From Xī Dàjiē go through the tunnel beneath and turn left.

Within sight of the similar Bell Tower, the Drum Tower is less visited and much quieter. It contains an 'exhibition' of Hùxiàn Farmer Paintings (*see* 'Shopping', p.137) and substantial gloomily varnished Chinese traditional furniture, all at prices well beyond reasonable. There are views to the north up Ānyuǎn Mén with a roofscape of how we foreigners would like China to look: curly-eaves, pigeon lofts, washing lines, a satellite dish or two. To the east the opposite, a vast underground shopping centre under construction. The tower suffered a major overhaul in 1996, which may give it the same atmosphere of fresh construction as the Bell Tower.

Dàyàn Tǎ (Big Goose Pagoda) & Dàcí'ēn Sì 大雁塔，大慈恩寺

Open 8.30–6; adm ¥13 ($2),
plus ¥25 ($3) to climb the pagoda.

The Dàcí'ēn Sì can be reached by minibus 501 from just west of the Bell Tower, and by bus 41 from the station.

The temple was originally built in AD 648–652 by Táng Crown Prince Lǐ Zhì to honour his mother the Empress Wén Dé. Having returned from his scripture-collecting trip to India, the Buddhist monk Xuánzàng requested the construction of a pagoda similar to those that he had seen on his travels, resulting in a plain tapering structure, intended to house the rare texts. Such was Xuánzàng's enthusiasm for the project, he is said to have carried bricks personally.

The temple has been destroyed and rebuilt several times, and in its Táng heyday it was the most important in China, with an added monastery that housed 300 monks. Its current scale dates from about 1466, although it was destroyed again several times after that. The pagoda was set ablaze on a few occasions and its top shaken off by an earthquake in 1556. During renovations it grew to its current seven storeys. Xuánzàng spent half the remainder of his life here translating scriptures with the help of assistants. He's credited with the translation of 75 texts in 1335 volumes, while still finding time to write *Notes on the Western Regions of the Great Táng* for the Emperor Tàizōng. Altogether he increased the amount of Buddhist literature in China by about 25 per cent, but differed with earlier translators on philosophical and textual points. Not all of his retranslations proved popular.

From the south entrance the path leads past bell and drum towers through two main halls containing Buddha and Arhat statues to the pagoda. The temple seems barely functional except as a tourist day trip, and self-conscious Chinese who have a vague idea about Buddhism giggle and dare each other to buy incense sticks. Those who look like they know what they are doing are probably Japanese visitors, bathing in smoke from the incense burners in ritual purification. The sign translated into English as 'Civilized Journey' has nothing to do with Xuánzàng but reminds the Chinese they shouldn't spit.

The pagoda is plain, elegant and with the interior atmosphere of a Victorian office block. The lintels of the four entrances on the ground floor are carved with Buddhist scenes and texts dating from the Táng, and as you enter, the tablets to the right and left contain writings on Buddhism by the Táng Emperors Tàizōng and Gāozōng. Once inside, the stairs to the right are the ones to climb. On the lower floors passages to each point of the compass contain photographs of other famous pagodas, then watercolours of scenes from *Journey to the West*, the fictionalized account of Xuánzàng's travels. At the top, you might be able to see the city wall, but that's often impossible, even from the much closer Little Goose Pagoda. The gaggle of miniature stupas that you can see below house the ashes of temple monks who officiated during the early Qīng dynasty.

To the east is the Táng Dynasty Arts Museum, belonging to the Xī'ān Garden Hotel. This is an introduction to China in Táng times, with a few antiquities. Save your energies for the History Museum instead.

Stupa, *Dagoba, Chorten,* or Pagoda?

The original purpose of stupas (the Sanskrit name) was to house the mortal remains of the historical Buddha—later of other key Buddhist saints—and served to commemorate key events in his life, being built at the place of his birth, death, first sermon, etc. Later, they housed sacred texts and images, or simply existed as symbols or reminders, sacred in their own right as supporting objects for meditation. Originally a hemisphere topped by an umbrellaed spire, the stupa assumed different shapes in different cultures, including the flask shapes of Tibetan monasteries such as Labrang and Kumbum, and at the White Dagoba Temple in Běijīng—'*dagoba*' is Sinhala for stupa, and the Tibetan word is *chorten*. By this stage of development, each part of the stupa, from the multiple levels of its now square plinth to the increased number of umbrellas or ridges on its spire, capped by a solar disc and crescent moon, was symbolic. All Buddhist processions proceed in the direction of the sun, and reverence is shown to a stupa or its contents by processing around it in a clockwise manner (the way you should also proceed around Buddhist temples).

In China, Japan and Korea, the stupa developed into the pagoda, a four- or eight-cornered tower of wood or brick, still often with a spire or ridged roof of similar symbolism, and doing the same job of housing relics or texts. Additionally, the pagoda claimed some kind of beneficial geomantic influence on its surroundings. They usually have an internal staircase, which makes you go clockwise as you climb, thus showing veneration as you ascend. The central pillar represents the Buddha and his position at the centre of the universe, and the passages or windows pointing towards the four points of the compass are associated with other individual Buddhas, and aid meditation. The multiple stories represent different worlds on the path to enlightenment, and the octagonal plan pagodas (such as the one at Fǎmén Sì outside Xī'ān) suggest the eight spokes of the wheel of *dharma*, the principle that what you do in one life affects what you are in the next.

Xī'ān Yǐngchéng (Xī'ān Film City)

Qín Gōngjiànjiè (Qín Palace) and Qínhànchéng (Qín–Hàn City)

西安影城

Open 9–6; adm ¥20 ($2.50).

The Film City is a short walk east of the Big Goose Pagoda, or can be reached directly from the station on bus 41.

Xī'ān's Film Studio achieved international status as the birthplace of work by a generation of post-Cultural Revolution cinamatographers and directors—in particular Zhāng Yìmóu, maker of *Red Sorghum*, *Jú Dòu*, *Raise the Red Lantern*, *Shànghǎi Triad* and others. Although it is a popular attraction for Chinese, few foreigners visit the Film City, and it should be understood that it is no high-tech Universal Studios-style theme park. As with all film and television sets, the first thought is how fake things look, and to wonder how they appear real on screen. The second, more worrying thought, is how similar the buildings look to supposedly historical and ancient sites that you have visited. Is China one big fake?

You receive two tickets, one for making a circuit beginning to your left as you enter (the Qín-Hàn City), and one for the Palace. The City is a jumble of lanes, castles, stockades, gates, banner-strewn hilltop forts, a waterwheel, ancient carts, and so on. The circuit crosses the route to the Palace via the upper floor of a gate which also has beautifully made models of various period buildings. You can be carried in a palanquin up to the Palace along an avenue of enormous guardian figures. The courtyard has a variety of military transport from horsecarts to rusting armoured cars, which look to be of genuine civil war vintage. Inside you can dress up, be made up, and have your photo taken on a partial set. One room on the left-hand side is littered with props, and on the right there is an exhibition of stills and posters, from films such as *Black Cannon Incident*, *Red Sorghum*, and *King of the Children*. Other entertainment includes a haunted house-cum-obstacle course full of skulls, snakes, waxwork corpses and wailing sound effects. From the rear of the clearly fake and incomplete Palace, you can look down on the main sound stages.

The walk from the north side of the Big Goose Pagoda to the Film City gives you a view of the widening gap between haves and have-nots. Compare the brand-new compound of guarded housing for the newly rich behind the Xī'ān Garden Hotel with the ragged peasants as you pass the terminus for their tractor/truck/motorbike cross-breeds.

Shǎnxī Lìshǐ Bówùguǎn (Shǎnxī History Museum)   陕西历史博物馆
Open 8.30–5.30; adm ¥38 ($5).

Those already disappointed by poor curatorial standards, poor display and discourteous staff at many Chinese museums will not be impressed by the claim that this is probably the best museum in China. Nevertheless, if you were to visit only one museum in the whole country, this should be it. It has a large, well-chosen collection, well-illuminated, with English introductions to every room and English labels on every item. It stands on Xiǎozhài Dōnglù in elegant modern buildings (designed by a 6th-generation descendant of the architect of Běijīng's Summer Palace, it is claimed), reached by bus 4 which runs down Jiěfàng Lù and Hépíng Lù. The museum needs several hours to savour, and is worth multiple visits to appreciate. There is a compulsory, free cloakroom for your bags at the entrance.

On the ground floor avoid the middle entrance ahead of you which is merely an overpriced shop, and take the left-hand one. There is a superb display of archaeological items in chronological order beginning 1.15 million years ago and proceeding to the Qīng: fossilized skulls, early tools, weaponry, cooking vessels, funerary objects. More unusual items include the equivalent of modern-day gold bath taps and two shoe soles made from jade. There is also a four-horse bronze chariot from the Qín mausoleum, four of the terracotta warriors themselves, and photographs of the sites from which items were retrieved, plentiful maps, and magnifying lenses to view smaller items.

Upstairs there are many funerary objects, including a green glazed model of a workshop from the Eastern Hàn, and a charming collection of ceramic camels including one from the Táng dynasty carrying a collection of musicians. Other impressive items include more than 300 miniature Míng figures which were only discovered in 1990. There's rare Táng glassware and evidence of the cosmopolitan nature of Táng Xī'ān in Arabic coins dating from AD 661 to 750. Supplementary material includes large wooden wall maps of Chinese territory under different dynasties such as the Hàn, diagrams of Silk Routes and other links, and of Zhāng Qiān's first and second trips.

Further side halls at ground level have extensive collections of porcelain and period costume.

Běilín Bówùguǎn ('Forest of Stelae')   碑林博物馆
Open 8.30–5.40; adm ¥30 ($4).

Also known as the 'Shǎnxī Provincial Museum', this is housed in a former Confucian temple not far from the Míngdé Mén (south gate), and best approached by walking east from Nán Dàjiē along the shop-lined Gǔ Wénhuà Jiē. Access to the city wall is opposite the entrance.

The temple was founded during the Sòng dynasty in 1090, and has an impressive gate, and fountains at the entrance. The central path through pleasant gardens is lined with small stone figures. The first hall on the left, 'The Exhibition of Ancient Buddhist Images' is, for once, an exhibition not a shop, and has an introduction in English. The items begin with the Northern and Southern dynasties (AD 420–589) and proceed through Suí and Táng (AD 581–907). Altogether more than 100 exhibits, including fine Buddhist statues and reliefs with photographs of their original locations, are intelligently and instructively arranged to show developments in style—the gradual Sinicization of originally alien figures, and absorption of Daoist and Confucian ideas.

Through the next gate a larger courtyard has the usual bell tower on the right, containing a 6-ton Táng bell from AD 711, while to the left a statue of a horse from AD 422 stands where the drum tower should be. It also contains six small pavilions, and the first stelae, some mounted on the back of stone turtles. A pavilion directly in front of the first main hall houses a square stele, dealing with filial piety, from AD 745. The Forest of Stelae was founded in 1087 (Northern Sòng), and the name forest is far from inept as you can walk amongst them, row upon row, mostly taller than you are. The idea may sound more interesting than the exhibition itself, but many of the stelae are pictorial, not solely covered in text, and have useful explanations in English. The earliest date from the Hàn dynasty.

Hall 1. Before the invention of printing, the introduction of copyists' errors into key texts was prevented by carving them in stone, from which rubbings could be made. The stelae in this hall preserve a number of the Chinese classics this way. Copies of Confucian texts were needed for those who wished to pass the Imperial Examinations—at times the only way to get on in Chinese society (other than corruption). 'The Analects', for instance, take both sides of each of 114 stones—more than 650,000 Chinese characters—which had to be memorized and sections regurgitated as answers to essay questions. All without a single mistaken character.

Hall 2. Most of the stelae are Táng, and to do with exchanges with foreign countries and outside influences. The best-known example is the tablet with the history of the first 150 years of Nestorian Christianity in China, dating the Nestorians' arrival to AD 635. Other stelae preserve examples of particularly fine calligraphy, designed to be both admired and reproduced—the fonts of their day. These stelae effectively offer a history of Chinese writing, and the Chinese use language to describe them which would put even the florid vocabulary of a wine connoisseur to shame. One style is described as 'vigorous and cautious'.

Rubbings are still being taken, and inevitably, there's a shop for them. 'Rubbing' is perhaps the wrong word. Moistened paper is hammered into the surface of the stone using wooden mallets, and colour patted on using a cloth-wrapped wooden disc. The sound of tapping and tamping echoes through the halls.

The stelae in **Hall 3** also demonstrate a wide variety of different writing styles, and some are intended as character primers, introducing and explaining, for instance, scripts with special uses such as seal script. Many stelae are capped with elaborate dragon sculptures.

Hall 4 has pictorial stelae with scenic views, maps of Táng Palaces, and a famous image of Confucius himself. One particularly popular stele for reproduction is a poem from 1716

which at first appears to be a picture of bamboo, but each cluster of leaves forms a character. To find this turn left upon entering and walk almost to the rear. In the right-hand-most corner of the hall, one tablet records the murder of 'Imperialist missionaries' in 1903. Another shows a map of land ownership after serious Yellow River flooding in 1842, and a further one has instructions on how to control the river, still one of China's main concerns.

To the usual 'no spitting' and 'no littering' signs are added 'no scribbling'.

To reach **Hall 5** double back to the left. Important edicts were often literally written in stone, and this hall has tablets concerning adminstration, and public works. **Hall 6** has poetry stelae and **Hall 7** has a calligraphy copy book, mostly on tablets. Another hall to south and west has a small but choice collection of Buddhist statuary.

Xiǎoyàntǎ (Little Goose Pagoda) and Jiànfú Sì
小雁塔，荐福寺

Open 9.30–8; adm ¥10 ($1.25), plus ¥10 ($1.25) to climb the pagoda.

The Jiànfú Sì, outside the city walls to the south, is entered from the rear (north) side, in Yǒuyì Xīlù, reached by bus 29 from the Bell Tower. Originally founded under a different name and on a different site in AD 684 and moved here at the end of the Táng dynasty, the temple was the storage place for Buddhist texts. Its collection of halls, pavilions and towers now surround the Lesser Wild Goose Pagoda, to give its name a more formal translation. The temple is not functional, many of the buildings now simply being shops, and while the two towers at the south end still actually contain their drum and bell, this is so you can be charged for striking them—supposedly bringing good luck (though not to your wallet).

The pagoda is a smaller and more slender version of its counterpart, but not in such a good state of repair. It's a gently tapering 15-tier tower of plain brick built between AD 707 and 709, deprived of its top by an earthquake in 1556. It's mounted by a narrow internal stair-case which is not to be attempted on a busy day. Enjoyment of the views from the tiny platform at the top is spoilt both by a pestering salesman with binoculars for hire and the usual pollution.

Qīngzhēn Dàsì (Great Mosque)
清真大寺

Open 8–6.30; adm ¥15 ($2).

The Great Mosque is in Huàjué Xiàng, a narrow left turn just north of the Drum Tower running parallel to Xī Dàjiē.

Originally founded during the Táng dynasty in AD 742, the mosque was extended and recon-structed in several subsequent dynasties and suffered surprisingly limited damage in the Cultural Revolution (1966–76). Reconstruction, which still continues, began in 1986. Some of the buildings remain in a slightly distressed state, and are actually more appealing to look at than other heavily restored temples.

Beyond a magnificent Míng entrance gate, there's a hall on the right full of ancient furniture and rubbings. The rooms on the left are used as residences, with much fine marquetry on view, particularly in the panels of the doors. A second stone gate has Arabic script both on itself and attendant stelae which record the mosque's history. The central courtyard has a triple-layer, blue-tiled, octagonal pagoda with green dragons, for use as a minaret, although no *muezzin* is allowed to call. The main buildings are clustered together at the rear. Side turnings lead to small shady courtyards with marquetry screens and walls covered in relief.

This is one of China's largest mosques, and an active one. A little decorum is appropriate, and access may be restricted on Fridays, the main Muslim day of prayer.

Bālùjūn Xī'ān Bànshìchù Jìniànguǎn (The Memorial Museum of the Eighth Route Army Xī'ān Office) 八路军西安办事处纪念馆

Open 9–5; adm ¥15 ($2).

The museum is in Běi Xīnjiē, in the northeast corner of the city.

One of the few memorials to events in China's modern history genuinely worth seeing. It has a whiff of the heroism of the Long March period rather than the propagandist posturing which followed. From 1936 to 1946, this collection of low grey and white buildings was first a secret communist base, then the liaison office for work with the Nationalists on the anti-Japanese front, following the Xī'ān Incident (*see* 'Huáqīng Chí', p.133). Time has been stopped at 10am on 10 Sept 1946, when the communists abandoned the office following the defeat of Japan and the resumption of hostilities with the Nationalists. It is as if the staff had only just left, right down to period furniture and equipment, and a secret radio transmitter in the basement. Many communist leaders visited, stayed or worked here, as did their foreign supporters and chroniclers, such as American journalist Edgar Snow and Canadian doctor Norman Bethune, and labels in English tell you who was who and who stayed where. There are many photographs from the period on display, including a pictorial history of China's involvement in the Second World War and of the civil war which returned after the expulsion of the Japanese.

Around Xī'ān

The plains around Xī'ān are acned with the burial mounds of Qín, Hàn, Suí, and Táng emperors, their family members and honoured courtiers, as well as innumerable temples. Some can be visited using ordinary public transport, but most hotels offer tours by car or taxi, with four possible routes, of which two are the most popular:

The **East Route** which includes Bànpō Neolithic Village, Qín Shǐ Huángdì's Tomb, the Museum of the Terracotta Warriors, and Huáqīng Hot Springs.

The **West Route** which includes the Xiányáng Museum, Qián Líng (Táng tombs), and Fǎmén Sì (temple).

The general speed of the tours is brisk but not excessively so.

East Route (Dōng Xiàn) 东线

Qín Bīngmǎyǒng Bówùguǎn (The Museum of Terracotta Warriors and Horses of Qín Shǐ Huángdì) 秦兵马俑博物馆

Open 8.30–5; adm ¥60 ($7.50), plus extra charges for various sections.

The warriors can be reached from the stand just east of the station by a choice of Japanese-built right-hand-drive buses: the 306 goes directly, and the 307 goes via Bànpō and Huáqīng, for ¥3.5. There are two types of entrance ticket. Foreigners are compelled to buy the theoretically all-inclusive ticket, but are still charged further entrance fees at Pit No.2 (¥20/$2.50), the film show (¥40/$5), and one of the museum buildings (¥15/$2). As you get off the bus you may be approached by men who tell you that you *must* leave your bag at a nearby hut or you will not be allowed in the museum—ignore these thieves.

Qín Shǐ Huángdì played toy soldiers on a megalomaniac scale. The first soldiers were discovered in March 1974 by peasants digging a well. Excavations began in 1976, and were kept largely secret until the first exhibition hall was opened in 1979. More and more finds were made until it became clear that several units of an entire army were deployed on the plain around the burial mound itself. At their most impressive in the largest hall, Pit 1, they stand eerily impassive, row upon row, with a solemnity that can reduce even Chinese tour groups to whispers. Despite the 'Eighth Wonder of the World' hype, and the widespread availability of photographs, few are disappointed by what has become an attraction to equal the Great Wall itself.

The King of the Qín state, having defeated six other states and unified them into the first version of China in 221 BC, named himself Qín Shǐ Huángdì, the first emperor. It is from this first imperial dynasty, the Qín, that we derive the word 'China'. Traditionally characterized as a book-burner and persecutor of scholars (although several subsequent dynasties and the communists themselves would qualify for the same label), who used cruel and severe punishments to enforce his draconian laws, Qín Shǐ Huángdì also conducted a European Union-style standardization of weights and measures, adopted a single currency, and enforced a single written standard for Chinese characters. Such actions established a Chinese identity, and although the Qín dynasty disintegrated in 207 BC, a mere three years after Shǐ Huángdì's death, central control was revived under the Hàn dynasty five years later.

The aircraft-hangar-like Pit 1 is still only partially excavated. Eleven corridors are thought to contain about 6000 figures and 40 chariots although many have yet to be fully brought to light. Some have been taken to various museums around China. The corridors were originally roofed with wood and covered over. The rotting of the timber caused the roofs to collapse, breaking and burying the figures. The warriors have an average height of about 1.8m, but the more senior the officer, the larger he is depicted. It was originally thought that each was modelled from a soldier alive at the time, but it seems that there is a limited number of varieties. However, there are still so many that the observer is unable to spot any two alike. Only slight traces remain of the figures' original bright paintwork, but the soldiers were discovered with the remains of their weapons, the bronze spearheads and swords still sharp, although wooden shafts and handles had long rotted away. The soldiers were made in separate pieces which were joined together with clay (a process known as *luting*) and fired intact except for their heads, which were added later.

As in the other pits photography is almost certain to lead to confiscation of your film.

Pits 2 and 3 were discovered in April 1976. Pit 2 has altogether 89 chariots, 356 horses and over 900 warriors, and enables you to see excavations in progress—slow and painstaking work with brushes, fingers and sieves. There are also several figures in glass cases for closer inspection. Pit 3 (which requires no extra ticket) was the Headquarters pit, with 68 warriors and one chariot.

Brilliant marketing ensures two peasants from the group who made the original find—both called Yáng but not related—are available on site. One is upstairs in the shop at Pit 2, the other in the shop at Pit 3. Both will autograph your souvenirs or be photographed with you. Now owlish and wrinkled, and with their identitity cards on display, their credibility is damaged by the fact that each claims to have been the very first to find the warriors.

A museum on the left as you enter contains samples of weapons and other items found in the pits, as well as the tools that were used in their construction. Most remarkable are chariots found in 1980 in a separate pit. Made of bronze and decorated with gold and silver, they are evidence of both superb artistry and advanced metallurgical skills of the time. Two further free museum rooms, on your left as you approach the gate on the way out, contain further figures (which can be photographed), and an excellent model, itself in clay, showing the process of manufacture of both warriors and horses. This itself is a minor masterpiece of life and activity, showing the artisans swarming over the horses and warriors which emerge in stages on a production line. Other models suggest the original brightly painted colour scheme of the figures.

A model at the entrance of Pit 1 shows the relationship between the buried army and the mound beneath which Qín Shǐ Huángdì is buried, and which it guards. Incredibly, given quite believable stories of immense riches buried with the emperor, this is said never to have been excavated, although signs of failed robberies have been discovered. The treasures inside are said to include a map of China in gold and silver, with rivers made of mercury. The reason why the tomb has remained inviolate may lie in stories of bows set up Indiana Jones-style to fire automatically at intruders, and other rumoured mysterious dangers. The mound is included in the East Route tour, and is passed by all buses to the terracottas. There is nothing to see and little to do except climb the mound and be pestered by souvenir sellers, for which you are charged an outrageous ¥15 ($2).

As China finally wakes up to the value of its archaeological heritage, other spectacular finds are coming to light. Another large set of pottery figures was recently discovered in Jiāngsū Province along with a substantial underground tomb complex belonging to a king of the Western Hàn dynasty of 206 BC–AD 24. Much of northwestern China is covered in a thick yellow dust blown in from the Gobi, which has formed a fertile soil technically called *loess*, and more commonly known as 'Yellow Earth'. In Gānsù and Shǎnxī it lies up to 30m deep, and has the remarkable quality of preserving the images of wooden items buried by it long after the wood has rotted. The presence of this soil is thus fortunate both for local farmers and for archaeologists, but not for the Chinese as a whole. This is the same soil that washes so easily away, makes the Yellow River yellow and, carried downstream, contributes to the abrupt changes of course and flooding that have killed millions over the centuries.

Bànpō Bówùguǎn (Bànpō Neolithic Village)

Open 8–6; adm ¥20 ($2.50).

半坡博物馆

Buses 11 and 42 from the railway station, bus 307 from the stand to the east of it (but *not* 306), and trolleybus 105 from north of the Bell Tower near the telephone office all go to Bànpō. The crossroads in the centre has signs pointing 120m right to the museum, a few minutes' walk away. The bus journey takes 25 mins and costs 8 *máo*.

The Bànpō site was discovered in 1953 and opened as a museum in 1958, surprising given that China was in the throes of the disastrous Great Leap Forward. Its rapid opening was no doubt aided by its interpretation as evidence of a proto-communist society and thus that Communism had quite naturally come into existence some 6000 years ago. The signs trumpeting this point of view have now disappeared, but one of the museum's leaflets still says of the people of Bànpō: 'They lived in a primitive communist society where there were no classes and thus no exploitation of man by man, worked collectively and divided amongst themselves what they had gained.' What was actually discovered was the remainder of a village of houses made from wattle-and-daub, partially sunk into the ground and surrounded by a moat and stockade. Dating from around 5000 BC onwards the village belonged to the Yǎngsháo culture, which was quite widespread across the Yellow River valley.

Begin with the exhibition hall on the left, which has an intro in English and items excavated from the site. The main hall at the rear covers part of the area excavated in detail, with the remains of 46 houses, 250 tombs and other buildings, covering 50,000 sq m in all, of which about 3000 sq m, all living quarters, are within the hall. Remains of buildings are mostly shown as raised ridges, and explanations in English suggest probable shapes of houses, one of which has been reconstructed. Occasional indications of the original ground level demonstrate the depth at which the houses were found, and other items on display include skeletal remains, and jars in which small children were buried. Despite its immense archaeological importance, the site is not of the greatest interest to the non-professional. Beware the huge mark-up at the gift shops of up to 15 times the correct price.

Walk back up to the main road and turn left to find buses to the Terracotta Warriors and Huáqīng hot springs. The 307 comes every half an hour and takes 30mins to reach Huáqīng. You can also haggle with passing minibuses.

Huáqīng Chí (Huáqīng Hot Springs)

Open 7–7; adm ¥30 ($4).

华清池

This ove-rated Chinese fun palace is a collection of halls, pavilions and walkways arranged around a number of pools and thermal springs. Its history is more interesting than the place itself.

There were buildings here possibly as early as the Western Zhōu (1050–771 BC), and a traditional story has Qín Shǐ Huángdì (reigned 221–210 BC) encountering a fairy, who in response to his approaches gave him a plague of boils, subsequently curing him with water from the spring. The Táng Emperor Xuánzōng (reigned AD 712–56) expanded the facilities considerably. His reign marked the high point of Táng culture and political power until, in the mid-740s, he became infatuated with a minor concubine, Yáng Guìfēi. The Jiǔlóng Tāng (Nine Dragon Pool) and the Guìfēi Chí were supposedly the sites at which they respectively bathed. Xuánzōng's dalliance and his appointment of Yáng family members to important posts led to factional fighting and a rebellion in which Cháng'ān was taken, forcing Xuánzōng to flee to Sìchuān. En route his soldiers mutinied and forced him to have both Yáng Guìfēi and her cousin, now chief minister, executed. The civil war raged on until 763 at the cost of millions of lives, to which the springs, despite elaborate claims of their health-giving properties, might be said to have contributed.

Nor was that their only involvement in affairs of state. In 1936 the Nationalist leader Chiang Kai-shek (Jiǎng Jièshí) was using Huáqīng as his headquarters in a campaign to destroy the communists in Shǎnxī before moving to deal with the Japanese invasion. He refused proposals from the communists that they should put their differences aside and form a united front against the invaders, despite support for that suggestion from some of his own generals, and student protests in Xī'ān itself. On 9 December in what came to be known as the **Xī'ān Incident**, one of his generals, the warlord Zhāng Xuéliáng, took matters into his own hands and at dawn units under his control stormed the Huáqīng compound where Chiang was staying, killing many bodyguards in a small fire fight. Chiang, convinced he was about to die, climbed over the rear wall, but was caught shivering on the hillside nearby. Zhāng's purpose, however, was to force consideration of a united front against the Japanese. But the communists waited for advice from Stalin, which was that only Chiang had the prestige to lead a combined assault on the Japanese. To prove his loyalty Zhāng went to Nánjīng with Chiang, was court-martialled and sentenced to ten years in prison, although this was quickly commuted to house arrest. The Nationalists again refused to make a commitment to a united front, but the pressure was taken off the communists' northern Shǎnxī stronghold, and more attention turned to the Japanese.

Bullet holes in the windows of the Wǔ Jiān Tīng (Five Room Hall) have been preserved as has the original furniture or that of the period. The five rooms include a guard house, Chiang's office, his bedroom, and his secretary's office, and there's a model of the cable-car-less hotsprings of the day with period photographs. You too can dress in period officer uniform (presumably imagining yourself as the officially heroic Zhāng), and be photographed outside the hall.

It's still possible to take a hot bath, although it's far from the exclusive experience it was in Táng days, and something foreigners rarely attempt. The baths are at 43°C, and 1–1½hrs in a private double room costs ¥120–150 ($15–19), a four-person room ¥400, and a sauna ¥60 ($7.50). A bath with the common herd is a mere ¥5. Various stalls sell the Huáqīng Chí brand Imperial Hot Spring Bath Liquid for ¥36 ($4.50).

West Route (Xī Xiàn)
西线

Longer and less popular, this nonetheless worthwhile tour has views of the lush and well-irrigated wheat and cotton fields around Xī'ān, booming peasant industries, and an unexpected neo-Gothic church standing in fields. Stops may include the Shèngpíngguǎn—halls of appallingly garish and stilted tableaux depicting scenes from the life of the Empress Wǔ—which should be avoided. Places on this route are harder to reach by public transport.

Xiányáng Bówùguǎn (Xiányáng Museum)
咸阳博物馆

Open 8–5.30; adm ¥12 ($1.50).

Xiányáng is 28km outside Xī'ān to the west, and the site of Xī'ān's airport. From Xī'ān take trolleybus 103 to its western terminus, and turn right into Hànchéng Běilù. Bus 59 to Xiányáng's railway station from across the road costs ¥2 (exact change needed). Trains to Xiányáng cost ¥3, and there are direct buses from the Xī'ān bus station opposite the railway station for ¥2.70. From the railway station in Xiányáng take the covered market street opposite and slightly on the right. At the other end cross Rénmín Dōnglù to Běi Dàjiē which is straight on, slightly to the left. At the T-junction turn right into Zhōngshān Jiē, and the museum is further up on the right, about 15 minutes' walk from the station altogether.

Xiányáng, on the opposite side of the Wèi river from Xī'ān, was once an imperial capital, but today is a small industrial town. The American archaeologist Langdon Warner, passing through in 1923, was unimpressed:

*For all its bold front on the bluff above the rushing river the town itself
was dejected enough. It did not need ten minutes in the streets to tell
the reason, for everywhere the little clay opium pipes were for sale and
in the shade of the temple enclosures lay bundles of rags which were
men with their heads on bricks, forgetting in merciful sleep that they
were doomed to be Chinese and in misery.*

Langdon Warner, *The Long Old Road in China,* 1926

One of the drugged slumberers turned out to be a policeman empowered to detect and arrest
all persons using or selling opium within the city limits. A temple he mentioned is at least now
being put to better use as a museum.

One of China's friendliest, it's housed in a Confucian temple of 1371, although most of the
buildings are more recent. There are signs of the temple's original function in an older courtyard to the rear. Altogether seven exhibition rooms hold around 5000 exhibits, if you count all
the figurines. The post-unification Qín capital and some of its pre-unification sites from around
350 BC were near Xiányáng and much of the collection is of Qín origin. It includes jade ware,
jewellery, architectural fragments and pottery figures, as well as an edict on copper said to
have been written by Qín Shǐ Huángdì himself. Items have good labels in English, and
supporting charts show Qín military movements, genealogy, and the unification of Chinese
weights, measures, coins and written characters.

However, the stars of the show are the figurines discovered in 1965 in a village called
Yángjiāwān, 20km to the east of Xiányáng. There are altogether 583 horsemen and 1965
standing figurine warriors, complete with pottery shields and miniature weapons, probably the
burial articles of a high-ranking general of the early (Western) Hàn dynasty. These are half-
metre-tall versions of their more famous counterparts, discovered ten years later. Both
mounted and foot soldiers come in light and heavy armour varieties. Their wooden weapons
have disappeared, but the front row have their pottery shields rewired to their bodies, others
lying stacked to the front and side of the display cabinets. Many figurines have patches of their
original red and blue colours, and signs of detailed painting of bridles and saddles. Photographs
show the unearthing of figurines, and informative explanations neither tell you what you can
see for yourself nor how you feel. A few figurines can also be seen in Běijīng's History
Museum, and the museum at the Màijī Shān caves outside Tiānshuǐ.

Táng Qián Líng (Táng Qián Tomb)

Adm ¥10 ($1.25).

唐乾陵

About 80km northwest of Xī'ān, this tomb is the centre piece of the group including the
Zhānghuái and Yǒngtài tombs (*see* below), and around 15 others.

This is the joint tomb of the Táng Emperor Gāozōng (AD 628–683) and the Empress Wǔ
Zétiān (624–705). Under Gāozōng China went through one of its periods of expansion, and
its borders were pushed further west to the Ferghana Valley. However, the costs of maintaining control, and an increasing military threat from both Tibetans and Turki tribes, led to a
crisis at the end of his reign. Gāozōng was physically weak, and the country was effectively
ruled for much of his reign by his second empress, Wǔ Zétiān. She began as a consort of
Gāozōng's father, became a nun, and then became a minor consort of Gāozōng himself. An

astute intriguer and political manipulator, she succeeded in replacing the legitimate empress, having her murdered. Following Gāozōng's death his heir, Zhōngzōng, proved too independent-minded, and Wǔ replaced him with his brother Ruìzōng, who was her puppet. In 690, she usurped the throne, establishing a new dynasty, the Zhōu, and became the only overt female ruler in Chinese history. Others such as Cíxǐ of the Qīng ruled quite effectively without title.

A broad imperial avenue or 'spirit way' runs between tower-topped hills, and imposing stone guardians: animals both mythical and real, two groups of headless figures, two large stone lions and twin stelae to the tomb mound, which remains unexcavated. The headless figures are political, representing the tribes on China's borders and representatives of foreign powers supposedly paying homage. Little changes in China; the headless state of the figures is said to be down to peasants who blamed the malevolent influence of the foreigners for local crop failures.

Of the two stelae, the left-hand one records Gāozōng's achievements, while the right-hand one, despite being covered in characters, is known as the 'blank stele'. Wǔ Zétiān decided that history should judge her, and the remarks now on view were added in the Sòng (AD 960–1279) and Jīn (1115–1234) dynasties. Wǔ Zétiān's bloody hands, somewhat arbitrary methods of government and, particularly in later life, the excesses of her personal favourites are decried now, but official communist histories tend to overlook these foibles due to Wǔ's promotion of meritocracy within the civil service. Wǔ recruited an elite through the state examinations which had begun during the Suí, and was astute in choosing good ministers whose influence lasted after her death. She decided that the Táng should resume power and had already nominated Zhōngzōng as her heir, when at an advanced age she was herself removed and her plans carried out sooner than she might have wished.

Zhānghuái Tàizǐ Mù (Tomb of Prince Zhānghuái)

Adm ¥10 ($1.25).

章怀太子墓

Prince Zhānghuái, Empress Wǔ's second son, spent a period in the hazardous post of heir-apparent, before she suspected him of plotting a coup, and banished him to Sìchuān. When she took the throne for herself, Wǔ sent an official to re-interrogate the prince, and he either exceeded his orders, or carried them out, in forcing him to commit suicide at the age of 32. Wǔ punished the official and rehabilitated her son. He was reburied in this tomb not far from his mother one year after her death.

A steep ramp with wall paintings leads down to the tomb chamber. The originals from higher up the passage are currently in the basement of the Shǎnxī History Museum and the lower glass-covered ones are in poor condition. The most famous and often reproduced show a polo game, possibly another Silk Route import and popular amongst the Táng aristocracy, and a group of maidens watching birds and catching cicadas. (Although cats and dogs are again popular as pets, you may still see and hear cicada-sellers with bicycle-loads of tiny cages.) An initial domed chamber has further paintings of attendants, courtiers and diplomats, and a short passage through a low carved black stone door leads to the burial chamber with a vast black stone tomb. Although the tomb was robbed, several hundred burial objects were recovered.

Yǒngtài Gōngzhǔ Mù (Tomb of Princess Yǒngtài)

永泰公主墓

Adm ¥10 ($1.25).

Yǒngtài was a granddaughter of Gāozōng and Wǔ, who fell out of favour with her grand-mother. She was put to death, along with her husband, in about AD 701, aged 17. A daughter of Zhōngzōng, she was granted her title after he took the throne, and reburied along with her husband in the Qián Líng area.

The tomb has a long ramp down past paintings of guardian beasts and warriors, multiple light wells, and shrine niches with pottery figures. It has been robbed many times, but archaeologists still recovered more than 1000 relics. The skeleton of a tomb robber and an iron axe suggest that he was either murdered or deliberately left behind by his companions.

An exhibition hall with an introduction in English has a model of the sarcophagus, murals taken from various Táng tombs, many figurines including a curious set of male and female ones, others in gold and jade, various tri-colour glaze items, and models of the Qián Líng and satellite tombs.

Fǎmén Sì

法门寺

Adm ¥12 ($1.50), and a further ¥10 ($1.25)
for the pagoda crypt.

About 120km from Xī'ān, this temple was constructed towards the end of the Eastern Hàn in around AD 147, added to by various dynasties, and under the Táng Emperor Gāozhōng, was expanded to include a large wooden stupa and 24 surrounding courtyards. The stupa was rebuilt on an ever larger scale several times but collapsed in 1569. It was rebuilt as a magnificent 47m-high, 13-layer brick octagon between 1579 and 1609, but earthquake damage in 1654 was left unrepaired until 1939, and it suffered partial collapse again in 1981. During consequent renovations an extensive crypt beneath the pagoda was rediscovered.

The temple was originally named the Ashoka Temple, after the Ghandaran King Ashoka (272–236 BC), who, following his conversion to Buddhism in 262 BC, arranged a distribution of relics of the Sakyamuni Buddha to various sites, including (supposedly) 19 in China. The morsels received by Fǎmén Sì were four slivers of finger bone. Having frequently been disinterred for viewing by various emperors, they lay forgotten for around 1100 years beneath the pagoda built to house them. The crypt houses a miniature stupa with a glass window where you kneel to view the main reliquary. Other sumptuous relics such as the bejewelled ten-layer casket in which one of the finger bones was found are on display too. Visitors can bow to a Buddha statue, having first paid money to a monk, after which a small gong is struck. The Chinese giggle self-consciously and dare each other to try this. Away from the tour groups, monks sit outside a standard residence block with an ornate roof, telling their rosaries, oblivious to anything else.

Xīngjiào Sì

兴教寺

Open 7–5; adm ¥10 ($1.25).

The temple is 50km southeast of Xī'ān, reached by bus 215 from South Gate (Míngdé Mén), which takes 30mins to reach its terminus, ¥2. Change to a minibus opposite, going in the direction of Yǐnzhèn (shortly after leaving you pass the monument to General Yáng, who was a conspirator with Zhāng Xuéliáng in the Xī'ān Incident—*see* 'Huáqīng Chí', p.133), and get off after about 20mins at a sign indicating Xīngjiào Sì 700m to the left, ¥1.8.

The temple is an important destination for Buddhists, housing at it does the remains of the expeditionary scholar-monk Xuánzàng. He continued travelling even after his death, going through several reburials, until his remains were finally brought to Xīngjiào Sì in AD 669. To the right as you enter and slightly uphill is a new stele marking Sino-Japanese friendship together with cherry trees presented by the Japanese. They have also paid for a new building at the rear of the centre of the complex, built in 1993 to contain a 10m sleeping Buddha. Of most interest is the five-storey pagoda housing Xuánzàng's remains and two smaller flanking pagodas housing those of two assistants, all pleasingly constructed of plain brick and restored in the Nationalist period. Climbing the hillside behind the temple gives pleasant views across a valley and down on the temple itself.

Other Sights

The expansionist Hàn Emperor Wǔdì, who initiated Chinese explorations to the west, is buried at the **Mào Líng**, about 40km northwest of Xī'ān, which like the Táng tombs has numerous satellites. A small museum has a collection of statuary from the area, and funerary objects that escaped grave-robbers. Further out in the same direction is a temple built where the Táng concubine **Yáng Guìfēi** met her end (*see* 'Huáqīng Chí', above).

Shopping

Musical instruments and Chinese opera **props and costumes** are available from several shops on the north side of Xī Dàjiē. The **signwriting alley**, Zhúbā Shì, which runs south of Xī Dàjiē not far from the Bell Tower, is busy with the stencilling of banners and the hammering of enormous brass characters nearly a metre high. These might give you excess baggage problems, but are a snip at around ¥300 ($36) depending on the number of strokes. Big copper etched and painted signs in two colours are around ¥250 ($30). There are also all kinds of badges and business cards, hotel signs, etc. for sale. In Xī Dàjiē there's a shop selling police paraphernalia including badges and insignia, illuminated hand-held stop signs, etc. This may account for the stories of widespread police impersonation.

Hùxiàn farmer paintings are a popular Xī'ān acquisition. Hùxiàn is a farming area southwest of Xī'ān that by now has probably produced more hectares of paintings than it usually has covered in crops. These are in complete contrast to traditional Chinese paintings in their brilliant colours and their bucolic subjects—village festivals, peasants at work in the fields, and strings of ducks. You can find these paintings on sale at almost every tourist site. In fact you can find *the same* paintings on sale. The official story is that the peasants made paintings to celebrate the construction of a reservoir and were so successful that centres were set up providing materials and training; there are now thousands of peasant painters. But more cynical Chinese (including those who sell the paintings) explain that paintings that prove popular are reproduced again and again in almost identical copies (as are almost all the paintings you will see in China—although some truly set themselves up only to be copies of famous works). Nonetheless, they make bright and attractive souvenirs, as long as it is understood that what you are buying is not unique, may not even have been painted by the artist of the original version, and perhaps not even by a farmer. Another nearby county produces painted pottery animals, also widely on display.

Covered markets such as **City God's Temple Market** (Chénghuángmiào Xiǎoshāngpǐn Shìcháng), running north from Xī Dàjiē just east of the Xījīng Bīnguǎn, have domestic utensils such as wooden coat hangers, knitting needles, cutlery and all kinds of stationery, as well as some of the world's most gaudy *májiàng* (mahjong) sets for around ¥65 ($8), and bags marked 'Hallods'. The temple itself is in a state of disrepair.

The Měishù Yīnyuè Shūdiàn on Xī Dàjiē just west of Nán Xīnjiē has all kinds of **artists' materials** at proper Chinese prices, and **art books** at the original publishers' prices. The History Museum catalogue can be bought here for ¥80 ($10) rather than the ¥200 ($24) asked at the museum. Also available here are posters of Chinese leaders and other communists, popular as souvenirs rather than how the originators would have wished.

The first alley to the west north of the Drum Tower (but not alongside it), **Huàjué Xiàng**, leading in a dog-leg to the Great Mosque, has assorted bric-a-brac of both real and doubtful antiquity and traditional Chinese gifts. These include Máo watches, old *májiàng* sets made from bone and bamboo, Nationalist paper money, Máo caps, Little Red Books (a compilation of Máo's thoughts particularly popular during the Cultural Revolution), steel exercise balls, 'jade', lacquered pens, boxed calligraphy sets, miniature abacuses, and 'chops', stamps carved with the characters of your name for use with sticky red ink as a seal. This is tourist-as-victim territory where the stallholders say 'Hello lookee?' in best Hollywood-Chinese style. The first asking price for any object will be at least five times the proper price, and often ten times, but the shady awning-hung alley makes a pleasant stroll on your way to the Great Mosque.

The Bēilín area has a small, semi-pedestrianized street to the east of Nán Dàjiē just inside the wall known as **Gǔwénhuà Jiē** (old culture street). Shops and stalls sell 'jade', paintings, paint brushes, rubbings, musical instruments and ceramics, and you can see calligraphers at work in the attractive restored or rebuilt traditional buildings.

Where to Stay

At any one time perhaps half of the hotels in Xī'ān seem to be undergoing upgrading or remodelling. Discounts are available during the off-season but due to Xī'ān's popularity not during March to September.

expensive

The **Hyatt** (Kǎiyuè Fàndiàn) is the best and only really de luxe hotel in the centre of Xī'ān at 158 Dōng Dàjiē, corner Hépíng Lù, straight down Jiěfàng Lù from the railway station, © 723 1234, @ 721 6799, US toll-free © 1-800 233 1234, UK © (0345) 581666, website www.travel.web.com. An interior atrium with greenery and waterfall shuts out Xī'ān's smog, and there are full facilities including business and fitness centres. Double rooms are $120–160, suites $220–1200, all plus 15% service and tax. There are Cantonese and Western restaurants, one specializing in Italian thin crust pizza, at Western prices. All major credit cards are accepted.

Xī'ān Garden Hotel (Tánghuá Bīnguǎn), 4 Dōngyànyǐn Lù, ✆ 526 1111, 📠 526 1998, is just east of the Big Goose Pagoda. A modern Japanese joint-venture hotel with correspondingly high standards of service, it is built in traditional style around a number of well-cared-for courtyard gardens, including a central one with pond and ducks. Its quietness makes up for its distance from the centre. Standard double $140, de luxe $220, $300 suite, all with plentiful Japanese-, Chinese- and English-speaking staff. 'Táng Dynasty' song and dance show with dinner $33. 15% service charge.

Solid, unimaginative, perfectly comfortable, the **Bell Tower Hotel** (Zhōnglóu Fàndiàn), ✆ 727 9200, 📠 721 8767, is under Holiday Inn management and has the best location in Xī'ān, adjacent to the Bell Tower, putting many sights and Xī'ān's throbbing shopping within easy walking distance. The hotel has reasonable Western and Chinese restaurants with Western prices, a good all-you-can-eat breakfast buffet, health club and disco. Doubles from $80 ($75 single occupancy) up to $230 for the penthouse, all plus 15%. There is also a branch of CYTS with on-line air ticket booking.

The **Hotel Royal Xī'ān** (Huángchéng Bīnguǎn) stands at 334 Dōng Dàjiē not far from the bell tower, ✆ 723 5311, 📠 723 5887, in the US and Canada ✆ (1-800) 645 5687, in the UK ✆ 0800 282502. This is a Nikko hotel—a perfectly comfortable standard international hotel with efficient Japanese management. Doubles are $90–100, suites $180–500, all plus 15% service charge. The banqueting hall offers a Táng-style dinner and show for $24, or show only for $9. All major credit cards are accepted.

moderate

The **Lónghǎi Dàjiǔdiàn**, 278 Jiěfàng Lù, ✆ 741 6090, 📠 742 0093, not far south of the railway station on the west side, is a shiny new hotel whose public areas are already showing signs of wear but which has pleasant bright rooms and staff who are trying hard to please. A standard double is ¥590 ($71), superior ¥680 ($82), and suites ¥980 to ¥2200 ($118–265), plus 15% city tax.

Once the main hotel in Xī'ān, the **Rénmín Dàshà**, on Dōng Xīnjiē, ✆ 721 5111, 📠 721 8152, has declined. Its palatial central blocks, built with Soviet technical assistance in the '60s, is flanked by two white-tiled monstrosities which have remained incomplete due to lack of funds for more than five years. Failing to compete, it has raised prices without improving, reducing its competitiveness yet further—typical old-style Chinese management. Doubles are $350 ($42), or ¥470 ($57) in the slightly more modern no.2 building. Suites are ¥650 ($78). There are four restaurants, an unreliable post office and a theatre offering opera highlights for ¥65 ($8).

The **Huáshāng Jiǔdiàn** (China Merchants Hotel) at 131 Hépíng Lù, ✆ 721 8988, 📠 721 8588, just south of the Hyatt, is a Hong Kong joint-venture schizoidly putting itself in the wrong place on the maps in some of its own literature. The service is poorer than at most joint-venture hotels, but the rooms are comfortable enough, and reasonably priced for Xī'ān at ¥390 ($47) for a double, and ¥980 ($118) for suites.

The **Mínshēng Dàjiǔdiàn**, 70 Nán Dàjiē, on the west side, ✆ 726 3133, 📠 726 3133, is a hotel, restaurant, and glitzy department store combined. Bizarrely, it offers plastic surgery, carried out by doctors from the Fourth Military Medical University, popular amongst Chinese wishing to remove the attractive epicanthic folds from their eyes and make them rounder—an important beauty point. The accommodation is of a higher standard than the China Merchants Hotel for much the same price: singles $320 ($39), doubles $390 ($47), and suites ¥1858 ($224).

Défācháng Jiǔdiàn in Píng'ān Shìcháng is on the north side of Dōng Dàjiē, one block east of the Bell Tower, ✆ 727 9247, @ 721 8683. Although in need of refurbishment, the hotel is well-positioned and good value for money. The restaurant has an excellent *jiǎozi* banquet (*see* 'Eating Out', below). Prices vary by season: single room ¥205–248 ($25–30), double ¥225–270 ($27–33), suite ¥405–485 ($49–58).

Xījīng Fàndiàn is on the north side of Xī Dàjiē, halfway to the West Gate, ✆ 721 0255, @ ext 8999. Similar to the Défācháng, all rooms have TV, aircon, phone and bath. Doubles are ¥177 ($22), ¥213 ($26) and ¥297 ($36), triples ¥213, suites from ¥438 ($53).

inexpensive

Wǔyī Bīnguǎn (May First Hotel) is on 351 Dōng Dàjiē, ✆ 721 5932, @ 721 3824. De luxe doubles cost ¥190, singles ¥132, and ¥150 for standard doubles—above average quality for this price range. It has a popular budget restaurant which was rebuilt in 1996.

For those staying briefly in Xī'ān, a good choice is the **Jiěfàng Fàndiàn**, 321 Jiěfàng Lù, across the square in front of the railway station on the left, ✆ 742 3829, @ 742 2619. Its proximity to the trains and to buses to the Terracotta Warriors, and the fact that it runs the best value tours, allow you to see more in less time. Doubles are ¥220 ($27) and ¥260 ($32), triples ¥280 ($34), quads $320 ($39), and suites $350 ($42). The cheapest beds are ¥80 ($10) in quads, and you can buy one bed in a double for ¥100 ($12) off season with a bit of haggling.

The **Shàngdé Bīnguǎn** is a little-known budget hotel on the west of Shàngdé Lù, a short walk from the railway station, ✆ 742 6164, @ 721 6287. It's more basic than the Jiěfàng (but better than the Flats of Rénmín), and as no one speaks English, it's much less busy, and a little cheaper: ¥180 ($22) for a double, ¥80 ($10) per bed in triples, all with bath.

University accommodation is sometimes a cheap option especially in larger Chinese cities. The **Northwest University Guesthouse** (Xībèi Dàxué Bīnguǎn), ✆ 721 1554, situated on a quiet and green campus just outside the city walls, is more upmarket than the Victory or the Flats of Rénmín, and recaptures the quietness of the Xī'ān of 10 years ago. In term time, doubles with bath are ¥160 ($20), triples with bath ¥165 ($20) or ¥55 ($7) per bed. Enter via the campus' west gate, reached by bus 205 from the railway station or 10 from the Yùxiángmén bus station (stop name Xībèi Dàxué). Turn first right, left at the T-junction, and next right, and the building is through the gate with a brass plate.

cheap

The **Rénmín Dàshà Gōngyù** (the People's Hotel Flats, usually known as the **Flats of Rénmín**), ✆ 625 2352, is the current backpackers' favourite, situated a little way outside the city wall to the northwest and reached by bus 9 from the railway station (stop name Xīnghuǒ Lù). There is competition between the plumbing and the staff to see which can be the more unreliable. In theory there is hot water between 9am and midnight. Dust from the nearby coal yard tends to get trekked into the building and the carpets, and the rooms are dank in the spring. There are two reasons to stay—Dad's Home Cooking and Mum's Home Cooking restaurants are nearby. Buses and minibuses run to the Drum Tower (501), and to the Big Goose Pagoda. Ageing doubles are ¥110 ($13.50), and slightly superior ones are ¥180 ($22). With a little persuasion off-season beds can be purchased individually for half the room price. Dorm beds are ¥40 ($5). All prices include a small and largely inedible Western or Chinese breakfast.

The **Victory Hotel** (Shènglì Fàndiàn), ✆ 789 3040, ✉ 789 3054, is on the corner of Yàntǎ Lù and Huánchéng Nánlù, just outside the city walls on the southeast side. This was once the backpacker favourite, and is still popular with younger Japanese. The staff is indifferent to whether you stay or not, as the condition of the rooms and other facilities shows—particularly the common showers. Beds in a double with bath are ¥70 ($8.50), in a common bath double ¥38 ($5) and ¥32, common bath triple ¥35 ($4.50) and ¥30 ($4), quad also ¥30. There's hot water 6pm–10pm.

Shǎnxī Institute of Mechanical Engineering Zhāodàisuǒ (Shǎnxī Jīxiè Xuéyuàn Zhāodàisuǒ), ✆ 721 1554, is the orangey building on the right 50m up the alley off Jīnhuā Nánlù opposite the east entrance to the university campus. Get there by bus no.8 from the Bell Tower, getting off at the stop called Jīnhuā Lù and walking north. This is very basic accommodation, but at only ¥14.30 ($2) for a bed in a wooden-bedded common bath triple, far and away the cheapest.

Eating Out

Xī'ān has vast numbers of conventional restaurants and standard noodle shops with menus to be found anywhere in China. Many of the more expensive hotels and glossy upmarket restaurants look to Xī'ān's former status as China's capital, attempting to revive or recreate extravagant Táng dynasty dishes, not always successfully. It also offers a wide range of local flavours; some, produced by its Huí minority population, will be found in almost every city westwards from here to Kashgar. Others are Hàn and Shǎnxī specific.

expensive

Several restaurants offer substantial banquets of bite-sized delicacies. The *jiǎozi* banquet at the **Défāchǎng Jiǔdiàn**'s restaurant (*open 11–2 and 5–8*) is something special, offering up to 22 different types of these steamed dumplings, delicately moulded into baskets of flowers, ducks, windmills, and so on with names like 'Phoenix Pearl'. The arrival of each bamboo steamer is accompanied by a little speech in Chinese about the design and content of each type of dumpling. Eat briskly to make sure that those in the later steamers are still hot. Banquets also include cold cuts and other snacks, and more conventional boiled *jiǎozi*. It is rounded off with a miniature hot pot attributed to the arrival of the Dowager Empress Cíxǐ in her flight from foreign armies breaking the Boxer siege of Běijīng's legation quarter. She wanted fast food, so the dumplings in the soup are particularly small. Banquet prices vary between ¥60 ($7.50) and ¥90 ($11), depending on how many varieties of *jiǎozi* you have. Beware of the early closing.

The **Báiwōniú Cāntīng** (Edible Snail Restaurant with English sign) is at 209 Xī Dàjiē. Its slightly grimy entrance and window display of slowly expiring fish are not exactly beguiling, but the Chinese speak well of it and its upstairs dining room is clean and comfortable. Snail dishes begin at ¥30 ($4); French roast snails and garlic snails are both ¥40 ($5). Keeping the supposedly French theme, they also serve bullfrog.

Lǎosūnjiā Fànzhuāng is on the south side of Dōng Dàjiē, just east of the Bank of China. Eating here is a bit of a performance, but well worth it. As you enter the ground floor pay ¥12.50 ($1.50) at a counter on your right, and collect a napkin, chopsticks, two tickets, a large bowl and two small round loaves. Find a table, and give the smaller ticket to the waitress who will return with a dish of garlic cloves steeped for one or two months in a mixture of sugar and vinegar, another of chili and fresh coriander, and a pot of tea. Meanwhile, wash your hands at the sink in the next room, then tear and crumble the bread into the smallest particles you can manage, filling your bowl. Using the clothes peg provided, clip the remaining ticket to the outside of the bowl and hand it to the waitress. She will return with the bowl topped up with a piping hot mutton stew, mixed with silk noodles, which the bread will have soaked up to a thick texture. Stir in coriander and chili to taste, and then struggle to finish this tasty and filling meal. This is called *Yángròu Pàomó* (there's a beef version, too). Upstairs are further rooms with higher prices and a larger menu. Incidental music is provided by the twittering of budgerigars from a cage in the foyer.

The three restaurants of the Jiǎ family are amongst the most famous in Xī'ān. Originally the three brothers worked together, but later opened their own restaurants. **Jiǎsān Fànguǎn** ('Jiǎ No.3 Restaurant'), in Xīyàng Jiē behind the Great Mosque, now has the best reputation. These restaurants serve a Huí-speciality floppy steamed dumpling called *Guàntāng Bāozi*, containing beef, lamb or 'three flavours'—a prawn, mushroom, lamb mix for ¥5 per steamer (*lóng*). The only other menu item is an unsweetened soup made from black rice for ¥0.50. The walls are hung with photographs of the proprietors with Chinese celebrities. The restaurant is on the north side of the street with several signs each including a Chinese three; next door, belonging to an elder brother (Jiǎ'èr), has lots of Chinese twos.

The Muslim quarter is packed with street stalls and small restaurants, often in buildings of considerable antiquity that have so far survived Xī'ān's modernization, serving thick, rope-like *lāmián* boiled, or chopped and fried, with spicy beef or lamb and peppers. Noodle variants include the Chinese version of *paste verde*. Look in Dàmàishì Jiē running north from Xī Dàjiē and other streets running off it. Large filling bowls are ¥4–6.

Standard Chinese *bāozi, jiǎozi, guōtiē* and noodles can be found in small restaurants everywhere, including several friendly ones in Xīyī Lù (the first right turn north of the Bell Tower). *Yī lóng bāozi* (one steamer of 10 dumplings) is ¥3.50, or you can buy half. On the corner of Xī Dàjiē and Jiěfàng Lù a stall sells kebabs (*shashlyk, kǎoròuchuàn*) for 5 *máo* a stick.

If you've come east from Central Asia and crave a change, there are **KFCs** on the west side of Jiěfàng Lù just north of the junction with Xī Dàjiē, and on the west side of Nán Dàjiē just north of the Míngdé Mén (South Gate). **Bob and Betty's**, opposite the Hotel Royal on Xī Dàjiē, has pizza for ¥9; *jiǎozi*, *bāozi*, and *diǎnxīn* (dim sum) from ¥4; excellent heavy rye bread to take away for ¥8, butter and pastries from ¥2, including croissants. Chinese children drag their parents in here as they would into McDonald's in the West (or Běijīng), and the seating is similarly plastic and fixed. Peasants stare in at the urbanized Chinese, everyone stares at the foreigner eating his Danish pastry, and The Carpenters warble in the background. Most Chinese are eating Chinese food. There are also burgers and bad coffee, and a hot pot section upstairs.

Xī Dàjiē also has two branches of **Singapore Fast Food**—the one of the north side is open 24hrs. These have menus in English, clearly marked prices, and small set meals for ¥10–15. There's another Singapore-style place next to the Lónghǎi Dàjiǔdiàn.

Those staying at the infamous Flats of Rénmín will find themselves orbiting around two restaurants, **Dad's Home Cooking**, and **Mum's Home Cooking**—if still there. Both offer basic Hàn cuisine and often amusing attempts at Western foods (hamburgers, french fries, scrambled eggs) that offer a welcome change from rice and noodles for the longer-term traveller. The staff are friendly, English-speaking and helpful, pointing visitors in the right direction for various sites, negotiating decent taxi fares, etc. Competition between the two is so fierce that staff meet trains and escort visitors to the Flats, pointing out their own premises on the way. These are probably the only restaurants in China where competition for foreign money has made the English-language menus carry *lower* prices than the Chinese-language ones. Assistance with buying rail tickets and free maps are all part of the service. In late 1996 the building housing both restaurants (they were next door to each other) was due to be redeveloped, and fierce negotiations were taking place for the right to take over a restaurant space inside the Flats. Don't let that stop you eating at both—whoever meets you at the station—and deciding for yourself which is the more friendly and more tolerant of your visits to the other one, and which has the better cooking.

Entertainment and Nightlife

The **Xī'ān Yìsú** theatre in the Huáyùnyuàn night club, with a neon sign at 270 Xīyī Lù, has occasional performances of Chinese opera with the audience in heavy carved chairs, chattering through the performance and spitting seed husks on the floor. The balcony is often deserted and gives a better view of the stage. Better than made-for-tourists highlight shows, this is the real thing, with elaborate costumes and make-up and nasal singing style. A complete opera is presented over a three-hour period. The only announcement of performances is on a sign hung near photographs of the performers well to the right of the entrance. Scrutinizing this usually produces someone who will try to help you. Tickets are ¥10 ($1.25). You may be the only foreigner in the audience and treated as part of the show by the rest.

The People's Theatre in Běi Dàjiē occasionally has opera but more often films.

For a little outdoor activity, go and roller-skate with the Chinese on appalling skates around the fountains at the junction of Nán Xīnjiē and Xī Xīnjiē for ¥2 per hour.

天水 Both rail and road routes to the west, having first crossed the Wèi Hé (river), follow its north bank, entering Gānsù Shěng (province) shortly before reaching Tiānshuǐ. The province is China's geographical centre, its capital Lánzhōu being almost equidistant from Xīnjiāng's western edge and the eastern seaboard. The emotional or cultural centre is considerably further east. Even though you are so close to China's ancient capital, you are already in a province much of whose territory spent extended periods out of Hàn control and which still has large areas where Muslim Huí people and other ethnic groups are in the majority. The build-up of industry and the Hàn population has come mostly since 1949. Tiānshuǐ, Gānsù's second-biggest city, is still considerably smaller than the major cities of more heavily populated provinces. Squeezed between mountains and the Wèi, it is inconveniently divided into two chunks, some 15km apart. The railway station is in the small section called Běidàoqū, and as this is the part of the town nearest to the magnificent Màijī Shān caves (the reason for visiting this otherwise nondescript city) it's best to find a hotel there. It is possible to arrive from Xī'ān by an overnight train, see the caves and continue onwards the same day.

Getting to and from Tiānshuǐ

by train

Despite Tiānshuǐ's size, it has limited allocations of tickets. Although all east- and westbound trains stop here, few actually start their journeys from Tiānshuǐ. To Gāngǔ the station staff prefer you to take a train at 07.30 or 13.15, ¥5. Be prepared to stand.

There are 14 westbound trains a day, all going at least as far as Lánzhōu. The best choice to there is the 509 since it starts at Tiānshuǐ, leaving at 07.15 and arriving at 20.43. There are also the 127 at 07.51, the 147 at 22.38, the 187 at 13.20, and the 203 at 04.58. To Xīníng via Lánzhōu directly, the best choice is the 275 at 00.14, arriving 14.17, which has an allocation of eight soft sleepers, three hard sleepers, and 50 hard seats. The 75 at 09.36, the 73 at 01.23, and the 177 at 06.41 all have hard seat allocations only, with most on the 73. To destinations beyond Lánzhōu, the 69 is an a/c train with no unreserved seating, and an allocation of only 15 hard seats, departing at 20.13 and going all the way to Ürümqi over two nights. The 143 goes to Ürümqi and Korla on alternate days at 05.38, with an allocation of four soft sleepers, six hard sleepers, and 150 hard seats. The 97 to Ürümqi at 12.08 has three hard sleepers, and the 53 at 17.20 and 113 at 16.31 have a few hard seats only. On all but the 69 you can risk buying an unreserved hard seat and upgrading.

The best allocations to Xī'ān are on the 204 with 12 soft sleepers, six hard sleepers and 200 hard sleepers, leaving at 22.56 and arriving at 06.10; the 74 with four soft sleepers, three hard sleepers and 60 hard seats, leaving Tiānshuǐ at 01.56 and arriving at 08.44; and the 276 at 00.08, with two soft sleepers, three hard sleepers and 50 hard seats. Some of the 14 eastbound trains bypass Xī'ān, turning south to Chéngdū. To Běijīng West the best choice is the 76 at 03.42, arriving 05.07 the next day, with two soft sleepers, six hard sleepers and 40 hard seats, or the 70 with 16 hard seats, leaving at 15.03 and arriving at 14.47 the next day. The 70 is the a/c train with no unreserved seating.

Buy sleeper tickets at window no.5; otherwise choose window no.1 and 2 for eastbound, and 3 and 4 for westbound trains.

by bus

There are occasional buses to Gāngǔ (one at 3pm) for the invented-on-the-spot price of ¥6. Walk away from the railway station up the road opposite past the Xīhuáng Dàshà and turn left at the first crossroads. The bus station is on the right. There are occasional buses from the railway station itself (larger ones on the right-hand side as you face it) but you'll have to bargain down from the foreigner price of ¥8. From the long-distance bus station in Qínchéng you pay ¥4.70. *See* 'Getting Around', below.

The Qínchéng bus station has buses to Lánzhōu at 6am (366km, ¥26.40/$3.50), Píngliáng at 7am (273km, ¥19.80/$2.50), to Gùyuán at 7am (273km, ¥20.20/$2.50), to Gāngǔ at 6am and 3.30pm, and to Wǔshān at 12 noon. The ticket office is upstairs.

Getting Around

A regular comfortable bus (no.6) (it shows videos) runs between the railway station in Běidàoqū, the bus station in Qínchéng, and Qínchéng centre for ¥2. There's a choice of hotels in walking distance of the railway station in Běidàoqū, which is anyway nearer Màijī Shān.

Tiānshuǐ © (0938)   Tourist Information

The six-figure Tiānshuǐ telephone numbers will probably add another digit before long.

There is a post office within sight of the no.6 bus stop in the centre of Qínchéng, and a Bank of China a short walk away. Save your administrative chores for Xī'ān, or larger towns to the west.

Around Tiānshuǐ

Màijī Shān Shíkū

Open 9–4; adm ¥31 ($4).

麦积山石窟

Màijī translates as 'haystack', after the odd shape of the mountain which stands apart from its conventionally shaped neighbours. Some Chinese say it's shaped like a *mántou*, a small steamed bun. 1742m high, its sheer, outward-leaning red cliffs are pine-topped, and riddled with hundreds of caves and niches, together with cliffside pavilions and several substantial Buddha statues. The Buddhas are not carved from the soft, red rock, but added to it. Some were hauled up by ropes in the 6th century, and their creamy colour makes them stand out.

Work on the caves was probably begun just before the Northern Wèi (AD 386–535), continued during the Western Wèi (535–57) and Northern Zhōu (557–81), with additions by almost every other dynasty up to the Táng (618–906), and late contributions by the Qīng

(1644–1911). The complex is China's fourth largest after those near Dūnhuáng, Luòyáng and Dàtóng, but none of these offer statuary and paintings of such a wide variety of styles (some unique to Màijī Shān) combined with scenery of such beauty. There are 194 caves extant, with thousands of clay and stone sculptures, and over 1000 sq m of mural painting. Being slightly off the main trade route, and the location of the the caves high up in the sheer sides of the American-muffin-shaped mountain, contributed to their preservation. Many were only ever accessible by wooden galleries cantilevered out from the cliff, and ledges and passages cut in the rock itself. These have been replaced with a tracery of metal stairways and galleries which make the mountain look like a large parcel wrapped up with string. Destruction by humans may for once have been slight, but fire and earth-

quake damage was substantial, and the damp climate, so unlike the arid air of the sites along the edge of deserts in Xīnjiāng, caused the paintings to deteriorate and fall off the walls. The sculptures that escaped the collapse of sections of cliff have traces of their original colouring still visible.

Minibuses run to Màijī Shān beginning very early in the morning from outside the railway station, ¥6. The trip of about 35km takes 1–1½ hours depending on the route chosen to drop passengers for intermediate stops. Most departures are before 8am, but buses continue to leave on demand until late morning. The main ticket office for the caves does not open until 9am, which may mean 9.30. To climb each of the spidery walkways around the face of the mountain, together with the walk up from the the bus, takes up to 2 hours, and there are other paths leading up adjacent mountains affording a view of the whole of Màijī Shān—bring a picnic. Most Chinese eat there, and, as the minibus drivers sleep through lunch, departure is usually about 1.30pm.

The bus stops at the ticket office, where you pay ¥6 for a scenery ticket just to let you into the area, and ends its run shortly afterwards, leaving you with a 10-minute walk to the entrance. The ticket office is on your right just before you see a set of stairs climbing up to your left. It's ¥25 ($3) for access to the museum and two separate routes around the caves. At the top of the stairs there is a square with the museum directly ahead.

The museum has a single 'Exhibition Hall for the Cream of Màijī Shān Art' with some fine statuary taken from the caves and which, for once, you can get close to (most statuary in the caves can only be viewed through grills). There are also paintings, and another set of the apparently inexhaustible Xiányáng pottery tomb figures (also on display in Xī'ān, Xiányáng and Běijīng).

Turn left at the top of the stairs and follow the path to reach the caves, leaving any bags (¥1) and cameras (¥2) at a hut you pass (compulsory). Three large white figures stand guard over your initial climb, mostly intact, apparently made by putting an outer clay coating on the rockface, linked by wooden staves to holes bored into the soft rock.

The first ticket takes you leftwards past a number of caves of varying sizes, many with statues similarly made. There are traces of remaining murals and reliefs, also made by putting clay on the walls and carving it. Concrete walkways connected by stairs lace the mountain and there are beautiful views across green valleys. Substantial chunks of fallen stone can be seen below. Some caves have the remains of the familiar 'thousand Buddhas', row upon row of tiny images. The caves are generally small with delicate statuary, especially the slender Northern Wèi figures with long necks and delicate faces, many still with traces of their original paintwork. Those of the Suí and later have fuller, fleshier, more typically Chinese forms. The galleries eventually lead to the feet of the three white figures, supposing they still had them, and later to side views of their large, plump, serene faces. One gallery on this route (no.9) has been completely walled in and you walk along as if inside the cave, very close to the sculptures. Many of the paintings here are still clear and intact. There is a wide variety of different styles, which, if followed in date order, would clearly demonstrate the gradual mutation of an Indian aesthetic into a Chinese one.

Eventually you come to the second entrance, which is above and to the right of your original starting point. It begins with some of the original stairs cut into the rock itself. The first cave was probably originally a larger space from which the front part has fallen away altogether with whatever building was in front of it, and it's followed by a gallery of 1m-high Buddhas, which probably once also had a substantial external covering. A further large cave retains traces of the original carved ceiling. There is a great deal of carved plaster on the exterior, and the statuary in the seven interior caves is in good condition, with portions of the original painted ceilings intact. Two side pillars are flanked by two large statues. One of the original tiny passages through the rock takes you to the next gallery, and on to the highest point of all. The stairways that link the galleries give dizzying views of the drop below your feet. The stairs are safe, firm and numerous—continuous backtracking is necessary up and down different stairs in order to explore all the possible corners. The way eventually leads to a further three large external figures, of which two survive (no.98). Cave no.191 on the far side has an impressive collection of reliefs including a remarkable winged figure with bulging eyes.

At the end, it's impressive to look back at where you've been. The Chinese hedge their bets on religion as usual, with Daoist fortune-tellers, palm-readers, and stalls with incense and firecrackers to set off outside cave 51 (at ground level), all doing brisk business.

Guides can be hired who can open a few of the caves for you but don't speak English. Hire is negotiable, but ¥200 ($24) is mentioned. ¥50 ($6) would be plenty unless you are in a large group. Many paths around the hills are worth exploring. Carrying on up the road past the ticket office and taking uphill paths to the left gives you excellent vantage points from which to view Màijī Shān itself.

There are two hotels that accept foreigners directly opposite the railway station, and another within 10–15 minutes' walk. The **Běidàoqū Zhèngfǔ Zhāodàisuǒ**, ✆ 736246, is an old building between two newer white-tiled ones. Walk to the far left-hand corner of the square, then cross the road and enter the gate to a courtyard. Reception is on your right. Carpeted doubles and triples with bath are ¥26 ($3.50) and ¥22 ($3) per bed, more basic doubles with equally basic bathrooms ¥18 ($2.50), and common bath doubles and quads go for ¥14 ($2) and ¥8. The new six-storey building on the right-hand corner of the road running directly away from the station is the **Xīhuáng Dàshà**, ✆ 731035 ext 217, with suites from ¥180 ($22), doubles and triples with bath for ¥48 ($6) and ¥36 ($4.50) per bed, and common bath quads for ¥14 ($2). The equally new and fractionally more up-market **Jīnróng Bīnguǎn** is straight past the Xīhuáng and on over the footbridge, then one block east (left), ✆ 731467 ext 8058. This has doubles with bath for ¥33 ($4) per bed, and triples with common bath for ¥26 ($3.50). There are also suites for ¥128 ($16).

Eating Out

There are plenty of restaurants. The one inside the Xīhuáng Dàshà has a standard menu of reasonable quality. Small ones with tables outside, to the left as you exit the railway station, have a variety of Hàn noodle dishes and other snacks. You can sit outside and entertain the Chinese or sit inside and entertain the flies. The street leading directly away from the station and the first right are a combination of pool hall and open-air Muslim food street at night, with local-flavour *jiǎozi*, filled with lamb and vegetables, and a murky-looking local form of hotpot with metal bowls set into tables heated from below.

Gāngǔ

甘谷 Gāngǔ is a small town, further west along the main route, which continues to follow the Wèi Hé. The railway is mostly on the north side, the road on the south. Gāngǔ can be crossed on foot in about 30 minutes and straddles the river, which looks like a torrent of chocolate milk. The town's roads are mostly dusty and unmetalled, but Hàn boulevardization is on its way. Visit Gāngǔ to see the group of temples and giant Buddha image known as Dàxiàng Sì ('Big Resemblance Temple'), strung spectacularly along a high ridge overlooking the town, and as yet rarely visited by travellers.

Getting to and from Gāngǔ
by train

Gāngǔ's railway station is a 10-minute walk from the bus station. All but the fastest trains stop here, about eight a day in each direction. You will have to purchase a hard seat and attempt to upgrade on the train. The possibility of standing all the way makes daylight trains best, but there's little choice. Going east the 178 at 04.03 reaches Xī'ān at 13.25, and the 188 at 16.14 arrives at 00.16. It's better to visit Tiānshuǐ, less than 1½ hours away, and continue from there. The best choice westwards to Lánzhōu is probably the 187 at 14.48 arriving at 21.34, or the 143 at 06.52 arriving at 13.04. There are two trains daily direct to Xīníng and two to Ürümqi.

To reach the town centre, turn right as you leave the railway station. After five minutes you will come to a square with the bridge over the Wèi visible to your left.

by bus

The bus station, on the banks of the Wèi next to the bridge, is rather larger than it needs to be, for some services have been superseded by private transport which leaves from the centre of town. There's a long-distance bus to Lánzhōu at 6am for ¥25 ($3), and services at 6am and around 11am to Luòmén (29km, ¥3) and Wǔshān (45km, ¥4). The 11am (from Tiānshuǐ) may arrive later and be crowded. The ticket office is reasonably sympathetic and helpful, only selling tickets after the bus has arrived. There are several morning departures to Tiānshuǐ (61km, ¥4.50), and frequent private minibuses from the main crossroads for the same price, as well as services to Línxià.

Getting Around

On foot, or by motorbike taxi. You ride in the sidecar, or pillion as you prefer, having bargained before setting out. ¥3 should get you from the railway station to the Nánlǐng Bīnguǎn, or ¥2 to the bus station or the centre of town.

Gāngǔ ☏ (0938)   Tourist Information

The main central crossroads is a 20-minute walk from the bus station. Everything you might need is strung out along this route. The post and telephone office is on the left 10 minutes along. Turning right at the main crossroads, marked on the right by a store that wishes it was a pagoda, brings you to an area of old backstreets, with the brick base of one of the original city gates and sections of the mud city walls still intact.

Dàxiàng Sì   大象寺

Open 8–6; adm ¥10 ($1.25).

From the bus station turn right up an uninviting muddy road, which turns left and eventually rises to the river bank. Follow that and when you can see an obvious footpath down to the mostly dry bed, take it and cross to the other side (there are several choices). Take the right fork and climb to the left-hand-side bank. Walk along that, and an enormous cliff-side Buddha will be visible across the fields. After the river crosses a road you'll see a traditional gate on the left and shortly a path down to it. If the river is in spate follow the road all the way to a cross-roads with a bridge to the right, and turn right under it. The temple entrance is on the left, a little way past what looks like an early attempt at a garden centre, brilliant with roses. Walking time is around 45 minutes; there are occasional minibuses from the centre of town, ¥2.

The ticket office is at the top of the first flight of stairs. A new concrete path with some traces of earlier routes follows the spine of a sharp and narrow ridge, with a number of small temples perched on it like swallows on a telephone line. Most of these are dilapidated and have the untidiness of active use, although one group, yellow-roofed and below the path to the right as you climb, is brand new. This demonstrates beautifully that the old skills of carving in relief on wood and painting detailed scenes on beams are not forgotten. Several other temples are undergoing renovation to which ordinary people are making considerable contributions by carrying up beams and other materials. The path meanders along the ridge, through and around the temples, until you reach the feet of the seated Buddha around 30m high, carved in the cliff. Until around 20 years ago this was protected by a substantial tower destroyed towards the end of the Cultural Revolution. The rock around the figure is perforated by large numbers of holes which once held the wooden beams. Originally the interior was covered with an elaborate tracery of delicate clay figures and clouds, now almost all destroyed, but the survivors are still impressive. Buddha himself has been given new feet, but the remainder was too substantial to sustain much damage. Traces of original paintwork remain, including a blue moustache and hair, and the position of his hands suggests preaching.

Beyond the Buddha are caves cut in the cliff-side, in which are traces of original murals but modern statuary. The views are increasingly impressive as you climb—the drop to the orderly fields and the specks of people in them being sheer. Just before the Buddha there is a stairway to the right through a passage cut in the rock itself. This leads to a cave undergoing restoration with substantial garish modern statuary. However, the monks are friendly and may invite you for tea.

The climb is the penitential trudge so beloved of Buddhism and Daoism, but the views across overgrazed hills on one side and fields and town on the other, make this one quite different. There's no tourist holiday-making feel here, and middle-aged ladies carrying beams to assist in the reconstruction suggest a degree of piety not usually encountered at Chinese temples. Despite the sale of tapes of chanting there's little commercialization except the welcome opportunity from time to time to sit and drink tea or egg soup under jerry-rigged awnings, and admire the view.

Where to Stay

Two choices: the cheapest is the very basic *zhāodàisuǒ* above the **bus station**, entered by the right-hand-most door at the front of the building (the side away from the river). The reception, such as it is, is on the fifth floor, and there is no lift. A bed in a standard concrete-floored wooden-bedded double is ¥12 ($1.50). There is one hotel, the **Nánlǐng Zhāodàisuǒ**, ℂ 622224, which likes to call itself a *bīnguǎn*, reached by walking to the main crossroads, turning right, then right again opposite the remains of the city gate. It's on the right shortly after taking a right fork. At least 20mins walk from the bus station, it's best tackled by motorcycle taxi. Moderately clean, and considerably more comfortable than the bus station, beds in rooms with bath cost: suites ¥80 ($10), singles ¥40 ($5), doubles ¥25 ($3) and ¥20 ($2.50). Common bath triples are ¥10 ($1.25), ¥8 and ¥5, depending if television is supplied.

Eating Out

A reasonable restaurant on the bridge side of the bus station serves standard Hàn dishes. There are also cheap Hàn and Muslim restaurants along the main street.

武山 The road to Wǔshān follows the steep banks of the Wèi, squeezed, with the railway line, between the river and the Qín Lǐng (mountains). Smaller than Gāngǔ, its rapid construction has not been matched by the process of metalling the roads. The street PA system is still in use, with occasional bursts of martial music and recordings of people doing bird impressions. Wǔshān is known locally for its lightly radioactive hot springs some distance outside town. There, people come to stay at the charmingly named Sanatorium of the Lánzhōu Railway Bureau. It also claims one of the world's largest deposits of 'mandarin duck jade', or serpentine, although the local version of 'night glowing cups' (*see* 'Jiǔquán', p.194) do not seem to be on sale. The main attraction is the trip into the Qín Lǐng to see the giant Buddha relief and accompanying caves and temples, rarely visited by foreigners.

Getting to and from Wǔshān

by train

Wǔshān is only half an hour by train from Gāngǔ and all the same trains stop here, except the 143 going west and the 144 going east.

by bus

There's a bus to Línxià at 10.30am, ¥22 ($3), which arrives from Tiānshuǐ and may be up to an hour late—buy your ticket in the morning. Helpful staff will ensure you get on the bus, which goes up the fork opposite the station. You may have to stand or take a wooden stool until someone gets off. There's a service to Lánzhōu which starts from Wǔshān at 9.30am, ¥23 ($3). Minibuses to Luòmén for ¥1 and Gāngǔ for ¥4 leave from the station when they are full.

Wǔshān ✆ *(09482)*   ### Getting Around and Tourist Information

The only street of interest is the one containing the bus station. Turning right out of it you pass several restaurants and shops, the Ruìlóng Fàndiàn on the left, and several street food-vendors. The government building is visible down a turning to the left after the post office on the right. This turning leads to the Xīnhuá Shūdiàn (nothing in English, no maps) and the Wǔshān Zhāodàisuǒ after veering to the right. There are no travel agencies, banks that know what traveller's cheques are, or policemen to extend your visa.

Around Wǔshān

Lāshāo Sì, Shuǐlián Dòng, and Qiānfó Dòng   拉梢寺, 水帘洞, 千佛洞

Adm ¥5.

These three sites—usually known collectively as Shuǐlián Dòng, the Water Curtain Cave—are 13km along a dry river bed from the town of Luòmén, approximately 15km from Wǔshān. From Gāngǔ you pass through Luòmén, and it's possible to arrive on the morning bus. Put your bags in the *zhāodàisuǒ* at the Luòmén bus station (very basic, ¥8 per bed), and then negotiate a *miàndī* from the town square. Alternatively, negotiate a *miàndī* to drive you there, taking your

bags with you, and to take you on to Wǔshān when you have seen the caves. The first asking price is ¥100 ($12), but there are several *miàndī* sitting round doing nothing and ¥40 ($5) is plenty for the caves only, ¥50 ($6) if you carry on (or return) to Wǔshān afterwards. If it rains you can't go to the caves at all. If it begins to rain heavily once there, head for the bus.

First see the Lāshāo Sì ('Pull away the branches temple'), referring to the piles of wood that carvers stood on to create the 60m Buddha and his companions represented in relief on the cliff face. They began work at the top, and shortened the wood pile as they worked down. The cliff-face has become an entire art gallery, with lions, deer, elephants and other figures in relief, some being made from plaster added to the cliff-face then carved and painted. Stairs lead up through the small temple, and around a rock and almost vertically to a gallery opposite the main Buddha, which allows you to view it at eye level. The figures are Northern Zhōu (Běi Zhōu AD 557–81), dating from around 559. The gallery, glued to the side of the cliff at a dizzying height, leads to a single small cave with Northern Zhōu figures. There is no charge, but at the temple there may be an attempt to extort a 'voluntary' donation, with hints that the door to the route further up will not be opened. If you prefer to avoid this, the cliff can be seen clearly from the path opposite up to the Shuǐlián Dòng.

Less than 15 minutes' walk, the path begins behind the ticket office (*open 10am until there's no one around*), to the right. It leads to a small bridge and winds round the mountainside, climbing slightly, past a small pavilion en route to the cave. A collection of small temples nestles right inside a large natural cave, which also contains a small waterfall, probably much more impressive after rain, but you can't visit it then. The temple gets its name from being supposedly hidden behind a curtain of water during rainy periods, but it's not clear whether this still happens. There are remains of paintings on the rock next to the path, which are suffering damage from passers-by (reminiscent of Langdon Warner's complaints about casual damage to the Mògāo Kū at Dūnhuáng). The temples are colourful, with roof ridges of heavily carved brick in the form of flowers, dragons and miniature pagodas. Access to the interiors is possible with a 'donation', although these are unremarkable. There's a pleasantly untidy and ramshackle air to the place indicating that it is not simply made for tourists. In the echoing quietness, the calls of the temple's own poultry mix with those of wild birds.

To reach the Qiānfó Dòng (Thousand Buddha Cave) walk up the dry river bed between the ticket office and the big Buddha, and turn left into a side valley indicated by Chinese characters painted on the rock with an arrow. Someone may have to go with you to unlock a gate. The paintings are in a natural cave at the head of this small gorge, and a new temple inside the cave is under construction.

Where to Stay

The **Wǔshān Zhāodàisuǒ**, also known as the Zhèngfǔ Zhāodàisuǒ, is in a state of confusion. Reception doesn't have a telephone, laughs at foreigners, and charges them double the ¥8, ¥10 ($1.25) and ¥12 ($1.50) prices displayed for beds in simple quads, triples and doubles with common bath, and the ¥27 ($3.50) per bed in large carpeted doubles with bath (¥50/$6 for the same size with a single bed), all plus ¥2 per person in tax. However, once you have moved into a room, the managers come to ask you if everything is all right and whether they can do anything for you, and the floor staff are also friendly. Evening hot water lasts only 15 minutes, however. The baths have no shower attachment and more rings than a sequoia. Arrive by going right out of the bus station and walking for 10 minutes, until a metalled left turn at the end of which you can see a government building. In front of this the road turns right, and it is on the right a little further down. Reception is on the left at the gate.

The **Ruìlóng Fàndiàn**, ✆ 22156, is much better. It only has concrete floors and the rooms are smaller, but they have large comfy beds and armchairs. Doubles with bright, clean bathrooms are ¥18 ($2.50) per bed, and hot water is available simply by asking. Beds in common bath doubles are ¥12 ($1.50), and in less comfortable triples ¥8. The staff are friendly, there is no doubling of prices, and the hotel is closer to the bus station. With your back to the bus station walk to the right, and keep looking left. After five minutes you will see the four-storey white-tile building behind some lower buildings on your left. It's up a small alley just past them.

Eating Out

There's nothing special, just the usual small, concrete-floored restaurants with the usual Hàn menus, and streetside snacks. Foreigners are rare here, so eat inside.

Línxià

临夏　Formerly an important stopping place on several Silk Route variations, a centre for Muslim scholarship, and a stepping stone for the religion's spread through Gānsù and beyond, Línxià is today an unimpressive little town, although still an important centre for trade. Locals claim it is the richest town in Gānsù due both to legitimate business and to the smuggling of drugs from Burma.

Reached by Arab missionaries in the 7th century, Línxià is still overwhelmingly Muslim (and within a Huí 'autonomous' prefecture), with a majority of Huí, and other Muslim groups such as the Dōngxiāng (Santa) and Bǎo'ān (Bonan). Few members of these minorities are easily identifiable, although Huí men wear their usual chef-like white hats, and women wear black cowls if married, green if not, sometimes over one of the white hats. The Bǎo'ān, one of China's least numerous minorities (fewer than 13,000), are more conservative still in dress, and possibly only identifiable by their decorated knives. Like their co-religionists the Uighurs further west, they are famous for the manufacture and discreet carrying of these, with a particular brass-bound style of handle to call their own. Only the Tibetans wear something approaching full-scale traditional costume—waistcoats and strings of beads, long heavy black skirts trimmed with bright colours, and sheepskin coats worn off the shoulder, their copious folds doubling as shopping baskets and suitcases. The Dōngxiāng have their own Altaic language but it lacks a written form. Many fled from here to the Ili region of Xīnjiāng in the 1960s to escape anti-religious persecution, prevented from entering the Kazak SSSR.

The town is dotted with mosques of no particular antiquity, following extensive destruction of the originals during the Cultural Revolution. Many have interesting minarets like open-sided pagodas, or giant multi-storeyed cake stands. As an important Muslim centre, Línxià's fame (at least with local Muslims) is in being the home town of the marauding Mǎ family, and especially of Mǎ Zhòngyīng. This incompetent warlord alternated between being an officer in the Nationalist army and an anti-Hàn separatist in the 1930s, briefly controlling the Tarim basin (see 'Ürümqi', p.243). Not surprisingly, he is usually omitted from Hàn histories of the area.

The local handicraft of carving brick dates from the Northern Sòng. Examples can be seen on temples and mosques, in the Hóng Yuán (park) in the city centre, and backstreet workshops.

At nearly 2000m above sea level, the nights in Línxià tend to be cool.

***

Getting to and from Línxià
by bus

The south bus station is the newest and biggest of the two in town, and may be the first or second you come to depending on the route. There are frequent direct buses from there to Xiàhé from 6.30am (107km, ¥7.70), Xīníng at 6am (271km, ¥20.50/$2.50), Wǔwēi at 12.30pm (423km, ¥30.50/$4), Lánzhōu west bus station (149km, ¥10.70/$1.25) and east station (156km, ¥11.20/$1.50), Yǒngjìng (for Bǐnglíng Sì) at 6am (256km, ¥18.40/$2.50), Wǔshān (287km, ¥19.90/$2.50), Luòmén (302km, ¥21/$2.50), Gāngǔ (332km, ¥23.10/$3), Tiānshuǐ (406km, ¥27.70/$3.50), and Yùmén in northwest Gānsù beyond Jiāyùguān (973km ¥70.10/$8.50). There are two alternative, longer, slightly more expensive routes to Xīníng.

If you have come via Wǔshān from Tiānshuǐ you will probably have your first encounter with the mandatory Gānsù bus insurance at Línxià. Foreigners who buy tickets must have this insurance at ¥30 ($4). The bus station will not sell you a ticket without it, but will let you board buses, where the driver will ask for a bribe of ¥50 ($6) to go to Xiàhé. Turn right out of the bus station and go straight on through Mínzú Cháng to the PICC (People's Insurance Company of China) office on your right in the next block, about 15 minutes' walk.

The main square in Línxià is Mínzú Cháng, 10 minutes north of the south bus station (to the right as you leave). The Bank of China on your right just after the first crossroads changes traveller's cheques but does not deal with cards. A little further on the left is a post and telephone office. The Xīnhuá Shūdiàn, the other side of the square, on the left doesn't have maps or English books.

Wànshòu Sì
(Běi Shān Gōngyuán)
万寿寺（北山公园）
Open daylight hours; adm ¥1.

This apparently inactive Daoist temple is up a muddy back street almost opposite the west bus station. Stairs lead up through a miscellany of ramshackle residences amongst the temples, all locked. The treat at the top is a recently renovated slender brick pagoda, with finely carved stonework around the base. Paths lace the mountainside to other temples, pavilions, restaurants, and tea houses. You can look out across the town and count the minarets. The grounds are alive with chipmunks who scutter away to avoid being made into pets or snacks.

Shopping

A street to the west of the Mínzú Cháng, confusingly called Běi Dàjiē (North St) and once containing a jumble of shops and and stalls, has now been redeveloped into a collection of the usual white tile monstrosities. However, shops have been reinstalled at ground level and you can buy Bǎo'ān knives, brassware, carpets, musical instruments, woven goods, animal skins, hats, ceramics, Tibetan boots, harnesses, saddles and all kinds of leatherware (better bought in Xiàhé).

Where to Stay

Línxià has many hotels for its size, both of the old-building old-thinking type, and the new white-tiled blue-glass variety where everything more-or-less works and the prices are the same for all. There are several hotels close to the south bus station, suitable both for budget travellers and for those looking for a little more comfort. Turning left out of the bus station, the large new **Línxià Bīnguǎn**, ✆ 211321, is one minute's walk down on the left, and has ornate suites with double bed for ¥252 ($30), single person suites for ¥152 ($19), comfortable doubles with shower for ¥82 ($10), similar triples and quads for ¥35 ($4.50) and ¥25 ($3) per bed, a bewildering variety of simple three-, four- and five-person rooms with common bath for ¥30 ($4), ¥18 ($2.50) and ¥15 ($2) per bed, and concrete-floor doubles with wooden beds for ¥20 ($2.50) per bed. Two minutes to the right of the bus station, the **Xīngdé Bīnguǎn**, ✆ 219449, is a small new hotel with large doubles (in the bay over the entrance) for ¥24 ($3) per bed, standard ones for ¥18 ($2.50), both with bath. You may be asked to pay for both beds if the hotel is busy, but this is resistible. There are also triples with common bath for ¥12 ($1.50) per bed. Both hotels have 24-hour hot water. Continuing past these two to the first crossroads, turn right and walk past the older building with the sign 'Lingxia Hotel' (*sic*), to the **Xīnghé Bīnguǎn** on the right, ✆ 219463 ext 220. It is similar to the Xīngdé, with suites for ¥88 ($11) and ¥80 ($10), doubles with bath for ¥48 ($6), and beds in triples without bath for ¥13 ($2). The most luxurious hotel is the new **Héhǎi Dàshà**, ✆ 217455, which is slightly more upmarket than the Línxià Bīnguǎn, with the usual plethora of beauty salons, restaurants, business centre, etc. Having transferred its management from an older, demolished building, it thinks you should pay ¥200 ($24) for a standard double only fractionally better than those in the Línxià Bīnguǎn (¥82/$10 there), when the Chinese pay half that. There are also triples for ¥60 ($7.50) per bed, and suites for ¥440. The **Línxià Fàndiàn**, however, has a new building going up on its site of a similar standard, which, they say, will have identical prices for Chinese and foreigners. Both hotels are in Hóngyuán Lù which is the second major left turn north of Mínzú Cháng. The Línxià Fàndiàn is on your left, the Héhǎi Dàshà shortly on your right.

Eating Out

For more comfort, eat at the restaurants in the Línxià Bīnguǎn and Héhǎi Dàshà. Muslim restaurants everywhere serve lamb *bāozi*, *jiǎozi*, and spicy noodle dishes.

Xiàhé

夏河 Xiàhé's buildings and people make it one of the most fascinating cities in China. It is a miniature Lhasa, containing the most important lamasery outside Tibet.

Línxià may be Muslim but to the south and west it is bordered by mountainous Tibetan 'autonomous' regions which reach to the borders of Sìchuān and Qīnghǎi provinces. Travelling southwest on the three-hour climb to Xiàhé, there's a visible change from villages with minarets to villages with prayer flags.

At 2900m, Xiàhé has grown up around the Labrang Monastery, one of the six most important monasteries of Tibetan Buddhism, only two of which, Labrang in Gānsù and Kumbum in Qīnghǎi, are outside Tibet itself. The town is really two villages linked by a single high street, parallelling the Dàxià Hé (river). The lower village is Hàn and Huí, and the road is lined with small shops serving the many Tibetan pilgrims who visit the monastery at the heart of the Tibetan village higher up. Minute weathered and wrinkled ladies of unbelievable antiquity shuffle around the pilgrim circuit spinning the large drum-shaped prayer wheels, clearly enraptured. The contrast between such devotion and the fidgety superstition encountered among Hàn visitors to Buddhist temples elsewhere is striking. As at the Jokang Temple in Lhasa and other major Lamaist sites, some of the Tibetans complete entire circuits of individual temples by repeatedly prostrating themselves at full length on the ground.

The shops in the linking street sell Buddhist devotional items but are often run by Huí. As canny traders they have made money from pilgrims to Labrang for centuries. After 10 minutes' walk up from the bus station the village becomes purely Tibetan, with mud-walled compounds, and Tibetan bread on sale in the street. The road cuts a tangent through the circular pilgrimage walk with its long low buildings containing hundreds of drum-shaped prayer-wheels, broken up by taller buildings with individual giant versions. These are provided with handles to avoid the wearing out of the prayer written on them, and some of the better-greased ones are kept almost perpetually in motion. Tibetans young and old go clockwise at a brisk pace, rosaries between their fingers or hand-held prayer-wheels a-swing. The route passes a golden stupa surrounded by prayer wheels, recrosses the main road and climbs up behind the main temple complex, passing two smaller white ones. A brief scramble up the hillside gives you views of the golden roofs and the red, brown, ochre and white walls of the monastery. Particularly beautiful in strong sunshine, it forms a backdrop for monks in crimson, vermilion and magenta robes.

Tibetan women pilgrims wear brightly coloured shirts, some floral, over which a darker wraparound dress trimmed with bright colours is often worn off one shoulder. Hair in braids long enough to sit on is sometimes looped together to keep them out of trouble. This ensemble is topped with a felt hat, strings of beads, and earrings of turquoise and coral. In the spring and early summer, the slopes of the surrounding Fèng Shān and Lóng Shān (Phoenix and Dragon Mountains) are carpeted with wildflowers, adding yet further colourfulness.

Getting to and from Xiàhé
by bus

To and from Línxià there are buses several times a day beginning at 6am (107km, ¥7.70), and frequent minibuses for ¥9, taking 3½ hours. The only direct bus to Lánzhōu starts at 7.20am (260km, ¥19.30/$2.50). There are also buses to Tóngrén in Qīnghǎi daily at 7.30am (107km, ¥10/$1.25), but the road is closed if there has been heavy rain. If closed, go to Shuāngchéng (87km away, ¥6.50 in a big bus, ¥7.50 in a small one) and change. Sight of travel insurance is required, but foreigners pay the normal price.

Getting Around

Xiàhé's main street runs gently uphill, with the bus station at the lower end. This is cluttered with motorbike taxis but these can be ignored, although they are useful if you want to go to as far as the Lābǔléng Bīnguǎn.

Xiàhé ℂ (09412)   Tourist Information

There's a travel agency in the Lābǔléng Bīnguǎn, but little need of its services. There are **no foreign exchange facilities** in Xiàhé; change money in Lánzhōu or Línxià. The uncooperative **post and telephone office** (*open 8–6*) is up from the bus station on the left, between the Friendship and White Conch Hotels. It will not let you send parcels unless you use its boxes, and claims not to provide a registration service. Phone calls from here are more than 50% more expensive than from some other places—¥44 per minute to Europe or North America. There are no fax facilities (although the Lābǔléng Bīnguǎn and Shuǐjīngshān Zhuāng have machines you may be able to use). There are film and developing shops up the main street (probably better left for a larger town). The Xīnhuá Shūdiàn is opposite the White Conch Hotel, but has no maps or English books. **Visa extensions** are easily obtained from the Visa Office of Xiàhé Public Security Station (*open Mon–Fri, 9–12 and 2.30–6*), opposite the Friendship Hotel and just up from the bus station on the right. Walk through the gate, cross the courtyard and the office is through the arch on the right. This office has an unusual interpretation of the rules. Instead of denying an extension until four days before your current visa expires, it thinks you must ask at least ten days before, or pay a fine. It will happily grant an extension two weeks or more before your current visa expires, and charges all foreigners a flat rate of ¥25 ($3). The **travel insurance** necessary to buy bus tickets is available from the PICC office down the turning next to the White Conch Hotel, on the left; ¥30 ($4).

Lābǔléng Sì (Labrang Monastery)

拉卜楞寺

Open 8.30–12 and 2.30–5; adm ¥22.50 ($3).

You will only be admitted to the monastery if with a tour guide organized for you as part of your admission fee. Unfortunately, and somewhat uncharitably, if you happen to miss the English-speaking one you will simply be added to a Hàn tour. (Genuine Tibetans wander around freely.) Go early. Tibetan and Chinese speakers able to phrase suitably polite requests may persuade the monks at the entrances to act as guides to individual buildings.

The monastery is the reason for the town's existence. It consists of a large number of Tibetan buildings, their golden roofs capped with the traditional images of the deer attending the Buddha's first sermon at Sarnath and the wheel of life and rebirth, as on all important Tibetan Buddhist buildings. From the rooftops monks produce long bass wails from immense horns to call the others to prayer, debate, and study. The monastery has around 1000 monks, and an atmosphere of mixed lightheartedness and extreme gravity. The younger monks are muscular and skittishly playful, and the seniors, wearing the plumed yellow hats of their order, are sober and thoughtful, but also given to the beaming smiles that make Tibetans the favourite people of China with almost all who meet them. The building interiors, the finest to be seen on the Silk Routes, are dimly lit by yak butter lamps and consequently smokey. They house yak butter sculpture, gleaming statuary, thousands of racked texts, tubular hangings, carpet-wrapped slender pillars, and ornate stupas containing the ashes of the five previous incarnations of the monastery's own reincarnating lama, Jiamuyang. (The current edition is said to be kept out of harm's way in Lánzhōu by the authorities.) Niches contain smaller reliquaries with the ashes of lama relatives and every wall is covered with paintings of Buddhist scenes. Treasures include a miniature dagoba studded with pearls and a *sutra* (concise Buddhist text) in letters of gold. When the halls reverberate with the monks' deep guttural chanting it is not difficult to imagine that you have suddenly been transported back to mediaeval times.

The monastery was begun by the first Jiamuyang, E'angsongzhe, in 1709. Amongst the residential and administrative buildings are six academic institutes, teaching exoteric Buddhism and religious philosophy, esoteric Buddhism, astronomy, geography, mathematics and medicine. There are also purely devotional buildings and a museum. The institutes are strongly rooted in the tradition of centuries, but the monks are far better informed about events, both in their own country and overseas, than most people in China, thanks to the pilgrims' grapevine and BBC World Service. The real world also penetrates the mystical atmosphere of the lamasery in other ways. Amongst the more traditional religious subjects of the intricate butter scultures there is a bizarre, but politically correct (in Hàn terms), reproduction of communist leaders reviewing a parade in Běijīng's Tiān'ānmén Square.

During the main religious festivals, the grasslands are dotted with pilgrim's tents. Determining when the festivals should take place is down to the astronomers, many guided by the lunar rather than solar calendars. The great Monlam festival takes place annually from the 4th to 16th days of the first lunar month, and includes 'sunning the Buddha'—hanging out a vast cloth image (*thangka*) on a terrace built for that purpose. There's also religious dancing, and a special butter sculpture show. Other festivals are held 1st–15th of the 7th lunar month, the 8th days of the 2nd and 7th lunar months, the 29th of the 9th lunar month, and during the 6th lunar month.

Around Xiàhé

There are some grasslands with grazing yak a one-hour cycle ride out of the village up the valley which are rapidly becoming a tourist spot, with refreshment tents and horse riding available. Bicycles are available for rent from several restaurants and hotels for ¥10 ($1.25) per day, plus a ¥200 ($24) deposit.

Shopping

Long rows of small shops sell devotional and practical items (a Tibetan probably wouldn't make this distinction), such as prayer wheels, cymbals, bells, cups for butter lamps, stamps for impressing Buddha shapes on butter pats, hats, fabrics, carpets, rugs, tents and awnings with attractive blue patterns on a white background. There's also coral and turquoise jewellery, and pictures of the late Panchen and other lamas. In the current climate only the monastery dares to display pictures of the allegedly secessionist Dalai Lama. As a result, within the precincts you may frequently be asked for copies of his picture. To be discovered with these in your luggage by Chinese officials would likely speed your departure from China, however. Tibetan clothing on sale includes rather smart Tibetan hats made from felt with a cowboy-like look. There are also saddles, leather goods, and shops for Muslims.

Where to Stay

Uphill from the bus station, the first hotel is the **Yǒuyì Bīnguǎn** (Friendship Hotel) on the left, ✆ 21593, a basic hotel with simple doubles with bath for ¥40 ($5) per bed, and ¥20 ($2.50) per bed in quads with common bath. Further up on the corner of the first left is the larger, new **Báihǎiluó Bīnguǎn** (White Conch Hotel), ✆ 29400, where the staff are eager to please, and the comfortable doubles with bath are good value at ¥40 ($5) per bed. Triples with common bath are ¥20 ($2.50) per bed, and suites ¥180 ($22). This is the best choice in this price range. Opposite is the older **Dàxià Bīnguǎn**, ✆ 21546, which is similar to the Yǒuyì, having doubles with bath for ¥40 ($5), common bath triples for

¥25 ($3), and quads for ¥16 ($2) per bed. Further up on the right, the **Shuǐjīngshān Zhuāng**, ✆ 21878, 📠 21368, another good new hotel, also has ¥40 ($5) per bed doubles with bathroom, larger doubles with bay windows for ¥100 ($12), and even larger suites for ¥120 ($15) per room. The hotel is white tiled with a green roof, and the left-hand entrance as you face it is the one for reception.

The best hotel in Xiàhé, the **Lābǔléng Bīnguǎn**, ✆ 21849, 📠 21328, suffers from being at the opposite end of town from the bus station, but is situated amongst fields and with views of the Tibetan part of the village. It has a Tibetan-style courtyard building with doubles with bath overlooking its interior garden for ¥200 ($24). Three-bed common bath dorms in the same building at ¥12 ($1.50) per bed are the best value for budget travellers, although there's not much space for anything else. There are also $300 ($36) doubles in concrete buildings shaped like Tibetan tents and painted with traditional blue patterns on white. A rear building has conventional doubles for ¥60 ($7.50). Take a motor tricycle or other transport from the bus station, or walk around 45mins through the Hàn–Huí and Tibetan villages, following the road as it swings to the left over a bridge. Take the first right turn and the hotel is just over a bridge on the left.

In the Tibetan village there are some rock-bottom places, like the **Lābǔléng Sì Zhāodàisuǒ**. Run by monks for Tibetan pilgrims, these may sometimes be cheaper, but are often as expensive as the hotels lower down, and less comfortable.

Eating Out

There are numerous small restaurants in the main street, many with English signs and menus, including Sìchuān, Huí and Tibetan. Dishes are normal price but rice, for some unknown reason, is often ¥3. There are friendly Tibetan-run restaurants with English menus on the first floor of a building just up from the White Conch Hotel, with a mixture of Tibetan, standard Hàn, and 'Western' food. There are similar restaurants uphill nearer the Tibetan part of the town. Try Tibetan yoghourt served with crunchy crystallized honey, and, if you wish, with *tsampa*—a paste of barley flour and yak butter, kneeded by hand, uncooked and possibly a source of stomach problems. The Tibetan version of *bāozi*, *momo*, are also widely available.

To Xīníng via Tóngrén

The bus takes 45mins to do the first 10km, steadily climbing up narrow valleys on an unmade but even road to views of permanently snow-capped mountains. The few villages have frames for drying grass at the roadside, and are Tibetan and Tǔ, with some Huí. All along are the white and blue tents of Tibetan nomads with guardian mastiffs, herds of yak, corkscrew-horned sheep, and hobbled horses, which have reduced the surrounding hillsides to a billiard-table-like smoothness. With luck you may see infant yak, Tibetan women milking yak, and shaggy, heavy-shouldered adult yak, some partly shorn, fleeing from the bus in an absurd scamper out of proportion to their bulk. After three hours there's a town with a small monastery, and almost every village has at least one dagoba. The two main passes are topped with prayer flags, and as spring progresses into summer the mountainsides are carpeted with blue, red, yellow, white and purple wildflowers. Through summer the grass grows ever lusher. Wildlife includes plump marmots, startled larks and a host of small birds. The bus occasionally wallows in mud, going uphill in first and downhill in no gear, engine off. Your travelling companions will be almost entirely Tibetans, counting their rosaries (what do they know about the driving that you don't?), chanting, and opening beer bottles with their teeth. The last hour is spent in sheer-sided grassless canyons, and the bus turns left for the few kilometres to Tóngrén itself, arriving after a total of 5½ hours or so. You are now in Qīnghǎi Shěng (Province).

Tóngrén is a small uninteresting town, but it's necessary to stop here because all the buses to Xīníng and the only bus to Xiàhé will have left by the time you arrive. Walking uphill from the bus station you immediately arrive at a junction with a statue of a horse. Ahead on the right is a cheap bathroomless *lǚshè* with ¥9 beds in doubles. Turning right at the statue, the old-style, overpriced Huángnán Bīnguǎn, ✆ (0973) 22688, is at the end of the street on the left. All prices are doubled for foreigners—a bed in a smelly concrete-floored standard double with bath will cost ¥66 ($8). A new building, going up opposite the far end of the street, which will offer a higher standard, but the same management. On the way there you pass the post and telephone office, quoting less than ¥20 ($2.50) per minute to the UK, and less than ¥18 ($2.50) to North America.

Buses from Tóngrén: the first Xīníng departure is at 7.30am (181km, ¥13.16/$2), and Línxià at 7am (183km, ¥16/$2). There are buses to Shuāngchéng (163km, ¥14.20/$2), and Xiàhé (104km, ¥10/$1.25) at 8am. There are later departures on most routes, but most are in the morning. Minibuses charge slightly more: ¥17 ($2) to Xīníng. Buy your ticket in advance. Although they are numbered, arrive early to ensure a seat. Xīníng is 5½ hours away.

Xīníng

西宁 Earlier this century, Qīnghǎi's almost unpopulated high grasslands were the home of nomadic Tibetans, Mongolians and others, with few permanent settlements. A village one day's march west of Xīníng was regarded as the 'last village in China', according to Peter Fleming who came this way from Lánzhōu in 1935 by mule. The people east of Xīníng:

> *...were indeed so poor that, when we were buying eggs and one egg dropped, there was a race—won by the most respectable-looking person present—to salvage the unbroken yolk. All along this road the standard of living is pitiably low, and a substantial proportion of the population lives for (and largely on) opium.*

Peter Fleming, *News from Tartary*, 1936

It's still one of the three poorest areas of China. Despite rapid industrialization in the Tsaidam Basin, nothing can alter the fact that, 'basin' or not, most of the province is plateau, with an average height of 4000m, long winters and minimal rainfall. The vast Qīnghǎi Hú (lake) is salt. Farming is limited to small areas, and those who have benefited from the new industrialization are mostly the more than a quarter of a million recent Hàn immigrants.

Fleming and his companion traveller Kini Maillart were held up in Xīníng pessimistically awaiting clearance to proceed westwards. Daytime entertainment consisted of reading detective fiction, hanging around a photographer's shop, and occasional visits to the Catholic and Protestant missions. The evening entertainment was to 'patch the fresh holes made in our paper windows by the fore-fingers of the curious'.

Qīnghǎi is now viewed as rich in ores and minerals, oil and natural gas, and has become a major generator of hydroelectric power. Its few towns and villages still seem backward, though, and Xīníng, the provincial capital and largest city, is of no great size, or much more entertaining than in Fleming's day.

He missed the most exciting period in Xīníng's history by 40 years. In 1895 one of several Dungan revolts spilled over from Gānsù, and the city fell to Muslim troops. By the end of the year, however, they were surrounded by troops from Běijīng. In January 1896 they sued for peace but were refused. Shortly afterwards Xīníng fell and a massacre provoked a general uprising of Dungans throughout Gānsù, spreading as far as Lop Nor on the edge of Kashgaria.

Getting to and from Xīníng

by air

The CAAC office (*open 8.30–12 and 2–5*), ✆ 817 4616, is on the north side of Bāyī Lù, 10 minutes' walk east of the Huàlóng Bīnguǎn. A bus connects with flights for ¥10 ($1.25). The airport is 29km to the east. Foreigners' tickets to Xī'ān are ¥710 ($86), Golmud ¥610 ($75), Běijīng ¥1630 ($196). CITS in the Xīníng Dàshà or Qīnghǎi Bīnguǎn can book tickets, as can the CYTS office near the Xīníng Bīnguǎn, for around ¥50 ($6) commission per ticket.

by train

The ticket office is well over to the right, as you face the railway station, in a separate building beyond another dealing with freight, and set back a little.

To Lánzhōu the best choice is the Lǚyóu2 at 08.15 arriving at 12.13. It can only be hoped that this is the future of Chinese railways. Clean and relatively fast, with efficient, polite staff and a free gift for every passenger (a noise-making toy, inevitably), it could only be improved by a reduction in the quantity of Richard Clayderman, The Carpenters, and *Mull of Kintyre*. Other choices include the 516 to Lánzhōu at 08.44 arr 15.48, and three trains that pass through both Lánzhōu and Xī'ān: the 74 to Qīngdǎo at 14.52, the 76 to Běijīng at 15.52 (arrives at 05.00 two days later), and the 178 at 16.30 to Shànghǎi. There's also the 276 to Xī'ān at 10.23 arr 07.55 the next day.

For those planning to go to Tibet there are the 507 to Golmud (Gē'ěrmù) at 07.30 arriving at 07.02 the next day, and the 303 at 17.20 arriving at 01.54.

by bus

There are buses to Lánzhōu at 7.30am (230km, ¥12.60/$1.50) but rail is better. There are three departures to Tóngrén from 8.30am (191km, ¥13.60/$2), four to Línxià beginning with 7.30am and 9.30am (266km, ¥16/$2). There are also buses to Zhāngyè at 7.30am (1½ days, 347km, ¥20.60/$2.50), Wǔwēi at 7.30am, not passing through Lánzhōu (7–8 hours, 362km ¥26.80/$3.50), and Shuāngchéng (246km, ¥15/$2).

If you plan to take the bus from Golmud to Lhasa, spare yourself and take the train to Golmud. By bus it's 781 long, uncomfortable kilometres for ¥42.80 ($5) before you even start the 36-hour epic from Golmud. Other immensely long trips include those to Dàcháidàn (715km, ¥53.80/$6.50) where you can change for Dūnhuáng, Chálěngkǒu also known as Lěnghú (865km, ¥49.90/$6), from where you connect to southwestern Xīnjiāng and, furthest of all, the real Lěnghú (975km, ¥73.50/$9), a long way from anywhere.

Ticket windows are mostly open 6.30am–9pm: no.5 for Lěnghú, Lánzhōu and Wǔwēi, no.4 for Línxià, and no.3 for Tóngrén.

Getting Around

Xīníng lines both banks of the Huáng Shuǐ and its tributaries. The centre of town is the crossroads (*dà shízì*) from which the inevitable Dōng, Nán, Xī, and Běi Dàjiē run. The railway station and bus station are close to each other at the east end of town on opposite sides of the river. Local bus services are frequent. Most useful are 1, which runs from the station past two hotels to the centre, and 9 from the station to the Xīníng Bīnguǎn. Fares are 5 *máo*. Taxis are plentiful, mostly *miàndī*, and use their meters.

Xīníng ☎ (0971)   *Tourist Information*

There is a branch of **CITS** in the Xīníng Dàshà, ☎ 814 9994 ext 4126, and one in the Qīnghǎi Bīnguǎn which run tours to places as near as Labrang Monastery (which you can easily reach by yourself), and as far away as Lhasa in Tibet, Dūnhuáng in Gānsù, and Bird Island (in Qīnghǎi Hú to the west and difficult to reach otherwise). For ticket booking go to **CYTS** in a small office on the west side of Běi Dàjiē just north of the Xīníng Bīnguǎn, ☎ 817 4616 (*open 8.30–12 and 2–5*). There is one main branch of the **Bank of China** which changes money—a tall, white, air-conditioned building on the north side of Dōngguān Dàjiē just west of the mosque (*open Mon–Fri, 8.30–12 and 2.30 –5*). The counter to the left labelled Foreign Trade Settlement is for foreign exchange, and the right-hand-most counter does credit card advances for 4% commission. The **post office** (*open 8.30–6.30*) is on the south side of the main crossroads (*dà shízì*). *Poste restante* is held at the counter on the right that sells envelopes, parcel boxes, and other stationery; postcode 810000. Buy stamps at counter no.6. The **telephone office** (*open 24 hours*) is upstairs from the post office. Calls to the US are ¥26.25 ($3.50) per minute, and to the UK ¥29.25 ($4), plus 10% service charge. The fax department is on the ground floor to one side of the post office (it's cheaper to fax from the Xīníng Bīnguǎn). There is a large **Xīnhuá Shūdiàn** diagonally opposite on the ground floor of a store called 'The Big Dipper', with Chinese maps ranging from ¥1 to ¥2.5, and a good selection of English books. Maps are also available at the railway station and from street vendors. **Film** is widely available, and there is a professional-looking Kodak developing shop just south of the post office on the west side of Nán Dàjiē. **Visa extensions** are available from a particularly helpful PSB with an English sign on the east side of Běi Dàjiē, a short walk north of the centre.

To Golmud

CHANGJIANG LU

H A

QI LU

2

XIGUAN DAJIE

BEI DAJIE

★ 3

HUANGHE LU

XI MEN

XI DAJIE

7

DA SHIZI

DONG DAJIE

5

6

NAN DAJIE

CHANGJIANG LU

C H

HUAYU

To Kumbum

Xīníng

For map key see over

Xīníng map key

北禅寺	1	Běichán Sì
中国青年旅行社	2	CYTS Zhōngguó Qīngnián Lǚxíngshè
公安局	3	PSB Gōng'ānjú
火车站	4	Railway station Huǒchēzhàn
	5	Buses to Kumbum
邮电局	6	Post and telephone office Yóudiànjú
新华书店	7	Xīnhuá Bookshop Xīnhuá Shūdiàn
中国银行	8	Bank of China Zhōngguó Yínháng
长途汽车站	9	Long-distance bus station Chángtú qìchēzhàn
清真大寺	10	Mosque Qīngzhēn Dàsì

HOTELS AND RESTAURANTS

西宁宾馆	A	Xīníng Bīnguǎn
永福宾馆	B	Yǒngfú Bīnguǎn
青海宾馆	C	Qīnghǎi Bīnguǎn
西宁大厦	D	Xīníng Dàshà
化隆宾馆	E	Huàlóng Bīnguǎn

STREET NAMES

八一路	Bāyī Lù
北大街	Běi Dàjiē
滨河路	Bīnhé Lù
长江路	Chángjiāng Lù
大十字	Dà Shízì
大众街	Dàzhòng Jiē
东大街	Dōng Dàjiē
东关大街	Dōngguān Dàjiē
黄河路	Huánghé Lù
湟中	Huángzhōng
花园南，北街	Huāyuán Nán/Běijiē
建国路	Jiànguó Lù
南大街	Nán Dàjiē
祁连路	Qí Lián Lù
七路	Qī Lù
五一路	Wǔyī Lù
西大街	Xī Dàjiē
西关大街	Xīguān Dàjiē
西门	Xī Mén

Běichán Sì　　　　　　　　北禅寺

Open 8–6; adm ¥3.

This small collection of cliffside Daoist temples, said to have originated in the 3rd century, is reached by walking north up Chángjiāng Lù across the river and turning left. Look for an entrance on your right with an arch through which you can see them. The steep staircase leading to the temples is less than 10 minutes' walk from the bridge, itself a 10-minute climb.

At the top turn left for the temples and around 20 small caves with statuary of the supposed founder of Daoism and the Eight Immortals, both crumblingly ancient and garishly modern, with some original painting intact. A gallery leads along the cliff and through occasional tunnels to other temples and caves undergoing renovation and open to those who make a suitable donation to the Daoist monk. Retrace your steps past the stairs and take an unmade path that climbs steeply past a ruined water channel to see a small five-storey brick pagoda with splendid views across the city—about a 15-minute climb. Halfway up, the man shouting 'Hello hello' at you is trying to indicate that you should pay ¥0.50 for another ticket.

Kumbum Tǎ'ěr Sì

Open 8.30–5; adm ¥21 ($2.50).

塔尔寺

The main reason for coming to Xīníng is to see one of the two great monasteries of the 'Yellow Hat' sect of Tibetan Buddhism to be found outside Tibet—Kumbum. Kumbum and Labrang in Xiàhé are in the top six, as any monk with whom you can communicate will enthuse.

The lamasery at Huángzhōng is reached by catching a bus or minibus from the road just to the east of Xīníng's sports centre, which is near Xīmén, directly west of the centre. Travel by buses 1 and 31 from the railway station area, and by the 2 from the Huàlóng Bīnguǎn and Xīníng Dàshà. Tickets are ¥5, and buses leave when they are full, which is more likely to happen earlier in the morning rather than later. It's a 26km, 45min journey. At Huángzhōng turn left out of the bus station, and at the T-junction turn left and keep walking on the left until you find two left turns together. Either will take you to the monastery. Taking the lower one, climb the stairs on the left-hand side to the bridge you see ahead of you and cross the road. The higher one slopes steadily to reach the same point. There are minibuses running from the bus station to the lamasery for 5 *máo*. The monks have a particular enthusiasm for taking the film of those who photograph inside the buildings, so do not attempt this. At the Hall of Butter Sculptures rolls of confiscated film are nailed up for all to see.

The Times correspondent Peter Fleming visited Kumbum in 1935.

> *Here, in the greatest temple, looking down from a high gallery upon the huddled chanting figures, I caught for a moment, and for the first time, something of that dark and powerful glamour with which Western superstition endows the sacred places of the East. I had been, as every traveller has, in many kinds of temples; never before in one where I had that tight, chill, tingling feeling which I suppose is something between spiritual awe and physical fear.*

Peter Fleming, *News from Tartary*, 1936.

Kumbum, being close to a major city and a railway line, has a more commercial atmosphere than its counterpart Labrang, although it is still a functioning monastery, and should not be missed. One benefit of larger numbers of visitors is that there is no compulsory guided tour. Another is that for once there are explanatory signs in English. Chinese tourists spin the prayer wheels just for fun. Your ticket entitles you to enter ten or so of the temples and halls sprawled over the hillside with residences, administrative buildings and stupas. These are thoughtfully numbered.

The importance of Kumbum lies in its connection to Tsongkhapa (1357–1419), the founder of the Gelugpa 'Yellow Hat' sect of Tibetan Buddhism or Lamaism, and known to the Chinese as Zōngkābā. According to legend he was born near here (although other authorities give his birthplace as Amdo in Tibet), and after his head was shaved at age seven, in preparation for a religious career, the scattered hair grew into a sandalwood tree, whose leaves carried his image. Born at a time when a fairly definitive edition of key Buddhist writings had been estab-lished, he went on to produce 18 volumes of commentary, plus instructions on meditation and other works. He was a reformer and responsible for the founding of several great monasteries in Tibet. Since the adoption of civil as well as religious authority by the Dalai Lama in the 17th century, his Gelugpa ('school of the virtuous') sect has been pre-eminent. Tsongkhapa's image can easily be recognized at Yellow Hat temples by his pointed hat with long ear flaps. According to legend, in 1379 Tsongkhapa's mother built a dagoba to mark his birthplace. A small lamasery was built not far away in 1560, which was joined by a hall to house a Maitreya statue after a visit by the third Dalai Lama in 1583. Enlarged and rebuilt many times, the monastery's buildings include a terrace for 'sunning the Buddha'—displaying a large image painted on cloth known as a *thangka* at certain festivals.

The ticket office is on your left if you have walked up, and on your right if you have been dropped by the minibus at the car park. With your back to the ticket office go up a path between the buildings to the left of and beyond the row of eight stupas to find the first stop. In addition to their function as storehouses for Buddhist texts and relics, stupas can also act as symbols of events in the life of the Sakyamuni Buddha, which is the role of these particular ones.

The **Lesser Temple of the Golden Roof**, constructed in 1692, was roofed in gold-plated bronze tiles after 1899. An interior balcony sports grotesquely distorted stuffed animals. A yak and a bear look down on tourists in a startled manner. Percussion with cymbals accompanies your visit, and there is a fine incense burner topped with a lion, belching the smoke from the interior. The building is well restored and hung with traditional blue and white awnings.

Go round the large stupa opposite the entrance to the Lesser Temple (known as the **Time Wheel Dagoba**), and on uphill to find the **Flower Temple** or Longevity Hall of 1717, with a small shady courtyard and finely decorated interior.

Across a small bridge and to the left, the **Holy Land of Mandela** contains a giant three-dimensional version of one of these visual representations of cosmic forces used to aid meditation.

The remaining halls are on your right as you continue uphill. What is open varies from time to time, so try to enter anything that looks as if it might be, and certainly anything with a numbered sign. One hall is currently undergoing reconstruction and will reopen as a museum.

The **Nine Roomed Hall** of 1592 is just one around a central courtyard, and contains statues of Dalai Lamas, Tsongkhapa and Bodhisattvas, and a courtyard for religious dances. The central space features three large seated figures and glass cases with hundreds of miniature ones. On the left a small temple with a stupa contains the ashes of the third Dalai Lama. Most halls have great tubs of waxy yak butter. At the right-hand corner is a doorway leading to the Grand Hall of the Golden Roof, built in 1379, and containing an 11m-high silver pagoda. It is worth paying the extra ¥3 for its brooding atmosphere, and sumptuous interior decorations. Its exterior walls are tiled in green with elaborate brass ties and either side are the smaller halls of Sakyamuni and Maitreya.

Higher up, the **Astronomy College** has racked texts, small statues, and coins and notes glued to the pillars using yak butter.

The **Hall of Butter Sculpture** now offers a permanent display (if anything so friable can be said to be permanent—an air-conditioning unit is used when the weather gets hot). These kaleidoscopic painted sculptures include myriad miniature figures of waxy delicacy and colossal psychedelic flowers. The rear has scenes of miniature monks, yellow hats and all, about their daily business.

Key festivals at Kumbum, which attract large numbers of Tibetan visitors, include 8th–15th of the 1st and 4th lunar month, 3rd–8th of the 6th lunar month, and 20th–26th of the 9th lunar month. If you can establish these dates by the solar calendar you are likely to see 'sunning the Buddha', elaborate religious dances, and mass chanting, accompanied by colourful fairs.

Qútán Sì

瞿昙寺

Open 9–6; adm ¥15 ($2).

This splendidly quiet Lamaist temple complex in Chinese style is about 20km outside Lèdū, a small town 65km east of Xīníng, altogether about 2½ hours by *miàndī*. Built in 1420 on the site of earlier buildings (main hall 1391), these plain stone buildings in a good solid state of repair have ten active monks. Beams are pleasingly weathered but their paintings and those on the walls are clear despite being unrestored, a rarity in China. The main attraction is a splendid mural gallery running around three sides of the compound. Mostly in good condition and also untouched by the heavy hand of restoration, murals depict scenes from the life of Buddha. Start left and go clockwise. There is an extra ¥20 ($2.50) charge for taking photos, and an extra ¥2 per person for a guide who will open a small museum and the main temple.

Lèdū can be reached by bus from Xīníng with 17 departures from 7.20am to 3pm, ¥3.50. Minibuses wait where the bus stops to take you to Qútán Sì for ¥2.50, departing when full.

Lèdū can also be used as a break point on the way between Xīníng and Lánzhōu, and can be reached by train as well as bus. The railway station is 1.5km out of town, but minibuses take you to the centre for ¥1. The Lèdū Zhāodàisuǒ behind a market in the centre of town has beds at ¥36 ($4.50) in singles, ¥18 ($2.50) in doubles, and ¥10 ($1.25) in four-bed rooms, all with common bath. A large shiny new *bīnguǎn* is nearing completion where the bus drops you.

Báimǎ Sì

白马寺

Open daylight hours; adm ¥1.

This is a temple clearly visible on the cliff-side 20 minutes' walk north of Píng'ān, a small town halfway between Xīníng and Lèdū, and the point where the road to Tóngrén turns south. It is supposed to mark the spot where a blind foal, having unknowingly kicked its mother over the cliff, regained its sight in time to see her fall and jumped over after her. Báimǎ Sì translates as White Horse Temple, and it's a small 8th-century temple of three storeys, with a good cliff-side location overlooking a Tibetan village immediately below, and Tǔ villages round about (most of the staff are Tǔ including the single monk). The temple is reached by a short climb up the red cliffs on not particularly steep paths. Píng'ān was the birthplace of the current Dalai Lama.

Where to Stay

expensive

The **Xīníng Dàshà**, ✆ 814 9995, has a number of buildings, the plushest of which have had a recent refit—on Jiānguó Lù 10 minutes' walk south across the river from the railway station, also reachable on bus no.1.

Suites are ¥258 ($31), ¥348 ($42) and singles ¥130 ($16); doubles with bath are ¥130 ($16), ¥182 ($22) and ¥234 ($28). More basic doubles are ¥66–104 ($8–12) per bed. Foreigners are unpopular and pay up to 2½ times Chinese prices.

Turn left at the Xīníng along Bāyī Lù to find the **Huàlóng Bīnguǎn**, a little way down on the right, ☎ 814 2090 ext 2112. This is a cheap (same price for foreigners and Chinese) and fairly new hotel, popular with minority traders, with a reasonable and cheap restaurant on the ground floor. There are single, double, and triple suites at ¥70 ($8.50), ¥38 ($5) and ¥28 ($3.50) per bed, doubles with bath from ¥22 ($3), and triples with common bath from ¥12 ($1.50). The private bathrooms have squat toilets.

The **Xīníng Bīnguǎn**, set back from Qī Lù, ☎ 823 8701, ✆ 823 798 ext 93, is reached by bus 9 from the railway station. The Soviet-style pile at the front only has offices; reception is in the newer building behind. There are rooms in older blocks behind that. Fairly good standard suites are $38, and doubles with bath $28 and $20. Good value triples with antique bathrooms and hot water three times a day are ¥38 ($5) per bed in building no.3 at the rear. This hotel accepts JCB cards only.

The **Yǒngfú Bīnguǎn**, opposite the bus station, just across the river from the railway station, ☎ 814 0230 ext 2026, is one of China's stranger hotels. Reception is on the ground floor but the rooms are several floors above levels of shopping and a roller disco. Everything is dirty and in very poor repair. Doubles with bath are ¥30 ($4) per bed, or there are rooms with a double bed for ¥70 ($8.50), singles for ¥50 ($6), and triples for ¥25 ($3) per bed all with bath. There are also small doubles and quads with bath at ¥25 ($3) per bed. The budget traveller is better off at the Huàlóng or Xīníng Bīnguǎn.

The **Qīnghǎi Bīnguǎn**, 20 Huánghé Lù, ☎ 814 4018, ✆ 814 4145, claims to be the most modern building in the province—a 21-storey, 395-room tower next to a conference centre, with standard doubles $48–60, and suites $65–80. Two 'Presidential' suites are $1200 and $1500. There are a dozen restaurants, business centre, karaoke, fitness centre, and other facilities. JCB cards are accepted. The hotel, southwest of the centre, can be reached by bus 22 from the station, or by taxi.

Eating Out

For more upmarket food the restaurants in the expensive hotels are best. Jiànguó Lù, leading away from the station, has cheap noodle and soup canteens, mostly Huí, and Běi Dàjiē has reasonable restaurants with standard Hàn menus. Tibetan food is available in an alley near the Yǒngfú Bīnguǎn, but despite the smiling friendliness of these places, get a clear price before consuming your *momo* and yak butter tea.

Lánzhōu to Hāmì

The Héxī Corridor

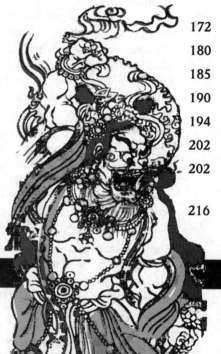

At Lánzhōu and Wǔwēi the various routes from Xī'ān were forced by nature to join into one main route. To the south lay the peaks of the Qílián or Nán Shān, and to the north stretched the Gobi Desert under a variety of different names, and occasional low ranges. Between them the intermittently green Héxī corridor ran northwest for more than 1200km, with a string of oasis towns, originally established during the expansionist Hàn dynasty as part of a successful military effort to drive off the mounted Xiōngnú; the concentration of trade through the one main route made them wealthy. Leading to China's edge, they also continued to benefit from military investment as border posts, except when, as under the Yuán and Táng, China's borders moved several thousand kilometres further away. During times of contraction they fell under the control of non-Hàn empires such as those of the Uighurs, Tibetans and Xī Xià.

Following the demise of the Silk Routes the oases became backwaters, and in modern times only Lánzhōu has grown into a sprawling, polluted metropolis. During the upheavals between 1911 and 1949 the 'Imperial Highway', as some called it, was rarely safe, and trade between Xīnjiāng and eastern China went by camel from near Ürümqi directly through Mongolia to Hohhot, avoiding Gānsù altogether. The arrival of rail links after 1949 brought the return of trade, and now several towns thrive on the processing and export of oil and mineral deposits in the Qílián Shān.

Although unattractive, Lánzhōu is the junction of routes to Níngxià, Qīnghǎi, and Tibetanized parts of southern Gānsù, and sees many visitors. Other smaller oasis towns are quieter, offering a diet of temples and pagodas founded during the Silk Route's Táng peak and maintained by pious merchants looking for protection against brigands, sandstorms, thirst and rapacious officials. Most of these are leapfrogged by modern travellers, who make Jiāyùguān's fort or Dūnhuáng's magnificent caves their next stop, after days of travelling by train through the mesmerizing landscape of the Gobi Desert's fringes.

Lánzhōu

兰州 Although once a major Silk Route staging post, the development of Lánzhōu as an industrial base following the communist victory in 1949 has obliterated traces of the small town of the past beneath a sprawling city, Gānsù's capital. Desperate tourism officials write of the air being full of the aroma of flowers, but its air is now heavy with pollutants from its traffic, refineries, petrochemical complexes, metal smelting operations, mills and other factories. Once a trading centre sufficiently successful to be known as Jīnchéng, 'Gold City', it now has more than two million people, and stretches along the banks of a now broad, shallow and sluggish Yellow River, groaning under the weight of its own atmospheric effluent. Some efforts are being made to improve the treacly atmosphere, and Lánzhōu is probably no worse than Xī'ān and Ürümqi.

In 1935 *The Times* correspondent Peter Fleming passed through, arriving by lorry from Xī'ān, and continuing by mule to Xīníng. In those days foreign visitors to Lánzhōu felt a long way from the 'real' China of the east coast treaty ports where most of them lived.

*The streets of Lanchow are romantic... The faces of the Moslems —
very influential, here as in Sian, though they form only ten per cent of
the population — are swarthy and fierce and almost hawk-like; most
of them wear white caps or turbans. Occasionally you see a Turki from
Sinkiang, a bearded, booted figure in a long chapan, with features so
Aryan and un-Mongoloid that he might almost have come from
the Caucasus.*

Peter Fleming, *News from Tartary*, 1936.

Lánzhōu still provides a preview of what's to come further west, although even in Fleming's day the Muslim influence was not what it had been, having borne the brunt of Chinese suppression of independence movements in the 1860s, with many thousands dead. In addition to its position between Xī'ān and China's western extremities, the city is also the junction between routes to Xīníng, and to Běijīng via Yínchuān and Hohhot. The trip to the Bǐnglíng Sì caves makes Lánzhōu worth a visit, but not a long one. If you are forced to stay a few days, there's some escape to be found at the Bái Tǎ Shān Gōngyuán (White Pagoda Park).

Getting to and from Lánzhōu

by air

The Air China office is just west of the 'Restaurant of Airline' near the Lánzhōu Fàndiàn, ✆ 884 0191, 901 7896 (*open 8.30–5.30*). The airport is 75km away, and the airport bus from the office costs ¥25 ($3). There are daily flights to Běijīng and Xī'ān, three times weekly to Dūnhuáng, four times to Ürümqi, and three to Jiāyùguān (via Dūnhuáng). It's probably better to book at the counter in the Lánzhōu Fàndiàn foyer, which has a computer terminal, no queues and no service charge.

by train

Touts (scalpers) accost foreigners at the ticket office pretending to be students. They'll ask you to buy tickets for them from the foreigners' allocation at window 12. If it doesn't occur to you to wonder why a 'student' wants to buy a hard or soft sleeper costing the equivalent of a few weeks' wages, then you'll find out when you see him selling the ticket for a profit outside the station later on. Buying sleeper tickets for most trains is not a problem from window 12, but go early in the morning three days before for any train that does not start at Lánzhōu.

The most convenient westbound train is the 143 at 13.16 (which comes from Xī'ān, and goes to Ürümqi and Korla on alternate days), but sleeper tickets are almost impossible to get, so it's a matter of buying a hard seat and upgrading on the train. This arrives at Wǔwēi at 21.09, Jiāyùguān at 06.50, Liǔyuán (for Dūnhuáng) at 13.36, Hāmì at 19.37, and Ürümqi at 06.32 or Korla at 13.54. Other options for long distances are the 243 at 17.00, which has a large allocation of seats since it starts at Lánzhōu, arr Zhāngyè at 06.44, Jiāyùguān at 11.28, Liǔyuán at 17.54, Turpan at 07.50 the next day, and Ürümqi at 10.43. For maximum comfort catch the the a/c 69, although this leaves at 02.08 and cannot be boarded without a reserved seat. Other westbound trains going to Ürümqi include the 97 at 19.10, and the 52/3 at 23.41.

Lánzhōu

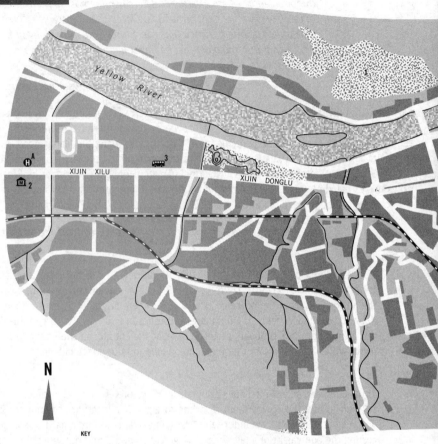

XIJIN XILU

XIJIN DONGLU

N

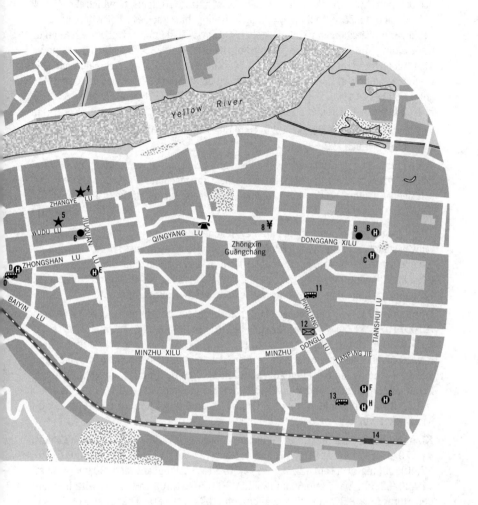

STREET NAMES

白银路	Báiyín Lù	天平街	Tiānpíng Jiē
东岗西路	Dōnggǎng Xīlù	天水路	Tiānshuǐ Lù
酒泉路	Jiǔquán Lù	武都路	Wǔdū Lù
民主西、东路	Mínzhǔ Xī/Dōnglù	西津西、东路	Xījīn Xī/Dōnglù
平凉路	Píngliáng Lù	张掖路	Zhāngyè Lù
七里河	Qīlǐhé bus stop	中山路	Zhōngshān Lù
庆阳路	Qìngyáng Lù	中心广场	Zhōngxīn Guǎngchǎng

Eastbound to Xī'ān (676km) there's a choice of at least 10 trains, of which the 71/74 at 19.08 and the 76 at 20.29 (continuing to Běijīng) have the best choice of seats, both starting from Lánzhōu and Xīníng on alternate days. Useful trains which reach Xī'ān in the evening and intermediate stops in daylight are the a/c 70 at 08.18 calling at Tiānshuǐ at 14.53, and the 51/54 at 10.14, calling at Tiānshuǐ at 16.25, although this reaches Xī'ān only at 23.18. If you want to get off at intermediate stops the best trains are the 111/114 at 08.51 (Wǔshān, Gāngǔ), and the 125/128 at 11.26 and 185/188 at 10.38 (Wǔshān, Luòmén, Gāngǔ), both of which start at Lánzhōu.

Trains northwards include the 202 to Hohhot at 19.46, the 44 to Běijīng at 09.58, and the 94 to Yínchuān at 22.37.

Train numbers are displayed in the relevant ticket windows. Carry film in your pockets when catching the train, as use of the X-ray machines is strictly enforced. The soft sleeper 'Guìbīn' section has a separate entrance to the left of the main one.

by bus

There are two main bus stations: the East (Qìchē Dōngzhàn) is a short walk from the railway station, and the West (Qìchē Xīzhàn) 30mins away by buses 1 or 6. Both have a tendency to charge foreigners double. There is also the Lánzhōu Qìchēzhàn, on the left a little way up Píngliáng Lù, past the Lánzhōu Dàshà, which doesn't overcharge. All stations require you to have insurance and to show your certificate.

Dōngzhàn: Most sleeper buses start from here, including those to Xī'ān at 6pm (¥100/107, $12/13—upper/lower berth), to Yínchuān at 7pm (¥70/75, $8.50/9.00), and to Píngliáng at 7pm (¥57/61, $7/$7.50). Buy tickets up to three days in advance at window no.8. There are daytime buses to Yínchuān, Gùyuán, and Gāngǔ (window no.6), Píngliáng and Xīníng (no.5), Tiānshuǐ (no.3), Zhāngyè, Dūnhuáng, Jiāyùguān, and Wǔwēi (8.30am and 3.30pm, ¥21/$2.50), and Jiǔquán, (no.2). It's also possible to travel to Ürümqi in around 44 hours for ¥110 ($13.50). Most ticket windows are open 6am–8pm.

Xīzhàn: There are buses to Wǔshān (281km, ¥12.90/$2), Gāngǔ (226km, ¥14.70/$2), Wǔwēi at 9am, 12, and 6.30pm (274km, ¥12.60/$2), Lèdū (161km, ¥7.40), Xīníng at 11am (223km, ¥10.30/$1.25), Píngliáng at 6.30am (419km, ¥19.20/$2.50), Xiàhé at 6.30am (256km, ¥11.70/$1.50), and Línxià with frequent departures from 8.30am until mid-afternoon (109km, ¥6.80). There's also one bus to Yǒngjìng at 7.30am for ¥10 ($1.25). Bus insurance is available here but with ¥10 or 25% commission.

Lánzhōu Qìchēzhàn: There are departures to Jiǔquán twice daily (¥53.40/$6.50), to Dūnhuáng at 5pm (¥82.60/$10), seven departures to Wǔwēi (¥20.30/$2.50), to Gāngǔ at 7am (¥24/$3), to Xīníng at 7am and 4pm (¥16.80/$2), to Tóngrén at 7.30am (¥25.80/$3), to Gùyuán at 6.30am (¥25.50/$3), to Yínchuān at 6.30am (¥38.20/$5), and six departures to Zhāngyè from 7am (¥37.30/$4.50).

Getting Around

Lánzhōu bus fares begin at ¥0.30. The most useful buses are the 1 from the railway station to west bus station (stop named Qīlǐhé, no.13 on route 1, 30mins) which passes the Lánzhōu Fàndiàn and Legend hotels and not far from the Guānghuá, and continues to the Provincial Museum and Huáyì Dàjiǔdiàn; and the 6 from the station which passes the post office, Bank of China, and along the shopping street of Zhāngyè Lù to the west bus station, museum, and Huáyì Dàjiǔdiàn. From the railway station to the west bus station is ¥0.40. *Miàndī* (minivans) are plentiful at ¥1 per km; flagfall ¥6. Other cars ¥1.4; flagfall ¥9.

Lánzhōu ✆ (0931)   Tourist Information

There are **travel agents** in every major hotel, running tours to all parts of Gānsù. Several run daily trips to the Bǐnglíng Sì Caves in high season, usually starting about 8am, but none really keeps track of the situation. One of the more friendly and efficient is West Asia Travel in room 121 of the Huáyì Dàjiǔdiàn, ✆ 233 3051, ✆ 233 0304, where there are several good English speakers. Most of these agents will also sell you the Gānsù bus insurance, but often for a considerable commission. Several of the major hotels have exchange counters but these only serve hotel guests, and in some cases close at weekends, as does the main **Bank of China** on the west side of Píngliáng Lù beyond Qìngyáng Lù (*open Mon–Fri 9.30–11.50 and 2.30–5.30*) and passed by bus 6. A new Bank of China tower is going up immediately south of the Lánzhōu Legend Hotel and this may well take over foreign exchange in the near future. The **post office** is on the corner of Mínzhǔ Dōnglù and Píngliáng Lù (*open 8–7 for mail, and 8–11 for telephone calls*). The *poste restante* counter is no.5 (closes randomly during the day); the postcode is 730000. **Telephone** calls to the US are ¥40 ($5) per minute, and ¥41 for England. To send facsimiles add ¥9.80 per page. At the 24-hour telegraph office in Qìngyáng Lù calls are ¥39 to the US, and ¥44 to the UK. **Film** is available at several department stores including those around the central square, Zhōngxīn Guǎngchǎng. **Maps** are available at the Wàiwén Shūdiàn (Foreign Languages Bookshop) in Jiǔquán Lù, which also has English books upstairs. **Visa extensions** are available from the city PSB in narrow Wǔdū Lù off Jiǔquán Lù near the bookshop (*open Mon–Fri 8–12 and 2.30–6*). The entrance is down the right-hand side of the building as you face it. Extensions can also be obtained from the provincial government offices at the top of Jiǔquán Lù on Zhāngyè Lù, same hours. The compulsory Gānsù bus insurance can be purchased at the **PICC** building, 150 Qìngyáng Lù, passed by the no.1 bus.

Shěng Bówùguǎn (Provincial Museum)   省博物馆

Open 9–12 and 2.30–5.30; closed Sun; adm ¥25 ($3).

Despite its superior title, this is no better than those in several other Gānsù towns, just considerably more expensive. The ground floor has a dull exhibition of Gānsù manufactures on the right, and the rest is used as a furniture store or locked up. The top floor has an exhibition devoted to the supposed triumphs of the revolution, but this is usually closed, too.

On the floor in between on the left there is a poorly presented and lit Silk Route exhibition laconically labelled in English, which begins with pottery from several thousand years ago, moving up to Qīng dynasty items. There are fine wooden animal tomb figures and other items from the Hàn dynasty Léitái tomb at Wǔwēi, of which the star is the small bronze of a galloping horse caught in mid-neigh, resting one foot on a swallow (the Tóng Bēn Mǎ). Reproductions of this horse are on sale in almost every tourist shop in China, so it's a surprise to find that most copies have improved on the original's spindly legs and tubby body. The horse is accompanied by a fine 40-piece set of bronze chariots and horsemen. The collection also has bamboo strips used to make up primitive scrolls, Táng dynasty tri-colour glazed figures, Buddhist paintings and statuary, and one room with a limited selection of items representing Gānsù's minorities, including beautifully illuminated Islamic texts.

Around Lánzhōu

Bǐnglíng Sì Shíkū

炳灵寺石窟

Most hotels have travel agents offering tours out here. The one public bus is the 7.30am departure from the west bus station for ¥10 ($1.25) which takes three hours to reach the reservoir port of Liújiāxiá outside the town of Yǒngjìng. Alternatively there are minibuses with departures beginning at 6.20am from near the Shènglì Bīnguǎn (Victory Hotel) for ¥7 and which take about 2½ hours. All drop you at the ticket office at the head of the road leading down to the reservoir. Foreigners are quickly corralled and have no chance to bargain for themselves—avoiding the ticket office and walking down the road only results in being directed to a second ticket office by a policeman. Large boats leave at around 10.30am after the public bus has arrived, taking up to three hours to reach the caves for ¥50 ($6). Small open outboard motorboats take about 1¼ hours for ¥70 ($8.50), and there are powerful covered motorboats with seats for 8–10 people (including the traditional stools in the aisle) which cover the distance in only 50mins for ¥80 ($10, but if you arrive in a group you can certainly bargain the price down by about ¥10 per person). Water levels in the reservoir depend on rainfall and demand for electricity, and can only be guaranteed to be high enough for the big boats in September and October, although they are often operational from June onwards. Taking the motorboats allows you easily to accomplish the trip in a day without using an organized tour from Lánzhōu. One seat in a minibus tour usually costs around ¥135 ($16.50), including big boat ticket and entrance fee (¥12/$1.50), and has the convenience of getting you picked up from your hotel. However, most agents don't bother to check about the water levels before sending you off on what may turn out to be a pointless trip. If boats full of Chinese seem to be departing when you have been told that water levels are too low, they are simply taking a ride to the main part of the reservoir well before the caves.

An alternative way to see the caves is to stay the night at Yǒngjìng, where there are three fairly cheap hotels, and return to Lánzhōu or continue to Línxià the next day.

Travelling by boat makes a pleasant change, but the scenery is mostly of interest only near the caves, where the water winds between steep, red, wind-eroded cliffs. After docking climb the steps and turn right. The foreigner price is ¥12 ($1.50, plus an optional ¥205/$25 to see the oldest cave, no.169). A path leads along the left-hand side of a narrow gully to the caves, where you can pick up a yellow hard hat to protect you from falling pebbles, since in places the cliffs overhang the path. There are 184 caves and niches dating from the Liáng (AD 502–57) to the Míng (1368–1644), the finest sculptures being from the Northern Zhōu (AD 557–81). There are small caves with paintings in fairly good condition, lines of smaller figures carved directly into the rock face, clay statues on wooden armatures, and post holes indicating external buildings now disappeared. Wooden galleries at a slightly higher level allow you to get very close to the carvings and statuary, although part of the staircase fell away some time ago. The large rock-cut seated Buddha is probably Táng; it is 27m high, and has a very Chinese plumpness and fleshiness, whereas the standing figures in cave 169 show strong Indian influences. This cave is claimed to be one of the oldest in China, and unusually for cave-temple sites is natural rather than man-made.

The site was finer before the building of the dam, which caused the water level to cover nearly 200 lower caves. If more time were allowed it would be possible to climb up the gully to a monastery with a small community of Tibetan monks, but boats are unwilling to stay more than an hour, which means that you need to move briskly to see even the main caves. Some visitors have found their way by early morning bus from Yǒngjìng to a village above the caves, and then walked down past the monastery, stopping for tea. It's still necessary to take a boat back, and the one-way fee is the same as the return—you're in a bad position for bargaining.

Although this is a pleasant day out, those with only a limited interest in caves would do better to save their energies for Tiānshuǐ, Dàtóng or Dūnhuáng.

Where to Stay

 Older Lánzhōu hotels have been undergoing face-lifts and correspondingly raised prices. They have, however, retained their double-pricing for foreigners, which has taken the cost of their rooms beyond those of newly built hotels with better facilities at every price level and more courteous staff. The cheapest beds in Lánzhōu are at Běijīng's level of prices, but give better value for money. Hotels in every price range can be found conveniently close to the railway station and east bus station.

expensive

The **Lánzhōu Fēitiān Dàjiǔdiàn** (Lánzhōu Legend Hotel) at the junction of Tiānshuǐ Lù and Dōnggǎng Xīlù, ✆ 888 2876, ✉ 888 7876, is a smartly run Singapore joint-venture tower with all the facilities of a standard international hotel. A double 'de luxe' room is ¥800 ($96); a larger one ¥900 ($109), and suites are ¥1700 ($205), ¥1900 ($229), and ¥7500 ($904), all plus 15% service charge. The hotel boasts a variety of bars and restaurants. The **Guānghuá Bīnguǎn**, 189 Guānghuá Lù, ✆ 843 6168, ✉ 846 4749, is a reasonably comfortable hotel with a good central location, although a little overpriced at ¥298 ($36) for a double and ¥428 ($52) for a suite, all plus 10%. A little haggling will produce an immediate removal of the service charge, and perhaps a further reduction in the room fee. Prices are the same for Chinese and foreigners. The health centre features a sauna and wave bath. The easiest entrance to find is that on Jiǔquán Lù. The old favourite was the **Lánzhōu Fàndiàn** (Lánzhōu Hotel), opposite the Legend, ✆ 841 6321, ✉ 841 8608, but while a face-lift has improved its appearance, it has not improved its manners. Most items you want appear to be *méiyǒu* (not have), and most staff *xiàbān* (off duty) whenever you most need them. Standard doubles are ¥420 ($51) for foreigners, with suites rising to ¥640 ($77). The hotel has a commission-free air ticket desk with its own computer.

moderate/inexpensive

The original Yǒuyì Bīnguǎn (Friendship Hotel) has had a partial face-lift which is still continuing, become a Hong Kong joint venture, and renamed itself the **Huáyì Dàjiǔdiàn**, at 14 Xījīn Xīlù, ✆ 233 3051, ✉ 233 0304. The hotel is inconveniently located in the west of the city, close to the west railway station, and has four blocks of differing standards containing 500 rooms and 10 restaurants. A standard double is ¥220 ($27), and there are reasonable common bath four-bed rooms in an older wing at ¥38 ($5) per bed.

The **Shènglì Bīnguǎn** (Victory Hotel) is a typically hopeless old-style double-price hotel, only noted because minibuses to Bǐnglíng Sì start from nearby, and to be avoided in favour of one of the following. The **Lánzhōu Dàshà**, ✆ 841 7177, 🖷 841 7210, conveniently opposite the railway station, is a tower with a variety of rooms: suites from ¥100 ($12) to ¥258 ($31), and doubles with bath from ¥90 ($11) to ¥160 ($20). There are also common bath doubles and triples for ¥56 ($7) and ¥35 ($4.50). Foreigners in the standard doubles seem to end up on the relative quiet of the 14th floor, and the ¥90 ($11) rooms are the best value for the middle-budget traveller. To the right and behind the Lánzhōu Dàshà, in Tiānshuǐ Lù, is the not particularly friendly or helpful **Yíngbīn Bīnguǎn**, ✆ 888 6552, 🖷 (in the service centre) 888 6776, with three blocks in varying conditions, although foreigners are not allowed to stay in the cheapest. The better condition rear building has suites for ¥160 ($20), doubles with bath for ¥120 ($15), and without for ¥60 ($7.50). The middle building has suites for ¥100 ($12), doubles with bath for ¥80 ($10), and triples without for ¥72 ($9). A better choice for the budget traveller would be the friendlier **Lánshān Bīnguǎn**, almost opposite, ✆ 861 7211, 🖷 ext 2108. The rooms here are simple but clean, with suites and doubles at ¥60 ($7.50) and ¥40 ($5) per bed, and common shower singles for ¥46 ($6) and ¥35 ($4.50); doubles ¥28 ($3.50), triples ¥20 ($2.50), and quads ¥16 ($2). There is even room for bargaining on some prices.

Eating Out

All the hotels sport restaurants, with decor and prices in proportion to their room rates. There are extensive noodle shops around the railway station, and in Tiānpíng Jiē, which links Píngliáng Lù and Tiānshuǐ Lù a short walk north of the railway station.

Wǔwēi

武威　The road and rail routes from Lánzhōu race each other northwest up a narrow river valley before emerging at the edge of the Tengger Desert (Ténggélǐ Shāmò), a Gobi sub-division, and arriving at Wǔwēi, the first large town in this direction. The last strands of more northerly routes join the mainstream here.

A military headquarters in the battle against the Xiōngnú as early as the time of the Hàn Emperor Wǔdì (reigned 141–87 BC), Wǔwēi was later three times the capital of minor Liáng dynasties (two of which were formed by non-Hàn peoples) between AD 317 and 439. In the 10th century Wǔwēi, like the other town up the Héxī Corridor, came under the control of the Xī Xià dynasty of the Tanguts (c. 1038–1227), a Tibetan-related people who threw off Chinese control and survived Sòng assaults, only to be obliterated by the Mongols around 1225–7. Hàn, Liáng and Xī Xià all left their mark on Wǔwēi. Polo called the city *Erguiul*, and placed it in 'the great Province of Tangut. The people consist of Nestorian Christians, Idolators, and worshippers of Mahommet'. There are still Uighurs, Huí, Manchus and other minorities in the area, and much of the territory between Lánzhōu and here is a Tibetan 'autonomous' county.

Like so many other Chinese towns, Wǔwēi had its city walls largely intact until the Cultural Revolution of 1966–76. Now only small chunks remain visible on Nán Dàjiē. It's a sleepy town, with warrens of mud-walled compounds behind the larger buildings of its few main streets, and its major sights are in walking distance of each other. While spectacular finds have been made here, particularly in the Léitái Hàn Mù (tomb), it's the finds rather than the sites that are spectacular. Foreign visitors are rare and attract a lot of attention, but for those looking for a day's break from the train, Wǔwēi is a good choice of stop. There's also the option of going east by rail, or more conveniently by road, directly to Zhōngwèi and Yínchuān.

Getting to and from Wǔwēi

by train

Private minibuses run from the bus station and just south of the centre to the railway station for ¥1 when trains are expected. Eastbound trains to Xī'ān include the 54 at 03.38, the 70 to Běijīng at 01.31, the 98 at 06.07, the 144 at 10.14, the 114 at 01.55. To Lánzhōu only there's the 522 at 21.20, and the 244 at 07.01.

There is a connecting line to Zhōngwèi avoiding Lánzhōu, but with inconvenient trains. Take the 682 at 16.00 to Wǔwēi Nán (south station) arr 16.27. Change to the 518 to Gāntáng which leaves at 17.15 and arrives at 21.45. Zhōngwèi is now 1½ hours away, and there's a train at 01.40.

Westbound to Ürümqi, trains include the 53 at 06.10, 69 at 09.01, 97 at 01.48, 143 at 20.15 (alternate days to Korla), 243 at 23.40, and the 113 at 07.08. The 501 at 08.05 will take you to Zhāngyè, Jiǔquán and Jiāyùguān.

The ticket office is on the right of the main entrance. The few sleepers and numbered seats are sold out quickly first thing in the morning three days before the date of travel. Other than asking a travel agent for assistance, buying an unnumbered seat and attempting to upgrade is probably your only choice. Lánzhōu, Zhāngyè, Jiǔquán and Jiāyùguān can all be reached in daylight hours, making a trip in a hard seat not too much of a burden. Lánzhōu tickets are ¥21 ($2.50), Jiāyùguān ¥37 ($4.50).

by bus

There are buses to Zhāngyè at 8am, 11am and 2pm (235km, ¥17/$2), Jiāyùguān at 9am, 2pm and 8pm (482km, ¥35/$4.50), Xīníng at 7am and 10am (362km, ¥27/$3.50), and Línxià at 10am (423km, ¥30.40/$4). There are buses to Lánzhōu approximately every half-hour from 7.30am, every hour in the afternoon, with some evening departures (291km, ¥20.30/$2.50). There are also buses to Píng'ān (326km, ¥24.50), Lèdū (299km, ¥22.40), Zhōngwèi (329km, ¥25.10/$3), and Yínchuān at 7am (¥37/$4.50). Private operators run buses to distant places such as Ānxī (751km), Hāmì (1104km), Turpan (1573km), and Ürümqi (1700km).

Getting Around

The centre of town is the crossroads where Dōng, Nán, Xī, and Běi Dàjiē meet. Wǔwēi is small enough to have no public transport. Miàndī have a flagfall of ¥6 and are ¥1 per km, larger cars mostly ¥9 and ¥1.4 per km. Most taxis are three-wheeler hybrids which will take you between the centre and the station for ¥3. There are also large numbers of motocyclists wanting you to ride pillion.

Wǔwēi ☏ (0935)   *Tourist Information*

The Tiānmǎ travel agency in the Tiānmǎ Bīnguǎn provides a limited range of expensive tours, and will buy rail and air tickets for a commission of ¥30 ($4) and ¥50 ($6) respectively. The **Bank of China** branch on the north side of Xī Dàjiē just east of the Tiānmǎ Bīnguǎn (*open Mon–Fri, 8–12 and 2.30–6; Sat am only*), will only deal with Visa and Amex traveller's cheques, and does not accept credit cards. The main **post office** (*open 8–6*) is on the west side of Běi Dàjiē just north of the centre, and the **telephone office** almost opposite but slightly further north (*open 8am–10pm*) has remarkably cheap rates by Chinese standards: only ¥18 ($2.50) per minute to the USA and ¥20 to the UK; add ¥6 per page for facsimiles. A good bi-lingual **map** is available from the foyer of the Liángzhōu Bīnguǎn, ¥2.5, and a Chinese-only one for ¥1 from the **Xīnhuá Shūdiàn** on the south side of Xī Dàjiē just west of the centre (opposite the small park) where you can also find a very small number of English-language novels. **Visa extensions** are available from the PSB office on the southeast corner of the centre, entrance on Dōng Dàjiē (*theoretically open Mon–Fri 8–12 and 2.30–6*). The main PICC office for the **travel insurance** necessary to buy bus tickets is a long way west of the centre, but there is an agent immediately east of the Liángzhōu Bīnguǎn.

Wén Miào   文庙
Open 8–11.40 and 2.30–5.30; adm ¥20 ($2.50).

Going past the Liángzhōu Bīnguǎn on Dōng Dàjiē, turn right down Jiànguó Lù, and then left at the T-junction down Xīn Qīngnián Xiàng.

Originally a Confucian temple built in 1437, claiming to be the largest and best preserved in Gānsù, the impressive halls, set around two courtyards, are now a museum with a diverse collection demonstrating Wǔwēi's varied history. A central pavilion has a striking Hàn dynasty mummified corpse and coffins, together with a skull in a box, hair intact and put up and held in place with a pin. In the same courtyard on the left a small hall holds numerous small pieces of statuary and stelae, including one with the feathery Xī Xià script on one side and Chinese characters on the other. This was of major assistance to linguists in deciphering the language, whose existence, along with that of the dynasty itself, was only rediscovered in the last 100 years.

Further to the left a second courtyard holds a history exhibition spread over four numbered buildings which begins with implements from 4000 BC, and proceeds through Hàn dynasty tomb figures to a centrepiece bronze set, the originals of which are now in Běijīng's History Museum. The third hall has photographs of the destroyed city walls. The interiors are dim, but the lights may be turned on if you badger the attendants enough—this is a 'don't bother me, I'm knitting' museum. Labels in English are limited to telling you what you can see for yourself ('A piece of paper'). The rearmost hall, a splendid building with a large sweeping roof, has Míng and Qīng painting on the ground floor and ceramics and a few tomb oddments upstairs. From its exterior gallery you can view the clouds of swallows around the museum's roofs, and see into mud-walled compounds around the rear.

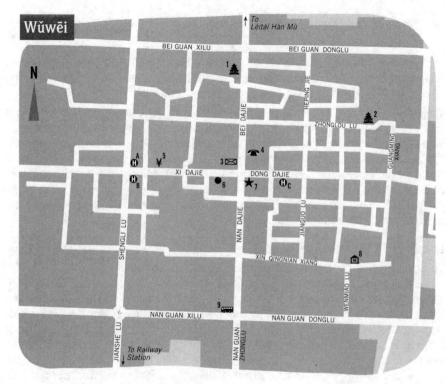

Wǔwēi

To
Léitái Hàn Mù

BEI GUAN XILU

BEI GUAN DONGLU

N

ZHONGLOU LU

BEI DAJIE

HEPING JIE

GUANGMING XIANG

¥ 5

A
H

3 ✉

✆ 4

H
B

XI DAJIE

DONG DAJIE

● 6

★ 7

H
C

SHENGLI LU

NAN DAJIE

JIANGUO LU

XIN QINGNIAN XIANG

8
M

WENMIAO LU

9

NAN GUAN XILU

NAN GUAN DONGLU

JIANSHE LU

To Railway
Station

NAN GUAN
ZHONGLU

	KEY			STREET NAMES	

罗什寺塔	1	Kumarajiva Pagoda Luóshí Sì Tǎ	北大街	Běi Dàjiē
古钟楼，大云寺	2	Gǔ Zhōnglóu and Dàyún Sì	北关东、西路	Běi Guān Dōng/Xīlù
邮局	3	Post office Yóujú	东大街	Dōng Dàjiē
电信楼	4	Telephone office Diànxìn lóu	光明巷	Guāngmíng Xiàng
中国银行	5	Bank of China Zhōngguó Yínháng	和平街	Hépíng Jiē
新华书店	6	Xīnhuá Bookshop Xīnhuá Shūdiàn	建国路	Jiànguó Lù
公安局	7	PSB Gōng'ānjú	建设路	Jiànshè Lù
文庙	8	Museum Wén Miào	南大街	Nán Dàjiē
武威汽车站	9	Bus station Wǔwēi Qìchēzhàn	南关中、东、西路	Nán Guān Zhōng/Dōng/Xīlù

HOTELS AND RESTAURANTS

天马宾馆	A	Tiānmǎ Bīnguǎn	胜利街	Shènglì Jiē
华丰饭店	B	Huáfēng Fàndiàn	文庙路	Wénmiào Lù
凉州宾馆	C	Liángzhōu Bīnguǎn	西大街	Xī Dàjiē
			新青年巷	Xīn Qīngnián Xiàng
			钟楼路	Zhōnglóu Lù

Gǔ Zhōnglóu and Dàyún Sì

Open 8–5; adm ¥10 ($1.25).

古钟楼，大云寺

Turn left out of the museum and left at the corner. Cross Dōng Dàjiē and go straight on up Guǎngmíng Xiàng, looking left until you see an opportunity to turn towards the Bell Tower down Zhōnglóu Lù (the *Gǔ* in the name simply means 'ancient').

The Bell Tower is part of a small temple group, the remains of an important Táng institution, now with a museum-like atmosphere and mostly used as a social centre. The Xī Xià stele in the Wén Miào was discovered here. A map on the wall of the right-hand side of the interior of the first hall indicates numerous small cave sites outside the town, but these are in a poor state of repair, and difficult to access. The tower can be climbed by a staircase which winds round the plinth. Wooden stairs lead to the upper floor where the *xiǎo zhōng* (daybreak bell) still hangs, covered in Buddhist images. The Kumarajiva Pagoda can be seen in the distance to the west, across a vista of mud-walled houses.

Luóshí Sì Tǎ (Kumarajiva Pagoda)

罗什寺塔

Turn right out of the temple and continue west along Zhōnglóu Lù crossing Hépíng Lù, and turn right up Běi Dàjiē. The pagoda's top can be seen to the left. It actually stands in the compound of a high-walled prison behind the PSB office, and the best view is from a gate in the north side. Kumarajiva was a Buddhist monk from Kuqa in Xīnjiāng, who became one of the most important translators of Buddhist texts from Sanskrit into Chinese, active in Xī'ān between around AD 402 and 413. Prior to this he taught in Wǔwēi and the 12-storey, 32m, octagonal, brick pagoda, hung with bells, was built later during the Táng to honour him. Part of his fame rests on his insistence on not translating the texts word for word, but on conveying the *meaning* of the Sanskrit, reducing the number of technical terms, and borrowing more familiar expressions that already existed in Chinese Daoism. Legend has it that he claimed that if his translations were free of distortion, his tongue would not rot after his death. The original purpose of pagodas was to house sacred texts and relics, and the same legend has it that this one houses Kumarijiva's still immaculate tongue.

Léitái Hàn Mù

Open 8–6; adm ¥20 ($2.50).

雷台汉墓

This tomb beneath a small group of temple buildings mounted on an earthen terrace is 20 minutes' walk north from the centre. At the major junction with Běiguān Xī and Dōnglù, you are about halfway there. Keep looking to the right and for a vertical sign with the Léitái characters on it. Turn right into a broad path immediately before a series of new shops.

In the first courtyard at the top of the stairs, the left-hand building contains a small exhibition of currency from cowrie shells to the coins of the Republic, and the rearmost hall contains some modern statues and a small collection of Xī Xià dynasty artefacts, mostly ceramics and small paintings on wooden tablets. Upstairs there are ceramics from other periods.

The terrace is thought to date from the Western Jīn (AD 265–316) while the halls themselves originally date from the Míng (1368–1644). The tomb below is Later (Eastern) Hàn, probably 2nd century, and belonged to an unknown Hàn official. Coming down from the terrace, turn left and walk around its base to find a door giving access to the tomb itself, which has a short concrete ramp leading to a series of brick-lined, small, domed chambers, connected by very low arches, and at the end a small set of replica tomb figures. Part of this space had long been used for storage, but the tomb itself was rediscovered only in 1969.

Where to Stay

Wŭwēi does have several new hotels usually willing to deal fairly with foreign visitors, but none is allowed to accept them. Only two older hotels do so, and both charge foreigners double prices. Attempts to negotiate these downwards are usually successful, but the staff become extremely exasperated at your stupidity: 'You can't pay that little because you're *foreign.*' The **Tiānmǎ Bīnguǎn**, 30mins walk north of the railway station at the junction of Dōng Dàjiē and Shènglì Lù, ✆ and ✆ 221 2356, is the better of the two hotels, but rarely full and with an absurd idea of what it can reasonably charge. First asking prices are ¥250 ($30) for an older double with bath but no lift, and which may be on the *6th* floor of the older of the hotel's two buildings. The newer building has a lift but a standard double is ¥388 ($47), a suite ¥522 ($63). There are triples with common bath in the older building for ¥180 ($22). Tough negotiation (but with a smile) may get you the older double for ¥130 ($16), and the newer for ¥150 ($18). There is hot water three times a day. Just east of the centre, the **Liángzhōu Bīnguǎn**, ✆ 221 2711, ✆ 221 3008, has a wider variety of choice in three buildings, but will only allow 'foreign guests' to pay $22 or ¥180 for a plain but acceptable double, $30 for a suite. The double can be negotiated down to around ¥120 ($15)—Chinese pay ¥98. The **Huáfēng Fàndiàn** on the opposite side of Xī Dàjiē from the Tiānmǎ is not licensed to accept foreigners, but may let you in for ¥66 ($8) per bed in a tiled-floor double—however you must pay for both beds.

Eating Out

There are plentiful standard Hàn restaurants, including a good one directly opposite the Liángzhōu Bīnguǎn which has upmarket atmosphere and service but reasonable prices. The most interesting food appears on almost the entire length of Xī Dàjiē at night, with excellent *guōtiē* (fried dumplings) for ¥3, quail egg soup, and all kinds of noodles, together with open-air karaoke stalls serving large mugs of Chinese lager.

Zhāngyè

张掖　　The road to Zhāngyè passes through areas long used for breeding the 'heavenly horses' which, after considerable military expenditure, were finally acquired by the Chinese from the petty kingdoms of Central Asia during the Hàn dynasty. The corridor is wide and lush enough to continue to support horse breeding.

Another military outpost established at the time of the Hàn Emperor Wǔdì, its position near the upper end of the Héxī corridor ensured that it prospered and declined along with the Silk Routes, and saw many famous visitors: Zhāng Qiān passed this way going to investigate the Western Regions for Wǔdì, and Bān Chāo came through later on his way to regain control of them. Buddhist monks Fǎxiǎn and Xuánzàng passed through on their way to look for Buddhist texts in India, and hosts of others passed by on their way to Cháng'ān (Xī'ān) with merchandise, especially during the Táng. Master merchant (or, at any rate, the son of one) Marco Polo is supposed to have spent a year here. Polo called Zhāngyè *Campichu*, his version of its ancient name of Gānzhōu. His description of the behaviour of the monks identified them as being the clergy of Tibetan Buddhism, from their observation of certain fasts. As at Wǔwēi, the people are described as Christian and Saracen, as well as Buddhist. In Polo's day the city was again part of a unified China under Mongol rule, but prior to that it had belonged to the Tanguts who had wrested it away from the Uighurs in 1031. The Mongols almost completely eliminated the Tanguts in around 1226. There are still Huí, Mǎn (Manchu), Tibetan and Yugur (Yùgù—'Yellow Uighur') minorities in the region today, as there are in most of the cities on this route, although the overwhelming majority is now Hàn.

Several of the late 19th- and early 20th-century archaeologists and explorers passed through, too: Stein in 1907 and 1914, Langdon Warner in 1926, and Hedin on more than one occasion, including 1933 and 1934 while he was surveying the feasibility of building a proper motor road along the old Silk Route for the Nationalist government in Nánjīng, which led to the building of the modern route. Today's Zhāngyè, having been industrialized, can no longer be admired as the pretty, green oasis that it once was, but the city is of a digestible size, its sights in easy walking distance of one another, and worth the attention of the modern traveller who wants less-visited destinations without too much inconvenience.

Getting to and from Zhāngyè

by train

All trains to and from Ürümqi stop at Zhāngyè, and so it is possible to go as far as Běijīng, Shànghǎi, Chéngdū, Xī'ān and many other cities without changing. *See* the Lánzhōu and Wǔwēi 'Getting to and from' sections for more details. However, Zhāngyè station is unwilling to sell you hard or soft sleepers, so the only option is to buy a hard seat ticket and hope to upgrade on the train.

by bus

There are buses to Lánzhōu (518km, ¥74.80), Dūnhuáng (630km, ¥90/$11), Ānxī (513km, ¥74.80/$9), Jiāyùguān (249km, ¥37/$4.50), Jiǔquán (249km, ¥33/$4), Wǔwēi (166km, ¥24.20/$3), all of which are twice the Chinese price, and assume you have already purchased the Gānsù insurance. There is also a tourist ticket to Mǎtí Sì (62km) for ¥12 *return*, but the South bus station sells the Chinese one-way tickets for ¥5.50. There are also more expensive sleeper buses on the longer routes. The main long-distance bus station is in the west almost opposite the Sùnán Mínzú Fàndiàn. Departures from the south bus station often call here, including those that go to Mǎtí.

Getting Around

Zhāngyè's centre is clearly marked by the Drum and Bell Tower. Built in 1507, this is the Héxī Corridor's largest, but it is not open for climbing and the passages beneath it are blocked and used as a bicycle shop. Almost everything of interest to the visitor is located south and west of here. From the main long-distance bus station turn right and then left after the Sùnán Mínzú Fàndiàn to see the Tower in front of you two blocks away to the east. All sights within the town are

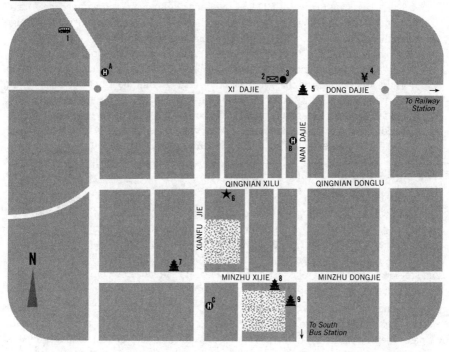

Zhāngyè

KEY

长途汽车站	1	Long-distance bus station Chángtú qìchēzhàn
邮电局	2	Post and telephone office Yóudiànjú
新华书店	3	Xīnhuá Bookshop Xīnhuá Shūdiàn
中国银行	4	Bank of China Zhōngguó Yínháng
鼓钟楼	5	Drum and Bell Tower Gǔ Zhōng Lóu
公安局	6	PSB Gōng'ānjú
万寿寺, 木塔	7	Wànshòu Sì, Mùtǎ
大佛寺	8	Dàfó Sì Big Buddha Temple
文化馆	9	Wénhuà Guǎn

HOTELS AND RESTAURANTS

肃南民族饭店	A	Sùnán Mínzú Fàndiàn
甘州宾馆	B	Gānzhōu Bīnguǎn
张掖宾馆	C	Zhāngyè Bīnguǎn

STREET NAMES

东、南、西大街	Dōng/Nán/Xī Dàjiē
民主东、西街	Mínzhǔ Dōng/Xījiē
青年东、西路	Qīngnián Dōng/Xīlù
县府街	Xiànfǔ Jiē

reachable on foot, but there are taxis, motortricycles, cycle rickshaws, and mutant hybrid vehicles outside the bus stations, railway stations and the hotels. These have neither meters nor any sense of honesty, so bargain hard. Minibuses run between the railway station, which is about 5km northeast of the centre, and the long-distance bus station for ¥1.

There is a local branch of **CITS** in the Zhāngyè Bīnguǎn, and another local travel agency in the Gānzhōu Bīnguǎn. The branch of the Bank of China which does **foreign exchange** is just east of the centre. The **post and telephone** office (Yóudiànjú) is on the same street, just west of the centre (*open for post 8am–8pm, and telephone 8am–9pm*). **Film** and developing are available at various shops around the post office. There are no **maps** of Zhāngyè, only of the district, from the Xīnhuá Shūdiàn next to the post office. A glossy sketch map of the area with photographs of major sights and a brief history in inaccurate English can be bought for ¥3 from the entrance to the Big Buddha Temple. **Visa extensions** and **permits** to visit Mǎtí Sì can be obtained from Room 220 on the fourth floor of the PSB building on Qīngnián Xīlù.

Dàfó Sì (Big Buddha Temple)   大佛寺

Open 8–6; adm ¥22.

This extensive temple with its multi-eaved buildings, which claims somewhat dubiously to be the largest in Gānsù, was begun in 1098 under the Xī Xià, and expanded further under the Míng and the Qīng. The main central building contains the largest reclining Buddha in China. Although its eyes are wide open, this 34.5m-long colossus, 7.5m wide at the shoulders, is for some reason often referred to as a sleeping Buddha. It is attended by upright statues of disciples and Buddhist saints (*luóhàn*, or, in Sanskrit, *Arhat*).

Legends about the temple say that it was Yuán Emperor Kublai Khan's birthplace, and that his mother was brought here to lie in state after her death. Both stories are mentioned (in Chinese—despite paying 3½ times the Chinese price to enter you will find nothing in English) in one hall to the left containing a small exhibition of archaeological finds from the area. There are also various stelae in the shadows of the temples. The buildings themselves have undergone heavy-handed restoration, and the site has been artificially disconnected from the stupa and other buildings in what is now the **Wénhuà Guǎn**.

To gain access turn right out of the temple and right along Nán Dàjiē. The buildings here, including several small pavilions, gates and halls, have been left unrestored in modern times, the finely detailed paintings on their panels and beams now flaking. The halls function as a social centre, and the ornate entrance gatehouse is used for showing martial arts videos. Old men play *májiàng* and Chinese chess (*xiàngqí*) at tables in shady corners.

Wànshòu Sì, Mù Tǎ   万寿寺, 木塔

Although the Longevity Temple has a main gate on Xiànfǔ Jiē it can only be reached through the yard of a school on its south side in Mínzhǔ Xījiē. Get the attention of the gatekeeper on the left as you enter, although as an object of unavoidable interest to swarms of children you'll probably already have it, and point at the pagoda which can be seen peering over the top of the school buildings, and which is the main point of interest. The wood and brick pagoda is an octagonal nine-storey tower, erected in AD 582, each corner decorated with dragon heads biting pearls. Both the pagoda and the adjacent temple buildings are decayed without being decrepit, and all are locked. The decay is somehow pleasing, and the lack of other visitors, guides, souvenir sellers and entrance fees delightful.

Mǎtí Sì (Horse's Hoof Temple)

马蹄寺

The village of Mǎtí is about 1¾ hours and 62km by bus from the south bus station (departs 3pm) or the main long-distance station (3.30pm). Aliens' Travel Permits (*wàiguórén lǚxíngzhèng*) must be bought from the same PSB office as that handling visa extensions (¥10/$1.25 per person). You will need to charter a taxi, use the services of CITS or similar, or stay two nights, since the bus back to Zhāngyè leaves at around 7am. Make sure your permit is made out for the right dates. There is basic bathroomless accommodation at various *lǚshè* for around ¥15 ($2) per person, including at the bus station itself. These are concrete-floored rooms with a door opening directly onto the bus yard, and a coal stove in each (Mǎtí is considerably higher and cooler than Zhāngyè). Hot water is provided in basins.

The temple is once again active, with visiting teachers from the Labrang Monastery at Xiàhé, and between 30 and 40 Buddhist lamas of the Tibetan Yellow Hat sect, who estimate that they receive fewer than 400 visitors per annum. The temple stands above the now mostly Hàn Mǎtí village. The road to the village runs beneath sandstone cliffs riddled with caves and mostly statueless niches, reached by narrow tracks. Although the main entrance is lower down, the main temple and its attendant buildings can be reached from a signed footpath leading from the centre of the village, winding around the cliff. The **Mǎtí Sì** itself is hewn from the cliff and features a glass-covered horseshoe-shaped mark in the stone of the floor, supposed to be the imprint of a supernatural steed indicating the place where a lamasery should be built. Aurel Stein visited here in 1914, as did the missionaries Mildred Cable and two sisters named French who passed up and down this route five times between 1923 and 1936. They commented on various treasures including a jewelled saddle and royal robe presented by the Qiánlóng emperor (1711–99), and a secret grotto containing the fantastic costumes used in Buddhist ceremonial dances. Most of the interior statuary is modern but traces of original fresco work from the Míng period survive on either side of the entrance. (Free, but donation welcome.) Other adjacent caves have only smashed remnants of their original statuary, or reproductions. Most interesting are the **Sānshísān Tiān Shíkū** (33 Heaven Caves), which resemble the Hanging Monastery near Dàtóng, except that connection between the temples is by steep tubular passages and stairwells cut through the rock itself, and for the nimble only. From below the tiny balconies appear to have been glued to the cliff-face. ¥3.

Despite the wrecking by Cultural Revolution vandals, this site is easy to reach and worth visiting, having an air of sincerity lacking at many more popular temples and cave sights.

Wooden pagoda, Wànshòu Sì

There are three hotels which accept foreigners. The plushest is the fairly new **Zhāngyè Bīnguǎn**, southwest of the centre, ☎ 212601, ✉ 213806, which is the tour group choice, with doubles with bath at ¥260 ($32), common bath triples at ¥40 ($5) per bed, and ¥30 ($4) in quads. The main reception is round to the right-hand side. The friendly **Gānzhōu Bīnguǎn** just south of the drum-bell tower in Nán Dàjiē, ☎ 214227, ✉ 212402, is fairly comfortable if simple, with suites at ¥128 ($16), common bath doubles at ¥28 ($3.50) per bed, triples ¥18 ($2.50) per bed, and quads ¥12 ($1.50). This is probably the best choice for the budget traveller, although the **Sùnán Mínzú Fàndiàn** is more convenient for the main bus station. This is a somewhat cheerless hotel, with suites for ¥70 ($8.50), common bath doubles for ¥46, triples with varying levels of comfort for ¥24–18 ($2–2.50), and quads for ¥14 ($2) per bed.

Food in Zhāngyè is simple. Each of the hotels has at least one dining room, that at the Sùnán Mínzú Fàndiàn having a separate entrance to the left. As usual, other restaurants have menus priced according to the quantity of mirror glass. The cheapest eating is at a row of standard Hàn restaurants and noodle shops opposite the main bus station.

Jiǔquán

酒泉 Benedict de Goës, a Jesuit lay brother from Lahore (1562–1607), breathed his last here after a five-year journey from Agra. Attempting to reach fellow Jesuits in Běijīng, he was swindled out of his money and died destitute. While the much earlier traveller William of Rubruck is said to have been the first to identify Cathay with the Seres of antiquity, de Goës is credited with finally confirming that the Cathay of ancient tradition and overland routes was the same place as the China which traders and his colleagues had reached by sea. The location of his grave is now unknown, but was said to have been marked only with a mound of stones.

Marco Polo called Jiǔquán 'Sukchur', his version of its alternative name of Sùzhōu, and commented on its famous rhubarb, another product to travel via the Silk Routes to the West. One tradition has it that when Genghis Khan was pillaging Tangut, one of his ministers would only take Chinese books and rhubarb, later achieving hero status by using it to save the lives of soldiers when an epidemic broke out in the army. In the 19th century the Qīng, perceiving the popularity of rhubarb with British troops, threatened to withdraw supplies in the belief that constipation would undermine the foreigners' military superiority.

The town was founded in around 121–115 BC, by Huò Qùbìng, the same Hàn general responsible for inflicting major defeats on the Xiōngnú 'barbarians'. The true facts of his life and military successes are embroidered with numerous folk tales, and he is credited with the naming of Jiǔquán. While Huò was here, the Emperor Wǔdì is said to have sent him a jar of wine in recognition of his achievements. To share the accolade he poured the wine into a local spring so that all his soldiers could taste it. Jiǔquán means 'Wine Spring'. Huò died at only 24, and is buried west of Xī'ān in a tomb said to resemble the Qílián Shān, the mountains he cleared of Xiōngnú to make the Héxī Corridor safe for traffic.

In modern times when Russia almost ran Xīnjiāng, its power extended as far as the establishment of a consulate here from 1881. Aurel Stein passed through in 1907 and again in 1914, and Langdon Warner spent ten days here in 1923. The most up-to-date aspect of Jiǔquán is its satellite launching centre, outside town and certainly *not* open to visitors. With its low labour and production costs, China has been able to undercut the launch prices of developed nations, but with mixed success. A Chinese spy satellite which fell back to earth in 1996 after only four years of use had a heat shield made from oak planks. However, by the end of 1996 China had successfully placed 10 foreign satellites in orbit and is expected to launch 30 more by the end of the century. Gānsù is rumoured to hold other military secrets.

Jiǔquán is a small but bustling town with the usual drum tower in the centre, and little to see. A more important administrative centre than better-known Jiāyùguān, it can easily be seen as a day, or half-day trip from there.

Getting to and from Jiǔquán

by air

The nearest airport is at Jiāyùguān, although there is a CAAC booking office next to the Jiǔquán Bīnguǎn.

by train

All trains in both directions stop at Jiǔquán, which is an important administrative centre. Buses to the railway station, 12km outside town, go from just to the west of the bus station, departing when full, for ¥1.

by bus

The main bus station is three blocks south of the centre on the corner of Nán Dàjiē and Jūnmín Tuánjié Lù. They may attempt to charge double or may forget until you are on the bus, in which case stand (or sit) your ground and refuse to pay—this is merely an initiative of individual xenophobes. There are local minibuses (*miànbāochē*) to Jiāyùguān from a corner two blocks to the west of the centre, ¥2.

There are buses to Lánzhōu at 10am, 4.30pm, 5.30pm, and 6.30pm (744km, ¥53.50), to Jiāyùguān (25km, ¥2), Ānxī (297km, ¥20.60/$2.50), Dūnhuáng at 8am and 11am (404km, ¥29), Zhāngyè (226km, ¥16.80/$2), and Wǔwēi (461km, ¥34.20).

Getting Around

The centre of town is clearly marked by the Bell Tower, and everything is within walking distance—the furthest destination is the park. There is one east–west bus route served by buses and minibuses for 5 *máo* flat fare, from just east of where the minibus from Jiāyùguān drops you and stops at the museum and the Jiǔquán Yuán.

Jiǔquán © (0937)   ### Tourist Information

There are local versions of **CITS** in both hotels. The **Bank of China** (*open 8–12 and 2.30–6*) is just north of the centre. They are unused to foreigners, and changing money can take a while. The **post and telephone** office (*open Mon–Fri, 8–7.30*) is on the northeast corner, **film and developing** and the **Xīnhuá Shūdiàn** with Chinese street maps of Jiǔquán and neighbouring cities can be found just to the west. The **PSB** is three blocks to the east (*open Mon-Fri 8.30–12 and 2.30–5.30*).

Zhōnglóu (Bell Tower) 钟楼

The tower marks the centre of this bustling town, and while it may not be possible to climb it (the gate to the stairs is on the east side), you can walk through the passages underneath, unlike the tower in Zhāngyè. This is a 1905 reconstruction of an earlier tower built on the site of a still earlier watchtower. Inscriptions on each side highlight what's to be found in each direction, reading right to left: the East greets China's mountains (or perhaps Huá Shān in particular—northeast of Xī'ān); the South gazes towards the Qílián Shān; the West reaches for Yīwú (an ancient name for Hāmì); the North towards the desert (the Gobi).

Jiǔquán Shì Bówùguǎn 酒泉市博物馆

Open 8–12 and 3–5, Sun 10–5; closed Sat; adm ¥3.

This small but interesting museum is 15mins walk east of the centre down Dōng Dàjiē, which turns into Gōngyuán Lù, and on the north side of the road. There is the usual presentation of local finds in chronological order with site photos and maps. The collection includes pottery, early bronzes, tomb figures, administrative orders on bamboo strips, Qīng ceramic figures, and coins. There are also reproductions of some of the splendid wall paintings from the Dōngjìn Bìhuà Mù, Eastern Jìn dynasty mural tomb (AD 317–420), and a model showing the layout. Unfortunately this tomb, one of a group of Wèi and Jìn tombs often known as Dìxià Huàláng ('Underground Art Gallery'), the major attraction of the area, has now been closed.

Jiǔquán Yuán 酒泉园

Open daylight hours; adm ¥3.

Another 10mins beyond the museum, this park was the location of the legendary wine donation incident after which the city is named. The source of the single spring (there were once three) is now walled, and flows into a small lake with a central island reached by a zigzag bridge (because various Chinese demons can only travel in straight lines). Otherwise this is the typical Chinese park once immensely popular but now losing out to television and video games, with a hall of mirrors, miniature railway, and some older former temple buildings occupied with other diversions, all with their own entrance fees. The park is pleasingly dismal and almost deserted in winter. On the walk there you pass, appropriately, a distillery.

Around Jiǔquán

Wénshū Shān Shíkū 文殊山石窟

The caves are about 15km outside the city to the south, and only reachable by taxi. These can be found parked in a group outside the department store at the northwest corner of the bell tower. Negotiating is difficult, and no-one will take you there, wait for an hour, and return for less than ¥80 ($10).

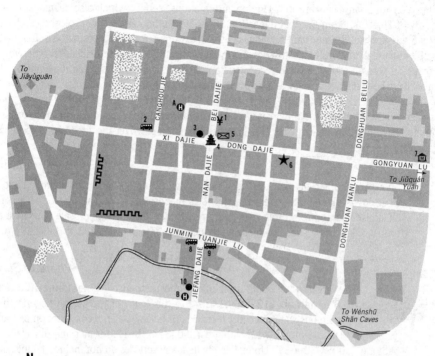

N

Jiǔquán

The Wénshū Shān caves are in a Uighur 'autonomous' county which also seems to have plenty of Tibetans. From the Wèi dynasties (386–557) to the Táng (618–906), the complex was the region's most important religious centre. The front part of the mountain is still dotted with temples, all modern reconstructions. The caves are at the rear, and reached by a network of narrow paths. Restoration and reconstruction are under way here, too, and some of the caves have been filled with new and garish statuary. Two caves are reasonably well preserved with clay Northern Wèi statuary, and Yuán and Míng murals, but this is really a trip for the specialist only. While for the time being entrance is free, the site is clearly being tarted up for promotion to tourists. A nearby military base casts an extra pall over the already depressingly gaunt hillside.

Shopping

Jiǔquán is another city that produces 'night-glowing cups'—traditional stemmed cups with bowls like slightly oversized thimbles made from jade. The black and green Qílián jade comes from three sites in the region, and the cups are on sale anywhere a tourist might pass. There's a factory producing them one block east of the centre on the south side of Dōng Dàjiē.

Where to Stay

The largest, most comfortable, and most expensive hotel is the **Jiǔquán Bīnguǎn**, ✆ 612554/614234, to the south of the centre beyond the main bus station, on the west side of Jiěfàng Dàjiē, a continuation of Nán Dàjiē. Doubles with bath are ¥200 ($24). Beds in triples and quads with bath are ¥60 ($7.50) each. Unfortunately its many services do not include telling the truth about anything if it might profit the hotel to lie. On those grounds at least, the **Jīnquán Bīnguǎn**, ✆ 612859/612271, is a better choice. Much more central, it's reached by walking north from the centre and taking the first left, or west from the centre and taking the first right. A double with bath is ¥180 ($22), a bed in a triple is ¥50 ($6), and in a seven-bed dorm ¥30 ($4).

Eating Out

Jiǔquán has a number of standard Hàn restaurants in Xī Dàjiē, Dōng Dàjiē on the way to the museum, and Nán Dàjiē around the bus station.

Jiāyùguān

嘉峪关 The missionaries Cable and French passed through Jiāyùguān in the 1920s and '30s, and described three types of people within the fortress walls: the resident traders who never left the place and took no interest in the outside world, the soldiers who hated such a remote posting and feared the desert, and the travellers who were on their way from all over China to its remotest frontier. At the time of the fort's construction in 1372, the Chinese viewed Jiāyùguān as marking the beginning of their version of the Wild West. It was much the same in Cable and French's time: Xīnjiāng was being ruled independently of the Nationalist government, there were frequent uprisings in Hāmì and beyond, and communication with Ürümqi was intermittent. The fort stood almost surrounded by great desert desolation, in which even the intrepid and emperor-defying monk Xuánzàng nearly lost heart and turned back. The fort guards a pass through the Qílián Shān and Hēi Shān, their high points spiky with beacon towers to warn of trouble coming from the west.

For much of Chinese history, after death by decapitation or strangulation, the next degree of punishment listed in the legal code was exile for life, with three levels of severity measured in *lǐ* (approximately half a kilometre). During the Qīng dynasty this was further refined to five levels and one supplementary level: very near banishment (2000 *lǐ*), nearby frontier (2500 *lǐ*), distant frontier (4000 *lǐ*), furthest frontier (4000 *lǐ*), a malarial region (also 4000 *lǐ*), and banishment to serve as a slave in a Manchu military post. In a country as large as China, exile did not mean going abroad, but it did mean going beyond the crowded and familiar world of the East, to areas full of hideous barbarians with big noses, repulsive customs, and incomprehensible languages. It often meant deportation up the funnel of the Héxī Corridor to be spat out into the emptiness beyond Jiāyùguān. It was not only criminals who passed through, but also those who had fallen foul of court intrigues or who were simply victims of China's brutal and corrupt justice system. The walls of Jiāyùguān represented their last view of China, and the more literary recorded their sorrows on its grey stones.

Jiāyùguān has been rapidly developing into a small industrial city where the cost of living and the wages are said to be higher even than Xī'ān. Further industrialization is expected with the building of a multi-billion-dollar steel plant, and many factories are set firmly between the city and its major attraction, Jiāyùguān Fort. Industry tends to gobble up the available electricity, and there are regular power cuts in the hotels, especially in winter. There is one long, broad, main street with most of the restaurants, hotels, shops and markets, and a quiet but prosperous air. Accommodation is plentiful and cheap, getting around is easy, and most visitors consider the elaborate and substantial Míng dynasty fort guarding one of the Great Wall's ends to be exactly their idea of China.

Getting to and from Jiāyùguān

by air

Jiāyùguān has summer air connections to Dūnhuáng (three times weekly) and Lánzhōu (daily) with onward connections to major cities elsewhere in China. The number of flights is sharply reduced in winter. The CAAC office (*open 8.30–12 and 2.30–6; closed Sun*) is on the west side of Xīnhuá Nánlù, just south of the main island. The airport is 15km outside town, and is reached by CAAC bus (¥6). Services from here go by the name of China Northwest Airlines, and a ticket to Dūnhuáng is ¥370.

by train

Jiāyùguān's station is 5km southwest of the city, and its staff are deeply uncooperative and unhelpful, although the situation is not helped by the fact that their allocation of hard and soft sleepers is very small, and only for certain trains. They will sell unnumbered hard seat tickets on the day of travel, which you can attempt to upgrade on the train itself (they only have six numbered hard seats per train). For anything else, having no *guānxì* (connections, influence) you had better rely on CITS. Their service charge is ¥40 ($5) per ticket, and the station charges a further ¥10 ($1.25) commission for doing its job. Give as many days' notice as possible. Hard sleepers to Ürümqi cost around ¥138 ($17), and to Lánzhōu around ¥108 ($13). Soft sleepers to Lánzhōu are around ¥172. There are six trains daily to Ürümqi. Going east there are departures to Shànghǎi (54), Xī'ān (98, 144 and 70, which continues to Běijīng), Lánzhōu (244, 502 and most other eastbound trains). The station is reached by bus no.1, or buses with *hǒuchēzhàn* written on the front, which take a similar route (¥1).

by bus

Jiāyùguān's bus station charges foreigners double for sleeper buses and Chinese prices for the rest. A sleeper bus to Lánzhōu is ¥180 ($22) for foreigners, plus ¥30–33 for the Gānsù insurance if you don't have it. The PICC building is diagonally opposite the Xióngguān Hotel but both they and the bus station prefer that you buy the insurance from travel agents at the Jiāyùguān or Chángchéng Hotels, hence the extra ¥3 commission. The bus station is on the junction of Lánxīn Gōnglù and Shènglì Nánlù, and is connected to the railway station by bus 1 and private minibuses (¥1). Other destinations include Ānxī (266km, ¥19.10/$2.50), four departures to Dūnhuáng from 9am (383km, ¥27.50/$3.50), five morning departures to Zhāngyè from 8.10am (250km, ¥18.50/$2.50), to Wǔwēi at 6.30am and 9am (485km, ¥35.80/¥4.50), five afternoon departures to Lánzhōu (765km, ¥56.50/$7) plus the sleeper bus at 6.10pm. There's also a bus direct to Línxià at 12 noon. Private minibuses to Jiǔquán run past the front of the bus station for ¥2 (extra for luggage if it's taking up seats). The ticket office opens at 6am and is supposed to stay open until 6.30pm but before that the bus station converts itself into a roller disco.

Getting Around

The centre of town is a roundabout with the Jiāyùguān Hotel and the City Post and Telecommunications Building (Shì Yóudiànjú). The roughly north–south road is Xīnhuá Běi/Nánlù, and the west–east is Xióngguān Xī/Dōnglù. There are three bus routes supported by minibuses (*miànbāochē*). Routes 1 and 2 both run north–south, the 1 going via the long-distance bus station, and the Qīngnián and Chángchéng Hotels, and ending at the railway station. The 2 goes straight south passing one block to the east of those hotels, and looping to terminate outside the more southerly Xīnhuá Shūdiàn. Route 3 goes west from the centre to the fort, but only runs in summer. Most trips are ¥1, but to the Fort, ¥2. Other options include taxis, pedicabs and motortricycles, all without meters. For taxis, minimum charges should be between ¥6 and ¥11 depending on the vehicle, and ¥1–2 per kilometre, but in fact you'll have to agree a price before setting out. Very hard bargaining may get you out to the fort and back for ¥40 ($5) with a one-hour wait. Bicycle hire is available from most hotels at ¥1 per hour, but the old boneshakers are very poorly maintained. The Jiāyùguān Hotel has similar bikes for ¥2 an hour, and slightly better ones for ¥3.

Jiāyùguān ℗ (0936)   Tourist Information

CITS, CTS, and CYTS have a joint venture in a new building on the east side of Shènglì Běilù, just north of Xióngguān Xīlù. They also have an office in the Jiāyùguān Bīnguǎn, run by the pleasant and efficient Qín Jiǎn (℗ 226598, ℗/℗ 226931, ℗ 222582). One-day tours are run which include the Overhanging Great Wall, the First Beacon Tower, the Museum and Jiāyùguān Pass for around ¥15 ($2) per person.

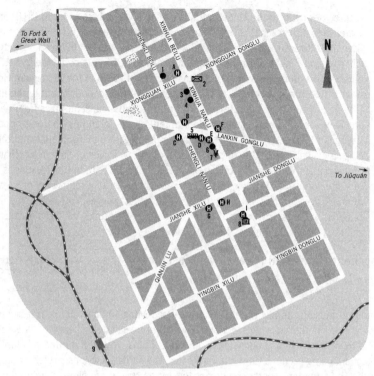

KEY

中国国际旅行社   1   CITS
Zhōngguó Guójì Lǚxíngshè

邮电局   2   Post and telephone office
Yóudiànjú

中国民航   3   CAAC
Zhōngguó Mínháng

新华书店   4   Xīnhuá Bookshop
Xīnhuá Shūdiàn

长途汽车站   5   Long-distance bus station
Chángtú qìchēzhàn

中国人民保险公司   6   PICC
Zhōngguó Rénmín Bǎoxiǎn Gōngsī

中国银行   7   Bank of China
Zhōngguó Yínháng

嘉峪关长城博物馆   8   Jiāyùguān Chángchéng Bówùguǎn

火车站   9   Railway station
Huǒchēzhàn

HOTELS AND RESTAURANTS

嘉峪关宾馆   A   Jiāyùguān Bīnguǎn

迎宾宾馆   B   Yíngbīn Bīnguǎn

物贸宾馆   C   Wùmào Bīnguǎn

嘉乐宾馆   D   Jiālè Bīnguǎn

交通宾馆   E   Jiāotōng Bīnguǎn

雄关宾馆   F   Xióngguān Bīnguǎn

长城宾馆   G   Chángchéng Bīnguǎn

青年宾馆   H   Qīngnián Bīnguǎn

旅游宾馆   I   Lǚyóu Bīnguǎn

STREET NAMES

建设西、东路   Jiànshè Xī/Dōnglù

兰新公路   Lánxīn Gōnglù

前进路   Qiánjìn Lù

胜利南、北路   Shènglì Nán/Běilù

新华南、北路   Xīnhuá Nán/Běilù

雄关西、东路   Xióngguān Xī/Dōnglù

迎宾东、西路   Yíngbīn Dōng/Xīlù

Jiāyùguān

A three-hour trip to the Underground Art Gallery Tomb costs ¥150 ($18) for an 18-seater bus, also reachable from Jiǔquán, and worth seeing if it reopens (meanwhile Jiǔquán Museum offers a sample). There is a competing travel agency in the Chángchéng Bīnguǎn. The shiny marble **Bank of China** (*open Mon–Fri 9.30–5.30, Sat 10–4*) is on the west side of Xīnhuá Nánlù just south of the Xióngguān Hotel. The **post office** (*open 8.30–7 daily*) is on the central roundabout opposite the Jiāyùguān Hotel and you can make **international phone calls** and send faxes from here. **Film** and developing are available in department stores including the one opposite the Jiāyùguān Hotel. A good Chinese-language **map** of Jiāyùguān, Jiǔquán and other local cities is available from the Xīnhuá Shūdiàn on the west side of Xīnhuá Nánlù just south of the centre. **Visa extensions** are available from the PSB, but its location is a matter of some confusion. While some policemen direct you to a temporary office about 10 minutes' walk to the west along Jiànshè Xīlù, others suggest you look in the Jiāyùguān Bīnguǎn, where there was no office at the time of writing. Ask CITS or your hotel to call the PSB and ask them where they are.

Chángchéng Bówùguǎn (Great Wall Museum) 嘉峪关长城博物馆

Open 8–12 and 2.30–6, Sat and Sun 10–4; adm ¥10 ($1.25).

This modern museum thinks it's a bit of crenellated Míng Great Wall itself. It begins with a thorough photographic survey of sections of wall and free-standing beacon towers of various ages and in various states of decomposition across China. A wall-mounted relief map shows various overlapping sections from different dates, the earliest sections stretching surprisingly far south. The attendant operates switches to turn on strings of coloured lights showing the different routes (Hàn dynasty green, newer Míng route red). Models, full-scale reproductions, and photographs show different wall construction methods. A staircase at the rear takes you upstairs to a section dealing with the Míng-era rerouted and reconditioned wall. A further large relief map shows the relationship of Jiāyùguān to remaining sections of different eras, neighbouring beacon towers and the fort. It's also possible to climb to the roof for a view across town.

Around Jiāyùguān

Jiāyùguān Chénglóu (Jiāyùguān Fort) 嘉峪关城楼

Open 8–12.30 and 2.30–6; adm ¥20 ($2.50).

Separated from downtown by a mixture of desert and industry, in summer the fort can be reached by minibus no.3 from Xióngguān Xīlù outside the Jiāyùguān Bīnguǎn, ¥1. Otherwise it's a 5km cycle ride or walk out on the Lánxīn Gōnglù, with a signposted right turn just after the railway bridge, and a left at the crossroads, although by this point the route is self-evident. The ticket office is on the left as you approach the outer walls.

If the most famous images of the Great Wall are those of its stone-clad and crenellated Míng dynasty sections, then Jiāyùguān Fort is perhaps the ultimate expression of this idea. Marking the end of the Míng dynasty rebuild, its triple-towered bulk resembles three of Xī'ān's city gates atop a knotted section of Wall. The final Míng sections run off towards the Qílián

mountains to the south and the Hēi Shān (Black Mountains) to the north, and make last surges up the mountainsides before petering out, as did Hàn influence at the time.

Entering the 10m-high 733m-long outer wall from the east, you first see a pavilion, theatre, and temple buildings, now mostly used to accommodate the staff, and then the first of the fort's three main 17m towers, each with three highly decorated storeys and flying eaves. Entrance to the entrapping rampart which projects in front of the gate tower, called the Guānghuà Mén, is from the south side, so that no direct frontal assault on the gate itself could be mounted, and fire could be poured down from four sides on attackers foolish enough to enter. Inside the inner wall, on the north side of the gate (turn right), the wall can be mounted by a ramp built to allow horses to be taken up to the battlements. At the corners and the halfway points of the north- and south-facing walls are further pavilioned watchtowers: the tower over the west gate, the Róuyuǎn Mén, with its own rampart extension and south-facing entrance point, exactly mirrors the gate in the east. Outside it, the outer wall comes much closer than it does on the east side, and is topped with its own tower directly in line with the other two, the Jiāyùguān Pass Gate, this time guarding a straight tunnel to the outside world. Cable and French noted that the residents preferred to avoid this gate, sometimes calling it the Gate of Sighs.

> The long archway was covered with writings, and anyone with suffi-
> cient knowledge to appreciate Chinese penmanship could see at once
> that these were the work of men of scholarship, who had fallen on an
> hour of deep distress. There were lines quoted from the Book of Odes,
> poems composed in the pure tradition of classic literature, and verses
> inspired by sorrow too heavy for the careful balance of literary values.

Mildred Cable with Francesca French, *The Gobi Desert*, 1942

These were the marks of those exiled for life. When Cable and French themselves left Jiāyùguān they were stopped by two soldiers, who led them to a place where a hollow had been made in the wall by the picking away of chunks of brick. One soldier told them, '"It is the custom that every traveller, as he goes outside the wall, should throw a stone at the fortress. If the stone rebounds he will come back safe and sound, but if not..." he left the doom unuttered.' The stones flung by the missionaries duly rebounded with a sound they described as 'like the cheeping of chicks'. Another popular story concerning the fort suggests a fine tradition of quantity surveying. The original builders are said to have calculated the number of bricks needed with such accuracy that when the fort was completed only one was remaining. This orphan brick can be seen sitting on a ledge on one side of the small tower overlooking the entrapping rampart outside the Róuyuǎn Mén.

Jiāyùguān Chángchéng ('Overhanging' Great Wall)　嘉峪关长城
Open daylight hours; ¥5.

The northwestern extremity of the Míng wall, built long after the fort in 1539 and completely restored in 1988, is about 6km north of it and is preceded by an unrestored section which can be followed along an uneven mud track. The original brick exterior of this section, like that of many others, was long ago taken away by peasants for building. Passages have been cut in the remains to allow tractors to pass through. When you reach a small village, turn right, and then left in the village itself when you see the final section of wall across the fields. This short section was completely reclad with brick in the Míng style and, starting off at desert level, climbs steeply up the appropriately named Hēi Shān or Black Mountains. The top gives impressive views of the emptiness surrounding the city.

Other Sights
Reaching all of these requires the use of a taxi or guided tour, or a lot of hard bicycling.

Hēi Shān Shí Kè Huàxiàng　黑山石刻画像
(Black Mountain Carved Portraits)
About 20km to the northwest of Jiāyùguān, a narrow gorge in the Hēi Shān is covered with carvings of hunters and their prey reminiscent of early European cave art, and probably made around the 5th–3rd century BC by the Yuèzhī people and the Xiōngnú who drove them out, until themselves temporarily evicted by Hàn general Huò Qùbìng (*see* p.190).

Dìxià Huàláng (Underground Art Gallery)　地下画廊
20km northeast of Jiāyùguān and closer to Jiǔquán, these small three-chambered brick-lined tombs have spectacularly decorated interiors, with images both on individual bricks and spread across large surfaces, showing scenes of daily life and dating from the Wèi (AD 220–65) and Jīn (265–420). The one tomb open to the public was recently closed due to fears of damage to the paintings. If it should reopen, CITS will know. There's a small display on the subject of the tombs at Jiǔquán Bówùguǎn.

Qīyī Bīngchuān (July 1st Glacier)　七一冰川
Beyond normal bicycling range at 116km southwest of Jiāyùguān, this is one of several Qílián Shān glaciers, supposedly named after the day it was 'discovered' in 1958. There's a trek along the edge of the glacier which is said to be more than 5000m above sea level. Warm clothing is advised, even at the height of summer.

Where to Stay

Jiāyùguān is another town where a host of new hotels now welcomes foreigners for the same prices as Chinese, offering better, brighter, cleaner rooms for as little as a quarter of the older, more decrepit, dirtier, and less friendly ones.

Of Jiāyùguān's older hotels, the plushest is the **Chángchéng Bīnguǎn** (Great Wall Hotel), ✆ 622 5266, ✉ 622 6306, on Jiànshè Xīlù, two blocks south of the bus station, and passed by buses from the railway station. It has postal and banking facilities and a travel service. Tour groups usually stay here. Doubles with bath are ¥200 ($24); triples ¥50 ($6) per bed, and quads ¥40 ($5). There are also dorm beds at ¥30 ($4). The building has pretensions to be a mini Jiāyùguān Fort, and contrasts oddly with the **Qīngnián Bīnguǎn** (Youth Hotel), ✆ 622 4671, opposite, which is a small, Disneyfied version of a European castle. This hotel was once the backpackers' favourite, but is becoming cagey about dormitories. Nevertheless it is bright and clean; beds in doubles are ¥50 ($6), and in triples ¥30 ($4), although you can do better in the new hotels. The **Jiāyùguān Bīnguǎn** on the central roundabout, ✆ 622 5804, ✉ 622 7174, is an older hotel undergoing the addition of a large extension. It's unusual in having hot water three times a day. Doubles with bath are ¥110 ($13.50) per bed (but they will try to make you buy the room), triples with common bath are ¥37, and basic quads ¥24. Some staff speak a little English and are friendly and polite, but at least one tells you frankly that she doesn't like foreigners. The rooms are dirty and the bathrooms unreliable. The **Xióngguān Bīnguǎn** should also be avoided. The few helpful staff are trampled on by the extremely discourteous majority, and in addition to the usual double price for foreigners, a ¥1 'service charge' is demanded for non-existent service.

Of the seven new hotels which opened in Jiāyùguān within a few months of each other in 1996, the simplest is the **Yíngbīn Bīnguǎn**, ✆ 628 3141, opposite the bus station. Bright, tiled doubles with bath are ¥30 ($4) per bed, and common bath triples ¥15 ($2). Diagonally opposite is the friendly, slightly more comfortable **Wùmào Bīnguǎn**, ✆ 622 7514, ✉ 622 6721, with suites for ¥240 ($29), doubles and triples with bath for ¥50 ($6) and ¥40 ($5) per bed, and common bath doubles for ¥20 ($2.50) per bed. Also near the bus station, the **Jiālè Bīnguǎn**, ✆ 623 4758, ✉ 628 1405, has doubles with bath for ¥35 ($4.50) per bed, and common bath doubles, triples and quads for ¥20 ($2.50), ¥15 ($2) and ¥12 ($1.50). The similar **Lǚyóu Bīnguǎn**, ✆ 628 6591, immediately north of the museum, has suites for ¥180 ($22), doubles with bath for ¥40 ($5) per bed, and common bath triples for ¥20 ($2.50). The **Jiāotōng Bīnguǎn**, ✆ 623 4407, on the corner of Lánxīn Gōnglù and Xīnhuá Nánlù, has suites for ¥288, doubles and triples with bath for ¥40 ($5) and ¥30 ($4). All of these have limited evening hot water for only an hour or two.

Eating Out

There are numerous Muslim and Hàn restaurants south of the centre, and restaurants in all the hotels. The one behind the Jiāyùguān Bīnguǎn was particularly pleasant, with friendly, efficient service, food prepared with more than the usual care, and low prices, but having recently expanded it seems to have gone downhill. It may nevertheless be worth investigating. Outside the hotels, the glitzier the exterior, the more you pay, but the quality of the food is not necessarily significantly better. The cheapest food is in the street market which crosses Xīnhuá Nánlù just north of the Xióngguān Bīnguǎn, with noodle restaurants, and small oval-shaped onion bread (*bǐng*) for sale, hot from the oven, in the market on the right-hand side of Xīnhuá Běilù beyond the Jiāyùguān Bīnguǎn, and on the corner of Xīnhuá Nánlù and Yíngbīn Dōnglù.

The Road to Dūnhuáng

At first the road from Jiāyùguān is bordered to the north by the aptly named Hēi Shān, Black Mountains, before these give way to the vast, flat, scrubby, peopleless emptiness, which exiled Chinese were right to fear. There are frequent beacon towers, some close to the road, and the occasional ruins of ancient cities. 50km beyond the new town of Yùmén Zhèn the road passes the still solid fortifications of a small town, possibly a garrison mentioned by Cable and French under the Mongolian name of Bulungir, thought to date back to one of the campaigns to regain control of Xīnjiāng in the 17th or 18th century. Once the campaign was over the town was abandoned. At the 1165km marker the less solid but immense sprawl of Qiáowān begins, which stretches for 10km alongside the road, and was built by the Qīng Emperor Kāngxī. On this route Cable and French also reported the existence of small, inward-looking villages which survived on selling thick crude oil from desert wells, and now several modern cities exist on refining oil from wells in the Qílián Shān, which is also piped to Lánzhōu.

After about six hours, you turn south off the road to Hāmì, and reach **Ānxī**, a possible base from which to visit the Yúlín Kū and Dōng Qiānfó Dòng (Elm Forest Caves, and East Thousand Buddha Caves) some 75 and 90km to the southeast respectively. However, Ānxī is not geared to receive visitors, and these caves are usually only open by special arrangement from the Dūnhuáng Research Institute. The bus conductress will be quite sure that you are getting off at the wrong place. There is a small, grim hotel opposite the bus station that will accept foreigners for between ¥8 and ¥14 per bed. Taxis are few, and prices quoted for the trip out to the caves high. (*See* p.212)

Beyond Ānxī there are further beacon towers to be seen and further fortifications at the 35km marker. The grimness of the landscape is relieved by the greenness of the Dūnhuáng oasis.

Dūnhuáng

敦煌　Dūnhuáng is mentioned by early visitors as being the first place where the east-bound traveller comes across Chinese peculiarities along with Chinese in any numbers. It's Táng name of Shāzhōu or 'sand district' describes it well, surrounded as it is by pebbly and sandy emptiness, and lapped by a sea of dunes.

Polo commented: 'The Idolators have a peculiar language, and are no traders, but live by their agriculture. They have a great many abbeys and minsters full of idols of sundry fashions, to which they pay great honour and reverence.' Amongst his many omissions were the nearby caves, the most extensive site in China, and a key stop for those entering and leaving the desert. It's odd, too, that he should describe the people as 'no traders', since Dūnhuáng stands at the mouth of the Héxī Corridor and was the meeting point of routes around the north and south of the Taklamakan; and while towns to the west might suffer from the increase in popularity of one route over that on which they sat, Dūnhuáng was almost assured of having merchandise continually changing hands and passing through. It was a place to acquire provisions before entering the desert and to rest after emerging from it.

The ruins of the original Hàn garrison town, founded in 121 BC, lie to the west and have mostly disappeared under the plough. Like the rest of the Héxī Corridor, Dūnhuáng subsequently came under Tibetan, Uighur and Xī Xià rule, slipping in and out of Chinese control until thoroughly resettled by the Qīng.

Modern Dūnhuáng is a town whose economy revolves around the tourism generated by the Mògāo caves, quite simply the most complete, least damaged, and most spectacular set in China. In a vain attempt to increase the number of nights visitors spend in the town additional tourist attractions have been developed, and some of the natural beauties of the nearby desert walled in so as to make the visitor pay to view them. Although the original connection to the southern route across the Lop desert is closed (and likely to remain so for the long half-life of certain radioactive materials), Dūnhuáng remains a major junction, with routes south and east to Xīníng in Qīnghǎi, south to Tibet, and south and west to Miran and Charklik.

Getting to and from Dūnhuáng

by air

The CAAC office is on the corner of Dōng Dàjiē and Dōnghuán Lù, close to the Dūnhuáng Bīnguǎn, © 882 2389 (*open 8.30–11.30 and 3–6*), and sells tickets for flights to Jiāyùguān (Wed and Sun, ¥370/$45) and Lánzhōu (daily and twice on Sundays, less in winter) (¥990/$120), and onwards to other major destinations. It runs a bus to the airport which is just past the turning to the Mògāo Caves, about 13km away, for ¥6.

by train

The station for Dūnhuáng is at Liǔyuán, 2½ to 3 hours and 130km away by bus or minibus, ¥10 ($1.25). Buses wait outside the station and drivers often accost travellers on the platform as they alight. Refuse demands for extra payment for baggage that you put on the roof. There are seven main westbound trains to Ürümqi (two of them going to Korla on alternate days), and six eastbound to Lánzhōu, four of which continue to Xī'ān, and one, the a/c 69, to Běijīng. To Ürümqi the most convenient train is the 143 at 13.59 which reaches Hāmì at 19.37, and Ürümqi at 06.32 the next morning. To Turpan the best train is the 243 at 18.08, which arrives at 07.50 the next day and reaches Ürümqi at 10.43. Buying tickets in Dūnhuáng involves using a travel agent, and the best way to proceed is via the people at John's Information Café.

by bus

The bus station is on Dīngzì Lù, close to a number of budget hotels. Minibus drivers from the railway station at Liǔyuán may drop you outside the Fóguāng Dàjiǔdiàn (which is a good choice for the budget traveller, but probably pays them commission). If you want to head to the Xīyù Bīnguǎn (Western Region Hotel) or elsewhere further south, insist on being taken to the bus station. There is *no* extra payment for this.

The bus station actually has an office for foreigners, and specializes in charging enormous amounts for the trip to Lhasa via Golmud (around ¥1200/$145). However, other tickets are available at standard Chinese prices (which you can check with the signs above the ticket windows in the main hall). If you use the Chinese ticket window you must still show your insurance, and will probably be accosted with demands to see your ticket as you wait for the bus. An attempt may then be made to charge you double unless you can show insurance. To pay normal prices for the trip to Golmud catch a minibus a few kilometres to Qǐlǐ from Xī Dàjiē near the junction with Xī Huánlù, and catch a morning departure from the station there. Make a dummy run to check times.

There are buses to and from Ānxī at 4pm (117km, ¥9), to Jiǔquán at 7.30am, 9am and 1pm (404km, ¥30/$4) which can also be used for reaching Jiāyùguān, Zhāngyè at 3.30pm (630km, ¥45.40/$6), Wǔwēi at 4.30pm (865km, ¥64,20/$8), and Lánzhōu at 8.30am and 10.30am (1148km, ¥82.20/$10). There are also buses to Hāmì (424km, ¥32.40/$4), Jiāyùguān at 11.30am, and eight departures a day to Liǔyuán (130km, ¥10/$1.25), plus various private minibuses, taking around three hours. Taking the road south from Dūnhuáng you can reach the southern Taklamakan route (with some difficulty) via Chálěngkǒu/Lěnghú (246km, ¥20/$2.50), and Huātǔgōu (536km, ¥43/$5.50), or eastwards to Xīníng (1052km, ¥84.30/$10.50).

Getting Around

The centre of town is a traffic island with the usual streets radiating to the points of the compass and named after them; Dōng, Nán, Xī, Běi Dàjiē, and most facilities and accommodation are within walking distance. The post and telephone office is here. There are **taxis** of various sizes, motortricycles and pedicabs, none of which have anything resembling a meter or much intention of sticking to any contract that you might make with them. For the trip to the Mògāo Kū take a minibus (see below), and for the other sights, walk or rent a bicycle. These are widely available at hotels, and at the English-menu restaurants strung out along the road between the Fēitiān and the Xīyù Bīnguǎn.

Dūnhuáng © (0937)   Tourist Information

There's a large branch of CITS next to the brand-new Dūnhuáng Guójì Fàndiàn in Dīngzì Lù, and agents in other hotels such as the Fēitiān and Jīnyè. The shiny new **Bank of China** (open Mon–Fri 9–12 and 3–6) is west of the junction between Míngshān Lù and Xī Dàjiē. The **post office** is at the main crossroads (open 8am–7pm). Collect poste restante mail from the counter straight ahead of you as you enter. The postcode for mail is 736200. International telephone calls can also be made here, rather pricily: USA ¥42 ($5) per minute, UK ¥47 ($6). **Film** is available at every tourist site, and at every department store, but in many cases superheated by Dūnhuáng's scorching summer weather, so choose wisely. **Maps** are available from hotel foyers, the Xīnhuá Shūdiàn east of the centre past the museum, and street vendors. Xīnhuá has very few English novels, but a good selection of books about the Mògāo Kū, which, unlike at the Cave Bookstore next to the museum, are at the proper publishers' prices. **Visa extensions** are available from the courteous and efficient PSB past the Bank of China on Xī Dàjiē (open Mon–Fri 8–12 and 2.30–6), at varying prices according to nationality. **Insurance** for Gānsù bus journeys is available from the foreigners' ticket office to the right of the main entrance of the bus station. If

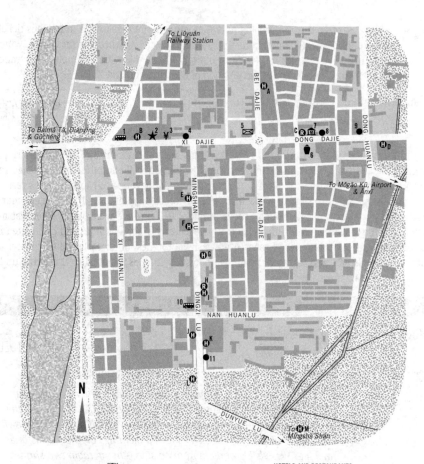

KEY

1	Buses to Qīlī
公安局	2 PSB Gōng'ānjú
中国银行	3 Bank of China Zhōngguó Yínháng
中国人民保险公司	4 PICC Zhōngguó Rénmín Bǎoxiǎn Gōngsī
邮电局	5 Post and telephone office Yóudiànjú
市场	6 Market Shìchǎng
县博物馆	7 County Museum Xiàn Bówùguǎn
新华书店	8 Xīnhuá Bookshop Xīnhuá Shūdiàn
中国民航	9 CAAC Zhōngguó Mínháng
长途汽车站	10 Long-distance bus station Chángtú qìchēzhàn
中国国际旅行社	11 CITS Zhōngguó Guójì Lǚxíngshè

Dūnhuáng

HOTELS AND RESTAURANTS

太阳能宾馆	A	Tàiyángnéng Bīnguǎn Solar Energy Hotel
悬泉宾馆	B	Xuánquán Bīngguǎn
	C	Manhattan Café
敦煌宾馆	D	Dūnhuáng Bīnguǎn
天缘饭店	E	Tiānyuán Fàndiàn
佛光大酒店	F	Fóguāng Dàjiǔdiàn
明珠宾馆	G	Míngzhū Bīnguǎn
	H	John's Information Café
飞天宾馆	I	Fēitiān Bīnguǎn
西域宾馆	J	Xīyù Bīnguǎn Western Region Hotel
敦煌国际饭店	K	Dūnhuáng International Hotel Dūnhuáng Guójì Fàndiàn
金叶宾馆	L	Jīnyè Bīnguǎn
敦煌山庄	M	Dūnhuáng Shān Zhuāng Silk Road Dūnhuáng Hotel

you've just arrived from Xīnjiāng note that you will not be allowed to buy bus tickets anywhere within the western half of Gānsù without showing this insurance, which costs ¥30 ($4) for 15 days. It's also available at the PICC (People's Insurance Company of China) office at the junction of Míngshān Lù and Xī Dàjiē.

Xiàn Bówùguǎn (County Museum) 县博物馆

Open summer, 8–6.30; winter, Mon–Fri
8–12 and 2.30–5.30; adm ¥15.

The museum is on the north side of Dōng Dàjiē just east of the centre. The retired airforce plane in the courtyard contrasts oddly with the Qīng dynasty bell and other ancient objects to be found there. The museum itself is drab compared to the new one at Mògāo, but its reasonably wide-ranging collection of finds from the region is supplemented with relief maps, diagrams and photographs (although little is in English). There are well-put-together displays devoted to the ancient sections of wall constructed mostly of reed bundles and discovered by Stein, as well as other bundles of reeds used as signal torches, other early military materials such as arrow heads, and instructions on bamboo-strip bundles identical to those dug up by Stein in watchtower rubbish heaps.

Around Dūnhuáng

Mògāo Kū (Mògāo Caves) 某高窟

Open 8.30–12 and 2–4; ¥80.

Even Aurel Stein, who saw most of the great sights of Turkestan, was impressed:

> *...hundreds of grottoes, large and small, honey combing in irregular tiers the sombre rock faces, from the foot of the cliff to the top of the precipice, and extending in close array for over half a mile. This bewildering multitude of grottoes all showed paintings on their walls or as much as was visible of them from outside. Among them two shrines containing colossal Buddha statues could at once be recognized; for in order to secure adequate space for the giant stucco images of the Buddhas, close on ninety feet high, a number of halls had been excavated one above the other, each providing light and access for a portion of the colossus.*

M. Aurel Stein, *Ancient Central Asia Tracks,* 1941

From early morning minibuses cruise the streets of Dūnhuáng searching for customers for the trip to Mògāo. Outside the peak season, having picked you up, they may continue to do figures-of-eight around Dūnhuáng's centre yelling their destination at anyone who looks unoccupied until as late as 10.30. The 25km trip to the site takes around 30 minutes which leaves little time to see the caves. Often the English-menu restaurants such as the Flavour Food and John's have minibus contacts, and when travellers are few it's better to get a group of six together and book a minibus with a fixed departure time (¥7 one way, ¥10 return).

From the car park where the minibus stops, walk further up the road to the new main entrance and reception building on your right. The brand-new and stylish modern building you pass on the left is the Japanese-designed and funded museum of the **Dūnhuáng Research**

Institute (*open 9–5; winter 9–4; adm ¥15*), one of China's best small museums. At ground-floor level eight of the best caves from different periods, seven of whose originals are not usually open to the public, have been completely reproduced by modern artists right down to the last crack in the murals. These include a reproduction of 275, the earliest cave and probably Northern Liáng from around AD 366, through 249 and 285 of the Western Wèi (AD 535–57), 419 of the Suí (589–618), 220 and 217 from the Táng (618–906), and no.3 from the Yuán (1279–1368). There's also one middle Táng period cave from the Yúlín Kū near Ānxī, which, along with several other sets of caves in the area, also falls under the Institute's administration. Unlike the real caves they are brightly lit, and there is time to consider the interiors in detail, and to move back and forth to make comparisons. There is also a small collection of finds from the caves including pieces from the famous hidden 'library cave', no.17. Upstairs there's an exhibition of Tibetan Buddhist statuary mostly made from bronze and precious metals, and removed by an enterprising curator from the clutches of Red Guards who had carried the statues out of Tibet to melt them down during the Cultural Revolution. This may eventually be displaced by further displays of items from Mògāo itself.

Ideally the museum should be seen first, but timing is not on your side. Guided tours are compulsory (and included in the price), but although some guides are lacklustre and indifferent, many are well informed, speak good English, and are able to do more than parrot a learned script. Other major languages including French, German, Japanese and Russian are also spoken. The site should be reached as early as possible in order to ensure that you can get a guide in the language of your choice. There are two types of ticket: the A ticket allows you to see caves in both the morning and the afternoon to a theoretical maximum of 40, although few people if any actually see that many. (The B ticket is only for sale to Chinese, and just gives them a high-speed race around a dozen caves.) There is talk that the museum entrance will eventually be included in the A ticket, although the price will almost certainly rise.

Traditionally the origins of the caves date to AD 366 when a passing monk, fleeing from famine elsewhere, saw a vision of multiple Buddhas in haloed glory, more prosaically explained by others as the light from the setting sun sparkling on a mineral-rich local mountain. Luckily for the history of art, this explanation did not occur to the monk, who, feeling himself to have received a revelation, cut the first cave. Subsequent ones were paid for by travellers praying for a safe journey outwards, and others giving thanks for a safe one inwards. Dūnhuáng's position at the edge of the desert and near the junction of two major routes meant that there were plentiful donors, and the Mògāo Kū grew into the largest set of caves on the Silk Routes.

Originally the caves were linked by rock-cut stairways and paths, many having elaborate antechambers, which eventually collapsed. These were replaced by wooden walkways which, following the abandonment of the caves, rotted away until the caves were rediscovered by a Daoist monk called Wáng in 1900. Many were unreachable without ropes and ladders, their interiors exposed to the elements, and others filled with wind-blown sand. Wáng appointed himself abbot, and set about raising funds for restoration and the provision of facilities for pilgrims. Today the caves are sealed with concrete, sometimes air-conditioned, all locked and connected by concrete walkways. The larger rock-cut Buddhas in triple-layered caves have had new buildings erected in front of them for protection. Anchoring grasses have been sown along the cliff-top and fences erected to prevent sand pouring off it. The selection of up to 40 caves open to the public varies from year to year, taken from a 200-odd subset of 492 now extant out of perhaps 1000 original caves (including storage and residential caves of little interest). For once the concentration isn't solely on money, and there is serious and sensible concern about damage. However, the 40 always include the 'library cave', allowing tour guides to moralize on theft, and those containing the giant Buddha figures—two upright (26m and 34.5m) and one recumbent (11m). Certain important closed caves can be opened by prior arrangement and the payment of sums in the region of $100 per cave. The caves function as an almost complete reference work to styles in cave design, painting, relief and sculpture in the round over more than 1000 years, and even though it's unusual for visitors to have time to see more than 30 caves at the most, these are sufficiently representative of the extravagant detail, quantity, and variety of the images. To see more is like trying to examine dozens of Sistine Chapels in a day.

The art at Dūnhuáng is primarily, but not exclusively, Buddhist. The 492 extant caves here, together with other contemporary sites in the region (Yúlín, the East and West Thousand Buddha caves), come to 570 in all. With that insistence on quantification which seems to characterize the Chinese approach to all their cultural heritage, the guides will doggedly tell you that there are more than 50,000 sq m of murals, and that discoveries in the caves amount to nearly 1000 paintings on silk and hemp, 3000 painted statues, 30,000 to 40,000 manuscripts, and other fragments of fabric and embroidery. The Chinese may be forgiven for being slightly vague about the manuscripts—most of them are no longer in China. The caves, however, are the most extensive, and their murals and statuary the least damaged, whether by Muslim iconoclasts or foreign archaeologists. Begun in *c.* AD 366, they were continuously extended during the Northern Wèi (386–535), Suí (589–618), and the Táng (618–907) periods, whose artistic achievements reached their peak here. Further building occurred during the Five Dynasties (907–960) and Sòng (960–1279) periods, mostly by enlarging existing caves, and the Yuán dynasty (1279–1368) saw the restoration of many more. By the Táng what might properly be called a fresco technique had been developed in which the paint was applied to a wet surface and dried with it, as opposed to painting on carefully prepared but dry surfaces which had been used before.

Following the Táng, and until the Mongol Yuán arrived, Chinese dynasties may have been in charge in central China, but not always in Dūnhuáng. Other ethnic groups left their mark, although these caves are rarely shown to the public. Inconveniently for Chinese politics, Dūnhuáng spent the best part of three centuries 'outside the wall'. The Tibetans ruled the region from the mid-7th to 9th centuries, until finally driven out by a local Hàn warlord. The Uighurs who had moved south into the Tarim Basin in the 840s took over Dūnhuáng in the early 10th century. Still Manichaeists, they had yet to learn to inflict damage on images of people, and they allowed the Hàn residents to continue as local rulers under their overall control. Mògāo also has some Manichaeist caves. Dūnhuáng was one of the Tangut Xī Xià dynasty's early acquisitions (1038–1227), and three caves are attributed to them, although these are redevelopments of earlier caves and almost indistinguishable from those of the Sòng.

Earlier paintings (the earliest may be from the Northern Liáng, AD 502–57) show strong Central Asian influences from the Kizil caves near Kuqa in Xīnjiāng, while later caves, such as the Táng cave no.220, show strong influence from the sophisticated painters of the Táng capital. Amongst the *jataka* stories (scenes from the various lives of the Buddha and his disciples) and other familiar Buddhist imagery is an extraordinary range of secular subjects.

Paintings often present a cartoon sequence of narrative, broken into individual cells not by lines but by landscape devices such as trees and mountains. Successive panels may often be read from right to left, by having events move from both left- and right-hand sides to the centre of a single panel, or by having a central scene with commentary panels around the centre. Merchants and envoys, many clearly foreign, are shown falling into the misadventures common to caravans crossing the wastes to reach Dūnhuáng, some with happy endings, some not (caves 45, 246, 420 and others). There are also depictions of historical events, such as Zhāng Qiān's departure for the Western Regions (cave 323), and portraits of kings, emperors (such as cave 220), and the donors (such as 329) whose gifts made the paintings possible. In statuary as well as painting figures gradually mutate from the slender Northern Wèi to the fleshier more solid Táng, and progress in use of line, perspective and colour. Persian and Indian facial features, stature and clothing gradually become more Sinicized, and a mixture of Central Asian and Chinese elements are fused into one style.

Politics and race are never far away from Chinese commentaries, and the possibility that a direction in Chinese art, even that done for an imported religion, could have been led by foreigners is too much for some Chinese commentators to swallow. They prefer to say that 'Dūnhuáng art is...based on Chinese tradition and created by the Chinese people after assimilating useful foreign elements into an expression of national characteristics and the distinctive style of the times'. Pro-communist morals are farcically and anachronistically drawn from assumptions about the equal division of land in farming scenes.

There are also variations in cave architecture, with Northern Wèi caves, for instance, having the carved central pillars also visible at Yúngǎng and elsewhere, and ceilings cut in imitation of wooden structures. In others the cave is designed simply to focus attention on a main statue and its attendant figures at the rear. The ceilings are usually richly decorated and indicative of heaven. The conglomerate of the cliff being too soft, three-dimensional sculpture was made of clay on wooden and straw armatures. Earlier three-dimensional sculpture was only one step away from relief, and only meant to be viewed from the front. During the Táng more natural sculpture viewable in the round was finally put together.

The Toss of a Coin

Whatever the combination of other caves open when you visit, you will certainly be shown the larger Buddhas, both Táng, and the most notorious cave, no.17, known as the 'Library Cave'. Walled up some time in the 11th century, it was only rediscovered in 1900 by Abbot Wáng. Inside were thousands of silk paintings, and paper manuscripts such as Buddhist sutras and legal documents, although many were in languages neither he nor anyone else could read, and which he began to give away.

In August 1903, the German archaeologist Albert von Le Coq and his team, having spent a few months excavating various sites around Turpan, were escaping from prickly heat in the relative cool of Komul (Hāmì). A passing trader gave them news of Wáng's find. Like other archaeologists, von Le Coq was used to being led on futile journeys by local people, but the thought of easily accessible and supposedly strange texts was attractive. But Dūnhuáng, then known as Shāzhōu, was 17 days' hot journeying from Hāmì, and von Le Coq had an appointment to meet his superior, Professor Grünwedel, in Kashgar only a month and a half later.

> So, somewhat in despair, I left the decision to Fate by tossing a Chinese dollar: heads win, tails lose! Tails. i.e. the inscription side, came uppermost, and I had my horse saddled and began our journey to Kashgar.

> Albert von Le Coq, *Buried Treasures of Chinese Turkestan*, 1928

Von Le Coq's low opinion of Grünwedel forms an unpleasant undertone to his book, and when his colleague was several weeks late in arriving at Kashgar, and then kept there longer by sickness, their relationship was not improved. The expedition had another programme to follow, and for the time being, Dūnhuáng was forgotten.

Four years later in May of 1907, Aurel Stein reached Dūnhuáng from tracing an ancient wall in the desert, and began careful negotiations with Abbot Wáng. Wáng was in need of funds but, fearful of losing his reputation for piety if it became publicly known that he had allowed the non-Buddhist Stein to remove manuscripts and paintings, he was inclined to part only with material that he could not read, and then only very tentatively. He was completely ignorant of the value of his hoard of material, discovered by accident and then locked up again. The tactful diplomacy of Stein's Chinese secretary, and Stein's own admiration for Xuánzàng, demonstrated by the fact that he had traced Xuánzàng's steps all the way from India, helped to smooth negotiations. The first bundle that Stein was allowed to inspect, smuggled to his tent under cover of darkness, turned out to contain material brought from India and later translated by Xuánzàng himself, centuries before. This was taken by the abbot to be a portent, and Stein was allowed to enter the hidden library to see for himself a trove of thousands of scrolls, fragments of manuscripts and paintings on silk, which the dry desert air had preserved almost perfectly. The fine Táng dynasty paintings were given little value by Wáng, and Stein was allowed to put many aside 'for further inspection'. He was careful not to show too much enthusiasm, confirming to the priest his indifference to the paintings. Stein worked through the day inspecting what he could.

After midnight Stein's secretary was allowed to bring the day's selections to his tent. They made further inspections daily, promising the vacillating abbot that a substantial donation would be made, and occasionally administering small doses of silver in the interim. The materials gathered on this visit together with those obtained four months later, including Chinese and Tibetan material, altogether came to 24 cases containing thousands of manuscripts and five more cases of paintings, for which he paid £130.

France's Paul Pelliot came later in 1908. Unlike Stein, Pelliot was a Sinologist with excellent Chinese. Working at high speed, and scanning perhaps 1000 texts per day, he was able to find valuable items more quickly than the less nimble Stein, who knew Sanskrit and Persian but not Chinese, and had to work with an interpreter. Following Pelliot's arrival at Běijīng in 1909 with his own haul, the Chinese government ordered the remainder of the library to be brought to the capital. On a return visit he made in 1914, Stein was told by Wáng that the materials had been very roughly packed in carts, and that substantial quantities had been pilfered even before the carts left Dūnhuáng, as well as en route, as had the sum of money sent by the government to compensate him for the loss of the papers. Stein was subsequently accosted in several towns by men muttering the equivalent of 'Psst! Wanna buy a sutra?' Stein records: 'In view of the official treatment his cherished store of Chinese rolls had suffered, [Wáng] expressed bitter regret at not having previously had the courage and wisdom to accept the big offer I had made through Chiang Ssu-yeh [Stein's secretary] for the whole collection en bloc.' In addition to the government's haul, a Japanese called Tachibana had taken away various materials in 1911, but Stein was still able to take a further five crates himself.

But that still was not the end of the hoard. The Russian Academician Sergei Oldenburg (who made his way around other Silk Road sites in 1909–10) came away from Dūnhuáng in January 1915 with several hundred scrolls and fragments, but even he was not the last of the foreigners. That honour went to the American Langdon Warner, who arrived in 1924 after the caves had been used to intern 400 fleeing White Russian soldiers. (According to Warner, the Chinese authorities were fearful, and having disarmed the soldiers and taken their horses, they imprisoned the commanding officer in Ürümqi, giving him enough opium to kill him reasonably swiftly.) Although envious of the achievements of his European counterparts, Warner had had scruples about removing murals wholesale.

> But it was with a shock that I traced, on the oval faces and calm mouths, the foul scratches of Slavic obsenity and the regimental numbers which Ivan and his polk [regiment] had left there.
>
> Langdon Warner, *The Long Old Road in China*, 1926

The sight of the soot from the prisoners' cooking fires and the casual damage inflicted accidentally by his own assistants helped Warner to overcome his reluctance. Cave 329 shows evidence of a rather unsuccessful attempt to take murals using a glueing process developed by Harvard chemists. A gap in cave 328 is evidence of his removal of a Táng statue.

Antiquities from Dūnhuáng are thus possibly more widely spread around the globe than those from any other site. Textiles, paintings and prints are now in the British Museum and British Library (Stein), as well as the Museum of Central Asian Antiquities in New Delhi (Stein), in the Musée Guimet and the Bibliothèque Nationale, Paris (Pelliot), the Tokyo National Museum, Japan (Tachibana and Otani), the National Museum of Korea (sold by Otani), the State Hermitage in St Petersburg (Oldenburg), and a few items at the Arthur M. Sackler Museum at Harvard (Warner). New discoveries are still being made: old paintings beneath newer layers and even previously unsuspected caves. The Institute regularly hosts international symposia, and many scholars and archaeologists are constantly at work. The question inevitably arises: should the manuscripts be given back? The British Museum's collection includes the oldest printed book in the world (actually a scroll), the *Diamond Sutra* of AD 868. Recently only five other fragments of Stein's massive haul were on view, the rest as buried below the streets of London as they were beneath Chinese sands. So far the Chinese are not asking. Off the record, some officials hint that they might. Others accept that had the documents not been carried away they would probably have been lost or destroyed by neglect, or stolen and distributed piecemeal in the upheavals between the end of the Qīng and the establishment of the Peoples' Republic, or ended up as firelighters for the Cultural Revolution's Red Guards. They are glad that the papers ended up safely overseas, professionally preserved, and open to scholars.

There are three other important caves sites in the region under the administration of the Institute and stylistically and historically of a group with Mògāo, which can be visited by special arrangement, perhaps eventually to be opened to the public. The **Xī Qiānfó Dòng** (West Thousand Buddha Caves), about 35km southwest of Dūnhuáng, overlooking the Dǎng Hé, have 16 extant caves, and the surviving murals include some stories not covered in those of Dūnhuáng. Cable and French, who visited the caves, described a precipitous path to a narrow ledge, rediscovered accidentally by a priest lost in a sandstorm. The **Chāngmǎ Dòng Qiānfó Dòng**, closer to Yùmén Zhèn than Dūnhuáng, are more numerous and in a broader valley, also with substantial murals, mostly Five Dynasties and Sòng in period. The **Yúlín Kū**, also well to the east and about 83km south of **Ānxī**, begun at about the same time as the Mògāo caves, have 41 major caves with large fine murals and hundreds of minor ones. There's another little-known set of **Dōng Qiānfó Dòng** (East Buddhist Caves) about 20km south of Ānxī, mostly of Xī Xià origin, and 20 in number (*see* p.202). If you are arranging to visit these caves, be clear about which you want to see.

Míngshā Shān and Yuèyá Quán (Singing Sand Mountains and Crescent Moon Spring) 鸣沙山, 月牙泉

Open daylight hours; adm ¥20 ($2.50).

The Míngshā Shān is a range of sand dunes 40km long, running in a line about 5km to the south of Dūnhuáng at its closest point and abruptly ending cultivation. Here a small lake produced by a spring sits improbably between high soft dunes; an image of refreshment surrounded by its exact opposite. Those who arrived by camel across the desert must have wondered if it was another mirage. What adds to the sands' fame is the noise-making quality of certain sections, a thundering rumble which can be activated by sliding down the sides of the dunes. The most popular time to visit the dunes is at sunrise or better still sunset, when the horizontal light emphasizes their wind-sculpted elegance, and turns them into giant geometrical shapes. This is everyone's idea of 'real' desert (except for the spring), and the highest dune rises to a towering 1715m above sea level. After this you can slide down and decide whether the noise you make more resembles the cry of a bird, animal or insect, or a ringing—varying translations of '*míng*', or the drum sound of most people's experience, and backed by the local myth of an army buried beneath your sliding bottom. Canadian scientists have recently discovered that the sounds (known as brontides) are produced by a silica gel coating on the sand grains when large numbers are rubbed together.

A once-active temple by the lake housed the missionaries Cable and French when they had been turned out of their accommodation in town by the ruffianly army of Mǎ Zhòngyīng (rebels to the Hàn, brigands to the local people, and independence fighters to modern campaigners for Xīnjiāng's self-determination). They revelled in the beauty, solitude and quietness of the place, and marvelled at the occasional drumming sound of the sand. Naively, Cable took some sand back to London but could not make it sound there.

These days the usual entrance point to the dunes has been walled up with a gate and a large fee is required to pass through it. An officious man with a flag waves down cyclists before a belt of tawdry souvenir shops, indicating an expensive bicycle park. The dunes are becoming covered in litter and pestering souvenir sellers, as well as those offering services such as paragliding (best done somewhere where regulation and safety certification are more genuine) and camel rides. The dunes can be approached from other directions, and entered by cycling round to the right or left, but a corrupt policeman loves to track down stray foreigners and lock them up in his office until they pay his 'fine'. The dunes are only 4km from town, and are reached by a short cycle ride to the south, following the road round to the left and over a bridge, and round to the right again, passing the Silk Road Hotel, at which point your destination is clearly visible. Minibuses leave from a turning off Dīngzì Lù near the bus station when full, and charge ¥2. A taxi to the dunes which waits for you and then returns should be no more than an outrageous ¥40 ($5), or around five times the normal rate per km.

Other Sights

The **Báimǎ Tǎ** (White Horse Pagoda) is another site connected with the translator-monk from Kuqa, Kumarajiva. Traditions vary, but they agree that his white horse died here, and the nine-tiered flask-shaped brick stupa stands on the spot. According to one version the horse merited the tower because it had safely brought the monk across the deserts, and another because Kumarajiva had a conversation with it in a dream the night it died. Leaving the city by Xī Dàjiē, the stupa can be found in fields about 4km out of town. Unprotected, it gives you an opportunity to guess what the Chinese characters for 'Kilroy was here' might be. Well beyond the stupa in the same direction lies the remains of the **Diànyǐng Gǔchéng** (Old City Film Set) built for a Japanese production in 1987. Heavily and misleadingly promoted to tourists just as the Old City (Gǔchéng), its fake walls are hardly worth the effort when you've got the real Jiāyùguān fort to see, and a better-preserved and still operational film location in Xī'ān. Minibuses run out to the site from near the bus station for ¥10 return, and the entrance fee is ¥15.

To the northwest and southwest of Dūnhuáng lie two fortified passes marking the original routes to the west around the north and south sides of the Lop desert. The **Yùmén Guān**, or Jade Gate Pass, about 102km away, was the route along which caravans from Khotan arrived, carrying cargos of valuable jade (although confusingly this is the northerly of the two). The shapeless but substantial mud walls of a Hàn dynasty fortified town remain standing, where Stein unearthed important evidence of Silk Route trade. He also rediscovered the remains of a brushwood wall and small garrison towers between the two passes and beyond. There is less to see at the **Yáng Guān** (aptly named 'Pass of the Sun'), 76km to the southwest, but there are the remains of a beacon tower. Reaching either site requires chartering a taxi or the assistance of a travel agency.

Where to Stay

As so frequently happens in China, over-optimistic tourism forecasting and a solipsistic approach to business planning has resulted in an oversupply of rooms in all but the summer high season. There is not necessarily any need to pay the first price asked.

expensive

The **Dūnhuáng Shān Zhuāng** (Silk Road Dūnhuáng Hotel) is an unusual Hong Kong-funded and managed hotel on Dūnyuè Lù, ✆ 882 5388, 📠 882 5366, halfway out to the entrance to the Míngshā Shān sand dunes, which tower over it. With the atmosphere of a film set only waiting for divisions of banner-waving extras, the hotel's imposing main building is a replica Chinese fortress, behind which are large courtyard buildings in a mixture of Hàn and Táng dynasty architectural styles. The courtyard suites begin at $250 rising to $1000, while standard rooms in the front building ('the castle') begin at $100 with suites at $150 to $300. A plainer, modern building behind has student bunks for $5, and more simply furnished but large and comfortable doubles for $43. There are several large restaurants in a courtyard building with good Western and Chinese menus, a theatre with dance performances and music, a night-time food market (popular with those returning past the hotel from watching the sunset at the dunes) and a weekend all-you-can-eat 'Genghis Khan' barbecue. All prices carry a 15% service charge, and all major credit cards are accepted.

moderate

For many years the hotel into which most tour groups have been bundled (including, in 1986, ambassadors from 73 countries) is the **Dūnhuáng Bīnguǎn**, at the east end of town on Dōng Dàjiē, ✆ 882 2415, which has older, refitted buildings on one side of the road, a newer building opposite, a theatre with made-for-tourists performances when numbers allow, a 'friendship store', disco hall, and so on. None of the rooms is reasonably priced: ¥500 ($60) for a suite, ¥400 ($48) and ¥300 ($36) for doubles, and beds in common bath doubles and triples for ¥40 ($5), all plus a special foreigner tax of ¥2 per person per day ('for security'). With similar prices, the new **Jīnyè Bīnguǎn**, ✆ 882 1470, 📠 882 1427, would be a better choice, as may the even newer **Dūnhuáng Guójì Fàndiàn** (Dūnhuáng International Hotel) when it opens, although there is ominous CITS involvement here. Another moderate hotel due to open shortly on Běi Dàjiē is the rebuild of the **Tàiyángnéng Bīnguǎn** (Solar Energy Hotel).

inexpensive

One older hotel worth considering is the **Xīyù Bīnguǎn** (Western Region Hotel) south of the bus station (turn right as you leave), ✆ 882 3017, which has long been the budget travellers' favourite, with doubles and triples at ¥50 ($6) and ¥40 ($5) per bed, and common bath triples and quads for ¥25 ($3) and ¥20 ($2.50); larger rooms ¥15 ($2). The staff are friendly and used to foreigners, but there are several new hotels offering cleaner and better-appointed rooms for the same prices or lower. The best choice is the **Fóguāng Dàjiǔdiàn**, ✆ 882 5040, outside which the minibus from Liǔyuán (probably on commission) may drop you. Beds in doubles are ¥50 ($6), triples ¥45 ($5.50), quads ¥35 ($4.50), all with bathrooms and *all day* hot water (all the remaining cheaper hotels have it evenings only). There are also suites at ¥120 ($15) per bed, and common bath triples for ¥25 ($3). All prices will be reduced for those planning to stay two or more nights. The nearby and similar **Tiānyuán Fàndiàn**, ✆ 882 2227, has doubles for ¥45 ($5.50) per bed, common bath doubles, triples and quads for ¥40 ($5), ¥30 ($4), and ¥20 ($2.50) per bed. Round the corner in Xī Dàjiē, the **Xuánquán Bīngguǎn**, ✆ 882 9005, has evening hot water for slightly longer than most, and also has the best bathrooms in this price range, with suites for ¥280 ($34), doubles with bath for ¥60 ($7.50) per bed, and common bath doubles and triples for ¥25 ($3) and ¥18 ($2.50) per bed. The cheapest beds of all are in the old dormitory building of the **Fēitiān Bīnguǎn**, ✆ 882 2377, ✆ 882 2311, at ¥15 ($2) per bed in six- to eight-bed rooms. Access to the common showers can sometimes be a problem as the staff seem to think they have priority. There's also the **Míngzhū Bīnguǎn** (Pearl Hotel), ✆ 882 2462: suites ¥60 ($7.50), doubles, triples and quads with bath ¥50 ($6) and ¥40 ($5), and common bath rooms ¥15 ($2) per bed.

Eating Out

The **Manhattan Café** has been opened by two enterprising New Yorkers and provides the only genuinely Western atmosphere to be found between Xī'ān's international hotels and Ürümqi's Holiday Inn, but even more so—it's quite possible to forget that you are in China at all. Safe-to-drink iced water appears automatically, there are properly chilled imported beers and fresh ground coffee, and the 100% Western menu is 100% Western quality. Prices are also Western but not extravagantly so. Snacks include freshly made banana bread and other cakes. The restaurant is set back from Dōng Dàjiē opposite the night market and close to the museum.

Dūnhuáng also boasts a branch of **John's Information Café**, ✆ 882 7000, with the same types of near-Western and Chinese foods found at his other Kashgar, Ürümqi and Turpan branches, and with practical information available from helpful, English-speaking staff, who also act as intermediaries with CITS for ticket purchases. This branch is in a shady outdoor spot outside the Fēitiān Hotel.

Across the road from the Fēitiān Bīnguǎn runs an almost continuous line of small, English-menu restaurants, most offering an assortment of Chinese and Western foods including breakfasts, and some specializing in Sichuanese food. Amongst the friendliest and best are the long-standing **Flavour Food Snack Bar** and **Shirley's**. The market on Dōng Dàjiē, which expands at night, boasts a number of small Huí and Hàn noodle restaurants, and snack stalls with *sānpàochá* (another version of the sweetened, fruity tea called *bābǎochá*), and bread pockets stuffed with fried pork.

Shopping and Entertainment

Most of the souvenir shops are down by Dūnhuáng Bīnguǎn with the JCB card signs which should warn you to shop elsewhere. Dūnhuáng produces a variety of T-shirts and batik clothing. There is a number of dubious 'antique' stores around, although Potato Valley Crafts near the Manhattan Café (and connected with it) has good pieces.

There's lively Chinese opera, done rustic style with the minimum of resources, every evening in a room across the courtyard behind the Manhattan Café, ¥3.

The route from Dūnhuáng to Hāmì is served by minibuses of considerable antiquity. When asked what time the bus will arrive, the bus station staff and the staff on the bus itself all reply, '*Bù yídìng*', which means 'not certain'. The meaning in this case appears to be 'not certain that it will get there at all', but it usually does so in about 9½ hours. Reflect that this is the trip that would have taken von Le Coq 17 days, had he decided to follow up the rumours of the hidden library. The bus first goes to the railhead at Liǔyuán in a little under three hours, before reversing direction slightly to return to the main road to Hāmì. Dūnhuáng's leafiness becomes scrubbiness, then gravelly emptiness, with the occasional low dune of wind-blown sand.

Heading west, the desert affords vistas of yellow-khaki sand, pink rock and grey gravel, until **Xīngxīngxiá** is reached at about the 3391km marker, with the remains of a fort, towers and other ruined fortifications, marking the border with Xīnjiāng. From the end of the Qīng dynasty in 1911 until the defeat of the Nationalists in 1949, Xīnjiāng was ruled almost as an independent fiefdom by a succession of warlords who only paid lip service to the Nánjīng government. The reign of the last was characterized by such paranoia that the border here was heavily patrolled, and no-one was allowed to leave the province without the personal permission of the governor. Those who were allowed in found it very difficult to leave. Passers-by were often press-ganged into the army, but in the seemingly limitless desert the only source of water ran through the narrow defile here, leaving travellers little choice.

Cable and French reported that the splintered grey rock had been carved so as to represent soldiers ready for action, amidst real soldiers who really were.

> *It is of precisely the same colour and shade as the Chinese soldiers'*
> *grey cotton uniform. Every day there was practice, when each man*
> *reached his appointed place and there stood motionless. The rock was*
> *covered with invisible soldiers and even the keenest eyes failed to*
> *distinguish between the man-like stone and the stone-like men.*

Mildred Cable with Francesca French, *The Gobi Desert*, 1942

Most routes in the Tarim Basin creep around the feet of the mountain ranges that almost surround it, but from Xīngxīngxiá to Hāmì the road crosses the narrow link between the Gobi and the Taklamakan, and for once there is no sheltering high ground. Although the pilgrim monk Xuánzàng left Dūnhuáng by the more direct ancient route through the Yáng Guān, it was on the way to Hāmì that he nearly gave up his expedition. Narrowly escaping death at the hands of a guide, he continued alone on horseback, used up all his water and became lost. Like the later Kumarijiva, he was possessed of a particularly intelligent horse, who after several thirsty days scented water and, ignoring his master's tugs on the reins, broke into a trot until he reached a small pool. Until recently herdsmen would still drive flocks of sheep on the old route between Hāmì and Dūnhuáng.

After a day spent almost entirely in the desert, Hāmì is a big splash of green and the smell of its wetness reaches through the bus windows. Mountains of its torpedo-like melons sit like ammunition dumps under awnings at the side of the road. Fields of sunflowers appear to scrutinize passing traffic.

Bird-seller, Ürümqi

Hāmì to Kashgar

The Northern Taklamakan Route

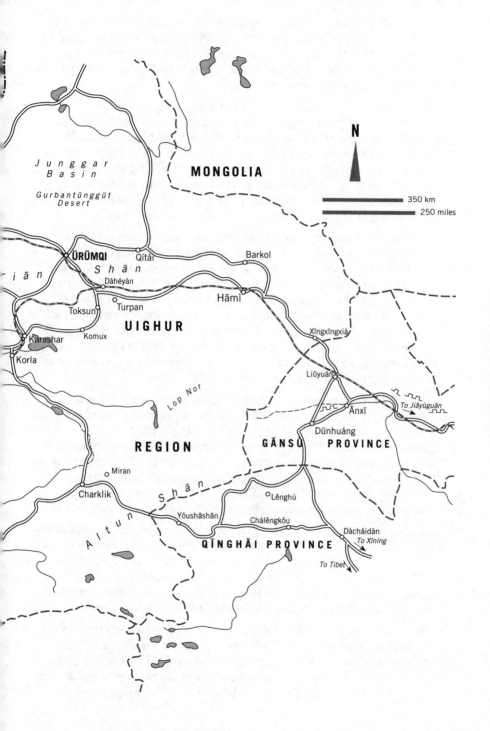

The Xīnjiāng Uighur Autonomous Region of China contains 1,646,800 sq km, a sixth of China's total land area, and is big enough to swallow a large part of Western Europe, or more than 20 per cent of the USA's 50 contiguous states. It contains one of the world's largest deserts, its second-highest mountain, and its second-deepest depression.

The region seems designed to be as inhospitable and inaccessible as possible. Almost completely surrounded by mountains, it is also divided by the Tiān Shān into two unequal parts—the top third, the Junggar Basin (Zhǔngéěr Péndì), which contains the Gurbantünggüt Desert (Gǔěrbāntōnggǔtè Shāmò), and the bottom two-thirds, the Tarim Basin (Tǎlǐmù Péndì), which contains the famously fearsome Taklamakan Desert (Tǎkèlāmǎgān Shāmò). Although a basin, most of it is 1000m above sea level, and suffers from sub-zero temperatures in winter nearly as unpleasant as its blazing summer heat.

To the north of Xīnjiāng are the relatively modest Altai mountains (Āěrtài Shān), the highest on Chinese territory being a mere 4374m (about 500m shorter than Mont Blanc). To the west the Pamirs and Karakorams include the world's second-highest mountain, the 6711m Qoghir (K2), and together with the Kūnlún and Altun (Āěrjīn Shān) ranges which lie to the south have an *average* elevation of around 6000 metres. As if to get the maximum contrast in one place, the comparatively tiny Turpan Basin drops to as low as 160m below sea level, an inland depth only surpassed by Israel's Dead Sea area. On the east side the Taklamakan Desert merges with the salt desert of Lop, and squeezes a sandy finger between mountain ranges to touch the Gobi.

Xīnjiāng has been gradually drying up for about 30,000 years, but in the 2nd century BC still supported animals now mostly only to be found in its southern neighbours, including lions, tigers, and elephants. Despite the manifest inhospitableness of its deserts, Xīnjiāng still has areas of grassland nearly as lush as those of Inner Mongolia, and a total of 320 rivers. One of these flows north to the Arctic, the rest draining into the various basins, and in most cases simply vanishing. Annual rainfall is low, and many of the rivers are formed from glacier meltwater, only appearing in any size for a few months each year.

In some areas water is brought from the feet of the mountains to the low-lying basins via underground channels called *karez*, preventing evaporation by the hot sun. Temperatures in the very low Turpan Basin, for example, can reach 48°C, but successful irrigation by this method has created a thriving fruit-growing area. Turpan grapes and Hāmì melons are prized country-wide, and other Xīnjiāng cities are famous for apricots, peaches, apples and pears.

The history of human affairs in Xīnjiāng was a matter of settler versus nomad. By 5000 years ago some of the peoples of the vast grasslands that stretched right across Europe and Asia and others from Persia had formed agricultural settlements in Xīnjiāng, and their descendants would go on to be city dwellers. There were also nomadic herdsmen who learned to ride horses in order to keep up with their flocks, and who would become the hordes that pillaged both the cities and the caravans that plied between them. For much of China's history its borders stopped at Jiāyùguān or Dūnhuáng, as the remains of various walls attest, although there were periodic shows of military strength along the Silk Routes to protect trade, and the remnants of watchtowers and garrison buildings are scattered around the Taklamakan and Lop Deserts' perimeters. During periods of Chinese control of Xīnjiāng, the lesson had to be learned again and again (and is still being learned) to let the hand of government rest lightly, or face bloody uprisings.

By the 20th century foreign powers were as much of a problem as rebellious local residents.

> *If it is untrue to say that at least four Powers are watching with the keenest interest the present situation in Sinkiang, it is only untrue because the present situation in Sinkiang is practically impossible to watch.*

Peter Fleming, News from Tartary, 1936

By Fleming's day, the horsemen who had watched and waited for opportunities to attack had been replaced by the equally watchful administrators, spies and diplomats of the Soviet and British empires. The Chinese were little more than watchers, too. Power lay in the hands of a Chinese governor, but one who paid little attention to the wishes of the Nationalist government of the day, and kept most of those who dared to enter the province from leaving again if he could, even including foreigners like Sven Hedin on government-sponsored expeditions. The Soviets, having discreetly provided him with the weaponry and support needed to resist Huí uprisings and keep himself in power, had control of trade, and many commentators expected Xīnjiāng to become part of the Soviet Union.

The Silk Routes, in ancient times already divided at Dūnhuáng, these days split into two further west at Korla. The southern route crosses the emptiness between the Lop and Takalamakan Deserts, and west through the oases at the feet of the Kūnlún Shān, swinging up to Kashgar at the western end of the Taklamakan (*see* **The Southern Taklamakan Route**, p.291). The northern route, often less travelled in ancient times than that of the south, but the more popular route now, hops between the mostly larger oases along the south side of the Tiān Shān along a better-quality highway. The railway line divides after Turpan, terminating at Ürümqi and Korla, until the extension to Kashgar currently under construction is complete, following the northern route.

Hāmì

哈密 Hāmì is a city of more than 300,000, and one of the few in Xīnjiāng that is majority Hàn—about two thirds. The remaining people are mostly Uighur (who form the majority in most other Xīnjiāng towns), with a few Huí, Uzbeks, Manchus, Tibetans, Yugur, Kazaks, Kyrgyz and Sibo, a mixture common in Xīnjiāng's oases.

Surrounded by desert, Hāmì survives on water brought along channels from the mountains called *karez*, a technology imported from the Middle East in ancient times. Its position on the main route to northern Xīnjiāng made it important for the control of both the Tarim and Junggar Basins, but even more than in the cities of the Héxī Corridor, Hàn control was intermittent, and Hāmì was sometimes an independent city-state fighting its own battles against its neighbour Turpan, or part of Uighur or post-Yuán dynasty Mongol empires. In 1482 the oasis was taken from the Jagatai Mongols by the Khitan Mongols with the support of China, then by the Turki Timurids in 1488, and retaken by the Khitans in 1489. Having Chinese support, the Khitans were forced to have a Chinese resident official, much as Kashmir and Gilgit were to have British political agents 400 years later. In 1493 both the resident and the lord of Hāmì were captured and held to ransom by the Timurids, causing the Míng (1368–1644) to suspend trade and expel Uighur traders from the market towns of the Héxī Corridor. Local anger against the Timurids was so great that they had to resign themselves to Hāmì's remaining under Mongol control, and thus under the sway of the Míng dynasty.

Although he passed by in the late 14th century, Polo probably didn't visit Hāmì, which he calls Camul, and which is still known as Kamul or Komul today. Nevertheless, his father and uncle may have visited on their earlier trip, and his book does devote one of its oft-quoted passages to the town:

> And it is the truth that if a foreigner comes to the house of one of these people to lodge, the host is delighted, and desires his wife to put herself entirely at the guest's disposal, whilst he himself gets out of the way, and comes back no more until the stranger shall have taken his departure. The guest may stay and enjoy the wife's society as long as he lists, whilst the husband has no shame in the matter, but indeed considers it an honour.

> Marco Polo, *The Travels*, Yule-Cordier edition

Under the Mongol Yuán dynasty, according to Polo, the people of Hāmì were forbidden from continuing this policy, but after three years they petitioned to be allowed to resume, on the grounds that the gods were no longer happy with them, and their fields were not fruitful. With disapproval they were allowed to reinstate 'their naughty custom'.

In 1887 the British explorer and Great Gamer Francis Younghusband passed through Hāmì. He had set off from Běijīng for Hohhot in Inner Mongolia, and then ventured overland by camel across the Gobi to Hāmì, a distance he estimated at 1255 miles (more than 2000km), and which took him 70 days. He was sharing surveying duties with the somewhat choleric Colonel Bell, who took a different route.

> ...we never met again till we arrived in India, and then Colonel Bell told me that he really had waited for me a whole day in Hāmì—this place in the middle of Central Asia, nearly two thousand miles from our starting-point—and, astonished at finding I had not turned up to date, had proceeded on his way to India.

> Captain Frank E. Younghusband, *The Heart of a Continent*, 1896

By the time of Younghusband's arrival Hāmì had become an important Chinese military base, having been used in the defeat of the rebel (or independence fighter) Yakub Beg, seven years before (see **Kashgar**, p.275). As with most other Xīnjiāng towns, when the Chinese took control they built themselves a new town outside the Turki town and the 'old town', and remained self-contained. Younghusband remarked upon a substantial wall surmounted by towers and, despite the demise of the Silk Routes long before, met Afghan and Andijani merchants (Andijan is now in Uzbekistan and Kyrgyzstan), and also an Arab.

The German archaeologist Albert von Le Coq visited in August 1905, calling Komul, 'the last Turkish place near the frontier of China proper'. Despite Chinese overlordship, von Le Coq discovered that he could not enter the town until specifically invited to do so by the hereditary king. He was given dinner in a palace full of Chinese and Khotani carpets, Chinese porcelain and Khotani jade, French clocks, Russian paraffin lamps, and a cuckoo clock. Despite the king's Muslim faith, he kept a good cellar of French champagne and Russian liqueurs, and the Germans had to work hard to keep up with him in consumption. Later they visited his summer residence to the northeast, and excavated Buddhist temples in the area. The missionaries Cable and French, who visited in 1930, entered the harem of a member of the royal family to meet various wives. They described the intrigues between the women, and how each was desperate to secure a future by bearing a son, otherwise enjoying a short period as favourite before being displaced by a younger new arrival.

The missionaries were staying in the king's summer palace when his death was announced. Xīnjiāng was under the weak and incompetent leadership of the warlord Jīn Shùrén, who was nominally responsible to the Nationalist government in Nánjīng, but who, like other governors during the Nationalist period (1911–49) largely went his own way. In a series of bold but foolish moves, he announced the end of the rule of the Hāmì kings and imprisoned the heir to the throne. He sent in teams of Hàn administrators, magistrates and tax collectors, who proceeded to give favour to Chinese residents at the expense of the Turki majority. The names of the districts around Hāmì were changed to those dating from the Hàn dynasty conquest of the region 2000 years before. There was growing dissent, but the Ürümqi government ignored messages of complaint. The final mistake was the seduction of a Uighur girl by what one account called 'a vile, pig-eating Chinese tax-collector'. A marriage was arranged but the couple's wedded bliss was short-lived. The same night the guards set to protect the house were attacked and killed, and the bride and bridegroom both murdered. In the rebellion that followed neighbouring oases also rose up against the Chinese, and Ürümqi was attacked several times. At the request of the Uighurs of Hāmì, led by the former king's Grand Vizier, Yolbas (Yollbars, Yulbaz) Khan, Mǎ Zhòngyīng (known as the 'Baby General' or 'Big Horse'), a Huí, was invited to help free Hāmì from Chinese oppression. The Chinese population withdrew into the citadel, was besieged by Mǎ's irregulars for six months, and attacked no less than 40 times, but without success. Mǎ became bored and withdrew, but much of Hāmì was left in ruins by this and subsequent actions. (For the full story of Mǎ, see pp.242–6).

The British diplomat Eric Teichman visited Hāmì in 1935, having come from Běijīng, through Hohhot, and across the Gobi by lorry.

> We visited the various local sights, the tombs of the Hami Princes, the ruins of the palace, the principal mosques, a Chinese temple called the Lung Wang Miao, which, held by the rebels, had been totally destroyed, and the Chiu Lung Shu ('Nine Dragon Tree'), the latter a famous

curiosity to all Chinese, nine venerable willows growing out of one root, but, like most of Hāmì, destroyed in the hostilities.

Eric Teichman, *Journey to Turkistan*, 1937

The Chinese were still in charge, but the Chinese administrator was now living in the old city and, in an arrangement characteristic of Xīnjiāng horse-trading, the rebellious Yolbas Khan had been appointed commander of the army and was based in the Chinese citadel. The Muslim city and the suburbs were simply heaps of rubble.

The centre of modern Hāmì looks just like the centre of every other Chinese city, now an industrialized producer of everything from steel, iron and cement to salt, pharmaceuticals and canned fruit. Wagons piled with coal can be seen at the railway station. However, Hāmì's centre is small and not unpleasant, and a short walk still brings you to the old town, a warren of adobe compounds hung with grape vines, and 100 per cent Uighur. There the tombs of the Muslim kings of Hāmì provide the main interest—their latticed windows and domed roofs containing several generations of the ruling family, their relatives and favoured ministers.

Imperial Melon Recipe

Hāmì is famous throughout China today not for uprisings and civil war, but for melons. It is almost impossible for a Chinese to say *guā*, 'melon', without saying *Hāmì guā*. More than 30 different varieties are grown here (some sources say 50 kinds), and their rich scent gusts around the streets.

Mountains of them can be found at every roadside in the region, and its difficult to imagine how so many can be eaten locally.

Their fame is partially attributed to the Emperor Kāngxī, said to be the first emperor to receive a tribute of the fruit. Most of the Chinese emperors are only known to us as aloof and impersonal beings, but early this century the diaries of perhaps the Qīng dynasty's most illustrious ruler were discovered in the Forbidden City. The historian Jonathan Spence translated the diary and interspresed sections with translations of Kāngxī's personal correspondence to make extended commentaries on various subjects in the emperor's own voice.

In 1697 while out on a campaign to defeat the bandit Galden, Kāngxī sent his Chief Eunuch the equivalent of a postcard, which included a note on local food:

> *Among the local produce that the Moslems of Hami sent to me along with the [captured] Galden bandits, only the sun-dried muskmelon had a really beautiful taste. I'm sending off some to you, but as I'm afraid you won't know what to do with it, I'll specifically write it out for you:*
>
> *After you have washed it clean in either cold or hot water, steep it in hot water (but only for a short time), and then eat it either cold or hot. It tastes fresh and the juice is like the honeyed juice of a dried peach. Where there are holes fill them up with little grapes.*

Jonathan Spence, *Emperor of China*, 1974

Up to the end of the Qīng dynasty in 1911, annual consignments were still being sliced, dried in Hāmì's parched air, and sent to the court, a journey of more than 100 days.

Getting to and from Hāmì
by train

The station is in the northwest corner of town, reached by bus 1 from the centre or 3 from the bus station. All trains going east and west stop at Hāmì, but tickets are not easy to obtain, in theory available one day in advance from 9am in the morning, but in fact mostly sold through the back door. The most convenient train to Ürümqi is the a/c 69, but there are only 10 hard seats available. There's also the evening 143 which goes to Korla and Ürümqi on alternate days. Hard seats are ¥55 ($7) to Ürümqi, ¥37 ($4.50) to Korla. Going east the a/c 70 is impossible to board unless you book through an agent, and departs at the inconvenient time of 04.19. The most convenient departures are the 144 to Xī'ān at 10.26 arriving at 09.36 after two nights, or the 98 at 08.24, arriving at Jiāyùguān 20.04, Zhāngyè 04.27, Wǔwēi 05.20, Lánzhōu 12.37, Tiānshuǐ 19.35. Dūnhuáng is best reached by bus. If the railway station has not yet been rebuilt, you will find the ticket office in a small building down a passage leading from the far left-hand corner of the square.

by bus

The bus station is within walking distance of the centre, and connected to the railway station by bus 3. There are departures to Ürümqi at 7am (¥59/$7.50) passing through Turpan, to Jiǔquán at 7am (¥51.50/$6.50) passing though Liǔyuán and Ānxī, to Dūnhuáng at 7am (¥34/$4), to Turpan at 8.30am (also ¥34). There is also a sleeper bus at 8.30pm to Ürümqi: upper berths ¥82 ($10), lower ¥92 ($11).

Getting Around

The centre of town is the junction between Tiān Shān Dōnglù and Zhōng Shān Běilù, with the post and telephone office, Xīnhuá Shūdiàn, two hotels, museum and bus station all within walking distance. The bus service in town is run entirely with minibuses, the most useful routes being the 1 which connects the railway station with the Shāngyè and Xīngcháng hotels (¥2), and the 3 which connects the railway station and the bus station. To see a taxi with its meter running is rare, but the minibus routes are convenient and the buses frequent, so there's little need for taxis anyway.

Hāmì ✆ (0902)   Tourist Information

NB: Watch out for Xīnjiāng time, two hours earlier than Běijīng time, which in Hāmì tends to be used only to explain delays. All times quoted in this book are in Běijīng time, which is used on timetables and all official documents and notices.

CITS is in building no.1 of the Hāmì Bīnguǎn, also known as the Hāmì Dìqū Zhāodàisuǒ. Their commission for the purchase of railway tickets is ¥30 ($4); air tickets (not from Hāmì) ¥50 ($6). The **Bank of China** (*open Mon–Fri, 9–1 and 4–8*) is a 5-minute walk south of the Shāngyè Bīnguǎn on Zhōng Shān Běilù, and the **post and telephone office** is just north of the same hotel (*open 9–1 and 5–8, Sun 9.30–4 for mail; telephone 24hrs*). Calls to the US are ¥31.50 per minute, and to the UK ¥35.60. For facsimiles add ¥6 to the telephone charges. **Film** can be found in the department stores at the centre. **Maps** in Chinese are available from the Xīnhuá

火车站	1	Railway station Huǒchēzhàn	邮电宾馆	A	Yóudiàn Bīnguǎn
长途汽车站	2	Long-distance bus station Chángtú qìchēzhàn	新星宾馆	B	Xīnxīng Bīnguǎn
哈密文物局	3	Hāmì Wénwùjú Hāmì Cultural Office Museum	加格达宾馆	C	Jiāgédá Bīnguǎn
盖斯墓	4	Tomb of Gài Sī Gàisī Mù	商业宾馆	D	Shāngyè Bīnguǎn
新华书店	5	Xīnhuá Bookshop Xīnhuá Shūdiàn	星长大酒店	E	Xīngcháng Dàjiǔdiàn
邮电局	6	Post and telephone office Yóudiànjú	哈密宾馆	F	Hāmì Bīnguǎn Hāmì Dìqū Zhāodàisuǒ
公安局	7	PSB Gōng'ānjú			
中国银行	8	Bank of China Zhōngguó Yínháng			
回王墓	9	Tombs of the Muslim Kings Húiwáng Mù			

Hāmì map key

STREET NAMES

爱国北路	Àiguó Běilu
光明路	Guāngmíng Lù
建国南、北路	Jiànguó Nán/Běilu
前进东路	Qiánjìn Dōnglù
天山东、南、西、北路	Tiān Shān Dōng/Nán/Xī/Běilù
文化路	Wénhuà Lù
中山南、北路	Zhōng Shān Nán/Běilù

Shūdiàn just north of the post office, and from hotel foyers, ¥1. The bookstore has half a dozen English titles at best. **Visa extensions** are available from the PSB's 'Section of Aliens and Entry-Exit Administration' (*open Mon–Fri, 9–1 and 5–8*), just south of the Xīngcháng Dàjiǔdiàn on Zhōng Shān Běilù.

Huíwáng Mù (Tombs of the Muslim Kings)   回王墓
Open approx. 9–7.30; ¥10 ($1.25).

The Muslim quarter (Huíchéng) is a short walk south of the Shāngyè Bīnguǎn down Zhōng Shān Nánlù, the no.1 bus terminating at its edge. Here an irregular net of narrow alleys sprawls in defiance of the rigid grid of the modern Hàn city, with walled courtyards and small mosques of adobe and brick, and donkey carts delivering melon mountains to roadside stalls. A walk of under 30mins brings you to the tombs, the road swinging round to the west (right), and passing a crossroads shortly before the entrance, which is on the left.

An ornate entrance in a modern brick outer wall surrounds an older mud enclosure containing a mosque with a brashly restored façade. Inside, its wooden roof is supported by painted and carved beams atop slender wooden columns only about three metres apart like an orchard. The walls are beautifully decorated with patterns, and with Koranic texts in Arabic script, illuminated by shafts of sunshine from four roof lights. The interior is only used at special festival periods such as Corban, and is otherwise inhabited by house martins doing elaborate

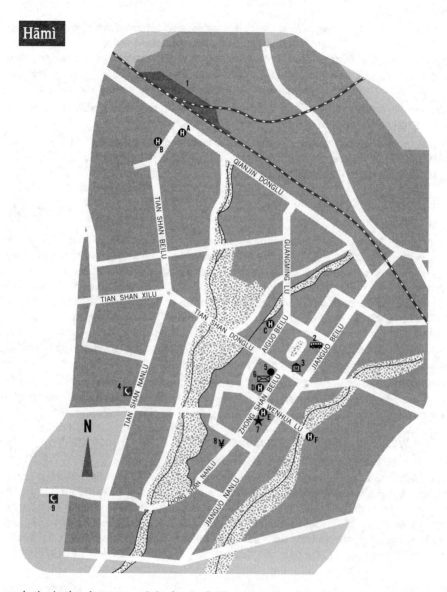

acrobatics in the gloom around the forest of pillars, and a cat. The exterior shows evidence of modernization, but this hasn't spoiled the solemn interior atmosphere.

Dominating the mosque is the substantial blue-tiled, dome-topped cube of the *mazar* containing a close huddle of tombs of Hāmì monarchs, who reigned from around 1697 to 1930, though often with other overlords. Some of the tombs are labelled in English and some in Japanese, but never both. The interior of the dome is elegant in blue and white, and standing inside it's difficult to believe that you are still on Chinese soil, rather than in the Middle East. Outside the *mazar* in the courtyard itself are the tombs of princes and other less senior family members, and beyond that two remarkable wooden pavilions (out of an original five), their exteriors supported by slim poles, and their roofs topped with round, octagonal and square roof lights. Further tombs occupy every inch of floor space, mostly those of prime ministers, although the left-hand building also contains the remains of the ninth king. Interiors are tiled or painted in blue and white and lit diffusely by delicately latticed windows.

The mosque is said to date from the early Qīng (late 17th century). The wooden pavilions are considerably more modern, one dating from 1902.

Albert von Le Coq was impressed by the tombs, and 'paid the customary fee which every traveller has to give, in proportion to his means, to this burial mosque; in my case it was ten Chinese dollars (about thirty-five shillings)'.

Gài Sī Mù (Tomb of Gài Sī) 盖斯墓
Open 7am–7.30pm; adm ¥5.

Returning to the crossroads and turning left (north) up Tiān Shān Nánlù, a ten-minute walk brings you to the tomb of Gài Sī on the left, in front of which is a graveyard of hump-shaped graves with spines of mud brick which look ready to crawl off somewhere. Gài Sī (Gess Ansari) was one of three legendary missionaries from Arab countries who arrived during the Táng. He died and was buried in Xīngxīngxiá, but his remains were scattered during the various civil wars in the area. The bits were regathered in 1945 and reburied here, but the building looks older. There is clear evidence that the man is still held in veneration, as the sarcophagus is substantial and draped with banners, and the floor carpeted. The interior is plain except for Koranic text in a band around the dome.

Walking back down to the crossroads you can try taking a short cut back to the centre of town, but if you enter the narrow alleys between small allotments and vine-hung courtyards, expect to get enjoyably lost. You are out of the rigidity of the Hàn grid-system here.

Hāmì Wénwùjú (Hāmì Cultural Office Museum) 哈密文物局

This museum is neither easy to find nor easy to get into. Its opening hours are erratic, and certainly do not include weekends. It is on the upper floors of a nondescript building with a library on the ground floor on the north side of Tiān Shān Dōnglù. An unusual element in the collection is one of the squat stone figures that function as a tombstone that can be seen at the Burana Tower outside Tokmok in Kyrgyzstan. There are also desiccated corpses from tomb sites around Hāmì, and burial artefacts similar to those more easily seen in Ürümqi. Recently some of the collection has been on loan to the Abakh Hoja Tomb in Kashgar.

Where to Stay

In Chinese Turkestan…good rest-houses are not numerous, and are not habitually kept clean and habitable.

Captain H. H. P. Deasy, *In Tibet and Chinese Turkestan*, 1901

Hāmì has a combination of older hotels that regard charging 'foreign guests' double as a matter of pride, and newer hotels only some of which have the same bad habits. Visitors to Hāmì being few, this overcharging can often be resisted and prices reduced. The hotels that do not overcharge are unfortunately not in good condition.

The conveniently located **Shāngyè Bīnguǎn** (Hāmì Trade Hotel) on Zhōng Shān Běilù, ✆ 223 1768, has had an exterior white-tile refit, but an interior redecoration is long overdue—the carpets are more cigarette burn than carpet, and filthy. Suites are ¥188 ($23), standard doubles ¥136 ($17) per bed, triples with bath ¥100 ($12) per bed, and there are common bath triples and six-bed rooms at ¥40 ($5) and ¥20 ($2.50). A cleaner, more comfortable, and more modern hotel is the **Jiāgédá Bīnguǎn**, Àiguó Běilù, ✆ 223 2140, which has signs saying 10% off for foreign guests, which means plus 100% less 10%, and insolence from the reception staff is free. The rooms are nevertheless the most comfortable rooms open to foreigners, and have 24-hour hot water. All rooms have baths: doubles ¥116 ($14), triples ¥270 ($33), quads $320 ($39). Buying by the bed is sometimes possible. The same rooms without air conditioning are about 10% cheaper. Diagonally opposite the Shāngyè, the **Xīngcháng Dàjiǔdiàn**, ✆ 223 0446, is new but deteriorating fast. The common bath triples at ¥25 ($3) per bed are the best value for the budget traveller, although cheaper beds are available at the hotel above the post office in the far left-hand corner of the square as you emerge from the railway station. The entrance is the left-hand-most door and the reception is one floor up. This, the **Yóudiàn Bīnguǎn**, ✆ 223 8052, is one of those basic transport hotels where it's necessary to duck when climbing the stairs. It has simple doubles with bath and a/c for ¥40 ($5) per bed, all the remaining rooms having common baths—singles and doubles at ¥30 ($4) per bed, triples ¥20 ($2.50) with a/c, ¥18 ($2.50) without, quads ¥16 ($2) and ¥12 ($1.50). A short walk straight on as you emerge from the station, the **Xīnxīng Bīnguǎn**, ✆ 223 3063, is fairly recent and in moderate condition, with suites at ¥120 ($15), and doubles, triples and quads at ¥40 ($5), ¥30 ($4) and ¥18 ($2.50) per bed, all with bath and fan.

Eating Out

Eating out in Hāmì is not particularly stimulating, but the food in most hotels is adequate. Cheap and simple restaurants with Uighur noodle dishes line Wénhuà Lù east of the Xīngcháng Bīnguǎn.

Turpan (Tǔlǔfān)

吐鲁番 The history of Turpan, like that of the other key Tarim oasis towns, tends to be repetitive. The constant struggle between 'barbarian' hordes from Mongolia, Central Asia and Tibet led to frequent exchanges of control between these nomads and the sedentary dynasties of Chinese and others. Like small shops on the border between the territories of rival street gangs, the Tarim oases always had people damaging the merchandise, frightening the customers, and demanding protection money.

The period following the first appearance of Chinese military control in the Tarim during the Hàn dynasty provides a good example. By 67 BC Turpan had given its allegiance back to the mounted nomadic Xiōngnú, and was subdued by a Chinese general. In 64 BC it went back to the Xiōngnú, but was reoccupied by the Chinese in 60 BC. When the Early (Former, Western) Hàn dynasty fell to the rebel-led single-emperor Xīn dynasty (AD 9–25), the Xiōngnú took back the Turpan area in AD 10. In AD 48, shortly after the Hàn restoration, the Xiōngnú became divided amongst themselves, giving the Hàn an opportunity to recover lost territory. They moved rapidly to make allies of the southern hordes, thus bringing Gānsù back under their influence, and allowing them access to the Tarim oases. In AD 73 the Hàn established a base at Hāmì, and set out to reconquer Turpan the following year.

The inhabitants of the western Tarim oases of those times were Indo-European. They spoke variants of a language related to Persian, Armenian and Slavic tongues, and some of them had blue eyes and red hair. Until the arrival of Turki peoples in the second half of the 8th century, these oases were extensions of Indian and Persian cultures, whereas Turpan, considerably further east, was more influenced by Chinese culture. In the periods between being under pressure from Xiōngnú or Hàn, these oases went their own way, invading each other, and building petty short-lived empires.

The most famous general of the Hàn reinvasion was Bān Chāo, thought by some commentators to be the most remarkable military mind that China has ever produced. General Bān kept the Tarim basin under control with a good intelligence network and a lot of courage and initiative, but with military resources usually significantly inferior to those of his opponents. He famously ensured the allegiance of one petty state by delivering the head of a Xiōngnú ambassador, intercepted en route, to its king. In AD 74 he beheaded the chief adviser of the king of Khotan in front of the startled monarch, and deposed the ruler of Kashgar. In 75 a general revolt against Chinese rule broke out, supported by the Xiōngnú, and Bān Chāo was besieged in Kashgar for a year by troops from Kuqa and Aksu. Meanwhile the Xiōngnú attacked Turpan. The Chinese court decided to recall its troops from this endlessly rebellious region, but Bān Chāo, reaching Khotan on his way home, defied his orders and returned to Kashgar, which had immediately fallen under Xiōngnú influence again, and beheaded the members of the pro-Xiōngnú faction. In AD 78, raising a mixed-race party of mercenaries, he recaptured Aksu and Turpan, beheading as he went. Throughout the 80s there were further rebellions with the men of Kashgar, Kuqa and Yarkand assisting each other, all subdued by force of arms or intelligence means. Major victories by other Chinese generals against the Xiōngnú in Mongolia in the early 90s led to the surrender of Turpan, Kuqa and Aksu in 91, after yet further rebellions. Karashar held out until AD 94 when it was attacked and its king beheaded.

Bān Chāo, who had kept his head when all around were losing theirs, retired in AD 102, and rebellions broke out again almost straight away. By AD 107 the Chinese court had had enough, and all the Tarim garrisons were withdrawn, as well as that at Hāmì. The Xiōngnú once again attacked Shānxī while Tibetans threatened the Gānsù corridor. In 119 the Chinese re-established the Hāmì garrison and regained control of Turpan, only to see the garrison massacred by a surprise Xiōngnú attack. In 123 the Chinese were back, and the Tarim was reconquered over the following four years. Despite the odd rebellion, the region stayed under control until China split into three kingdoms at the end of the Hàn, and a long period of civil war followed.

This strife continued while Turki and Mongol groups took over from the Xiōngnú, the expansionist Táng dynasty took Chinese control far into modern-day Kyrgyzstan and Kazakstan, and the Mongols of Genghis Khan and his successors took control of the Chinese and almost everyone else. Militant Islam eventually wiped out the Indo-European Buddhist civilizations of the Tarim, but in around AD 630, when the pilgrim Xuánzàng passed through, Turpan was enthusiastically Buddhist, and he was welcomed by the king, who insisted that he stay in

Turpan rather than continue his journey. Xuánzàng eventually had to begin a hunger strike in order to get his freedom. Allowed to leave, he was sent on his way with letters of introduction to 24 other kingdoms, and vast amounts of riches.

The first European to visit Turpan since Jesuit Benedict de Goës passed through in 1604 was probably a German-Russian botanist, Dr A. Regel, who visited Gāochāng in 1878, considering it a late Roman settlement, not a view widely adopted elsewhere.

Modern Turpan is both a small town and a major tourist destination with all the usual vices that that combination entails. Everyone from street fruit-sellers to the post office employees mark up prices for tourists, and many restaurants have English menus with no prices, or no qualms about adding up to 30% to the bill if they think they can get away with it. Shopping at the Uighur market and eating at Uighur restaurants brings some relief. Travel out to the various ancient cities, caves and other sights around Turpan is easy and cheap to arrange, and the city has an atmosphere different from most other cities in China, and even from others in Xīnjiāng. This is created both by the majority Uighur population and by the grape vines which are trained to grow over the streets on arches of wire, turning them into cool green tunnels.

The city of Turpan lies in the second-deepest inland depression in the world, with more than 4000 sq km of land below sea level, some of it more than 100m down (only Israel's Dead Sea is lower). Anciently called Huǒzhōu—'Land of Fire'—the region is a series of splashes of green in a gravelly desert.

The Chinese administrator Aitchen K. Wu passed through Turpan in 1933.

> *The market often goes on all night long—while in the daytime the streets are deserted, every one having 'gone to earth' in the caves...The hot wind is worse than anything that can be imagined, shrivelling the skin, scorching the eyes; and the direct rays of the sun carry death. It is a proverbial saying, not much exaggerated, that the people bake their dough cakes by sticking them on the wall of the huts.*

Aitchen K. Wu, *Turkistan Tumult*, 1940

The climate has not changed, although a vast tree-planting programme to Turpan's northwest has helped to break the power of the wind. The shops' interiors are caves of blackness compared to the glare outside. While the local people are not now quite as nocturnal as they once were, as in Hāmì many businesses are shut between 2pm and 5pm, reopening until 8pm.

Turpan survives with the assistance of *karez*, covered water channels that bring meltwater from the mountains to the north and west into the Turpan basin, together with Tiān Shān waters that, having been absorbed by the desert, resurface at the foot of the Flaming Mountains as the land drops away into the Turpan Depression. The missionaries, Mildred Cable and Francesca French, commented: 'The expense of caring for the *karez* is very heavy, but Turfan produces such phenomenal crops of fruit, grain, and cotton that any expenditure on irrigation is justified.' Turpan's speciality is grapes, and almost every house has a drying tower for turning them into the seedless raisins famous throughout China.

Turpan's main attractions are the plentiful ancient sites in the area, all easily reached by minibus. All are within long-standing cultivated areas, or near villages, and have never been abandoned completely.

公安局	1	PSB Gōng'ānjú	高昌宾馆	A	Gāochāng Bīnguǎn
吐鲁番博物馆	2	Tǔlǔfān Bówùguǎn	绿洲宾馆	B	Lùzhōu Bīnguǎn Oasis Hotel
邮电局	3	Post and telephone office Yóudiànjú	吐鲁番饭店	C	Tǔlǔfān Fàndiàn Turpan Hotel
长途汽车站	4	Long-distance bus station Chángtú qìchēzhàn	交通宾馆	D	Jiāotōng Bīnguǎn
新华书店	5	Xīnhuá Bookshop Xīnhuá Shūdiàn		E	English menu restaurants
中国银行	6	Bank of China Zhōngguó Yínháng	颐园宾馆	F	Yíyuán Bīnguǎn
	7	Buses to Tuyoq	粮贸宾馆	G	Liángmào Bīnguǎn
市场	8	Market Shìchǎng		H	John's Information Café
			吐鲁番宾馆	I	Tǔlǔfān Bīnguǎn Turpan Hotel

Turpan map key

Getting to and from Turpan
by train

The station for Turpan is at Dàhéyàn, 49km away, and also known as Tǔlǔfān Zhàn (Turpan Station). Minibuses connect the station with Turpan's bus station, which leave only when full, take just over an hour, and charge 'foreign guests' ¥10 ($1.25). To reach Dàhéyàn's bus station walk uphill from the railway station and take the first major right turn. The bus station is a few minutes' walk away on the left. For those who arrive in the middle of the night, there is reputedly a tolerable hotel reached by turning left at the same junction.

All trains east and west stop at Dàhéyàn. The only way to buy tickets while in Turpan is from CITS in the Oasis Hotel, or possibly through the local branch of John's Information Café, where the current timetable should also be available. Trips to Ürümqi are best made by bus. The timing of the 143 to Korla (on alternate days) is not good either, as it leaves Dàhéyàn at 03.52, arriving 13.54. There are six trains to the east (the 54/51, 70, 98, 114/111, 144 and 244) all going at least as far as Lánzhōu, and all except the 244 going to Xī'ān or beyond. Hāmì is best reached by bus, and for Dūnhuáng (Liǔyuán station) the best train is the comfortable a/c 70, which leaves at 21.06 and arrives at 09.33. There's also the 114/111 which leaves at 18.06 and arrives at 07.03; other trains leave in the middle of the night.

by bus

There are sleeper buses to Kashgar three times weekly, and buses to points in between, such as Korla and Kuqa, and to places east such as Hāmì and Dūnhuáng (summer only—otherwise change at Hāmì). There are buses to Ürümqi approximately every 30 minutes for ¥11 ($1.50), some of which are expresses costing ¥15 ($2), although foreigners are sometimes asked to pay double. The bus station is just west of the centre on the north side of Lǎochéng Lù.

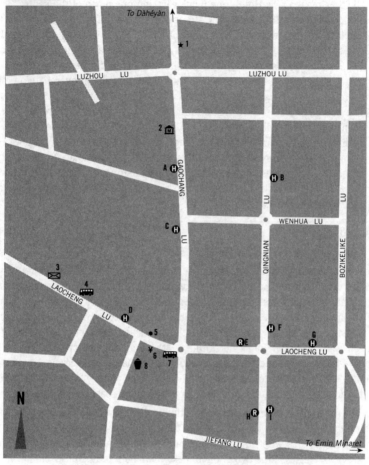

Turpan

To Dàhéyàn

★ 1

LUZHOU LU   LUZHOU LU

2 🏛

A Ⓗ GAOCHANG LU

Ⓗ B

C Ⓗ LU

WENHUA LU

QINGNIAN LU

BOZIKELIKE LU

3 ✉

LAOCHENG

4 🚌

D Ⓗ

● 5

Ⓗ F

Ⓡ E

Ⓗ G

LAOCHENG LU

¥ 6

🚌 7

🛍 8

N

Ⓡ Ⓗ
H I

JIEFANG LU

To Emin Minaret

STREET NAMES

柏孜克里克路	Bózīkèlǐkè Lù	老城路	Lǎochéng Lù
高昌路	Gāochāng Lù	绿洲、东、中、西路	Lùzhōu Dōng/Zhōng/Xīlù
解放路	Jiěfàng Lù	青年路	Qīngnián Lù
		文化路	Wénhuà Lù

Getting Around

The centre of Turpan is a traffic island between the main hotels and most other useful points. Turpan is small and everything is within walking distance of the centre. The main sights are all outside town and need a taxi, minibus or bicycle. Minibus drivers wait at the bus station, outside the hotels, and even knock on your door at regular intervals to sell you one-day tours to eight standard places, or the combination of your choice.

CITS is in the Oasis Hotel, one block east and one north of the centre. There is a branch of **John's Information Café** opposite the Tǔlǔfān Bīnguǎn, where information is more freely available. The **Bank of China** (*open 9–1 and 5–8*) is on the south side of Lǎochéng Lù just west of the centre. The **post and telephone office** (*open 9–12 and 5–8, less in winter*) is on the north side, further west beyond the bus station. There is an international counter which insists on overcharging foreigners even for basic letters by assuming without weighing that all letters are overweight. The *poste restante* service is also unreliable, but what letters there are that haven't been sent back are in a drawer of the right-hand desk behind the counter. **Film** is available in the department stores. There are **maps** of the inaccurate but colourful variety available from the ground floor of the Xīnhuá Shūdiàn on the north side of Lǎochéng Lù just west of the centre. **Visa extensions** are available from the PSB on the east side of Gāochāng Lù, two and a half blocks north of the centre (*irregular hours; closed weekends*).

Tǔlǔfān Bówùguǎn

吐鲁番博物馆

Open 9–1 and 3.30–7; adm ¥12 ($1.50).

The museum is on the west side of Gāochāng Lù two blocks north of the centre. Its shiny exterior belies the shabby and poorly lit interior typical of most Chinese museums, but there is a small collection of items from various sites around Turpan on the ground floor and in one upstairs room which is worth seeing. The exhibits are arranged in roughly chronological order, and demonstrate the preserving qualities of the area's arid atmosphere. Amongst the most striking are 2300-year-old items of clothing, 4th- and 5th-century toys from Gāochāng (including a wooden tiger and cow, and a whole detachment of military figures), a clay drum containing a skull and other remains, and *diǎnxīn* (more commonly known in the West as dim sum), almost identical to modern dumplings but 14 centuries past their sell-by date.

Upstairs are five corpses from Gāochāng, mostly 8th century, remarkably well-preserved and with hair intact. A man who was head of the Gāochāng army, and who died in AD 558, lies preserved alongside his wife. In death his beard and sunken cheeks give him a Sir Walter Raleigh look, but effigies of the two of them make them both prosperously plump.

Around Turpan

The sights outside Turpan are usually all visited in one day, with a break during the hottest hours. The eight sights on most tours are the ancient city of Jiāohé, the Emin Minaret, the Flaming Mountains (Huǒyàn Shān), the *karez* irrigation channels, the ancient city of Gāochāng, Grape Valley, the Astana Tombs, and Bezeklik Caves, sometimes with the addition of a visit to the town's not particularly interesting mosque. Several of these sights are overrated, but as private minibus operators charge about ¥50 ($6) per person, the whole day trip is good value. The CITS air-conditioned version with English-speaking guide is also worth considering, as there is little information in English at the sites themselves. What information is displayed in English is mostly intended to establish through lies or omission that the Hàn have been continuously in charge of the area almost since the beginning of time.

Shorter tours can be arranged, too. Gāochāng and Astana both stand below the Flaming Mountains, and Bezeklik is in them, so missing the turning to the designated Flaming Mountain photo-opportunity spot is no great loss. The *karez* system is impressive; Turpan is hung with grapes, and the bus from Dàhéyàn passes fields full of vines, so Grape Valley can be missed, too. If you accept Gāochāng as representative of the ancient cities, then a half-day tour of Gāochāng, Astana, Bezeklik and Emin is a good choice. For those on a budget, both Emin and Jiāohé are in boneshaker bicycle range of Turpan.

Gāochāng (Karakhoja) and Jiāohé (Yarkhoto) 高昌, 交河

Adm to each site ¥13 ($2).

Having been built of mud and adobe brick, many of Xīnjiāng's ancient Silk Route cities have now been reduced to plains of low-lying shapeless mounds, with only the remains of outer city walls and the odd featureless drum of mud to suggest human agency in an obvious way. Few are reachable by metalled roads. Gāochāng and Jiāohé's substantial size and ease of access place them amongst the most important and interesting Silk Route ruins.

Gāochāng is about 40km east of Turpan. The German archaeologist Albert von Le Coq arrived at Gāochāng in November 1904:

> *The old town is an enormous square, covering about a square mile or 256 acres. The massive old wall in many places is still in good preservation. It is almost 22 yards high and made out of stamped mud in the fashion common even at the present time from Persia to China. Numerous towers—there are still seventy of them existing—strengthen this wall, which diminishes its solidity towards the top, but which in the lower part is so massive that the builders could have arranged whole suites of rooms within its bulk, especially near the gates.*

> Albert von Le Coq, *Buried Treasures of Chinese Turkestan*, 1928

The walls are as impressive as when Le Coq saw them, although the continuous process of destruction begun long before he arrived has continued, and many more of the buildings which he identified as being temples, monasteries or tombs have been destroyed. The missionaries Cable and French saw farmers hacking at the buildings with pickaxes, and streams were diverted through the site in order to bring it under cultivation, ending the dryness necessary to preserve buildings and documents alike. Von Le Coq discovered a library in a Manichaean shrine which had been completely destroyed by water. Peasants' ploughs brought many treasures to light, and Cable and French took away a variety of small items, observing children playing with beads they had found amongst the ruins, and their canny mothers pressing any ancient pots they unearthed into modern service. Peasants would scrape paintings from walls for use as fertilizer, and documents discovered were often destroyed for fear of their images of humans, or other material perhaps heretical to the Muslim faith. Von Le Coq met a man who had thrown a whole library of books he discovered, amounting to several cartloads, into the river. The finder was afraid 'of the unholy nature of the writings and, secondly, that the Chinese might use the discovery as a pretext for fresh extortions'.

As von Le Coq commented, 'The Chinese, acting as officials in the country, pay no attention to this destruction; they are all Confucians, and despise Buddhism as the religion of the "small folk".' Matters do not seem to have improved greatly in modern times. Despite having theoretically been under government protection since 1961, cultivation within the walls continues, and there are signs of digging which suggest that the hunt for treasures is not yet over. Farm vehicles have free passage through the site, and visitors are allowed to clamber all over the remaining ruins without restraint, with rapid erosion the result.

Objects discovered at Gāochāng proved to be more Chinese in style than at most other Central Asian sites, although the city and surrounding state was founded by the non-Hàn Northern Liáng dynasty (AD 397–439), who were later absorbed by the equally non-Hàn Northern Wèi (AD 386–585). It passed to the Uighurs in about AD 800, and to the Xī Xià people about 200 years later. Von Le Coq identified the architecture as being of Iranian and Indian origin, although the remaining ruins, however large, are difficult for the untrained eye to identify.

Le Coq did make two particularly interesting discoveries. In one building he excavated he found 'the remains of a great mural painting, representing a man over life-size in the dress of a Manichaean priest, surrounded by Manichaean monks (*electi*) and nuns (*electae*) also dressed in the white garb of their order.' It was not previously thought that the Manichaeans had religious buildings adorned with paintings. The mural can now be seen in Berlin.

A second discovery was somewhat more gruesome:

> We broke open the floor, found the remains of the old domed roof, and then came suddenly upon confused heaps of piled up corpses of at least some hundred murdered men. Judging from their clothing they were Buddhist monks … skin, hair, the dried-up eyes, and the frightful wounds which had caused their death, were in many cases intact and recognizable. One skull especially had been split from the top of the head to the teeth with a frightful sabre cut.

Albert von Le Coq, *Buried Treasures of Chinese Turkestan*, 1928

Von Le Coq attributes this to religious persecution in the middle of the 9th century. The city was eventually abandoned during local wars in the 14th century.

Gāochāng was so rich a site that although Aurel Stein did not arrive until 1914, after there had been two German expeditions and continuous destructive operations by the peasants, he found numerous metal objects and papers, together with coins dating his finds to the Sòng dynasty. Von Le Coq also took away recordings of local singing, and even hedgehogs he found rustling amongst his photographic papers.

Donkey carts will take you for a 3km ride through the ruins for ¥10 ($1.25) per person.

Jiāohé is only 10km from Turpan, and can be reached by bicycle. It was founded earlier than Gāochāng, and was one of the small city-states discovered by Zhāng Qiān during his investigations in the time of the Hàn dynasty. It was at different times a Hàn military base, occupied by Tibetans, ruled over by Gāochāng, and under Uighur and Mongol control. The site was abandoned during the Yuán dynasty, and most of the remains are probably Táng. The city is similar in scale to Gāochāng but more spectacular in location on a raised terrace between two ravines, which do the job of city walls. Some of the ruins have more shape than those at Gāochāng, and a clear main street from the southern entrance leads to the remains of a Buddhist temple.

Bózīkèlǐkè Qiānfódòng (Bezeklik Caves)
Adm ¥17 ($2).

柏孜克里克千佛洞

The site is about 8km northwest of Gāochāng, and en route you can admire the 'Flaming Mountains' whose barren sides do glow impressively red if seen in the late afternoon horizontal light. The 57 surviving caves are reached by descending from the ticket office by a modern stairway to the interior of a narrow river-carved ravine. Most were once decorated with wall paintings, but the majority of these were removed to Berlin by von Le Coq, who also unearthed two libraries here. A few years later in 1914, Aurel Stein took further works for what is now the National Museum in Delhi.

Perhaps more than at any other cave site, the huge vacant spaces created by sawing giant jigsaw puzzle pieces from the walls give the foreign visitor pause for thought—there is so little left. Von Le Coq had no qualms about the wholesale removal of any antiquities he could discover, although his superior, the older and more cautious Professor Grünwedel, did not agree. Stein did think twice:

> *For centuries the frescoes had been liable to casual injury at the hands of iconoclast Mohammedan visitors. During recent years they had been exposed to further damage from local people, who in vandal fashion cut out small pieces for sale to Europeans. Careful systematic removal therefore presented the only means under existing conditions of saving as many characteristic specimens as possible of these fine remains of Buddhist pictorial art as developed in Central Asia.*

M. Aurel Stein, *Ancient Central Asia Tracks*, 1941

Today only a few caves are open to the public, and these are in dismal condition. The site resembles a popular beach after a day at the height of the holiday season. There is litter everywhere, and sometimes empty beer bottles are stacked in odd corners of the caves.

Āsītǎnā Mùqún (Astana Graves)
Adm ¥10 ($1.25).

阿斯塔那墓群

There are more than 400 tombs scattered around the plain here, identifiable only by shallow mounds of earth. Three can be entered, and the gatekeeper or his young son will show you around. These feature a narrow ramp leading down to a single chamber with painted walls. The first two tombs are empty, but the third has its original corpses in situ, although now under glass.

Stein opened numerous tombs here in 1914 (as did Russian, French and Japanese expeditions at other times). He dated the burials from the beginning of the 7th to the second quarter of the 8th century, although local literature puts the earliest burial at AD 273. He removed silks, documents used as fillers in the coffins, and substantial amounts of objects buried with the dead, including a painted wooden statue of one of the horses so prized by the Hàn, now in the British Museum.

Émǐn Tǎ or Sūgōng Tǎ (Emin Minaret) 额敏塔，苏公塔

Open 9am–9pm; adm ¥15.

The roughly 40m-high brick minaret is actually part of a large mosque, built in 1778. The minaret has an elegant conical shape, its bricks laid in patterns that make it look knitted. Until a few years ago it could be climbed, but no longer. The mosque's dusty and gloomy interior is still the setting for religious services on Fridays, when entrance may be restricted.

Tuyoq (Tǔyùgōu) 吐峪沟

The 100 per cent Uighur village of Tuyoq is not usually included in minibus tours, but can be added by arrangement. There is one bus every afternoon to Tuyoq for ¥10 ($1.25). Private minibuses which also run in the afternoon wait outside the Bank of China. Return buses leave in the morning, but unusually (and probably unofficially) it's possible to stay with local people in simple accommodation for about ¥40 ($5) including meals.

Cable and French were reminded of Tuscany, and little has changed since their visit, save for the introduction of a small hydroelectric plant. The cluster of mud and adobe buildings that make up the village stand at the entrance to a narrow valley, with a stream that supplies its water. Above the stream to the left at the point where the valley begins to narrow stands a walled compound housing a damaged mosque. Following the stream on the right- or left-hand side up the valley, using footpaths or the edges of man-made watercourses, you come to a few caves first on the left, and then a number high on the right where the valley turns left, reached after about 10 minutes. Here it also narrows sharply, and has been dammed, making further progress impossible. Altogether there are about 46 extant caves, but when von Le Coq visited in 1905, 'on the giddy heights of a terrace, there used to be a very large monastery that, like similar buildings in Tibet, clung, as might a swallows nest, on the almost perpendicular slope of the mountain-side'. The monastery fell down during an earthquake in 1916. He removed two sacks of 8th- and 9th-century manuscripts and embroideries.

The main caves, thought to be the oldest in the area, can only be reached with a steep scramble up the cliff, and are locked, the guardian not being easily found. Nine of the caves are said to have the remains of murals (Stein removed some pieces in 1914). The largest cave in the area is regarded as particularly holy by local Muslims, and there are a number of legends concerning it, one of which was recounted by Cable and French. It is supposed to house seven sleeping men, wandering pilgrims who finally despaired of humanity and lay down to sleep until matters improved. After a thousand years they emerged to find that things were even worse than before, and decided to return to their slumbers. A little dog asked for permission to join them on the grounds that it was also a creature of Allah, and now sleeps there, too. Were they to emerge today it's possible to imagine that they would find little changed, except the addition of the hydroelectric plant, and indeed getting into the caves is not the main point of visiting the village (the key-holder is reputed to invent large sums as entrance fees).

The valley is extremely quiet, and the birds consequently seem to have powerful singing voices. The village is almost completely free of any pretension to modernity. While the daily bus provides access to Turpan's markets both for buying and selling, it brings few visitors from the outside world, and seems slightly out of place.

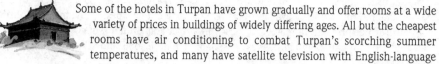

Where to Stay

Some of the hotels in Turpan have grown gradually and offer rooms at a wide variety of prices in buildings of widely differing ages. All but the cheapest rooms have air conditioning to combat Turpan's scorching summer temperatures, and many have satellite television with English-language programming. Summer water shortages may sometimes limit the availability of showers to a few hours a day. Prices for some rooms may drop to as little as one-third in the low season.

expensive

The best hotel is the **Lùzhōu Bīnguǎn** (Oasis Hotel), ✆ 522491, @ 523348, which has doubles with bath from ¥350/$42. Both this hotel and the **Tǔlǔfān Bīnguǎn** (Turpan Hotel), ✆ 522301, @ 523262, 15 minutes' walk south, have several build-ings arranged around green spaces, the Turpan Hotel's grape-hung cold drinks area being particularly pleasant. Double rooms in its new wing are ¥380 ($46). The **Tǔlǔfān Fàndiàn** (another Turpan Hotel), ✆ 522147, @ 522336, north of the bus station, is less appealing in location and layout, but has smart doubles in its new wing from ¥320 ($39). Enter through the gate at the right-hand end of the building to find the newer wing and reception across the car park. All these hotels, and the **Gāochāng Bīnguǎn**, ✆ 523229, a little further north, have suites at between ¥300 ($36) and ¥680 (¥82). Walk round to the right-hand side to find the entrance, or walk through the restaurant at the front of the building if it is open.

moderate

The **Tǔlǔfān Bīnguǎn** also has an older Muslim-style wing, where a triple with bath and day-long hot water costs ¥90 ($11) per bed. The **Tǔlǔfān Fàndiàn** has older doubles from ¥80 ($10) per bed. The new **Yíyuán Bīnguǎn**, ✆ 522170, between the Oasis and the Tǔlǔfān Bīnguǎn, has smart doubles for ¥90 ($11) per bed, as does the **Gāochāng** for ¥75 ($9). The **Jiāotōng Bīnguǎn** next to the bus station, ✆ 523238, has basic doubles with bath for ¥80 ($10) per bed, and triple rooms with bath for ¥40 ($5) per bed. The **Liángmào Bīnguǎn** (Grain Trade Hotel), ✆ 522448, one block east of the centre, has doubles and five-bed rooms with bath for ¥80 ($10) per bed.

inexpensive

There are dorms in the older buildings of the Tǔlǔfān Bīnguǎn (from ¥20/$2.50), the Oasis (four beds, ¥22 /$3), the Tǔlǔfān Fàndiàn (four beds, from ¥24/$3), the Jiāotōng (three beds, ¥36; four beds ¥24/$3, larger rooms ¥16/$2), and the Liángmào (four beds, ¥20/$2.50).

Eating Out

Each hotel has its own restaurant, and sometimes several, as in the case of the Oasis Hotel. Restaurants here have no hesitation in upping the prices between order and bill. There are a number of Hàn and Uighur restau-rants at different levels just east of the centre, some with English menus. One or two of these are dubious, leaving prices off their English menus, but most serve perfectly satisfactory if unexciting food. Uighur noodle dishes and bread are available at street-side stalls in front of tiny noodle restaurants immediately to the east of the bus station. Fruit is widely available on street corners, but cheapest in the market. **John's Information Café** (a relative of those in Kashgar and Ürümqi), opposite the entrance to the Tǔlǔfān Bīnguǎn, serves reasonable Chinese food and Chinese attempts at Western food.

The Roads to Turpan and Ürümqi

Neither has a good reputation. The route to Turpan heads west to Toksun (Tuōkèxùn) and then south, crossing a spur of the Tiān Shān through the Toksun Gorges, which Eric Teichman, en route by truck in 1935, was advised by Serat, a Mongol acting as a guide, and who had been this way with Sven Hedin only a few years before, was 'the worst place on the whole route from Peking to Kashgar'. Another inheritance from Hedin was an older lorry, nicknamed 'Edsel' after the member of the Ford family who had originally donated it to Hedin's road surveying expedition, and which had crossed China twice already. This finally met its end here, stripping the teeth one by one from its differential on the struggle through the gorges, and coasting down to Komux (Kùmǐshí) on the other side, to become permanently immobile. Teichman was not enthusiastic about his enforced bivouac:

> *The night was cold, our lodging wretched, and I felt depressed, wishing the journey over and strain of waiting for the unexpected at an end... The Sinkiang deserts are more sterile and forbidding even than the Gobi and, in all my asiatic wanderings I cannot recall a more depressing resting-place than dirty, ruined Kumush.*

> Eric Teichman, *Journey to Turkistan*, 1937

The Ford was gutted and abandoned, and various equipment that could no longer be carried was given away. Those who find it impossible to pack light may be heartened to know that Teichman's party had carried a cast-iron kitchen stove across the deserts of Mongolia and Xīnjiāng. This, with other odds and ends, was bequeathed to the village headman, who was not head of much, since at Hedin's estimate only four families lived there. As Teichman noted, many other travellers had difficulties at the Toksun Gorges, too: an earlier venture with tractors (the Hardt-Citroën expedition) took ten hours to do a mile, and Sven Hedin with Fords (including the ill-fated 'Edsel') got through, but only very slowly. In fact on one occasion on an urgent trip to rescue one member of the expedition who had been bitten by a pig, the car in which Hedin was travelling got stuck as a rainstorm began, and was only saved from being washed away as the stream rapidly swelled by the driving skills of Serat, who must have wondered why he was doomed to bring odd foreigners through such a dismal place so many times. Hedin cursed the despotic Xīnjiāng governor of the day, Jīn Shùrén, who while milking the populace had spent not a penny on the roads. As Teichman remarked, the Toksun road hadn't improved since Younghusband took a day to do 1½ miles with a cart in 1887. Teichman's newer Ford truck, which became part of the equipment of the British consulate at Kashgar, was later to become another victim of the Toksun Gorges, on the return from a trip to Ürümqi made by the last British Consul-General, Eric Shipton. Cracking a cylinder head on the climb, it didn't make it over the top and rolled back down to be abandoned at Toksun.

The route north to Ürümqi also involves following a stream through a gorge, although, as with the route to Korla, travelling in the stream bed is no longer necessary, and the winding road now offers a pleasant change from the monotony of the desert.

Ürümqi (Wūlǔmùqǐ)

乌鲁木齐 Ürümqi has long suffered from poor reviews:

Sven Hedin: 'No one leaves the town with regret, and it is full of people who are only there because they cannot get permission to leave, and may not leave without permission.'

Eric Teichman: 'That there is something gloomy dark and sinister about the Ürümqi atmosphere is something that no one who has resided there is likely to deny.'

Albert von Le Coq praised the substantial architecture of some of the buildings belonging to Chinese secret societies, but remarked that otherwise Ürümqi looked just like any other Chinese town. He was not impressed to find an execution in progress in the main street, in which a man standing on a raised board had his head firmly fixed between two planks. The foot board was lowered a little every day, and the execution thus took eight days to carry out. 'The traffic went on as usual past this barbaric apparatus, and a melon-dealer was selling his juicy fruit with no concern for his neighbour's misery.'

Owen Lattimore, arriving by camel caravan from Hohhot, regretted the passing of his easygoing times in the desert, and the formality that enforced him to behave and dress like a foreigner, and thus become remote from the local people. After a meal of unaccustomed elegance with the Irish postmaster and his wife, he went back to his inn, '...a servant going before me with a lantern, because that is the rule, after the city gates have been closed, and both of us provided with sticks, to fend off the packs of curs which patrol the empty streets.'

Aitchen K. Wu: 'Tihwa [the Qīng name for Ürümqi] had for centuries been notorious for its floods, and was spoken of as the town in the desert where camels are drowned in the streets.'

Today Hedin would find many Hàn who would leave immediately for the east if only they could get permission, and Kazaks, Kyrgyz, Uighurs and others who would join their families and co-religionists in the neighbouring newly minted states of Kazakstan and Kyrgyzstan, if the Chinese would let them out. Teichman's remark on gloom might now be taken to refer to Ürümqi's polluted atmosphere. There are no longer packs of curs, but local people have a sense of increasing lawlessness. Ürümqi is not representative of Xīnjiāng, and is an island of Hàn people and typical Hàn architecture in an ocean of 12 minority peoples, who form the majority in most other Xīnjiāng cities and towns.

'The golden season of this city is from May to September, when flowers are all in blossom and various kinds of melons and fruits are in season sending forth fragrance everywhere in the city', says one Chinese guide book of Ürümqi. The only things sending forth fragrance are the factories and vehicles which together make even breathing in Ürümqi unpleasant. As you stroll down Guāngmíng Lù to Jiànkāng Lù choking in the traffic fumes that turn the sky grey-blue, you may wonder why one is called 'Bright Street' and the other 'Healthy Street'. Ürümqi is the boom town of China's northwest, with glossy office and hotel towers springing up everywhere, and smoking factory chimneys sprouting amongst the tenement housing. Every other building seems to be a restaurant, and the rest are clothes shops or computer game arcades. The city is in a permanent shopping frenzy and even pedestrian underpasses are crammed with stalls. There is life late into the night, with food available until well after 12am, numerous discos, and ubiquitous open-air snooker tables. Neighbouring Almaty and Bishkek may be national capitals, but they are backwaters in comparison. Even Lánzhōu, the capital of Gānsù province and much nearer the Chinese heartlands, has less buzz than Ürümqi, and you'll reach Xī'ān before finding the same frenzy of activity.

Shipton was right. Ürümqi is still a typical Hàn Chinese city with precious little to distinguish it architecturally from others thousands of miles away, except the occasional mosque. Uighurs, Huí (Chinese muslims, also known as Dungans), Kazaks, and other minorities can be found however, particularly in markets, at food stalls, and in restaurants marked *Qīngzhēn* (pure truth)—Mandarin for Muslim. At night part of Zhōng Shān Lù in the heart of the Hàn city becomes a massive minority open-air food festival, open until midnight.

Until recent times Ürümqi was decidedly Uighur. The Chinese administrator Aitchen K. Wu was here in the 1930s.

> *In the Chinese quarter all was familiar to me, the walled yamens, the neat wooden houses, the seething bazaars. This was China as I knew it; but within a distance of a few yards I was plunged into an alien atmosphere. Here was the vigorous life of a city of the southern steppes, where Turk and Tartar meet—the mosque, the market, the endless rows of stalls. And passing beyond the fortifications I came into another world, the bare spaciousness of a Russian market town, the walled compound of the Soviet Consulate serving as its focus, from which it straggled to the south.*

> Aitchen K. Wu, *Turkistan Tumult*, 1940

Now the Chinese authorities are doing everything they can to encourage reluctant Hàn to move to Xīnjiāng, and have succeeded in turning Ürümqi from a Uighur city with a Chinese quarter into a Chinese city with a Uighur quarter, around the Èrdàoqiáo Market. Of the Russians there is now little sign outside the Aeroflot office, and small groups of traders on the Almaty to Ürümqi train.

Warlord vs. Warlord

Following the end of the Manchu Qīng dynasty in 1911/12, Xīnjiāng was ruled by a series of administrators who, although nominally loyal to the new republic, ran the region as an independent fiefdom. In the case of the first, Yáng Zēngxīn, his independence was more a result of the Nationalist government's inability to offer him any assistance, or often even to communicate with him, due to problems in the east or uprisings in between. Yáng was much praised by commentators of the time as an astute administrator who kept a lid on ethnic tensions with very limited military resources. After the Russian revolution 30–40,000 White Russians entered Xīnjiāng and could easily have taken over, but they were kept under control by Yáng with deft diplomacy and only 10,000 men. Inevitably, modern communist histories portray him as a vicious autocrat. Yáng was assassinated at a banquet on 7 July 1928 (*see* 'Eating Out', p.257).

His successor, Jīn Shùrén, reviled by all commentators, was incompetent and despotic, putting relatives into positions of power, and his valet in command of a regiment. He raised taxes, monopolized the most profitable trades, issued valueless paper money, sealed off Xīnjiāng from China, placed spies everywhere, forbade travel without a permit signed by him personally, and was the cause of various revolts. He abolished the monarchy in Hāmì, taking cultivated land there from Turkis and giving it to Hàn peasants arriving from Gānsù (*see* **Hāmì**, p.223), setting off a province-wide revolt that was to lead to his own downfall.

At this time there were a number of Huí (Chinese Muslim) generals and warlords of unpredictable loyalty and behaviour, who controlled large areas of Gānsù, Qīnghǎi and Níngxià. Like the Hàn governors of Xīnjiāng, they often gave nominal allegiance to the Nationalist government, but only to bolster their own legitimacy while they enjoyed the benefits of power. The warlords were known as the five horses, sharing the surname Mǎ, meaning horse, a popular surname amongst Huí, being a Chinese contraction of *Mohammed*. In the '30s the most charismatic and notorious was Mǎ Zhòngyīng, who was an active bandit and army leader from his late teens, thus known as the 'Baby General', and, as his fame grew, 'Big Horse'.

Mǎ Zhòngyīng was born in Línxià and became at only 17 a general in the army of another Mǎ at Xīníng. When another warlord, the 'Christian General' Féng Yùxiáng, was waging war in Gānsù, Mǎ Zhòngyīng revolted, marched to Línxià with several thousand men and besieged the town for eight months, until the town was relieved by reinforcements from Féng's army. Mǎ then became a bandit chief, travelling up and down the 'Imperial Highway' through Gānsù, trying and failing to stir up further rebellion, and murdering around 6000 people in the process. In 1929–30, while Mǎ was robbing in Níngxià, the governor-general of Gānsù had his father executed as an act of vengeance for Mǎ's rebellion, thus increasing Mǎ's already bitter hatred of the Chinese. Nevertheless, the Nationalists needed any allies they could get, and in 1930 Mǎ was admitted to Chiang Kai-shek's military academy in Nánjīng. After three months there, he went to Zhōngwèi and reassembled his soldiers, and the Governor-General of Gānsù made him Commander-In-Chief at Zhāngyè, in command of Western Gānsù. He conscripted local people into an army of more than 10,000, but when his restless nature led him to show signs of independence from authority, another Mǎ was sent to suppress him.

It was at this low point in his bloody career that he received a request from Hāmì Chancellor Yolbas Khan to come and help with the uprising at Hāmì, now a joint-Turki-Kyrgyz effort. Raising a poorly supplied force of 500 men Mǎ marched them through a long stretch of desert from Ānxī to Hāmì by main force of personality. The commandant of Barkol (to the north of Hāmì) went over to him and provided ammunition, and he began a siege of Hāmì's Chinese garrison, but lost interest after six months. In February 1932 he arrived at Jiǔquán, and was again given office by the desperate Nationalists, spending a year raising fresh recruits.

Following the relief of Hāmì, Governor Jīn sent Shèng Shìcái, his military commander, on pacification operations, and he travelled around the province reducing various towns to ashes, and fighting an engagement against Big Horse's adjutant, another Mǎ (Shímíng). In the winter of 1932–3 Mǎ Shímíng headed for Ürümqi, won one engagement with Jīn's troops but lost a second and had to retreat. In January 1933 the two Mǎs advanced together, slaughtering any Chinese they met. Jīn did little to organize a defence, but there was a strict curfew.

Russian émigrés did most of the work of repelling the attacks when they came. On 21 February there was intense fighting in the streets of the western suburbs which continued for several days, the whole area finally being set ablaze by the Russians. Hedin says 6000 noncombatants died. The rebel forces then blockaded the town, attempting to starve it into submission, and Jīn's brother confiscated all wheat in order to sell it back for huge sums. Without the émigrés Ürümqi would have been lost, but Jīn feared all foreigners, and deliberately kept them poorly supplied and armed, keeping the best *matériel* for Chinese troops and sending the Russians to the most dangerous positions.

On 12 April 1933 White Russian officers took it upon themselves to stage a coup d'état on the grounds of Jīn Shùrén's incompetence. They drove back Jīn's bodyguards, while he escaped over the back wall of his compound disguised as an ordinary soldier. The Russians had no intention of taking overall control, and temporary political and military councils were formed under the chairmenship of Chinese. Aitchen K. Wu, somewhat reluctantly at first, became secretary. The immediate problem, other than staving off the marauding Mǎs, was to inform Shèng, the Chinese military commander in the field against them, and to send a full account to the Nánjīng government. Jīn Shùrén headed for Chuguchak (Tǎchéng) intending to regroup and retake Ürümqi, and put every White Russian in the region to death. He never succeeded, and returned to Nánjīng, deemed by the government to have resigned his post.

The education minister was elected in his place, and military commander Shèng was provisionally appointed military governor. The Turkis were promised good government and requested to lay down their arms, but were refused any senior government posts and so began to rearm. In May 1933, 'Big Horse' was once more asked to give assistance, and he again resigned from government authority, taking control of an area east of Ürümqi. The Ürümqi government offered him control of eastern Xīnjiāng and of Hāmì, but Mǎ would not be bought off, and advanced. He was engaged by mostly Russian government forces halfway to Ürümqi, and was on the point of winning a decisive victory when a sudden storm, for which his troops were ill-equipped, bogged down his cavalry. At the same time, government troops driven out of Manchuria by the Japanese invasion, who had travelled west through Soviet territory, arrived to strengthen Shèng's forces. The combination gave Mǎ a decisive defeat. 1000 of his troops were killed and the rest ran away. Mǎ was not pursued, however, and he had a chance to regroup, taking Turpan and gaining control of Hāmì, Korla and Kuqa and thus effectively the whole of Xīnjiāng south of the Tiān Shān.

Wu, who had been busying himself during the various sieges with running a Red Cross service and burying the many combatants and non-combatants dead of wounds or starvation, was sent to negotiate with Mǎ at Hāmì. He carried letters offering Mǎ the opportunity to pacify the remainder of the south of Xīnjiāng, and finish off the bandits and other independent groups around Khotan. This was a calculated gamble, for while it would relieve the pressure on Ürümqi and allow it to rebuild its defences, it would also give Mǎ the opportunity to build his forces to greater strengths in an empire he might build for himself in the south.

Legends were bound to grow up around so charismatic a figure as Mǎ, said always to be in the thick of the fighting and often the first to scale the walls during an attack. He was strict about Islamic dietary regulation, carried a rifle like a common soldier, and would play football with his men. Yet he personally shot soldiers guilty of misdemeanours, and would order the slaughter of entire towns that resisted him. If to his charisma he could have added patience and humanity, a truly independent Turkestan might have emerged from the chaos of the Nationalist period, which the Chinese would have found difficult to reacquire after 1949.

Mildred Cable was forced to heal one of Mǎ's wounds, and was a witness to his callousness and flippancy. To Wu he showed another side of his personality:

> *I saw that his face was thin, his eyes very bright. His figure was perfectly proportioned, having that trained look seen on racehorses of the finest breed... The care with which he read the letters puzzled me. I should have felt no surprise had he tossed them contemptuously aside, the strong, bluff, soldier, impatient of scribblings. But no, he pored over them with every appearance of intense concentration. I realized that today he was a scholar, seeking to impress upon me that in matters of the pen he was my equal. Tomorrow he might be a savage warlord of the great plains ordering the execution of a thousand innocent victims. But today he was the great ruler, wise in matters of diplomacy.*

Aitchen K. Wu, Turkistan Tumult, 1940

Wu tried to sow uncertainty and to undermine the confidence of Mǎ, and by his own account succeeded. His final verdict was that force of personality was Mǎ's best quality, but that he was ignorant of strategy and lacked political judgement. However, while Mǎ and Wu talked, other uprisings were taking place.

The governor of Ili, faced with a combined Huí-Kyrgyz revolt, came over to Mǎ, and in November marched south. Communication between him and Mǎ, which was intercepted, revealed disloyal generals amongst the Manchurians and Russians, who were promptly arrested. The Ili governor marched south from Gulja to Aksu, but was caught in a snowstorm on the way, his army freezing and deserting en masse. He shot himself. Mǎ suddenly pushed forward on 12 January and another siege of Ürümqi began, which looked likely to bring about its final reduction. But in an arrangement parallel to US involvement in Cambodia, Soviet advisors, armour and aircraft, all without markings, came to Shèng's aid. Mǎ was bombed into retreat, and government troops attacked Turpan and Karashar in order to cut him off. In early 1934 he retreated in good order to Kashgar, to become involved in the factional fighting taking place there. He then mysteriously disappeared, and was rumoured to be a guest of the Soviet Union.

Peter Fleming and Ella Maillart, passing along the southern Taklamakan route, were to meet yet another Mǎ, a half-brother of Mǎ Zhòngyīng, and were permitted to see a photograph of 'Big Horse' taken after his departure to Russia. He was wearing the uniform of a cavalry officer in the Soviet Red Army, and exile seemed to be suiting him well.

Shèng's Reign of Terror

At this point, Shèng, deciding that three of the council were plotting against the government, had them shot, and took overall control, receiving the token blessing of Nánjīng.

At the time of Teichman's visit to Ürümqi in 1935, Shèng Shìcái was following the example of his post-revolutionary predecessors and running the province independently of other authorities. Teichman and the then British consul-general from Kashgar, Colonel Thompson Glover, spent days in negotiations with the governor over the future of British-Indian trade with Xīnjiāng, and the position of British subjects resident there.

Initially reformist, Shèng's regime became more and more corrupt and bloody. It is estimated that between 80,000 and 100,000 people were killed before he fled in fear of his life to Chóngqìng, the capital following the Japanese capture of Nánjīng, in 1944. He increasingly looked to the Soviet Union for trade, aid and military support. However, Soviet assistance began to dwindle at the start of the Second World War, and he began to make more of his notional relationship with the Nationalist government. Soviet trading missions and troops were withdrawn, and US and British consulates were opened to counter the Soviet influence, which by 1943 had almost completely evaporated.

The Nationalist government hardly welcomed Shèng's arrival in Chóngqìng. He had signed secret treaties with the Soviets giving them almost complete control of trade in Xīnjiāng in return for arms, and was placed under arrest.

Getting to and from Ürümqi

In 1948, shortly before the final closure of the British Consulate in Kashgar, the wife of the last consul, Diana Shipton, came to Ürümqi and boarded a Chinese flight to Shànghǎi, which left once a fortnight. The passengers sat with their backs to the small round windows, and their luggage, limited to 30lbs each, was piled up between them. Most of the Chinese passengers were violently ill during the flight. The trip took 48 hours in a Dakota with an American pilot, who occasionally invited Shipton into the cockpit. 'I gazed down with interested awe on to communist-held territory' she remarked, '—it looked exactly the same as the rest of the country.'

by air

Four airlines operate **international flights** to and from Ürümqi. Check-in times are usually two hours before departure, and departure taxes of ¥90 ($11) for international flights are payable at the airport or when you buy your ticket. **China Xīnjiāng Airlines** (CAAC in effect) flies to **Novosibirsk** (¥1300/$157) and on to **Moscow** (¥2270/$274) on Fridays. Boarding is not permitted unless you already hold a Russian visa. **Aeroflot** also flies to Novosibirsk and Moscow ($280) on Tuesdays, with connections to destinations worldwide, and since the office has a ticketing terminal you can buy these tickets in Ürümqi. No visa is required if you simply change planes at Moscow, but if you have an onward ticket and want to see the town, transit visas can be purchased in the transit lounge in Moscow's Sheremetyevo Airport. They start from $18 for 6 hours, running up to $110 for 72 hours, but ask Aeroflot for the latest prices. It is also possible to buy tourist visas at the airport if accommodation is purchased at the same time, although this is expensive. You will need three photographs.

There are three flights a week to and from **Almaty**. CAAC flies there and back on Mondays and Fridays, leaving Ürümqi at 9.50am Běijīng time, and you must have a Kazak visa before buying a ticket. **Kazak Airlines** flies on Tuesdays, leaving Ürümqi at 5pm. CAAC charges ¥1660 one way; Kazak Airlines $111. Their office is also able to issue three-day transit visas for $15 (issued in seven days) or $30 (issued in three days). You must have the visa of another CIS country or an onward air ticket from Almaty to a country beyond the CIS. Two-week tourist visas may also be possible for the same prices, but only if you can produce visa support, and they have received a corresponding fax or telex. One photograph is needed.

At the time of going to press Kyrgyz Airlines had just started a flight to Bishkek on Tuesdays, but the location of the ticketing office was unknown. Try asking Kazak Airlines or look for a parallel China Xīnjiāng Airlines flight, which will probably be more expensive. CXA and Aeroflot will almost certainly deny the existence of the Kazak and Kyrgyz flights, as will travel agents.

Air China also flies to **Islamabad** on Sundays for ¥2270 ($274). A Pakistani visa is necessary, and the nearest place in China to get it is Běijīng.

Ürümqi is the Xīnjiāng hub for CAAC's domestic network, with daily flights to Kashgar (6.50pm Běijīng time; ¥1220/$147), Běijīng (¥2550/$307), Xī'ān (¥2090/$252), Guǎngzhōu (¥3420/$412), Lánzhōu (¥1610/$194) and regular ones to Khotan (Hétián), Yīníng (Gulja, ¥560/$65), Korla (Kùěrlè, ¥400/$48), and via Korla to Charchan (Qiěmò, ¥750/$90), and Kuqa, and many other destinations. Domestic departure tax of ¥50 ($6) is payable at the airport, or when paying for tickets.

China Xīnjiāng Airlines has offices on the east side of Yǒuhǎo Nánlù just north of the post office (*open 9–9*), ✆ 481 4668, and on the west side of Chángjiāng Lù just south of Hēilóngjiāng Lù (*open 10–1.30 and 4–7*), ✆ 581 3782; look for the sign one floor up. The second office is quieter and has a friendly English speaker. The main office has a separate counter for foreigners. Payment can only be made in RMB cash, but US$ traveller's cheques and other cash can be exchanged in the main office. Buses to the airport leave from there two hours before each flight for ¥6.

Kazak Airlines has an office at 31 Kūnmíng Lù, well to the north, and one block to the east of Běijīng Nánlù, and best found by taxi (*open Mon, Tues, Thurs and Fri, 10–1 for visas and tickets, and 4–7 for tickets only*). The opening times seem to change frequently, but English is spoken so call ahead, ✆ 382 1207 (tickets) and ✆ and 🖷 382 1203 (visas). To reach the office by bus, take no.2, and ask for the stop called Dàzhàigōu, one stop north of the Hotel World Plaza. Walk north and turn right into Qīngdǎo Dōnglù. Kūnmíng Lù is a left turn. Payment for all services is in US$ cash notes of 1990 or later date, which can be obtained from the Bank of China.

Aeroflot is in the Overseas Chinese Hotel, ✆ 286 8326/7 (*open Mon–Sat 10–1 and 3–7*). Payment is in $US cash.

by train

For trains to Almaty, *see* 'To Kazakstan by Road and Rail', p.259.

As Ürümqi is the starting point for all trains going east it should be easier than at any other Xīnjiāng city except Korla to buy tickets of all classes for all trains, but there is no foreigner ticket window, the queues are long, and there is a lot of tout (scalper) activity. Non-Chinese-speaking visitors would be wise to use an agent to buy the tickets—even some of them blench at the thought, or ask ¥200 ($24) commission. *See* 'Tourist Information' below. Unless you plan to spend a week or more in Ürümqi, make your booking soon after arrival. There are trains to all points down the line to Xī'ān (144, 11.30pm), and it's also possible to go as far as Běijīng via Xī'ān (the a/c 70, 6.20pm), Chéngdū (144/111, 3.13pm), and even Shànghǎi (54, 8.20pm) without changing. Almost all of these trains, and others, pass through Lánzhōu and Xī'ān.

If you want to try booking hard or soft sleepers for yourself, go to window no.11 or 12, but for the Lǚyóu3/2 to Korla go to window 9, and for the a/c 70 to Běijīng try window 8. Ticket windows are typically open 10–1.30, 3.30–7.30, and 9–11.30.

The hard seat/sleeper waiting room is at the top of the left-hand staircase, and the soft sleeper one through the doors on the landing halfway up. The waiting room for international trains is on the right on the ground floor. Larger baggage is X-rayed on the way into the station in a manner unlikely to be film-safe.

by bus

For buses to Almaty, *see* 'To Kazakstan by Road and Rail', p.259.

In 1935, when Eric Teichman delivered a battered Ford truck to the British consulate in Kashgar, and thereafter it was used several times to get to Ürümqi and back by various consuls, reducing the eight-week horseback ride to eight days of suffering on uneven roads constantly broken up by meltwater streams from the Tiān Shān. The journey has now been reduced to around 40 hours of constant driving.

The long-distance bus station (*chángtú qìchēzhàn*) is at the west end of Hēilóngjiāng Lù. There are sleeper buses to Kashgar (1474km, about 40hrs, ¥199/$24 for the best place), and points en route around the north side of the Taklamakan: Korla (470km), Kuqa (751km), and Aksu (1009km). There are buses to the north of Ürümqi to Tǎchéng (637km) and other destinations.

Window 1 has sleepers for Yīníng (680km, ¥95/$11.50 on top, ¥108/$13 below), and 2 has seats (¥68, $8.50); 3 has tickets for Kuqa (Kùchē), Kashgar (Kāshí), Karghalik (Yèchéng), Yarkand (Shāchē), Khotan (Hétián), and points in between. Window 7 has tickets for Hāmì (seats ¥82/$10, sleepers ¥123/$15 bottom, ¥103/$12.50 top); 8 for Lánzhōu (sleeper ¥180/$22), Hāmì and Almaty (Ālāmùtú), and will often give foreigners a hand when the jostle at other windows is too much.

An alternative route to Kuqa involves taking the bus to west to Gulja (Yīníng). Sleeper bus tickets south from there over the mountains are about ¥120 ($15.50, although some are asked to pay double), and there are ordinary buses departing at 8.30am, which take two days, breaking the journey for the night at the fairly high and thus chilly town of Bayanbulak (Bāyīnbùlǔkè) halfway to Kuqa, ¥72 or ¥144 ($9 or $18). It may also be possible to get off the Ürümqi to Gulja bus at Kuytun (Kuítún), a crossroads with the road from Kuqa, and catch a bus more directly south.

Buses to **Turpan** (Tǔlǔfān) go from the main bus station (¥11/$1.50 to ¥15/$2 depending on size and speed, 187km, 4–5hrs). There are also buses from outside the Turpan Affairs Office at the Èrdàoqiáo market, but these often charge foreigners double (if you let them). Buses coming from Turpan and continuing to destinations beyond Ürümqi may drop you two blocks south of the Huáqiáo Bīnguǎn at the terminus for buses 1 and 7 (see 'Getting Around', below).

The bus station on the left-hand side of the square in front of the railway station (as you face it) has buses to many of the same destinations for the same prices. The small bus station opposite the Ürümqi Bīnguǎn in Qiántángjiāng Lù, the **Liùyùn Kāshí Qìchēzhàn**, has 14 departures a day to Kashgar for charges slightly higher than those of the main bus station. There's a small exterior ticket window just to the right of the main entrance.

Getting Around

Ürümqi is much more spread out than maps suggest, but public and private transport is plentiful. Bus fares range between ¥0.20 and ¥0.50, depending on the distance travelled. Private *miànbāochē* (minibuses) and buses with the same numbers as public ones charge up to double, but if they ask for more, or if the figures creep into *kuài* rather than *máo*, just get off the bus.

The most useful routes are the 2, which starts from the railway station and goes north, passing a China Xīnjiāng Airlines (CXA) office, the turning to the bus station, the main post office (neat the Hóng Shān Bīnguǎn), the Peafowl Hotel, another CXA office, the Kūnlún Bīnguǎn, the Hotel World Plaza, and near the Kazak Airlines office.

The 7 runs past the Huáqiáo Bīnguǎn and Aeroflot office, the west end of the Èrdàoqiáo market, the telephone office, the Hóng Shān Bīnguǎn, and the Peafowl Hotel and CAAC office.

The 1 runs past the east end of the Èrdàoqiáo market, within walking distance of the Grand Islam Hotel, then passes the Bogda Hotel, the Hóng Shān, and follows the route of the 2 as far as the Kūnlún Bīnguǎn.

The are plentiful metered **taxis** for ¥1.3 per km with a minimum charge of ¥10 ($1.25). Reject any that have no meters or refuse to start them.

Bicycle hire is available from some hotels but with Ürümqi's dense traffic, and denser pollution, cycling is not recommended.

Ürümqi℗ (0991)   ***Tourist Information***

CITS is in its own building next to the Holiday Inn, ℗ 282 6719, and has an office in the Hóng Shān, ℗ 281 6018 ext 122, along with **CYTS** (more reliable than most) and two other private agencies, some with astronomical charges. The Overseas Chinese Hotel has **CTS**, and the Xīnjiāng Fàndiàn the **Xīnjiāng Nature Travel Service**. All the agencies will book tickets for fees ranging from ¥20 ($2.50) to ¥50 ($6), but some will lie about the ticket price in order to increase their income, so ask all of them to tell you the ticket price and commission separately, and initiate an auction until you get the lowest price. Even the usually unhelpful Hóng Shān posts a notice disclaiming responsibility for the actions of agents with offices in the hotel, and the local tourism bureau also has a warning notice and a helpful (but non-English-speaking) complaints office in the hotel on the ground floor just behind reception. Book tickets for yourself if

区博物馆	1	Region Museum Qū Bówùguǎn	昆仑宾馆	A	Kūnlún Bīnguǎn
红山公园	2	Hóng Shān Park Hóng Shān Gōngyuán	孔雀大厦	B	Kǒngquè Dàshà Peafowl Hotel
新疆航空公司	3	China Xīnjiāng Airlines Xīnjiāng Hángkōng Gōngsī	博格达宾馆	C	Bógédá Bīnguǎn
红山市场	4	Hóng Shān market Hóng Shān Shìchǎng		D	John's Information Café and Tom's Café
红山商场	5	Hóng Shān Shāngchǎng department store, bookshop inside	红山宾馆	E	Hóng Shān Bīnguǎn, CYTS, etc.
邮电局	6	Post and telephone office Yóudiànjú		F	Dumpling shops
中国银行	7	Bank of China Zhōngguó Yínháng	假日大酒店	G	Holiday Inn Jiàrì Dàjiǔdiàn
	8	Buses to Heavenly Lake	城市大酒店	H	Chéngshì Dàjiǔdiàn City Hotel
中国国际旅行社	9	CITS Zhōngguó Guójì Lǚxíngshè	伊斯兰大饭店	I	Yīsīlán Dàfàndiàn Grand Islam Hotel
人民公园	10	Rénmín Gōngyuán	华联新疆商业大厦	J	Huálián Xīnjiāng Shāngyè Dàshà Xīnjiāng Commercial Hotel
公安局	11	PSB Gōng'ānjú	天马大酒店	K	Tiānmǎ Dàjiǔdiàn
长途汽车站	12	Long-distance bus station Chángtú qìchēzhàn	琦那尔饭店	L	Qínà'ěr Fàndiàn
新疆航空公司	13	China Xīnjiāng Airlines Xīnjiāng Hángkōng Gōngsī	新疆饭店	M	Xīnjiāng Fàndiàn
市电信局	14	City Telephone Office Shì Diànxìnjú	华侨宾馆	N	Huáqiáo Bīnguǎn and Aeroflot Overseas Chinese Hotel
外文书店	15	Foreign Languages Bookshop Wàiwén Shūdiàn	环球大酒店	O	Hotel World Plaza Huánqiú Dàjiǔguǎn
中国银行	16	Bank of China Zhōngguó Yínháng			
新华书店	17	Xīnhuá Bookshop Xīnhuá Shūdiàn			
六运喀什汽车站	18	Liùyùn Kāshí Qìchēzhàn Buses to Kashgar			
	19	Buses to Turpan			
二道桥市场	20	Èrdàoqiáo Market			
清真寺	21	Mosque Qīngzhēn Sì			
火车站	22	Railway station Huǒchēzhàn			
	23	Railway bus station			

Ürümqi map key

you can—acquiring air tickets, Almaty rail tickets, other rail tickets out of season, and bus tickets is not usually more of a problem than anywhere else. For tours, shop around. For further advice try the Ürümqi branch of **John's Information Café**, ✆ 231 0191, where you can find genuinely free information from fairly reliable people over a cup of coffee, and a ticket booking service which usually delivers. Oddly, one of the cheapest ticket agencies is the **Xīnjiāng Folk Custom Travel Service** in the Holiday Inn. For domestic rail tickets give as much notice as possible, making a booking as soon as you arrive in Ürümqi. The most useful branches of the **Bank of China** (*open Mon–Fri, 10–1 and 3.30–6.30*) are the ones opposite the post office on the south side of Guāngmíng Lù, and on the corner of Rénmín Lù and Jiěfàng Nánlù. Both sell the US$ needed for travelling to Almaty, but if you want to use a credit card it's best to go to the Rénmín Lù branch. There are also money exchange facilities in some hotels, and unlike most others the **Holiday Inn** is courteous enough to allow non-residents to exchange up to $200 or so if they are not short of cash themselves. Black-market money changers offer RMB *yuán* for cash dollars outside the main Bank of China, in front of the railway station, and in the pedestrian underpass just in front of the main post office. They are much cleverer at this business than you, and you can

Ürümqi

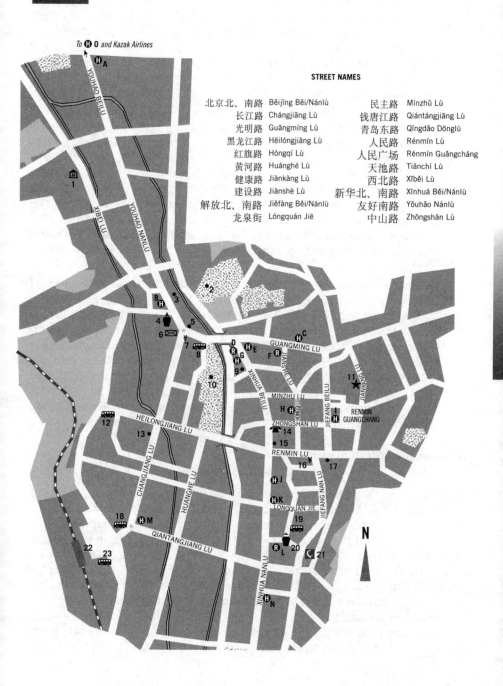

To H O and Kazak Airlines

YOUHAO BEILU

A

STREET NAMES

北京北、南路	Běijīng Běi/Nánlù	民主路	Mínzhǔ Lù
长江路	Chángjiāng Lù	钱唐江路	Qiántángjiāng Lù
光明路	Guāngmíng Lù	青岛东路	Qīngdǎo Dōnglù
黑龙江路	Hēilóngjiāng Lù	人民路	Rénmín Lù
红旗路	Hóngqí Lù	人民广场	Rénmín Guǎngchǎng
黄河路	Huánghé Lù	天池路	Tiānchí Lù
健康路	Jiànkàng Lù	西北路	Xīběi Lù
建设路	Jiànshè Lù	新华北、南路	Xīnhuá Běi/Nánlù
解放北、南路	Jiěfàng Běi/Nánlù	友好南路	Yǒuhǎo Nánlù
龙泉街	Lóngquán Jiē	中山路	Zhōngshān Lù

251

expect to be short-changed and given fake notes if you try this. The most useful **post office** (*open 10–8*) is on the west side of the large traffic island where Chángjiāng Lù meets Yǒuhǎo Nánlù and Guāngmíng Lù, 5 to 10 minutes' walk west of the Hóng Shān. This is where the *poste restante* mail ends up, at the last counter but one on the right, and is kept for one month (¥1.5 for each item collected). The postcode is 830000. **International telephone calls** can be made from the Holiday Inn's business centre, other major hotels, John's Information Café, or much more cheaply at the **city telephone office** (Shì Diànxìnjú) at the junction of Zhōng Shān Lù and Xīnhuá Běilù, open 24 hours (UK ¥35.46 per minute, USA ¥31.50, fax minimum 3 minutes plus ¥10/$1.25 per page).

Film and developing are widely available, but your best choice is probably the Bālù Gōngsī, on the south side of Guāngmíng Lù east of the Bank of China, which has a large stock including several types of slide film, kept in a fridge. It can also develop both print and slide film. Fuji slide film is ¥76 ($9.50), Kodak ¥48 ($6), and Kodak print film cheaper than in most of Xīnjiāng at ¥19.60 ($2.50). Slide developing takes 24 hours and costs ¥20 ($2.50). Prints take 4 hours and cost ¥5 plus ¥0.60 per print. **Passport photographs** for Kazak and Russian visas are widely available, including at the shop with Fuji signs on the north side of Zhōng Shān Lù just east of the junction with Hóngqí Lù.

Maps, guides and postcards can be bought from the shop in the foyer of the Huáqiáo Bīnguǎn, from the Xīnhuá Shūdiàn on the left-hand side of the ground floor of the big department store on the north side of Guāngmíng Lù opposite the Bank of China, and from the large Xīnhuá Shūdiàn at the junction of Rénmín Lù and Jiěfàng Nánlù opposite the other Bank of China. Cheap editions of **novels in English** ranging from George Eliot to *Jaws* are also available from the fourth floor of this shop, and from the Wàiwén Shūdiàn (Foreign Languages Bookshop) at 14 Xīnhuá Běilù (third floor), on the east side of the street just north of the junction with Zhōng Shān Lù. **Visa extensions** are available from the PSB at the junction of Jiànkàng Lù and Mínzhǔ Lù (*open Mon–Fri, 10–2; Mon, Tues and Thurs, 3.30–7.30*).

Qū Bówùguǎn (Region Museum) 区博物馆

Open 9.30–7.30; adm to three sections ¥15 ($2), ¥5, ¥5.

The exhibition on the left-hand side of the ground floor (¥5) is devoted to Xīnjiāng's minorities, and includes yurts in three different styles, stuffed sheep, displays of costume, musical instruments, traditional weapons, other utensils, and a reproduction of a traditional Kazak wooden house, faintly reminiscent of the Museum of Kazak Musical Instruments in Almaty. The exhibition on the right (¥5) is of archaeological items from various Silk Route sites around the Tarim Basin, including desert sites it is not usually possible to visit. There are displays of pottery and human remains, and photographs of archaeological sites, indifferently presented, but offering an introduction to Silk Route archaeology for those who've just arrived in China from Pakistan or Kazakstan, although as usual there's nothing written in English. The exhibition also features a map at which you can push the buttons to light up trade routes of different periods. Those who have been in other museums on the way from Xī'ān should go straight to the eerie exhibition of corpses from various Xīnjiāng tombs around Charchan (Qiěmò), Lóulán and Hāmì, as much as 4000 years old (¥15). Their remarkable state of preservation is due both to the natural drying effect of burial in a desert, and by additional artificial means at the time of burial. Particularly moving is the corpse of a tiny baby, with small stones placed where its eyes once were, and a sheep's breast to hand, used as a dummy. Not even the usual atmosphere of neglect can overpower the effect of this row of ancient bodies.

Political after Death

Bodies have been unearthed from the Taklamakan since the 1970s, but now some are being left in the ground both because the technology at China's museums is inadequate for preserving them, and for reasons of political sensitivity. There has been resistance to letting foreign archaeologists examine fabrics and other artefacts found with the bodies, as these have been found to use techniques similar to those in use in Europe at the same time, stressing the Western rather than Eastern origins of the indigenous cultures.

Rather than simply being institutions for the preservation and display of historical arte-facts, Chinese museums are part of the non-stop barrage of crude propaganda aimed at Hàn Chinese, the ethnic minorities within China's current borders, and, to a lesser extent, foreign visitors. Introductions in Chinese are usually aggressively inclusive ('this is our country's...'), and full of uninformative generalizations and paeans to the great-ness and longevity of Hàn culture. This is particularly true in museums in minority areas, where ideas of 'our country' may vary from the official line. Those artefacts which are undeniably of non-Hàn origin are often labelled as being evidence of minority prosperity under Chinese rule, as demonstrating Hàn cultural influence, or as samples of items sent as tribute to the Chinese court.

Hàn claims for their continuing rule over minority areas are often based on the argu-ment that they ruled there in some early historical period or other, and so they are entitled to rule now. Hàn artefacts in museums are often labelled as showing that the Chinese were present in the area at the time of the artefact, ignoring the fact that the Hàn may have been an unwelcome minority kept in place by military force, or that they were usually driven out. Most recently this feeble reasoning has been applied to the dispute with Vietnam, the Philippines, and others over ownership of the South China Sea Paracel Islands. A Chinese naval expedition claimed to have found Táng dynasty items there and it was asserted that therefore the islands must be Chinese.

These clumsy arguments may work for ordinary Chinese, who have no other sources of information, and who have little or no sympathy for non-Hàn peoples anyway, but in Xīnjiāng they tend to rebound. There is no denying both that the high-cheekboned bodies in the Ürümqi Region Museum are Caucasian, and that they were buried many hundreds of years before the Hàn can claim to have ventured into the area. The 'we were here first' argument may be fatuous, but the Hàn started it, and now members of Xīnjiāng's Turki minorities claim descent from the museum's dead, using the same reasoning to claim their right to self-determination.

Hóng Shān Gōngyuán (Hóng Shān Park)

红山公园

Open daylight hours; adm ¥20.

> *A favourite excursion, for an hour or two between the morning diplo-matic wrangle and the evening banquet, was to the public park, below the Red Temple pagoda and across the bridge on the Ili road. Here there was an ornate pavilion, a crude statue of the late governor of Sinkiang, Yáng Tseng-hsin, and pleasure grounds, round which we used to wander, feeding the wild animals, specimens of the T'ian Shan fauna, a bear, wild ass, wapiti, deer, wolves, foxes, and the like.*
>
> Eric Teichman, *Journey to Turkistan*, 1937

This pagoda-topped hill was a major strategic point in the attempts to overwhelm Ürümqi by the Muslim leader Mǎ Zhòngyīng in the 1930s, potentially providing the perfect position from which to fire down into the city. Today it's like many other public parks in China, with heavy-handed restoration of buildings (usually following damage inflicted by neglect or active destruction during some political campaign) mixed with the self-Disneyfication of concrete moon gates, and a garish funfair. In the daytime you can peer down through the pollution at the nonstop construction, and at night you can peer up at a temple and pagoda tastelessly outlined with lightbulbs. Built in 1788, the solid brick nine-level tower is a mere eight metres high, and is said to have the purpose of preventing a dragon from interfering with the river below, thus known as the Zhènlóng Tǎ, or 'Suppressing Dragon' pagoda. The temples on the hill were all burnt down in the civil wars, and the current building is a modern construction. There is a cable car and a boating lake, and there are other sideshows and fairground attrac-tions such as a ferris wheel, in the unlikely event that you have found your experience of China so far too anodyne. Despite the outrageous entrance fee for foreigners there is a further ¥4 charge to enter the temple. **Rénmín Park** is quieter and prettier, and only ¥2.

Around Ürümqi

Heaven Lake (Tiān Chí)

天池

The lake can be reached by a minibus from outside the Hóng Shān Bīnguǎn, which departs at 8am daily and returns at 4pm; ¥15 ($2) each way, but there are occasional attempts to cheat. It takes three hours there, and 2½ back. A better alternative is to take the Chinese bus from the entrance to Rénmín Park, a few minutes' walk from the Hóng Shān, for ¥25 ($3) return. Tickets are on sale from 8.30am and the bus leaves at 9am, arriving back at Ürümqi at 5.30pm.

Young Kazaks haunt the Hóng Shān Hotel's forecourt and John's Information Café, offering accommodation in yurts near the lakeside. Several families now do this professionally: they are geared to the needs of foreigners, genuinely friendly, and often talented in traditional singing and dancing (those of one Rashid and his sister have been particularly recommended). It's typi-cally ¥20 ($2.50) to stay and ¥20 ($2.50) for three meals), but you can also just go and walk from yurt to yurt negotiating your price. There is a charge of ¥15 ($2) to enter the site.

There are the usual diversions for the Chinese tourists who also flock there, and who have spread litter over much of the area, such as dressing up in Kazak costume to be photographed. After the return buses have left in mid-afternoon, things become quieter.

A Chinese poet described the scenery around Tiān Chí as masculine, and the hills and plains beneath as womanish. There are views on the way of Mt Bogda (Bógēdá Fēng), more than 5000m high, with a 5km-long, 2km-wide glacier. The lake tends to disappoint because it has been over-promoted, and it is certainly not worth travelling to Ürümqi specifically for the trip.

Another similar day trip is to **Báiyáng Gōu** (White Poplar Gully) in the mountains about 75km south of Ürümqi, where there are further yurts, opportunities to ride Kazak horses, and a pretty 20m waterfall amidst lush scenery. Buses leave from outside the entrance to Rénmín Park for ¥20 ($2.50) return.

Where to Stay

As Xīnjiāng's capital and a major trading centre, Ürümqi is seething with hotels, but relatively few are open to foreigners, and many operate at Běijīng price levels. Shiny new towers are taking over from the older monoliths, but with a gradual fading away of budget accommodation. In the off-season some hotels publicly drop their prices, and at almost all of them a little haggling can produce results, if done with a smile. New up- and middle-market hotels are opening all the time which will probably bring prices down, but the situation for the budget traveller remains poor, as the cheaper new hotels do not accept foreigners.

expensive

The **Ürümqi Holiday Inn** (Jiàrì Dàjiǔdiàn) on Xīnhuá Běilù, ✆ 281 8788, ☎ 281 7422, is undoubtedly the best hotel in western China, and for the travel-weary who have come west from Běijīng or Xī'ān overland it's an oasis of real coffee, real-ish service, live music, and all-you-can-eat breakfast buffets (¥106 including service charge and tax). Standard double rooms start from $96 or ¥986 rising to the Presidential Suite at $285 or ¥2986, plus 15% service charge and 3% tax. Facilities include a disco (¥45/$5.50, 'ladies' and hotel residents free, smart casual dress code), an 'English' bar with waitresses in tartan, three restaurants including a 24hr Western one, and a business centre. All major credit cards are accepted.

The nearest in quality to the Holiday Inn and with similar facilities plus a pool and revolving restaurant is the Hong Kong joint-venture **Hotel World Plaza** (Huánqiú Dàjiǔguǎn) well to the north at 2 Běijīng Nánlù, ✆ 383 6400, ☎ 383 6399. Doubles start at ¥750 ($90), rising to ¥1390 ($168) for a superior suite, also plus 18% in surcharges. Major credit cards accepted.

moderate

The best value for money in this price range is the brand new 22-storey **Chéngshì Dàjiǔdiàn** (City Hotel), ✆ 230 9911, ☎ 283 3338, on the west side of Hóngqí Lù. Lower floors are occupied by a department store, restaurants, disco and offices, and bedrooms are on the relative quiet of the 13th floor upwards. Comfortable standard doubles are between ¥360 ($44) and ¥400 ($48) depending on size, singles ¥280

($34), and there are de luxe rooms and suites between ¥560 ($68) and ¥760 ($92), all plus 15%. All major credit cards are accepted.

Older but acceptable is the **Kǒngquè Dàshà** (Peafowl Hotel) in Yǒuhǎo Nánlù, opposite the CAAC office, ✆ 432 2988, ✉ 432 2943. Doubles with bath are ¥238 ($29), and triples with bath ¥70 ($8.50) per bed, all plus ¥2 per person tax. They may be unwilling to part with a cheaper bed in the off season.

The **Yīsīlán Dàfàndiàn** (Grand Islam Hotel), also centrally located in Rénmín Guǎngchǎng, ✆ 282 8360, ✉ 281 1513, is friendly and has comfortable doubles with bath for ¥480 ($58).

The **Huáqiáo Bīnguǎn** (Overseas Chinese Hotel), a little way to the south on Xīnhuá Nánlù, ✆ 286 0793, ✉ 286 2279, was once the top hotel in town, and still takes itself very seriously, with one new and one old building, karaoke bar, Hàn and Uighur restaurants, a souvenir bookshop and the Aeroflot office. Double rooms in the new building are ¥350 ($42), and in the old one ¥200 ($24). The City Hotel is a better choice for this price.

In the same direction as the World Plaza but not so far north, at the top end of Běijīng Běilù, is the cavernous, Soviet-style, and somewhat overpriced **Kūnlún Bīnguǎn**, ✆ 481 1403, ✉ 484 0213, reached by bus 2 from the railway station. Doubles with shower are from ¥480 ($58). At this price the Yīsīlán Dàfàndiàn is a better choice.

inexpensive

The centrally located **Hóng Shān Bīnguǎn**, ✆ 282 4761, has fanless doubles from ¥150 ($18) and dorm beds from ¥25 ($3, eight sofas in a meeting room and ten mattresses on the floor). Long the most popular hotel with independent travellers, it is nevertheless unfriendly and overpriced, with absurdly long queues for the common showers which are in a separate building, and a poor, gloomy restaurant. The reception staff have grown considerably more friendly than they used to be, but still use every possible art including economy with the truth to drive you into a more highly priced room, when even the cheaper beds are already 80% more expensive for 'foreign guests' than they are for Chinese. Unfortunately at rock-bottom prices there are few alternatives, and they know it. The floor staff are amiable enough but do everything in slow motion, and there are bathrooms which have had broken showers for at least four years. Do not look under the beds or behind the furniture as certainly none of the staff have done this for a considerable period of time.

The **Huálián Xīnjiāng Shāngyè Dàshà** (Xīnjiāng Commercial Hotel), ✆ 281 5531, ✉ 282 1513, is a tower two blocks south of the telephone office on Xīnhuá Nánlù, and much better value for money than the Hóng Shān, with all-day hot water, fairly friendly staff, good-sized doubles with better bathrooms for ¥150 ($18), and smaller doubles with shower for ¥100 ($12), as high as 15 floors above Ürümqi's bustle, with corresponding views and relative quiet. There are also quads with bath for ¥60 ($7.50) per bed. Add ¥4 city tax per room per day. The slightly more expensive **Tiānmǎ Dàjiǔdiàn**, ✆ 282 1922, at 80 Lóngquán Jiē, on the corner of Xīnhuá Nánlù, is also significantly cleaner and better than the Hóng Shān, with good doubles for ¥180 ($22) and large ones for ¥200 ($24). There are triples with bath for ¥260 ($32) and suites for ¥400 ($48). On the 8th floor or so you're well clear of the traffic and it's much quieter, too. This hotel's karaoke bar and disco is safely buried underground, and popular with Uighurs.

A few minutes further east of the Hóng Shān, the slightly glitzier **Bógédá Bīnguǎn** (Bogda Hotel), at 10 Guāngmíng Lù, ✆ 281 5238, ✉ 282 3910 ext 4101, is much less friendly than it used to be, and its four-bed ¥40 ($5) dorms are almost always 'full'. You will be offered a ¥380 ($46) double room (100% mark-up for foreigners) instead. At least the restaurant is good. An alternative but slightly rowdy option is the huge **Xīnjiāng Fàndiàn**, popular with Pakistani traders, ✆ 585 2511, ✉ 581 1354 (dorm beds from ¥30/$4), conveniently located near the railway station.

Eating Out

Dining out in Xīnjiāng can be dangerous. The wily Chinese general Bān Chāo, who used intelligence, diplomatic acumen, and a great deal of nerve to gain control of most of Xīnjiāng in the 9th century, drove the Indo-European king of Kashgar from his seat in AD 87. The king pretended to be willing to submit to Bān Chāo, and requested the opportunity to make obeisance. Arriving with a strong force of cavalry, he planned a surprise attack. Bān Chāo, not so easily deceived, invited him to a banquet, and after a few cups of wine, seized the king and beheaded him at the dinner table. This began a tradition. 1850 years later, Governor Yáng, who had detected a plot against himself, held a banquet in Ürümqi.

> When the cups had been filled a few times the Governor suddenly rose and left the hall. This action aroused no suspicion since it was known that Yáng cared little for wine. But in a few minutes he returned, followed by a soldier who held concealed behind his back a long curved sword. The Governor paused behind the seat of Hsia Ting, one of the principal malcontents. Then in a cold, even casual voice speaking typical Yunnanese dialect, he said: 'Behead Hsia Ting!'

> Aitchen K. Wu, *Turkistan Tumult*, 1940

Seconds later, the clothes of his neighbours, who cowered in terror, were spattered with the luckless diner's blood. The governor calmly assured them that his difference of opinion with the one guest had nothing to do with the others, and ordered more wine to be poured, again leaving the room. He returned with another soldier at his side, and taking up position behind another diner, again ordered his execution. In this case, the victim, guessing that his plot had been discovered, ducked and fled wounded from the room. His screams informed the remaining guests that he had been caught not far outside.

This was not the end of deadly dinner parties. On 7 July, 1928, in what was thus called the 'Double Seven Incident', at a banquet whose guests included the Soviet consul-general, Yáng himself was shot seven times as a toast was drunk. This was a coup organized by a young rival, partially the result of his determination not to meet the same fate as the earlier diners, but who himself did not survive the incident long.

A few years later the journalist Peter Fleming was entertained to dinner at the Soviet consulate in Kashgar.

> *You never know what may happen at a banquet in Kashgar, and each of our official hosts had prudently brought his own bodyguard. Turki and Chinese soldiers lounged everywhere; automatic rifles and executioners' swords were much in evidence, and the Mauser pistols of the waiters knocked ominously against the back of your chair as they leant over you with the dishes...*
>
> *Nobody was assassinated.*

Peter Fleming, News from Tartary, 1936

expensive–moderate

All the expensive hotels have restaurants that take themselves very seriously. For those craving a change to Western food, the 24-hour restaurant with breakfast, lunch and dinner buffets in the **Holiday Inn** is irresistible. For a truly Uighur atmosphere with an excellent menu of Muslim and Chinese food, the **Qínàěr Fàndiàn** in the Èrdàoqiáo market at Tiānchí Lù 73 also features bursts of live Uighur pop music and traditional dance performances by a Uighur woman. The small dance floor fills with ballroom-dancing Uighurs, and foreigners are made very welcome. Around ¥50 ($6) per head for a good meal.

inexpensive

The restaurant behind the **Bógédá Bīnguǎn** (*not* the one to the left of the main entrance—go through the foyer and out the other side of the building) has a menu which includes good sizzling Sìchuān food and popular Cantonese dishes as well as Uighur ones for around ¥15 ($2) to ¥20 ($2.50) per meat dish. At the north end of Jiànshè Lù almost opposite the same hotel is a group of Shànghǎi-style dumpling shops serving beef and lamb dumplings for ¥0.60 to ¥0.80 each. Chinese attempts at Western food along with a cheap Chinese menu are available at **John's Information Café**, opposite the Hóng Shān Hotel. A few doors east the Pastry Shop has changed its name to **Tom's Café**, dropped its cakes and taken to attempts at pizza and burgers, but for prices that suggest you may as well go next door to the Holiday Inn.

At night a group of stalls run by people from a variety of minorities magically appears on the south side of Zhōng Shān Lù just east of the junction with Hóngqí Lù, and stays until nearly midnight. At the Èrdàoqiáo market *shashlyk*, *pulau*, noodles, and nan bread are available until around 8pm. At the Hóng Shān market to the right of the post office there's excellent cheap Muslim food all day, and late opening food stalls are scattered around pavements everywhere.

Shopping and Entertainment

Ürümqi's department stores, however large, and however many, only contain the same goods as everywhere else. Xīnjiāng souvenirs such as Yengisar knives, a wide variety of hats, and locally made carpets can all be bought in or near the Èrdàoqiáo market. If you are going to Kashgar then shop there instead, as there's a better choice and lower prices at the Sunday Bazaar. Ürümqi is the best place in Xīnjiāng to restock on Western toiletries, chocolate and biscuits in its many department stores, such as the Hóng Shān Shāngchǎng and its neighbours, opposite the post office.

To Kazakstan by Rail and Road

by train

There are two trains a week to **Almaty** (Ālāmùtú), one Chinese which leaves on Saturdays, and one Kazak which leaves on Mondays, both at 11pm Běijīng time, arriving at 4.30am Moscow time (7.30am Kazak time, two hours earlier than Běijīng time). Much of the middle day is taken up with Kazak customs thievery, multiple searches of the train and other nonsense. Whether or not you have a Russian or other CIS visa which theoretically allows you three days' transit through Kazakstan, the border guards may have other ideas. It pays to buy a Kazak transit visa if you can, especially as the station may refuse to sell you a ticket if you don't have one. If you have another CIS visa or an air ticket out of Almaty, Kazak transit visas are available from the Kazak Airlines office—*see* 'by air', p.246.

To buy tickets, enter the station in the centre, turn right and walk through the waiting room to find the international ticket window in the far right-hand corner (*open 10–3 and 5–7*). Tickets for the Saturday Chinese train are ¥588 ($71) in hard sleeper and ¥1130 ($136) in soft sleeper. However, the hard sleepers are the same four-berth compartments called soft sleeper elsewhere in China, and the soft sleepers have only two beds, a comfy chair, and a small washroom shared with the next compartment. Tickets for the Monday Kazak train are ¥505 ($61) and ¥860 ($104) respectively. The Kazak train is widely preferred for being in better condition and having a better restaurant car, but plenty of provisions should be taken, just in case.

The train arrives at Almaty I on Monday and Wednesday mornings at 5.05am Moscow time, 8.05am Kazak time (7.05am in winter). Stay on to Almaty II, 5.25am (8.25/7.25am), unless you want to go straight to the airport, which is closer to Almaty I, taking a taxi (around 250t), or bus 42. Almaty I and II are connected by buses 30 and 34, and trolleybuses 5 and 6.

Trains *from* Almaty arrive at 9.30am Běijīng time on Mondays and Wednesdays.

See p.444 for customs information and more on this route.

by bus

Sleeper buses to **Almaty** (Ālāmùtú) run daily except Saturdays, leaving Ürümqi at 5pm and crossing the border the next morning. The trip takes at least 24 hours, and costs ¥460 ($56), insurance included, or $50 plus ¥10 ($1.25) insurance one-way.

The ticket window is no.8 (*open 7–7, one hour later in winter*), and tickets can be bought up to one day in advance.

It's only ¥150 ($18) by the Almaty bus overnight to Khorgos (Huòěrgásī), and some have used this as a cheaper, if trickier route to Almaty, completing the journey on local transport. Yet more cheaply, you can take a bus to Gulja (Yīníng) for ¥103 ($12.50), getting off at either Gulja (680km) or Qīngshuǐhé, which is before the bus doubles back to Gulja and closer to the border, but which has fewer taxis and buses and less room for negotiation. From Gulja there are buses for ¥10 ($1.25) or ¥15 ($2) to the border. There is another bus which shuttles the 3km or so between the border posts for ¥10 ($1.25). The border is open 8.30–4 Kazak time, which is two hours earlier than Běijīng time (one hour earlier in summer), but closed on Saturday afternoons and Sundays. Taxi drivers will ask for $10 to take you to the nearest town in Kazakstan which is Zharkant, formerly Panfilov, but you may be lucky enough to find a bus, and from there you can get another local bus to Almaty.

Korla (Kùěrlè)

库尔勒 The route southwest from Ürümqi crosses back over the Tiān Shān, passing wind farms, returning much of the way back to Turpan before heading west to struggle through the Toksun Gorges and turn south, passing through Karashar (various spellings, Chinese name Yānqí) to Korla, after about 470km. Afternoon sleeper buses from Ürümqi arrive at about 5am.

Karashar was an important trading town on the Silk Route north of the Taklamakan, but has little to offer the modern visitor, although many of the 19th- and 20th-century explorers and archaeologists from the West passed through it, remarking on its fortifications and its fame as a production centre for ponies and mushrooms. It sits on the edge of a marshy lake, Bagrash Kol (Bósīténg Hú), Xīnjiāng's largest, fed by Tiān Shān meltwater and, unusually for Xīnjiāng, fresh not salt. Karashar was once the centre of a local kingdom with its own distinctive blend of western and eastern culture, a link with Kuqa to the west, and Miran and Khotan to the south and, like them, with influence from Buddhist Gandhara in modern-day Pakistan. Like these, too, it changed hands frequently between the Hàn, Tibetans, Indo-Europeans, Turkis and Mongols, all of whom can still be found in the region. Younghusband, passing through in 1887, remarked on the Huí (Dungans). 'These Tunganis (they called themselves Tungani without my asking who they were) are not distinguishable in features from an ordinary Chinaman, but they seem cleaner and more respectable than the Chinese about here, who appear to be the scum of the central provinces of China proper.' Xīnjiāng is still China's Siberia, and used as a dumping ground for criminals and other undesirables.

Ancient buildings known as the *Ming-oi* (one thousand dwellings) and cave-temple sites provided 'a splendid harvest of manuscripts, pictures, and pieces of sculpture' (von Le Coq 1905), and 'plentiful archaeological spoil', 'a great quantity of excellent small statues in stucco', and 'interesting fresco panels' (Stein 1907), now to be seen in Berlin and London.

In the early '90s Korla, famous for pears, was still a small, sleepy and friendly town and, before the arrival of sleeper buses, a necessary overnight stop on the road between Ürümqi and Kashgar. It has since gone through rapid development and lost its innocence, apparently developing a deep dislike for foreigners on the way. Some hotels charge as much as 350% of the

Chinese price for indifferent accommodation, and the bus station charges double. Some street vendors like to ask five times the normal price for bread and other sundries. The charmlessness of the inhabitants is matched by that of the architecture, but Korla does represent an opportunity to change between train and bus, and thereby to avoid visiting Ürümqi altogether.

Korla is currently the southern terminus at the west end of the Nánjiāng (South Xīnjiāng) railway line, but Prime Minister Lǐ Péng came personally to Korla in September 1996 to break the ground for an extension to Kashgar. This is due to be completed by the end of the Ninth Five-Year Plan (the year 2000). By the end of 1997 it should have reached Kuqa, making a visit to Korla completely unnecessary. Lǐ Péng remarked that the railway line '...would boost confidence in the Communist Party among ethnic minorities'—some hope. In fact it is likely to do the opposite, probably meaning a rise in the Hàn population in western Xīnjiāng, which may result in Uighur unrest.

Korla had originally the same layout as other Hàn-occupied Turki towns, with the Hàn isolating themselves in a separate compound at some distance from the original town, but this has all been obliterated by the modern city. There are many Mongols in the area, descendants of those originally granted land by the Qīng Emperor Qiánlóng in the 18th century. They still spend their summers in the Tiān Shān pastures and winters in the lusher ground near Bagrash Kol, having little influence on Korla. Sven Hedin's road surveying expedition bumped into the retreating troops of Mǎ Zhòngyīng here in 1934, and was kept under house arrest while planes clandestinely provided by the Soviets bombed the town. The ruins of an earlier version of Korla can be found 80km to the west, but with not enough left above ground to make the trip worthwhile. Korla's most notable sight is the Tiě Mén Guān (Iron Gate Pass), a rebuilt Chinese fortified gate also well outside town.

Korla has flights six days a week (not Thurs) to and from Ürümqi on 18-seat Twin Otters (¥400/$48), which fly low, giving excellent views of the arid mountains, the marshy Bagrash Kol, and the endless expanse of desert. On Wed and Sat the flights continue to Kuqa (Kùchē), and on the other days to Charchan (Qiěmò) on the southern side of the Taklamakan.

The nearest railway station is the north one (*huǒchē běizhàn*), reached by turning left out of the bus station and left along Tiān Shān Xīlù. The schedule will change as soon as the extension to Kuqa is open, but at present the Lǔ4/1 leaves for Ürümqi at 21.00, arriving at Turpan at 06.17, and Ürümqi at 08.53. The 144 leaves for Xī'ān and all points in between at 15.54, arriving at Turpan at 02.15. The air ticket office is at the airport, ✆ 215 1333.

Korla bus station has connections to Ürümqi (471km, ¥90/$11, 15hrs), Turpan (386km, ¥45/$5.50, about 20hrs—the journey can also be broken at Toksun), Dàhéyàn (357km), Khotan (Hétián, 1512km), Kashgar (Kāshí, 1003km). Going anti-clockwise around the desert there are buses to Charklik (Ruòqiāng, 493km, at least 15hrs), and Charchan (Qiěmò, 794km, ¥71/$9). All tickets are double price for foreigners going east or west on the northern route around the Taklamakan, but not (yet) if you want to go south.

The most comfortable hotel is the vastly overpriced **Bāyīnguōléng Bīnguǎn**, ✆ (0996) 202 4441, where a triple with bath, for instance, is ¥580 ($70) per room (the Chinese pay ¥50/$6 per bed). This is on the east side of town, 30mins walk from the bus station, and further still from the railway station, and best approached by taxi. There are two hotels at the bus station—the **Jiāotōng Lǚzhuāng**, and the newer **Yuǎndōng Bīnguǎn** (Far East Hotel) with beds in primitive common bath rooms from ¥20 ($2.50), rising to reasonable doubles but at the unreasonable foreigner double price of ¥100 ($12) per bed. The best value is the **Dōngfāng Bīnguǎn**, reached in five minutes' walk from the bus station, turning right out of the building and crossing the bridge. The hotel is on the right at the end of the road. Here is a variety of common bath beds from ¥15 ($2, eight beds), up to large old-fashioned doubles with bath for ¥67.50 ($8.50) per bed (only 50% more than the Chinese price).

Kuqa (Kùchē)

库车 From Korla to Kuqa the desert is shy, often screened from the road by rows of slender poplars, or by distant plantations. Oases are frequent, but long and thin, clinging to the road. Only just before Kuqa are there stretches of the tussocky emptiness which characterize the desert along the northern route. At Lúntái, about halfway between Korla and Kuqa, a new road opened in 1995 crosses the desert south to Niya (Mínfēng), but there is as yet no public transport on this route, which is devoid of habitation for its whole length. You can charter a taxi (with difficulty) and travel agents in Kashgar and elsewhere offer guided tours using this road.

Kuqa is squeezed between the aridity of the Tarim Basin and the remote heights of the Tiān Shān, but meltwater keeps it fertile. Anciently known to the Chinese as Qiūcí, at the time of the Hàn dynasty it was one of the largest states of the Western Regions, and became a military outpost during Hàn expansion into the region. Its main cultural influences came from Persia and the Graeco-Indian Ghandara, rather than China. Its Indo-European population produced the Buddhist art that was to influence that of every town on the route from here to Xī'ān, and which still adorns the walls of nearby cave-temple sites, the most complete outside Dūnhuáng. This thriving Buddhist centre translated texts from Sanskrit into the local language, and actively promoted the spread of Buddhism to other Tarim oases and on to China itself.

The Kuqan Buddhist scholar **Kumarijiva** (AD 344–413) came from a family of Indian origin, which had held high office in the town. Kumarajiva's father wanted to become a Buddhist monk, but the king made him remain in office, giving him his sister in marriage. Kumarijiva was taken to Kashmir by his mother while still a boy, to be instructed in Indian literature and Buddhism, and later studied in Kashgar. Returning to Kuqa with a Kashmiri teacher, he had two grandsons of the king of Yarkand as his disciples. Taken to China by an invading general in around AD 383, he won respect there as a translator and teacher. The general, who had probably previously considered all the occupants of the Tarim oases to be barbarians, was said to be amazed at the splendour of Kuqan palaces, although the comments of the pilgrim Xuánzàng, who passed through in around AD 630, suggest the culture was only just reaching its peak 250 years later. There may have been as many as 100 temples and 5000 monks. Kuqa also had its own distinctive style of music, which became very popular in China during the Táng.

Like much else in Xīnjiāng, Kuqa was frequently out of touch with the Chinese heartland, as in AD 670 during the early Táng dynasty, when Tibetans took control of large areas. Later Kuqa became a satellite of the Western Liáo dynasty until being swallowed up by Genghis Khan in 1218. It returned to independence after the Míng had driven out the Yuán from China proper, until the arrival of Qīng military incursions and the foundation of Xīnjiāng.

The modern town has an unfinished, disorderly look, with a backwater air more common to the oases of the southern route. It consists of typical overly broad Hàn streets, perhaps six blocks by four, which dwindle into small lanes, except on the main highway itself, and the typical Uighur warren of the old town, like a growth on one side. The majority here are Uighurs, followed by Hàn, with a number of Huí, Kyrgyz, Manchus, Uzbeks, Mongolians, Russians and Sibos in the area, totalling about 350,000 people. Kuqa has a surprising amount of both agriculture and industry to keep these people occupied, although like so many other Xīnjiāng towns, its most famous product is a fruit; in this case the apricot.

Getting to and from Kuqa

by air

There are flights to and from Ürümqi on Wednesdays and Saturdays. The booking office is at Kuqa airport, ✆ 712 2051, but there is high demand for tickets for the small plane. There are no flights directly to Kashgar.

by train

The Nánjiāng railway line is expected to reach Kuqa from Korla in late 1997, and eventually to connect to Kashgar.

by bus

The bus station charges foreigners double, and its spectacular rudeness is a jarring reminder of how almost all ticket offices used to be just a few years ago. No buses to Kashgar start from here, so there's no guarantee of being able to board sleeper buses, soft seat or hard seat buses that come through from Korla. There are frequent departures west to Aksu, however, which offers a greater choice of buses. Westbound there are buses to Korla and Ürümqi, plus whatever else you can squeeze onto that's coming from Kashgar. Although the Kuqa travel agency for some reason denies it, there are also buses north to Gulja (Yīníng), through beautiful mountain scenery. Sir T. Douglas Forsyth, leader of two trade missions to the rebel leader Yakub Beg (see **Kashgar**, p.275) commented on this route, 'The road by this pass crosses an enormous glacier, which is interrupted by vast fissures and massive banks, and unless constantly kept open by gangs of labourers, becomes speedily impassable.' Today, however, the problem is avoided by use of a tunnel.

Getting Around

Taxis are essential to visit the sites out of town, but are without meters. Horse-drawn carts still take the role of buses, travelling between the long-distance bus station and the old town, although this can be walked in about 15 minutes.

Kuqa ✆ (0997)   Tourist Information

Xīnjiāng Kuqa International Travel Service (CITS in effect) is on the third floor of the Tóngdá Bīnguǎn, ✆ and ✉ 712 2524, and offers trips to Kizil and other sites. The first asking price for a car to Kizil with a slight diversion to Kizil Kara and the beacon tower is ¥300 ($36), but this is negotiable down to ¥250 ($30). You can arrange this for yourself for ¥200 ($24) in a small car, or ¥150 ($18) in a *miàndī* (minivan). They can also book rail tickets from Korla with a few days' notice (¥50/$6 commission) or plane tickets from Kuqa to Korla or Ürümqi (¥30/$4). The **Bank of China** (*open summer 9.30–8 and winter 10–7.30*) is on the corner of the second major right turn, walking

west from the bus station—a short way up the road you can see a traditional Chinese gate, but this is a dead end. The bank is capable of handling traveller's cheques and credit card withdrawals. The **post office** (*open 9.30–8*) is reached up the third right-hand turn and left at the **Xīnhuá Shūdiàn** (which has nothing you want), and the **telephone office** (*open summer 9.30am–12am and winter 10am–12am*) immediately west of it. The **Foreign Affairs Office** (Wàibàn), which deals with accommodation at the Kizil site and permission to visit Kumtura, is in the same block on the opposite side of the road. Calls to the USA are cheap for China at ¥16 ($2) per minute, the UK ¥19 ($2.50) per minute, all plus 20% service charge. There are **no maps** of Kuqa, and there is **no visa extension service**. Extensions are said by the PSB to be available in Aksu, but you would be wiser to wait until Kashgar, Korla, Ürümqi or Turpan, depending on your route.

Friday Bazaar (Xīngqīwǔ Dàshìchǎng)　星期五大市场

Kuqa's old town is similar to that of Kashgar and Hāmì, a tangle of lanes of mud and adobe houses tacked untidily onto the Hàn city's grid. The bazaar is like Khotan's insofar as it takes place in the streets of the old town to the west, but partly spills over into the new one, too. Every Uighur town has its bazaar, but Kuqa's is the only one on a Friday, which is the best day to chose to be in the town, as people pour in from remote hamlets by transport both modern and medieval. Horse carts act as buses between the old and newer parts of town, although these are only 15 minutes' walk apart, heading west along the main highway and taking an obvious left fork. The old town also sports small mosques and the tomb of Molena Ashidin Hoja, a 14th-century Islamic preacher originally from Bokhara whose father had converted the Khan of Aksu to Islam, and who spearheaded compulsory conversions of the Mongol Buddhist state of Kuqa, leading to the suppression of Buddhism.

Around Kuqa

Kizil Thousand Buddha Caves (Kèzǐěr Qiānfódòng)　克孜尔千佛洞

Adm ticket A ¥45 ($5.50), tickets A and B ¥90 ($11).

Access to the caves is possible with any ease only by booking a tour through a travel agent, or hiring a taxi yourself for the 73km trip. For the hardy only, an alternative method would be to take a bus going to Báichéng and get off at the turning to the caves after about 60km, leaving a very hot 11km walk to the site, and the same back to flag down passing buses on the main road. A hotel at the site can be booked through the foreign affairs office in Kuqa, © 712 2479. Foreigner prices for doubles with bath are from ¥150 ($18), and triples ¥160 ($20). Common bath triples are ¥25 ($3) per bed. There's also an over-priced restaurant.

The site is extensive, and visitors have the option to see a collection of the caves nearest the entrance (ticket A), or both those and another group a short walk further down the valley (ticket B). There are fewer caves in the second group, but the best paintings open to the public are there. Those without a special enthusiasm for cave temples should save themselves for Dūnhuáng, but for those with an interest in more remote and less-visited sites, or in the transmission of Buddhist ideas and art from west to east, this is a must.

A few kilometres outside Kuqa heading north from the main highway there's a right turn to the **Kizil Kara Beacon Tower** (Kèzīěrgǎhā Fēnghuǒtái), hidden behind a cement factory. This is a chance to get up close to one of the highest and most intact of the earthen beacon towers of the region, not a squat pyramid with a levelled top like so many others but a proper tower about 13m high, with evidence of an internal wooden structure and an abobe brick top. Two lines of beacons cross Kuqa county, one parallel to the highway, and the other along the base of the Tiān Shān. This tower is Ozymandian and forlorn. One kilometre beyond the tower are the **Kizil Kara Caves** (Kèzīěrgǎhā Shíkū), a set of 46, few of which are open for viewing and with little in the way of painting remaining.

The road to the main Kizil caves heads north and winds through an area of red rocks that look as if they have been whipped and folded like so much meringue, before arriving on flatter land closer to the Tiān Shān. The caves are burrowed into cliffs overlooking water, a type of location already familiar to those travelling west from Xī'ān, but the Muzart River valley is prettier and greener than most. The last 11km from the main road to the caves is uneven, and ends with an impressive plunge down the cliff side to the river. Buy your ticket(s) at the entrance gate and then walk on to a modern building on the right to sign the visitors' book and collect a guide who will show you round. No English is spoken. On the path up to the first cave there is a compulsory bag deposit for all bags and cameras, for which you will be charged ¥2 per item on collection. Photography inside the caves is possible, but for a charge of around $150.

The Kizil caves are some of the earliest and, despite visits by various Western and Japanese expeditions in the early part of the century, retain a large number of murals (more than 5000 sq m according to some Chinese guide books, 10,000 sq m according to others) and many of them are in good condition. There were originally 236 caves, although far fewer are still intact, fewer still having paintings, and unfortunately many of the best are not opened for the casual visitor. The most famous of these is cave 38, known as the Cave of Musicians, portraying 28 of them playing lutes, harps and drums, including a flute-blowing *apsara*. The statuary from the site either graces foreign museums or was smashed long ago, with the exception of a small statue in a cave only rediscovered in 1973. More than any other site, their principal subjects are the *jataka* stories of the former lives of the Buddha, and much opportunity is taken to illustrate the murals with scenes of the music and dancing for which the prosperous Kuqa kingdom was famous. The wealthy Buddhists who donated money are portrayed standing among the watching crowds. The earliest caves are 3rd century, and the paintings increase in sophistication until the 4th and 5th centuries, strongly influencing the earliest caves at Dūnhuáng. Construction continued right up to the 14th-century Yuán and

Míng, when Buddhism was supplanted by Islam. Many of the caves are cut with a large central pillar at the rear, functioning as a stupa, with passages around it, and this design also spread eastwards to various other sites.

Despite the aridity of the area and the intense heat, the cliffs wind round a green and pretty oasis on the bank of the Muzart River, with some cultivation and fruit trees, exactly as described by von Le Coq when he visited nearly 100 years ago. The caves are on various levels, and although once connected by long passages cut on the rock itself and almost invisible from the river, are now reached by modern concrete walkways and iron balconies, the caves being sealed to protect the murals.

There is some variation in the choice of caves that will be shown, but not as much as at Dūnhuáng. In cave 8, as in most other caves, large portions of mural have been removed from the walls, and on the ceiling the repeated small Buddha images ('thousand Buddha') have lost their gold clothing, scratched away for sale elsewhere, although the remaining colours are still very bright. Cave 10, formerly a residential cave, has nothing on the walls except a brief essay in Chinese criticizing Stein and von Le Coq, responsible for the removal of many paintings. Cave 17 has a 6th-century ceiling which is bright and largely intact although large sections of wall painting are missing. As in most of the other caves, the Buddhist scenes are heavily blue, black and green, with a portrait of a sleeping Buddha at the rear of the central pillar. Cave 27 is 8th century, with niches now bereft of statuary, paintings almost all gone, and a roof once elaborately carved but now damaged. Cave 32 is 6th century with a few remnants of painting, but to one side are large niches, one of which once housed a 16m seated Buddha. Cave 47, 4th century, once housed a large recumbent Buddha, and post holes indicate that there was a protective building and further statuary attached to walls. Neighbouring cave 48 next door has a U-shaped passage with very Islamic damage to paintings—mainly eyes and faces missing. 5th-century cave 77 also formerly housed a recumbent Buddha in its rear passage, where some paintings remain. Cave 80 is 7th century, with substantial amounts of painting in mixed condition. Here, intriguingly, is Cyrillic graffiti from 1934, suggesting that the Dūnhuáng caves may not have been the only ones offering shelter to White Russian fugitives. In this cave, too, selective damage has been inflicted on eyes or faces as a whole, revealing the vandal as someone with an Islamic distaste for representations of the human form.

The caves are in groups connected by paths over rough land, and visitors must force their way through areas of high reeds. The chill of the caves' interiors is a shock after the hot and thirsty work of walking between them in the sunshine, and it takes time for the eyes to adjust.

The group B caves are a short walk further on down the valley, passing dozens of other caves not open to the public. Cave 190 is 8–9th century with paintings in good condition, as if to suggest that no-one could be bothered to walk this far, whether for theft of gold, religion-inspired vandalism, or wholesale removal on archaeological grounds. The paintings here have more red, the original colour of some of the black in the group A caves, now oxidized. Cave 188 next door has almost all its paintings intact, and the adjacent niche 187 has figures with distinctly Indian clothing. 7th-century caves 186 and 184 are very small with little left inside. Caves 167 and 165 have roof designs reminiscent of Gojal and Hunza buildings, and some floral design not seen in other caves.

Few if any scenic sites in China are without their legends, and there is an oft-repeated story about Kizil. During the Western Hàn dynasty the king of Qiūcí had a beautiful daughter who fell in love with a commoner. To prevent their marriage the king set the young man an impossible task—to cut 1000 caves in homage to Buddha within three years. The young man successfully cut 999 caves before dying of exhaustion. The princess wept, and the two lovers turned into two peaks, Mounts Mingwudag and Qaoldag, which stand over the site, the princess' tears represented by a small spring and stream that still flows through the valley.

Fisticuffs and Foxtail Saws

In the early 1900s, with magnificent finds being reported to scientific societies in Britain, France, Germany and Russia, an antiques race was developing amongst the major powers, with talk of 'spheres of influence' coming from the padded armchairs of smoke-filled rooms, in an art-historian's version of the Great Game.

Professor Grünwedel, von Le Coq's superior, made an informal agreement with two Russian scholars, Radloff and Salemann, that the Germans should work the more recent areas of the Turpan district, and the Russians the older ones around Kuqa. While in Ürümqi in late 1904, von Le Coq discovered that the Russian consular agent of the day knew nothing of this agreement, and was about to conduct excavations in the 'German sphere' on his government's instructions. Le Coq took this as evidence that the agreement was null and void, but being discovered digging at Simsim, close to Kuqa, by the Russian Beresovsky brothers, was threatened with expulsion by force of arms. The Germans smoothed things over and retreated, realizing that the Russians lacked the ability to remove large-scale wall paintings, which the Germans could retrieve later, and left to investigate the more promising Kizil sites. The first foreigners to visit Kizil and remove antiquities may have been those of the Japanese Otani mission in 1902–3, but in January 1905 Grünwedel and von Le Coq staked a claim to the Kizil caves in anticipation of the arrival of other parties, by hiring the only dwelling for miles, and set off for a few weeks' work at Kumtura (*see* below).

When the German team returned, their technique for removing large murals was used to good effect: '...the harvest was exceedingly satisfactory,' wrote von Le Coq. For the Kizil paintings a surface was applied to the rock walls made of a mixture of camel dung, straw and other vegetable fibres, which was smoothed out, and then a thin coat of stucco applied on top. To remove the paintings intact required considerable teamwork. First the type of transport to be used was considered, which affected the size of packing case to be chosen. A sharp knife was then used to cut round the section of mural to be removed, and if this was too large, to cut it into segments which could later be reassembled, jigsaw puzzle-like, in Berlin. Care was taken to cut round figures and other important subjects. If the painted surface was already loose, men with boards held it in place. Next it was necessary to hack a hole in the rock at one corner of the chosen section, using a pickaxe or hammer and chisel where there was no room to swing, to allow for the insertion of the most important tool, a foxtail saw, which, worked in behind the painted surface, was used to cut it from the wall. The top edge of the painting was then allowed to perform an arc as the whole surface was lowered slowly until face down on a previously prepared board. It was then packed in layers of springy reeds, cotton and felt, boxed and eventually transferred to the nearest railhead, which was then Andizhan. The German team's hallmark of a hole in the cave wall next to a blank area can easily be identified here, at Bezeklik near Turpan, and at other sites.

Other archaeological tools were equally as inventive, if less orthodox. The walls of one temple at Kizil were covered in an inch-thick layer of white mould, but von Le Coq had a solution. 'I fetched Chinese brandy—no European can drink it—and washed down all the walls with a sponge.'

The visit was not without its excitements of a less academic kind, including an earthquake. Von Le Coq and the others rushed outside only to be threatened by falling rocks. Grünwedel had instinctively crawled deeper into the cave where he was working, risking burial alive, but no one was hurt. Later von Le Coq nearly came to an early end when a large rock silently detached itself from the wall of one cave and buried itself in the ground where he had been standing only moments before. Further research at that cave was abandoned.

Finds other than the paintings, in which von Le Coq noticed European styles of clothing (although he assumed design influences had flowed both west and east from Turkey and Persia), and statuary with Hellenic influences, included a small library of documents and evidence of the monkish diet, in the form of vegetable seeds, millet, dried fruits and beans. Despite being free of other foreign archaeological teams, not everything went the Germans' way, however. While working in one cave, they noticed two old women digging away at mounds of earth on the other side of the stream. Never generous of spirit, and certainly unable to see any parallel with his own occupation, von Le Coq complained about having to pay the large price of nine shillings to the women for one hundred sheets of Tocharian and Indian manuscripts.

The eventual winner was Berlin's Museum für Indische Kunst, where the spoils of several expeditions are now magnificently displayed.

Kumtura Kùmùtǔlǎ Shíkū 库木吐喇石窟

This site, at the mouth of the Muzart River somewhat closer to Kuqa, was also thoroughly picked over by foreign archaeologists, but still has significant quantities of murals in place, and some statuary. The caves were constructed in three bursts, mostly between the 5th and 11th centuries, and there are about 112 extant. New caves were still being discovered as late as 1979. Divided into two groups, northern and southern, the five northernmost caves are unusual in being connected by a hidden passage.

Access to the Kumtura site is still restricted, and costs ¥400 ($48), by arrangement with the Foreign Affairs Office or a travel agent.

Other Sights

Ruins of several cities stand in the area. Of an earlier version of Kuqa just west of the centre, only a few walls and three mounds remain, while at Subash (Sūbāshí Gǔchéng), about 20km north, there are the remains of a 4th-century town, including a large Buddhist temple. Another cave temple site, only accessible with special permission from the Foreign Affairs Office, is Simsim (Sēnmùsāimǔ Shíkū), about 46km northwest of Kuqa, consisting of 52 caves with 19 fairly intact.

Hotel managers in Kuqa are no doubt dreaming of the day when the town becomes the main point of exchange between road and railway, and when prices will rise.

Tour groups generally end up in the **Qiūcí Bīnguǎn**, about 15mins walk west of the bus station (turn right along the main highway), ✆ 712 2005, ✆ 712 5115. This is the most comfortable and expensive until new buildings open at the Sīlù Bīnguǎn. Overpriced singles and doubles with tiled floors and bathrooms are ¥280 ($34) per room, triples and quads ¥100 ($12) per bed, triples with common bath are ¥52 ($6.50) per bed. There's morning and evening hot water. The **Sīlù Bīnguǎn** (Silk Road Hotel), ✆ 712 2901, was once the best hotel in town, and is reached up the fourth right-hand turn west of the bus station, about 15mins walk, and has a new block under construction. The older buildings are the choice of cadre 'conferences' and have doubles with bath at ¥62 ($7.50) per bed, quads without at ¥22 ($3), and suites for ¥92 ($11), which are being replaced by the newer buildings. The **Kuqa Bīnguǎn**, ✆ 712 2844, is a short way down a left turn just beyond the Sīlù. This is a small hotel with various low-rise buildings around an ill-kept central garden. All rooms have baths: doubles are ¥70 ($8.50) per bed, triples ¥60 ($7.50), quads ¥60 ($7.50), and there's a five-bed room for ¥120 ($15) with two connected rooms plus bath— haggling will get you individual beds here, too, if demand is low. There's all-day hot water. The **Qìchēzhàn Zhāodàisuǒ** at the bus station (also known as the Jiāotōng Bīnguǎn) is decrepit and filthy, with unhelpful and lazy staff, but cheap. Doubles are ¥15 ($2) with a fan which may or may not work, and ¥13 per bed without. Triples are ¥10 ($1.25), quads ¥8, and larger rooms ¥5 per bed. All have common bathrooms and the worst kind of toilets. The **Tóngdá Bīnguǎn**, ✆ 712 2539, just west of the bus station on the opposite side of the highway, is a much better choice for the budget traveller. The reception is in the rear building, with smart, bright double rooms, at ¥72 ($9) per bed (with bath), and ¥64 ($8) per bed (with shower). There are cheaper rooms in an older building at the front: doubles with bath are ¥28 ($3.50), with common bath ¥20 ($2.50), and there's an assortment of triples and doubles of various sizes at between ¥33 ($4) and ¥58 ($7) per bed. There's hot water 10.30am–2pm.

Eating Out

There are plentiful noodle restaurants around the bus station, and stalls with Uighur nan bread, pilau, fried snacks, etc. The restaurant in the Tóngdá Bīnguǎn's rear building has a standard Hàn menu.

The Road to Kashgar

Beyond Kuqa the desert reappears, deceptively green, but deadly nonetheless. The gravelly emptiness is broken by small lumps of khaki sand, topped and anchored by tenacious scrub, repeated endlessly to a flat horizon. Hour after hour the view to the south is relentlessly repetitive, while to the north the foothills of the Tiān Shān sometimes tiptoe up to the road, and again retreat. The larger peaks behind are for most of the year obscured by the dust-laden air, which renders everything flat and washed out. The air through open vehicle windows is like the hot breath of a convection oven.

From time to time the road is broken up as if the desert has come to take a bite out of it, caused partly by drifting sand, or by sudden heavy rain in the mountains which has run down to overwhelm the road for a few hours, before disappearing into the dessicated landscape or evaporating. Otherwise the road is mostly good, but with such vast distances involved some section or other is always under repair, and buses are forced to take long detours across the desert itself. The British diplomat Eric Teichman came this way in 1935.

> In the middle of the desert we drove through an empty town, called
> Old Chilan, a weird and eerie spot, completely lifeless, the mud
> houses, mosques and city walls crumbling to dust. Apparently the water
> supply had failed and the inhabitants had moved out—an epitome of
> the history of many Central Asian cities.
>
> Eric Teichman, *Journey to Turkistan*, 1937

The remains of walls and buildings often appear briefly in the windows, particularly to the south, and dwindle rapidly to nothing. The first major town is **Aksu** (Ākèsū), 255km and 5–6 hours from Kuqa, once a major Buddhist centre, later famous for its walnuts and leather goods, now too modern to be of much interest to the visitor and more concerned with developing neighbouring mineral deposits. A broad, strong meltwater river flows through multiple natural and man-made channels west of the centre.

On such a long trip you are almost certain to see at least one sunset over the desert, and will watch khakis turn gradually to pinks, and then to moonlight greys. Buses to destinations on the southern route often turn off to **Bāchǔ** (Maralbashi), about 150km before Kashgar, and cut across directly to Yarkand (Shāchē). Aurel Stein crossed the desert this way in 1908, and he, von Le Coq (1905), and the French archaeologist Pelliot all worked at cave sites at nearby Tumchuk. 40km before Kashgar you reach **Artux** (Ātúshí), the capital of a Kyrgyz Autonomous Prefecture. Outside the town is the Tomb of Sutuq Bughra Khan, said to be the first ruler of Kashgar to convert to Islam. Younghusband noticed here a large canal which was said to have been begun by Yakub Beg before the end of his short-lived independent Turkestan (*see* p.275), but not completed. Buses arrive in Kashgar at all times of the day and night, but around 16–18 hours and 723km after leaving Kuqa, 11–12 hours after leaving Aksu, they trundle into Xīnjiāng's most famous oasis town.

Kashgar to Dūnhuáng/Korla

The Southern Taklamakan Route

Kashgar is a place of video arcades and donkey carts; old men with white beards in traditional Uighur fur-trimmed hats, long coats and boots, carrying televisions; and younger Uighur men in sour-coloured suits and flat caps looking like escapees from sepia photographs of turn-of-the-century mill workers. China seems to have had little impact on this modern-medieval city, which contains one of the world's great bazaars—a meeting place for all of Xīnjiāng's Muslim minorities and their neighbours from Pakistan and the CIS. You are still likely to be awoken by the braying of donkeys and the jingling of bell-hung harnesses, as much as by the hooting and clattering of trucks.

Intermittent Chinese rule over Kashgar has always been marked by their assumption of superiority over an alien people. One expression of this was in architecture and, as in other Tarim towns, when taking control the Chinese built themselves separate new quarters. Now the usual rigid grid of post-1949 socialist modernism is attempting to surround the Uighur old town, but a number of more elegant buildings with both Islamic and Russian influences survive. The old city remains a warren of mud brick, coloured tile and over-hanging balconies, and on one street a small section of the original city wall remains tucked away behind hotels and office buildings.

Travelling south and east from Kashgar along the edge of the Kūnlún mountains puts you in good company. General Zhāng Qiān came this way on his return to China in 126 BC carrying news of foreign lands to the Hàn dynasty court. The Buddhist pilgrim Fǎxiǎn came west in search of Buddhist texts in AD 400, and Xuánzàng took further texts back this way from India in AD 644. Marco Polo supposedly took the route in 1273, and many travelling as late as the early 20th century carried his book as the only available guide.

The late 19th century saw not only professional soldiers, diplomats, geographers, and spies venture over the Karakorams and into Turkestan, but also an ever-increasing number of private individuals, eager for adventure in one of the world's last unmapped regions. Eastern Turkestan and its neighbour Tibet were constantly in the British newspapers, with speculation about Russian occupation. Intrepid amateur map-makers saw chances for glory:

> *Like other British officers smitten with the exploration fever, I had had difficulty in obtaining sufficient leave of absence from my regiment, but in March, 1897, owing to trouble arising from an unhealthy liver, I found it necessary to resign my commission and quit India for good.*

Captain H. P. Deasy, *In Tibet and Chinese Turkestan*, 1901

Deasy's health may have been too poor for him to continue to serve as a soldier, but his liver didn't prevent him from travelling over the Khunjerab Pass, down to Khotan, and in and out of Tibet over the Kūnlún Mountains, surveying as he went. He set off from Srinagar in 1897, travelled over 5300 miles, and returned to India in 1899, promptly collapsing with 'malarial fever, congestion of the liver, sciatica, rheumatism, and gout'.

Though less travelled of late, this southern route was the route by which Buddhism first reached China, resulting in a string of Buddhist centres in towns now long abandoned to the desert. As the Tarim Basin has dried, the route has crept ever closer to the Kūnlún Shān, the mountains marking the border with Tibet. The oasis towns see few visitors, transport can be unreliable, and the desert sometimes pounces on the road and reclaims it. Recently reopened to foreigners, the route lacks major sites, but the Uighur way of life has been almost as perfectly preserved as the desiccated artefacts discovered in the archaeological gold rush of the early 20th century.

Kashgar (Kāshí)

喀什 Sunday is market day, but only for the biggest market and the one with the most livestock. Every day is market day in the old town, and there's constant bustle on all the roads in and out of Kashgar, with truck-loads of melons. Small grey and black donkeys led by grey-haired Uighurs in black coats pull carts with basket-loads of tomatoes in fluorescent reds, perhaps with a little girl in brilliant pink perched on the rear. Men lead bleating, wobbly-bottomed sheep through the streets on pieces of rope.

Despite its remoteness Kashgar has long thrived as the junction of routes around both sides of the Taklamakan, from Tibet, India, Afghanistan and Russia. The opening of the Torugart and Khunjerab crossings has once again turned Kashgar into an international crossroads, and there is always talk of further options to come: the Irkestam route to Osh; perhaps a link to Tajikistan. Some Pakistanis treat Kashgar as a kind of Bangkok, with forbidden entertainment such as alcohol and women discreetly but widely available. Brothels, disguised as video parlours, come and go, and so do marriages. There is a long tradition of flexibility in this area, and of young ladies called *chaukans* willing to contract temporary alliances or marriages with traders when their camel convoys were in port, seen as dissolved once the caravans had disappeared over the horizon. Hàn residents sneer, and claim that it is a matter of pride for Uighurs to have as many marriages as possible. Diana Shipton, wife of the last British consul, remarked of Turki women in the 1940s that, 'Divorce was a simple matter and changing husbands seemed to be another of their pastimes.' Evenings and weekends are regularly enlivened by the sound of wedding convoys of vehicles carrying traditional Uighur bands.

Like Marx and Proust, Polo is more often quoted than read: one historian cited Polo as claiming that Kashgar was the birthplace of the Swedes. Kashgar Prefecture is now 93 per cent Uighur, 6 per cent Hàn, with a scattering of Tajik, Kyrgyz, Uzbek, Kazak, Tartar, Xībó, Manchu, Mongol, Daur, and Huí 'nationalities'.

After the year 2000 the railway will certainly bring more visitors, more hotels will be built to house them, and more Hàn will arrive to run the hotels and other tourist services. There may be unrest. For now the Hàn are less confident than in Ürümqi and, even if born in Kashgar, more likely to think of themselves as from the same province as their parents. For many this is the remotest corner of exile from real China, and some advocate giving Xīnjiāng independence, seeing it as a drain on the money-making east. So no one forgets who's in charge, one of China's larger remaining Máo statues stands guard not far from Idkah Square.

History

Far enough west to be within the reach of the Chinese only at the times of their greatest strength, Kashgar has mostly gone its own way, either as an independent city-state or as the capital of larger areas of the Tarim Basin, under Turki or Mongol control. Nearly all the more famous Silk Route travellers passed through, reporting Muslim or Buddhist civilizations, depending on the times. Hàn dynasty general Zhāng Qiān visited Kashgar in about 126 BC in his search for allies to help the Hàn defeat the marauding Xiōngnú, noting Kashgar as just one of many walled cities around the rim of the Tarim Basin. Chinese military hero Bān Chāo, the first to put the region under formal Chinese control from AD 73, used Kashgar as his headquarters.

In the competition to 'prove' to whom Kashgar belongs, Chinese histories and guide books allow you to imagine that Hàn armies and settlers never left again. Equally, some opponents base their claims for an independent 'Eastern Turkestan' on the straight noses of 2000-year-old desiccated corpses dug up from various points around the desert. After the Hàn Kashgar was under an assortment of different rulers, including the Western Turkish Khanate; it was reclaimed by the Táng dynasty, which was followed by the Kharakanids, and the Khitan Mongol Xī Liáo dynasty. It was one of Genghis Khan's first conquests, later becoming part of the fiefdom of his son Chagatai, and part of the Mongol Yuán dynasty's territory.

The monk Xuánzàng noticed intense Buddhist activity in AD 644, but passing through in around 1273 (if he did) Marco Polo reported:

> Cascar is a region lying between north-east and east, and constituted a kingdom in former days, but now it is subject to the Great Kaan. The people worship Mahommet. There are a good number of towns and villages, but the greatest and finest is Cascar itself. The inhabitants live by trade and handicrafts; they have beautiful gardens and vineyards, and fine estates, and grow a great deal of cotton. From this country many merchants go forth about the world on trading journeys. The natives are a wretched, niggardly set of people; they eat and drink in miserable fashion. There are in the country many Nestorian Christians, who have churches of their own. The people of the country have a peculiar language, and the territory extends for five days' journey.

Marco Polo, *The Travels*, 13th century (Yule-Cordier edition)

The Míng, who followed, were weaker and more inward-looking, and it was not until the Qīng (1644–1911) that China once again took an interest in the territories to its northwest. Xīnjiāng's first proper inclusion into China came during the reign of the Emperor Qiánlóng (1736–99). His weapon was a Manchu bannerman named Zhàohuì (1708–64), who after enduring all the traditional banes of invading Chinese armies—defections, murder of his emissaries, long marches in difficult terrain, and shortages that reduced his troops to cannibalism—took Kashgar and Yarkand in 1759, slaughtering the remaining Dungan (Chinese muslim or Huí) troops with great cruelty. When Zhàohuì returned to Běijīng, the emperor came out beyond the city gates to welcome him in person, an almost unparalleled honour.

The Qīng administrators proved intolerant, calling the local Turkis 'turban heads' (*chántóu*, which can still occasionally be heard), and kept themselves aloof in a separate new city, insisting on the use of Chinese language and customs in all administrative matters. In an extension of their usual 'use barbarian to fight barbarian' policy, they employed locals as tax collectors, and were content as long as they were given what they expected. They asked no questions as to how the taxes might have been raised or what extra monies the collectors might have taken for themselves. Noisy ceremonies, such as that of firing a gun when the senior Chinese official left his *yámen* (office-cum-court), were designed to impress, and as a reminder of just who was in charge. Younghusband remarked of local governors:

> *In whatever part of the Chinese Empire you visit an official, you will always find both his residence and his official dress precisely the same: the loose blue silk jacket and petticoat, and either the mushroom hat in summer, or the pork pie hat in winter.*

Captain Frank E. Younghusband, *The Heart of a Continent*, 1896

Regrettably, the plumage of Chinese officials is less dazzling these days, but their administration is equally as indifferent to local opinion, despite window-dressing to the contrary. With this degree of tact, it is not surprising that the Qīng faced multiple uprisings throughout Xīnjiāng and Gānsù, the most serious of which, that of the Khokandi adventurer Yakub Beg, resulted from 1866 to 1877 in the declaration of an independent Kashgaria (another name for the Tarim Basin and its settled oases), ruled, of course, from Kashgar.

Great Game Players in Kashgar

In 1886 a tea planter called **Robert Shaw**, attracted as much by the thought of profit as by the romance of hide-and-seek with the Russians in unexplored lands which usually motivated travel in the region at that time, set out from Ladakh on his own initiative to be the first Englishman ever to enter Kashgar. Shaw had in mind that the adventurer Yakub Beg, who had cut a large part of Turkestan free from Chinese rule, had also cut it off from supplies of useful commodities. He had visions of caravans crossing the Karakorams and Pamirs from India, laden with British goods, to the exclusion of Russian products. Knowing the issues involved in entering unknown territory ruled by an oriental despot, he planned carefully, making contact through intermediaries, and taking lavish gifts. The only European to precede him in modern times, a German called Adolph Schlagentweit, had passed through Yarkand and been murdered near Kashgar in 1857.

En route, Shaw was horrified to discover that he was in competition with a well-known Great Game player and explorer, **George Hayward** (later to meet with an assassin's knife on a lonely mountain top, and be made a patriotic hero by the British press, *see* 'Gilgit', p.493). The two exchanged messages on the fly, with Shaw trying to convince Hayward, who seemed ill-prepared and who was not expected by Yakub Beg, to avoid compromising his expedition. On 14 October 1886 they met to discuss terms, but Hayward, on a mission for the Royal Geographical Society, refused to turn back. They compromised: Shaw was to go ahead and prepare the way, and Hayward, who had intended to get to Yarkand disguised as an Afghan, to show more stiff upper lip, and travel 'in the character of an Englishman', as Shaw put it.

Hayward failed to keep to the agreement, turning up as Shaw was engaged in delicate negotiations near the border. Allowed eventually to proceed, Shaw spent Christmas at Yarkand, and reached Kashgar to meet Yakub Beg in early 1869. Despite expressions of friendship and of delight at the gifts brought by Shaw, Yakub kept him under house arrest for three months without further audience. Shaw discovered that Hayward had arrived and was also under arrest, and the two managed to exchange secret messages. Shaw was initially unaware that he had been beaten to Kashgar by four months by a Russian with the gift of 1000 rifles, and Yakub Beg was performing a delicate tightrope walk between his two superpower neighbours, the British empire and the Russian, before deciding which to call his friend. The Russians, while eager to secure trade, were not willing to gamble on his continued existence and risk Běijīng's wrath by formally recognizing his new state (an entertaining parallel to the pussyfooting of modern Western states on issues that might compromise their access to China's exploding economy). In April the profuse expressions of undying amity towards Shaw were renewed as Yakub decided to turn to Britain for support, and Shaw finally left Kashgar on 9 April, returning to India to find himself something of a hero. Despite his difficult relationship with their own explorer, he received the Royal Geographical Society's Gold Medal. Shaw gave up tea planting for life as a freelance administrator, and was later appointed Political Agent in Yarkand.

Shaw's risky journey was to inspire his ambitious nephew Francis Younghusband, who eventually travelled to Kashgar by the same route, and later led the British invasion of Tibet in a search for wholly imaginary Russians. Younghusband dedicated his book, *The Heart of a Continent*: 'To the memory of my mother, through whom, as the sister of Robert Shaw, I inherited the spirit of exploration.'

The Viceroy of India, Lord Mayo, who took up office in Calcutta in 1869, also wanted to send British goods, and thought that Kashgaria could serve as a buffer state between British India and the Russians. In 1872 the Russians, having earlier occupied the Ili region to prevent Muslim rebellion spreading to their recently acquired Central Asia possessions, forced Yakub into a trading agreement, and two British trade missions ended in failure. In a repeat of the Hàn dynasty defeat of the Ferghanans and subsequent similar Tarim episodes, the emotionally fuelled uprising was defeated by cooler long-term planning on the part of the Chinese. In 1877 Yakub asked for a British representative to be sent, but by December the Chinese army which had been advancing upon him for nearly three years was in Kashgar, and he was dead. Younghusband, passing through Kashgar for the first time in 1887, heard the story of Kashgar's fall from an Afghan in the service of the Chinese government:

> At the time the Chinese re-took Kasgar he was in the town, and said there was practically no fighting. Yakoob Beg had died, or been poisoned, away westward some weeks before...there was no one to lead the defence... What soldiers there were, when they heard the Chinese were close to the town, hastily threw aside their uniforms or disguises as soldiers, and, assuming the dress of cultivators, walked about the fields in a lamb-like and innocent manner. The Chinese entered the town, and everything went on as if nothing had happened—the shopkeeper sold his wares, and the countryman ploughed his fields, totally indifferent as to who was or who was not in power in Kashgar.

Captain Frank E. Younghusband, *The Heart of a Continent*, 1896

In 1884, in an attempt to reduce further Russian incursions, the Chinese announced that the region now had the status of a province, although this neither prevented further rebellions in Kashgar, or stopped the Russians virtually governing Xīnjiāng until 1949. The construction of the Turk-Sib railway in 1931 put Kashgar a mere two weeks from Moscow, while it was at least three months from Běijīng, and at least six weeks from the nearest Indian railhead.

Uprisings and Croquet Parties (Russia vs. Britain)

The 1864 Treaty of Tarbatagai and the 1881 Treaty of St Petersburg turned over large areas of nominally Qīng territory north of Issyk-Kul to the Russians, and granted them preferential trading terms. In November 1882 the Russians set up a consulate in Kashgar; a British trade representative followed two years later. Kashgar was the centre for local government and, although subordinate to the new provincial capital at Ürümqi, was so far from it as to go its own way in many matters. In the 1890s it had a population of about 40,000, rather less than the 60,000 of Yarkand, nearer to India and thus a greater trading centre, as the main routes then went west from Yarkand to Tashkurgan, or south over two passes direct to Leh.

The reconquest of the Tarim oases turned out to be one of the dying gasps of the Qīng dynasty, which had to deal with uprisings and loss of control in territory rather closer to home. By the 1890s there were only 7–8000 troops in the whole of Xīnjiāng, derided by passing travellers as being cowardly and ill-disciplined, but good at gardening. The occupants of the two consulates strove for influence over the senior Chinese Amban (official), the Dàotāi. The Russian consul, **Petrovsky**, combined a forceful personality with the threat of Cossack forces just over the nearby border to cow the Chinese into submission. He ran a network of spies and informants who indulged in cloak and dagger operations such as intercepting mail, and he constantly conspired to have his British counterpart expelled from Kashgar. In promoting trade he had the advantage both of tax concessions and the shorter and easier route that Russian goods had to travel from Russia's recently acquired Central Asian possessions, compared to the arduous trek over perilous passes of the Karakorams and Pamirs faced by British traders from India. It was widely assumed by foreign observers that the Russians were only looking for an excuse to take Xīnjiāng, as they seemed to treat it virtually as a colony. Petrovsky once boasted to an English traveller that the Dàotāi did precisely as he was told, and should he prove reluctant the threat of a whipping changed his mind.

His British opposite number, **George Macartney**, was just 24 when he arrived in 1890 as an assistant and translator to Captain Younghusband. The purpose of their visit was to encourage the Chinese to back up militarily their claim to Somatash in the Pamirs on the edge of Afghanistan, which would close up a gap between Afghan and Chinese territory, reducing the chances of a Russian advance on India. Having drawn a few lines arbitrarily on a map, Younghusband was convinced that he had solved the British-Afghan-Russian-Chinese boundary problems, but he was a failure at the diplomacy needed to deal with the Chinese, and considered himself above Petrovsky's subterfuges. Restless, he bought a yurt and slept in the garden, and before long departed for more active duties elsewhere, leaving Macartney in charge at this isolated outpost of the British Empire for a further 27 years until 1918.

Macartney was the product of a Scottish father and Chinese mother (of whom he never spoke), who had been brought up in China until he was 10, given a public school education in England, and taken a degree from a French university. Coincidentally he was distantly related to the Lord Macartney who had been sent to China in 1793 by George III. Fluent in Mandarin, French, Turki, Persian, Hindustani (and English), he was on the way to a post in the Burmese civil service when diverted to travel with Younghusband. Quiet, modest and reserved about his achievements, he was the volatile Petrovsky's opposite, once turning down an opportunity for a clandestine read of the Russian's mail.

He began his time in Kashgar under the disadvantage of having neither Petrovsky's military back-up, nor official consular status (until 1908). Instead, Macartney won his battles with his intimate knowledge of Chinese procedure and customs, and fluency in Mandarin. He gradually built up a relationship with the Dàotāi which allowed him to advise the governor on the best responses to Petrovsky's threats, his main aim being to avoid allowing the Chinese to give the Russians the excuse they wanted to bring in more troops. The Ambans were both vacillating and corrupt. Macartney helped them to steer a safe course between Russian aggression, local discontent, and the changing fortunes of Běijīng.

The Chinese Opium Wars had had as their result a number of 'unequal treaties' which affected life even in faraway Kashgar. One of these enshrined the principle of extra-territoriality, which made most Westerners in China subject to the laws and law officers of their own countries rather than to those of the Chinese. Much of Macartney's time was spent in adjudication and punishment of British subjects, mostly Hindu moneylenders or other traders from India. He also succeeded in releasing many slaves, assisted the boundary commission of 1895 (which was tackling the problems that Younghusband had left unsolved), and visited Hunza to assist with the delicate negotiations following the British annexation of the valley.

The European community in Kashgar was tiny, consisting of the consular staff and a few missionaries, although Macartney eventually added to it by bringing out a wife and having children. Catherine Macartney later produced a book, *An English Lady in Chinese Turkestan*, full of diplomatic dinner parties, struggles with servants and gardening. This limited social life was also part of the Russian-British front. One of Petrovsky's weapons was the imagined slight, and despite the smallness of the European community there were long periods when he refused to speak to Macartney at all. Following an exchange of magazines, the Russian consulate found a copy of *Punch* which made a joke at the expense of the Tsar, and there followed a silence of more than two and a half years. Younghusband's calling at the Russian consulate in the morning rather than the afternoon was also taken as a major insult. Petrovsky would go to considerable lengths to discomfort those he disliked. He successfully campaigned to have a missionary deprived of his house, and asked Macartney to return a pane of glass he had lent him—at the time the only one the British had, the rest of the windows being covered in oiled paper. He once accused Macartney of importing arms, when he had in fact been doing so himself, and of aiding Cossacks to sell Russian government property.

During this period several of the explorers and archaeologists who were to bring the early Buddhist civilizations of the Tarim basin to light, including Hedin, Stein, von Le Coq and Pelliot, passed through Kashgar, staying at one consulate and usually dining at least once at the other. There was frequent praise for the comforts and hospitality of the British Consulate, and the delightful gardens. Few had anything good to say about Petrovsky, although Swedish pioneer explorer Sven Hedin described him as 'my good old friend', and commented on 'the well-nigh omnipotent influence which he enjoys in East Turkestan'. Petrovsky lent Hedin some Cossacks, and arranged for his mail to reach him in the desert using four special couriers.

Younghusband, who was to despise Petrovsky when he got to know him better, initially found him an interesting man, commenting in 1887 on his first visit to Kashgar:

> *The talk turned on India, and I was astonished to find how well acquainted M. Petrovsky was with that country.... On the Central Asian question he spoke very freely, and said that we English always suspected the Russians of designs upon India, but that in reality nothing was further from their minds.*

Captain Frank E. Younghusband, *The Heart of a Continent*, 1896

Younghusband, one of the major proponents of anti-Russian scaremongering 'forward policy', differed in his opinion.

In 1894, Japanese advances in northeast China threatened Russian designs in the Amur River, and Russian military spending in Xīnjiāng was cut, leaving the consulates in Kashgar exposed to increasing Dungan (Huí) unrest. Petrovsky became correspondingly more affable, even paying a social visit to the British. After his departure things became easier, and for a while later, following the Russian revolution, the Russian consulate was unmanned until a consul sympathetic to the Bolsheviks was installed.

The effects of the 1911 Chinese revolution were sluggish in reaching the country's outer regions, and did not arrive in Kashgar until the spring of 1912, preceded by rumours of the murder of Chinese officials in neighbouring towns, mostly by other Chinese. Kashgar followed the same pattern, the excuse of 'revolution' being used for the settling of personal grievances, in this case the mob being led by a recalcitrant pork butcher and a barber. Some officials were murdered in their beds; others took refuge in the British consulate compound, along with the other European residents, who expected attack at any moment. Macartney and his brother, who was visiting, made arrangements for the despatch of the women and children, in case the under-armed defenders of the consulate (which included a nurse with a kitchen knife, and another with a syringe full of acid) should be overwhelmed. Eventually a Russian regiment arrived to restore order, and the revolutionaries went quiet. A few surviving Chinese officials and their relatives emerged from bakers' ovens and rooftops where they had been hidden by friendly Uighurs, and in due course the pork butcher and the barber were themselves appropriately butchered by beheading.

By 1915 all was back to normal. While the Macartneys took leave, Sir Percy Sykes and his sister Ella stood in, attending tea parties, playing tennis and croquet. 'Every one "spooned" and pushed the balls into position in a way contrary to every rule of up-to-date croquet and got quite excited over the games.' As with Great Games, so with small: cheating was essential.

In his 28 years in Kashgar, Macartney outlasted four Russians consuls, passing a stream of information on Russian activities and his views on their intentions to the Indian government. Catherine Macartney's much praised gardens are now covered in concrete and the Chini Bagh Hotel buildings. Macartney finally persuaded the authorities to build him a proper consulate in 1913, and a few of the buildings remain behind the hotel. The site of the Russian consulate now houses the Sèmǎn Hotel, but a number of the old buildings remain at the rear.

The consulates survived the uprisings that swept through the area in the 1930s, which were as much civil wars between Kyrgyz, other Turkis and Dungans (Huí), as anti-Chinese rebellions. In 1933 the Turkis had control of old Kashgar while the Dungans were besieged in the Chinese new city. The Dungan general Mǎ Zhòngyīng ('Big Horse', *see* p.243), driven south following his defeat near Ürümqi, arrived in early 1934 and drove out the Turkis, only to be driven out himself by a pursuing army of combined Russians, Manchus and Turkis. Mrs Thompson-Glover, wife of the British consul of the time, was hit in the shoulder while standing on the verandah of the residence. The Dungan troops retreated to Khotan, and Mā disappeared to Russia, not to be seen again. *The Times* correspondent, Peter Fleming, arriving from Xī'ān around the southern route in 1935, found almost all the southern oases under the control of Dungan troops, but relative serenity in Kashgar. He took his first bath in five and a half months, sat in comfortable armchairs, drank cool drinks while listening to the gramophone, played football with the Hunzakut guards, and swam in the Russian consulate's pool. Both consulates closed following the formation of the People's Republic in 1949.

Getting to and from Kashgar

Everyone comes to Kashgar for the Sunday Bazaar, and Sunday night and Monday transportation out of town is often heavily booked. This is not usually a problem on the route to Pakistan, where extra buses are laid on as necessary.

by air

Kashgar's only air connection is to Ürümqi. Throughout most of the year China Xīnjiāng Airways flies daily from Ürümqi to Kashgar and back (flight time 1hr 40mins; ¥1265/$152 one way), leaving Ürümqi at 6pm Běijīng time and Kashgar at 9pm; on some days there are two flights. In winter, the frequency falls to three flights a week unless there is exceptional demand. The unhelpful Kashgar CAAC office, ☏ 282 2113 (*open 10–1.30 and 3.30–7.30*) is next to the People's Park's south entrance at 49 Jiěfàng Nánlù. An airport bus leaves here at 6.30pm every day there is a flight and takes 25 minutes, or you can take public bus no.2 from Idkah Sq.

by bus

For international transport *see* 'To Pakistan via the Khunjerab Pass', p.288, and 'To Kyrgyzstan via the Torugart Pass', p.289.

The main long-distance bus station is on Jiěfàng Nánlù. Foreigners are charged double prices for buses from Kashgar, and there are individuals who roam the ticket hall and who follow you onto the bus to make sure that the 'right' price has been paid. To add confusion, starting times tend to be half an hour later in winter, and tickets are stamped with Xīnjiāng time, although the time you are told to come to the station is usually given in Běijīng time. Until the railway is completed, long-distance sleeper buses remain the fastest and most comfortable way to get round the Taklamakan.

Going north around the Taklamakan: Sleeper buses to Ürümqi are twice the price of those in the opposite direction at ¥382 ($46) upper berth and ¥424 ($51) lower berth for the 1474km, with two departures daily, and two departures with seats, all passing through Aksu (468km), Kuqa (723km), and Korla (1003km). There are two other departures daily to Korla; upper berths are ¥232 ($28), lower ¥280 ($34). In the summer buses go the 1374km to Turpan direct on Mon, Wed, and Fri, and daily to Dàhéyàn, from where you can take minibuses or taxis to Turpan. There are also daily departures to Gulja (Yīníng) which turn north over the mountains at Kuqa, 1644km.

Going south round the Taklamakan: There's a daily bus directly to Keriya (Yútián, 687km), passing through Yengisar (Yīngjíshā, 68km, 9 departures, ¥10/$1.20),

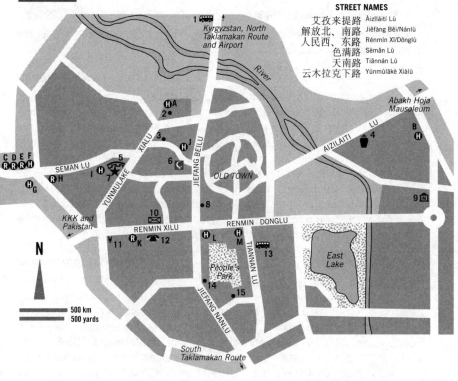

Kashgar

Kyrgyzstan, North
Taklamakan Route
and Airport

River

Abakh Hoja
Mausoleum

SEMAN LU

XILU

JIEFANG BEILU

AIZILAITI LU

YUNMULAKE

OLD TOWN

KKK and
Pakistan

RENMIN XILU

RENMIN DONGLU

TIANNAN LU

People's
Park

East
Lake

JIEFANG NANLU

South
Taklamakan Route

N

500 km
500 yards

Yarkand (Shāchē, 192km, 7 departures), Karghalik (Yèchéng, 254km, 5 departures), and Khotan (Hétián, 509km, 2 departures, ¥72/$9), which is 17 hours away.

There are also local buses to Tashkurgan for ¥40 ($5) on Mon, Wed, and Fri, 291km.

Go to windows 2, 3, or 4 for tickets to southern Taklamakan destinations, 5 for the northern route and Gulja, and 6 or 7 for Tashkurgan.

Getting Around

Kashgar is divided into four quarters by the north–south Jiěfàng Běilù/Nánlù and the west–east Rénmín Xīlù/Dōnglù. The most useful form of transport in Kashgar is the bicycle, as the buses are infrequent, and routes don't cater for the visitor (an exception is minibus 9, which runs from the Sèmǎn Bīnguǎn, past the Chini Bagh, and connects to the small bus station for the Kyrgyz border). Bicycle rental is ¥2 (24¢) per hour from the Sèmǎn Hotel, and ¥1.5 (18¢) from the Chini Bagh. Taxis have 'broken' meters, so fix the price first. Motorbike taxis (up to two people ride in the sidecar) are cheaper and more amenable. Jeeps and minibuses can be hired from agents at most major hotels and through John's Information Café, or flag them down in the street and haggle yourself.

Kashgar ✆ (0998)   ### Tourist Information

CITS (*open 10–2 and 3.30–7.30*) is in the Chini Bagh Hotel, ✆ 282 5390 or 282 3087, 📠 282 2525. One or two staff speak English, and information is freely given. Sometimes you will be told, 'Just negotiate a taxi for yourself, it's cheaper than with us' (and probably more reliable). CITS has a particularly poor reputation for getting people across the Torugart in either direction. **John's Information Café**, ✆ 282 4186, 📠 282 2861, is the best place to ask all basic questions over reasonable food. John will arrange purchase of bus and plane tickets for ¥25 ($3) per bus ticket or ¥50 ($6) per plane ticket, and jeeps to sites outside town, to the new Torugart border post, to Karakol Lake, and more distant destinations. Sometimes he can obtain tickets when flights are 'sold out', and get sleeper bus tickets around 25% cheaper than the bus station foreigners' price. Permits for crossing the Torugart Pass into China can be arranged for around ¥3–400 ($36–48), with about two weeks' notice, and collection from the new border post for about ¥300. In general his services are cheaper, more reliable, and more friendly than the other agencies, and, unlike CITS, he has a reputation to protect. He also runs a free shuttle bus to the Sunday bazaar during the high season. **Xīnjiāng Kashgar Mountaineering Association**, 8 Tǐyù Lù, ✆ 282 680, 📠 282 2957, runs a vast range of expensive mountaineering, skiing, and trekking tours. They can arrange collection from the old Torugart border post by jeep ($200 *per person*), and the permit to ensure that you can cross into China ($60 *per person*).

Note: If you fax any of these agencies, especially from Central Asia, use large type, block capitals, and write all numbers (including phone numbers) out in full words, as transmissions are often garbled. All will be happy to fax you back a quote, eventually.

The **Bank of China** (*open summer Mon–Fri, 9.30–1.30 and 4–7; winter 10–2 and 3.30–6.30, summer and winter Sat and Sun 11–3*) is on Rénmín Xīlù and in the foyers of major hotels such as the Chini Bagh and Sèmǎn with a variety of opening hours. Note that the main Bank of China is particularly reluctant to change Rénmínbì back to US dollars, or to give US dollars for traveller's cheques. If you are going to Kyrgyzstan via the Torugart Pass you will find the bank at the new border post erratic at best, so insist; or try the Sèmǎn Bīnguǎn. You will need plentiful amounts of US dollars in cash, and bills larger than $1 should 1990 or later. You can draw Rénmínbì cash on Amex, Visa, Mastercard and JCB. The minimum amount is ¥1200 ($145) and the maximum is whatever your credit limit will stand. There is 4% commission, plus whatever your credit card charges you. Allow plenty of time for this. *Poste restante* and international postage are all handled from a counter upstairs on the right at the **post office** (*yóudiàn dàlóu*) on the north side of Rénmín Lù at the first small junction east of the Bank of China (*open 9.30–1 and 4–8, Sat and Sun 12–5, slight variations in winter*). Mail is kept fairly reliably for one month. Some of the hotels also have postal services. **International telephone calls** can be made from the Sèmǎn Bīnguǎn Business Centre (*open 10am–11.30pm*), ✆ 282 2129, and other businesses around town with signs in English. The cheapest option for both phone and fax is the communications building (*diànxìn dàlóu*) opposite the post office, ✆ 282 1212 (*open 10–8*). US and Britain are both ¥35 ($4.25) per minute, and Kyrgyzstan ¥32 ($3.90). Facsimiles are everywhere at least three times the price of phone calls (e.g ¥113.10/$13.70 per page to Europe at the communications building, ¥180/$21.70 at the Sèmǎn—possibly China's most expensive prices). The communications building will charge you for phone time if your fax fails to go through (about ¥37/$4.50 per minute) but the Sèmǎn only charges if the fax goes through completely. If faxing CIS countries where transmission often fails, definitely choose the Sèmǎn. (Telex is better than fax or phone to Kyrgyzstan, available at the post office and for the same prices at CITS— ¥80/$9.70 per minute.) Receiving faxes costs ¥15 (¥1.80) per page at the Sèmǎn, but ¥9 ($1.10) at the communications building. **Film and developing** are available at a photo store on the east side of Jiěfàng Beilu just south of Idkah Sq (*open 10–8.30*): 36-shot Kodak ¥23 ($2.80); developing ¥4 (50¢), plus ¥1 (12¢) per print. There is also a camera store opposite the post office. English language **books** are hard to find in Kashgar—the Xīnhuá Shūdiàn further south on Jiěfàng Běilù has nothing you want, and the staff would prefer you not to bother them even if it has. CITS and hotel foyers have impractical and inaccurate **maps** of Kashgar and environs for ¥5 (60¢). One month **visa extensions** are available from the well-organized PSB on Yúnmùlākè Xiàlù south of the Chini Bagh (*open Mon–Fri, 10–7*), but only in the last four days before your existing visa expires. The right-hand-most entrance is the Aliens department. Occasionally, in the absence of the right officer, applicants are sent to the Foreign Affairs office, which is considerably less helpful, but will issue extensions if pressed.

Kashgar Sunday Great Bazaar (Kāshí Xīngqītiān Dàshìcháng)　喀什星期天大市场

Sunday is no day of rest but Kashgar's busiest, and the town empties as residents and visitors join rivers of arrivals from neighbouring areas flowing to the Sunday Great Bazaar. It has been modernized in recent years, and some activities put under cover, but the remainder is still a sprawl of bleating animals and haggling Uighurs. There are warrens of cool awning-hung alleys with a constant murmur of offer and counter-offer, and open areas of blazing sunlight, hoofbeats and shouted commands, as diminutive boys test-drive horses and carts.

The market site (*màoyìshìcháng*) is in the northeast corner of the city, about 20 minutes' walk from the Chini Bagh Hotel. A trip with a motorcycle and sidecar should cost no more than ¥5 (60¢), but still 200 or 300 metres from the site you are likely to encounter a donkey cart traffic jam which you will have to negotiate on foot anyway.

The sign on the main entrance (which you have to go round, rather than through) says 'Kashgar International Trade Market of Central and Western Asia', and for once in China, this boast of internationalism is not idle. Although there is trading here all week, on Sundays from around 10am until mid-afternoon the market is a crush of country people, brought by streams of donkey carts, and joined by bus- and taxi-loads of Pakistanis, Uzbeks, Kyrgyz and Kazaks.

You can buy Chinese boom boxes and Russian optical equipment; lengths of gaudy fabric and every kind of clothing that polyester can make; spices, foodstuffs, and medicines manufactured from unidentifiable parts of equally unidentifiable animals; baskets and woven screens; shoes, boots, hats, coats, and furs; camels, goats, sheep, and horses; billiard tables, wooden chests covered in fake brass, and garishly painted cabinets and cribs; knives, dishes, pots, and pans; carts to take it all away in, donkeys to pull them, and leather harnesses to connect the two.

Take plenty of film and go early for better light and and the best of the livestock market. Retire under awnings for local bread, tea, and snacks when the day gets too hot.

Idkah Mosque (Àitígǎěr Qīngzhēnsì)　艾提尕尔清真寺

Entrance to the main hall costs ¥3 (36¢); to take photographs anywhere inside the gate costs ¥5 (60¢).

Originally built in 1442, although extended and remodelled since then, the mosque's main gate dominates Idkah Square, the heart both of Kashgar and of Uighur China. The mosque is not so much an attraction in itself as relief from the bustle in the square outside, except on Fridays when the opposite is true. The prayer hall's wooden roof is supported by more than 100 interior and exterior pillars, and together with the leafy courtyard is said to be able to hold up to 20,000 people, making it Xīnjiāng's largest mosque. The interior is unspectacular.

For those not stopping in the smaller oasis towns of the Tarim basin, the backstreets of Kashgar to the east of Idkah Square offer some of the most accessible portions of ordinary Uighur life, with food stalls, small wood- and metal-working workshops, and colourful balconies teetering over narrow alleys. Shops and stalls sell furs, knives, hats and carpets seven days a week.

Abakh Hoja Mausoleum (Ābākèhéjiā Mù)

阿巴克和加墓

Open 7.30–6; adm ¥15 ($1.80),
plus ¥2 (24¢) to take photographs.

Outside town beyond the market, about 3km and 20–30 minutes by bicycle, the mausoleum is set amongst a patchwork of fields and graveyards on the left of Aizīláití Lù. The domed tomb hall is covered in an assortment of blue and green tiles, and contains a huddle of unlabelled tombs which take up almost the entire space of its cool interior, and are said to contain a total of 72 bodies from five generations of the same family of political and religious leaders. The tomb building was built by second-generation Abakh to honour his father, probably around 1640. Other buildings include halls for teaching and prayer. Somewhere nearby is said to be the now unmarked grave of Yakub Beg, the leader of a temporarily independent Kashgaria in the 19th century, and a man the Chinese would rather you forgot.

There are temporary exhibitions in a building behind the ticket desk, currently items from the Cultural Office Museum in Hāmì, including the 3200-year-old corpse of a 40-year-old man in the foetal position, and looking as if made from old papier-mâché. Tickets are a further ¥6 (70¢).

The Legend of the Xiāngfēi

The tomb is more commonly known to Hàn as the Xiāngfēi Mù, or tomb of the Fragrant Concubine, a beloved Uighur concubine of the Emperor Qiánlóng (1711–99), and a Hoja family descendant, named Iparhan. Her tomb is a smaller one in the back row. Mystical Hàn versions of the Xiāngfěi's story have her naturally emitting a pleasant fragrance, and more prosaic Uighur ones describe her as fond of wearing a sprig of oleaster in her hair. Born in 1734, she was chosen to be an imperial consort at the age of 22, but only sent to the court on certain conditions, including that her remains be returned to Kashgar for burial after she died. Alternatively, she was the wife of a rebellious Kashgar chieftain and part of the spoils carried off for the emperor by Zhàohuì after the bloody quelling of a Muslim uprising in 1759. Or yet again her elder brother helped in the quelling of the rebellion, and when summoned to the Qīng court to be created duke, he took his younger sister with him. She was talent-spotted, subsequently rising rapidly up the hierarchy of concubinage from Distinguished Lady, through Junior Imperial Consort, to Imperial Consort.

All accounts have Qiánlóng heartbroken at her death, despite her supposed iciness towards him. She either committed suicide rather than sleep with the emperor, or committed it at the age of 29 on the instruction of the emperor's mother, or died naturally of old age at 55. 120 guards are supposed to have accompanied her remains back to Kashgar for burial in the Hoja family tomb, but archaeologists say that she was buried with other Qīng family members in the Eastern Qīng tombs in Héběi Province, thousands of kilometres away. A coffin labelled in Arabic and with strands of fair hair inside has been unearthed there. Never ones to let truth or lack of hard evidence get in the way of a good story, the Chinese have labelled a palanquin just inside the tomb on the left as being the one that brought her coffin to Kashgar, although it is clearly neither of imperial quality nor of sufficient antiquity.

Around Kashgar

There are several ancient city sites around Kashgar, the nearest of which is **Hanoi** (Hǎnnuòyī Gǔchéng), 38km northeast of town on a bad road (jeep preferred, ¥250/$30). This Táng dynasty predecessor to Kashgar is about 1km by 3km of crumbling walls, and the most significant remains are those of the nearby 12m-high **Mor Buddhist Pagoda**, an almost featureless drum of mud. The few visitors make deep impressions in the soft earth, scattering lizards as they walk, and causing further rapid erosion. There are ticketing problems here: ¥5 (60¢) per person just outside the site, but a further ¥10 each extorted by stone-throwing Uighur peasants. The problem seems to be that both Kashgar and Artux authorities claim jurisdiction. Repeated complaints to the police have produced no results.

The **Sānxiāndòng** (Three Immortals Caves), 20km north of Kashgar, are only worth seeing if you are trying to complete the set of Buddhist caves in China. High up in a cliff face, traces of paintings can be seen if you squint, or take binoculars. Earlier visitors used to persuade the local fire service to bring ladders so they could climb up to look more closely. It might even be possible to do this today—most things can be arranged in China if you have enough rénmínbì.

The **tomb of Mohammed Kashgari**, about 50 km to the southwest, is a less-decorated version of the Abakh Hoja Tomb. Kashgari was an 11th-century Uighur scholar who gave his name to Kashgar, and is honoured for his compilation of a Turkic dictionary. Alternatively known as 'The Tomb of Honourable Scholars', it also contains a library of texts contributed by various Islamic intellectuals. Jeep ¥250 ($30).

Where to Stay

Since 1996 Kashgar hotels have been asked to charge guests a ¥1 per person per night city tax. Kashgar now has an oversupply of hotels, and most prices are negotiable at all but the highest of peak seasons.

expensive

The **Kāshí Bīnguǎn** (**Kashgar Hotel**), ✆ 282 2368, 🖷 282 4679, to the east end of Rénmín Dōnglù, turn left past the museum, is a collection of buildings around green spaces, with the atmosphere of a modern university on an out-of-town campus. Doubles with bathroom are ¥350 ($42) and there are Chinese and Western restaurants.

moderate/inexpensive

The **Sèmǎn Hotel** (Sèmǎn Bīnguǎn) at the junction of Sèmǎn Lù and Rénmín Xīlù, ✆ 282 2129, is one of China's oddest. It occupies some of the former Russian consulate (No.2 Building), a new building in front (No.1 Building), and another one across the road (No.3 Building). The new building looks like a giant slice of overdecorated birthday cake, and the rooms have bizarre triangular and trapezoidal shapes. The foyer has an old colonial style, complete with ceiling fans. The disintegrating elegance of the high-ceilinged old buildings are popular with budget travellers, whereas traders go for the very reasonably priced doubles in the standard Chinese building. Doubles are ¥280 ($34) in the new building, and ¥160 ($19) in the disintegrating elegance of the old one, or ¥60 ($7) without bath. New and overly bright 12-bed dormitories have beds at ¥15 ($2) per bed, but the old dormitories are preferred as they have enormous baths in their albeit decrepit bathrooms; ¥20 ($2.50) per bed from two beds per room upwards. The cluster of old buildings at the rear include a theatre used for Uighur song and dance performances when ordered by groups, a hairdresser, souvenir shops, and a pleasant open-air restaurant. The hotel also has a business centre, and a karaoke bar with a limited Western selection. The best value beds are in building No.3, which has its own reception, and has doubles with bath for ¥40 ($5) per bed, sometimes reducible to ¥30 ($4). Staff at the main reception may be reluctant to admit the existence of cheaper beds if the hotel is not full.

In contrast, the gradual expansion of the **Chini Bagh Hotel** (Qínǐwǎkè Bīnguǎn), Yúnmùlākè Xiàlù, ✆ 282 2103, has almost obliterated any signs of the British Consulate which used to occupy the site, although the former consular residence behind houses a restaurant. The buses to and from Pakistan terminate here, and it's popular with Pakistani traders—women should be a little cautious as they would in Pakistan itself. Chinese dislike of foreigners tends to grow in proportion to the darkness of the foreigners' skin colour, and there have been occasional outbreaks of inter-racial fisticuffs here. In the winter, after the Sèmǎn has closed down, the Chini Bagh becomes the main budget traveller hotel. Doubles in the new but already disintegrating international wing (which has its own reception) are ¥280 ($34), but individual beds in comfortable hot water quads in the main building are ¥40 ($5). The main branch of CITS is in one of the buildings at the front, on the left as you enter.

The **Kāshí Huáqiáo Bīnguǎn** (Overseas Chinese Hotel), ✆ 283 2480, opposite the Sèmǎn Hotel, is Kashgar's newest, with bright and clean large doubles with double bed for ¥280 ($34), smaller ones with two beds for ¥200 ($24) with a balcony overlooking the bustling junction, and standard ones for ¥150 ($18), all plus ¥1 per person one-time insurance fee. Prices are negotiable to a low of ¥150 and in desperate times to ¥30 ($4) per bed—the best value in Kashgar if you can get it. 24-hour hot water.

The **Silk Road Hotel** on the south side of Sèmǎn Lù halfway between the Sèmǎn and the Chini Bagh, ✆ 282 2004, has now also become largely Pakistani. Beds in reasonable three-bed rooms are ¥20 ($2.50), and larger dorms ¥15 ($2), but the bathrooms are primitive and smelly. The rear of the hotel overlooks a chunk of the old city wall.

Close to the bus station on the south side of Rénmín Dōnglù, the **Tiānnán Fàndiàn**, ✆ 282 2211, has doubles with bathroom from ¥60 ($7.50) per bed, with common bath from ¥30 ($4), and quads without bath for ¥16 ($2) per bed. Beware the restaurant and café where you will be charged double for being foreign. Two blocks west at Jiěfàng Nánlù 1, the **Rénmín Fàndiàn**, ✆ 282 4785, is central and friendly, but not as good value or as interesting as the Sèmǎn. A bed in a triple with its own bathroom is ¥53 ($6.50) and dorm beds are ¥16 ($2) in a nine-bed room. Primitive but colourful, the **Noor Bish Hotel**, ✆ 282 3092, is a concrete version of a traditional Uighur building tucked away on the left as you walk from the Chini Bagh to the Idkah Mosque. Only Uighur is spoken, unless a Pakistani guest can act as a translator, but dorm bed prices are negotiable and may be as little as ¥10 or ¥12 ($1.50).

All the larger hotels have reasonable restaurants. The vine-hung space with a concrete penguin at the rear of the Sèmăn is a pleasant place to have lunch on a hot day, but these days has been abandoned in favour of the newer restaurants opposite the hotel's side entrance: **Daniel's Restaurant**, the **Sèmăn Road Restaurant**, and best of all the **Oasis Restaurant** (formerly Limin Restaurant), all featuring English menus, some Western dishes, and all standard Hàn dishes except those using pork. Due to Muslim sensibilities the nearest pig is probably in Ürümqi. In Sèmăn Building No.3, **John's Information Café** has a similar menu, a willingness to tackle larger speciality dishes with a bit of notice, and free travel information from English-speaking staff. **Uighur food** is available at street-side restaurants throughout the old town, on the smaller roads leading to Idkah Square, in the covered market leading north from the square, and at night in the square itself. The **European Sweet Foods Market Section**, on the left going towards the square before the Noor Bish Hotel, has eggy local biscuits, pastries, and cakes, and is a good place to stock up for the long bus journeys.

Upmarket Chinese food is served at the **Western Dynasty Great Wall Hotel** (which is not a hotel) on Rénmín Xīlù not far from the communications building. The atmosphere is that of a good Chinese restaurant in the West, and prices match.

To Pakistan via the Khunjerab Pass

Going from Kashgar to **Pakistan** (Bājīsītán), a bus leaves for Sost every morning between April and October when the pass is open, the dates often varying from year to year according to the weather. It goes from the yard on the left-hand side of the main building of the Chini Bagh Hotel. Tickets are available from the hotel foyer; ¥275 ($33). The official departure time is 11am, but this is just when the customs office opens and the fun begins. First show your passport and your copy of the customs declaration form you received on the way into China to the person at the left window, show your baggage to the people with the scales at the rear of the bus, then pay ¥2 at the right-hand office inside the customs building, taking your luggage to the loaders. They will also take your ticket and passport, which will be returned as you board the bus. You will not have access to your luggage at Tashkurgan, where you spend the night, so take essentials with you. From November to March, when there may be no bus, smaller vehicles holding up to six people can be rented for ¥3000 ($362) or so, weather permitting.

Immediately upon setting out from Tashkurgan the next morning the bus pulls into the customs post, for what is usually a straightforward procedure. There is an opportunity to convert any last remaining ¥RMB into rupees at branches of the Bank of China and the National Bank of Pakistan. There are at least four further passport checks between here and Sost, which usually involve getting down from the bus. Arrival at Sost, all being well, is at around 3pm Pakistani time (4pm Xīnjiāng time, 6pm Běijīng time). *See* 'Sost', p.507.

A local bus leaves for Tashkurgan from Kashgar on Mon, Wed, and Fri mornings from the main bus station for ¥40 ($5). To get on the international bus to Sost at Tashkurgan costs ¥202 ($25).

To Kyrgyzstan via the Torugart Pass

Paul Nazaroff, fugitive from the Bolshevik revolution, coming over the Torugart in 1919, commented, 'Of all the roads leading to Kashgar, or in general from the civilised world into Central Asia, this is the best, most convenient, shortest, easiest, cheapest, and it would not be difficult to improve it into a good carriage road, so as to connect up the railway systems of Europe with the very heart of Central Asia.' More than 80 years later these improvements are still awaited. Start early, and expect this to take up a whole day.

Leaving China, public and private transport now runs to the new border post (Xīnkǒu'àn), a mere 63km from Kashgar on the road to Wuqa (Wūqià). Minibuses run from the tiny Běidàqiáo Chēzhàn (bus station) (15 minutes' walk from the Chini Bagh hotel) in Jiěfàng Běilù opposite the Dìqū Rénmín Yīyuàn (District People's Hospital), or ride on minibus no.9 from the Sèmǎn Hotel or Chini Bagh for ¥1. They leave from 8.30am throughout the day when full, and cost ¥9 ($1.10), although the ticket office (on the right as you enter the alley) will attempt to charge you ¥18 ($2.20). It takes around two hours to travel the 63km. Quotes from agents for transport by minibus or taxi to the new border post vary from ¥200 ($24) to ¥300 ($36), although you can arrange a taxi for yourself for about ¥150 ($18, less than an hour). You must get out of your vehicle for a passport check at a barrier just before the new post.

The border is open Mon–Fri, 10–1 and 4.30–6, Běijīng time; closed all weekends and Chinese and Kyrgyz public holidays (see p.27). You will not be allowed to continue to the old border post without a valid CIS visa. Following customs and immigration formalities, minibuses take you to the old post 104km further on for ¥100 ($12). These are decrepit and travel in tandem, so you may have to wait some time until both are full. CITS will provide a vehicle holding up to five people from Kashgar to the old post for ¥1200 ($145) and including the necessary vehicle permit. A few days' notice is preferred. The pass is open all year round, but a CITS jeep or similar will be needed in the winter as the minibuses cannot deal with serious weather. If in doubt make a reconnaissance trip to the new post before you want to leave from Kashgar, as no-one in the town will know whether the minibuses are running and most travel agents will not tell you the truth. You are not allowed to hitch or take any other form of transport.

The road on the Chinese side through closed Kyrgyz minority villages mostly follows small river valleys. Although it is currently unmade, surfacing is in preparation. It climbs gently, fairly fast and even and should take about 2½ hours, except that the minibuses are prone to break down. Only in the final few kilometres do snow-capped peaks loom out of the dusty atmosphere.

The old border post at Torugart is a remote place of smashed buildings. Here passports are collected before you descend from your vehicle, and you begin negotiations for transport to take you on to the Kyrgyz post or further. Once agreement has been reached with car, jeep or bus, the next job is to attract the border official with the passports to your vehicle so that he can hand them back and see you off into no-man's land. $100 is the first asking price for a ride to Bishkek (but make sure that you agree per *vehicle* and not per person). Better prices are available beyond the Kyrgyz post. To get as far as that, the cheapest option is $5, 50 som, or ¥40 by bus, but this is usually the last to leave. If you have arranged to be collected by a Kyrgyz travel company, they will usually collect you here and take you over the pass, often smoothing your way through Kyrgyz immigration procedures. The road over the pass, through a symbolic arch, is unmade, and it takes 20 bumpy minutes to travel the 12km or so to the

Kyrgyz side. Some people have crossed the border on foot, but the Chinese guards are not keen on this.

In summer Kyrgyz time is the same as Xīnjiāng time, two hours earlier than Běijīng time, and in the winter three hours earlier. The Kyrgyz customs hall is a typically Soviet building of marble tiles and decrepitude. Whereas the Chinese customs are usually staightforward and even friendly, the approach to the Kyrgyz is one of supplicant to high priest. A tidy line forms for the passport check, the first you'll have seen since entering China. If you have a Kyrgyz but no other CIS visa, the Kyrgyz are happier if you can show how you are planning to get out of Kyrgyzstan. Saying that you plan to fly from Almaty, for instance, is usually enough, but have your air ticket ready to show them just in case. Beyond immigration, the door straight ahead is for customs, and is opened intermittently to admit not more than two people at a time.

When it does open ask for a declaration form (*deklaratsy*) and take *two*, and complete both, because the customs officers will keep one for themselves. These are in Russian and (possibly) Kyrgyz only. One of the bored soldiers standing around asking for cigarettes will probably offer to help. If not, the first five spaces require your name, your nationality, 'China', 'Kyrgyzstan', and 'tourist'. The answers to all the following questions I to V is 'no' (no weapons, no narcotics, no poisons, no antiques or art, etc.) The boxed section is for the currency you are carrying: line one is for US dollars, two for pounds sterling, three for French francs, and four for Deutschmarks. Add other currency amounts in the lines underneath. The answer to question VI is 'no' (no currency or negotiables belonging to anyone else). Add the date bottom left and sign bottom right. Overleaf list valuables such as cameras with brand name.

When finally admitted you will probably face three officials who would like an opportunity to separate you from some money, although they are slightly more chary of you than of their own citizens or of the Chinese, to whom they like to give a hard time. You must get your copy of the declaration form stamped to take away, or you will almost certainly face difficulties leaving the CIS. They will attempt to extort 5 som for the second form, regardless of the fact that it's their job to give it to you, and that you are unlikely to be carrying any som, having just arrived from China. This is a good time not to be able to speak Russian or Kyrgyz, although the extortion only amounts to 45¢ or so; politely, and with a smile, insist on your rights. This also reduces the chance that they will bother to search your baggage, since you are obviously not to be trifled with. A few moments of smiling incomprehension with a few repeated requests in English and it will all be over.

Once outside you will probably find a motley collection of ancient vehicles, although fewer than at the Chinese Torugart post, all still demanding $100 per person to take you to Bishkek. Stand your ground—you should pay much less than this, and certainly no more than half. Some of these people may be here to collect friends or family returning from China, and *any* hard currency payment will be welcome. Other options include going only as far as Naryn, or even just to At-Bashi, which both have buses to Bishkek. It's also possible to negotiate with trucks, which is best done while they wait in line at the checkpoint immediately before the Kyrgyz post. For assistance with this, make friends with local people on the way from the Chinese side. If all else fails you can stay cheaply in caravans a few minutes' walk down the road, or at the depressing hotel at the border itself (20–25 som/$2) and try your luck the next day. Be prepared for cold at night, even in summer. You're only just over the top of a 3752m pass.

For the rest of the trip to Bishkek *see* pp.462–4. Collection by jeep allows you to reach Bishkek the same day, or better still, to take the turning to Tash-Rabat, and the jeep track to Son-Kul, with overnight camping. There's also the possibility of visiting Issyk-kul (*see* Cadogan's guide to *Central Asia*). All this can be arranged by fax, phone or preferably telex from Kashgar. For details of Bishkek agents, *see* p.452.

Note: For information on arriving in China from Kyrgyzstan, *see* 'To China via the Torugart Pass' p.460.

Via Irkeshtam

Every year it is rumoured that the route to Osh via Irkeshtam is open, said to be reachable by continuing west from the new border post rather than north to Torugart. The Chinese say it isn't open, and the Kyrgyz say it is, and maps contradict each other about road layouts. Some minibuses passing the new border on the way to Wuqa continue to Wūlǔkèqiàdī, the town nearest to the border, but check whether this is an open town before proceeding.

The route is older and easier than the Torugart one, and was that taken by 'Hatter' Bailey on his ill-fated trip to Tashkent in 1918, and often used by Western archaeologists and consuls going to Kashgar from the nearest railhead at Andizhan. Macartney returned to Kashgar with his new wife this way in 1898, and found a white fort on a hilltop with an officer, 100 Cossacks, and a customs official. They were given hospitality and entertained with stories of smugglers who induced their ponies to swallow lumps of coral before reaching the customs post, and then hurried on so as to be able to search the droppings without suspicion. But not everything was quite so jolly. The officer went outside at night to fire a pistol to scare away wolves, and on another occasion there were further frights on the Kyrgyz side:

> *Then we saw ahead of us and a little lower down, in a gloomy valley, a caravan of horses and men, the horses still standing but frozen to death, overcome probably by a blizzard. And there were the vultures at their ghastly work, picking the skeletons clean.*

Lady Macartney, *An English Lady in Chinese Turkestan*, 1931

For the time being, it is better to contend with the lesser struggles of the Torugart route.

The Southern Taklamakan Route

Yengisar (Yīngjíshā)

英吉沙 If you tell anyone in Kashgar that you are going to Yengisar they will say, 'Are you going to buy a knife?' as the town is famous for making those discreetly carried by most Uighur men. Going south, the road is bordered by cultivated land and screened by trees, with only occasional vistas of the scrubby emptiness to the east. Long, low sand dunes occasionally sit isolated in fields on the west side of the road. After 68km (1¼ hours, ¥8/$1) you arrive at **Yengisar**, a thoroughly Uighur town. As in other areas with a high proportion of minorities, many towns on this road, Yengisar included, still have propaganda loudspeakers in their main streets, which occasionally burst into life with a bizarre mixture of incomprehensible announcements, martial music, and exotica such as a whistled version of Elton John's *Your Song*. If your bus terminates in Yengisar, walk on a further kilometre to the main crossroads, identifiable by its larger buildings including an Islamicized department store, and turn right. 200m down, again on the right, the large building with the gift shop next to the gate is the **Yengisar Bīnguǎn**, which has triples with bath for ¥25 ($3) per bed, no hot water, and depressing bathrooms. Go past the hotel to the next junction, turn left to get to the main bazaar, and left again to find the **Daggers Factory**. Here you can see the entire process of manufacture by hand, from the hammering of glowing metal and the flying sparks of grinders to the delicate process of decorating the handles.

From Yengisar it is 125km and 2½ hours to **Yarkand** (Shāchē), reached by returning to the bus station and taking a bus (¥10/$1.20) or minibus (¥16/$2). These leave when full. Just outside Yengisar, a small lake appears on the west side, contrasting oddly with the barren mud and dunes to the east, and followed by the usually dry beds of meltwater rivers.

Yarkand (Shāchē)

莎车

Yarkand, December 9th.—Congratulate me on being able to date a letter to you from Yarkand, where we arrived yesterday in perfect safety. You who know how I had longed for that moment can realise the satisfaction with which I passed through the gate of the city, the first Englishman that has ever succeeded in doing so.

Robert Shaw, *Visits to High Tartary, Yarkand and Kashgar*, 1871

So wrote Dharamsala tea planter Robert Shaw in 1868, on an expedition to meet Yakub Beg in his capital Kashgar, following his formation of an independent Kashgaria. Shaw later returned after Yakub's demise to be a political agent for the government of India. Yarkand then had a population of about 60,000 and was a more important commercial town than Kashgar. Most travellers from India came through Yarkand on their way to Kashgar: the route from the Khunjerab and Mintaka passes went east from Tashkurgan rather than north, and the more direct route from Leh, now blocked due to disputes over the border, was more popular. The road directly from Tashkurgan is also closed to foreigners, and there is no public transport.

Yarkand had a sizeable population of Hindu money-lenders, whose uneasy relationship with their clients was complicated by the fact that most of these were Muslims. Since the Hindus were British citizens they were responsible to the consul in Kashgar or his agents rather than to any Chinese amban (magistrate), and when religious rioting broke out in Yarkand in 1907 it was the British consul Macartney who had to defuse the situation and punish them.

Many of the people in the area were Andijanis (from modern-day Kyrgyzstan and Uzbekistan). Macartney's Russian opposite number, Petrovsky, claimed that since their home territories had been annexed by Russia earlier in the century, they were Russians and offered Russian nationality and passports to all who would take them, in the hope that Chinese harassment of these new citizens would give him the excuse to bring Cossacks to Kashgar and beyond to 'protect' them. This was not in fact managed until the time of his successor, Sokov, around 1912.

Marco Polo, explorer Sven Hedin, and Sir Percy and Ella Sykes (who covered for Macartney while he was in England in 1915) all commented on the prevalence of goitre amongst Yarkand's Turki population, putting the cause down to bad water. The Chinese were thought to escape the disease because they boiled all their drinking water, although goitre is caused by iodine deficiency. Even now the disease has not vanished, and a few individuals can be seen with huge pouches at their throats. The problem is not unique to the area, and in 1996 the government began a campaign to supply 800,000 women and 2.5 million children with iodine supplements in Shǎnxī province, after a *partial* head count revealed 300,000 goitre sufferers and 520,000 suffering from mental health problems caused by lack of iodine.

At Yarkand the bus turns right and then left into the bus station. Returning to the main road and turning right brings you to the **Yerkan Hotel** (Shāchē Bīnguǎn) on the left just before the town's central crossroads. Doubles in the new wing are ¥200 ($24) per bed, and there are antique dorms with a prison-like atmosphere in the neighbouring building for ¥16 ($2) per bed. In the same building you will find the Yerkan Travel Service, offering overpriced but convenient tours around town, out to a silkworm breeding centre, and to an ancient watch-tower some 20km into the desert. There's also a basic *lǚshè* opposite the bus station with beds from ¥15. The main sights in town you can easily walk to yourself. Go past the hotel, and one block beyond the next junction, turn left to find several impressive Islamic buildings including the **Aminashahan Memorial Mausoleum** (in honour of a 16th-century master of Uighur music), and the **Aletun Mosque**. Behind the mosque is the substantial **Aletun Graveyard**—a wilderness of loaf-shaped tombs, mostly of mud brick, but some covered with blue and white tiles. Go early in the morning to find whole families kneeling and chanting at the graves of their ancestors, and women sweeping the dust from the tombs of deceased relatives. This side of the town is a warren of mud-brick walled courtyards with ornate doors occasionally ajar offering glimpses of old men drinking tea and young men trying to start motorbikes.

Minibuses leave every 45 minutes or so from the bus station to Karghalik, 1½ to 2 hours and ¥5 (60¢) away through 62km of almost consistent cultivation.

Shortly after leaving you cross the Yarkand River, followed by Aurel Stein in 1908 when he made a 200km desert crossing from here to Bāchǔ, just off the road from Kashgar to Aksu, in five days. The route is now paved and passes through the tiny town of Markit from where, in 1895, Sven Hedin set off on his disastrous crossing that cost the lives of several men and camels. No wonder then, when the portentously named Joint British-Chinese Taklamakan Desert Crossing party also chose to set out from here in 1993, that amidst the firecrackers, confetti, releasing of doves, speeches and gifts of the official send-off, many ordinary local people were in tears and begged them not to go.

It was also from near Markit that on his second trip in 1899, Sven Hedin began the unlikely-sounding project of exploring the desert by boat. He bought one in Yarkand, and built another smaller one for exploring shallow areas. He travelled down the river until it froze, playing Strauss on a portable gramophone and making an immense map.

Karghalik (Yèchéng)

叶城   The hotel at the **bus station** has basic triples from ¥24 ($3) per bed with shared bath. Go out of the long-distance bus station and turn right to find a local bus station with minibuses for ¥2 to **Arba**, which is the end of the run, just outside Karghalik. Here is the main point to pick up trucks for the illegal journey to **Tibet**, and there is a guesthouse with beds for a negotiable ¥20 ($2.50). Karghalik is also the first base for Chinese expeditions to K2. If you are staying in Karghalik, continue past the local bus station for two blocks and turn left onto Wénhuà Lù to find the plain and simple **Yèchéng Bīnguǎn**, with

beds from ¥16 ($2) upwards. Walk on and turn right into Jiěfàng Lù to find the central **Jama Masjid** (mosque), founded in 1408, an impressive bulk topped by a green-tiled dome, and with a finely painted interior. The old market streets around the mosque are colourful,with garish carpets for sale at the main entrance of the mosque.

There are several buses daily to **Khotan** (Hétián) from 9.30am onwards; 5½–6hrs, 265km, and ¥30–36 ($4.50) depending on the bus. Beyond Yèchéng the road becomes truly bleak. Wind-blown dunes snuggle up to the road and threaten to engulf it, and on both sides the flat, toneless scrub and sand seem limitless. This is everyone's idea of a desert, with water mirages and dust devils seeming to follow the bus. Occasional slight curves in the road are a welcome novelty. From time to time Uighurs persuade the driver to stop, perhaps at a point where a cart track leads away from the road, and they climb down from the bus to be left abandoned in emptiness, rapidly dwindling to dots in the rear window. After 80km and 1½ hours there is finally some green at the turn-off to **Píshān**, but the desert soon reclaims the road's boundaries, threatening the road itself, until **Karakax** (Mòyù), about 25km before Khotan, where there are tidy cultivated fields of corn, cotton and rice. Snowy mountains of picked cotton rear over the walls of storage yards, mud-walled dwellings grow more frequent, and eventually the bleak, tiled modernity of a Chinese town centre appears with its standard concrete buildings.

Between here and Khotan once stood the Pigeon Shrine at Zawa.

There in the midst of the sand lay a graveyard marked by poles on which hung fluttering rags and bits of sheepskin, and near by was a tiny mosque with fretted wooden door and window and some low buildings, the roofs of which were crowded with grey pigeons. Legend has it that the Imam Shakir Padshah, trying to convert the Buddhist inhabitants of the country to Islam by the drastic agency of the sword, fell here in battle against the army of Khotan and was buried in the little cemetery...two doves flew forth from the heart of the dead saint and became the ancestors of the swarms of sacred pigeons that we saw.

Miss Ella and Brigadier-General Sir Percy Sykes,
Through Deserts and Oases of Central Asia, 1920

Even Stein, passing here after one his expeditions, paused to feed the birds.

和田 Khotan is a compact fusion of a few overly-broad Chinese streets and the warren of the Uighur old town, where dense throngs gather in the streets for Khotan's lively Sunday market. To the south the Kūnlún Shān are at their most toothy, and include the 7282m Mt Muztag, but sight of even its immense bulk is hidden by the dusty air.

History

Stein was cheered by his first arrival in Khotan:

> From there [the first Khotani village] *onwards there lay an unbroken succession of gardens, hamlets and carefully cultivated fields on both sides. The road itself is flanked by shady avenues of poplars and willows for almost its whole length. Autumn had just turned the leaves yellow and red on most of the trees, and after the monotonous khaki of the desert marches this display of colour was doubly cheerful.*
>
> Sir M. A. Stein, *Sand-Buried Ruins of Khotan*, 1903

Khotan was once a major Buddhist centre, and the desert around is dotted with ruined and now near-featureless cities, former capitals of the kingdom of Khotan (or Yuteen/Yútián), and mostly inaccessible. Fǎxiǎn, here in about AD 401, described a purely Buddhist population, with monks amounting to 'several myriads', all receiving their food from a common store. Each house had a substantial *tope* (dagoba) in front, and Fǎxiǎn stayed in a monastery of 3000 monks, one of several in the vicinity. He was present for a two-week-long Buddhist festival, including a vast procession of images, at the feet of which the king abased himself.

According to the account of Xuánzàng, Khotan was the first place outside China to learn the art of silk-making, the seeds of mulberry trees and the silkworms themselves being concealed in the head-dress of a Chinese princess coming to marry a Khotani king. A later 10th-century king is depicted on the walls of cave no.97 at Dūnhuáng. Xuánzàng also mentions carpet manufacture, so it's another point against supposedly sharp-eyed merchant Polo that he mentions neither silk nor carpets, and dismisses Khotan in a single paragraph.

Rumours that earlier versions of Khotan still existed reached the West in 1855 from one of the *pundits*, Indians employed by the British government in India as secret agents to map the uncharted regions of Central Asia and Tibet using the equivalent of the secret radio pen: surveying equipment hidden in walking sticks and prayer wheels. As pawns in the Great Game, they were also to report on Russian activity in the regions they surveyed, but one Mohamed-i-Hameed also mentioned having heard rumours of ruins near Khotan during a six-month stay in Yarkand. His report was followed up in 1866–7 without official permission by an Englishman called William Johnson, who thus became the first of a series of Westerners to visit the Khotani ruins. At the time of Johnson's visit the population was a sizeable 40,000. He entered the city at the invitation of the Khan, who then kept him hostage for a short time in the hope that that would bring British troops to help him against the Russians. After the Xīnjiāng-wide revolt of 1863 the area came under the rule of Habib-ullah, who was subsequently murdered by Yakub Beg in January 1867.

Stein made several visits to Khotani sites from 1901, naming Yotkan as the site of the ancient capital of the region, occupied from the 1st century AD until the arrival of Islam in the 8th century. He discovered Roman coins from the time of the Emperor Valens (AD 364–78) and paintings of figures dating from the 2nd and 3rd centuries showed strong Gandharan influences which were passed on to those at Dàtóng's Yúngǎng caves. The British Museum has a collection of wooden plaques and terracotta figures brought back by Stein. Larger sculptures were left in place, buried again in the sand. Five years later when Stein visited the site again, all the statues had been smashed by Chinese treasure hunters.

There are 24 rivers of various sizes in the Khotan area, many of them carrying Khotan's most famous product, jade, first mentioned in Chinese histories during the Hàn dynasty in the time of the Emperor Wǔdì (140–86 BC). A jade image of the Buddha was sent from Khotan to the imperial court in AD 541. Later Islamicized Turki groups were said to have had no interest in the material but to have recognized the demand from the east, and the Yùmén (Jade Gate) near Dūnhuáng was so named for the shipments that passed through it. Jade workers and hawkers alike today appear to be still mostly Hàn.

Like all the towns on the fringes of the Taklamakan, Khotan's greenness and its abundant crops (it's particularly famous for honey peaches) have always depended upon careful water management. Many early Western commentators put what they perceived as the laziness of the sedentary Turkis down to the ease of cultivation in the oasis towns: the seasonal meltwaters of the Kūnlún Shān and Tiān Shān offered far more predictable supplies of moisture than the rainfall essential to success elsewhere. The oases on both sides of the Taklamakan still produce vast quantities of fruit, but these days demand for water tends to exceed supply. 1965 and 1993 were both drought years, and investigators on the Khotan River discovered that while the current was the same or greater near the headwaters in the Kūnlún, lower down in the desert beyond Khotan the current in 1993 was only a quarter of what it had been in the earlier year. The annual volumes of meltwater rivers are unpredictable, and there is no proper co-ordination of their use, or overall plan, so that new irrigation schemes at higher levels are starving longer-established ones of needed water. The lessons of the lost cities further out in the desert, many of which were abandoned for lack of water, have not been learned.

The Book Factory

As important as the reports of ancient ruins in setting off the competitive archaeological free-for-all of the early 20th century were the ancient documents in unknown scripts which, from around 1889, began accidentally to make their way into British and other hands. The first was a document from a tower near Kuqa dug up instead of more obvious booty by disappointed treasure hunters, and which was bought by a passing Briton, Lieutenant Bower. After others had declared it indecipherable it was decoded by the doyen of oriental linguists, Dr Rudolph Hoernle, and declared to be one of the oldest written documents yet discovered anywhere. As other material from the same source trickled out through the hands of the British and Russian consuls, it became clear that, if relatively casual treasure-hunting could turn up such riches, organized archaeological expeditions might turn up a great deal more. Taklamakan treasure hunters learned quickly that good money could be had for mouldy scribbles on tree bark and other media, and the number of documents arriving at Kashgar began to grow. Amongst them were scripts with wholly unknown characters, which were studied in detail, and became the pride of collections in London, Paris, and St Petersburg. They resulted in large tomes of academic analysis, particularly by Dr Hoernle.

By the time Aurel Stein arrived in the Taklamakan for his first trip in 1900–1, he was already suspicious of the documents with the unknown characters, all of which had been brought to Kashgar by one particular treasure-hunter, Islam Akhun. Stein failed to find these mysterious characters in any of the documents he personally unearthed. Furthermore, the sites at which Stein had made his finds differed completely from those described by Akhun in interviews with Macartney. Akhun had disappeared when Stein arrived, but in April 1901, Stein initiated a 'semi-antiquarian, semi-judicial inquiry'. He confided his concerns that Akhun was a forger to the ever-helpful Amban of Khotan, who duly produced the treasure seeker on 25 April. In his possession had been found sheets of artificially discoloured paper, covered in the unknown characters seen on documents recently sold by him in Kashgar.

Akhun now claimed to have merely been the middle man, selling books and papers brought by others, who had now absconded or died. Stein had already made it clear that he would not press charges with the Chinese Amban, for he was aware that that would lead to torture, and tried to convince Akhun to change his story but without success. The Khotani was eventually caught out by his claim not to have visited any of the sites where the papers with unknown characters had been found. Stein had with him verbatim transcriptions of the depositions that Akhun had made to Macartney at the time of sale, complete with detailed accounts of his treasure-seeking activities. It had not occurred to Akhun that his lies might have been so thoroughly recorded and preserved. Gradually, with further pressure, he revealed the whole truth.

Prior to 1894 he had collected old coins and other antiques that turned up in Khotan villages, but hearing of the value that foreigners placed on ancient manuscripts, and not wishing to submit himself to the hardships of desert travel and excavation, he had hit on the plan of forging the materials, first by handwriting and then by setting up a production line using wood-block printing. At first he had attempted to imitate other old characters and the first book produced had been sold to an assistant of Macartney's in 1895. 'Though the forgers never succeeded in producing a text showing consecutively the characters of any known script, yet their earliest fabrications were executed with an amount of care and ingenuity which might well deceive for a time even expert scholars in Europe,' remarks Stein, clearly preparing a defence for friend and patron Hoernle whose reputation was to be severely damaged by these revelations. He also hints at others' embarrassment: 'The facsimile of an "ancient Khotan manuscript" which appears in the German edition of Dr. Sven Hedin's work, "Through Asia", is a conveniently accessible illustration of the factory's produce in a somewhat later and less careful phase of its working.' In other words, it's not surprising that Hoernle was deceived by the earlier, better works when Hedin was deceived by later, shoddier ones.

Perceiving that the Europeans could not read the characters on the documents, Akhun began to invent his own, as did other assistants in the process, producing a variety of scripts. The transfer of production to wood-block printing speeded up the amount of money-making material that could be produced. Modern paper was stained with the product of a local tree, written or printed upon, then hung up over a fire to be 'aged' by smoke. The binding process was less convincing, says Stein, 'for the coarse imitation of European volumes which is unmistakable in the case of most of the later products, as well as the utter unsuitability of the fastenings employed (usually pegs of copper or twists of paper), would a priori have justified grave suspicions as to their genuineness.' Either he is indulging in a little hindsight, or scholars should have spotted the forgeries earlier. The final stage was to apply a liberal coating of sand, often so thickly that a clothes brush was needed to remove it by the excited collector.

Stein let Akhun off with a warning, taking some satisfaction in the thought that he had already received fairly brutal punishment for other crimes, admitting himself amused by Akhun's witty repartee, and describing him as a man of exceptional intelligence. For his part Akhun was impressed to find that he was internationally famous, and fascinated by the photogravure plates of his handiwork accompanying the text in Dr Hoernle's report. 'How much more proud would he have felt,' commented Stein, 'if he could but have seen, as I did a few months later, the fine morocco bindings with which a number of his block-printed Codices had been honoured in a great European library!'

It's not clear how things ever went that far. In addition to Stein's disquiet about bindings, there was already considerable scepticism about Akhun's general reliability. He had been denounced by Macartney for posing as his representative in the search for enslaved British Indian citizens, and been punished. In 1897 Deasy arranged for Akhun to provide him with guides to see a promised ancient city not yet seen by other foreigners. After only two days the 'guides' were lost, and one admitted that he had never been that far into the desert in his life. Deasy ordered a return, not having prepared for a lengthy stay and found that the only way to get back was to follow the traces of their inward journey. Upon his return, Akhun had disappeared, but at Deasy's request he was apprehended and brought to Khotan, where the Amban sentenced him to wear the cangue, 'a large, square board, weighing about 30lbs, around his neck for a month'. Akhun had also previously been found to have forged a note to an Afgan aksakal (commercial attaché) purporting to be from Captain Deasy, and had thus obtained money from him.

But what is perhaps most astonishing is that in 1897 Deasy heard a detailed rumour of the book factory from one of the Swedish missionaries also known to Macartney, who had heard it from the servant of a Persian missionary, who had been told it by the son of one of the conspirators.

Samples of Islam Akhun's handiwork are still preserved at the British Library.

Getting to and from Khotan

by air

The airport is 10 kilometres from Khotan, and an airport bus (¥2) leaves the CAAC ticket office in Bōsītǎn Nánlù (a little north of the Hétián Hotel) at 2.30pm on Mon, Wed and Fri to catch the only flight, which goes to Ürümqi for ¥1250 ($150) at 5pm. The ticket office, ℗ 282 2178, is open 10–1 and 4–7.

by bus

Going east: there is one bus a day at 9.30am to Keriya (Yútián, 177km, ¥12.50/ $1.50, 4–5hrs) and to Niya (Mínfēng, 294km, ¥20.90/$2.50, about 10hrs), and there

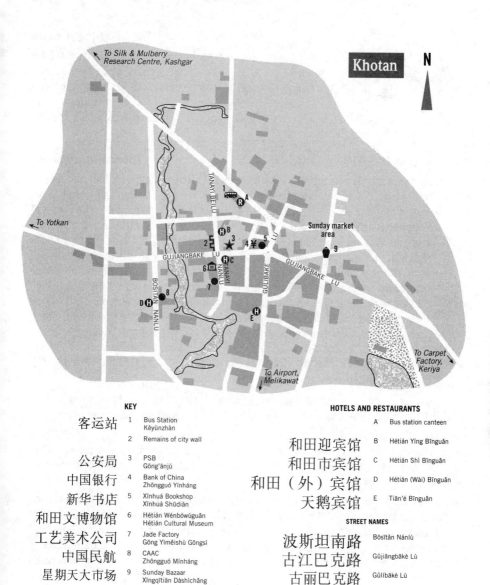

To Silk & Mulberry
Research Centre, Kashgar

Khotan

N

To Yotkan

TANAYI BEILU

Sunday market
area

GUJIANGBAKE LU

GUJIANGBAKE LU

GULIBAKE LU

TANAYI NANLU

BOSTAN NANLU

To Carpet
Factory,
Keriya

To Airport,
Melikawat

KEY

客运站   1   Bus Station
          Kèyùnzhàn

          2   Remains of city wall

公安局   3   PSB
          Gōng'ānjú

中国银行   4   Bank of China
          Zhōngguó Yínháng

新华书店   5   Xīnhuá Bookshop
          Xīnhuá Shūdiàn

和田文博物馆 6   Hétián Wénbówùguǎn
          Hétián Cultural Museum

工艺美术公司 7   Jade Factory
          Gōng Yìměishù Gōngsī

中国民航   8   CAAC
          Zhōngguó Mínháng

星期天大市场 9   Sunday Bazaar
          Xīngqītiān Dàshìchǎng

HOTELS AND RESTAURANTS

   A   Bus station canteen

和田迎宾馆   B   Hétián Yíng Bīnguǎn

和田市宾馆   C   Hétián Shì Bīnguǎn

和田（外）宾馆 D   Hétián (Wài) Bīnguǎn

天鹅宾馆   E   Tiān'é Bīnguǎn

STREET NAMES

波斯坦南路   Bōsītǎn Nánlù

古江巴克路   Gǔjiāngbākè Lù

古丽巴克路   Gǔlìbākè Lù

塔纳依南，北路 Tǎnàyī Nán/Běilù

---

are buses on Mon, Tues, Wed, Thurs, and Sat to Charchan (Qiěmò, 603km,
¥36.80/$4.50). Going west: there is one bus a day to Karghalik, and two to Kashgar
(509km, ¥39.60/$5, about 10hrs), leaving at 7am and 7.30pm. There are also four or
five buses a day to Ürümqi, 1983km away. Minibuses leave throughout the day to the
nearer destinations only when full, so you may have to wait one or two hours.

The centre of town is the roundabout where east–west Gǔjiāngbākè Lù meets north–south Gǔlíbākè Lù. Central Khotan can easily be seen on foot. Taxis infest the bus station and hotel forecourts. The price per kilometre (¥1.30) is written on a side window, and all display a number you can call in case of complaint, but this is unlikely to be necessary. Minibuses are useful for getting to the carpet and silk factories.

Khotan ✆ (0903)   *Tourist Information*

There is a travel company at the gatehouse of the Hétián Guesthouse, and you may be able to extract information while they try to sell you tours. The **Bank of China**, is just west of the town centre on Gǔjiāngbākè Lù (*open 9.30–1.30 and 4–8*). The **post and telephone office** (*open 8.30–8.30*) is opposite the bank. **Film** is available from department stores including the one just west of the Bank of China (36-shot Kodak ¥25/$3), and there is photo developing opposite. There are no **maps** of Khotan, although the Xīnhuá Shūdiàn next to the bank has a few Xīnjiāng postcards. **Visa extensions** are available from the aliens office of the PSB just west of the bank, which hardly ever seems to be open. Go round the back and knock at the door, and if you get no response complain in the main building. They will simply tell you to come back later. This is your last chance, however, before Korla, Dūnhuáng or Kashgar.

Hétián Wénbówùguǎn (Hétián Cultural Museum)   和田文博物馆

Open Mon–Fri, 9.30–1.30; adm ¥3.

The opening hours of this small museum (fully called the Hétián Historical Relics and Ancient Corpses Exhibit) are erratic, as is the entrance price, which is not stamped on the tickets.

Some of the treasures that Stein found were of too great a size to be carted away. As apologists for the wholesale transportation of treasures to foreign countries are likely to point out, when Stein returned to the site in question he found that the statues had been re-exposed and then smashed by those looking for treasure inside.

The two upstairs rooms comprising the museum contain relics from various sites around Khotan, including samples of the kind of finds that excited Aurel Stein, such as a variety of scripts written on bamboo strips and wood. There are samples of coins and figurines, and carved beams from ancient houses. Most interesting are two corpses, similar to those in Ürümqi, and one of the coffins, made without nails, and with a faded but elaborately painted exterior.

Jade Factory (Gōng Yìměishù Gōngsì)   工艺美术公司

Open hours erratic; Mon–Fri from 10am; free adm.

Just south of the museum, the Jade Factory is more of a cottage industry, with one small room of workers turning, polishing and carving small pieces of green jade. Simply walk in. There are jade shops in the same building, and upstairs above the workshop.

Zhāng Qiān is said to have been the first to bring back news of Khotan jade to China in 138 BC. Although jade is something we think of as essentially Chinese, China proper has always had to import its jade from Khotan and Yarkand. The name is commonly used to refer to two different stones very similar in appearance—nephrite and jadeite. Athough they have different chemical compositions they are difficult to tell apart even after carving and polishing. Khotan and Yarkand have long been the principal sources of supply of nephrite, while jadeite has been imported from Burma and sometimes Siberia.

Sunday Bazaar (Xīngqītiān Dàshìchǎng) 星期天大市场

Go east from the centre and almost immediately fork left.
By the time you reach the next junction you are in the Uighur heart of town, as opposed to the Chinese one. Although trade goes on every day, the streets are choked with livestock and people all day on Sunday in a local version of Kashgar's more famous bazaar. Particularly colourful elements include 'wheel of fortune' gambling tables (operators will not to be photographed), and rat-poison sellers with samples of their work on display.

Around Khotan

Silk and Mulberry Research Centre (Sīsāng Yánjiūsuǒ) 丝桑研究所

You pass the Centre on your right as you arrive from Karghalik about 6km out of town. Take a no.1 bus from just north of the centre or from outside the bus station to its terminus, and walk back a few yards. The gleaming building at the front is mainly offices, and the silk manufacture goes on in older buildings behind. The simplest way to go is by arrangement with the Hétián City Travel Agency in the Hétián Yíng Bīnguǎn, but if you go independently and walk into the front of the main building someone may offer to show you around in hope of a substantial xiǎofèi (tip). Whether you pay this is up to you, but to find the right buildings is difficult. Take the road to the left of the main building and turn right to find a small gatehouse. If you are allowed to continue, turn left at the second junction, and the first building on your right is the main hall for unreeling the thread from the steamed cocoons.

From the near-medieval street scenes of the bazaar, you now enter an early industrial age. Each room is distinctly atmospheric, often with clouds of steam, and the throb, rattle, and clank of machinery. You can see the whole process from selecting and sorting the cocoons, through steaming and loosening the silk, reeling it in and finally weaving it into fabrics. Everything is run by large amounts of female labour, with not a computer in sight, and few guards or safety devices on the machines. Most impressive are the looms weaving the patterned material, which read the pattern from long swathes of punched paper. After visiting the weaving rooms you will understand why some people in China shout all the time.

The factory can produce up to 1.2 million metres of silk fabrics per year, about 60 per cent of which goes for export, although this is in decline. There is a shop in the main building, but little of the silk ends up as tasteful final products, and prices are what they think they can get away with charging you. You'll do better in the markets of Běijīng.

Carpet Factory (Dìtǎnchǎng) 地毯厂

The Xīnjiāng Hétián Carpet Factory is just north of the road to Charchan on the eastern bank of the Jade Dragon Kashgar River (Yùlóng Kāshí Hé). Take bus no.2 almost from outside the Hétián Shì Bīnguǎn to its terminus (¥0.50), and then the no.3, which termi-nates at the factory gate (¥0.60), about 4km from Khotan (although the sign says 6km).

No-one seems to mind as you simply wander around. The first big building on your right is the main carpet-making hall, filled with the murmuring of Uighur women, who sit on benches in front of the great carpet looms making each individual knot by hand. Their gentle chatter mixes with the sound of sharp knives cutting yarn and the rush of combs. Many of the carpets are exquisite, and inevitably there's a shop beyond the main hall, but no-one bothers you there either. Great swathes of washed raw wool lie drying in the sun and smelling like a pack of wet dogs, and neighbouring buildings contain the machines for washing the wool, and combing and spinning it. Local sheep are said to have the medium-coarse wool perfect for making carpets, and 400 people make around 7000 sq m of carpet here a year.

Ancient Cities

Aurel Stein excavated a number of sites using Khotan as a base, but some are as much as 200km away. The most accessible are **Yotkan** (Yāotègān), 10km to the west, and **Melikawat** (Mǎlìkèwǎtè), 26km south. Neither has much left standing, Yotkan being threatened by agri-culture, and Melikawat a flat plain strewn with potsherds and only the vaguest remains of buildings. In contrast to the earlier part of the century when Khotanis were experts in finding ancient sites and digging for treasure, few local people be they Hàn or Uighur now seem to have any idea where these sites are. Of the two they are more likely to know Yotkan. Both require taxi rides. Melikawat is reached by driving to the airport, out to the runway, turning left and then driving along it (there are only three flights a week). Continuing straight on down an unmade road and interrogating local people from time to time, you eventually swing right across the desert, and drop down unexpectedly to a cultivated area by a small hydroelec-tric plant. The site is straight on through a small village, a total of 16km beyond the airport.

Shopping

Not much has changed since Captain Deasy passed through in the 1890s, remarking on Khotan's cottage industries: 'These comprise carpet-weaving, silk-weaving, the making of felt rugs, and the cutting and polishing of jade... Jade of the best quality is very rare and can be obtained only in small pieces, such as are suitable for rings.'

There are many places to buy jade, but as usual, the advice is caveat emptor. The stall holders aren't waving and shouting at you (and not at the locals) because they like foreigners, but because they know a mug when they see one. If you are determined to buy jade, have a reputable supplier in your own country show you pieces of various quality and tell you prices before you leave for China. In Khotan, visit first the shops with marked prices adjacent to the jade factory, then those on the south side of Gǔjiāngbākè Lù west of the Hétián Shì Bīnguǎn, and finally the street stalls east of the same hotel, before making a purchase. Don't buy silk from the silk factory but from wherever you see it properly priced. The shop at the carpet factory has marked prices on many items, but also the ominous 'Authorised Tour Unit' sign on the door. However, carpets of this quality are not easily found in Xīnjiāng, mostly ending up in the bigger centres, and probably at higher prices still. Look for prices before leaving home, and bargain hard to get the shop price well down from the first asking price.

Where to Stay

expensive

The **Hétián Wàibīnguǎn** (Hétián Hotel), ✆ 282 3564, is in Bōsītǎn Nánlù, two blocks west and one south of the centre, and signposted from the main road as you enter Khotan from the west. This hotel, which looks like the result of an encounter between a Muslim architect and a bathroom tile surplus store, is the most comfortable in Khotan. Doubles with bath are ¥260 ($31), and beds in triples also with bath are ¥100 ($12). Beds in doubles with common bath are ¥60 ($7.50). There is a Muslim restaurant. The Hétián Yíng Bīnguǎn (*see* below) has some luxury singles at ¥280 ($34), and doubles at ¥180 ($22) per bed. A brand-new hotel just east of the Hétián City Guesthouse, labelled unspecifically a 'Sino Foreign Joint Venture', will probably be open by the time you reach Khotan.

moderate/inexpensive

The **Bus Station Hotel** is rude and unfriendly, and has the usual basic, concrete-floored, bus station-quality rooms, from ¥16 ($2) per bed upwards, but there is a small and friendly Hàn canteen just outside. Reportedly a better cheap option is the **Tiān'é Bīnguǎn**, two blocks south of the main roundabout on the west side of Gǔlíbākè Lù, with beds in doubles with bath for ¥31 ($4), and common bath triples and quads for ¥16 ($2) and ¥11 ($1.50). Turn left out of the bus station and first left for one and a half blocks to find the **Hétián Yíng Bīnguǎn** (Hétián Guesthouse) in Tǎnǎi Lù, ✆ 282 2630, with decaying but atmospheric four-bed dorms from ¥25 ($3) per bed. Doubles cost ¥72 ($9) per bed with bath, ¥42 ($5) per bed in triples and ¥32 ($4) in quads with common bath. The shared bathrooms have very hot water from 10pm to midnight daily, but are amongst the most decrepit that you will see in China. The rooms are in an assortment of buildings arranged around trees and a rose garden, and there are Hàn and Muslim restaurants, although these have separate double price menus for foreigners (still only in Chinese). The more modern **Hétián Shì Bīnguǎn** (Hétián City Guesthouse) is one block west of the centre and just south of the Hétián Guesthouse, ✆ 282 3809 or 282 6101. Doubles with telephone and TV and bathroom are ¥80 ($10) per bed, triples and quads with shared bath are ¥42 ($5) and ¥28 ($3.50) per bed respectively.

Eating Out

Small Uighur restaurants with *nan* and *shashlyk* line the road just south of the Hétián Guesthouse in Tǎnǎi Lù. At night the whole street becomes a Uighur food fair, with the usual range of *pulao*, dumplings, *laghman*, etc. Cheap Hàn meals are available at several restaurants around town. As elsewhere in China, blue mirror glass is a popular decoration around the entrances—the more there is, the higher the price. The Hàn canteen to the left of the bus station is basic and friendly; the one just to the south of the Hétián Yíng Bīnguǎn slaps on imaginary charges for chopsticks, tea, and anything else they can think of. The restaurants in the major hotels are fine, although beware the pricing of those in the Hétián Yíng Bīnguǎn.

Traditional Uighur architecture, Khotan

From Khotan to Charklik

Khotan and the earlier sites of the next few towns you pass through lay within the borders of the ancient state of Yútián. Most of the modern towns have crumbling desert counterparts, mostly on the far older and now buried route to the north. Ventures to these sites in recent times, such as the British Taklamakan crossing expedition and semi-private expeditions with Japanese funding, have often found these sites little disturbed since Stein visited.

> *It was an exciting moment; evidence of Stein's excavations were clear to see but more had been uncovered by the wind since he first dug there. Around lay all the paraphernalia of daily life in this garrison city, abandoned over 1,000 years ago... In the remains of the old fort we found a board from a game of chinese chess; Stein had found the pieces for a similar game in 1903.*
>
> Barney White-Spunner, *An Uncrossed Desert,* Wexas Travel, 1994

Travelling east from Khotan you enter an area as yet little visited by foreigners, because until recently to travel here was illegal and could lead to arrest. Few bus stations or hotels have higher prices for foreigners, local people of all types often seem quite pleased to see visitors, and even most private businesses and market stalls forget to overcharge. Many Uighurs speak no Chinese at all, and most hotels are even less likely to have English speakers than those elsewhere in China. There is less officialdom: do your money changing and visa extensions in Kashgar, Khotan, Korla or Dūnhuáng. The post offices are unused to dealing with overseas mail. The towns are small and have little in the way of formal sights, and the hotels often have only cold running water with no bathrooms at all (hot water is provided in kettles, dishes or buckets). Primitive toilets are on the opposite side of the courtyard—a mercy for the nose, at least. The biggest, brightest buildings are usually those of the police station, the People's Insurance Company of China, and the Construction Bank. However, there is more chance of seeing normal Uighur life, and the quiet provincial atmosphere of these places makes them enjoyable stops. The desolation between towns is itself spectacular.

From Khotan cultivated fields and trees keep the desert at bay for a while, but for most of the first 100km the landcape returns to its usual khaki flatness with occasional soft dunes and the dry beds of meltwater rivers, fed in season by the dust-obscured Kūnlún range to the south. About 77km before Keriya the greenness returns, with belts of tall grasses more reminiscent of steppe than desert. The road is not so good east of Hétián, and the buses dither more. Allow about 4½ hours for the 177km to Keriya (¥10.20/$1.25). You may find yourself sharing the interior of the bus with a sheep or goat, or both.

Just before the bus station at **Keriya** (Yútián), there is an enormous statue of Máo shaking hands with a hatted, coated, and booted Uighur ancient. In contrast to anthropological norms, and what is known of Máo's stature, the Chairman has carefully been rendered larger in height than the Uighur, and beams down on him with a slightly threatening smile.

Keriya (Yútián)

于田 Much of Marco Polo's treatment of the southern route is dull, and little more than a merchant's shopping list, but at Keriya, which he calls Pein, there is a passage which never fails to give a frisson to commentators. 'But they have a custom I must relate. If the husband of any woman go away upon a journey and remain away for more than 20 days, as soon as that term is past the woman may marry another man, and the husband also may then marry whom he pleases.'

Some commentators suggest that slightly racier passages such as this owe more to ghostwriter Rustichello's knowing what holds the reader's attention than the degree of importance Polo placed on such information. Throughout Central Asia, stopping places for caravans, the desert equivalent of seaports, probably had the same arrangement.

The older Keriya out in the desert was Xuánzàng's first stop after he left Khotan on his way back to China, and one of the meeting points for the 1993 Taklamakan expedition's crossing and back-up parties. Peter Fleming, arriving at the newer town by donkey from the east, found the first faint whiffs of civilization: an Indian acting as British trade agent who possessed an umbrella, a gramophone, oil lamps from Tashkent, and a cuckoo clock, which was used to summon his exhausted visitors to breakfast.

The Chinese side of town is on the south side of the road, with a few Hàn and Uighur restaurants and broad streets, almost empty of people. In contrast on the north side there are pleasant lanes of tree-shaded courtyard houses. The only place to stay is at the rear of the bus station; ¥10 ($1.20) per bed in a quad. There are no bathrooms but a kettle of cold water and bowls are provided. The lady with the keys lives in the cottages on your right as you leave the rear of the bus station. There are frequent buses and minibuses to Khotan, but buses to Niya (¥7, 2½hrs, 117km) and Charchan (¥32/$4, up to 14hrs) are less frequent. Catch the buses at 8am or 9am or risk waiting 3–4 hours for a minibus to depart.

Taking the Treasures

Stein praised Hedin as the pioneer of Taklamakan exploration, but subsequent archaeologists praised Stein, since he was an archaeologist who understood the importance of his discoveries and Hedin was simply a geographer and explorer. It is Stein, too, who receives most criticism from the Chinese.

Despite claims by them that they were robbed, Stein was given extensive help by Chinese Ambans whom he often praises in his writings. They only became interested in his hauls from the desert when rumours developed that he had found considerable amounts of gold. Showing that he had mainly found ancient texts and other artefacts cleared his way to return with what he had. As usual, greed was potentially the only obstacle.

In a final meeting with the Amban in Keriya, Stein praised his guide, Ibrahim, who had been the first to find vitally important documents on wood, and who led Stein to the source. 'So the Amban publicly lauded him and promised to reward him with a comfortable berth and good emoluments.' Posts were also given to others recommended by Stein, which he attributes to pious support for his attempts to trace the monk Xuánzàng's path. Stein's activities were hardly cloak and dagger.

The desert returns after you leave Keriya, and dunes periodically threaten the road.

Niya (Mínfēng)

民丰 Niya (Mínfēng) is even smaller than Keriya, its centre, a short walk beyond the bus station, marked by a pillar with a quotation from Máo. Its older counterpart is over 150km out into the desert. The 1993 expedition found some new buildings missed by Stein to the west. Early in 1901 he had found substantial numbers of wooden tablets in the cursive Kharoshthi writing in a remarkably well-preserved state. The tablets turned out to be official orders written in an early Indian language using the script—a language that was a long way from its original home. In addition to excavating buildings, Stein also removed more than 200 documents on wood from a rubbish tip. Digging into these became one of his favoured methods of investigation: 'For three long working days I had to inhale the odours of this antique dirt and litter, still pungent after so many centuries.' He returned for a second visit in 1906 and was excited to find clear connections with the art of Greece and Rome in images on clay seals. Further digging brought to light hundreds more documents, many in a perfect state of preservation. Most of these are now buried again beneath the British Museum, but at least preserved, and open to scholars. A Sino-Japanese team found a new site 40km to the north of Niya in 1997, with 2500-year-old relics including bronze crucibles and knives, stone sickles, pottery and bone beads.

The small **Hotel of the Mínfēng County Committee of the Communist Party** (turn right at the Máo quote pillar) has doubles for ¥60 ($7.50). The new Uighur-run **Lǚshè** at the bus station has beds in quads for as little as ¥6 (no washing facilities), and doubles with bath for ¥25 ($3). The **Niya Hotel** is reached by turning right out of the bus station and taking the first right, with comfortable doubles for a negotiable ¥70 ($8.50). Buses to Keriya are daily, but no buses to Charchan start at Niya. The bus from Keriya passes through at about 12 noon, but while some days it is half-empty, on others it is extremely full, and you may not be able to board. There's also a bus from Khotan which stays overnight at Niya and starts at about

7.30am, but not every day. On a good day Charchan is 307km, 7½ hours, and ¥20 away. On a bad one it's ¥33 ($4) and 12 hours, depending on who's selling the ticket and the state of the bus.

Beyond Niya the road deteriorates, not aided by the fact that the whole route from here to Korla is gradually being rebuilt. Long diversions across areas of grassland with twisted, desiccated and pollarded trees make the trip feel like a safari. Trucks that took wrong turnings lie sunk up to their axles in mud. Concrete houses with two sides missing are actually bridges awaiting the building of embankments to carry the road. The desert appears in all its possible moods: wind-sculpted soft dunes, hard ones fixed by bushes and resembling old ruins, plains of flat scrub with the occasional trees only serving to emphasize the emptiness, and areas of salt-smeared ribbed sand that look as if the tide has just gone out. The only habitations are tiny one-donkey towns, and the occasional depot for road maintenance crews. After about 4 hours and 126km there is a stop for food, Muslim-style only, at a tiny hamlet with one pool table.

Charchan (Qiěmò)

且末 Charchan (sometimes Cherchen) is slightly, but only slightly, bigger than Niya, with one central crossroads, and no particular sights, but seems to be one of the friendliest places in Xīnjiāng. In the daytime Uighur men sit in the street with small, brilliant-eyed buzzards on their arms, used for catching rabbits.

Polo mentions Charchan as being a jade-producing town, and reports, 'When an army passes through the land, the people escape with their wives, children, and cattle a distance of two or three days' journey into the sandy waste; and knowing the spots where water is to be had, they are able to live there, and to keep their cattle alive, whilst it is impossible to discover them; for the wind immediately blows the sand over their track.' Several meltwater rivers feed the Charchan oasis before disappearing into the desert, but their terminal areas create an unexpected area of forest seen by the 1993 expedition.

Charchan is tiny. On the northeast corner of the central crossroads is a restaurant and bar used for Uighur wedding receptions at weekends, called the **Mirage Inn**. On the northwest corner upstairs is a night club, and nearby there's a basic, bathroomless guesthouse with beds for ¥6 . About 200m to the west is the exceptionally friendly and new **Wàibīnguǎn**, which has triples with bath at ¥25 ($3) per bed, and triples without for ¥15 ($2). Hot water comes in buckets, but the primitive toilets are across the yard. The hotel also has a reasonable restaurant. Go east from the junction and left (north) at the first crossroads to find the airport. Just before it is the **Muztagh Hotel**, ✆ (0996) 762 2687, the most comfortable hotel in town, with not entirely reliable evening hot water. There are luxury singles for ¥180 ($22) and ¥360 ($44), doubles at ¥80 ($10) per bed, and triples at ¥60 ($7.50) per bed, all with bathrooms and fans. Some members of staff try to revise the price upwards after the first night. There is a restaurant but it's not always staffed. The main purpose of this hotel is to provide accommodation to foreign and Chinese bigwigs from the oil wells about 200km into the desert the night before they fly out to Ürümqi. Giant supply trucks with 1.75m-diameter wheels park behind the Wàibīnguǎn, surprisingly quietly. The flights from Charchan are on an 18-seat Twin Otter, which flies to Korla and on to Ürümqi on Mon, Wed, Fri, and Sun mornings. Go to the airport early in the morning of the day before you want to fly to buy your ticket. Tickets are ¥400 ($48) to Korla, ¥750 ($90) to Ürümqi. The ticket office is at the airport, ✆ 762 2547.

One and a half blocks north of the junction on the left is the bus station, but the rooms here are not open to foreigners. Buses go to Niya and beyond to Khotan, but not every day. Buy your ticket the day before in the early afternoon. There are daily buses going west, and east to Charklik (Ruòqiāng), all at 7.30am. Occasionally travellers are told that there are no buses to Charklik but only to Korla. If you want to go to Charklik ignore this and insist—there is only one road and it goes through there. The post office is just south of the junction (*open 10–2 and 3.30–7.30*), and before it are two or three reasonable restaurants.

Charklik (Ruòqiāng) is about 10 hours, 304km, and ¥28.70 ($3.50) away, and Korla ¥63 ($8) and a further 16 hours or so, beginning the following morning. Attempts have been made to prevent the dunes from smothering the road by sowing anchoring grasses in a crosshatch pattern which makes them seem quilted. But neither these nor fences of brushwood bundles have prevented the wind from occasionally covering the road in sand, leaving buses wallowing and floundering. You may get your first clear view of the peaks to the south, never far away from the southern route but usually lost in the dust haze. These are the Altun (Āěrjīn) range, which run northeast from the Kūnlún to form the border between Xīnjiāng and Qīnghǎi. The beds of seasonal rivers become more frequent and seem to delight in ignoring the bridges built for them to pass under, simply demolishing the road instead. Vehicles are sent on long detours across the flat desert. In periods of bad weather, or when the sand dunes have been on the move, this can lengthen the trip to as much as 17 or even 24 hours, with the bus having frequently to be dug and pushed out of sand traps. There is almost nothing at all on the road until the small oasis of Wasa, about 263km from Charchan, although there is a break for lunch at the solitary restaurant (noodles, noodles, or noodles) at a road repair depot.

Charklik (Ruòqiāng)

若羌 Ruòqiāng is also the name of the county, which at 200,000 sq km is China's largest, and big enough to swallow several European countries or US states, although rather emptier of life than either. The ancient county seat of crumbling mud has clear inner and outer walls, and is about 6km southeast of the modern town. Potsherds, fragments of fabric, and even the odd bone are still to be found.

The bus stops not at the bus station but at the deeply unfriendly **Ruòqiāng Bīnguǎn**. Buses to Charchan (Qiěmò) also leave from here, the town's only comfortable hotel, although the staff may try to persuade you that the only way out is to take their jeep for ¥1000 ($120). There are beds at ¥8, ¥10, and ¥12, but they will refuse to sell you anything cheaper than a ¥50 ($6) bed in a dismal triple. There are also beds for ¥100 ($12) and ¥150 ($18). The stickers on the door suggest that the Joint British-Chinese Taklamakan Desert Crossing stayed here in 1993. Following the crossing's completion they were feted, and the Union Jack paraded through the streets. Lacking such a warm reception, the budget traveller can walk out of the hotel and turn right; turn left at the junction and go straight over the next one. The bus station is on the left and just past it on the right is a basic *zhāodàisuǒ* (hostel), with beds in doubles or dorms for ¥15 ($2). The Uighur manager knows how much you have to pay at the hotel, and will not bargain. He claims he has to pay the PSB ¥5 per person per night. Whether this is a bribe or legal payment, or even true, is a matter for debate. Just back past the bus station there is a friendly shop with a pool table outside, and almost opposite an equally friendly restaurant with good food. Another basic hostel near the mosque has been reported, and if the PSB tries to make you stay at the Bīnguǎn but you plead poverty, this is where you may be put.

Charklik is also the headquarters of the Altun Mountain Nature Reserve, established in 1983, consisting of 45,000 sq km of basin between the Altun and Kūnlún mountains at an average elevation of 4000m. Wild yak, wild ass, gazelle, Tibetan antelope, argali, bharal, snow leopard, lynx, brown bear, vulture, snow cock and bar-headed goose can be found: a living pharmacopoeia and gourmet menu. There has been talk of reintroducing *Equus przewalskii* here, a species of wild horse now extinct except in zoos, and named after the Russian explorer who made five expeditions in Mongolia, Gānsù, Tibet and Xīnjiāng between 1871 and 1885, earning himself international acclaim and near-heroic status in Russia. But some foreign conservation organizations have claimed that this reserve has no integrity and that both illegal gold-prospecting and hunting are still taking place, and they have withdrawn their support.

To Korla and Dūnhuáng

From Charklik there are daily buses north to **Korla** (Kùěrlè). An alternative route, only for the hardy, lies east through Qīnghǎi Province and up to Dūnhuáng in Gānsù. The oasis town and ancient city of Miran can be visited on the way to Dūnhuáng, or as a day trip from Charklik.

To Korla

Korla (*see* p.260) is 483km, ¥35.50 ($4.50) and 15 hours away, the road much the same as that between Charchan and Charklik, and subject to interruption by substantial amounts of sand. The area is politically sensitive, particularly because of the nuclear test site at Lop to the east. China carried out more than 40 nuclear tests from 1964 to 1996, and has developed the world's fourth-largest nuclear weapons stockpile, including missiles, bombs and artillery shells, estimated to be the equivalent of 16,000 Hiroshima bombs. Anti-nuclear campaigners Greenpeace estimated that around 50 kilos of plutonium-239 were released during testing, with about half as much again still present at the testing site.

Human rights campaigners claim that the local populace suffered widespread casualties and birth defects from fallout, and wondered why China's continued testing didn't attract the same level of international condemnation that France's 1995/6 series did. The answer lies in trade, presumably. China unexpectedly exploded its final bomb in July 1996, three months earlier than publicized, and joined the self-imposed moratorium on tests the next day.

The Lop desert had been a no-go area for centuries before the Chinese acquired nuclear technology. Although relatively small, this salt desert, crossed by the main southern route, appears to have been regarded as the most frightening of all. The Buddhist traveller Fǎxiǎn commented, 'In the Desert there are a great many evil demons; there are also sirocco winds, which kill all who encounter them. There are no birds or beasts to be seen; but as far as the eye can reach, the route is marked out by the bleached bones of men who have perished in the attempt to cross.' Polo offered more elaborate ghost stories:

> But there is a marvellous thing related of this desert, which is that when travellers are on the move by night, and one of them chances to lag behind or to fall asleep or the like, when he tries to gain his company again he will hear spirits talking, and will suppose them to be his comrades.
>
> Marco Polo, *The Travels*, 13th century (Yule-Cordier edition)

Better stay on the bus.

Another local mystery was the salt lake of Lop, **Lop Nor**. The Russian explorer, Nicolai Przhevalsky, arriving here well ahead of the rest of the European pack in 1877, discovered that the lake was 100 miles away from where Chinese geographers had placed it since ancient times. This sparked considerable debate. Queen Victoria's Geographer Royal declared that this discovery had 'the same geographical importance as the reaching of the North Pole or the crossing of Africa'. Others, including the German geographer von Richthofen (coiner of the expression 'Silk Route'), disagreed. Lop Nor was a salt lake, and Hedin had found a completely different freshwater one. On later visits Przhevalsky, now internationally famous for his exploits, confirmed his own conclusions, but still not to von Richthofen's satisfaction. The issue was decided by Sven Hedin who visited the lake in 1895 and 1900. It was exactly where Przhevalsky had claimed, but there was also a dry bed further north in the traditional location. Hedin noted the shallowness of the Tarim river at this point and the tendency of debris and silt to build up. He concluded that the river had changed course, and was about to do so again. Returning to the area in 1928 he found both river and lake in their original places.

In 1907 Stein set off from Miran to travel around the south side of the Lop Nor area on a lesser trade route to Dūnhuáng than the one that went further north via the ancient city of Lóulán. This route was forgotten when Chinese power in the region waned, and had to be rediscovered with each reconquest. The saltiness of the land and wells made it only practical to travel this way in the winter, when large quantities of fresh water could be more easily carried in the form of ice, the technique favoured by Stein himself in all his desert explorations. Marco Polo claimed that this 380 mile-long route took 28 stages, but the indefatigable Stein did it in 17, and without seeing a single human being. En route he made his most astonishing discovery to date, an ancient and long-forgotten extension of China's defensive walls made from bundles of reeds and stamped clay. This first section was over 50 miles long, and later investigation showed it to be around 400 miles altogether. From refuse heaps near its watch towers, Stein turned up Chinese records on wood from the Former (Early) Hàn dynasty—the oldest written Chinese documents so far discovered, dating from 1st century AD.

Stein also visited Lóulán, ancient capital of a substantial state during the early Hàn. Until modern times, the year in China was given as the name of current emperor's reign and the number of years of his occupation of the throne (like calling 1999 'Clinton 7'). Digging in rubbish heaps as usual, Stein found a document dated by reign but with a date 14 years after the Chinese emperor in question had died, indicating that Lóulán was at times completely cut off from the Chinese mainstream. Despite this, Chinese records show that a substantial amount of trade came this way from Dūnhuáng, a distance of about 120 miles of waterless and treeless ground. Stein found remains of wool tapestries with Hellenistic designs confirming that the trade was far from just one-way—the Silk Routes were also Wool Routes. Stein found the exact way to Dūnhuáng by a bizarre piece of good fortune.

> *The last traces of dead vegetation marking the termination of the ancient delta had long been left behind when we suddenly found the old route line plainly marked by two-hundred-odd Chinese copper coins strewing the dismal ground of salt-encrusted clay for a distance of about thirty yards. They lay in a well-defined line running from northeast to southwest. The coins, square-holed, were all of the Han type and*

*seemed as if fresh from a mint. Clearly they had got loose from the
string which tied them, and gradually dropped out through an opening
of the bag or case in which they were being carried by some convoy.*

Sir Aurel Stein, *On Ancient Central Asian Tracks*, 1941

To Dūnhuáng via Miran and Shímiánkuàng

Miran (Mǐlán) is 74km and two hours to the east and can be visited as a day trip from
Charklik if you decide to go north to Korla. There is a daily minibus at about 9.30am from the
main bus station, and tickets (¥12/$1.50) are sold just before the bus departs. It leaves Miran
at around 4pm to return to Charklik. From Charklik there are buses going further east through
Miran to Shímiánkuàng (¥40/$5, 273km), but not every day. Alternatively, try the post office
van, which goes at around 9am every two or three days, passing through Miran on the way,
also ¥40. Buy your ticket at the post office the day before. It seats 10 at best, depending on the
amount of mail and whatever else the driver decides to take. The buses for Charchan leave
from the Ruòqiāng Bīnguǎn, where you also buy your ticket.

Miran (Mǐlán)

米兰   Miran is a tiny oasis town reached on a road which is in parts less a road than a
line which vehicles have collectively decided to take. Its centre is an inverted T-
junction whose perpendicular arm quickly peters out into an area of attractive tree-lined lanes
between orchards. Flocks of pigeons with whistles attached to them circle overhead creating
an eerie moaning, and the grunting and squealing of pigs tells you that although you are still in
Xīnjiāng you are truly back in Hàn China.

At the base of the T is a compound containing on the left as you enter the **Sānshíliù
Tuánchǎng Zhāodàisuǒ** (36 Tuánchǎng is also the name for Miran on some Chinese maps),
the only place to stay in town (¥15/$2 per bed in a basic quad, ¥10 for a set meal in the
restaurant), and on the right the local PSB. This is where you apply for a permit to visit the old
Miran ruins (Mǐlán Gǔchéng), although if the relevant officer is away you will be told to return
to Charklik (Ruòqiāng) and apply there. Try Charklik first if you are coming that way, and you
will probably be told to apply in Miran. In the absence of a permit-issuing officer another
policeman may offer to take you there in a jeep, but his first asking price for this service will be
¥300 ($36) per person. The site is only 9km away. Transport can also be negotiated in
Charklik, but neither there nor in Miran is there much choice. The daily minibus from
Charklik may agree to take you there for ¥100 ($12) after dropping off passengers in Miran.
However, if you stay in Miran there is nothing to stop you walking or cycling, although you
will have to negotiate the loan of a bicycle from some friendly person. There is one other
minibus in Miran which may be available for hire. Turn left (west) out of the *zhāodàisuǒ*
compound and continue walking for about 3–5 minutes until you see a pale blue door to an
ordinary house on your left. Knock. This bus also goes east to Shímiánkuàng when there are
enough passengers to justify it, which may be less than once a week (¥30/$4).

Also at the T-junction is a vast department store with a disco on top, dominating this tiny
town. At night the sound of tuneless karaoke, ballroom dancing competitions, or disco easily
penetrate the walls of your room. To see what is going on, go round to the back of the building
to the left-hand side and climb up to the third floor, or to a further room at roof level.

Xuánzàng visited both Miran and Charklik in AD 645. The ruins were rediscovered by Sven Hedin in 1900, and visited by Stein in 1907 and 1914, when he dug into refuse pits again, finding Tibetan documents showing that there had been a Tibetan garrison there in the 8th to 9th centuries. The route through Miran was then the main link between the oases of the southern Tarim and Dūnhuáng, and Chinese histories prefer to let you think that there was constant Chinese control from the Hàn dynasty onwards, ignoring Stein's conclusions:

> The absence of even the slightest scrap of Chinese writing among all these records is a significant indication of the total disappearance of Chinese influence and control in the Tarim basin from the last third of the eighth century onward. But, on the other hand, a crumpled-up little package of papers in 'Runic' Turkish script supplies distinct proof that this distant corner, too, of the Tarim basin had seen something of those valiant Western Turk tribes who, whether as allies or as rivals of the Tibetans, had a main share in bringing down Chinese domination in Central Asia.

Sir Aurel Stein, *On Ancient Central Asian Tracks*, 1941

The ruins of Miran proved to be almost a reference work on the movement of peoples and exchange of ideas along the Silk Routes. In addition to Tibetan and Turki writing, Stein discovered what are thought to be the earliest surviving wall paintings in the area, 3rd century or earlier, with clear Western classical influences. He was astonished to find pictures of winged angels (Buddhist *apsaras*): 'Much in the vivacious look of the large fully opened eyes, in the expression of the small dimpled lips, etc., brought back to my mind the fine portrait heads of Greek girls and youths to be seen on painted panels from mummies of the Ptolemaic and Roman periods found in Egypt.'

Paintings from Miran are divided between Delhi and London.

Today the site still has more above ground than most of the ancient cities on the southern route, including small sections of the 8th-century Tibetan garrison and city walls, and 3rd-century shrines and *viharas* (residences for monks), excavated by Stein. In recent years Chinese archaeologists have removed those which Stein left behind as too damaged.

Other options for leaving Miran include a bus which goes to **Shímiánkuàng** taking factory workers. Its departures are unscheduled, and may be only once a week. If you see a large bus doing nothing near the department store, talk to the driver, but if there are too many workers to transport, everyone else is thrown off. The only English speaker in town is a teacher at the Middle School just to the west of the centre. If you bother the PSB enough they will summon her to translate. Otherwise you can get on the post office bus from Ruòqiāng when it passes through Miran sometime between 10am and 11am on Monday, Wednesday, and Friday (¥30/$4, pay the driver) if there are spare seats. The bus is a long-wheelbase Běijīng jeep which travels in convoy with a truck (which will probably carry your luggage) and takes 5½ hours. If all these fail, returning to Ruòqiāng by the afternoon minibuses and starting again for Shímiánkuàng the next day may be the only option, and probably less trouble. From here on there is considerable confusion about names: maps contradict each other and show roads that do not exist. Shímiánkuàng is sometimes known as Mangnai or Mángyá, and maps have an assortment of other Mangnai variants dotted around the area.

The road to Shímiánkuàng is narrow and winding, crossing the Altun mountains by a 3800m pass. Looking back you can see where you were half an hour before, one kilometre distant but 10 kilometres by road. At one point the road disappears and vehicles descend into a dry river bed. From the pass and for a while afterwards there are views of the apparently endless snow-covered peaks of Tibet to the south. If you travel by post office jeep, extra excitement may be provided by the determined lunacy of the driving. Russian explorer Nikolai Przhevalsky was the first European to visit these mountains in 1872, unexpectedly finding them to be 200 miles further north than Western geographers had previously thought.

Shímiánkuàng

石棉矿 **Shímiánkuàng** is one of China's more out-of-the-way and less charming towns, its name translating as Asbestos Deposit. Its sole purpose is the production of asbestos, and the ground regularly shakes from explosions less than a kilometre away which throw tons of rock high into the air, clouds of dust drifting over the town. Those who live and work there are surprised to see you, particularly workers who, despite their masks, have eyebrows and hair matted with asbestos dust. Asbestos was an ancient Silk Route product, but the real southern Silk Routes ran to the north of the Altun mountains, via Lóulán.

Marco Polo proudly announced that he had discovered the substance from which salamanders are made, and that the salamander was not a beast, but a substance found in the earth (or in the case of Shímiánkuàng in the air and on people's faces).

> *Any other account of the matter is fabulous nonsense. And I may add that they have at Rome a napkin of this stuff, which the Grand Kaan sent to the Pope to make a wrapper for the Holy Sudarium* [face cloth] *of Jesus Christ.*

> Marco Polo, *The Travels*, 13th century (Yule-Cordier edition)

Fabulous nonsense in itself because the Vatican has no knowledge of such a thing.

The only place to stay is the *zhāodàisuǒ* (hostel) where you will be dropped off. A bed in a four-bed room with television is ¥20 ($2.50) per bed; without, ¥10. There are no bathrooms. The staff are quite friendly, but in league with the truck drivers who provide one of the ways out. They will find out for you what transport is leaving from the factory, but they think that you should pay the drivers' first asking price of ¥200 ($24) per person for the ride to Dūnhuáng with an overnight stay in Lěnghú. You may get the price reduced to ¥100 ($12), but then the driver may decide that that means you ride on top of the bags of asbestos.

All will tell you that there is no other transport, but this is not true. A red bus leaves for Huātǔgōu, the next town of any size, at around 12.30 to 1pm daily from the far end of Shímiánkuàng, about 1km away. Keep walking through the town and telling everyone you pass that you want to go to Huātǔgōu, so that you are pointed in the right direction. Buy your ticket on the bus, ¥14 ($1.75). The 71km ride takes about two hours. The best way to get to Charklik or Miran is by the post office jeep, on Tuesday, Thursday, and Saturday. The post office is nearly opposite the *zhāodàisuǒ*.

On the way to **Huātǔgōu** you cross into Qīnghǎi Province. Huātǔgōu is also aptly named Yóushāshān—Oil Sand Mountain. Larger than Shímiánkuàng, it contains mainly oil processing and storage facilities, and is nearly as grim. The only place to stay is at the bus station, where beds are either ¥8 or ¥12 ($1.50) in primitive rooms with a small coal stove. Ask to see the guest book to make sure that you are paying the right price, or you will be overcharged by the old woman who runs the place, and who also encourages the bus ticket sellers to charge more for the bus, whispering clumsily behind her hand. The only reason to go to Huātǔgōu is to get a bus to somewhere else, but there are interesting possibilities. There are buses to Dūnhuáng roughly every other day (536km, all day, ¥40/$5), to Golmud (Gěěrmù) several times a month (more than 700km, all day, ¥60/$7), and to Xīníng daily (two days). If the bus you want is not available, take the Xīníng bus and change at Lěnghú (also known as Chálěngkǒu, 328km, ¥30/$4, and there's another Lěnghú further north) for Dūnhuáng (a further 206km, ¥25/$3), or at Dàcháidàn (433km) for Golmud.

The bus trundles uneventfully for the morning across the Tsaidan Basin to Lěnghú (Cold Lake), another unprepossessing town, from where occasional buses and more frequent private minibuses run to Dūnhuáng, taking the rest of the day (¥25/$3). The road to Dūnhuáng heads east for 109km before turning north to cross the Nán Shān into Gānsù Province via the Dàngjīn Pass. A 5798m Āěrjīn peak is just to the west. Before Dūnhuáng, the road winds through spectacularly high wind-sculpted dunes, and passes the 'Old City' film set as it enters the suburbs.

The Yellow River Route

Běijīng to Lánzhōu

The Great Wall at **Bādálǐng**

315

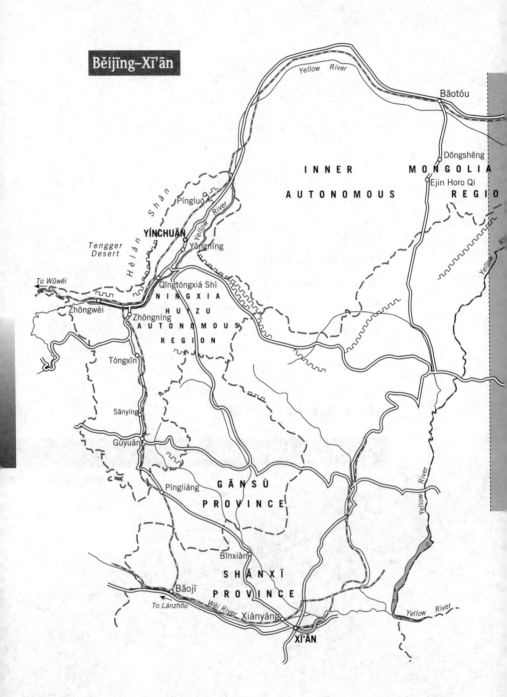

Běijīng–Xī'ān

Yellow River

Bāotóu

Dōngshēng

INNER MONGOLIA

AUTONOMOUS Ejin Horo Qi REGIO

Hèlán Shān

Pízluó

Píngluó

YÍNCHUĀN

Tengger Desert

Yŏngníng

Yellow River

To Wŭwēi

Qīngtóngxiá Shì

NINGXIA

Zhōngwèi

HUÍZU

Zhōngníng

AUTONOMOUS

REGION

Tóngxīn

Sānyíng

Yellow River

Gùyuán

Píngliáng

GĀNSÙ

PROVINCE

Bīnxiàn

SHĀNXĪ

Bǎojī

PROVINCE

To Lánzhōu

Wèi River

Xiányáng

Yellow River

XĪ'ĀN

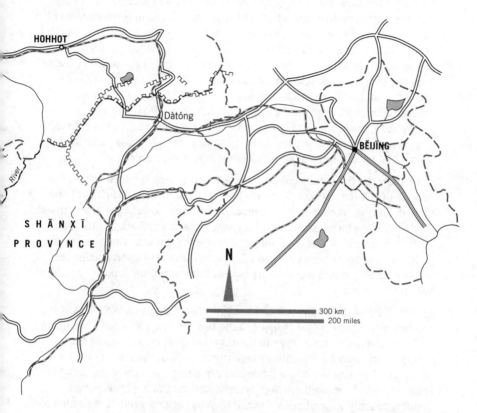

At night the sound of bells was heard, faint and hard to distinguish in the distance. Slowly it grew clearer, and its rhythm betrayed the measured step of camels. It came nearer and nearer, and when the first bell passed our tent its sound was loud and piercing. The others followed in due order, and finally we heard the last bell of the last camel in the caravan. I listened, moved by these old familiar bells, the special melody of the caravan routes for a thousand years past, around which which the whole desert life of traveller, driver, merchant unfolds its varied and fascinating pictures.

Sven Hedin, *The Silk Road*, 1938

Landing at Běijīng's Capital Airport and driving down the highway into the smoggy, stationary city, it may occur to modern Marco Polos that the only similarity between their situation and that of those who once arrived by camel caravan, is that their vehicles are nose-to-tail. Where is *real* China?

Of course, the Běijīng of traffic jams and 24-hour, seven-day construction is a reflection of modern China's slow transformation to a 'socialist market economy', and as 'real' as it gets. Whereas political motives once led to the levelling of historic buildings as symbols of old ways of thought, now the old-fashioned profit motive works both to the same end, and to restore some of the few ancient sites that remain in order to attract tourist hard currency. Not unreasonably, Běijīng residents would rather have a new apartment with a private toilet than the picturesque remnant of a courtyard house with overly aromatic public facilities, so ancient domestic architecture is continuously disappearing, too. But tucked away behind shoddily built towers, in the shadow of on-ramps and overpasses, round the corner from a branch of McDonald's, down a lane too narrow for cars, a glimpse of a steep tiled roof or of a carved lintel over a sagging doorway shows the sufficiently inquisitive visitor that not all traces of ancient Běijīng have passed away.

Then there are the great icons of Chinese tourism—the Imperial Palace, the Temple of Heaven, and the Great Wall, all far from hidden, and all not to be missed. Stuffed, mounted, and on display, like trophies that have been through the hands of an inept taxidermist, they have a rigidity and artificiality about them that scarcely seems 'real' either. But peering through windows, investigating the remoter corners of even busy tourist sites, and always taking the smaller turning, can produce surprises. In Běijīng atmosphere must be stalked and hunted down.

Leaving Běijīng for Dàtóng you cross a section of Míng Great Wall, and follow the Dowager Empress Cíxǐ as in 1900 she fled the vengeful armies coming to the relief of foreigners besieged in the Legation Quarter. She would scarcely recognize the now heavily industrial northern plain or the rebuilt city, but evidence of ancient Silk Route influences remain in the form of the Buddhist cave temples of the Northern Wèi dynasty. Beyond Dàtóng life becomes gentler, and visitors fewer. Even in the friendly regional capitals of Hohhot and Yínchuān, the streets are less crowded and life less hectic. The days are long, hot and dry, although the wind can bring scouring Gobi sand, and the rare rainfall leaves yellow patches on all it touches. The modern road and railways follow the soupy Yellow River, thick with the loess soil made from centuries of wind-deposited Gobi sand. Outside the summer peak there is an oversupply of accommodation, and all but a few hotels see foreigners as simply welcome customers, and charge them the same prices as Chinese. It may no longer be possible to cross the Gobi by camel to Xīnjiāng, but the ancient trail to Lánzhōu, now a rail and road route following the once navigable Yellow River, is still a byway through pleasant backwater capitals with many unusual and little visited sights. Turning off at Zhōngwèi to follow the road down the spine of Níngxià leads you through even more remote and rural areas, and makes a fascinating alternative route to Xī'ān.

北京 **History**

At the time of the Silk Routes' peak under the Táng dynasty, Běijīng had not yet been conceived, although there had been settlements in the area for thousands of years. A minor capital of lesser dynasties, such as the Mongol-speaking Khitan Liáo (907–1125), and the Jurchen Tartar Jīn (1115–1234), it was under the Mongol Yuán dynasty that Běijīng, then known as Dàdū (Great Capital) by the Chinese but called Khanbalik by its founders, finally became the full-scale capital of a large empire, built alongside the existing settlement. Captured by Genghis Khan in 1215, it was adopted as his chief residence by Khubilai Khan in 1264, and the new city was founded in 1271. The Silk Routes' point of origin had been Xī'ān, but now they and routes running considerably further north served the purpose of both trade and the communications that kept the vast Mongol empire intact. All roads led to Dàdū in the winter, and to the summer capital of Shàngdū (the Xanadu of Coleridge, and today's Dolon Nor in Inner Mongolia) when the Great Khan was there.

The Mongol design gave the shape to modern-day Běijīng, a rectangle with a north–south central axis, of which the Imperial residence was the heart. An immense wall ran round the city with corner turrets and three gates to each side, topped with 'palaces' according to Polo.

When the Yuán fell, the Míng set up their capital at Nánjīng, and Dàdū was renamed Běipíng (Northern Peace). The third Míng emperor, Yǒnglè (reigned 1403–25), rebuilt the city on a slightly smaller scale than that of the Mongols, and moved the capital back there in 1420, and renamed it Běijīng, 'Northern Capital'. Yǒnglè repaired the existing walls, but reduced the overall size by cutting off part of the northern side of the Mongol city with a new wall, leaving the traditionally central bell and drum towers north of the new focal point. Most of the original building of the Forbidden City and several other major monuments dates from his reign.

The Manchu Qīng dynasty, arriving in 1644, left the Míng city much as it was, a series of walls within walls. At the heart lay the walled Imperial Palace or 'Forbidden City', surrounded by the Imperial City whose walls enclosed what is now Běi Hǎi Gōngyuán (park) and the still inaccessible Zhōngnán Hǎi government compound to the west. Its Hòu Mén (rear gate) was halfway to the bell and drum towers to the north, and the walls ran down modern-day Běihéyàn Dàjiē to the east, and halfway down what is now Tiān'ān Mén Guǎngchǎng (Square) to a now-vanished gate. Around all of this stood the massive outer walls of what foreigners called the Tartar City, which the Manchus had taken for themselves and their troops. Roughly square, its 16m-high walls, said to be wide enough for four chariots to run abreast on them, were pierced with two tower-topped gates on each of its west, north and east sides. The south wall had three gates, the middle of which, the Zhèngyáng Mén or Qián Mén (Front Gate), straddled the city's axis, a north–south line running through the centre of the Forbidden City's main gates and buildings, and through the drum and bell towers. The south wall of the Tartar City was the north wall of another, slightly wider city, whose other three walls were lower but still substantial. The central gate of its southern wall, the Yǒngdìng Mén, also lay on the main axis, and stood between the Tiāntán (Temple of Heaven) and its now vanished counterpart, the Temple of Agriculture. This second, smaller city was the Chinese quarter of Běijīng.

Barbarians at the Gates

The Chinese suppression of the import of opium gave Britain an excuse to go to war with China. The Chinese had continued through the 18th and 19th centuries to regard foreigners as inferior, and all trade as merely the offering of tribute. The country's Qīng-enforced purdah had left it ignorant of foreign technological developments and militarily backward. The Opium War of 1840–2 was largely a string of easy victories for the British, and ended with Chinese capitulation and the Treaty of Nánjīng, which forced China to open up yet further to contact with the despised foreigners at designated treaty ports. This was also the agreement which gave Britain Hong Kong, and marked the beginning of a century of unequal treaties with foreign powers. The Chinese were reluctant to enforce their side, and a petty incident involving the boarding of a ship suspected of piracy in 1856 led to the Arrow War (named after the ship in question), in which further British military activity forced on the Chinese the Treaty of Tiānjīn of 1858. This opened up yet further areas for trade, and compelled the Chinese to accept the residence of foreign diplomats in Běijīng. (Another clause forbade the Chinese from using the character *yí*, 'barbarian', in documents relating to the British.) Further reluctance on the part of the Manchus to sign the treaty in Běijīng and to accept the permanent residence of foreign diplomats to which they had already agreed led to further engagements and the occupation of Běijīng in 1860 by Anglo-French forces. These burned down the Summer Palace and drove the Qīng emperor into exile in Manchuria (where he was struck dead by lightning). Another agreement, the Conventions of Běijīng, reduced Manchu sovereignty over China yet further.

Modern Běijīng

1911 saw the end of Qīng power, although the final abdication of the last emperor, still a child, did not come until 1912, and he continued to live in the Forbidden City until 1924. The Nationalist government returned the capital to Nánjīng, and Běijīng to its old name, Běipíng, and it was during this period that the city went into decline. The authors of one 1930s guide book complained that while many ancient buildings had been vandalized, allowed to fall into disrepair, or were now covered in political slogans, some had been destroyed on official orders.

> The loss by vandalism and utter neglect has been proceeding at such a rate that, on repeated occasions, buildings and historical monuments have actually disappeared while the authors were still writing about them.

L. C. Arlington and William Lewisohn, *In Search of Old Peking*, 1935

The Japanese occupied the city between 1937 and the end of the Second World War, but did little damage, revering its remaining palaces and temples, still far more numerous than today. The communists returned the city to capital status, Máo announcing the creation of the People's Republic from atop the Tiān'ān Mén on 1 October 1949, and they then proceeded to destroy most of what was left. During the years that followed ancient temples and halls were turned into military camps and factories. A huge influx of people turned courtyard houses that had once held single families and their servants into home for dozens. The city walls that had stood since Yuán and Míng times were completely torn down, leaving only the occasional gate tower standing isolated and pointless. The stone from the walls was used to line a system of tunnels into which the population could theoretically run in case of nuclear attack, and no doubt be tidily vaporized all in one place, as well as a secret system connecting the Great Hall of the People and the government residential compound of Zhōngnán Hăi with an escape route to the west. The line of the walls of the Tartar City was replaced below ground by more tunnels, those of the metro's circle line, several of whose stops are named after now-vanished gates. Above ground the perimeter line of the Tartar and Chinese cities is followed by the second ring road, still clearly showing the wider bulge of the Chinese city in the south.

The few English signs at Běijīng's sights are loquacious in their indictment of the foreign troops who inflicted damage in 1860 and 1900, but remarkably reticent about the rather larger-scale efforts of the Chinese themselves. The scale of the destruction of China's heritage is indicated by recently announced plans to make Běijīng one of the world's top tourist attractions within 15 years. While much of this plan consists of vague intentions to improve the environment and infrastructure, socialism is never seen to advance without concrete figures. By 2001, 45 ancient sites are to be restored at a cost of ¥200 million, bringing the number of officially designated tourist sites from 105 to 150 (24 of 'national level'), although even the most obsessive visitor will currently have difficulty finding more than a fraction of that amount, unless he or she includes such joys as the Dōngbiàn Mén Overpass, hymned in one Chinese guide book ('821,000 square metres of road surface along with 60 bridges embracing a total length of 97,290 metres'). Even a 115m section of the city wall is being rebuilt, 30,000 of the original bricks, their Míng dynasty kiln marks still visible, having been returned following an appeal. By 2010 the number of restored sites will supposedly have tripled to 350, demonstrating what a treasure house pre-communist Běijīng must have been. 20 new museums are to be built, including a new Capital Museum to display the treasures stored beneath the Forbidden City, bringing the city's total to 110, although even Chinese-produced guide books list considerably fewer. That new museums at Xī'ān and Shànghăi have won international attention is undoubtedly a factor in this programme of culture-by-numbers. The modern guide book writer may be faced with a problem exactly opposite to that of Arlington and Lewisohn, quoted above, as numbers of ancient buildings rapidly emerge from obscurity as factories, and new museums sprout faster than the pen can follow.

Getting to and from Běijīng
by air

Airport information, ✆ 6456 3604/3107.

Despite the rapid growth in China's economy, Běijīng's small Capital Airport is no Narita, JFK, or Heathrow, although redevelopment is gradually removing its musty, third-world atmosphere. A new terminal building, four times the size of the current one, is under construction.

Most hotels have desks that will book airport taxis for substantial sums. Buses to the airport go from the front of the Aviation Building (Mínháng Dàlóu) on the north side Fùxīngmén Nèi Dàjiē, just east of Xīdān metro station at least every half an hour from 5.30am to 7pm. Each bus leaves as it is full, taking 45mins to 1hr to reach the airport for ¥12 ($1.50). Buy your ticket from a counter inside a door at the right-hand end of the building.

Airport tax must be paid at the windows just inside the departure area. Customs checks and X-rays are next, before check-in.

Amongst the desks in the arrivals hall are two offering comfortable bus services into the centre. One with a green sign with yellow characters to your right as you leave, next to the Huayi Hotel's stand, is the bus to Xīdān, ¥12 ($1.50). CITS, slightly to the left, also has a bus to Běijīng station and routes passing various metro stations and hotels, listed in English, all ¥12. These run 8am–9.30pm. Major hotels also have desks here, all somewhat incompetently staffed, some with no information about the hotels they represent, and even willing to offer you information about their competitors. The CITS desk claims to be able to offer you a discount on many of these hotels, but negotiation should be possible at all of the desks, however upmarket the hotel.

There are public telephones at the right- and left-hand ends of the building. Departures are upstairs, along with baggage storage, IDD telephone and fax, and an Air China information desk which is slightly less chaotic than the arrivals one. There's also Chinese regional airline representation and the offices of overseas airlines on both the departures level and the one above (which also has some quieter lavatories). There's a branch of the Bank of China at the rear on the right-hand end of the departures level.

by train

Train information, ✆ 6563 4432/4452.

Běijīng now has two major stations of importance to visitors, Běijīng Zhàn and Běijīng Xī Zhàn (west), and two minor ones of equally minor importance, Běijīng Běi Zhàn (north, also known as Xīzhí Mén Zhàn), and Běijīng Nán Zhàn (south, also known as Yǒngdìng Mén Zhàn).

Běijīng Zhàn is for the time being still the main Běijīng station, and the one nearest the centre. The broad space in front of the station is often occupied by a sea of peasants, and the part in front of the main entrance is fenced off. Tickets are checked at the fence, but the foreigners' ticket windows are inside the station itself. Those obviously not Hàn can simply walk through with confidence, and will not be stopped; others should be prepared to show their passports if not already ticket holders. 'I'm going to buy tickets' is '*Wǒ qù mǎi piào*'. Baggage is X-rayed upon entering the building, so keep film in your pockets. The ticket office (*open 5.30–7.30, 8–12, 1.30–5.30, and 7–12 midnight*) is at the rear of the main hall on the left and through the international waiting room. Advance booking is a maximum of four days in advance including the day of booking and the day of travel. Before 8am and after 4.30pm however, you can only book for the same and sometimes the next day. First obtain a ticket booking form from the left-hand-most window, and complete it before attempting to buy a ticket. Refunds are available up to two hours before departure, with a deduction of 20% of the ticket value (minimum ¥10/$1.25).

Getting to and from Běijīng Zhàn. The station has its own metro station (Ⓜ Běijīng Zhàn), and whatever your destination you should use the metro to go as far as you can towards it. The second and third stops to the west, Qián Mén and Hépíng Mén, are handy for shopping, eating, and moderate hotels, and Qián Mén offers an interchange to buses running south. One stop east, Jiànguó Mén, is near a number of more expensive hotels and the Friendship Store, and an interchange for buses running east–west. Useful buses include the 209 which goes to Běijīng Xī Zhàn via Qián Mén and Hépíng Mén. The tè1 ('special 1') runs from just north of Běijīng Zhàn (straight ahead as you exit) along Jiànguó Mén Wài Dàjiē past several major hotels. The 20 runs down Qián Mén to the Nán Zhàn, not far from many of the moderate and budget hotels. Minibuses at the front of the station will take you directly to the Xī Zhàn for ¥5.

Long-distance trains leave from Běijīng Zhàn if they are going anywhere except the southwest or west. Trains relevant to the routes in this book include the 89 to Hohhot, dep 18.53, arr 06.48 (not every day); the 95 to Dàtóng dep 23.21, arr 06.46; the 295 to Bāotóu dep 21.17, arr Dàtóng 05.20, Hohhot 10.33, and Bāotóu East 12.59; and the 77 to Yínchuān dep 17.00, arr Dàtóng 00.29, Hohhot 05.13, Bāotóu East 07.34, and Yínchuān 17.17. The 43 provides an alternative to Lánzhōu from the more conventional route via Xī'ān, dep 11.01, arr Dàtóng 18.16, Hohhot 23.02, Bāotóu East 01.17, Yínchuān 10.58, Zhōngwèi 14.10, and Lánzhōu 21.18. There is also a train to Bādálǐng near the Great Wall at 08.50 for ¥11 ($1.50).

Typical fares (but expect these to have increased) for hard seat, hard sleeper, and soft sleeper: Dàtóng ¥53 ($6.50), ¥107 ($13), ¥161 ($19.50); Hohhot ¥90 ($11), ¥168 ($21) ¥253 ($31); Bāotóu ¥111 ($13.50), ¥207 ($25), ¥311 ($38); Yínchuān ¥163 ($20), ¥299 ($36), ¥457 ($55).

There are left-luggage lockers in the international waiting room for ¥10 ($1.25) per day, or ¥8 for a smaller one. Timetables in Chinese are sold for ¥7. When you arrive to take any domestic train, show your ticket to someone at the top or bottom of the escalators in the main hall to be pointed to the right waiting room. Most are upstairs.

International departures all go from Běijīng Zhàn, but **international tickets** are not sold here. Some travel agencies will lead you to believe either that access to international tickets is difficult to get, or that only they have access. In fact it's usually easy to buy tickets for yourself from four to five days before often right up to the day of departure, even in the summer, and several of the international ticket office staff speak reasonable English. The office is in the Běijīng Guójì Fàndiàn (Běijīng International Hotel, *open Mon–Fri, 8.30–12, 1.30–5; Sat and Sun, 9–11, 2–4*), ✆ 6512 0507, ✆ 6512 0503. From the main entrance go round to the left-hand side and look for a brass plate; the nondescript door next to it is the one for railway tickets. (There is a glitzy CITS international air ticket office inside the main entrance. This is not it.) To buy tickets you must show your passport or a photocopy of the information page.

On international trains the lowest level of accommodation is equivalent to soft sleeper in China (but sometimes referred to as hard), and the luxury class has two berths in a compartment with a comfy chair and a washroom shared between two compartments. Where there are three classes, the middle one is simply soft sleeper plus a few decorative details, and both the cheaper and the more expensive classes are better value for money.

The **Trans-Manchurian to Moscow** is Russian-run, and heads to China's northeast before crossing directly to Russian territory. The trains are Russian and leave at 07.40 on Wed, for ¥2562 ($309) soft sleeper, ¥3365 ($405) de luxe, arriving in Moscow the following Monday, 7865km later, at 17.25.

The Chinese-run **Trans-Mongolian to Moscow** heads more directly north, passing through Outer Mongolia before entering Russia, and departs at 20.32 on Fri and Sat for ¥1636 ($197) soft sleeper, and ¥2569 ($310) de luxe, arriving in Moscow the following Thurs and Fri at 20.30.

Ulan Batar (Wūlánbātuō) can by reached by the Trans-Manchurian, or by its own train at 7.40am on Saturdays, for ¥773 ($73) soft sleeper and ¥1081 ($130) de luxe.

Pyongyang (Píngrǎng) has a weekly train which may be Chinese or Korean, leaving on Saturdays at 16.48. The Chinese train has two classes for ¥959 ($116) and ¥677 ($82), and the Korean three classes for ¥599 ($73), ¥831 ($100), and ¥915 ($112).

Moonsky Star or Monkey Business, 4th Floor, West Building, Běijīng Commercial Business Complex on the second ring road in the southwest, ✆ 329 2244 ext 4408, can offer tickets with breaks in the journey, and tours of Mongolia and the Baikal area of Siberia, although these are expensive. Sample prices include $385 to Moscow through Mongolia including the first night's accommodation; or $845 including a six-day stopover in Mongolia; $795 including three days in Irkutsk, and so on. They also offer the route via Ürümqi, Almaty and Tashkent to Moscow for $1200 including the first night in Moscow, or a 14-day trip to Kazakstan via Mongolia, Siberia and the Turk-Sib line for $1650.

The brand-new **Běijīng Xī Zhàn** (West Station) is one of the most impressive and most vulgar buildings in Běijīng—a post-modern assemblage of popular motifs from China's architectural past, with hints of arrow tower and Forbidden City all out of scale both with each other and with a vast arch in the centre. Opened in early 1996 after three years' construction work by 20,000 people at a cost of ¥5 billion (more than $600 million—equivalent to about two-thirds of China's total annual spending on education), this is the kind of building that makes the visitor wonder whether giving aid to China would be necessary if the government altered its priorities. When the second phase of construction is completed in 2000, the station is expected to handle about three times the capacity of Běijīng Zhàn. Trains from here now run to the southwest and west, including Xī'ān, Lánzhōu and Ürümqi.

Getting to and from Běijīng Xī Zhàn. The nearest metro station for the Xī Zhàn is Ⓜ Jūnshì Bówùguǎn, three stops west of the Ⓜ Fùxīng Mén exchange station. Take the east exit on the south side and walk west, taking the first left turn at the lights down Yángfángdiàn Lù—about 15mins walk altogether, or catch any bus on the opposite side of Yángfángdiàn Lù.

Several buses start from stands signposted to your right in English and Chinese as you leave the station, well below ground level. The 52 runs straight along Cháng'ān Jiē across the top of Tiān'ān Mén and along Jiànguó Mén Dàjiē. The 21 runs to Xīzhí Mén Nán Dàjiē just south of Běijīng Běi Zhàn. The 320 runs north nearly as far as Běijīng Dàxué (Běijīng University). There's also a minibus direct to the Summer Palace.

Outside the station at ground level (reached by a spiral ramp) the 212 goes to Qián Mén (marked 'to square'), the tè5 ('special 5') is an express double-decker which runs to the Zoo in one direction (where you can change for most of the universities and the Summer Palace) and to Běijīng Nán Zhàn in the other. Going south it passes usefully close to the some of the moderate and cheaper hotels south of Qián Mén, stopping near the junction of Nán Xīnhuá Jiē and Zhūshìkǒu Xī Dàjiē. The 209 goes to Běijīng Zhàn via Hépíng Mén and Qián Mén. The tè1 runs to just north of Běijīng Zhàn and on down Jiànguó Mén Wài Dàjiē past several major hotels. After a 15-minute walk west to the junction with the third ring road, you can catch the 324 which travels around it south to the Jīnghuá Fàndiàn (although taking the tè5 to the south station and changing to the 40 on the opposite side of the canalized river may be more reliable).

The left-luggage office is straight in front of you as you emerge from the platforms. As you arrive at the station take the spiral ramp down to the lower levels outside the building on the left, and look for signs.

The foreigners' ticket office is through the main entrance, where all baggage is X-rayed. Go up the escalators ahead of you and turn left (*open 8–12 and 1–6, and right through the night 7.30pm–7am*). The soft sleeper waiting room is also at this level.

Undoubtedly the best train to catch to Xī'ān and on northwest to Ürümqi is the 69, the new alternative to the Trans-Siberian trains, but air-conditioned, with video screens in hard sleepers (Jackie Chan and other Hong Kong action movies). Leaving Běijīng Xī Zhàn at 21.17, it arrives at Xī'ān at 14.20, Lánzhōu 02.19, Wǔwēi 10.05, Zhāngyè 15.13, Jiāyùguān 19.29, Liǔyuán (for Dūnhuáng) 01.14, Hāmì 06.37, Tǔlǔfān 14.06, and Ürümqi at 16.45 after a total of four days. An international train runs from here to Almaty in Kazakstan from where there are trains on to Moscow and beyond (*see* pp.259 and 424). Other useful trains include the 75 at 09.16 arriving Xī'ān 03.04, and Lánzhōu at 16.31, continuing to Xīníng on alternate days, arriving 21.26. Better for Xī'ān is the 41 at 13.23 arriving at Xī'ān at 06.17.

Běijīng Xī Zhàn also receives trains direct from Hong Kong on a brand-new line opened in 1996.

Fares are: from Běijīng Xī Zhàn on the a/c 69, hard seat (reserved places only—no unreserved seating), hard sleeper, soft sleeper, to Xī'ān ¥152 ($19), ¥279 ($34), ¥428 ($52)—on normal trains ¥240 ($29). Some other 'normal' fares: Lánzhōu ¥121 ($15), ¥241 ($29), ¥401 ($49); Turpan ¥200 ($24), ¥393 ($48), ¥659 ($80); Ürümqi ¥204 ($25), ¥400 ($48), ¥672 ($81).

Běijīng Běi Zhàn (north, also known as Xīzhí Mén) is on the circle line at ⊕ Xīzhí Mén, and has an early morning train to the Bādálǐng Great Wall, and the occasional train to Dàtóng and beyond. The **Běijīng Nán Zhàn** (south, also known as Yǒngdìng Mén Zhàn), is reached by the tè5 from Běijīng Xī Zhàn, and the 20 from Běijīng Zhàn. For those staying at budget accommodation in the south, and wanting to take the route through Inner Mongolia, it may also be worth considering one of the few trains that leave from here.

by bus

Běijīng has several bus stations scattered around its third and second ring roads, but leaving Běijīng by train is considerably more convenient. The Dōng Zhí Mén Chángtú Qìchēzhàn, northeast of Dōng Zhí Mén, has buses to towns and villages near Great Wall sites (*see* below).

airlines

Almost all the world's major airlines and many of the minor ones now fly to Bĕijīng. The following list is not exhaustive, and the frequencies when given are for the summer peak— there may be fewer flights at other times.

Aeroflot flies to Moscow and on to almost everywhere. Hotel Bĕijīng-Toronto, Jiànguó Mén Wài Dàjiē, ✆ 6500 2412.

Chinese international flights are mostly a considerable improvement on domestic ones. Tickets for both can be found at the Aviation Building, 15 Xī Cháng'ān Jiē, ✆ 6601 7755, 📠 6601 7585. International ticketing is on the ground floor, and domestic upstairs (more information below). **Air China**'s destinations include London, Paris, Berlin, Stockholm, Sydney, Melbourne, Vancouver, San Francisco and New York. **China Eastern** flies to Brussels, Munich, Madrid, Los Angeles, Seattle and Chicago. **China Southern** flies to Amsterdam. There are also Chinese flights to all Asian destinations (except Táiwān).

Air France flies to Paris and beyond. China World Trade Centre, ✆ 6505 1818.

Air New Zealand flies to Auckland three times weekly from *Hong Kong*; call in HK ✆ (852) 2524 8606.

Alitalia flies twice weekly to Rome and on to multiple European destinations. Jiànguó Fàndiàn, Jiànguó Mén Wài Dàjiē, ✆ 6591 8468.

ANA flies daily to Tokyo, and once a week to Osaka with connections to Europe, Australia, and the US east and west coasts. China World Trade Centre, ✆ 6505 3311.

Asiana flies daily except Saturday to Seoul, and on to five US destinations, Vienna, Brussels, Sydney, and many Asian cities. Jiànguó Mén Wài Dàjiē just west of the China World Trade Centre, ✆ 6506 1118.

British Airways flies to London Heathrow three times a week, with connections world-wide. SCITE Tower, Room 210, 2nd Floor, Jiànguŏ Mén Wài Dàjiē, ✆ 6512 4070.

Canadian Airlines flies to Vancouver four times weekly with connections to major Canadian and other North American cities. Lufthansa Centre, ✆ 6463 7901–5, 📠 6463 7906.

Dragonair flies to Hong Kong twice daily with Cathay Pacific connections to Australia, New Zealand, Europe and North America. China World Trade Centre, ✆ 6505 4343.

Finnair, CVIK Tower Room 204, 22 Jiànguó Mén Wài Dàjiē, ✆ 6512 7180/1, 📠 6512 7182.

Garuda Indonesia flies twice weekly to Jakarta via Guăngzhōu. China World Trade Centre, ✆ 6505 2901-3, 📠 6505 2904.

Japan Airlines has flights to Tokyo, Osaka and Nagoya. Chángfùgōng Fàndiàn (Hotel New Otani) office section, 26 Jiànguó Mén Wài Dàjiē, ✆ 6513 0888.

KLM flies twice weekly to Amsterdam with rapid connections at Schipol airport to a wide range of destinations worldwide. China World Trade Centre, ✆ 6505 3505, 📠 6505 1855.

Korean Airlines flies four times weekly to Seoul and with connections to Europe, North America and Australasia. China World Trade Centre, ✆ 6505 1047.

Lufthansa flies to Frankfurt daily with connections to an immense worldwide network. Lufthansa Centre, ✆ 6465 4488.

Malaysian Airlines flies five times a week to Kuala Lumpur, with connections to Europe. China World Trade Centre, ✆ 6505 2681.

Northwest Airlines flies non-stop to Detroit, as well as to LA and Tokyo, ✆ 6505 3505, 🖷 6505 5147.

Quantas flies twice weekly to Sydney via Shànghǎi. Lufthansa Centre, ✆ 6467 4794.

SAS flies four times weekly to Copenhagen. CVIK Tower, 22 Jiànguó Mén Wài Dàjiē, ✆ 6512 0575/6.

Singapore Airlines flies once or twice daily to Singapore with connections to London, Paris, Amsterdam, Australasia, and US west and east coasts. East Wing, China World Trade Centre, ✆ 6505 2233, 🖷 6505 1178.

Thai Airways International flies fives times a week to Bangkok with good onwards connections, ✆ 6512 3881, 6460 8899.

United Airlines flies to major US cities via Tokyo. Lufthansa Centre, ✆ 6463 1111.

Those looking for cheaper flights should investigate the airlines of intermediate countries, which may provide slower but considerably cheaper links via their own capitals. Amongst less familiar airlines flying to Běijīng are **Ethiopia Airlines**, ✆ 6505 0314; **Iran Air**, ✆ 6512 4940; **LOT Polish Airlines** (to Warsaw every Friday), ✆ 500 7799 2002; and **PIA**, ✆ 6505 2256.

Domestic and international tickets for Chinese airlines can be bought through agents or at the Aviation Building (Mínháng Dàlóu), 15 Xī Cháng'ān Jiē (Ⓜ Xīdān, just east on the north side of the road), ✆ 6601 7755, 🖷 6601 7585. International ticketing is on the ground floor, and domestic upstairs. As Chinese airlines only accept cash, there is a branch of the Bank of China upstairs, too (*open Mon–Fri, 9–11 and 12–8; Sat and Sun 3–8*). China Southern, Eastern, Xīnhuá, United, Sìchuān, North, Southwest, Northwest, Xīnjiāng, Zhèjiāng, and Xiàmén Airlines are all represented here. You can buy a complete domestic and international timetable for ¥10 ($1.25). Turn left as you enter and ask at the counter on the left.

Two alternative booking numbers for Chinese airlines: domestic ✆ 6601 3336, international ✆ 6601 6667.

There are direct flights from Běijīng to every major city in China, including the following Silk Route towns: Bāotóu (1–3 times daily), Hohhot (1–3 times daily), Lánzhōu (2–3 times daily, and on to Dūnhuáng three times a week), Ürümqi (daily), Xī'ān (at least seven times daily), Xīníng (three times a week), Yínchuān (daily).

CITS offices also act as ticket agents for Chinese airlines and for JAL, ANA, Northwest and United. CITS is at 103 Fùxīngmén Wài Dàjiē, ℰ 6603 9321, ℰ 6603 9320; China World Trade Centre, ℰ 6505 3775, ℰ 6505 3105; Běijīng International Hotel, ℰ 6512 0507, ℰ 6512 0503, and elsewhere. There is no commission on airline ticket sales.

embassies

There are two principal diplomatic enclaves: the Rìtán Embassy Area (Rìtán Shǐguǎnqū), which is north of the Friendship Store, and the Sānlǐtún Embassy Area (Sānlǐtún Shǐguǎnqū) which is further to the northeast towards the Lufthansa Centre, although there are one or two escapees.

Onward visas:

Kazakstan: 9 Sānlǐtún Dōng Liù Jiē, Sānlǐtún, ℰ 6532 6182, ℰ 6532 6183 (*open Tues and Fri, 8.30am–12 noon*). Transit visas available if you hold another CIS visa (in which case a transit visa is not necessary, but is still advisable) or an air ticket from Almaty, $15. Tourist visas $25 for 2 weeks, but only with an invitation (*see* p.8). Payment in 1990 or later $US cash only. One photograph is needed.

Kyrgyzstan: Section 1, 4th Floor, Tǎyuán Diplomatic Office Building, 14 Liàngmǎhé Nánlù, Sānlǐtún, ℰ 6532 6458, ℰ 6532 6459 (*open Mon–Fri, 8–6*). Tourist visas are valid for up to 2 months, and cost $60. Two photographs are needed. Invitations are not usually necessary, but can be purchased if needed (*see* p.8).

Mongolia: 2 Xiùshuǐ Běidàjiē, Rìtán, ℰ 6532 1810, ℰ 6532 5045. Transit visas are $15, tourist $25.

Pakistan: 1 Dōng Zhí Mén Wài Dàjiē, Sānlǐtún, ℰ 6532 2558 (*open Mon–Fri, 9–4*). Visa fees vary according to nationality (UK ¥472/$57) and are usually available later the same day. Two photographs are needed.

Russia: 4 Dōng Zhí Mén Běi Zhōngjiē, ℰ 6532 1267, ℰ 6532 4853 (*open Mon–Fri, 9–1*). To buy a tourist visa you must prove that you have booked accommodation. No visa is required if you simply change planes at Moscow, but if you have an onward ticket and want to see the town, transit visas can be purchased in the transit lounge in Moscow's Sheremetyevo Airport. They start from $18 for 6 hours, running up to $110 for 72 hours, but ask Aeroflot for the latest prices, since these are liable to change at short notice. It is also possible to buy tourist visas at the airport if accommodation is purchased at the same time, although this will be very expensive. Aeroflot staff advise making visa arrangements before leaving Běijīng if possible. A three-day transit will only cost $40 if bought in Běijīng, a tourist visa $50. You will need three photographs.

Passport photos are widely available at shops with the Polaroid sign. There's a large photo studio with an English sign just east of the Lotteria restaurant at the top of Qián Mén, and another in the basement of the China World Trade Centre. About ¥25 ($3) for four.

In case of emergency:

Australia: 15 Dōng Zhí Mén Wài Dàjiē, Sānlǐtún, ℰ 6532 2331–7, ℰ 6532 4605
Canada: 16 Dōng Zhí Mén Wài Dàjiē, Sānlǐtún, ℰ 6532 3536, ℰ 6532 4072
France: 3 Sānlǐtún Dōng Wǔ Jiē, Sānlǐtún, ℰ 6532 1331, ℰ 6501 4872

Germany: 5 Dōng Zhí Mén Wài Dàjiē, Sānlǐtún, ✆ 6532 2161, 🖷 6532 5336
Italy: 2 Sānlǐtún Dōng Èr Jiē, Sānlǐtún, ✆ 6532 2131
Japan: 7 Rìtán Lù, Rìtán, ✆ 6532 2361
New Zealand: 1 Rìtán Dōng Èr Jiē, Rìtán, ✆ 6532 2731–4, 🖷 6532 4317
USA: 3 Xiùshuǐ Běi Jiē, Rìtán, ✆ 6532 3431 🖷 6532 3831
UK: 11 Guānghuá Lù, Rìtán, ✆ 6532 1961–5, 🖷 6532 1939 ext 239

maps and books

Maps in English and Chinese or Chinese only are available in bookshops throughout the city (several in Qián Mén Dàjiē alone), from street vendors at railway stations, and at tourist sites for ¥2.5 to ¥3. The clearest of these is the Hong Kong produced *Beijing—The Latest Tourist Map*, which also has an English key. There are also much more detailed Chinese-only street directories such as the Běijīng Shēnghuó Dìtúcè, ¥9. The four-storey Foreign Languages Bookstore (Wàiwén Shūdiàn) on the west side of Wángfǔjǐng (no.235) has an immense stock of novels and other materials in English and other languages.

money

Travellers' cheques can be most easily exchanged at the Friendship Store (*open daily, 9–9*). Useful branches of the Bank of China include those next to the Wénxuān Bīnguǎn, Nán Xīnhuá Jiē, ⓜ Hépíng Mén (*open Mon–Fri, 9–12 and 1.30–5*), rear counter, window 8. The main office is the building with a clock on top directly west of the Mausoleum (*open Mon–Thurs, 9–12 and 1–4, Fri 9–12 and 1–3.30*) in an alley called Xī Jiāomín Xiàng. There's another branch on the ground floor of CVIK building on the south side of Jiànguó Mén Wài Dàjiē, west of the Friendship Store (*open daily 9–12 and 1–6.30*). The CITIC Industrial Bank on the ground floor of the CITIC building immediately to the west of the Friendship Store will issue cash against major credit cards (*open Mon–Fri, 9–12 and 1–4*). American Express in the China World Trade Centre, ✆ 6505 2888, 🖷 6505 4972 (*open Mon–Fri, 9–5, Sat 9–12*), has one of its own cash machines that will issue ¥RMB cash and $US travellers' cheques to card-holders who know their PIN (24 hours). Personal cheques guaranteed by the card can be cashed for a combination of $US cash and traveller's cheques at certain banks in Běijīng and other major cities including the CITIC Industrial Bank, the amount depending upon the card held (ask Amex for a list).

photographic

Film and camera shops are numerous in every major shopping street, and passport photos are widely available from various Polaroid-signed sites, also at a large photoshop just east of the top of Qián Mén, where shots are taken in an upstairs studio with proper lighting. In the basement of the China World Trade Centre four polaroid shots are available for ¥25 ($3).

post office and telephones

The **Jiànguó Mén Post and Telecommunication Office** (Jiànguó Mén Yóudiànjú), a block north of Jiànguó Mén up Cháoyáng Mén Nán Dàjiē, is the main post office for foreigners (*open 8–7*), and the one where *poste restante* mail ends up. The counter is half-way down on the left where incoming mail sits on a desk in three boxes. There is the usual

¥1.5 charge per item to pick up. The postcode is 100600. To claim parcels you must show your passport, and you may have to open the parcel in front of the staff if requested. The parcel counter is at the rear on the right (*open Mon–Fri, 9–5*). There are numerous useful small post offices dotted around: in the basement of the China World Trade Centre (*open 9–6*), on the east side of Wángfǔjǐng Dàjiē, just east of the Telegraph Building on the south side of Xī Cháng'ān Jiē (*open 8.30–7*), and just to the east of the Hépíng Mén roast duck restaurant on the south side of Qián Mén Xī Dàjiē (*open 8.30–6.30*).

International telephone services are offered by even the cheapest hotels, though sometimes from a cabin in the foyer, and at substantial mark-ups above the already expensive International Telegraph and Telephone Service Hall (Diànbào Diànhuà Gōngyètīng), which is at Ⓜ Xīdān, just east of the Aviation building on the north side of Qián Mén Xī Dàjiē (*open 24hrs*). Here you can also send and receive email during the day at counter 16 (btoyy@public.bta.net.cn). ¥10 ($1.25) to send, ¥4 to receive, using a primitive DOS text editor and Windows communications software. Expect your mail to be read by curious staff.

Internet access is also available at the Sentiment Bar, 1 North 8 Building, Sānlǐtún Běilù, ☎ 6415 3691 for ¥82 ($10) per hour (*open 5.30pm–1am*), and in the café on the second floor of the Běijīng Concert Hall, although if there's a concert taking place, you can't get access without buying a ticket. Call for opening times, ☎ 6605 5846.

travel agents

Even the cheapest hotels in Běijīng have **travel agents** who can make local travel arrangements, albeit at a higher price than they charge Chinese for the same service and often at many multiples of the cost of using local transport for the same purpose. A tour to the Míng Tombs and Bādálǐng Great Wall, for instance, can cost up to ¥500 ($60) per person, including entrance tickets and lunch, but you can do much the same thing yourself by bus for only ¥16 in bus fares, ¥60 ($7.50) in entrance tickets, and whatever you choose to spend on lunch (take a picnic). These agents can also book air and train tickets for commissions ranging from nothing (usually air tickets) to ¥100 ($12) per ticket, something which is also easy to do for yourself in Běijīng.

Special services laid on by these agencies include the *hútòng* tour. Dung cleaners still have to walk up alleys too narrow for the dung carts and shoulder 50kg buckets of human waste, delivering it to villages close to Běijīng for use on the fields, and earning nearly double the typical worker's salary—around ¥800 ($96) monthly. Compare this to the ¥180 ($22) you can pay to take a half-day 'To the Hútòng Tour' on foot and by bicycle rickshaw. Call ☎ 6525 4263 if your legs and your sense of proportion have both failed you.

visa extensions

Visa extensions are available from the Wàiguórén Qiānzhèng Bànshìchù office of the PSB at 85 Běi Chízi Dàjiē, which runs up the east side of the Forbidden City, ☎ 6525 2729 (*open Mon–Fri, 8.30–11.30 and 1–5*). There have occasionally been some problems with corrupt policemen here. If you are told that you must go to a travel agency and pay ¥800 for your extension, politely insist on your rights, involve other policemen in the discussion, or get the extension in another town.

Běijīng's heart is Tiān'ān Mén and the vast square to its south, surrounded by four concentric ring roads, the fourth of which is still under construction, a few kilometres out in nearly green space. Most of the main sights are within the second ring road, budget accommodation is out on the third, and the fourth will only be crossed when venturing to the Great Wall, the Marco Polo Bridge, or the Summer Palace. Most major streets run north to south or east to west, parallel to the sides of Tiān'ān Mén Square, often running straight for several kilometres and changing name several times.

by metro

Unless it means going absurdly far out of your way, always use the metro to travel as much of your route as possible. There are two lines: an east–west 17km 'First Line' which opened in 1970, and a circle line which follows the route of the second ring road, opened in 1984. It finally occurred to someone that since these lines cross there should be an interchange between them, and this opened three years later (Ⓜ Fùxīng Mén). Signs in pīnyīn indicate exits and the nearest sights, cross-track signs tell you the next station in each direction, and on the trains long announcements in Chinese end with the name of the next stop in English. Buy your ticket at a window below ground just before the final stairs to the platform, and have it torn by offering the short end to the ticket collector and hanging on to the rest. Make sure you get your half back. There is a ¥2 flat fare, and exchange between the two lines is permitted without further charge. The east–west line currently terminates at Xīdān, one stop east of the interchange, but is being extended a further 12km or so along Cháng'ān Jiē past another exchange at Ⓜ Jiànguó Mén, and on out to the east along Jiànguó Mén Wài Dàjiē.

by bus

Buses within the city and with numbers lower than 100 have a flat fare of ¥0.50 for all but the longest trips. Trolleybuses, numbering 101 upwards, are the same. Other buses in the 200 series around town, and the 300+ series for suburban transport, begin at ¥0.50, and then go up in units of ¥0.30 according to distance travelled. Express buses *tè* (special) 1–5 have flat fares of around ¥5 depending on route (these are sometimes double-deckers). On bus stop signs, the black number is the route number and the red number is merely the number of the stop. Exchange points with which you are likely to become familiar include the Zoo, Qián Mén and Běijīng Zhàn. Běijīng blocks are exhaustingly long, and bus stops far apart. Small wars break out in the search for seats, but unless you are willing to pile in and crush your share of children and old ladies (both capable of looking after themselves, as your ribs will discover), you will not often be boarding buses. The chaos has been somewhat relieved by the arrival in recent years of minibuses running the same routes for about twice the price.

by taxi

Taxis are legion. The cheapest are small and usually yellow or white minivans (*miàndī*), at ¥1 per km with a flagfall of ¥10 ($1.25). With other cabs, flagfall is ¥4

To Summer Palace **N**

To Marco Polo Bridge

THIRD RING ROAD

XI ZHI MEN WAI DAJIE

XI ZHI MEN NAN DAJIE

XISI BEI DAJIE

XISI NAN DAJIE

XIDAN BEI DAJIE

XUANWU MEN NEI DAJIE

YANGFANG TIAN

FUXINGMEN WAI DAJIE

FUXINGMEN NEI DAJIE

XI CHA

RONGXIAN HUTONG

XUANWU MEN XI DAJIE

XUANWU MEN DONG DAJIE

NAN XINHUA JIE

XUANWU MEN NAN XINHUA JIE

SECOND RING

NAN SAN HUAN XILU

Běijīng map key

HOTELS AND RESTAURANTS

黑土地酒家	A	Hēi Tǔdì Jiǔjiā
竹园宾馆	B	Zhúyuán Bīnguǎn Bamboo Garden Hotel
北京燕莎中心凯宾馆斯基饭店	C	Kempinski Hotel Běijīng Lufthansa Centre Běijīng Yànshāzhōngxīn Kǎibīnguǎn Sījī Fàndiàn
	D	Hard Rock Café
砂锅居饭庄	E	Shāguōjū Fànzhuāng
北京饭店	F	Běijīng Hotel Běijīng Fàndiàn
国际饭店	G	International Hotel Guójī Fàndiàn
京伦饭店	H	Jīnglún Fàndiàn Hotel Běijīng-Toronto
四川饭店	I	Sìchuān Fàndiàn
三峡酒楼	J	Sānxiá Jiǔlóu
格兰云天大酒店	K	Gélányúntiān Dàjiǔdiàn Grand Skylight Hotel
文轩宾馆	L	Wénxuān Bīnguǎn
全聚德	M	Quánjùdé Roast duck
老舍茶馆	N	Lǎo Shě Cháguǎn
卡巴快餐厅	O	Australian Kebab House Kǎbā Kuàicāntīng

肯德鸡	O	Kentucky Fried Chicken Kěndé Jī
麦当劳	O	McDonald's Màidāngláo
全聚德	O	Quánjùdé Roast duck
大磨坊面包店	O	Vie de France Dàmófáng Miànbāodiàn
全聚德	P	Quánjùdé roast duck
都一处烧麦馆	Q	Dūyīchù Shāomàiguǎn
丰泽园饭店	R	Fēngzéyuán Fàndiàn
东方饭店	S	Dōngfāng Fàndiàn
前门饭店	T	Qián Mén Fàndiàn
景泰宾馆	U	Jǐngtài Bīnguǎn
京华饭店	V	Jīnghuá Fàndiàn
王府井大饭店	W	Wángfǔjǐng Grand Hotel Wángfǔjǐng Dàfàndiàn
天伦王朝饭店	X	Tiānlún Wángcháo Fàndiàn Tiānlún Dynasty Hotel
长富宫饭店	Y	Chángfùgōng Fàndiàn Hotel New Otani
远东饭店	Z	Yuǎndōng Fàndiàn Far East Hotel

STREET & BUS STOP NAMES

安乐林路	Ānlèlín Lù	南新华街	Nán Xīnhuá Jiē
北长街	Běi Cháng Jie	蒲黄榆	Púhuángyú
北池子大街	Běi Chízi Dàjiē	蒲黄榆路	Púhuángyú Lù
北新华街	Běi Xīnhuá Jiē	前门大街	Qián Mén Dàjiē
朝阳门南、北大街	Cháoyáng Mén Nán/Běidàjiē	前门东、西大街	Qián Mén Dōng/Xī Dàjiē
崇文门外大街	Chóngwén Mén Wài Dàjiē	日坛使馆区	Rìtán Shǐguǎnqū (diplomatic enclave)
大栅栏街	Dàzhàlán Jiē	绒线胡同	Róngxiàn Hútòng
地安门外大街	Dì'ān Mén Wài Dàjiē	三里屯北路	Sānlǐtún Běilù
东长安街	Dōng Cháng'ān Jiē	三里屯使馆区	Sānlǐtún Shǐguǎnqū (diplomatic enclave)
东交民巷	Dōng Jiāomín Xiàng	天安门广场	Tiān'ān Mén Guǎngchǎng (square)
东三环北路	Dōng Sān Huán Běilù	天坛东、北路	Tiāntán Dōng/Běilù
东四北大街	Dōngsì Běi Dàjiē	铁树斜街	Tiěshù Xiéjiē
东直门北大街	Dōng Zhí Mén Běi Dàjiē	王府井大街	Wángfǔjǐng Dàjiē
东直门北中街	Dōng Zhí Mén Běi Zhōngjiē	万明路	Wànmíng Lù
东直门外大街	Dōng Zhí Mén Wài Dàjiē	小十桥胡同	Xiǎoshíqiáo Hútòng
复兴门内、外大街	Fùxīngmén Nèi/Wài Dàjiē	西长安街	Xī Cháng'ān Jiē
缸瓦市	Gāngwǎ Shì	西交民巷	Xī Jiāomín Xiàng
光华路	Guānghuá Lù	西四南、北大街	Xìsì Nán/Běi Dàjiē
国子监街	Guózǐjiān Jiē	西直门外、南大街	Xī Zhí Mén Wài/Nán Dàjiē
和平里东街	Hépínglǐ Dōngjiē	西单北大街	Xīdān Běidàjiē
建国门内、外大街	Jiànguó Mén Nèi/Wài Dàjiē	西四南、北大街	Xìsì Nán/Běidàjiē
景山前街	Jǐngshān Qián Jiē	秀水北大街	Xiùshuǐ Běidàjiē
旧鼓楼路	Jiùgǔlóu Lù	宣武门内、东、西大街	Xuānwǔ Mén Nèi/Dōng/Xī Dàjiē
亮马河南路	Liàngmǎhé Nánlù	洋桥	Yáng Qiáo
亮马桥路	Liàngmǎqiáo Lù	羊坊店路	Yángfángdiàn Lù
琉璃厂	Liúlichǎng	永安路	Yǒng'ān Lù
琉璃井	Liúlíjǐng	永定门内、外大街	Yǒngdīng Mén Nèi/Wài Dàjiē
南长街	Nán Cháng Jiē	雍和宫大街	Yōnghégōng Dàjiē
南池子大街	Nán Chízi Dàjiē	珠市口东、西大街	Zhūshìkǒu Dōng/Xī Dàjiē
南三环西路	Nán Sān Huán Xīlù		

plus 4km at the rate per km written on the side window, with rare exceptions the cheapest and rarest being ¥1.4 per km (thus flagfall is ¥9.60). The majority are small, red cars (*xiàlì*). The meters run about 30% faster at night (legally). As usual, do not accept rides from taxi drivers who approach you at the airport, the Aviation Building or railway stations, and where possible walk out a little distance before flagging a cab; otherwise be prepared to face all the range of tricks—speedy meters, 'broken' meters, getting 'lost', 'misunderstanding', 'no change', and, most shockingly for those who remember the China of only a few years ago, 'You want girl? Drugs?' Some types of taxi, *miàndī* in particular, are not allowed up Xīdān and some other major shopping streets at certain hours. Always carry an open map on your lap so that the driver thinks you are following the route, even if you are not.

If you do have a bad experience, try calling these taxi complaints numbers, ☎ 6601 2620, 6834 4238, 6701 6181.

by bicycle or cycle rickshaw

Bicycles are usually available for hire at the cheaper hotels, typically for ¥10 ($1.25) per day, but Běijīng's heavy traffic means that you are risking your life, although doing so with millions of Chinese. If you stay in Běijīng for a week it is highly likely that you will see an accident involving a cyclist and a vehicle. Always park in designated spots (wherever you see a vista of bicycles in a roped-off part of the pavement, ¥0.20), and nowhere else, or your bike is unlikely to be there when you get back.

For a foreign visitor a ride in a **cycle rickshaw** (pedicab) *always* end in tears. If you don't fix a price in advance, ¥200 ($24) will be demanded for half a kilometre. If you do fix a price, either you will not be taken to your destination or a much higher price will be demanded for an incomprehensible reason when you arrive. The average worker is being paid around ¥450 per month, not per 15mins. A typical price quoted to a Chinese for the run from Qián Mén to Wángfǔjǐng is ¥10 ($1.25). Why waste your time when a *miàndī* will take you there much quicker for the same price and be happy to take your money for such a short run? Spare yourself.

Běijīng ☎ (010)   **Tourist Information**

Visitors to Běijīng should be wary of all tourist services. Běijīng has a Tourist Hotline, open 24 hours, ☎ 6513 0828, which is for assistance and complaints, but don't expect miracles. Other information lines where you may find English speakers are: train information ☎ 6563 4432/4452, airport information ☎ 6456 3604/3107, taxi complaints ☎ 6601 2620, 6834 4238, 6701 6181.

China Daily, free at the Friendship Store and in the foyers of larger hotels, has information on what's on in Běijīng, as does the weekly *Běijīng Weekend*—published by *China Daily* and available on Fridays in the same locations—which has almost no news or politics, just entertainment features. *Běijīng Scene*, an amateur weekly produced by foreign residents, is available free at American Express and ex-pat watering holes such as burger bars and pubs (*see* 'Eating Out', p.369), with information on acrobatics and theatre as well as jazz, rock and amateur dramatics.

Tiān'ān Mén Guǎngchǎng (Square)   天安门广场

An agoraphobic's nightmare, Tiān'ān Mén Square, one of the world's largest man-made open spaces, is full for most of the day with happy holiday-making crowds flying kites, taking each other's photographs, and in the case of those from out of town, marvelling to find themselves at the country's very heart. A kite-tail of a queue to see China's one-man Madame Tussaud's, the embalmed Máo, edges slowly forward. At the edges crowds gape both at the grim buildings symbolizing the current 'dictatorship of the proletariat', and at the ornate relics of the imperial past. The square and its contents are utterly fascinating both as propaganda through town planning and as a sobering lesson in modern Chinese history.

On the north side lies the **Tiān'ān Mén** (Gate of Heavenly Peace) after which the square is named, the entrance to the 800-year-old palace of the emperors, and from the balcony of which Máo declared the formation of the People's Republic of China on 1 October 1949. On the west side lies the **Great Hall of the People** (Rénmín Dàhuìtáng), the venue for set-piece government meetings where in a mockery of consultation and democracy, delegates largely rubber-stamp what has been decided for them. On the east side the **Museum of Chinese History** and the Museum of the Revolution enshrine the official view of what happened in Chinese ancient and modern history (subject to revision without notice). The south side has some of the few remains still standing of the ancient city walls destroyed in the 1960s as part of Máo's 'Great Leap Forward' campaign, victims of the communists' desire to make their own mark on Běijīng. These, the double towers of the **Zhèngyáng Mén**, are more commonly known as the Qián Mén or 'Front Gate'. Within the square are the **Monument to the People's Heroes** (Rénmín Yīngxióng Jìniànbēi), an involuntary tribute to the manipulation of history the government would have the masses think important, and the **Chairman Máo Memorial Hall**, containing the embalmed corpse of the 'Great Helmsman' who so often directed the ship onto the rocks.

The square has long been the venue both for carefully staged political set pieces (military reviews, demonstrations in support of Máo), and spontaneous outbursts of dissent. Long before the violent suppression of the Democracy Movement was beamed around the world by television on 4 June 1989, the square had a history of mass political protest. The May Fourth movement of 1919 saw 3000 students gathered to protest at the provision of the Treaty of Versailles which had given parts of China occupied by Germany to Japan at the end of the First World War. While not being able to send troops, China had sent several thousand labourers to France who had freed Europeans to go to the front. Expecting the return of occupied territory, they discovered that the Chinese president had earlier acquiesced to the passing of the territory to Japan in return for its support in the war. They marched towards the foreign legations where gates and guards barred them from entry. On 9 December 1935 thousands of students rallied to protest at the Nationalist government's impotence against Japanese aggression. They were hosed with water and clubbed, but the following week almost 30,000 people reappeared. On 5 April 1976 demonstrations begun the previous day swelled to over 100,000 mourning the death of the disgraced moderate Zhōu Ēnlái, and by implication criticizing Máo and the 'Gang of Four' who were running the Cultural Revolution which had hounded him. Threats over loudspeakers frightened most away, but in the evening several hundred of those still in the square were arrested and later sent to prison camps.

It was the death of another moderate, Hú Yàobāng, which set off the demonstrations of 1989. Initially prevented from taking violent action by the visit of Mikhail Gorbachev, then leader of the Soviet Union, tanks and soldiers were sent into the square once he had departed on the night of 4 June, an incident known as Liù Sì ('Six Four') after the date. As with every other figure ever quoted about China, the numbers of those who died in the square vary from thousands (supporters of the movement) to none (the Chinese government—on the grounds that if any died it was in Cháng'ān Jiē which runs across the top of the square, along which many fled).

Tiān'ān Mén 天安门

Open 9–5.30; adm ¥30.

Since the source of all power in China once resided behind this gate, it is not surprising that the gate has become a symbol of power itself. Those who have replaced the emperors have felt the need to be seen here, and the gate appears on coins, official seals and insignia, and other symbols of power. It has a history similar to most of the wooden buildings in Běijīng (and indeed in China as a whole). Originally built in 1417, it burned down 1456, was rebuilt in 1651, and was set ablaze again in 1644 by the peasant armies who had ended the Míng as they were chased out by the Qīng. Rebuilt in 1651 it no doubt went through numerous further restorations up to a complete replacement of the roof in 1984.

Of the five arched bridges leading to it from the square, the middle one was for the emperor alone, as was the central door, where Máo's portrait now hangs. That to the right was for senior officials, and the left for military advisors. The way in is often blocked by Chinese trying to stick coins to the doors for luck, but beyond on the left is an office for tickets to climb the gate. You can look across the square (although this can be done considerably more cheaply from the Zhèngyáng Mén to the south) and pretend to be China's first president Yuán Shìkǎi reviewing celebrations of his appointment in 1912 (in those daysSun Yatsen's portrait hung where Máo's does now). Alternatively you can be Máo announcing the formation of the People's Republic in 1949 or reviewing the Red Guards who were to damage or destroy most of what you will want to see while in China. The last ticket is sold at 5pm.

Two dragon-carved pillars called *huábiǎo* stand in front of the gate, and two behind. These are often to be found at important sites (there are two at the Marco Polo bridge), and imperial residences. Topped either with a mythical animal called a *hòu*, or with Chinese lions, and with cloud-shaped projections, they are ornamental descendants of boards established by early emperors inviting criticism of and comment on their policies. Here tradition has it that the animals facing south on top of the outer pair have their mouths open, supposedly to report to the emperor any misdeeds of his officials when he returned. The inner pair face north to the interior of the palace with closed mouths to indicate the need for silence on the emperor's whereabouts when he left the palace incognito. It is said that one of the last Qīng emperors, Tóngzhì (reigned 1862–74) would go secretly to the pleasure quarters of the Chinese city, and later died of syphilis, which was indeed hushed up.

Rénmín Yīngxióng Jìniànbēi (Monument to the People's Heroes) 人民英雄纪念碑

One of the first acts of the communists following their occupation of Běijīng was to ordain the construction of this massive 38m-high monument, although it took until 1958 to complete.

Official policy says that the story of modern China is that of revolution and anti-imperialist struggle, but the government has had to distort history to find enough heroes to fill the monument's eight relief panels. One portrays the campaign to prevent the importation of opium in 1840, seen as marking the beginning of modern history. The destruction of opium at Canton was undertaken by anti-opium commissioner Lín Zéxú acting on the orders of the Qīng emperor, member of a 300-year-old foreign dynasty, and thus hardly a revolutionary or an anti-imperialist. Another panel celebrates the Tàipíng Rebellion which, while certainly anti-Manchu, lacked populist revolutionary qualities. The Tàipíng took control of large areas of China which they ruled from Nánjīng between 1853 and 1864. There was a pooling of funds and common granaries, but the movement was pseudo-Christian, formed by one Hóng Xiùquán, who believed himself to be the younger brother of Jesus Christ.

Zhōngguó Lìshǐ Bówùguǎn (History Museum)   中国历史博物馆

Open 8.30–4.30; closed Mon; adm ¥5.

The ticket office is on the right under the arches, and the last ticket is sold at 3.30pm.

This is the museum of China's greatest hits, so it is unfortunate the gloomy interior with its poorly lit exhibits makes you more conscious of China's impoverishment than of the splendours of its cultural heritage, and creates the kind of atmosphere that may have driven you out of museums as a child. China's rich cultural history results from the continuous occupation of one area by a single culture for longer than anywhere else in the world, and this is a large museum on two floors. Almost the only English labels are those dividing the building into sections that suit the government's interpretation, such as 'The Age of Slaves'. Silk Route items include terracotta warriors from Xī'ān, and tomb figurines from Xiányáng, but the star of the collection is a remarkable burial suit made from hundreds of pieces of jade linked together by gold wire (sometimes the only illuminated item in the whole museum). It is worth paying ¥5 just to see this, but those with limited tolerance of museums might otherwise save their energies for the Capital Museum in the Confucius Temple (*see* p.353).

The neighbouring **Museum of the Revolution** has often been closed for revision, historical 'truth' always being the handmaiden of political necessity. Its role has changed more recently to housing exhibitions giving distorted comment on contemporary events, such as the return of Hong Kong (1997) and Macao (1999) to Chinese sovereignty. It's not worth the effort unless you are a student of propaganda.

Máo Zhǔxí Jìniàntáng (Chairman Mao Memorial Hall)   毛主席纪念堂

Open Mon–Sat, 8.30–11.30 and Mon, Wed, Fri, 2–4; adm free.

The 'Máo-soleum' is grotesquely popular so go very early, and without bags or cameras (which are not allowed inside, although they may be deposited at huts on the east side of the building). It's a long slow shuffle to enter, which seems to turn into a brisker shuffle when you finally get to Máo, and you quickly find yourself out in the sunshine again with the souvenir vendors. Máo died in 1976, having caused, according to one estimate, nearly 38 million people to predecease him. Pumped with 22 litres of formaldehyde after his death, and now kept underground and refrigerated, he's hydraulically brought up for the adoration of the masses during opening hours.

Máo's current status is ambiguous. The oft-parroted official position is incomprehensible: Máo was 70 per cent right and 30 per cent wrong. This is the nearest that there will probably ever be to public criticism of the Communist Party's pin-up boy, a man whose social experiments caused so much misery, death and destruction. Today Máo, the great suppressor of all who disagreed with him, has become a useful tool for dissent against his heirs. In Máo's day there was little conventional crime, prostitution or drug use, and jobs were guaranteed for life. There are those who loudly praise these achievements, and express nostalgia for purer, simpler times: a safe way to criticize the current leaders for the rise in criminal activity, heroin addiction, unemployment, corruption and naked greed.

Zhèngyáng Mén, Zhèngyáng Mén Jiànlóu 正阳门，箭楼

Open 8–5.30 (last ticket 5pm);
adm ¥5, and open 8.30–4; adm ¥3, respectively.

The 'Straight Towards the Sun Gate', more commonly known as the Qián Mén or 'Front Gate', was once part of the Tartar City wall, the Jiànlóu (Arrow Tower) standing on a semi-circular projection, which had side gates for the common people and a central gate for the emperor's use only. The existing Qián Mén road loop was the result of Qián Mén Dàjiē splitting into two roads which ran round either side of the semi-circular enceinte, and turned into the lesser gates. The two towers still stand in line with Tiān'ān Mén and the key buildings of the Forbidden City, and formed one of three entrances from the Chinese City to the Tartar City. Any invader fighting his way into the interior courtyard would face fire from both towers while he attempted to break down the second gate. The originals were constructed in 1420 and 1439, but the outer Jiànlóu was burned down by the Boxers in 1900. The inner Zhèngyáng Mén was later accidentally reduced to ashes by the occupying foreign troops. Since the Qián Mén was the main gate of the Tartar City, the towers were promptly rebuilt, but increasing motor traffic led to adjustments in 1916, in which the outer enceinte and tower were completely torn down, and replaced by the modern tower, which even by the '30s was being used to display local handicrafts, as today. By that time, too, railway termini had been built by foreign companies on either side of Qián Mén, whose brick towers can still be identified.

Běijīng's gates were closed at dusk with the beating of gongs and loud cries from the guards to alert those who wanted to pass through. Alone amongst them, the Zhèngyáng Mén was re-opened for a few minutes after midnight, to allow officials to return from the theatres, tea houses and the more sensual pleasures of Dàzhàlan Jiē in time for the imperial audience, which would take place in the small hours of the morning.

These two towers are now the most easily accessible parts of the tiny remaining fragments of all Běijīng's walls. The Zhèngyáng Mén, which overlooks the Chairman Máo Memorial Hall, can be entered from its west or east end. Once on the plinth, an excellent exhibition in the ground floor of the tower has early photographs of Běijīng. The early 20th-century street life had a vigour which has only very recently returned. There are pictures of old shops in the Qián Mén area which are being torn down even as you look at the images, and of the old Qián Mén railway stations when just built. Other subjects include early ice skating, street festivals, major churches unsurrounded by modern clutter and before their conversion to other purposes, the broad boulevards without highrises alongside, and the post-Boxer Legation Quarter in its alien splendour. Most have English labels except those with controversial subjects, such as an opium den or prostitution. Unfortunately, just as there are modern counterparts of the street vendors and rickshaws shown in the photographs, so prostitution and drug use are now on the rise, and censorship won't make the problems go away. In general, though, these are pictures of the China many visitors would like to find

On three higher floors are the inevitable noisy shop and dusty displays on topics such as Chinese tea. For a further ¥3 you can emerge onto the highest balcony of the tower, but the view is much the same. To the north crowds stream from their view of Chairman Máo, and to the south there's a roofscape of Qián Mén *hútòngs*.

The 38m-high **Jiànlóu**, with its 94 windows for shooting arrows, gives you better views over Qián Mén but usually contains only exhibitions of paintings for sale, and it is not possible to climb higher. The eaves and narrow brick windows are the favoured homes of so many swallows you may wonder if it supplies the nests for the soup of local restaurants. (The genuine nest is actually that of a kind of sea swallow, and usually imported from Malaysia.) Enter from the south side, buying a ticket on the left and then walking around the left-hand side of the tower to find the stairs.

Legation Quarter

The area behind the Museum of History was the Legation Quarter. Having examined the photographs in the Zhèngyáng Mén, go for a stroll along Dōng Jiāomín Xiàng off the east side of Tiān'ān Mén Square. Some of the banks, hospitals and legation buildings still standing have become the residences of senior officials or been taken over by unnamable ministries, and the area is somewhat blank on modern maps.

Gùgōng Bówùyuàn (Palace Museum) 故宫博物院

Open 8.30–4.30; adm ¥55 ($7).
Your ¥55 is for a tào piào *('set' or all-inclusive ticket), which gives you free entry to the special exhibition halls (Clock and Watches, Jewellery, etc.), but the last ticket is sold at 3.30pm, which is also the time the special exhibition halls close, and no warning or refund will be given.*

Begin the day here: the light is better for photography, and seeing all the corners of the palace open to the public and admiring all the exhibitions can take several hours. It's also possible to pay a further ¥30 ($4) for an acoustiguide with up to two headsets. In English the voice is that of Roger Moore at his most lugubrious. The audio tour takes about 1½ hours, and the route follows the central axis of the palace (and of Běijīng) through the largest ceremonial halls; the audio equipment can be returned at the rear entrance. However, even if you take the tour you should return to the exhibition halls it does not cover, and to the smaller halls on either side which were offices and the residences of concubines.

Having passed through the Tiān'ān Mén don't be confused into buying a ticket at the first booth you see on the left, unless you want to climb it (*see* above). The ticket office for the Palace Museum is some way ahead, down a path lined with souvenir vendors, through another gate (the Duān Mén—Gate of Correct Deportment), and across the moat, to the right of the enormous Wǔ Mén (Meridian Gate), which is the main entrance. Guides will hassle you to take their services, but few have much grasp of their subject, and they are not recommended. One benefit of your ¥55 ticket (Chinese pay ¥20) is that you have an express entrance, the right-hand-most door of the Wǔ Mén, where you can also pick up your audio-tour, Forbidden City baseball cap, mug or CD-ROM. On the right just before entering there is a place to deposit bags, but this is not compulsory.

The Imperial Palace was originally constructed over a period of 14 years, and said to have involved 100,000 artisans (but this is the kind of round figure the Chinese love to use when they just mean 'many'). The palace was completed in 1420, and the Míng Emperor Yǒnglè moved here shortly afterwards, the first of 24 Míng and Qīng emperors to live in the palace up to 1924, kept secure by its 10m-high walls, surrounded by a moat. Wild figures of up to 9000 are given for the number of rooms in what is still the largest and best-preserved group of historic buildings in China, occupying approximately 1km by 0.75km.

Encouraged to visit China by the American archaeologist and art historian Langdon Warner, Sinophile George Kates lived in Běijīng between 1933 and 1941, in the style of a member of the Chinese scholarly class. While there, he was determined to see as much as possible of the Forbidden City, which then had only small areas open to the public, entered separately from the north and south ends.

> *It was a pursuit, almost a wooing; it carried me through the seasons; it became an absorption. After two or three years, some weed-overgrown courtyard, apparently destined to remain sealed for ever with a rusty Chinese padlock, through chinks in whose rotting doorways I had long peered in vain, would one day be wide open, while unconcerned masons went about some simple task. My reward would then be great.*

> George N. Kates, *The Years that Were Fat*, 1952

Kates eventually obtained a pass to use the two libraries then located in the palace, which allowed him a quarter of a mile further in than most visitors, he estimated. Few today will have the time that Kates had to devote to sleuthing, but by following him around the edges of courtyards, by peering through windows and loosely chained doors, and by taking every side turning that you find, you will discover dusty rooms, and overgrown peeling corners with crumbling stonework. Many freshly arrived in China will be shocked that such a major monument could be allowed to decay, but the heavily restored towering palaces and broad open spaces on the main axis, impressive as they are, are comparatively lacking in atmosphere. It is in the smaller, more human spaces of the residential quarters, a more luxurious version of the *hùtóng* of the outside world, that the ghosts of drowned concubines and Machiavellian eunuchs must reside.

Most of the palace's original treasures are long gone, however. In 1933 the Nationalist government took those neither previously looted nor removed by the departing imperial household, for safe-keeping in the new capital of Nánjīng. When, following their defeat in the civil war, the Nationalists retreated to Táiwān, the treasures retreated, too, and are now on display in possibly the world's finest museum of oriental art, in Táiběi (Taipei). What is now on display in the palace has mostly been gathered from other sources, and much is poorly displayed behind glass in dimly-lit interiors, obscured by smears from the noses of every visitor since the place was opened.

The palace itself is an architectural reference work, full of elements that you will see repeated in palace after palace, and in other imperial buildings on the Silk Routes.

Most of the halls have yellow **roof tiles**, a colour that could only be used with imperial consent. Green tiled buildings belonged to princes, although upon attaining maturity they were usually required to live elsewhere. The palace libraries had black tiled roofs, the colour being associated with water and seen as an aid to fire-fighting. Those buildings reserved for functionaries had the same grey tiles as buildings throughout the rest of China.

The huge wooden doors from the Tiān'ān Mén onwards are studded with large golden **knobs**. These have been likened to golden fish eyes, bowls, mushrooms and *mántou*, Chinese steamed bread rolls. One story has it that they were inspired by conches, symbols of tightness and security. The number of knobs, usually arranged nine by nine, seven by seven, or five by five, indicates the rank of the door.

Looking up you'll see **ceramic figures** on the spine and eaves of the roof of each building. The two beasts facing inwards along the spine of each roof are water dragons, supposed to resist the attacks of lightning and fire. A row of ceramic figures runs down the eaves: at the tip the figure of a man followed by a succession of animal figures. Traditionally the figure is the tyrannical prince of an early pre-Qín state who was overthrown by the combined forces of his neighbours and hanged from the roof of his palace. The people erected images of the prince on their roofs, mounted on a chicken unable to fly down to the ground below, and with a fearsome dragon (called a *chīwěn*) at his back to prevent escape over the roof. The other figures are said to date from the time of the Forbidden City's builder, Yǒnglè, and can include another lesser dragon, phoenix, lion, unicorn and celestial horse, with the *chīwěn* always last. Often the middle figures are all lions.

The large dog-like creatures to either side of the main entrances of major buildings throughout China are **guardian lions**. The beast on the right is male, his right paw placed on top of a ball, said either to represent the world, or to be full of milk supplied by the female. She sits on the left, a cub lying on its back beneath her left paw, apparently taking suck from one of her claws. Most of these lions are stone, but look out for a particularly fine bronze pair within the Forbidden City.

Several of the palaces sit atop marble plinths of up to three layers, with beautifully carved balustrades, and projecting water spouts carved in the shape of dragons. The main pillars are single tree trunks, heavily lacquered in red, the colour of prosperity, used also for the walls. All the important buildings on the main axis face south, giving them maximum sunshine. They were heated with braziers of charcoal, different quantities being allotted to members of the imperial household according to rank, the careless handling of which caused many fires.

The major halls run straight north and have brief introduction signs in English.

The **Wǔ Mén** or Meridian Gate where you buy your ticket is the main entrance to the Forbidden City proper, also called Five Phoenix Tower, with five pavilions on top. In the early days of the Palace Museum these were used as exhibition space, but the gate cannot be climbed now. Drums on top were struck when the emperors visited the ancestral temple (on the right as you walk up from Tiān'ān Mén and now converted into the Working People's Cultural Palace). Trips to the Temple of Heaven were marked with the striking of bells. Ceremonies performed here included the announcement of the calendar, and the punishment of lax or unfortunate officials, many of whom would die from their beatings. Of the five doors, the middle was for the emperor alone, the right for senior civil officials, the left for senior military advisers, and the outer gates for the few others allowed in.

Beyond the Meridian Gate, offices on the right originally housed the imperial secretariat and historians, and those on the left translators. Behind them were the only other two side gates, used by civil and military officials when coming for the emperor's pre-dawn audiences. Crossing a stream by one of five bridges matching the gate's five doors, you reach the **Tàihé Mén**, or Gate of Supreme Harmony. During the Míng dynasty this was used for imperial consultations, which under the Qīng were handled further in the city.

Beyond the gate is the largest courtyard in the palace, capable of holding a vast throng of officials and administrators on ceremonial occasions. The paving tiles are said to be 15 layers deep to prevent anyone tunnelling in from the outside. Storage areas run down either side, and around the courtyard are large vats for storing water to aid in fire fighting, which are numerous throughout the palace. Fires were not always accidental: the eunuchs were able to benefit by stealing the contents of buildings before setting them alight, and by fiddling the repair bills.

Across the courtyard is the first of three halls that form the palace's centrepiece, raised on triple-layer plinths, on which stand large, bronze incense burners. The **Tàihé Diàn** or Hall or Supreme Harmony was where the emperor sat to review the prostrations of his court at the celebrations of solstices, birthdays, the new year, etc. Behind it, the smaller **Zhōnghé Diàn** (Hall of Middle Harmony) was the antechamber where the emperor made his preparations for the ceremonies. The Emperor Guāngxù was arrested here on the orders of Dowager Empress Cíxǐ.

Behind this is the **Bǎohé Diàn** (Hall of Preserving Harmony), which was used to receive the princes of vassal states, on New Year's Eve for banquets for high officials, and for the highest level imperial civil service examinations, which began during the Táng and were held every three years right up until 1905. At the rear of the hall is the most magnificent of the marble ramps that run up the middle of the stairs to the palaces. These are carved with intertwined dragons of remarkable complexity, and this one is nearly 17m long and said to weigh as much as 200 tons. It was made in the Míng and brought to Běijīng on a combination of rollers and a path made from ice. It was recarved during the Qīng in 1761.

The buildings straddling the Bǎohé Diàn are often used for exhibitions of art from various dynasties, including ceramics, bronzes and stonework from other imperial palaces, as well as calligraphy, watercolours, Buddhist statuary and the ubiquitous terracottas from Xī'ān. These are not well signposted and are easily missed. Start on the right-hand (east) side as you face the hall. Making your way from room to room you pass from one courtyard to the next.

At this point the audio tour will take you straight on, but it's better to turn left (west) into an area of smaller halls that function as offices and residences, where the scale is more human. There is considerably more atmosphere in these labyrinthine corridors and interconnected courtyards which echo in a more luxurious and orderly fashion the *hútòng* (alleys) outside. Several residences have been refurnished roughly in the style of the late Qīng, but the original materials are mostly in Taipei. Amongst them, the **Yǎngxīn Diàn** (Hall of Mental Cultivation) was the main living and working space for the emperors, and has a magnificent ceiling sculpture of a dragon playing with a pearl. While some of the last Qīng emperors gave audiences to officials in this room, the Dowager Empress Cíxǐ controlled matters from behind a screen.

The End of the Emperors

Cíxǐ was born in 1835, the daughter of a minor Qīng official, and was one of 28 Manchu girls selected for the Emperor Xiánfēng (reigned 1851–61). She was made a concubine of the fifth rank at the age of 17, and later gave birth to a son, something the Empress Cí'ān had failed to do, and was raised to the second rank. Following the emperor's death in 1861, Cíxǐ, Cí'ān, and the dead emperor's brother perpetrated a coup which installed the six-year-old Tóngzhì emperor in 1862, and named Cíxǐ Dowager Empress. The two women both sat behind the screen, but Cí'ān died suddenly in 1881 after eating some cakes sent to her by Cíxǐ, who then became sole puppet-mistress. When Tóngzhì died in 1874, leaving her without a puppet, she manoeuvred her sister's child onto the throne in 1875 so that she could remain in power as regent. The new Emperor Guāngxù was only four years old. He came of age in 1890, and began to plan political reforms that might have saved the Qīng but which were resisted by Cíxǐ. Guāngxù planned to throw off Cíxǐ's control and asked Yuán Shìkǎi, head of a new Chinese army, to arrest her. Instead Yuán revealed his plans, and Guāngxù was imprisoned on an island in Zhōngnán Hǎi in 1898. Cíxǐ issued an edict claiming that he had asked her to take control, and put several of his advisors to death. Guāngxù met an early end from smallpox in 1908, which is also said to have taken place in this hall (although the Palace of Heavenly Purity is also named as the place). Shortly before she died, aged 73, Cíxǐ placed the three-year-old infant Pǔyí on the throne as Emperor Xūantǒng. His reign was short, and it was in the Hall of Mental Cultivation on 12 February 1912 that he issued an edict recognizing the Republic of China and abdicating. The republic's first president was Yuán Shìkǎi.

The emperor and his entourage continued to live in part of the Forbidden City until forced to leave in 1924, eventually taking refuge in the Japanese-occupied Manchuria, once the family's home region, where Pǔyí was made a puppet emperor of the imaginary state of Manchukuo by the Japanese.

After wandering around various smaller halls you can return to the rear of the Hall of Preserving Harmony, and continue north up the main axis. The **Qiánqīng Mén** (Gate of Heavenly Purity), leading to the inner court and built in 1429, was rebuilt in 1655, but it's said to have been the only building not to have been destroyed at least once since then, and thus the oldest in the whole palace. Sometimes used for giving audiences by the Míng emperors, the gate did not originally form such a solid block between the larger ceremonial halls and the inner palace. The connecting walls to either side were extended by Yuán Shìkǎi once the emperor had abdicated and been confined to the residential quarters.

Unlike its luckier neighbour, the **Qiánqīng Gōng** (Palace of Heavenly Purity), through the gate, is said to have burned down and been rebuilt at least three times. Living quarters for emperors during the Míng and early Qīng, it was later used as an audience chamber. The Emperor Guāngxù's secret discussions about reform are said to have taken place here, and it was here that he gave his fatal briefing to Yuán Shìkǎi. Foreign envoys were received here under the terms of the post-Boxer protocol. Being barbarians, they had not previously been allowed to sully the Imperial Palace, and had been received in a hall in what is now Zhōngnán Hǎi. The last emperor carried out all his ceremonial duties here and it was also the site of his wedding ceremony in December 1922. This and the following two halls have the same relationship as the three large 'Harmony' ceremonial halls but on a much smaller scale and in reverse order.

The **Jiāotài Diàn** (Hall of Union and Peace or Hall of Vigorous Fertility) was the throne room of the empresses, who held various celebrations here. The 25 jade seals of imperial authority were also kept here from the time of Qiánlóng onwards.

The **Kūnníng Gōng** (Palace of Earthly Tranquillity) was the living quarters of the Míng empresses. It was reconstructed and divided under the Qīng for use in Manchu shaman religious ceremonies.

At the **Kūnníng Mén** (Gate of Earthly Tranquillity) behind the Palace there's an exhibition of Qīng toys on the right. These are mostly musical boxes and automata. Some are exquisite steam-powered contraptions which much have been the most expensive of their time.

The rear courtyard is known as **Yùhuā Yuán** (Imperial Flower Garden) with small temples, ancient bamboo, and an enormous rock garden topped by a small pavilion. One pavilion on the west side was the home of the English tutor of the last emperor, Sir Reginald Johnston, and furnished with heavy Victorian furniture, Nottingham lace curtains, and Axminster carpets to make him comfortable. Johnston, an American woman who taught the empress, and the imperial couple, would have *al fresco* lunches here in the garden.

The **Shénwǔ Mén** (Gate of Military Prowess) is now the rear gate of the Forbidden City, and unlike the rest can be climbed. The well-put-together exhibition on top has photographs of less accessible parts of the complex, cutaway models showing the internal construction of some of the buildings, and a complete scale model allowing you to work out where you've just been, and just how much is still not open to the public. The palace wall stretches away, overgrown and inaccessible, to the corner arrow towers.

Returning south down the east side of the Earthly Tranquillity section, there are various exhibitions in halls formerly functioning as the residences of concubines, each group contained within its own walls.

The **Hall of Arts and Crafts** (Gōngyìměishù Guǎn) is in fact two halls with displays of finely carved jade, and two further halls to the east containing enamel ware.

The **Clock and Watch Exhibition Hall** (Zhōngbiǎo Guǎn, formerly the Palace of Eternal Harmony) contains 185 timepieces of which 51 are Chinese and 83 British, mostly 18th century, with US and French contributions. Some of the emperors were avid collectors (at one point a clock factory was set up in the palace), and many of the clocks were gifts from those hoping to gain favour at court. While the Chinese were probably the inventors of the world's first escapement mechanism, during their self-imposed isolation they slipped behind Western technology. The clocks are now well lit and displayed, and a video shows them in operation, many being more automaton than clock. Perhaps the most impressive is a British clock with the figure of a man holding a calligraphy brush, who writes eight characters meaning 'People come from various places to pay their respects to the emperor'. Another clock is towed in a circle by an exquisite miniature mechanical elephant, which waves its trunk and rolls its eyes. Some clocks are miniature palaces or pagodas of silver, gold, enamel and precious stones.

Tào piào or no, there is a separate charge of ¥2 for compulsory polystyrene overshoes supposedly to protect the floor (and which you can keep for use at the Hall of Jewellery where the same rule applies). Whether the overshoes have any real success in protecting the bricks is moot, since the staff are only interested in collecting the money and not in making visitors wear them, and many just carry the shoes to show they have paid.

Further to the south and east are the Treasure Halls, labelled **Hall of Jewellery** (Zhēnbǎoguǎn), occupying a number of halls constructed for the retirement of the Qiánlóng Emperor (reigned 1736–95) who abdicated at the age of 85 in favour of his son. If he had reigned one more year he would have been on the throne as long as his grandfather, Kāngxī, but he thought this would show disrespect. These buildings have suitable names such as Hall of Imperial Zenith and Palace of Peaceful Old Age, but Qiánlóng did not have long to enjoy them, dying four years later. They remained unused for 100 years until Cíxǐ nominally retired to them when Guāngxù reached his majority in 1899. It was here, too, that her body rested for a year after her death, awaiting an auspicious burial date.

On the way in you pass the **Jiǔlóngbì** or Nine Dragon Screen, 6m high and 31m long, origi- nally built in 1773. The dragons writhe in relief from an assemblage of large tiles, one of which is said to be a wooden copy hurriedly created to replace a tile broken during assembly, but which could not be replaced before inspection. There's another nine dragon screen in Běihǎi Gōngyuán, and one in Dàtóng.

The two jewellery halls have ornate swords, knives, saddles, costume, musical instruments, miniature jewelled pagodas, imperial seals, perfume holders, and other extravagant items, including an extraordinary woven ivory mat. Three halls beyond these to the north contain other treasures but are also worth inspecting in their own right, and are preserved much as they were in Qiánlóng's day. The first has magnificently carved doors on either side of its inte- rior, and the second houses two enormous pieces of jade, one carved into a dragon-covered bowl, the other into a mountain scene nearly 2m high. Intricate screen doors with inset painted panels run round the interior on two levels. Behind the third hall lies an area of several small courtyards, overgrown and unrestored, where the visitor can search out details such as a moon gate (circular entranceway) inset with mother of pearl. On the left (west) side is the **Níngshòu Gōng Huāyuán** (Flower Garden of the Palace of Peaceful Old Age), with paths winding between small, secluded pavilions, trees, and rockeries—one of the most pleasant areas of the entire complex. One of the pavilions contains a snaking water channel for floating wine cups, where the retired emperor played literary drinking games.

It was in these halls that the hurried conferences of Cíxǐ and her court took place as the foreign armies approached Běijīng during the Boxer Rebellion of 1900. At the rear (north) side is the gate she used to flee her quarters along with the Emperor Guāngxù, called the Zhēnshùn Mén (Gate of Faithful Obedience).

Guāngxù's wedding, arranged by Cíxǐ, was said, despite the decayed state of the dynasty, to have cost 5.5 million taels of silver (1 tael = 38g). Nevertheless, Guāngxù is said to have slept with his wife only once, prefering a concubine called the Zhēnfēi, usually known as the Pearl Concubine. As Cíxǐ was leaving for Xī'ān, the Zhēnfēi came to protest. There are many versions of what happened next. The official version has her a martyr to her comparatively enlightened political views, and her support of the emperor's moves for reform. Other accounts simply have her demanding to be taken with the emperor although the other concu- bines were being left behind. Cíxǐ had her thrown down the well here, perhaps in front of the horrified emperor (a not unusual end for troublesome concubines). While the terms of reparations were being worked out with foreign powers during the following months, Cíxǐ issued a decree praising the Zhēnfēi for her loyalty in committing suicide when unable to catch up with the departing court.

Behind the Zhēnshùn Mén a passage leads west to the main exit on the north side, and you can cross the road to see the Jǐngshān Gōngyuán. Alternatively you can return to the entrance to this section at the Nine Dragon Screen and leave the palace through the Tiān'ān Mén.

Jǐngshān Gōngyuán
Open 6am–9pm; adm ¥0.30.

景山公园

'Prospect Park' is directly behind the Forbidden City's rear entrance, and reached by bus 5 from Qián Mén, but for those who haven't been exhausted by traversing the vast interior of the palace it's simpler to cross to the park directly from there. It can also be seen first, the palace being entered by the rear gate. Until this century the two were connected directly to the palace, but the walls were pulled down and a road driven through during the Nationalist period.

Different stories have the hill either constructed on a base of coal or used as a storage place for it, and it is often known as Méi Shān, or Coal Hill. Built by the Míng Emperor Yǒnglè (reigned 1403–24), it is mostly made from the earth dug out to make the palace's moat. It's topped by five pavilions which originally date from 1750, and which once held Buddha statues which were all either looted or destroyed in 1900.

A variety of paths climb the green and shady hillside, and the central pavilion at the top gives views south over the yellow roofscape of the Forbidden City, and to Běi Hǎi ('North Sea', actually a lake) with its stupa to the west. Between the two stands Zhōngnán Hǎi ('Middle and South Seas'), where the Chinese leaders, although so much loved by the people, have always felt it necessary to lock themselves safely away. Originally of a piece with Běi Hǎi, and within the walls of the Imperial City, the lakes were the playground of Liáo, Jīn, Yuán, Míng and Qīng dynasty emperors. Now the southern two lakes and their pavilions are separated by a road and high walls, and are the closely guarded headquarters of the Central Committee of the Chinese Communist Party, and the State Council of the People's Republic of China.

The hall below on the north side once housed portraits of the emperors, and is now part of the Běijīng's Children's Palace. Its neighbour to the east is where the bodies of the emperors lay in state while final preparations were made for their burial.

On the east side of the hill's base can be found the stump of a locust tree (a *sophora, cassia,* or *acacia,* depending on whose view you take, also known as a scholar tree). The last Míng emperor, Chóngzhēn, hanged himself here using his own belt on 25 April 1644 as rebel peasants took over Běijīng, and shortly before they were evicted again by the Qīng armies arriving from Manchuria. During the Qīng dynasty the tree was treated like a criminal since it had been an accessory to the murder of an emperor, and a large iron chain was placed around it. It was known as the *zuì huái*—'guilty *sophora*'. (One of the gates at the rear of the palace also used to carry a wooden scaffold resembling a cangue, the heavy board placed around the necks of certain criminals—*see* 'The Book Factory' pp.296–9—a punishment for having allowed the emperor to leave to go to his death.) The chain is said to have been removed in the looting following the Boxer Rebellion, but the tree survived until the Cultural Revolution when it was hacked to pieces, only the stunted stump remaining. A new tree was planted in 1981, although how this is supposed to replace the historical authenticity of the original is not clear.

Tiāntán Gōngyuán (Temple of Heaven Park)

天坛公园

Open April–Sept, 6am–10pm; Oct–Mar, 6am–9pm; adm ¥30 ($4).

Foreigners are not allowed to buy the ticket for the park entrance only (*mén piào*, ¥0.50), but the ¥30 all-inclusive ticket (*tào piào*) allows access to all the halls without further charge. The park can be entered from the north (trolleybus 106 from Dōngdān Běidàjiē or Běijīng Nán Zhàn—stop Tiāntán Běi Mén), west (bus 17 from the west side of Qián Mén, also the 2 and the 20—stop Tiāntán), or south sides (bicycle from the southern budget accommodation, with care).

Tiāntán was constructed at the same period as the Forbidden City by the Míng Emperor Yǒnglè and completed in around 1420. Tiāntán actually means 'Altar of Heaven', and it was the site of the emperors' winter solstice sacrifices and prayers for a good harvest, and as much off-limits to ordinary Chinese as the Forbidden City itself. Now it's a recreational facility for the local *lǎobǎixìng* ('old hundred names'—ordinary people) who pay ¥0.50 to come in and fly kites, practise *tàijíquán* and martial arts, sing opera, and play traditional musical instruments—activities which tend to add to the attraction for the foreign visitor. The buildings, altars and enclosures have the themes of earth, signified by square shapes, and heaven, signified by round ones. The outer wall of Tiāntán Gōngyuán is square on the south side and rounded on the north, and some of the interior enclosures follow the same plan.

Entering from the north, the first major building is the perfectly circular **Qínián Diàn** (Hall of Prayer for Good Harvests) which is possibly the most beautiful ancient building in Běijīng. It is painted in blue, green and gold, its ground floor surrounded by red latticed doors The triple-layered roofs are a deep blue, reflecting its heavenly focus, and topped with a large gold knob. It stands on a triple-layered marble terrace, and is heavily decorated both internally and externally, a superb dragon-phoenix relief in the centre of the ceiling being mirrored by a natural marble circular slab on the floor. The hall is entirely constructed of wood without the use of nails, and its roof is supported by 28 pillars, including four of particularly massive girth, all made from single tree trunks. It was struck by lightning and burned down in 1889, and has been restored several times following its rebuild. The hall was used for displaying the tablets of the emperor's ancestors, and for ceremonies before he proceeded to the sacrificial altar. Only swallows enter now, and perform acrobatics around the pillars of the interior.

Small halls on the east and west sides of the compound were once used for the worship of various weather-influencing gods, but now the one to the east houses a small exhibition of Chinese traditional musical instruments, and a model of a Chinese orchestra in full swing with recorded accompaniment. The west one is a gift shop.

Just south of here a path leads to the west and to the **Zhāi Gōng** or Palace of Abstinence, where the emperor, having fasted for three days, spent the night before the ceremonial sacrifice. The palace is like a Forbidden City in miniature, walled and moated (although the moat is now dry), and inside you can see a model of an emperor duly abstaining. In the northeast corner there is a two-storey bell tower, built in 1742, and you can pay ¥1 to climb the short but very narrow staircase and strike the bell.

Returning to the Hall of Prayer for Good Harvests, a broad, raised walk leads south to the second main group of buildings. The **Huángqióngyǔ** (Imperial Vault of Heaven), a lower, round building used for storing material used in the ceremony, is enclosed in a perfectly circular wall. This is said to function in the same way as the Whispering Gallery at St Paul's, London, or that at the Duomo in Florence, reflecting the sound of words spoken near the wall to listeners also near it but some distance away or even on the opposite side of the enclosure. Visitors who have been a few days in China may already be wondering whether there is such a person as a quiet Chinese, and it is impossible to find the conditions to test the effect. Once they pressed their ears against the wall itself, but are now prevented from doing so by a fence. Instead they shout loudly enough at it to ensure that their voices are heard on the other side of Běijīng, let alone the other side of the compound.

Leading from the base of the stairs to the hall is a row of three stones. To stand on one and clap produces the expected single echo, but to repeat the action on the second produces two echoes, and the third three. The compound is full day-long of the sound of desultory applause as many experiment, and none gives way to the others.

The final major feature is the **Huán Qiū** (usually known as the Circular Mound, although the *huán* character is not the one for *ring*, but for *mediate*). This, not the visitor-attracting Hall of Prayer, was the focus of the site, where the complicated three-part ceremony of supplication took place, culminating with the burning of a bullock killed earlier. The multiple-layered round altar is enclosed in both round and square walls, symbolizing the earth's appeal to heaven. Buildings to the east held the sacrificial implements, the tents that covered the ceremony itself, and were where the butchering of the animal took place.

Gǔ Guānxiàngtái (Old Observatory) 古观象台

Open 9–11.30 and 1–4.30; closed Mon and Tues; adm ¥10 ($1.25).

Chinese observations of the heavens go back as far as 1300 BC, and recordings of supernovae and the passage of Halley's Comet are still being used in astronomical research today. Accurate clocks, essential for proper astronomical and calendrical calculation, were also invented in China, the escapement mechanism being known from at least the 8th century AD. The method of giving co-ordinates to stars universally used today is one invented by the Chinese, which superseded in the West a different technique invented by the ancient Greeks. Nevertheless, by the end of the Míng the Chinese were still unable accurately to reconcile the 29.5 day lunar month, and the 365.25-day solar year. The calendar was a mess, and help was needed from more accurate Western instruments and more advanced mathematics.

The observatory can claim to be one of the oldest in the world, having been established around 1279–96 during the Mongol Yuán dynasty, nearly 300 years before Europe was to have a similar institution, using instruments brought to the city during the Jīn dynasty (1115–1234). When the Míng established their capital in Nánjīng in 1368 the instruments went there, but when the Emperor Yǒnglè returned the capital to Běijīng, he thought it would be disrespectful to the first emperor, buried in Nánjīng, to bring the instruments back. He therefore had copies of some of them made in wood, which then served as the models for new bronze versions. The current observatory is of approximately the same size and scale as a building erected on the same or nearly the same site during the Míng, probably around 1522.

Matteo Ricci (1552–1610) was the first Jesuit to receive permission to reside in Běijīng. Sympathetic to Chinese civilization, he acquired a detailed knowledge of classical and spoken Chinese, and impressed the emperor and Chinese intellectuals with his prodigious memory and scientific skills. He won imperial favour through his map-making and clock-regulating, and imported Western clocks and other high-tech items to use as gifts, and to get him past hostile eunuchs. Another Jesuit, Adam Schall von Bell, correctly predicted the 1624 solar eclipse, and was appointed to the Board for Calendar Regulation. Although the Qīng deposed the Míng in 1644, Schall remained in favour, and was appointed president of the Board by the first Qīng emperor.

Kāngxī, the second Qīng emperor (reigned 1661–1722), having been taught by Schall, appointed another Jesuit, Ferdinand Verbiest, to assist in reforming the calendar. According to some accounts, when the matter was debated before the emperor by ministers and princes, the Manchus were in favour of Verbiest, while the Chinese officials would rather have had a faulty calendar than one tainted by foreigners (an argument which must have needed tactful phrasing to present to the foreign Manchus). To correct the calendar, Verbiest had to cut out a month, which provoked widespread anti-foreign feeling at its supposed theft.

Verbiest was in charge of the Imperial Astronomical Bureau from 1662 to 1722, and super-vised the construction of a collection of Western measuring instruments, which remained with their Chinese counterparts at the observatory until after the Boxer Rebellion of 1900. Following the occupation of Běijīng by foreign powers, the French suddenly remembered that some of the instruments had been given to China by Louis XIV, and proposed to take them away as spoils of war. The Germans objected, since the observatory was in the 'German sector', and insisted that the instruments belonged to them. In fact Louis had donated one, an altazimuth, but in the end five went to the French Legation until the French were shamed into returning them in 1902, and six went for display in Potsdam, half-scale copies having been made and left in their place. One minor benefit to China of the Treaty of Versailles which marked the end of the First World War was the instruments' return in 1921. Half of them were to make yet another journey when they were removed to Nánjīng by the Nationalists in 1933 to prevent them from falling into the hands of the Japanese. Although Nánjīng itself was later overrun, they are still on display there.

The remaining instruments stand on a 17m-high plinth once reachable by a link from the now-vanished Tartar City wall. The building is now entered at ground level, and a right turn brings you to a courtyard with reproductions of early instruments. The first hall on the right has a well-displayed exhibition of early Chinese astronomical observation with English explanations. The instrument platform is reached by a brick staircase opposite the courtyard. Eight of the massive bronze instruments remain, up to 2m in diameter, including an ecliptic armilla, altaz-imuth, quadrant, azimuth theodolite, sextant and equatorial armilla. Each has an explanation of its purpose in English, and all are impressive due both to their size and decoration, with supporting struts often cast as writhing dragons. A small garden at the rear contains what may be one of the half-scale instruments made by the Germans.

Yōnghé Gōng (Lama Temple)

Open 9–4.30; adm ¥10 ($1.25).

雍和宫

The 116 bus runs straight north from the northeast corner of Tiāntán Gōngyuán through Chóngwén Mén. Get off at the stop called Yōnghé Gōng in Yōnghé Gōng Dàjiē. It's better if possible to take the metro to Yōnghé Gōng. Leave by the south exit and turn left, then immediately left, and the entrance is about 200m further. Bus 13 runs from Xīsì Dàjiē, north of Xīdān. Get off at stop no.21.

Although usually known as the Lama Temple, Yōnghé Gōng means 'The Palace of Peace and Harmony', and was built during the reign of the Qīng Emperor Kāngxī in 1694 as the residence of his fourth son, who later became the third Qīng emperor to rule from Běijīng (Yōngzhèng—reigned 1723–35). The palace was converted to a lamasery during the reign of Qiánlóng in 1744. It now functions partly as a genuine place of worship and teaching for around 80 monks and innumerable visitors, and partly as a vehicle for Chinese propaganda concerning Tibet.

Their former role as an imperial residence has left the main halls of the Lama Temple with the same yellow roofs as the Imperial Palace, and with the same figures on the eaves. Running south to north, these increase in size and importance, ending with the towering and impressive Wànfú Gé (Pavilion of Ten Thousand Fortunes), with its aerial passages to side halls.

Passing throught the first courtyard with its drum tower, bell tower and stelae pavilions, you reach the Tiānwáng Diàn (Hall of the Heavenly Kings) with the four statues found at all Chinese Buddhist and Lamaist temples. The next courtyard is bordered with halls for teaching various disciplines such as mathematics, plus halls for exoteric (public) doctrines, teachers originally coming from an inner circle of adepts. As elsewhere Esoteric Buddhism is represented by statues of larger males figures enjoying sexual pleasure with smaller female ones, although due to official prudery these are usually draped. The courtyard contains a substantial and ornate incense burner, dating from 1747, and a pavilion housing a single four-language stele carved with Qiánlóng's views on Buddhism, its Chinese characters in his handwriting.

Ahead is the Yōnghé Gōng after which the whole temple is now known, with bronze and gold statues of the past, present (Sakyamuni, in the middle), and future Buddhas, along with two of Sakyamuni's favourite students and the 18 *luóhàn* (saints).

Beyond is the Yǒngyòu Diàn (Hall of Eternal Blessing) with further figures, and through that the main hall of the complex, the Fǎlún Diàn (Hall of the Wheel of Law). Despite the constant chatter of visitors, this cross-shaped hall is gloomily atmospheric, lined with racks of cloth-wrapped religious texts, and dominated by a 6m-high bronze of Tsongkhapa (Zōngkābā), the founder of the 'Yellow Hat' sect of reformed lamaism to which this temple belongs. Closer examination of the walls reveals their covering of painted scenes, while rows of kneeling places lit by Ikea-style desk lamps shows the hall's continuing purpose as a place of teaching. At the rear behind Tsongkhapa is an elaborate carving, 'The Mountain of the 500 Arhats'.

The smaller halls to the left and right of the Yǒngyòu Diàn are entered from the rear, and contain exhibitions which require a separate ticket (¥3 for the two). The left (west) side hall contains Qiánlóng's court dress and crown, and, perhaps inappropriately for a Buddhist temple, the gun and sword he used when out hunting. Other Buddhist ceremonial items include masks used in religious dances, and an enormous rosary with beads the size of cricket balls or softballs. The hall on the east side is named after the Panchen Lama, the most senior reincarnation after the Dalai Lama, whose last adult version resided in Běijīng and did much as he was told. The hall contains an exhibition about Tibetan Buddhism, whose aim is to show, falsely, that Tibet has always been subservient to China, and suggesting that Běijīng always authorized the appointment of the new Dalai Lama and other important reincarnations. There are paintings and photographs of all of the Dalai and Panchen lamas and of other important monasteries, as well as gold and bronze statuary and other valuable and beautiful religious items.

The rearmost hall accessible to the public is the three-storey Wànfú Gé (Pavilion of Ten Thousand Fortunes) with flying buttress-like foot passages forming connections to two side halls. It contains a serene 26m-high Maitreya (future) Buddha statue carved from a single white sandalwood trunk and transported all the way from Tibet as a gift to Qiánlóng from the seventh Dalai Lama. Its copper-coloured bulk is hung with scarves of respect, and enclosed by three stories of galleries with many more statues. For once in China fact replaces hyperbole— there is an incongruous testament to the statue's uniqueness in a brass reproduction of a *Guinness Book of Records* certificate displayed outside.

Shǒudū Bówùguǎn (Capital Museum and Confucius Temple)   首都博物馆

Open 8–5; adm ¥10 ($1.25).

The temple is about 60m down Guózǐjiān Jiē (Imperial College Street), a turning off Yōnghé Gōng Dàjiē almost opposite the entrance to the Lama Temple.

Confucius having until recently been one of the Communist Party's *bêtes noires*, the Kǒng Miào (Temple of Confucius) is more usually known as the Capital Museum. A fine collection of locally discovered artefacts housed in buildings on the right-hand (east) side.

This relatively little-visited temple group is pleasantly quiet compared to the neighbouring Lama Temple. Around the first courtyard stand 198 stelae bearing the names of all those who passed the highest level triennial civil service exam. Altogether the stelae carry 51,624 names, places of origin, and position numbers, from the Yuán, Míng and Qīng dynasties. The Yuán, like the later Qīng, learned that to conquer China on horseback was one thing, but it could not be governed without adopting Chinese ways, and using Chinese administrative skills. It was a Mongol emperor who in 1307 conferred on Confucius the title 'Sage of Great Accomplishment', the highest title he was ever awarded although Confucius (551–479 BC) had been dead for nearly 1800 years. It was the Mongols, too, who built the original temple in the 13th century, but the stelae listing the graduates of their day were removed and buried by the Míng, who probably considered that examinations held under barbarian rulers did not count. These were rediscovered and re-erected in the time of the Qīng Emperor Kāngxī, who also restored the buildings in 1689. Another restoration was carried out under Qiánlóng, who replaced the roofs with imperial yellow tiles.

Various pavilions in the second courtyard are in a poor state of repair and roughly bricked up, their roofs more heavily overgrown with grasses than most other temples. Statues of Confucius and his principle commentators stand around, with cypress trees of considerable antiquity, one nearly 700 years old.

Much of the site, formerly connected to the Imperial College to the west, is no longer open to the public. The emperor would come annually to the college to expound the classics to the scholars, and his representatives would come several times a year to the temple for ceremonies in honour of Confucius, especially on the sage's birthday. The main hall of the temple, the **Dàchéng Diàn** (Hall of Great Perfection) stands on a broad terrace and contains a central shrine to Confucius, surrounded by a think-tank of tributes to 60 top scholars. The hall also contains a number of Chinese classical musical instruments (and often someone playing them), as well as incense burners and other artefacts.

A passage at the rear left-hand corner of the compound gives access to the **Qiánlóng Stone Scriptures**, similar to Xī'ān's Forest of Stelae, with the stones arranged in five long rows in a long shed which nevertheless has a certain library-like quality. These are the classics produced by Confucius and his students during the Spring and Autumn period (770–475 BC) and other texts which were the subjects of the imperial examinations. The stones originate from the desire of one man to produce a perfect copy of these classics, amounting to some 630,000 characters, which he undertook between 1726 and 1738. His finished version was presented to Qiánlóng who later had them thoroughly proofread and caused them to be carved on stelae in around 1790. 189 stelae contain the text and the 190th is a copy of the emperor's order that the work be undertaken. The stones were relocated from the neighbouring Imperial College and restored in 1988.

The buildings on the east of the main hall house the **Capital Museum**, an exhibition of the history of Běijīng from Paleolithic times onwards, well lit and presented, and with English introductions. Běijīng may not have become China's major capital until the time of the Mongols, but many earlier dynasties left their mark in the form of funerary objects, coin and seals, Buddhist devotional objects, and fine ceramics. The exhibition ends with copies of ancient maps and modern aerial photographs of the city.

Civil Service Examinations

The Chinese are generally credited with the invention of a meritocratic civil service with entrance based on examination. Lists of successful candidates have survived from as early as 165 BC, and the Chinese model is thought to have led to the introduction of civil service exams in Britain in the 19th century, where senior civil servants are still labelled 'Mandarins', and later in the U.S. The examination system would collapse when the country did, but revived under the Táng it ran almost continuously in different forms until abolished by decree in 1905. At its best it allowed candidates from families without *guānxī* (connections or influence) to compete fairly with those more powerful, but for much of the time candidates' names were left on their papers, and patronage was as important as examination success. Given the years and sometimes decades of study necessary, access remained open only to those families who could afford to pay to support a candidate's studies. By the Míng and Qīng the requirements of the examinations were driving the entire education system. Success guaranteed social advancement, employment as an official, and the resulting opportunities for enrichment through means both legitimate and corrupt.

It was first necessary to pass an examination at district level, graduates of which were exempt from enforced labour (such as on containing the Yellow River) and corporal punishment. They also qualified to take the triennial examinations at the provincial capital. Success here led to the triennial metropolitan examination in Běijīng, the results of which were confirmed by an examination in the Imperial Palace itself. In later years other intermediate qualifying examinations were added, as well as separate tests for military candidates.

Papers involved writing commentaries on the Confucian classics, literary composition, and the drafting of memorials in favour of a particular policy, supported by quotations from the classics. In later times handwriting was also taken into account, and to write a single character incorrectly could be fatal to a candidate's chances. They were put into cells at special locked examination halls for up to three days at a time, and it was widely believed that their past misdeeds would come back to haunt them, often in the form of the ghosts of those they had harmed. The stress was sometimes too much, and candidates would run mad, or be found hanging in their cells.

In a continuing backwards march from the anti-intellectual, anti-specialist stance of the Máo years, the government has announced that by the year 2000 all civil servants will once again be recruited by examination, although it's probably fair to say that a knowledge of Confucius is less likely to be of assistance than a willingness to toe the party line. New graduates will probably be more concerned to see their names written on pay cheques than on stelae.

Běi Hǎi Gōngyuán (Běi Hǎi Park)   北海公园

Park open 6–9; adm ¥0.50; halls and temples open 9–5; adm ¥10 ($1.25).

Non-Chinese-speaking foreigners may find it difficult to buy the park entrance ticket (*mén piào*), as opposed to the all-inclusive ticket (*tài piào*). The south entrance to the park is a short walk west of Jǐngshān Gōngyuán, and just northwest of the Forbidden City.

This lake called the 'North Sea' was first dug out and the artificial hills created during the Tartar Jīn dynasty in about 1179, and remodelled during the Yuán by Khubilai (the white dagoba is mentioned by Polo). Extensive buildings were added by the Míng Emperor Yǒnglè during Běijīng's overall redesign. Běi Hǎi is now a very popular park for local people, with boating activities and radio-controlled model speedboats on the lake. It is not a place for quiet contemplation.

Inside the south entrance and just to the left, the **Tuánchéng** (Round City), in a mixed state of repair, is a raised circular terrace, topped with several small buildings. A pavilion contains an enormous jade urn, claimed to weigh 3500 kilos, and carved with sea monsters on the outside and poetry on the inside. Used as a wine jar by Khubilai Khan, it was somehow purged during the Míng, and ended up as a pickling vat. Rediscovered and rehabilitated by Qiánlóng who bought it for 1000 ounces of silver, it was placed in its present position in 1749. Also worth noting is the **Chéngguāng Diàn** (Hall for Receiving Light), which houses a 1.5m-high statue of Buddha, made from 'white jade' and which originated in Burma. There are several cypresses around the City thought to be as much as 800 years old.

The striking white, flask-shaped dagoba, visible from various high points around Běijīng, stands atop an island reached by a bridge from near the south entrance. A steep climb through the halls of the **Yǒng'ān Sì** (Temple of Eternal Peace) leads to the dagoba, which was originally built in 1651 and twice reconstructed following earthquake damage. The temple buildings have bronze and wooden statues of Buddhas, Bodhisattvas, Arhats, Panchen and Dalai Lamas, and the guardian deity of Běijīng (who clearly hasn't been doing much of a job).

The north shore of the lake has further temples, and Běijīng's second Nine Dragon Screen (the other is in the Forbidden City).

Yíhé Yuán (Summer Palace)   颐和园

Open daylight hours, adm ¥35 ($4.50).

The Summer Palace is about 10km northwest of central Běijīng, and most easily reached by minibus from outside the Bank of China in Xī Jiāomín Xiàng, just off the west side of Tiān'ān Mén Square (¥6).

Not all of the individual museums, temples, and halls are included in the comparatively over-priced *tào piào*, and all have shorter opening hours than the park itself.

Sometimes known as the 'New Summer Palace', this collection of halls, pavilions and temples beside the large Kūnmíng Hú (lake), overlooked by Wànshòu Shān (Longevity Hill), was a favourite haunt of the Dowager Empress Cíxǐ, who preferred it to the Forbidden City, and named it Yíhé Yuán (roughly 'Garden of Health and Harmony'), following reconstruction in 1888. Although the gardens had long existed, and major landscaping and construction work had been undertaken by the indefatigable Qiánlóng in 1751, it was a lesser, subsidiary site, compared to the Yuánmíng Yuán (Garden of Perfect Brightness) which stretches to the north-east. Both were destroyed by British and French troops during the occupation of Běijīng in 1860, but the 'old' palace went swiftly back under the plough, and there are now only a few remains of what George Kates called 'Européenerie'—neo-Baroque buildings of stone and Chinese glazed tile, built by the Jesuits at the request of Qiánlóng.

Inexcusable as it was, the troops' destruction of the Summer Palace on the orders of Lord Elgin was intended to punish the dynasty for failing to adhere to its treaties. It was China as a

whole that suffered as Cíxǐ spent vast amounts of her country's limited funds to rebuild the southwestern section where destruction had been less complete, including money that should have been spent on a modern navy. What little conscience she had led her to open a token school for naval officers, and to build her most lasting monument, the **Marble Boat**. From the entrance to the east, this is reached by following the shore north and west through and past many halls and pavilions and along the **Long Corridor**, more than 700m of it, and every beam painted with a landscape. The base of the boat had already been carved from an offshore rock, and Cíxǐ added its ornate marble superstructure.

South of the entrance is the graceful **Seventeen Arch Bridge**, which crosses to a small island. The total area of the park and lake is about 290 hectares, and it is possible to spend several hours of climbing and walking around the lake. Various ferries cross from one point to another (double fare for foreigners), and near the entrance there is a maelstrom of pedalos and other leisure craft, ice-cream stalls and other amusements. Walking west from the Marble Boat or south from the Seventeen Arch Bridge will bring you before long to quieter areas and lesser lakes. A full circumnavigation is possible, but allow about half a day.

Around Běijīng

The Great Wall (Wànlǐ Cháng Chéng) 万里长城

The Great Wall was begun in the Warring States period (475–221 BC) as a series of earthworks erected by individual kingdoms as a defence against each other as well as from invasions from the north. The Qín (221–207 BC) unified them into a single coordinated system at the time of a particularly dangerous confederation of Xiōngnú tribes. Some Chinese histories claim that a fifth of the population, one million people, were involuntarily involved in its construction. The success of the wall depended upon large quantities of manpower, which was not always available either under the Qín or succeeding dynasties. The wall was extended under the Hàn (206 BC–AD 220), some sections reaching as far as Xīnjiāng, and was extensively repaired under the Suí (AD 589–618). The familiar, stone-clad, crenellated wall dates only from the Míng (1368–1644) whose extensive repairs and reinforcements also involved a partial rerouting. The length of the Great Wall is almost impossible to calculate. Figures from 2400km to 5000km are quoted for the Míng wall, which runs from Shānhǎiguān in the east to Jiāyùguān in the west, crossing the Yellow River several times. The higher estimate is perhaps due to an overly literal translation of *Wànlǐ*, '10,000 *lǐ*', where a *lǐ* is about 0.5km, although *wàn* is often just a Chinese way of saying 'rather a lot'. In some areas there are two or even three overlapping walls, and many sections lie separate and disconnected from the main route. One Great Wall ticket has a claim of 6000km.

The Míng wall has an average height of 8m and an average width of 6m, is made of rubble and earth clad with stone, and topped with brick, broken up by brick watchtowers, about 12m square and 12m high. Most of it is completely dilapidated with little more than the core remaining, peasants having carted off the stone for their own houses. Several sections near Běijīng have been completely restored, and several more are due to open during the life of this book.

Almost every hotel in Běijīng offers tours to one Great Wall destination or another. This often only means finding a taxi for you and adding a large mark-up, although at some you may arrange a minibus for a group of hotel guests with an English-speaking guide, and provide lunch. Typical charges are around ¥300 ($36) per person to the nearest site at Bādálǐng, less as numbers increase.

It is ironic that the Wall, once used to keep barbarians out, is now used to draw them into China. Foreign money has been donated to help repair the Wall, too, and for once the Chinese acknowledge this with plaques at various sites.

On the Wall there is little protection from sun or wind, so dress appropriately, and take suntan lotion and drinking water.

Bādálǐng   八达岭长城
Adm ¥30 ($4) or ¥35 ($4.50).

This is the nearest Great Wall site to Běijīng (about 64km away), reachable by public bus from Qián Mén in about 2hrs for ¥8. It is the most popular with Chinese tourists, the most commercialized, and the most crowded, having also been open longer than any other. The same buses that take you to the wall then run to the Míng tombs for ¥2, and on to Qián Mén for a further ¥6. The buses leave from 6am (6.30am in winter) to 10am, arriving back between 1.30pm and 5.30pm (5pm in winter). A similar and less crowded service is run from Xī Zhí Mén from right outside the metro stop of the same name. The higher entrance price entitles you to a souvenir ticket with a plastic coin.

Once everyone was very enthusiastic about Bādálǐng, but now there are other sections open it has fallen out of fashion at least with independent travellers, although the site's natural beauty and the Wall's acrobatic behaviour remain the same. Wherever possible it runs through mountainous or hilly areas and, as here, never fails to climb the steepest slopes to the highest points, even if that means doubling and redoubling back on itself. At Bādálǐng it is possible to stand on the Wall and turn through 180 degrees with some part of it at varying distances in view through every degree. Admittedly the area around Bādálǐng might well be renamed the Great Wall Shopping Experience, heaving as it is with T-shirt sellers, but once on the Wall itself, steep climbs to left and right soon thin out the crowds, and in either direction, 30 minutes' effort will bring you to unrepaired sections with very few people about, although a little caution is needed as there have been reports of muggings by peasants here.

Míng Tombs (Shísān Líng)   十三陵
Adm ¥30 ($4).

Organized tours to Bādálǐng always include a visit to the 'Thirteen Tombs', built to house the corpses of all but three of the Míng emperors and their empresses. Usually only one tomb is visited (although three are open). This takes 45mins by bus from Bādálǐng.

The Dìng Líng (Tomb of Security) was built for the 13th Míng Emperor Wànlì, who died in 1620, aged 57. The tomb was begun when the emperor was only 22, taking six years and eight million taels of silver to construct. Wànlì had two wives only the second of whom bore him a son, and who predeceased him by several years. Not an empress, she could not be buried in the Dìng Líng, and was buried in a nearby tomb for imperial concubines. Wànlì's son, Tàichāng, died less than a month after taking the throne, and was succeeded by his own son, Tiānqǐ, who moved his grandmother into the Dìng Líng. The buildings above ground were damaged in the peasant uprising which helped to bring down the Míng in 1644, but were restored by the Qīng Emperor Qiánlóng. They burnt down again in the early 20th century, and the tomb itself was excavated 1956–8. There is a pleasing path behind the tower which makes a complete circuit around the cypress-topped mound.

The tomb is entered from the rear down a deep staircase to seven largely empty interlocking chambers, with an atmosphere reminiscent of Victorian railway stations, although one contains marble thrones. A slightly shorter climb up at the end brings you back to the original blue-tiled entrance gate known as the Soul Tower, housing a large red stele. Small exhibitions in side halls are little more than excuses for souvenir shops.

Those who really wish to see the site, including the spirit way—a long paved avenue lined with the statues of guardian animals—and to investigate the tomb valleys in more detail, including the overgrown upper portions of the other tombs, should charter transport especially for this purpose. The other two tombs open to the public are the Cháng Líng of the Emperor Yǒnglè, the first and largest of the Míng tombs, and the Zhāo Líng of 9th Emperor Lóngqìng (reigned 1567–72).

Sīmǎtái

司马台长城

Adm ¥25 ($3).

There are no special tourist buses to this site, but there is public transport from Xī Zhí Mén or Dōng Zhí Mén bus stations (just northeast of Ⓜ Dōng Zhí Mén). Catch a very early morning bus to Mìyún, for ¥6. A clamour of taxi and minibus drivers will surround you, and careful negotiations are necessary. The taxis are too unreliable to be worth considering. A seat in a minibus can be had for about ¥20, but make sure that you are being taken to the *entrance to the Wall*, and not just to a nearby village. To return to Běijīng will involve hitching a ride with a returning tour group, or similar minibus negotiations, but with far less choice, so begin early. You must be back at Mìyún before 4pm if you hope to catch a bus back to Běijīng. The Jīnghuá Fàndiàn runs minibus tours every other day for ¥80 ($10) per person return.

Alarmingly described on the ticket as being 'the most dangerous part of the Great Wall' and at 120km northwest of Běijīng the farthest of the sites visited from Běijīng, this section is less visited than most, although it seems to be preparing for mainstream tourism, with the reconstruction of long sections and the installation of a cable car. The 'danger' is in the ease of access to sections both unrestored and very steep and narrow, where outer stones have disappeared to leave a barrierless raised walkway. The towers are partially ruined and heavily weathered, and entered by balancing on wobbly piles of stones. There's a 30min walk from the ticket office to the Wall, where it plunges down both sides of a steep valley to be cut by a stream, and where it can be climbed. The stream having now been dammed, it's possible to travel part of the way by boat, and a bridge has been constructed to connect the two banks. The wall on the left-hand side of the valley is in a better state of repair, but the right-hand 'dangerous' side is the choice of most visitors. This section was built in the early reign of Míng Emperor Hóngwǔ (1368–99). As at Bādálǐng the less limber can take the cable car up.

Lúgōu Qiáo (Marco Polo Bridge) and Wǎnpíng Chéng

卢沟桥，宛平城

Open 8–5.30; adm ¥6 (bridge), ¥5 (city walls).

The bridge is reached by taking bus 6, which passes the north gate of Tiāntán, and proceeds west from the junction of Zhūshìkǒu Xī Dàjiē and Nán Xīnhuá Jiē. Get off at the terminus (Liùlǐ Qiáo Nánlǐ) and catch the 339 suburban bus. Tell the conductor 'Lúgōu Qiáo' and the bus will drop you just before the new road bridge (Lúgōu Xīn Qiáo, 30mins, ¥1.10). Continue walking in the same direction as the bus and then turn right along the river bank to reach the bridge, about a 5min walk.

Lúgōu Qiáo means 'Reed Ditch Bridge', and the bridge has gained its English name through being mentioned in Polo's *The Travels*. It was originally built between 1189 and 1194, and thoroughly restored after being partially washed away in 1698. Two imperial stelae under stone canopies carved with dragons stand at either end of the bridge, accompanied by two *hòu*-topped *huábiǎo* (*see* p.338). One stele celebrates the rebuilding, and the other, in the calligraphy of the Qīng Emperor Qiánlóng (reigned 1736–96) celebrates the bridge's beauty with the characters *Lúgōu xiǎo yuè*—'moon at dawn over Lúgōu'—one of a traditional list of the eight most scenic spots of the region, all of which were graced with Qiánlóng stelae. The eleven-arched white marble bridge has balustrades down either side, each upright topped with lions which appear to be individual. Local tradition has it that attempting to count the lions will drive you mad. Polo has 1200 (but he has them at the base of the uprights as well as at the top), and modern guide books give numbers varying between 140 and 485, although there seem to be 120, so perhaps the tradition is right (in which case 120 is wrong, and this writer is a lunatic, too).

The little town of **Wǎnpíng**, opposite the near end of the bridge, has now outgrown its city walls, but they remain the most intact that you will see on the Silk Routes. Like a miniature Xī'ān, down to the double tower arrangement at the west and east gates, it's all in good repair, although stone bases indicate that there were once other towers at the corners and north and south sides. Passing under the double west gate to enter the town, turn left to find the ticket office and stairs up to the top. A pleasant 30mins walk will give you roofscapes of the older interior *hútòng* and more modern exterior ones, and bring you back the same point having made a complete circuit.

Was Polo Here?

Polo's description of the bridge is typical of most of his descriptions of China—as much wrong as right. He gives the number of arches as 24, not 11, and makes other mistakes in describing a bridge generally agreed to have survived largely unchanged since its construction.

Following the publication of Frances Wood's entertaining book, *Did Marco Polo go to China?*, or rather since the companion television documentary was broadcast, popular imagination has finally caught up with what some academics have being saying for years: probably not.

Wills and other legal documents give convincing evidence that he existed, and the mention in one of them of a Mongol *laissez-passer* seems to suggest that there was some contact between the family and the Mongols. According to *The Travels*, in around 1260 two Venetian merchants, Niccolò and Maffeo Polo set off for the Crimea looking for new markets. They then adventurously proceeded to the Volga where the lord of the Western Tartars (a sub-division of the Mongol empire) had his capital. A civil war which broke out between this khan and one of his neighbours prevented the Polos from returning to the Crimea, so they sought refuge at the court of a third khan in Bokhara. They were given the opportunity to join a mission to the Great Khan, Khubilai, and ventured to his pre-Běijīng capital of Karakorum in Mongolia. He sent them to the pope asking for 100 teachers who could speak convincingly about Christianity, and provided a safe-conduct in the form of a gold tablet. The Polos got back in 1269, to find Christendom pope-less due to the death of Clement IV the previous year. In 1271, no new pope having been elected, the Polos returned to Acre and enlisted the support of the papal legate there, who gave them letters explaining why they had been unable to fulfil their mission. They had not long set off when they were recalled. The new pope turned out to be none other than the same legate, now Gregory X, who gave them full diplomatic credentials but at such short notice could only find two missionaries rather than 100, and even these dropped out. Undeterred, the Polos set off again, and it was only on this second occasion and at the age of 17 that Marco joined his father and uncle on a trip that was to last 20 years.

The Polos left China in 1292 by a sea route through the Malay Straits, arriving back in Venice in 1295. Fighting on behalf of Venice against Genoa in the sea battle of Cursola in 1298, Marco was taken prisoner and probably not released until the following year. While in captivity he had little to do but talk about his travels. One of his companions in prison was a well-known romance writer called Rustichello who set down what Polo had to say. Rustichello was not the greatest of writers, and those sections that did not fall into his usual experience come across as little more than a merchant's shopping list. Very little of the book comes vividly to life, and where Rustichello's florid pen takes over from the laconic Polo, he has no scruples about lifting passages from his earlier work and dropping them wholesale into *The Travels*, although these insertions become fewer as the narrative proceeds to less well-known territory.

The success of *The Travels* probably lay in its coverage of such a large part of the world at a time when there was a great eagerness to know more. Although there were many other published accounts of travel to the Far East, the Polos went further, and took some routes of which no other European was to leave records for nearly 600 years. There are more than 80 Polo manuscripts extant, in a variety of languages, and scholars still dispute about the original language used by Rustichello, although most now think that it was an Italianized form of French. Few of the manuscripts are entirely alike, various hands having perhaps added some passages, or deleted others.

The evidence against Polo is substantial, although the jury is still out. While in China Marco is supposed to have undertaken various offices for the khan, yet he fails to appear in any Chinese records, although other foreign travellers do. These travellers also appear in each other's notes, while the Polos do not. The narrative begins with a description of a route and a sequence of places visited, but by the time China is reached this has largely descended into confusion, and many an incautious commentator claims Marco's presence in a town where a more careful reading of the text would suggest that a hearsay description is being offered. There is far too little material in the book to cover the whole period of time supposedly spent away, and much of the historical material is contradicted by other sources. Major omissions include the Great Wall, tea (unknown in Europe at the time), the bound feet of all but the poorest of Chinese women, and the Chinese script, so different from the phonetic systems familar to Europeans.

It will take a long time for the idea of Polo to fade or change, as so much hyperbole has been expended on him over the centuries, and he serves as a symbol of adventurous travel, and east-west contacts. Chinese guide books claim Polo caused Chinese noodles and *jiǎozi* to appear in Italy as spaghetti and ravioli. (Some Italians claim the transmission was in the opposite direction.) The truth is probably that pasta was Turki in origin and travelled to both west and east.

The Marco Polo Bridge Incident

The bridge's role in modern history is as the site for what might be described as the opening battle of the Second World War. The peace protocol at the end of the Boxer Rebellion entitled the Japanese to station 1350 troops in the area of Běijīng and Tiānjīn to ensure that the route to the sea, which had been blocked during the Rebellion, was kept open. By July 1937 Japan had more than five times the permitted number of soldiers in the area, was conducting manoeuvres beyond the agreed territorial limits, and looking for an excuse to take control of the lines issuing from the Fēngtái railway junction, one of which almost touches the northeast corner of Wǎnpíng's walls. On 7 July the Japanese used the excuse of a missing soldier to bombard Wǎnpíng, and on 9 July attacked it, but without success. The Nationalists sent troops north from Nánjīng, the Japanese sent reinforcements, and by the end of July had occupied both Běijīng and Tiānjīn. The Marco Polo Bridge Incident marked the beginning of the war known in China as the Anti-Japanese War of 1937–45. A museum to the war now stands at the far end of the bridge.

Shopping

Xīdān Běidàjiē, Wángfǔjǐng Dàjiē and Qián Mén Dàjiē are the main shopping streets, with multiple department stores, speciality stores and restaurants. These are the places to look for practical items, and to some degree souvenirs. Many *hútòng* have small groceries and convenience stores open long hours.

Perhaps the most attractive area for shopping is Liúlichǎng (named after a tile factory that once existed in the area), where old buildings have been restored and rebuilt to house **antiques and art materials shops**. This makes for a pleasant two-hour browse, even if you don't shop. *Caveat emptor*: almost every shop window sports credit card signs, and there's a healthy understanding of the depth of foreign as opposed to domestic pockets. Some antiques are freshly manufactured. Nevertheless, there's a large selection of cloisonné, lacquerware, ceramics and painting, as well as theatre puppets, old clocks and watches, and vast amounts of bric-a-brac. The Běijīng Fine Arts Publishing House at no.4 on the west side has **guides and art books** about many Silk Route destinations sold at the proper cover price rather than the tourist mark-up. Further up the ancient books bookshop (Gǔjí Shūdiàn) has sets of out-of-print books, including reproductions of the entire collections of Dūnhuáng papers in

St Petersburg, London, Delhi and Paris from ¥3800 per volume. Opposite, an artists' materials shop has an inkstone the size of a double bed for ¥1.3 million (plus considerable excess baggage charges should you choose to fly it home). More portable goods include blank fans for painting on, oil paints, pastels, and other media, pestles and mortars, etc. The eastern half of the street also has a good bookshop on the corner of Nán Xīnhuá Jiē, with a neighbouring stationery/art equipment shop through which is a **second-hand bookshop** with many foreign-language books rescued from the libraries of embassies and private collections. There's also a flea market, with Běijīng attempts to cash in on the peasant art so wildly successful in Xī'ān, Cultural Revolution memorabilia (Máo watches, little red books), and much else.

Although there are stores in Nán Xīnhuá Jiē near Liúlichǎng which sell **silk**, there's a much better choice and considerably lower prices at the Friendship Store and neighbouring silk market. The ground floor has imported electronics, cosmetics, Western newpapers and magazines, carpets, and a bakery and imported foods store at the rear. Upstairs is mostly clothing, and a wide selection of good quality silk at marked (but still haggleable) prices lower than other tourist stores. Expect at least a 10% discount and push for 20% if you purchase in quantity. One option is to look at clothing and carpets here, feeling the quality of the silk, then walk east to the Xiùshuǐ Dōngjiē silk market and see if you can find the same or better items.

The market is a narrow and shady awning-hung alley between the Friendship Store and Jiànguó Hotel, running north from Jiànguó Mén Wài Dàjiē immediately west of the junction with Dōngdàqiáo Lù. It's full of Chinese nymphettes shopping for fake Hermès, Lauren, Chanel, Givenchy and DKNY, and if you're confident that you can tell real silk from polyester this is the place to shop for made-up goods. There's no need to be a nymphette yourself—Western sizes are available. Examine all goods very carefully for flaws as neither styles nor quality of manufacture are always up to Western standards. Russians and Eastern Europeans shop in bulk here, making frequent return trips on the real Silk Route of today, the Trans-Siberian railway line. Bargain hard but amiably—prices should be 40% cheaper than in tourist stores. There are silk and wool carpets on sale in shops at the rear, but you should have a good look at those in the Friendship Store (take at least 10% off marked prices), and have some knowledge of prices at home, before starting to bargain.

Prices for silk may drop further as China starts to explore its domestic market, overseas sales having been undermined by foreign competitors who produce a product of more consistent quality, falling 10% in 1994 and a further 40% in 1995. New silk markets are expected to open in Běijīng shortly to develop domestic sales. Ask your hotel staff.

A market just inside the wall of Tiāntán at the northeast corner and entered from there has a spectacular display of **ceramics**, including a vast choice of teapots, bowls, jars, vases, dishes and plates, from the miniature to the bigger than you. The Hóngqiáo Market of **antiques and curios** used to be huddled against the same wall, but has now moved to the top floor of a new building opposite. On the way up you pass stalls of electronics, watches, clothing and bags. Popular items here include the Cultural Revolution clocks, featuring red-cheeked Red Guards, one of whom waves her arm with a little red book while the second hand sports a soaring aeroplane.

Not everything is fake. The basement of the China World Trade Centre has Balenciaga and other fashion houses, as well as imported fast foods. One has a sign saying 'You're in Paris', but really you're in Hong Kong, which is where the Chinese get their idea of Paris from. There's also a branch of the Hong Kong Wellcome supermarket chain. The Běijīng Lufthansa Centre Yǒuyì Shopping City also has imported foods and goods including Italian, German, French and Korean restaurants, and counters with perfume, lighters and luggage. The CVIK building almost opposite the Friendship Store has Dior and Cartier for more than you would pay at home. Who in China has ¥28,000 ($3374) to spend on a watch?

Where to Stay

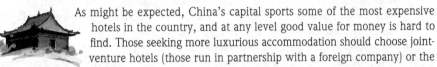

As might be expected, China's capital sports some of the most expensive hotels in the country, and at any level good value for money is hard to find. Those seeking more luxurious accommodation should choose joint-venture hotels (those run in partnership with a foreign company) or the usual recognized international chains, however bland and 'un-Chinese' they may be. Those staying in self-designated five-star Chinese hotels in Běijīng can find themselves in a room whose corners seem not to have been vacuumed or swept since the place was built, and with a decaying bathroom. This is almost to be expected in a Chinese three star, but is unacceptable in $200-per-night hotels.

Most of the better up-market hotels have desks at the airport arrivals hall and provide connections straight to their doors, although the staff are surprisingly incompetent and seem capable of little more than dealing with guests who already have reservations. The CITS desk there claims to be able to book rooms at a discount, so compare prices. There is currently an oversupply of accommodation for most of the year, barring major conferences, so haggle, even for the very best hotel. Newly opened Chinese and joint-venture hotels often offer rooms at up to half the price of their competitors for several months, and new ones are opening all the time. Many of the older hotels are undergoing major renovation with or without shutting, and without reducing their prices or otherwise compensating their guests.

Staying within reach of Tiān'ān Mén is recommended, since this marks the centre of Běijīng, has several of the city's major sights, and is well-connected by bus and metro. The hotels listed below are concentrated in three areas: more luxurious hotels in the shopping area of Wángfǔjǐng Dàjiē, and along Jiànguó Mén Wài Dàjiē east of the Forbidden City; mid-price hotels in the restaurant-packed Qián Mén area south and west of Tiān'ān Mén; and the budget hotels an unavoidable 30min bus journey further south.

expensive

The **Kempinski Hotel Běijīng Lufthansa Center** (Běijīng Yànshāzhōngxīn Kǎibīnguǎn Sìjī Fàndiàn), 50 Liàngmǎqiáo Lù, ✆ 6465 3388, @ 6465 3366, is a Korean/German/Chinese joint-venture, part of a shopping mall and apartment complex, and largely oriented towards up-market business dealings. Doubles are from $270, and suites from $410 to $2400, all plus 15%. Although a little far from the centre, there are so many Western restaurants and other facilities nearby that this is the place to go if you want to forget completely that you are in China. Bookings can be made to toll-free numbers in North America, ☎ (1-800) 426 3135, and the UK ☎ (0800) 868588.

The **Chángfùgōng Fàndiàn** (Hotel New Otani), 26 Jiànguó Mén Wài Dàjiē, ☎ 6512 5555, ☏ 6513 9810, has a beautiful internal garden and is popular with Japanese tour groups and Japanese major travel agents. Well-appointed and with every possible facility, the hotel is east of the observatory on the south side of the road. Single rooms are from $180, doubles from $200, and suites from $300 to $650. Probably the best choice in this price range. Plus ¥6 tax and 15% service.

The **Wángfǔjǐng Grand Hotel** (Wángfǔjǐng Dàfàndiàn), 57 Wángfǔjǐng Dàjiē, ☎ 6522 1188, ☏ 6522 3816, is a brand new Singapore-Chinese joint venture hotel, offering better value for money that most of the others in Wángfǔjǐng. Doubles are a highly negotiable $180–200, and suites $300–1800, all plus 15% and ¥6 per person tax. Facilities include a pool, sauna and a business centre.

Tiānlún Wángcháo Fàndiàn (Tiānlún Dynasty Hotel), 50 Wángfǔjǐng Dàjiē, ☎ 6513 8888, ☏ 6513 7866, has rooms around four sides of a large internal atrium with street café-style tables surrounded by restaurants and other facilities, all attempting to be European. Those rooms facing inwards tend to be both cool and quiet. Doubles are ¥1280 (¥154), suites ¥2000 (¥241) and ¥2600 ($314).

One Chinese-run hotel worth considering is the **Běijīng Guójì Fàndiàn** (Běijīng International Hotel), 9 Jiànguó Mén Nèi Dàjiē ☎ 6512 6688, ☏ 6512 9972, a 29-storey tower topped by a revolving restaurant just north of Běijīng Station, and with every possible facility from business centre to swimming pool and billiard room. Standard single rooms are $85, and doubles $120, with suites from $140 to $1000, all plus 15% service charge, and government tax of ¥6 per person per night. Multiple restaurants include one for vegetarians.

The Japanese often seem to lead in getting the best out of their local staff. The **Jīnglún Fàndiàn** (Hotel Běijīng-Toronto), 3 Jiànguó Mén Wài Dàjiē, ☎ 6500 2266, ☏ 6500 2022, is a Japanese (Nikko) joint-venture hotel, close to the Friendship Store, with good service and full facilities. Doubles are $140 to $180, and suites $210 to $230, all plus 15% service charge. Breakfast is included. Toll-free in North America ☎ (1-800) 645 5687, UK ☎ (0800) 282502.

The **Zhúyuán Bīnguǎn** (Bamboo Garden Hotel), 24 Xiǎoshíqiáo, Jiùgúlóu Lù, ☎ 6403 2229, ☏ 6403 2077, has considerably more style than most hotels in China. A mixture of old and discreet modern buildings set around a pretty garden that once belonged to a Qīng eunuch and subsequently to a Qīng Minister of Posts, the hotel has several rooms furnished in an interpretation of Míng style. That it was later the home of the architect of China's spy system, a posthumously disgraced supporter of Máo, is oddly not mentioned in the hotel's publicity material. Despite the emphasis on tradition, there are modern facilities such as IDD telephone and satellite TV. Single rooms are ¥420 ($51), doubles are from ¥600 ($73) to ¥766 ($93) depending upon garden view and size, and suites are ¥1148 ($138), all plus ¥6 per person city tax.

Once the best address before the upstart joint-venture hotels arrived, but still popular, and the most centrally located, large and relatively upmarket hotel, the **Běijīng**

Fàndiàn (Běijīng Hotel), 33 Dōng Cháng'ān Jiē, ☎ 6513 7766, 🖷 6513 7703, is a Soviet-influenced central mansion with two connected and more (but not much more) modern buildings of different dates. It stands on the site of the second Hôtel de Pékin, built after the Boxer Rebellion had severely damaged the first, and run by an enterprising Swiss who with his American wife took an active part in the fighting. When the first block of the modern building went up in 1974, it was discovered that a sniper would be able to fire from the top storey across the Forbidden City into the Zhōngnán Hǎi compound of the party leaders. The top storey was demolished and an ugly office block built overlooking the city from the compound so as further to block the view of would-be assassins. A Friendship Store-style operation stretches the entire width of the ground floor of the central building. The cheapest rooms are in the West Building at $110, and in the others at $160. Suites range from $280 to $680, all plus 10% service charge.

moderate

Dōngfāng Fàndiàn is situated at 11 Wànmíng Lù, a south turning off Zhūshìkǒu Xī Dàjiē west of Qián Mén Dàjiē, ☎ 6301 4466, 🖷 6304 4801. Within an easy walk of the Tiāntán (Temple of Heaven) north entrance, and a short ride from Tiān'ān Mén Square, this relatively plush tower has views from the upper floors towards the park. Standard doubles with in-room IDD are ¥630 ($76), and good size suites ¥750 ($92) rising to ¥2688 ($324) for those who want space to do business. There's also ¥6 per person per day city tax.

The **Fēngzéyuán Fàndiàn**, 83 Zhūshìkǒu Xī Dàjiē, just west of Qián Mén, ☎ 6318 6688, 🖷 6308 4271, is a new piece of pink post-modernism without Chinese touches except in the marble-lined foyer water garden, and reachable by any southbound bus down Qián Mén Dàjiē, or walkable in about 30 mins. The hotel is only a short walk from Tiāntán Gōngyuán, with a labyrinth of *hútòng* leading to the Dàzhàlan area at its rear. Standard doubles are ¥438 ($53), and suites ¥618 ($75).

The **Yuǎndōng Fàndiàn** (Far East Hotel), 90 Tiěshù Xiéjiē, ☎ 6301 8811, 🖷 6301 8233, is amongst the small *hútòngs* west of Qián Mén and east of Hépíng Mén, conveniently within walking distance of Ⓜ Hépíng Mén and Ⓜ Qián Mén, Tiān'ān Mén Square and Tiāntán, enabling several of Běijīng's major sights to be seen on foot, and offering easy access to many others via the metro. The reception staff leave something to be desired, but the floor staff are friendly and work hard to keep the rooms clean, although most are in need of redecoration. ¥298 ($36) for a standard double, ¥398 ($48) for a superior one. If you walk south from Ⓜ Hépíng Mén, after about 10mins you will see a sign to the left.

The **Gélányún Dàjiǔdìan** (Grand Skylight Hotel), 45 Běi Xīnhuá Jiē, ☎ 6607 1166, 🖷 6605 3705, Ⓜ Hépíng Mén, is a new hotel diagonally opposite the Hépíng Mén Quánjùdé Kǎoyādiàn roast duck restaurant, and a short walk west of Tiān'ān Mén. This is a friendly hotel that's the best deal in this price range and area: doubles are ¥300 ($36) to ¥400 ($48), and suites at ¥600 ($73), all negotiable, plus 10%.

Close by on the south side of Xuānwǔ Mén Dōng Dàjiē, the slightly overpriced **Wénxuān Bīnguǎn**, 1 Nán Xīnhuá Jiē, opposite the south entrance to Ⓜ Hépíng Mén,

✆ 6301 9832, ✆ 6318 8182, is much the same but more expensive: ¥458 ($56) to ¥498 ($60) for doubles, ¥888 ($107) to ¥1380 ($167) for suites, all plus 15%.

inexpensive

The common bath triples for ¥168 ($21) at the **Yuǎndōng Fàndiàn** (*see* above) are worth considering both for the *hútòng* atmosphere, and to avoid long bus trips to the south. There is a disco and karaoke bar on the same floor, but nevertheless this is a good deal. There are also a few bathroomless triangular-shaped doubles on upper floors for ¥90 ($11) which are not listed on the board at the reception, but which are excellent value for money.

The **Jīnghuá Fàndiàn** in Yǒngdìng Mén Wài on the south side of the third ring road (Nán Sān Huán Xīlù), ✆ 6722 2211, is the cornerstone of a rapidly growing empire run by the managers here, John and Su, along with a travel business. In addition to the Jīnghuá they have access to rooms at other nearby hotels and are opening other new places themselves, such as the Hǎixīng (Sea Star Hotel). Cheapness is the most attractive aspect of the Jīnghuá, beds being crammed into the dorms, many of which are in the basement. Inspect before choosing between the ¥26 ($3.50), ¥28 ($3.50), or ¥35 ($4.50) beds. Double rooms with bath range from ¥170 ($21) to ¥230 ($28). John and Su also sell Great Wall, opera, and acrobat tours tailor-made for backpackers, but you pay for the convenience: ¥80 ($10) for a trip to Simatai, for instance. If they don't have one in the Jīnghuá, they'll find you one somewhere else. There's cheap food both in a restaurant outside the hotel, and in neighbouring streets. The hotel is a 10-minute walk west of the terminus of bus 2, which runs down Wángfǔjǐng Dàjiē then down Qián Mén Dàjiē. Or from Ⓜ Hépíng Mén take the 14 south down Nán Xīnhuá Jiē to the stop called Yáng Qiáo, and walk five minutes east.

The **Jīngtài Bīnguǎn**, Ānlèlín Lù, ✆ 6722 4675, is also well to the south. Almost all budget hotels in China were once like this, with lazy and hostile floor staff, while those at the reception are bare-faced liars. 'I've been working here for eight years and we've never had triples.' Beds in these supposedly non-existent rooms with common bath cost ¥75 ($9), and with bath but almost no window ¥90 ($11). Basic doubles are ¥82 ($10), with bath and a/c ¥120 ($15), and larger rooms are ¥150 ($18). Bus 43 passes just west of Běijīng Zhàn, running down Chóngwén Mén Wài Dàjiē, and down the east side of Tiāntán. Get off one stop after the bus turns into Ānlèlín Lù at the junction with Jǐngtài Lù. Continue walking west on the south side of the road, and the hotel is down an alley with a small branch of the Construction Bank of China on the corner (MC and Visa signs). Bus 45 runs from Ⓜ Hépíng Mén and along Ānlèlín Lù. Get off at the stop called Liúlíjǐng halfway along. The 39 runs from Běijīng Zhàn past the east end of Ānlèlín Lù. Get off at the stop called Púhuángyú. Ānlèlín Lù has street food and a lively market.

Eating Out

Restaurants are so numerous and food in general so good, that only a small selection of the possibilities can be listed below, but you should not fear experimentation. Food away from the main tourist areas and in the *hútòng* (alleys) is cheap and plentiful.

Běijīng's most famous dish is **roast duck** (Běijīng Kǎoyā), available as everything from polystyrene box take-away, to multiple course banquet, especially concentrated in the Qián Mén area, but spread throughout Běijīng. Běijīng duck is roasted in a manner which largely separates the skin from the meat and makes it remarkably crispy. A dish of carved meat and skin is served or the bird is carved for you at the table. You are also provided with sliced onions, plum sauce, and a pile of small pancakes. Smear the pancake with a little sauce and place a few greens near one edge (or dip the greens in the sauce and use them for smearing). Put pieces of duck on top of the greens and roll the whole thing up. The meal is usually followed by duck soup, and can be accompanied if you wish by extra dishes involving every other part of the duck except the feathers.

The sign of a large concrete duck in a chef's hat is an indication of the ever-expanding **Quánjùdé** chain, of which some branches are better than others. The staff are quite keen that you should order the ¥126 ($15.50) 'lucky' duck on the menu's first page, which you are taken to select for yourself and upon which you may write your name (or something else). This then takes 50 mins to roast and bring to the table, where it is carved for you, the carcass being taken away to make the soup which will follow. While waiting you can sample just about every other part of the duck if you wish from roast duck hearts to duck webs in mustard sauce at a wide range of prices. On the second page of the menu in Chinese only you will find roast duck for ¥98 ($12). This is exactly the same meal, except that it comes more quickly and ready-sliced. In either case you pay a further ¥2 for plum sauce and sliced spring onions, and ¥2 for a fairly liberal supply of pancakes.

The best-known branch is in Qián Mén Dàjiē, one of the most famous restaurants in Běijīng until private restaurants began to open a few years ago, and there's another just west in Qián Mén Xīdàjiē. Better than either is the branch a little further west still, outside ❶ Hépíng Mén on the corner of Nán Xīnhuá Jiē. In the *hútòng* south of Qián Mén you can eat Běijīng duck for only about ¥30 ($4), or order the cooked meat by weight.

Another famous meal that Běijīng has made its own is **Mongolian Hotpot** (*huǒguō*). For a detailed description, *see* **Hohhot** p.391. Hot pot restaurants are easily identified by the pictures of UFO-like pots in the window. Prices vary widely from very cheap in the *hútòng*, to self-evidently more expensive in the glossier main street restaurants, also depending what you choose to put in it, and the side dishes chosen.

A considerably less well-known Běijīng dish might be called the Cultural Revolution's leftovers. The Cultural Revolution (1966–76), inspired by Máo Zédōng's struggles to re-establish himself in the face of criticism from his colleagues for the failure of the Great Leap Forward and other campaigns, brought the education system in China to a standstill following the disgrace and sometimes murder of intellectuals and teachers, and saw millions of people sent to the countryside to be 're-educated' by the peasants. After Máo's death, many found it impossible to return home without the connections to find jobs and accommodation for them.

In recent years a few returnees have opened restaurants to commemorate this period, serving the same plain peasant food they ate in those frugal times, and providing a way for those who have returned to try to contact lost friends. One of the best known is **Hēi Tǔdì Jiǔjiā** (Black Earth Restaurant), which serves plain peasant fare from the northeastern province of Hēilóngjiāng, where the owner was sent for his re-education. The food may be plain, but it's not without interest (try the pork with sour cabbage), and the restaurant has become very popular with Běijīng residents. The walls of the ground floor are adorned with various collectively written poems and statements expressing considerable bitterness. Upstairs there is a display of posters from the period in praise of Máo, and propaganda photographs of happy work units, their display deeply ironic, but impervious to criticism by officials. To reach the restaurant take the metro to Ⓜ Yōnghégōng. Take the west and then the north exit, turn left along the canal, and first left into Hépínglǐ Dōngjiē. The restaurant is five minutes' walk up on the left.

The **Shāguōjū Fànzhuāng** is more than 250 years old and possibly the oldest restaurant in Běijīng, although the current building is modern. It does for pigs what the duck restaurants do for ducks, giving you every part of them except the grunts, these being provided by your fellow diners. Amongst a large menu of nothing but pork, their best-known dish is Shāguōbáiròu, layers of pork slices baked with apple and silk noodles in a clay pot which is then brought directly to your table, together with a bowl of dipping sauce made from *dòufu* (tofu), chives, and pepper oil, which give it a creamy, red colour (¥26.10/$3.50). The restaurant's origins are said to lie in giving a more useful afterlife to pigs slaughtered in ceremonies by the emperors. It's on the east side of Xīsì Nándàjiē, a northern continuation of Xīdān Běidàjiē, and reached by the 22 bus from Qián Mén to the stop called Gāngwǎ Shì.

Dūyíchù Shāomàiguǎn serves Shāndōng-style wheaty steamed dumplings (*shāomài*) for ¥20 per *lóng* (steamer), which gives you about two dozen with mixed fillings, and jugs of cold beer for ¥5. Tasty and filling. There's a wider Shāndōng menu available upstairs. The restaurant is on the east side of Qián Mén Dàjiē almost opposite the turning to Dàzhàlan Jiē.

foreign food

Foreign fast food has standard Western prices, but seems expensive compared to the tasty and usually more nutritious Chinese food you can get for the same money. However, the choice for those who are craving a change is extensive.

Bìsàkè (Pizza Hut) can be found in several locations including Zhūshìkǒu Xī Dàjiē, the Friendship Store, and in Xīdān near the junction with Xī Cháng'ān Jiē. On the south side of Qián Mén Xījiē a clutch of fast-food restaurants include KFC (Kěndé Jī— the first foreign chain to open in China), McDonald's (Màidāngláo), the Australian Kebab House (Kābā Kuàicāntīng), and Vie de France (Dàmòfáng Miànbāodiàn). Those in search of real but affordable coffee will find the best at the Australian Kebab House, made with real milk for ¥4. The Chinese regard **McDonald's** as *haute cuisine*, and the main branch on the corner of Wángfǔjǐng Dàjiē and Dōng Cháng'ān Jiē was almost always full. The branch closed at the beginning of 1997, and will eventually reopen inside the new centre, 150m to the north. There are several other branches, including in Tiāntán Dōnglù off the southeast corner of Tiāntán, and in Xīdān Běi Dàjiē. **Vie de France**, also in Xī Cháng'ān Jiē at Xīdān, has passable croissants, pastries and bread.

Baskin Robbins is in Xīdān and at the Friendship Store. Xīdān also boasts several Chinese attempts at the Western fast-food format, such as a fast food roast duck restaurant near the Xī Cháng'ān Jiē junction.

Slightly more upmarket, **TGI Friday's** is on the third ring road in the northeast at 19 Dōng Sān Huán Běilù. The **Hard Rock Café**, just south of the Běijīng Lufthansa Centre, has the usual menu of burgers for around ¥68 ($8.50), plus the odd local dish such as Hunanese Chicken.

other

The **Bànpō Huǒguō Píjiǔcūn** (Banpo Primitive Hotpot Beer Hut), an imitation cave in a basement opposite the Wángfǔjǐng Grand Hotel in Wángfǔjǐng Dàjiē, is worth mentioning not so much for its bizarre menu, which includes scorpions, locusts, cicadas, ants, worms, poplar, willow and prickly ash, but as an example of what drives visitors away from China. An advertising leaflet offers a 10% discount which never appears, and the English-language menu has prices double those of the Chinese language one, which mysteriously disappears when you ask to see it. The fennel dumplings are rather good, but unless you enjoy being discrimated against and abused, this restaurant should be boycotted.

One of the best-known Sìchuān restaurants was the **Sìchuān Fàndiàn**, but it has emerged from a recent renovation as the members-only **Běijīng Club**. A little to the east on the south side of the same *hútòng* at no.76 is the **Sānxiá Jiǔlóu**, another good Sìchuān restaurant, unused to dealing with foreigners, but friendly and with standard prices. Imitating its more prestigious neighbour, it has waiters in traditional costume who refill your tea cup from an ornate, long-spouted, copper tea pot. Not all Sìchuān food is spicily hot. Try the subtly flavoured smoked duck (*zhāng chá quán yā*, ¥50/$6 for a half duck), and pork on a sizzling crispy rice base (*guō bā ròu piàn*, ¥17/$2).

Entertainment and Nightlife

Check *China Daily* and *Běijīng Weekend* for announcements of performances of all kinds, and ask your hotel staff to check in the Chinese-language papers.

The **Lǎo Shě Cháguǎn**, in the Dà Wǎn Chá building, 2 Qián Mén Xījiē on the south side, ✆ 6304 6334/6303 6830, claims to recreate 'what life was like in a Běijīng tea house of the bygone days'—apparently a combination of extracts from Chinese opera, acrobatics, magic shows and ballad singing. Performances begin at 7.40pm and finish at 9.20pm daily, and tickets are between ¥40 ($5) and ¥130 ($16), depending on proximity to the stage. Patrons are seated eight to a table, and tickets include tea and pastries. George Bush, Henry Kissinger and Lǐ Péng have all preceded you here. The 'tea house' is two floors up, and opposite its theatre has a smaller room which serves a variety of China's more famous teas with live music for ¥10 ($1.25) in the afternoons, and reasonable roast duck in the evenings for ¥68 ($8). Other tea houses have been opening in imitation of the profitable Lǎo Shě including the Tiānqiáo Teahouse, 113 Tiānqiáo Nándàjiē (on the west side of Tiāntán), ✆ 6304 0617, which has a similar combination of martial arts, acrobatics and Běijīng opera, but in an older building.

The Gloria Plaza Hotel, just south of the Chángfùgōng Fàndiàn (Hotel New Otani), has a tacky dinner and dance show from 6.30 to 9.30 nightly including banquet for $25 plus 15%, ✆ 6515 8855.

Full-length **operas** are performed in considerably greater style at the Zhèngyìcí Theatre, immediately south of the Hépíngmén Roast Duck Restaurant, ✆ 6303 6233/4. One of four ancient theatres in Běijīng, this is the only one to reopen for opera, being 340 years old. Originally a temple in the Míng (1368–1644), it was subsequently converted into a theatre by some of the founding artists of Běijīng Opera (a relatively modern hybrid of other forms). A young successful restaurateur took control of the theatre in 1995, and it reopened in 1996. Most performers are the best students from the China School of Běijīng Opera. Performances are at 7.15pm daily, and seats are at tables arranged in a courtyard. Tickets are ¥150 ($18), and there are no subtitles for foreigners.

Most visitors who simply want selections of Běijīng opera usually end up at the theatre in the Qián Mén Hotel, 175 Yǒng'ān Lù, ✆ 6301 6688 ext 8986. Tickets are from ¥20 ($2.50, but often 'sold out' for foreigners) to ¥100 ($12). There are occasional surtitles in English to explain the action.

The Běijīng Yīnyuètīng (Běijīng Concert Hall) in Běi Xīnhuá Jiē, ✆ 6605 7006, 6605 5812, claims to have the only pipe organ in China, and hosts a variety of performances of both **Western and Chinese classical music**. Tickets range in price from ¥20 ($2.50) to ¥200 ($24), depending on the event, most of which begin at 7.30pm. Traditional Chinese music can also be heard at the Sānwèi Bookstore for ¥30 ($4) on Saturday evenings at 7pm. The venue is off Xīdān opposite the Mínzú Hotel, ✆ 6601 3204.

Other choices include acrobatics at the Cháoyáng Theatre, 36 Dōng Sān Huán Běilù, ✆ 6507 2421 (7.15pm daily, ¥60/$7.50), and the Jīnglún Puppet Art Theatre, 4th floor Jīnglún Fàndiàn, ✆ 6500 2266 ext 8111.

Dàtóng

大同　A thousand metres above sea level on the loess plateau, the area around Dàtóng is a major coal-producing centre, and heavily industrialized. The town dates back to the Warring States period (475–221 BC), and in AD 398 became the capital of the Northern Wèi (AD 386–535) until around AD 493, and was later a capital of the Liáo and Jīn dynasties. The Wèi were of Turki stock, whose empire grew to cover most of northern China, and who became more and more Sinicized in the process, intermarrying with Chinese and adopting Chinese as their official language. They responded enthusiastically to the Buddhist influences that came along the Silk Routes, and during their stay in Dàtóng carved out the caves at Yúngǎng, a bus ride from the modern city. These, and a monastery glued to the side of a sheer cliff, make the city worth visiting. Within the town itself, a few pieces of ancient wall and two monasteries are almost all that remain of Dàtóng's pre-industrial history.

Many tour groups visit Dàtóng as a day trip, arriving overnight from Běijīng by train, visiting the Hanging Monastery and Yúngǎng caves by minibus, and returning overnight the next night. Independent travellers using public transport will find it difficult to visit both in one day, and there is enough in the town which can be seen the same day as the caves to make a two-day stay in this otherwise depressing town worthwhile.

Dàtóng key

Getting to and from Dàtóng

by air

Having been ejected from the airfield it shared with the military, Dàtóng is in the process of building an airport for itself and there are currently no flights. The Dàtóng Air Service Co (Dàtóng Hángkōng Fúwù Gōngsī), in Nánguān Nánjiē, sells tickets for flights from Běijīng with rail connections from Dàtóng.

by train

Ticket allocations even for hard seats are few and far between. Use CITS for a commission of around ¥50 ($6) soft sleeper, ¥40 ($5) hard sleeper, or ¥10 ($1.25) hard seat per ticket—even they have difficulties. There's a ticket office for hard seat only in the centre of town available up to three days before. CITS is in the railway station and at the Yúngǎng Bīnguǎn.

The best choice to Hohhot is the 157/156 at 09.36 arriving 14.23. This continues to Bāotóu, arriving at 16.49. The 173/176 leaves at 11.12, arriving Hohhot at 15.52, and Bāotóu East at 18.24. The most comfortable train is the a/c 43 departing at 18.35, which arrives during the night in Hohhot and Bāotóu, but is convenient for Yínchuān where it arrives at 10.58, carrying on to Zhōngwèi (arr 14.10) and Lánzhōu (arr 21.18).

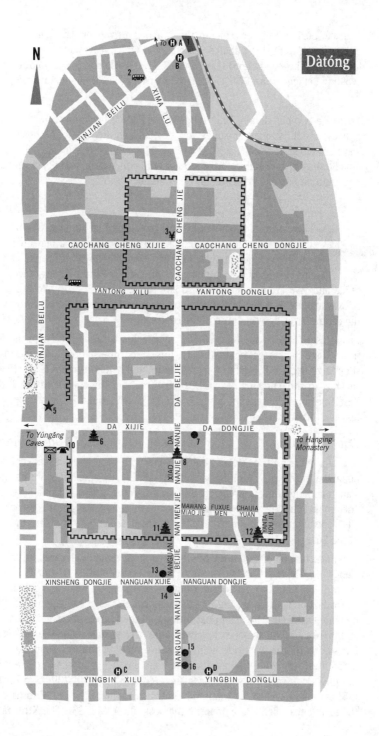

N

To ⊕ A
⊕ B

2 🚌

XINJIAN BEILU

XIMA LU

CAOCHANG CHENG JIE

3 ¥

CAOCHANG CHENG XIJIE   CAOCHANG CHENG DONGJIE

4 🚌

YANTONG XILU   YANTONG DONGLU

XINJIAN BEILU

DA BEIJIE

★ 5

DA XIJIE   DA DONGJIE

To Yúngǎng
Caves

6

● 7

To Hanging
Monastery

10
9

8

DA NANJIE

XIAO NANJIE

NAN MEN JIE

MAWANG   FUXUE   CHAIJIA
MIAO JIE   MEN   YUAN

11

12

NANTA HOU JIE

NANGUAN BEIJIE

13 ●

XINSHENG DONGJIE   NANGUAN XIJIE   NANGUAN DONGJIE

14 ●

NANGUAN NANJIE

15 ●
16 ●

⊕ C   ⊕ D

YINGBIN XILU   YINGBIN DONGLU

Trains to Běijīng are inconveniently timed, either arriving or leaving in the small hours of the morning. The best choice is the a/c 44 which leaves at 12.15 arriving 21.17, followed by the 296 at 05.08, arriving 13.35. It's also possible to go directly to Xī'ān avoiding Běijīng on the 174/175 at 16.20, arriving 11.22 the next morning.

by bus

There are two bus stations in Dàtóng. The old one is five minutes' walk south of the railway station (straight ahead as you exit, and on the right), and buses to Hohhot leave at 7.20am for ¥20 ($2.50). To reach the new bus station take bus 2 or 15 from outside the railway station to the stop called Dìqū Yīyuàn, walk back and turn right into Yàntóng Xīlù and walk east for two minutes.

Getting Around

The centre of town would once have been the battered Drum Tower, but it's now one block north and further west, where a big square has been built at the junction of Dà Xījiē and Xīnjiàn Běilù, which runs south from the station. Much of the shopping lies on Dà Xījiē, and the post office, telephone office and PSB are at or near the square, which is passed by two buses from the railway station. Accommodation is either close to the station, which is to the north of the centre, or well to the south of the centre.

Buses inside Dàtóng are a flat ¥0.50, payable into a slot as you board the bus at the front. Have the correct change ready. Bus 2 from the station takes you to the main shopping area, the PSB (stop 7 going south), and its far terminus is where you catch the bus to the Yúngāng caves. Bus 15 runs from the station to the Dàtóng and Yúngāng Hotels. Buses start around 6am and finish around 7.30pm. Taxis are meterless and tiresome.

Dàtóng ✆ (0352)   Tourist Information

For once there's a friendly and helpful CITS with good English speakers, led by the amiable Gāo Jīnwǔ, which has an almost continually open office inside the railway station and often meets foreigners from trains. The staff try perhaps a little too hard to encourage you to take one of their tours, but in general this office is what most other CITS operations should aim to beat. If they are closed at the station call the main office in the Yúngāng Bīnguǎn, ✆ 502 4176/502 8326, ✉ 502 2046.

The main branch of the **Bank of China** is inconveniently located on the corner of Cāochǎng Chéng Jiē and Cāochǎng Chéng Xījiē (*open 8–12 and 2.30–6, 5.30 in winter*). Take bus 4 or14 from the station, or 4 from Dà Xījiē, and get off at the stop called Sìzhōng. The Yúngāng Bīnguǎn also has a foreign exchange desk which may help non-residents. The main **post office** is in the square (*open 8–6.30, 6 in winter*), and there's a useful sub-branch between the railway station and the old long-distance bus station on the west side, with the same opening hours. Telephone calls can be made from a building to the left of the main post office marked 'toll service' (*open 6am–12 midnight*). Calls to Canada are ¥26.25 ($3.50), UK ¥29.55 ($4), US ¥39.45 ($5) per minute. There's a minimum 3mins charge to send a fax. **Film** is available in the main department store opposite the post office, ¥22 ($3). The **Xīnhuá Shūdiàn** close to the Yúngǎng Bīnguǎn has **maps** of Dàtóng, and further north the **Wàiwén Shūdiàn** has a small collection of English literature. **Visa extensions** are available from the friendly and helpful PSB's 'Exit Entry Administrative Dept' (*open 8–12 and 2.30–5.30*: '*chàbuduō*', says the officer, meaning 'more or less'—leave it until half an hour after opening times and no later than half an hour before closing to arrive). The office is on Xīnjiàn Běilù, immediately north of the department store. The visa office is on the right as you enter.

Jiǔlóng Bì (Nine Dragon Screen) 九龙壁

Open 8–6.30; adm ¥6.

The Nine Dragon Screen is in Dà Dōngjiē, east of the centre.

Nine dragons writhe in relief on large tiles of green and yellow visible from the entrance and perhaps not really worth the entry fee, especially if you are planning to visit the Forbidden City or Běi Hǎi Park in Běijīng, where you will find close relatives. This one is Míng, built around 1392, and about 45m long. It originally stood in front of the home of an imperial prince, long gone, and as the ticket helpfully adds, 'It has had boo years his fory' [sic]. A few stelae in the courtyard have received modern additions from builders working nearby.

Shànhuà Sì 善化寺

Open 8.30–5.30; adm ¥12 .

The temple is down a dusty slope on the east side of Nán Mén Jiē just inside some remains of the city's gappy wall.

Many of the ancient buildings in Dàtóng have even more of an uncared-for air than most in China. At the Táng-founded Shànhuà Sì there are three main halls, originally 12th-century Jīn dynasty, restored in the Míng, but the rearmost and largest is undergoing a substantial reconstruction and is roped off. Of the two halls that you can still visit, the first contains the four celestial king guardian figures, huge and horrible, and the second little of interest beyond its elaborate beams. The interiors of both are covered in the dust of centuries, and most of the life is provided by members of the martin family whose offerings liberally dot the walls.

Through moon gates to one side lie an iron statue of an ox which has seen better days, architectural odds and ends, a budget version of the Nine Dragon Screen with only five dragons, and a two-storey pavilion full of builders' rubbish.

To the north of Shànhuà Sì stands the three-storey squat **Drum Tower** in a dilapidated condition and not open to the public, now the centre of a traffic island.

Pagoda Bǎo Tǎ or Yàn Tǎ 宝塔, 雁塔

Returning north towards the Drum Tower from visiting Shànhuà Sì, turn right into Mǎwáng Miào Jiē, which becomes Fǔxué Mén, then Cháijiā Yuán. Turn right into Yàntǎ Hòu Jiē and the miniature tower can be seen ahead. This is a small, seven-storey, octagonal, bell-hung, brick pagoda on top of a short section of restored wall. If the gates are locked try knocking at the first gate around the corner to the left. Local people will advise you just to climb over the gate.

Huáyán Sì 华严寺

Open 8.30–5.30; adm ¥8 to each of two parts.

The temple is in two parts, both down an alley off the south side of Dà Xījiē, east of the post office. As you enter the compound, the Upper Monastery is on the right, and the Lower straight ahead.

The Upper and Lower temples were originally built during the Liáo dynasty (907–1125), and two of them have survived to modern times, amongst the most ancient temple buildings in China. A slightly later and very large Jīn dynasty hall is the centre of the Upper Monastery but has been undergoing major repairs for several years, which have been halted due to lack of funds. Nevertheless it remains the most atmospheric of the halls at Huáyán Sì, its interior covered in detailed painting and with much statuary, and there is monkish activity. The Lower Monastery, however, contains the most significant hall, the Buddhist Bhagavat Storage Hall, which was constructed in 1038 to resemble an imperial palace. It contains 5m-high clay statues, accompanied by a remarkable two-storey bookcase for storing sutras, which runs round three sides of the building, and which is built as an extended temple in miniature, complete with hip-and-gable roofs supported by elaborate brackets, two parts at the rear being connected by an elaborate arch. The rest of the Lower buildings smack of substantial restoration and are faintly sterile. The entrance ticket promises a Dàtóng City Museum, but the exhibits have long been closed.

Around Dàtóng

The two important sites are the Hanging Monastery and the Yúngǎng caves (one of the most important sets in China). CITS has a convenient tour that covers both, which includes the services of an English-speaking guide, and leaves at 9am every morning for ¥100 ($12). Pay for your own lunch and entrance fees. There are several other little-known sights around Dàtóng, most of which are difficult to reach without hiring special transport. An exception is the **Mù Tǎ**, an impressive and stately octagonal wooden pagoda, said to have been built without the assistance of nails, and located about 73km south of Dàtóng, which can be reached by public bus, leaving at 7.30am from the old bus station (2hrs, ¥7).

Xuánkōng Sì (Hanging Monastery) 悬空寺

Open 7 to 7 daily; ¥20 ($2.50).

The CITS ¥100 ($12) one-day tour includes the monastery. Otherwise visitors are supposed to take a tourist bus from the new bus station at 8am daily for ¥30 ($4) return. However, Chinese minibuses wait outside the old bus station leaving when full, and take three hours to reach a village near the monastery. Negotiation is necessary to get the price down to a reasonable ¥8, and you may still be asked for an extra ¥7 to travel the final few km to the monastery itself. A ride all the way back to Dàtóng may nevertheless be only ¥7 altogether.

A handful of delicate temples connected by narrow stairways and walkways are glued to the side of a sheer cliff, apparently supported by slender poles, although these have more of a decorative than structural function since the beams on which the temples sit go far back into the cliff. Daoism, Buddhism and Confucianism are all represented here, in one case all three in one temple. There is little to see inside the tiny halls, but one very small building has a Buddha whose face you can touch for luck, although this has not been lucky for the Buddha itself, now worn away by the passage of many hands. One hall boasts a fine clay and wood tracery of flying and suspended figures totally suited to the monastery's own suspension, and one of the Daoist halls has a particularly fine tracery of dragons in relief.

The temple was elevated to avoid damage from the river below which was prone to floods but is now dammed. Despite this and nearby industrialization, all carefully excluded from the photographs CITS and others may show you, this is an unusual and interesting temple well worth visiting.

Yúngǎng Shíkū

Open 8–6, adm ¥25 ($3).

云冈石窟

Take bus 2 from the railway station to its terminus (¥0.50) then bus 3 to the caves (¥0.80). Several caves have reasonable introductions in English.

About 16km west of Dàtóng, the 53 caves were mostly cut out beween AD 460 and 494, during the Northern Wèi as compensation by one emperor for his predecessor's persecution of Buddhists. 20 of the caves are large, and contain sizable figures, as might be expected in an enterprise conducted under direct imperial supervision. As with many other sites, the long angularity of the earlier statues, based on an aesthetic imported with Buddhism itself, becomes softened and rounded by a native Chinese tone, even as the Wèi themselves adopted Hàn language and customs, and a few later caves were carved AD 500–35, long after the Northern Wèi capital had moved to Luòyáng and a mature style had been developed.

The caves are in three groups spread across nearly one kilometre of cliff, 1–4 in the east, 5–13 in the middle, and 14–53 in the west. A reported 51,000 statues range in height from a few centimetres to over 17m. The earliest caves, such as no.20, are not temples or chapels, but large niches scarcely able to contain their giant occupants, in this case an early 14m-high seated Buddha, although part of the cliff and the front of the niche have in fact fallen away. The flat folds of the mantle and other details show links with caves outside Kuqa, thousands of kilometres to the west in Xīnjiāng. Cave 6, probably executed shortly before AD 494, has a central pagoda-shaped pillar as well as all four walls smothered in painted relief of Buddhas, Bodhisattvas, *apsaras*, and other beings. Many panels, arranged in rows, provide cartoon-like narrative of the life of the Sakyamuni Buddha. The remains of brilliant paintwork are the result of a Qīng dynasty retouching.

There are other large Buddhas both exposed to the elements and enclosed, and plentiful spectacular relief in other caves, too. The larger statues were carved from top to bottom, and early cave 17 has one that didn't quite come off. An overly elongated torso left the sculptors carving the feet well below ground level.

Where to Stay

There are few hotels that accept foreigners in Dàtóng. CITS has contracts with the two nearest ones, the Fēitiān and the Tiělù Dìèr Zhāodàisuǒ, so if you want anything better than a dormitory bed and unless you arrive in the middle of the night, talk to them first.

The **Fēitiān Bīnguǎn**, ✆ 602 2133 ext 2222, is the newish tower on the left as you leave the railway station. Doubles are ¥225 ($27), suites ¥400 ($48), triples ¥245 ($30), and there are bathroomless quads for ¥220 ($27). This is a busy hotel, and if you arrive alone you will have to pay for two beds in a double. It's a standard mid-range Chinese hotel, but clean, bright and quite friendly, and the best choice for all but the budget traveller. Furthermore, CITS can get you in for a lower price, so speak to them at the railway station first.

The **Tiělù Dìèr Zhāodàisuǒ**, ✆ 205 1440, is a walk west from the station. Turn right out of the main building and left after five minutes down a small street flanked by a long blue-painted wall, taking the first right into a large compound. The Zhāodàisuǒ is diagonally across from you, pale green and red in colour, beyond the statue of an ox. When the price of dorms at the older hotels had reached ¥82 ($10), CITS persuaded this hotel rather against its will to open to foreigners. If this is your first encounter with a *zhāodàisuǒ*, expect hard wooden beds on concrete floors. The changing of bedlinen and supplies of hot water work to an arcane lunar calendar inexplicable even by the staff, who have occasionally been known to clean the rooms. A bed in a quad is ¥40 ($5) on the 6th or 7th floors, and there's no lift. Lower-level more comfortable carpeted doubles with bath are ¥82 ($10) per bed, triples ¥60 ($7.50), all with bath, and there are 'luxury' singles for ¥200 ($24). Again, CITS may be able to offer you rooms above dormitory level somewhat cheaper.

The **Yúngǎng Bīnguǎn** and **Dàtóng Bīnguǎn** are on the opposite side of town from the railway station, both reachable by bus 15. Get off at the first stop after the bus turns left for the Dàtóng, and one stop later for the Yúngǎng. Both have grubby but functional doubles, but the Dàtóng apparently includes arrogance and lying in its training courses for staff. The Yúngǎng Bīnguǎn, ✆ 502 1601, ☎ 502 4727, has more facilities, including 24hr hot water, sauna, money exchange, post office, two restaurants, a bar and uniformed staff to call the lifts for you. Doubles are ¥400 ($48), suites ¥600 ($73). Overpriced, but cheaper than the Dàtóng Bīnguǎn.

Eating Out

Food in Dàtóng is not particularly exciting, but there are as many functional restaurants as anywhere else. There is a row of acceptable eating places opposite the Yúngǎng. Cheap food is available at restaurants outside the gate of the Railway Zhāodàisuǒ compound (add up prices as you order), near the crossroads with the bus station, and in the lane leading to Huáyán Sì.

Hohhot (Hūhéhàotè)

呼和浩特

A Westerner going through Siberia or even Turkestan to Mongolia feels that he is passing from alien to still more alien people: but the average Westerner entering Mongolia from China feels that he has emerged from a totally incomprehensible race among a race with whom good-fellowship is understood in equal terms.

Owen Lattimore, *The Desert Road to Turkestan,* 1929

Lattimore, a man able to speak Chinese like a native, and highly sympathetic to both Mongols and Chinese, was certainly not 'the average Westerner'. The problem for visitors to Inner Mongolia today is to find any Mongols whose good fellowship can be tested.

At the end of the march we came upon country cultivated by Chinamen, who here, as nearly all along the borders of Mongolia, are encroaching on the Mongols, and gradually driving them out of the best country back to the desert. The slack, easy-going Mongol cannot stand before the pushing, industrious Chinaman; so back and back he goes.

Captain Frank E. Younghusband, *The Heart of a Continent,* 1896

All Western commentators write so sympathetically about the Mongols that it's hard to connect them with the fearsome horsemen who ruled the continent a few centuries earlier.

As in Xīnjiāng, the government has made efforts to keep independence problems at a minimum, both by designating the region 'autonomous', and by inducing as many Hàn as possible to live there. Inner Mongolia's proximity to the Chinese heartlands has made this an easier task to accomplish, and the Mongols now number merely 2.7 million in a population of more than 20 million. Much of the region consists of steppe 1000m above sea level, with a loop of more fertile land around the Yellow River where lie the cities, the transport links, the best farmland and the Hàn. To the west the region is increasingly arid, invaded from the north by the Gobi desert. Winters are cold, and there's little rainfall.

Outer Mongolia was under the control of the Manchus, but with the breakdown of central government at the end of the Qīng dynasty largely went its own way, and like Xīnjiāng came more under the influence of Russia. In 1919–20 the Chinese made diplomatic and military efforts to assert control, only to be driven out by White Russians, providing the pretext for

Bolshevik forces to enter and establish an 'independent' communist republic, which the Soviet Union forced China to accept in 1924. Independence for Inner Mongolia was mooted, and in 1933 Mongol princes gathered at Bǎilíng Miào north of Hohhot to discuss autonomy, but Inner Mongolia was shortly afterwards annexed by the Japanese.

Bāotóu has become a major industrial area, but the region's grasslands, with soil too poor to support conventional farming, are still home to vast flocks, and Inner Mongolia is China's largest producer of sheep and goat wool, and cashmere. Considerable effort has been put into wresting usable farmland from the desert, with the building of wind-breaks and fences, and the planting of grasses and hundreds of thousands of trees.

Younghusband's description of Hohhot (once known to the Chinese as Guīhuà) is still accurate, except for the Mongol prince:

> Kwei-hwa-cheng used originally to be a Mongol town. It is even now included in Mongolia, and there is a Mongol prince resident in the place; but no one would believe that it was not Chinese, for it is occupied almost exclusively by Chinamen, and the Mongols are relegated to the outskirts. There are, however, some fine Buddhist temples and a large number of Mongol lamas in the city.

> Captain Frank E. Younghusband, *The Heart of a Continent*, 1896

Despite its status as the capital of the Inner Mongolia Autonomous Region, Hohhot is neither large nor polluted, and enjoys a largely dry warm and sunny climate with cool evenings. In spite of the presence of Mongolian script on public buildings (also the left-hand-most script on the rear of Chinese banknotes), it seems to be a largely Mongol-free zone, except at the temples, some of the market areas and at the minorities department store. But even Hàn Chinese cannot tell some Mongols apart from some Hàn.

The Chinese regard the history of Hohhot as beginning with its adoption by the Wànlì emperor of the Míng in 1573, but it had long been a Mongol trading centre, and is usually identified with the city of Tenduc, mentioned by Polo four centuries earlier. As in Xīnjiāng, the Qīng built a new and separate city for themselves alongside the old and garrisoned it with Manchu troops, partially to tax the traders and to keep an eye on the camel caravans arriving from the west. The eventual arrival of a railway line from Běijīng confirmed Hohhot's status as the terminus for caravans from areas all around the Yellow River, and from Xīnjiāng on the other side of the Gobi. Several temples were established at the time of Wànlì, some housing the reincarnating lamas of the faith the Mongols' had learned from the Tibetans, and their numbers increased with the city's prosperity. Two Lazarist missionaries, Evariste-Régis Huc and Joseph Gabet, passing through in 1846, commented on the extent of the religious community.

> In the Blue Town there exist five great Lamaseries, each inhabited by more than 2,000 Lamas; besides these, they reckon fifteen less considerable establishments—branches, as it were, of the former. The number of regular Lamas resident in this city may fairly be stated at 20,000.

> Huc and Gabet, *Travels in Tartary, Thibet and China, 1844–1846*, 1850

Perhaps one in every two or three male Mongolians became a lama. Vastly fewer in numbers now, their remaining temples are still particularly fine, and constitute Hohhot's major attractions. There's also a sizeable Huí population, but their ancient mosque is not usually open to the public.

The Long and Winding Road

When the camel man has done up his little bundle, he shambles away out of the city as if he were expecting to stroll home within half an hour; but he plods on until he finds the camp where the caravan waits behind the hills with its camels at pasture, until its complement of loads be filled; when camp is broken, he plods away again until he fetches up in Central Asia; for the men of his calling, by leaving their houses and pitching tents, depart with no more ado from the civilization of telegraphs and newspapers, bayonets and martial law, into a secret and distant land of which they only know the doors.

Owen Lattimore, *The Desert Road to Turkestan*, 1929

The caravans brought hides and wool to the east, and took manufactured goods to the west. At Hohhot's markets the camel men, identifiable by their weathered appearance, their clothing of sheep and fox fur, and by a certain slouch caused by sleeping semi-upright on a moving camel, bought the rope, casks, saddles and other tackle necessary to continue their hazardous trade. In addition to the dangers of bad weather and mistaken navigation, they faced corrupt customs officials, bandits and opium smugglers (the Chinese had learned the cultivation of the opium poppy for themselves).

The main route west followed the Yellow River for part or all of its loop in multiple parallel tracks around to Bāotóu, followed by missionaries Huc and Gabet, Russian explorer Przhevalsky, and others. It then split into routes to every part of Gānsù. In the late 19th and early 20th centuries the ancient trading routes further north running from Hohhot to Xīnjiāng were investigated by several parties of Westerners. **Francis Younghusband**, later to play the Great Game in the Pamirs and Karakorams, set out from Hohhot on 24 April 1887 on a surveying expedition. Caravans assembled and departed monthly during the winter reaching Xīnjiāng in 80–90 days, or turning off for Hāmì, as Younghusband did, and arriving there after 70 days, having travelled around 2000km. Younghusband's route took him on what was known as the 'Great Road', which passed through part of Outer Mongolia.

American **Owen Lattimore**, who left Hohhot on 20 August 1926, had given up his job working for a Tiānjīn trading company to investigate the route by which some of the wool it dealt with arrived. Outer Mongolia had now achieved a spurious independence, and crossing the border laid caravans open to the attentions of almost equally rapacious tribesmen and officials. Whereas the old 'Great Road' had been relatively flat, lush and populated, the caravans were now following what Lattimore called the 'Winding Road' which stayed within China's borders, but was stony, unpopulated, with passes to cross, and salty water supplies. He arrived at Qítái, east of Ürümqi and the western terminus of the caravans, 137 days and a little more than 2500km later.

Sven Hedin's pioneering expeditions in Xīnjiāng, which helped to set off the archaeological free-for-all of the early 20th century, did not seem to be a cause of friction between him and the Nationalist authorities who came to power after 1911. In 1933, having advised the government that proper motor roads and a railway from the Chinese heartlands to Xīnjiāng were vital to prevent its going the way of Tibet, Outer Mongolia and Manchuria (under Japanese control), all de facto independent of central authority, he found himself appointed 'adviser to the Ministry of Railways'. He was commissioned to survey both a motor road to replace the camel routes across the Gobi, and a road along the 'Imperial Highway' through Lánzhōu to Xī'ān. His equipment was three Ford lorries and a Ford sedan (which was destroyed in Hohhot in a collision with a train and had to be replaced). Camels were still necessary, 40 of them loaded with petrol drums being sent ahead to create a refuelling dump halfway across the desert.

Hedin's party, which included several other Swedes, set off from Hohhot on 10 November 1933. Meltwater rivers rising in Gānsù's Nán Shān run north to near the Outer Mongolian border bisecting the Chinese Gobi, ending in a small group of lakes which vary in size according to the season, and near which lie the ruins of Karakhoto (Hēichéng—the 'black city'). Russian archaeologists had discovered the city in 1908 and in doing so rediscovered the forgotten Xī Xià dynasty. Aurel Stein and Langdon Warner later made discoveries there, but approached the city by following the water courses north. While the original camel route ran well to the north of the lakes, and Lattimore on the more southerly 'Winding Road' was able to ford the rivers that fed them, the lorries had to swing north to avoid the marshy ground. Reaching the town after 90 days, rather slower than Younghusband, they found it destroyed by civil war. The remainder of Hedin's trip was even more hair-raising, as his party narrowly avoided execution by rebels, and suffered the commandeering of their vehicles and forced detention. Nevertheless, when they finally did return down the 'Imperial Highway', the report made by Hedin was to lead to the construction of first a road then a railway which have helped to keep Xīnjiāng under Chinese control ever since.

Eric Teichman, an official from the British Legation in Běijīng, also made a motorized assault on the ancient camel routes, mainly because the cart track through Lánzhōu was unsafe due to the communists. Like Hedin sending an advance train of petrol-laden camels, he left Hohhot on 18 September 1935, and followed Lattimore's route until forced to turn north to avoid soft sand. Crossing the Mongolian border for a short time he arrived at the lakes and swung round the top before heading south until he crossed a camel trail leading to Hāmì, arriving after 34 days and a little more than 1900km.

> So long as Kuei-hua [Hohhot] stands where caravans and freight trains exchange their cargoes, the old life will retain its vigor. In our time, though every outward freight the caravans carry goes to work changes in Mongolia and Chinese Turkestan, they carry them in the old timeless way, as if no white man had ever come to Asia. Yet their doom is on them. When, in a time deferred but inevitable,—for time in China goes by the half-century,—those who have learned from the foreigner shall have carried the railway through to Nīng-hsia and Lan Chou, the business of the caravans will decline into an affair of peddlers...

> Owen Lattimore, *The Desert Road to Turkestan*, 1929

The railway was extended to Lánzhōu in 1958, and the camel caravans are no more.

by air

There is a flight from Hohhot to Ulan Batar in Outer Mongolia with MIAT Mongolian Airlines every Monday and Thursday departing at 12.20pm. Tickets are $130 or ¥1144, plus around ¥10 ($1.25) per kilo of baggage, which perhaps indicates that this is a major trading flight. Tickets must be booked between one month and seven days in advance, and paid for at least 24 hours before the flight. There are onward connections to Kazakstan, Russia, Japan and South Korea; ✆ 495 2026/901 9835/496 3590 (not that anyone will necessarily answer these numbers, and it's better to go in person), ✆ 495 2015. Tickets must be booked at least 7 days in advance and paid for at least 24 hours in advance in cash. MIAT shares its offices with a Mongolian consulate (Měngǔguó Lǐngshìguǎn—*open Mon, Wed, Fri, 9–12*), ✆ 495 3254 (maybe). No English and not necessarily even any Chinese is spoken. Visas are $50. To reach the office take bus 2 from the railway station, to the last but one stop, Měngwén Yìnshuāchǎng. Getting off the bus walk back in the direction you've come and take the first left at the junction with Dōngyíng Nánjiē. The consulate and airline offices are 10 mins' walk down on the right-hand side.

There are between one and three flights daily to Běijīng for ¥470 ($57). The ticket office is in Xīlínguōlè Běilù, just north of the junction with Zhōng Shān Lù, ✆ 696 4103. The airport is about 15km out of town, and reached by bus from the CAAC office.

by train

Trains towards Běijīng are the 44 at 7.26 arr 19.50, the 90 at 18.16 arr 6.20, the 264 at 21.37 arr 10.34, the 296 at 23.58 arr 13.32. It's also possible to travel to lesser Běijīng stations, although often at inconvenient times. The 442 runs to Běijīng South at 11.32 arr 4.31, as does the 158 at 12.50 arr 3.37. The 92 runs to Běijīng North at 9.31 arr 21.56. The 44 stops in Dàtóng at 11.58, the 90 at 22.42, the 92 at 14.10, the 158 at 17.42, the 264 at 02.14, the 296 at 04.53, and the 442 at 18.56.

The 174 runs directly to Xī'ān at 11.10, calling at Dàtóng at 15.57, and reaching Xī'ān at 11.22 the next day.

Trains to Bāotóu Dōng Zhàn (East Station) include the 173 at 16.04 arr 18.24; the 157 at 14.35 arr 16.49, the 201 at 09.24 arr 12.12, the 263 at 04.40 arr 07.20, the 295 at 10.45 arr 12.59, and the 441 at 18.06 arr 21.22. All continue to Bāotóu Zhàn a few minutes later. The 43 at 23.14 goes all the way to Lánzhōu, arr East Bāotóu 01.17, Yínchuān 10.54, and Lánzhōu 21.18.

Ticket windows are mostly open all day with an early evening break. Buy tickets for Dàtóng at windows 7, 9 and 10, Běijīng windows 7–10, and westbound at windows 1–4. The easiest trains to buy tickets for are the 90 and 92 to Běijīng, and the 201 to Lánzhōu, all of which start in Hohhot.

The 305/304 international train runs from Hohhot to Ulan Batar on Sun and Wed, leaving at 22.24 and arriving at 10.45 the next morning. (The train entering China from Ulan Batar is the 332/276.)

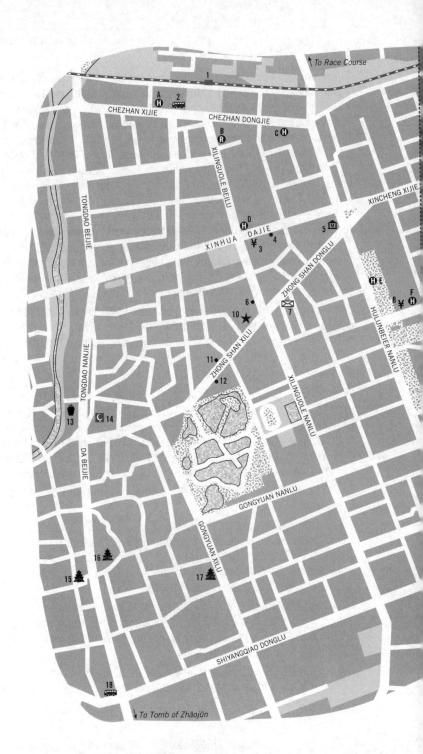

To Race Course

1

A Ⓗ 2

CHEZHAN XIJIE   CHEZHAN DONGJIE

B Ⓡ   C Ⓗ

XINCHENG XIJIE

XILINGUOLE BEILU

TONGDAO BEIJIE

D Ⓗ
XINHUA   DAJIE   5 Ⓜ
¥3 • 4

ZHONG SHAN DONGLU

Ⓗ E
8 ¥ Ⓗ F

HULUNBEIER NANLU

6 •
10 ★   ✉ 7

ZHONG SHAN XILU

TONGDAO NANJIE

11 •
• 12

XILINGUOLE NANLU

13 ●   ☪ 14

DA BEIJIE

GONGYUAN NANLU

16 🏯
15 🏯   17 🏯

GONGYUAN XILU

GONGYUAN XILU

18 🚌

SHIYANGQIAO DONGLU

↓ To Tomb of Zhāojūn

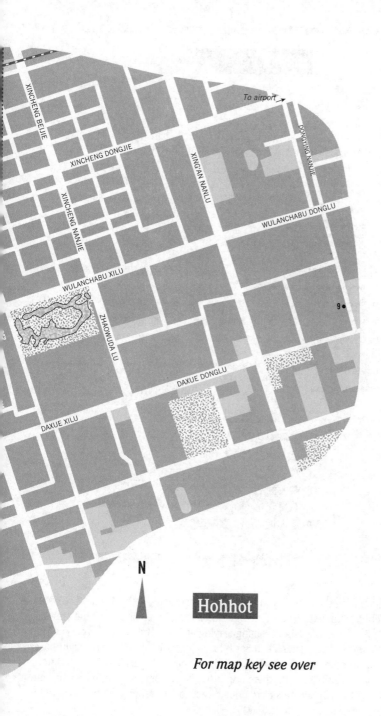

To airport

XINCHENG BEILIE

XINCHENG DONGJIE

XINCHENG NANJIE

XING'AN NANLU

DONGYING NANJIE

WULANCHABU DONGLU

WULANCHABU XILU

ZHAOWUDA LU

9

DAXUE DONGLU

DAXUE XILU

N

Hohhot

For map key see over

Hohhot map key

KEY		STREET & BUS STOP NAMES	
火车站	1 Railway station Huǒchēzhàn	大北街	Dà Běijiē
长途汽车站	2 Long-distance bus station Chángtú qìchēzhàn	大学东、西路	Dàxué Dōng/Xīlù
中国银行	3 Bank of China Zhōngguó Yínháng	东影南街	Dōngyǐng Nánjiē
外文书店	4 Foreign Languages Bookshop Wàiwén Shūdiàn	车站东、西街	Chēzhàn Dōng/Xījiē
内蒙古博物馆	5 Inner Mongolia Museum Nèi Měnggǔ Bówùguǎn	公园南路	Gōngyuán Nánlù
民航售票处	6 Air ticket office Mínháng Shòupiàochù	呼伦见尔南、北路	Hūlúnbèièr Nán/Běilù
邮电局	7 Post and telephone office Yóudiànjú	蒙文印刷厂	Měngwén Yìnshuāchǎng
中国银行	8 Bank of China Zhōngguó Yínháng	赛马场	Sàimǎ Chǎng
蒙古国领事馆	9 Mongolian Consulate Měnggǔguó Lǐngshìguǎn	石羊桥东路	Shíyángqiáo Dōnglù
公安局	10 PSB Gōng'ānjú	通道南、北街	Tōngdào Nán/Běijiē
民族商场	11 Minorities Department Store Mínzú Shāngchǎng	乌兰察布东、西路	Wūlánchábù Dōng/Xīlù
天元商厦	12 Tiānyuán Shāngshà department store	小什字	Xiǎo Shízì
滨河路鸟市场	13 Bird Market Bīnhé Lù Niǎo Shìchǎng	锡林郭勒南、北路	Xīlínguōlè Nán/Běilù
清真寺	14 Mosque Qīngzhēnsì	新城东、南、西、北街	Xīnchéng Dōng/Nán/Xī/Běijiē
席力图召	15 Xílìtú Zhào	兴安南路	Xing'an Nánlù
大召	16 Dà Zhào	新华大街	Xīnhuá Dàjiē
五塔寺	17 Wǔtǎ Sì	昭乌达路	Zhāowūdá Lù
	18 Buses to Zhāojūn Mù	中山东、西路	Zhōng Shān Dōng/Xīlù

HOTELS AND RESTAURANTS

王府饭店	A	Wángfǔ Fàndiàn
三和星大酒家	B	Sānhéxīng Dàjiǔjiā
八一宾馆	C	Bāyī Bīnguǎn
昭君大酒店	D	Zhāo Jūn Dàjiǔdiàn
新城宾馆	E	Xīnchéng Bīnguǎn
内蒙古饭店	F	Nèiměnggǔ Fàndiàn Inner Mongolia Hotel

by bus

The bus station is on the right as you leave the railway station, the ticket office on the left as you enter, although tickets for some buses can also be bought at the entrance to each bay. Bay 5 has the 189 to Běijīng leaving at 7.15am daily, plus 1pm on Mon and Fri and 8am on Tues, Thurs, and Sat (9hrs, ¥50/$6). There are also night buses (¥75/$9), but in each case the train would be a better choice. The 119 to Dàtóng leaves from bay 7 (¥23/$3), and there are buses every 15mins or so to Bāotóu from bays 1 and 2 (¥14/$2). There's also a bus direct to Dōngshèng every morning for ¥23 ($3).

Getting Around

Buses within the city are frequent and not usually crowded. Fares are all a flat ¥0.50, payable as you board and with no change given except for one or two which still start as low as ¥0.30 (see the signs of a hand holding money at the stops). **Taxis** have meters but don't use them. In any kind of taxi, short journeys around town are ¥10 ($1.25), and longer ones ¥15 ($2), as long as you don't want a receipt (*Wǒ bú yào fāpiào*). Check with hotel staff to what degree these rates have gone up but don't pay a *fēn* more than they say. As usual taxis waiting at the station and outside hotels are more likely to give you difficulties. A whole day out to the grasslands etc. costs ¥200 ($24).

Hohhot ✆ (0471)   Tourist Information

Hohhot is thick with **travel agents** whose main purpose is to offer high-priced low-quality tours to the grasslands around the city. The Inner Mongolia Hotel has its own travel agency, ✆ 696 4233 ext 8169, 🖷 696 1479, and CITS is there, too, ✆ 696 4233. CITS also has a ticket booking service there but its main office is now in the new Wángfǔ Fàndiàn, ✆ 695 0323. The main **Bank of China** branch is on Xīnhuá Dàjiē (*open 7.30–11.30 and 2.30–5.30; winter 8–12 and 2–5*) but the Zhāo Jūn Dàjiǔdiàn, opposite, will change money at the weekends. Another small branch just west of the Inner Mongolia Hotel also does foreign exchange (*open Mon–Fri, 7.30–6.30; winter 8–6*). The **post and telephone office** on Zhōng Shān Lù does have a *poste restante* service, but is puzzled by it as mail is very rarely received. However, this seems to mean that they do keep it, and in fact never send it back if uncollected. The postcode is 010020. The counter for both *poste restante* and international mail is on the right as you go in, for telephone calls on the left. The largest **Xīnhuá Shūdiàn** and the **Wàiwén Shūdiàn** are together just east of the main Bank of China, with maps in English and Chinese, and a very limited selection of English books. The PSB is in the building to the right of no.39 Zhōng Shān Xīlù (*open Mon–Fri, 8–12 and 2.30–6.30*). The visa office is immediately to your left as you enter the compound.

Stupa, Xílìtú Zhào

Xílìtú Zhào

席力图召

Open 8–6; adm ¥6.

The nearest bus stop for both Xílìtú and Dà Zhào is called Xiǎo Shízì on route 6. Cross to the east side of the road, turn right, and left up the first alley. Take the 4 or 19 along Zhōng Shān Lù to their terminus at the junction with Dà Běijiē, and change to the 6 or walk south.

Built during the reign of Míng Emperor Wànlì (1572–1620), this is an active temple in which you may see monks leading the faithful in a chanting procession around the courtyard, while to one side tourists dress up to be photographed. Stelae pavilions show further imperial interest in the form of two stelae carrying descriptions of Kāngxī's victory over the rebel Galden (*see* p.71). The interior has worn floorboards, pillars wrapped in dusty dragon carpets, and beams largely unrestored and covered in Tibetan writing, and is stacked with drums and other religious paraphernalia. The fourth Dalai Lama is said to have studied here as a child.

A large white stupa, an inverted goblet on a stepped base, is the largest in Inner Mongolia, the relic it houses visible through a glass panel in the base.

Dà Zhào

大召

Open 8 to 6.30; adm ¥6.

From the south entrance of Xílìtú Zhào turn right and cross the main road into the alley directly opposite, turning left at the end and following the lane round to the right to find the entrance to Dà Zhào. These lanes are packed with shops selling spices and other goods.

Constructed in 1580 by a local khan who had travelled to meet the third Dalai Lama in Qīnghǎi, Dà Zhào claims to be the oldest lamasery in Inner Mongolia, and its most magnificent. While the first halls have the atmosphere of a tourist attraction, and one has been converted into a shop, there are some fine statues of monstrous skull-bedecked guardian figures, stubby-armed Buddhas hung with scarves. and the founder of Yellow Hat Buddhism. The rear hall is magnificent, and the tourist atmosphere is left behind in the dusty, incense-laden air of a functioning temple. The Qīng Emperor Qiánlóng visited here leaving an inscription, and the roof is tiled in imperial yellow. The interior walls are covered in finely painted scenes of the life of Buddha, and the pillars are painted with dragons. Around two principal columns at the rear wind two of the most spectacular carved dragons you'll see in China, all fangs and claws, and covered in gilt. They protect a Buddha statue reputedly of solid silver, the lamasery's great treasure. The interior combination of carvings, paintings, statuary, hangings and lanterns, complemented by fine relief and carved beams on the exterior, make this the finest single temple building on this route.

Wǔtǎ Sì (Five Pagodas Temple)

五塔寺

Open 8–6.30; adm ¥4.

The Lamasery of the Five Towers is the finest and the most famous: here it is that the Hobilgan lives—that is, a grand Lama—who after having been identified with the substance of Buddha, has already undergone several times the process of transmigration.

Huc and Gabet, *Travels in Tartary, Thibet and China, 1844–1846*, 1850

The temple housing the five pagodas was originally built in 1727, but little remains except the pagodas themselves. An unusual solid square stone structure, striped with ridges of tile, is topped by five miniature pagodas, four smaller ones at the corners around a central larger spire, which can be reached by a narrow internal staircase. The building is covered with inscriptions in Tibetan, Mongolian and Chinese characters, and finely carved stone relief including more than 1500 images of Buddha. Inside the entrance stands what is said to be China's oldest star map (actually in Mongolian) carved in stone. According to legend some of Buddha's ashes are buried within the pagoda.

Nèi Měnggǔ Bówùguǎn 内蒙古博物馆

Opening hours unpredictable; adm ¥8.

The museum's most famous exhibit is a mammoth skeleton, which is accompanied by an assortment of Mongolian traditional costume, and artefacts from the region's archaeological sites.

Bīnhé Lù Niǎo Shìchǎng (Bird Market) 滨河路鸟市场

Up a small side street just north of the junction of Tōngdào Nánjiē and Zhōngshān Xīlù lies Hohhot's biggest bird market. The trade in larks here has a long history, and the area was once known as 'Land of the Larks'.

> *In the early summer, when the nestlings are old enough to be kept alive but not yet able to fly, the Chinese come in hundreds to catch them. A bird market is opened in Kuei-hua, where a brisk trade is done in the very early mornings, before other markets have opened. Before the time of the railway, men used to come all the way from Shan-tung on foot to catch larks; or buy them in the market, returning with as many as they could carry in two baskets slung from a pole.*

> Owen Lattimore, *The Desert Road to Turkestan*, 1929

Although there was a great demand for these delicate-voiced song birds in the Chinese heartlands, catching, selling and buying them had, as Lattimore put it, 'all the fascination of a gamble'. The baby birds were lifted directly from their nests in the grasslands, but those that grew into females were set free. The value of the remainder depended upon their abilities, and while a bird of moderate voice might be improved by hanging his cage next to that of a proven soloist, worth as much as thirty dollars, some would perpetually fail their auditions, and be worth only a few cents.

Although not large, the market has now revived after a period of suppression when owning pets was dangerously bourgeois. Weekends are busiest, but there's no longer any need to go first thing in the morning, and even in the afternoon you will find freshly captured baby larks in boxes, and novice singers hung next to proven performers in the traditional ornate cages, all singing their hearts out while flapping their wings. Small boys grip baby larks in their hot little hands, which they themselves have caught and brought to the market. The first asking price on a good singer is ¥800 ($96), and there are other birds with vocal abilities on sale, too, including mynah birds and various pretty finches.

Zhāojūn Mù (Tomb of Zhāojūn)

昭君墓

Open 8–7; winter 8–6; adm ¥10.

The tomb is merely an unexcavated pavilion-topped grassy mound about 9km south of Hohhot, reached by taking bus 1 from the station to its terminus in the southwest corner of the city, and then bus 14 (40mins, ¥0.70–¥1). A taxi should cost around ¥20 ($2.50) one way.

The 30m-high mound takes five minutes to climb, and gives views towards the surrounding villages and hills. The story of the mound is slightly more interesting than the sight itself, and dates from 33 BC. A Hàn dynasty imperial concubine, Zhāojūn was one of many imperial consorts of different periods who were sent to marry leaders of neighbouring states and thus cement peaceful alliances. In this case the lucky bridegroom was a Xiōngnú chieftain, and peace with the marauding horsemen would be short-lived. More prudish and politically correct accounts praise Zhāojūn as a kind of minor imperial librarian who heroically volunteered to be a peace envoy. If she was caught sleeping with a barbarian today, of course, she'd be in big trouble with the police, and this is all 'peace and friendship between the two nationalities' political hokum. No-one knows who's buried here.

Cǎoyuán (Grasslands)

草原

Trips to neighbouring grasslands are offered by all of Hohhot's many travel agents, with one- or two-day tours of dubious quality for ¥500–1000 ($60–120) per person (rather more if you are by yourself). Overnight accommodation is in made-for-tourists yurts on concrete plinths with bathrooms. If it's real nomads and tent-dwellers you're looking for, you'll find them in Gānsù or Xīnjiāng rather than here. With a little haggling you can charter a taxi for a day trip to take you to the nearest grasslands at Xilamulun, about 90km away, for ¥200 ($24). This is considerably more than most drivers would earn on the average day, so don't be abashed if the ones outside your hotel, used to fleecing foreigners, ask for four times as much. Stop taxis in the street the day before you want to go until you get the right price. The time to visit is during the Naadam festival, usually some time in August, when real Mongols gather for horse racing, wrestling, archery, and to buy and sell at a large fair.

Shopping

Zhōngshān Xīlù sports the Mínzú Shāngchǎng, a minorities department store-cum-market, which has mostly the same goods as the other department stores in the same street, but sold by Mongols. It also has a few stalls with shoes and costumes, brassware and daggers. Other shops in the same street sell furs and leather goods. Slightly further west, the shiny new Tiānyuán Shāngshà store has the best selection of biscuits, coffee, and other items useful to travellers as well as the locally made Měngǔ Wáng grain spirit, and other colourfully packaged Chinese alcoholic drinks.

Where to Stay

For once in China the visitor is spoilt for choice. Several of the hotels in Hohhot have reception and floor staff who are nothing less than charming, and there are good hotels in all price ranges at which foreigners and Chinese pay the same prices. The one exception on all counts is the Hūhéhàotè Bīnguǎn (Hohhot Hotel), which will not be mentioned again.

The **Zhāo Jūn Dàjiǔdiàn**, 11 Xīnhuá Dàjiē, ✆ 696 2211, ✉ 696 8825, is Hohhot's flashiest, but still friendly, with multiple restaurants (Mongolian, Sìchuān and Western, including the 'Windsor Castle'), billiard room, fitness centre, and a nightclub full of ball-room-dancing PSB officers. There's also a ticket office and a foreign exchange facility which does serve non-residents. Doubles have IDD and a/c, and start from ¥500 ($60). Suites, which unusually for China have minibars, are ¥660 ($80).

The newest hotel is the **Wángfǔ Fàndiàn**, opened in May 1996, 1 Chēzhàn Xījie, ✆ 696 4531, conveniently located next to the bus station and railway station, but reasonably well sealed against the noise. Sparkling doubles are ¥120 ($15), larger ones ¥160 ($20), and suites ¥240 ($29). Although it will no doubt deteriorate rapidly and prices will rise, it's worth looking in here first if you are not on a tight budget.

The **Nèiménggǔ Fàndiàn** (Inner Mongolia Hotel) is on Wūlánchábù Xīlù, ✆ 696 4233, ✉ 696 1479, in better condition and cleaner than most in this price range. The 16-floor block also houses restaurants, travel agents and a nightclub. The a/c double rooms, which have above-average bathrooms, cost ¥420 ($51), and there are suites from ¥520 ($63) to ¥1200 ($145). Triples with bath cost ¥130 ($16) per bed.

The **Xīnchéng Bīnguǎn** in Hūlúnbèiěr Nán/Běilù, ✆ 696 3322 ext 8188, ✉ 696 3141, consists of a number of buildings arranged around a central green space and beyond. The reception building is on the right through the gates. Beds in comfortable bathroomless quads with TV and telephone are ¥40 ($5). The common baths are basic but functional, and the friendly and helpful staff work hard to keep everything clean and working. There is 24hr hot water. All the remaining rooms have bathrooms, ¥55 ($7) per bed in triples (overall best value for the not too rock-bottom budget traveller), and ¥82 ($10) per bed in doubles. More luxurious rooms are ¥280 ($34), ¥300 ($36) per room, or ¥500 ($60) for a suite.

The somewhat gloomy **Bāyī Bīnguǎn** on the south side of Chēzhàn Dōngjiē, ✆ 695 6688, won't let you buy a single bed in a double, but if you are by yourself try haggling. Doubles with bath are ¥180 ($22), suites ¥400 ($48). There's 24hr hot water. Somewhat musty in atmosphere but clean enough—you stay in the smartest block only. There's an unusual tiled Máo screen in the courtyard at the rear.

Eating Out

When in the capital of Inner Mongolia, try the Mongols' most famous dish, the **hotpot** (*huǒguō*). The pot itself is a large chimney-like device with a charcoal fire in the base, ringed by a channel containing soup, which can be divided into two compartments, for spicy and milder flavours. The menu consists of a variety of foods which arrive cut into thin slices. The essential ingredient is lamb in marbled rolled up slices, to which you can add various vegetables, a close relative of black pudding, lamb tripe, bean curd, noodles, and many other items. Take whatever you want to eat and put it in the bubbling soup, retrieving it when cooked, which only takes a few moments, especially as the soup gets hotter and hotter as the meal progresses. Cooked items can be dipped into a creamy sauce made from sesame paste, fragrant garlic and fermented bean curd, to which you can add pepper oil and fresh coriander if you wish. Other local specialities include cold stewed donkey slices with vinegar to dip them in, various brittle versions of cheese, and 'milk skin' (*bá sī nǎi pí*)—balls of a relative of cottage cheese in hot sugar, which you dip in cold water to harden before eating.

When you've finished cooking, spoon the hot liquid from the pot into the bowl containing the remains of the dipping sauce, add any remaining vegetables, and treat as a soup. There are many hotpot restaurants in Hohhot. A particularly good one is the **Sānhéxīng Dàjiǔjiā**, at 170 Xīlínguōlè Běilù. The cost will be around ¥25 (¥3) per person upwards, depending on what is chosen. If you'd like to see hotpot in action but prefer something more conventional for yourself, the restaurant also serves Běijīng dishes, roast duck, etc.

The key element that makes Mongolian food different from Chinese food, other than its emphasis on lamb, is the use of milk and its buttery and cheesy derivatives. Outside the race course, north of the station in Hūlúnbèiěr Běilù, reached by bus 13 from Zhōng Shān Lù to stop Sàimǎ Chǎng, you can eat Mongolian food in a concrete version of a yurt. Take off your shoes and sit cross-legged on the platform. Begin with a bowl of milky tea to which you add lumps of butter of varying hues, a variety of cheeses in different stages of desiccation, and sugar. The remainder of the meal is made up of various parts of the lamb including its liver, delivered in large chunks from which you carve pieces to eat using the sharp dagger provided for each person. There are a number of dipping sauces including one made from chilis and one from chives, and more straightforward dishes such as lamb *jiǎozi*, and Xīnjiāng-style kebabs of small lumps of peppery beef. Around ¥40 ($5) per person for a big meal. The same food is also available at numerous conventional restaurants around the centre.

The narrow streets around the Dà Zhào, Xílìtú Zhào, and mosque have cheap noodle and *jiǎozi* shops, some little more than shacks, but the food is hot and tasty.

Bāotóu

包头 A modern city with any history of Silk Route and Yellow River trade completely obliterated, Bāotóu has good, cheap hotels to serve the businessmen visiting its smoky production lines. What buys you a bed in a dormitory in Hohhot will buy you a bed in a double with bath in Bāotóu.

There's nothing whatsoever to see in Bāotóu itself, but outside to the north is a fine temple (yet another claiming be the largest in China), and the city is a convenient starting point for Dōngshèng and Genghis Khan's mausoleum. Those who have travelled from Hohhot directly to Dōngshèng will almost certainly need to spend at least a night here before proceeding to Yínchuān. The city is sprawled across 20km or so and with two railway stations, but the only part that you will probably need to deal with is the east section, called Dōng Hé (East River). This has hotels, shops, a long-distance bus station, and post office, all within walking distance of Bāotóu East railway station (the first you come to when arriving from the direction of Běijīng).

Getting to and from Bāotóu

by air

There's an air ticket booking office in the otherwise avoidable Dōng Hé Bīnguǎn (mouldy and decaying with rude staff and double prices), on the left straight up Nán Mén Wài Dàjiē from the station past the Běi Yáng Fàndiàn. There are flights once or twice daily to Běijīng, twice weekly to Xī'ān (Wed and Sun), and to one or two other major Chinese cities. The proper CAAC office (*open 8–12 and 2–6*) is on the south side of Gāngtiě Dàjiē in Kūn Qū (West Bāotóu), and the bus stops outside just after the television tower on the left as you come from the east.

by train

All trains stop at Bāotóu Dōng Zhàn (East Station) and Bāotóu Zhàn. The times quoted here are from the East Station.

Towards Lánzhōu: the 201 at 12.42 arriving Yínchuān 23.03, and Lánzhōu 10.43; the 77 at 07.48 arriving Yínchuān at 17.17; the a/c 43 at 01.29, arriving Yínchuān 10.54, and Lánzhōu 21.28.

Towards Běijīng: the a/c 44 at 05.58, arriving Hohhot 07.13, Dàtóng 12.15, and Běijīng 19.50; the 78 at 20.54, arriving Dàtóng 04.10, and Běijīng 12.22; the 296 at 21.15, arriving Dàtóng 05.08, and Běijīng 13.32; the 264 at 19.58, arriving Dàtóng 02.29, and Běijīng 10.34; the 442 at 07.41, arriving Dàtóng 18.56, and Běijīng South 04.31; the 158 at 10.24, arriving Dàtóng 17.42, Běijīng South at 03.04.

To Xī'ān there's the 174 at 08.43, arriving Dàtóng 15.57, Xī'ān 11.22.

The easiest tickets to buy are those for the westbound 296, 264 and 158, and the 174 to Xī'ān, which all start from Bāotóu. Since the a/c 43 and 44 are the most expensive trains it's usually possible to buy a hard seat and upgrade to hard or soft sleeper on the train without too much difficulty (an ordinary hard sleeper to Běijīng is around ¥111/$13.50, an a/c one is ¥177/$22). Hard seat tickets are available from 7.30pm on the same evening at window 6, which is also the window for all hard and soft sleeper purchases. For train 201 to Lánzhōu whatever's left from Hohhot's allocation is put on sale at 11.30am on the day of departure. There's a single hard sleeper ticket on sale the day before.

by bus

The bus station is directly opposite the railway station. Tickets go on sale from 5.30am. There are buses to Yínchuān at 6.30am (602km, 12hrs, ¥58/$7), to Hohhot every 20mins (150km, ¥10/$1.25), and to Dàtóng there are several departures from 7am (385km).

Getting Around

There's little point in the visitor straying beyond the immediate areas of the hotel and railway and bus stations, unless there are specific visa extension, CITS, book purchase or money exchange tasks to perform. For those who need to go to the main area of West Bāotóu—Kūndūlún Qū, usually abbreviated to Kūn Qū—bus 5 leaves from the far end of the square in front of the bus station, and travels up Nán Mén Wài Dàjiē before turning west.

Bāotóu ℭ (0472)

Tourist Information

CITS is in the Bāotóu Bīnguǎn in Kūn Qū, room 321 in the west wing, ℭ 515 6655 ext 833, 🖂 515 1075. Bus 5 stops outside in Gāngtiě Dàjiē, West Bāotóu's main east–west boulevard. (This hotel is more used to foreigners, but also used to charging them ridiculous prices for ageing facilities.) They can book train tickets for ¥50 ($6) from the *west* station, and plane tickets for ¥20 ($2.50). They will rent their minibus for vast prices for trips to Wǔdāng Zhào and the Xilamulun grasslands. The main **Bank of China** is two blocks east and one stop earlier (*open 8–12 and 2.30–6.30; winter 8–12 and 2–6*). The **post and telephone office** is in Huánchéng Lù (*open 8.30–7*). **Film** is available at the department stores around the junction of Nán Mén Wài Dàjiē and Huánchéng Lù. Chinese-only maps are available at the railway station, and at the **Xīnhuá Shūdiàn**, a 10min walk west of the Bāotóu Bīnguǎn, or two more bus stops on bus 5 and walk back a little way. **Visa extensions** are available from the PSB (*open Mon–Fri 8.30–12 and 2.30–6.30*), which has its main entrance just east of the book shop on Gāngtiě Dàjiē, but whose visa office, with an English sign, is in the alley called Wūlán Dào parallel to the north. If there's no sign of life during opening hours, go through the passage to the left and in the rear entrance of the building, climb to room 330 two floors up, and knock. This is another office that sees so few foreigners it may forget to charge any more than the flat rate whatever your nationality.

Around Bāotóu

Chéngjísīhán Líng (Genghis Khan Mausoleum)   成吉思汗陵

Open 7.30–6; adm ¥24.

The Mausoleum is reached by taking a bus to the small industrial town of Dōngshèng. There are departures every 20–30 minutes (110km, 3hrs, ¥10/$1.25, or ¥14 by minibus). In Dōngshèng change to a bus to the Mausoleum (2hrs, ¥7, or minibus ¥10), usually calling at the village of Ejin Horo Qi (Yījīn Huòluò Qí). An early start is necessary to get back to Bāotóu the same day—the last bus back to Bāotóu from Dōngshèng leaves around 5pm. The first big bus to Dōngshèng is at 6.30am. Alternatively, a taxi from Dōngshèng to wait and take you back will be around ¥60 ($7.50) depending on your negotiating skills. A taxi for the day to take you all the way from Bāotóu, wait, and return will be ¥150 ($18) to ¥200 ($24).

The road crosses the Yellow River and heads south, and is full of lorries bringing huge loads of coal coming to feed the iron and steel furnaces, and empty lorries speeding back again. Wrecks litter the sides of the road, and this is one occasion when sitting further back in the bus might be a good idea. Local people who ask visitors why they aren't frightened of the occasional earthquake here don't seem to have done their sums, since the annual slaughter on this road alone must be considerably greater than the earthquake-related deaths for the entire region. The scenery is a mixture of open water and sand dunes, cultivated land and tundra, and, nearer the Mausoleum itself, of open grassland.

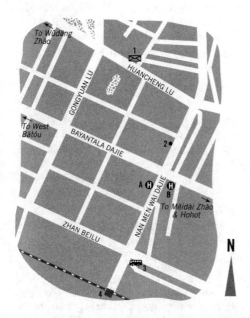

To Wǔdāng Zhào

GONGYUAN LU

HUANCHENG LU

To West Bǎtóu

BAYANTALA DAJIE

NAN MEN WAI DAJIE

To Měidài Zhào & Hohot

ZHAN BEILU

N

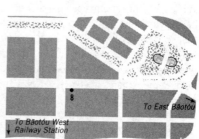

KEY

邮电局	1	Post and telephone office Yóudiànjú
民航售票处	2	Air ticket office Mínháng Shòupiàochù
长途汽车站	3	Long-distance bus station Chángtú qìchēzhàn
包头东站	4	East Bāotóu Railway station Bāotóu Dōngzhàn

HOTELS AND RESTAURANTS

北洋宾馆	A	Běiyáng Bīnguǎn
金桥宾馆	B	Jīnqiáo Bīnguǎn

STREET NAMES

巴彦塔拉大街	Bāyàntǎlā Dàjiē
公园路	Gōngyuán Lù
环城路	Huánchéng Lù
南门外大街	Nán Mén Wài Dàjiē
站北路	Zhàn Běilù

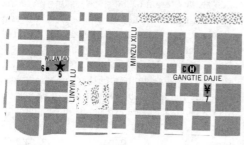

WULAN DAO

MINZU XILU

LINYIN LU

GANGTIE DAJIE

To Bāotóu West Railway Station

To East Bāotóu

KEY

公安局	5	PSB Gōng'ānjú
新华书店	6	Xīnhuá Bookshop Xīnhuá Shūdiàn
中国银行	7	Bank of China Zhōngguó Yínháng
民航售票处	8	Air ticket office Mínháng Shòupiàochù

HOTELS AND RESTAURANTS

包头宾馆	C	Bāotóu Bīnguǎn

STREET NAMES

钢铁大街	Gāngtiě Dàjiē
林荫路	Línyīn Lù
民族西路	Mínzú Xīlù
乌兰道	Wūlán Dào

West Bāotóu

Genghis Khan was born the son of the chieftain of the Kiyat tribe in the early 1160s somewhere on the Mongolian plateau, and named Temüjen. His tribe disintegrated while he was still a boy, after enemies poisoned his father. Brought up by his mother alone, he re-established his clan, only to have his wife stolen in a raid by a tribe called the Merkit. Forming an alliance with a third tribe he defeated the Merkit, marking the beginning of a rise to power that saw him elected leader of the reformed Kiyat in 1189. In 1206 he called a *khuriltai*, or meeting of tribal leaders, at which he was given the title of Genghis Khan—Emperor of Emperors. In 1209 his forces attacked the Xī Xià state, extracting submission, tribute and a princess in marriage. The next to receive attention were the Jīn, who had been the Mongols' overlords for nearly 100 years.

By 1214 the Mongols were knocking at the gates of the Jīn capital near modern-day Běijīng, again receiving tribute and princesses. In 1217 expansion began to the west, and by 1220 Bukhara, Samarkand, and many other Central Asia city-states had fallen, each being given the opportunity to surrender unconditionally or face complete obliteration. Genghis's forces continued through Georgia and Azerbaijan to the west end of the Black Sea. Before dying in 1226 on his way to pulverize the newly rebellious Xī Xià, Genghis divided his vast empire into three khanates, under the control of his first three sons. He was buried at a secret location in the Ordos grasslands of Mongolia, but he subsequently moved around nearly as much in death as in life, ending up at a site slightly south of the modern one. He was moved again to escape the Japanese occupation of China in 1939, visiting points in Gānsù and Qīnghǎi (including the Kumbum Lamasery or Tǎ'ěr Sì) before settling back here.

The domes of the Mausoleum are visible from the road, and several paths lead across from it. The bus can also drop you at the beginning of the road to the site just on the other side of the village. The ticket office is near a concrete arch at the bottom of the slope leading up to the halls, which are three connected, domed, modern pavilions tiled in blue and yellow and topped with yellow knobs. These only date from 1956, and had to be substantially repaired following damage in the Cultural Revolution. The central hall, its roof supported by dragon-wrapped pillars, holds a statue of the great man, behind which are roughly yurt-shaped tents, holding the remains of Genghis, wives and brothers. On altars in front of them stand offerings of brick tea, butter and alcohol. Halls to the left and right contain the remains of Genghis's fourth son and his wife, who were Khubilai Khan's parents, as well as a saddle decorated with silver, a silver (and supposedly miraculous) milk pail and other ware, weapons, and Mongolian coins which either belonged to Genghis or are contemporary with him. The walls are painted with idealized images of Mongol court life—even the camels seem to be smiling.

If you haven't yet met Mongolians, here you will, either working at the Mausoleum or coming to pay their respects, some from Outer Mongolia. Looking back from the halls down the slope, to your left are *obo*—sacred cairns made from stones brought by visitors. In the distance a small dagoba marks an earlier location of the shrine, and back down the slope a small exhibition hall is really just an excuse for a shop.

Your ticket also includes a visit to the 'Temporary Imperial Palace of Genghis Khan'. Turn left out of the gate and walk for ten minutes down a sandy track, to find three film-set style pavilions, where you can dress up as the khan and be photographed sitting on a throne, with one or two camels looking on in a suitably cynical way. Large carts and a reviewing stand are used in festivals held here.

If you decide to spend the night in Dōngshèng, there is a reasonable choice of accommodation. Turn right out of the long-distance bus station, first right towards a dead end, and the second building on the right is the **Jiāolián Dàjiǔjiā**, ✆ (0477) 325122. This is a basic bus station hotel with a reasonable cheap restaurant. Suites, unusually, have a double bed, and are ¥130 ($16). Doubles with bath are ¥70 ($8.50) with double bed, or ¥35 ($4.50) per bed with twin beds. If you haven't yet developed an imperviousness to Chinese noise, try to get a room away from the nightclub. Better hotels in Dōngshèng are often full, so you might end up here anyway. Turn right out of the bus station and carry straight on to find the more comfortable **Dōngshèng Dàjiǔdiàn**, ✆ (0477) 327333, on the right. Doubles are ¥120 ($15) and suites ¥360 ($44) per room, triples ¥60 ($7.50) per bed all with bath, and common bath quads are ¥25 ($3) per bed. Turn right and the older, simpler, and best budget option **Wàimào Bīnguǎn**, ✆ (0477) 325379, is a few minutes down on the left. There are doubles and triples with bath for ¥26 ($3.50) and ¥21 ($2.50) per bed, and quads with common bath for ¥10 ($1.25). They also have suites for ¥105 ($13), and a three-bed suite for ¥160 ($20). If all else fails, try the **Mínzú Fàndiàn**, ✆ (0477) 323629, suites ¥180 ($22), doubles ¥60 ($7.50) per bed, singles ¥110 ($13.50), all at foreigners' double prices, and not particularly welcoming.

There's a direct bus to Hohhot at 8.15am for ¥26 ($3.50). There's also a road directly west to a junction with the route around the Yellow River at a point about 100km north of Yínchuān, but no public transport seems to go this way.

Wǔdāng Zhào

五当召

Open 8.30–6; adm ¥10 ($1.25).

Bus 7 runs to the lamasery in the summer only, leaving from outside the bus station at 10.30 and returning at 4.30. Minibuses leave from the same point year round, mostly by 8 or 9am, and can also be flagged down as they drive up Nán Mén Wài Dàjiē (62km, 2hrs, ¥10/$1.25).

The lamasery is about 70km northeast, in the foothills of mountains with some remnants of their covering of pine and cypress, and was built during the reign of Qīng Emperor Qiánlóng in 1749. There are still more than 50 active monks here, but they seem less well-informed than their colleagues in monasteries nearer Tibet.

The lamasery is a set of Tibetan-style buildings with slab-like frontages, narrow windows, and beautifully and elaborately painted exteriors rising one behind the other up a hillside. A route around the site is marked and the buildings open for viewing are numbered in order. Climbing stairs up the narrow passages between buildings you might momentarily fool yourself that you are in Tibet. The second hall can be entered and is in active use for prayer, with a dimly lit finely painted interior, Buddhist texts wrapped up in yellow cloth on rows of shelves, dragon-carpet-wrapped square pillars, and an uneven stone floor. Allow time for your eyes to adjust. The fourth hall has wonderfully detailed gruesome statuary of monstrous multi-eyed, multi-headed, and multi-armed figures, garlanded with human skulls. Here the dragons around the pillars are in striking relief, with added three-dimensional heads. Similar images are painted on the walls, and the entrance doors are painted with pictures of hanging blood-spattered naked corpses. The fifth hall is on two levels, with endless small Buddha statues in glass cases, each individually wrapped in fabric and wearing a yellow hat. A large statue is adorned with scarves to scale. The following small temple contains beautifully worked reliquaries in the shape of miniature dagobas, containing the ashes of previous incarnations of the temple's reincarnating 'living Buddhas'. Hall no.8 (which may have a crimson-clad doorkeeper monk playing tetris on a Nintendo machine) has a finely carved exterior.

The liveliest time here is during the Mani Fair which begins on the 24th day of the 7th lunar month.

Měidài Zhào 美岱召

Open 7.30–7; adm ¥10 ($1.25).

Bus 6 runs here in summer from outside the bus station, or take any Hohhot bus. The temple is just off the road from Hohhot, and can be visited from there, or as a stopover on the way to or from Bāotóu if your luggage is light enough. The entrance way is marked by a modern arch at the roadside, from where it's a 10min walk to the lamasery. A new expressway under construction might make reaching the monastery more difficult in future insofar as vehicles taking it may not be able to stop to drop you off.

Unlike its larger counterpart and contemporary, Měidài Zhào is inactive, and maintained for tourists and the benefit of those employed to look after it. The gate of the main temple must be unlocked by the guardian. The emptiness is eloquent, but the beautifully painted interior has been reasonably well preserved, and the high roof is supported by particularly slender pillars, which seem guarded by the statues which stand in front of them. One small pavilion has an esoteric Buddha which for once is not wrapped up, and right at the rear there's a three-storey temple with three Buddhas. From the top of the walls you can also see that the compound has been invaded by modern residence buildings, a concrete yurt, hideous pieces of modern statuary and other junk.

Returning to the road it's easy to flag down buses in either direction.

Where to Stay

Bāotóu's industrialization runs to the names of its hotels, which include the charmingly titled Bāotóu Aluminium Smelter Hotel. Hotels in Bāotóu add ¥1 police tax, 5% construction tax, and ¥1 insurance.

The **Běiyáng Bīnguǎn** (North Sea Hotel), © 417 5656 ext 822, ◎ 417 1440, is the nine-storey tower visible up the road straight ahead from Bāotóu East railway station on the left-hand side—white with yellow, blue and red coloured stripes. Suites are ¥198 ($24), doubles with bath are ¥82 ($10) and ¥60 ($7.50) per room, and there are common bath triples and quads for ¥20 ($2.50) and ¥18 per bed respectively.

Turn right into Bāyàntǎlā Dàjiē just past the Běiyáng to find the **Jīnqiáo Bīnguǎn** © 417 1616, ◎ 417 1616 ext 8518, above a furniture store. Suites of ever-increasing size are ¥180 ($22), ¥200 ($24), ¥280 ($34) per room, doubles ¥40 ($5) and ¥60 ($7.50), triples ¥30 ($4), and quins ¥25 ($3) per bed all with bath. New, bright, and clean, it is perhaps slightly better value than the Běiyáng.

Eating Out

The Běiyáng has a moderate restaurant entered to the left of the main entrance and one floor up. There's cheap food in multiple noodle and dumpling shops near the bus and railway stations.

Yínchuān

银川   Yínchuān is the capital of one of the poorest regions of China, the Níngxià Huí Autonomous Region. Unlike Ūrūmqi and Hohhot, the city still has a majority of 'autonomous' people—Yínchuān is approximately 60 per cent Huí, 30 per cent Hàn, and 10 per cent Mongolian. Neither crowded nor particularly polluted, and enjoying a warm, sunny and dry climate, Yínchuān is one of China's more pleasant cities, and it's a good choice for a few days' relaxation between bus and train jouneys, if you have the time. The hotels have relatively friendly and helpful staff, and charge the same price for foreigners as for Chinese. The main sights in town are all but one in easy walking distance of each other, and there are several easy and pleasant day trips available using either taxis or public transport. Eating out is also cheap, and there is considerable variety. The summer days are scorchingly hot, but the evenings are cool, and pavement tables appear at which you can sit and drink beer or yoghurt, and watch an air traffic controller's nightmare of swallows swooping around the ornate Drum Tower.

Yínchuān is thought to date from around the 5th century, and stood on one of several trade routes passing through different parts of the province. New discoveries of Roman porcelain and glassware were made south of the city in 1996, in the tomb of a Sogdian migrant who became a Táng dynasty official. Several unusual monuments in and near the city date from its importance during the long-forgotten Xī Xià (Western Xià) dynasty of c. AD 1038–1227.

Much of Níngxià is extremely arid, and there is a relocation programme under way to move 746,000 people to lusher areas of the province, although so far it has taken more than ten years to move a quarter of that number. Other projects designed to alleviate the region's backwardness and poverty include the construction of a major canal to transport Níngxià's coal to the east coast, and others to tame and divert the Yellow River, the obsession of thousands of years, in order to convert desert areas to fertile farmland. A new railway line connecting Yínchuān to the main west route near Xī'ān was opened in 1996.

Getting to and from Yínchuān

by air

The ticket office is at 16 Mínzú Běijiē (*open 8–6*), © 602 2143/602 2085. There are flights to Běijīng daily for ¥1040 ($125) taking around 1hr 50mins, and to Ūrūmqi on Tues and Sat. Other destinations include Shànghǎi, Guǎngzhōu, Chéngdū, Xī'ān (daily) and Dūnhuáng. A bus service leaves from the office about two hours before each flight, ¥4.

by train

Trains towards Lánzhōu: the 201 at 20.17 arr 10.43, the a/c 43 at 11.12 arr 21.20, the 531 at 07.30 arr 21.56, Lǚ3 at 20.38 arr 7.00. Of these the 531 and Lǚ3 start at Yínchuān, and there are larger allocations of tickets. Trains towards Běijīng: the 78 at 11.20 arr 12.22, the a/c 44 at 19.44 arr 19.50, all calling at Bāotóu, Hohhot and Dàtóng. The 202 runs to Hohhot at 06.50 arr 20.15. Of these the 78 starts at Yínchuān.

Trains following the new railway line down Níngxià to Xī'ān via Bǎojī also start at Yínchuān. Train 207/208 leaves at 18.18 daily, probably calling at Zhōngwèi and then every intermediate station on the 846km to Xī'ān (*see* **Zhōngwèi to Xī'ān**, p.410).

KEY

中国国际旅行社   1   CITS
Zhōngguó Guójì Lǚxíngshè

中国银行   2   Bank of China
Zhōngguó Yínháng

电信大楼   3   Telephone office
Diànxìn dàlóu

民航售票处   4   Air ticket office
Mínháng Shòupiàochù

邮局   5   Post office
Yóujú

玉皇阁   6   Yùhuáng Gé

外文书店   7   Foreign Languages Bookshop
Wàiwén Shūdiàn

鼓楼   8   Drum Tower
Gǔ Lóu

承天寺，宁夏博物馆   9   Chéngtiān Sì
and Níngxià Bówùguǎn

南门楼   10   Nán Mén Lóu

长途汽车站   11   Long-distance bus station
Chángtú qìchēzhàn

公安局   12   PSB
Gōng'ānjú

海宝塔寺   13   Hǎibǎo Tǎ Sì

HOTELS AND RESTAURANTS

宁夏国际饭店   A   Níngxià Guójì Fàndiàn
International Hotel

银川饭店   B   Yínchuān Fàndiàn

绿岛饭店   C   Lǜdǎo Fàndiàn
Green Island Hotel

金桥宾馆   D   Jīnqiáo Bīnguǎn

大宝饺子馆   E   Dàbǎo Jiǎoziguǎn
and cheap restaurants

宁丰宾馆   F   Níngfēng Bīnguǎn

银川宾馆   G   Yínchuān Bīnguǎn

喜可登快餐厅   H   Xǐkědēng Kuàicāntīng

露露快餐厅   I   Lùlù Kuàicāntīng

  J   Huí restaurants

Yínchuān map key

The railway station ticket windows are mostly open in four bursts: 6am–8am, 8.40am–11.30am, 3pm–5pm, and 6pm–11.30pm.

by bus

Yínchuān's bus station is on Shènglì Běilù in the southeast corner of the old city (*open 6.30–5*). Use ticket counter 3 for Pínglúo, 5 for Bāotóu, 7 for Zhōngwèi, 8 for for Tiānshuǐ, Bǎojī, Xīníng, Tóngxīn and Lánzhōu, and 9 for booking up to three days in advance.

There are buses to Bāotóu at 6.20am (602km, ¥46.80/$6), Qīngtóngxiá Zhèn (76km, ¥6), three departures to Zhōngwèi from 8am (173km, ¥12.70/$2), to Tóngxīn at 2pm (218km, ¥15.20/$2), seven departures to Gùyuán from 7.30am (342km, ¥24.50/$3), Píngliáng (434km, ¥31.60/$4), and six departures to Xiányáng (718km) and Xī'ān (746km) from 6.30am (¥61/$7.50). A sleeper bus to Xī'ān leaves at 4.30pm (¥111/$13.50). There are also buses to Tiānshuǐ at 6am (595km, ¥44.70/$5.50), and Bǎojī at 6am (633km, ¥46.80/$6). Two buses daily go to Lánzhōu (514km, ¥30.80/$4).

Getting Around

Yínchuān has a new and an old town, but everything of interest except the railway station and airport are in the old town a few kilometres east of the station. **Buses** charge from ¥0.30 according to distance. Bus 1 goes from outside the railway station through the new and old towns and passes most of the hotels mentioned below, to the long-distance bus station (¥0.70, 15–20 minutes), and there are plentiful faster minibuses running the same route for ¥1. The old town is no longer old, but its street plan is on a more human scale than that of the newer town. With the exception of the Běi Tǎ, everything in the old town is within easy

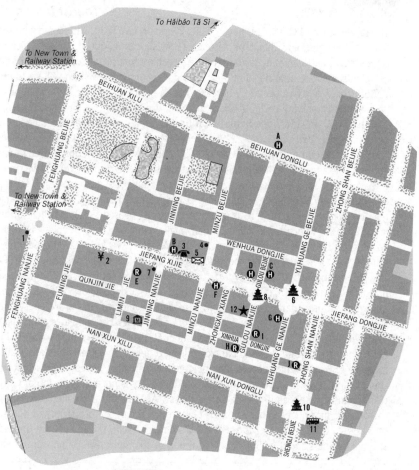

Yínchuān

STREET NAMES

北环东、西路	Běihuán Dōng/Xī Lù	南熏东、西路	Nán Xūn Dōng/Xīlù
富宁街	Fùníng Jiē	前进街	Qiánjìn Jiē
鼓楼南、北街	Gǔlóu Nán/Běijiē	胜利北街	Shènglì Běijiē
凤凰南、北街	Fènghuáng Nán/Běijiē	文化东街	Wénhuà Dōngjiē
解放东、西街	Jiěfàng Dōng/Xījiē	新华东街	Xīnhuá Dōngjiē
进宁南、北街	Jìnníng Nán/Běijiē	玉皇阁南、北街	Yùhuáng Gé Nán/Běijiē
利民街	Lìmín Jiē	中山南、北街	Zhōng Shān Nán/Běijiē
民族南、北街	Mínzú Nán/Běijiē	中心巷	Zhōngxīn Xiàng

walking distance of the hotels. **Bicycle** hire is available from the Yínchuān Fàndiàn and some other hotels for around ¥3 for four hours. The centre is the Drum Tower at the junction of Jiěfàng Xījiē and Dōngjiē, and Gǔ Lóu Běijiē and Nánjiē. **Taxis** use their meters, with a flagfall equivalent to 8km at the price per km written on the side window.

Yínchuān ✆ (0951)   **Tourist Information**

The local branch of **CITS**, 150 Jiěfàng Xījiē, ✆ and 🖷 504 3734, has people who speak reasonable English and charge unreasonable prices for tours outside town, which only represent value for money if you are in a sizeable group. They do have an off-road vehicle for more remote sites but their idea of a good price to visit the Xī Xià tombs is ¥1880 ($227) for five people, whereas you can do it yourself for ¥90 ($11) or less, with a little bargaining with a *miàndì* (minivan) driver. Their fee for booking plane or train tickets is ¥50 ($6). The **Bank of China** on the south side of Jiěfàng Xījiē just east of Fùníng Jiē (*open 9–12 and 2.30–6; winter 9–12 and 2–5.30*) handles traveller's' cheques and credit card withdrawals without problems. The main **post office** is on the corner of Jiěfàng Xījiē and Mínzú Běijiē just west of the Drum Tower (*open summer 8–7, winter 8–6.30*). The staff here are sticklers for procedure and their favourite expression is *bù xíng* ('not acceptable'). Using ordinary hotel envelopes for overseas mail is *bù xíng*, wrapping parcels in brown paper as opposed to sewing them up with fabric is *bù xíng*. Persistence will eventually make them *xíng*, but to avoid wasting time and energy, buy your airmail envelopes at the post office, ¥0.20 each. They say they do not have a *poste restante* service, but if you want to risk it the postcode is 750001. The **telephone office** is slightly further west and somewhat expensive: ¥42 ($5) per minute to the UK, ¥37 ($4.50) to the USA, with a deposit of ¥200 ($24); faxes minimum 3mins charge. In Yínchuān **film** and developing shops are everywhere, including just east of the Drum Tower on the north side. The railway station and the **Wàiwén Shūdiàn**, almost opposite the Yínchuān Fàndiàn, have **maps** with old and new Yínchuān on one side and Níngxià on the other. **Visa extensions** are available from the PSB's exit-entry department, hidden down an alley with the PSB symbol over the entrance squeezed between two department stores on the west side of Gǔ Lóu Nánjiē, immediately south of the Drum Tower. At the end of the alley turn left, and the office is in the far left-hand corner. Go through the door, turn right and it's at the end of the corridor (*open Mon–Fri, 8–12 and 2.30–6.30*). The staff are unused to seeing foreigners and it will probably require more than one visit to find someone in.

Gǔ Lóu (Drum Tower)   鼓楼
Open 8–12 and 3–6; adm ¥2.

Yínchuān has perhaps a slightly over-practical approach to the management of its city centre sights. The plinth of the Drum Tower is hung with advertising for banks, and that of the Nán Mén Lóu is used by local shops for storage, while the rooms in the Yùhuáng Gé are offices.

The Drum Tower has three storeys on a high, square brick base, surrounded by four smaller towers in the by now familiar format. The plinth can be climbed from the east side, although the central tower itself, with particularly curly upturned eaves, cannot. It is occasionally used as an art gallery, and this, for once, is not a euphemism for 'shop'.

Yùhuáng Gé 玉皇阁

Just to the east, the *gé* (pavilion) is a larger rectangular version of the Drum Tower, entered from the north up a stairway which winds round to the west. In recent years it has been used to house a small exhibition of bodies exhumed from nearby tombs, now removed. A central two-storey tower sits amidst a cluster of smaller towers, bizarrely housing offices full of computers. There are views over the town similar to those from the Drum Tower, but for free.

Nán Mén Lóu 南门楼

The South Gate tower sits in a square outside the bus station, and is Běijīng's Tiān'ān Mén in miniature, complete with flanking reviewing stands, 'Long live the People's Republic' signs, and Máo portrait.

Chéngtiān Sì and Níngxià Bówùguǎn 承天寺，宁夏博物馆

Open 8.30–12 and 3–6 daily;
adm ¥20 ($2.50).

The temple, in Jìnníng Nánjiē, contains a tall pagoda and the Níngxià Bówùguǎn, which is mostly dedicated to Xī Xià dynasty artefacts.

The brick, bell-hung pagoda (which can be seen by itself for ¥6 before the temple opens or during the afternoon break) was originally built during the Xī Xià dynasty in 1050, and restored in 1738 and 1820. It's a steep climb up the narrow stairways of its 11 storeys to the top, rewarded by clear views across the city's roofscape of shoddy apartment buildings to the countryside beyond, punctuated by more ancient buildings.

The pagoda stands in a courtyard of more modern buildings, some of which contain the museum of Xī Xià artefacts, although one old gatehouse remains with some fine stone relief.

The Xī Xià (Western Xià, *c.* AD 990–1227) were of a stock related to the Tibetans known as Tanguts, but who adopted numerous institutions of the Táng, while forming the junior partners in an alliance with the Liáo to keep the Sòng at bay, for several decades receiving bribes from the Sòng to keep the peace. Having once submitted to the Mongols, they later rebelled, and in 1226 Genghis Khan is said personally to have led the attacks that extinguished the dynasty which had lasted for twelve emperors (although he fell ill and died before the final assault).

The resulting destruction and slaughter contributed to the omission of the dynasty from historical records until the 20th century. Two buildings on the south side of the courtyard house an exhibition of Xī Xià items discovered in various sites around Yínchuān and elsewhere in Xī Xià territory, which once included almost all of modern-day Gānsù and Níngxià, much of Inner Mongolia, and parts of Xīnjiāng and Shānxī. Items on display include ceramics, statuary, architectural fragments and documents in Xī Xià script, with a good explanation in English of its relation to Chinese script and how it works. The general introduction to the museum ties itself in knots wanting to tell you both that this was a *Chinese* dynasty, that it was blessed by the Táng, and yet that it was founded by people who survive as the Dōngxiāng (Santa) minority today. The end of the exhibition has a small collection of Buddhist items, and a map of Xī Xià sites, with some photographs, including a black and white one of Karakhoto (Hēichéng), visited by both Aurel Stein and Langdon Warner. The Buddhist relics include various finely made heads, paintings and miniature pagodas.

Běi Tǎ or Hǎibǎo Tǎ Sì   北塔，海宝塔寺

Open daily 8–6; adm ¥4, plus ¥5 to climb pagoda.

A 20min bicycle ride or brief taxi journey to the north of town, this temple is undergoing substantial restoration with somewhat strident paint. It houses a highly unusual brick pagoda with a cross-shaped ground plan. 11 storeys and 54m high, it was originally erected around AD 407–24, and restored several times in the 18th century. One of the rear temple buildings contains a 7m sleeping Buddha.

Around Yínchuān

The countryside around Yínchuān is nearly as littered with tombs, pagodas and temples as that around Xī'ān, but much less well known and less frequently visited. Many are spectacular and in good condition, and make easy and pleasant day trips from Yínchuān.

Xī Xià Wáng Líng   西夏王陵

Visiting the tombs requires a taxi, and you can do this trip on the meter, or negotiate for a fixed price. For the half-day ¥90 ($11) is about right for a *miàndì*, which can hold six. There is neither ticket office nor entrance fee.

Promoted by China's tourism agencies as the nation's answer to the pyramids, these tombs of the Xī Xià emperors are not nearly as impressive, but certainly unique. A dusty area of 40 sq km on the edge of low mountains is dotted with mounds of various sizes including substantial pyramidal tombs with their own surrounding mud fortifications, some with corner watch-towers inhabited by owls. The plain is scattered with the remnants of tiles, layers of which can be seen like sandwich filling in the tombs, and which once were probably eaves on an outer casing of some kind. The tapering shape of the remains is probably just a matter of wind erosion, but they remain squat and massive, some as much as 15m high. Nine larger tombs are thought to be those of the emperors, and a further 200 or so of other worthies.

Qīngtóngxiá Yìbǎilíngbātǎ (108 Dagobas)   青铜峡一百零八塔

Open daylight hours; adm ¥7.

These are at Qīngtóngxiá Zhèn, 76km south of Yínchuān, and can be seen in a single trip with the Nàjiāhù Qīngzhēnsì, an active mosque at Yǒngníng, 20km south of Yínchuān on the same road. The easiest method is to board the 153 bus at 9am (there are other departures at 12.50pm and 4pm). The trip takes about 1hr 45mins. While this is a direct bus, you may be asked to change to another at Qīngtóngxiá Shì, but you will not need to buy another ticket.

The bus will drop you at a junction in the centre of town. The walk from here is part of the pleasure of visiting the dagobas. Take the turning to the right. Reaching the gates of the hydro-electric plant after five minutes, turn left walking slightly uphill, then right, reaching a major dam after another five minutes. A ferry crosses the Yellow River from below you to the left when there are enough people, for ¥10 ($1.25) return, and there are smaller craft with outboard motors, too.

If the guard on the dam is in a good mood you may be allowed to cross it on foot, which takes a further five minutes. At the far end turn left, walk round smaller sluice gates, and then take any sheep track leading up the hill to find paths that lead down again to fields on the banks of the river. Follow the track through the fields, altogether about 25 minutes, but a pleasant walk.

An alternative is to get off the bus as it reaches a single-track girder bridge two or three minutes after the cement plant, and before Qīngtóngxiá Zhèn. Walk back and take paths leading to two footbridges, one of which also carries large pipes and, having crossed, turn left following a cement road round to the same sluice gates mentioned above. This takes about 20 minutes.

The 108 small squat dagobas resembling inverted goblets are arranged in 12 ever-decreasing rows rising up the hillside, including a single larger dagoba at the top, behind which is a small temple with modern Buddhist clay figures. Having undergone substantial repairs the brick dagobas are in excellent condition, and topped with metal caps. The date of their original construction is unknown, but they are the only ones of their kind in China. The views from the top across the fields and the river valley are pretty. Bring a picnic. Returning either to the town centre or the bridge, flag down any passing bus, and change at Qīngtóngxiá Shì.

Nàjiāhù Qīngzhēnsì   纳家户清真寺

There are frequent buses to Yǒngníng (20km, ¥1.50), or you can stop off on your way back from the 108 Dagobas, about 1hr 20mins after leaving Qīngtóngxiá Shì. The mosque is a signposted 10mins walk west of the main road. It has an impressive triple-arched three-storeyed entrance gate flanked by twin towers. The keepers are friendly and if asked politely will show you the quiet and pleasant interior, as long as it's not Friday, when demand for space far exceeds capacity. Originally built in 1525 during the Míng, this is one of the oldest mosques in Níngxià. The village in

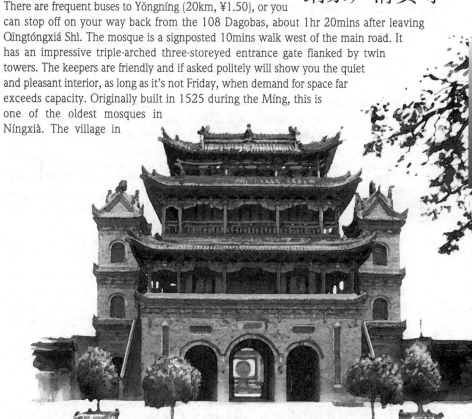

which it stands has 5000 inhabitants, 97 per cent Huí, and 60 per cent from the same Nà family after which both mosque and village are named.

Píngluó Yùhuáng Gé 平罗玉皇阁

Open 8–6; adm ¥0.50 park, ¥2 pavilion.

Bus 129 runs to Píngluó with four departures beginning at 7am (1½hrs, 59km, ¥4.40). Emerging from the bus station, turn left towards the small but elegant drum tower and go straight on until you see what appears to be a collection of temples on your left, but which is in fact one mass on three levels. Unfortunately this is inside a public park, and it's inadvisable to visit at weekends unless you want to be one of the exhibits and be followed around the complex like the Pied Piper of Hamlyn by groups of people who are pretending not to follow you.

This is a smaller but still impressive version of Zhōngwèi's Gāo Miào. Double and triple layered pavilions and halls are connected by aerial walkways making an impressive assembly of interlocking and overlapping roofs. The upper levels of the rearmost hall and connected walkways to other pavilions can be reached by climbing the left-hand stairs at the very rear. The halls have modern or recently repainted statuary, and feature figures from Buddhism, Daoism and Confucianism (probably Míng).

There are two other brick pagodas similar in scale to those in Yínchuān to be seen en route. One is immediately outside Píngluó, and the other at the 1197km marker about 37km from Yínchuān, both on the east side of the road.

Shopping

Waistcoats lined with the fluffy wool of one-month-old lambs, and coats made from fox fur appear to be the local specialities, the latter not likely to win you many friends at home. There are multiple department stores along Jiěfàng Xījiē and around the junction of Xīnhuá Dōngjiē and Gǔ Lóu Nánjiē.

Where to Stay

Hotels in Yínchuān are plentiful and friendly, and do not charge foreigners extra. City construction and other taxes amount to a total of 16%, which are included in the room rate unless indicated.

The **Níngxià Guójì Fàndiàn** (International Hotel), 25 Běihuán Xī Lù, © 602 8688, @ 609 1808, is where tour groups usually stay, and has fairly efficient service and full facilities. The doormen know how to say 'Good afternoon' in English, and the room rates are half what you would pay for similar quality in Běijīng. The 169 rooms are slightly unusual in having parquet floors, also a/c, refrigerators, etc. Doubles are ¥280 ($34) to ¥380 ($46), and suites ¥680 ($82) to ¥2800 ($338), all plus 10% service charge, and include breakfast. All major credit cards accepted.

The centrally located **Yínchuān Bīnguǎn**, 50–52 Yùhuáng Gé Nánjiē, just south of the Yùhuáng Gé, is easily identified by its odd neoclassical portico, © 602 8783, @ 607 2918. Its new north building is the newest hotel in town, with central a/c, well-appointed bathrooms, and all the usual facilities. Good-sized suites are ¥218 ($27) to ¥256 ($31). A well-furnished standard double is ¥220 ($27), and a four-bed room with common bath is ¥120 ($15), which at ¥30 per person is probably the best cheap deal in town. There are even cheaper rooms in the older south wing, doubles with bath for ¥70 ($8.50), triples ¥90 ($11), common bath triples and quads for ¥63 ($8) and ¥76 ($9.50) respectively. Add 16% in taxes to these prices.

The **Lǚdǎo Fàndiàn** (Green Island Hotel), 7 Gǔlóu Běijiē just north of the Drum Tower, ✆ 601 1666, 📠 603 1961, is bright, clean, friendly and efficient; standard doubles ¥198 ($24), suites ¥398 ($48), and superior rooms ¥800 ($96); all plus 10% service and 10% development tax but including breakfast. Cantonese, Běijīng and Sichuanese cuisine, and a serve-yourself hotpot available. Mastercard and Visa accepted.

The **Níngfēng Bīnguǎn**, on the south side of Jiěfàng Dōngjiē west of the drum tower, ✆ 602 8898, 📠 602 7224, has 16 floors of standard doubles and singles for ¥208.80, and suites from ¥324.80, with in-room refrigerator and a two-storey restaurant serving Muslim, hotpot and some Western foods. Visa and MC accepted.

The **Yínchuān Fàndiàn**, ✆ 602 5058, 📠 602 5602, is exceptionally friendly and helpful, the only problem being the proximity of two karaoke bars, one with occasional live bands. It has some of the cheapest beds but no restaurant to speak of, although there are many nearby. Doubles cost ¥168 ($21), ¥108 ($13), ¥98 ($12), triples ¥120 ($15), large singles made by taking one bed out of a double ¥82 ($10) and ¥85 ($10.50), doubles with no bath ¥50 ($6), ¥48 ($6), triples with no bath ¥60 ($7.50), singles ¥40 ($5), ¥28 ($3.50).

The plain **Jīnqiáo Bīnguǎn** is just down a small alley on the north side of Jiěfàng Dōngjiē on the right, ✆ 602 6431 ext 337, has larger triples and doubles for ¥105 ($13), and smaller ones for ¥82 ($10), all with bath. Suites ¥198 ($24).

Eating Out

expensive

If you have adapted to the idea that the Chinese eat chicken feet and duck webs, the restaurant at the **International Hotel** gives you the opportunity to try the next stage—braised camel paw at ¥238 ($29) per paw. Other exotica include crucian carp, *filet mignon*, 'red-cooked' rabbit, simmered ox penis (¥20/$2.50), and stir-fried spiced camel shreds (¥58/$7). There's also real coffee available for ¥10 ($1.25), all plus 15% service charge.

moderate

If you haven't yet tried hotpot, the restaurant at the **Green Island Hotel** makes it convenient and easy. There's a flat ¥38 ($5) charge, and you help yourself to the ingredients of your choice from a buffet. If in doubt about what you're eating, there are a number of helpful English-speaking staff in the hotel.

inexpensive

There are several cheap hole-in-the-wall restaurants in Lìmín Jiē, some with tables outside, mostly serving *làmiàn* for around ¥2.50. There are excellent piping-hot plump lamb-filled *jiǎozi* at the **Dàbǎo Jiǎoziguǎn** on the left immediately past the first right-hand turning as you walk south, run by a friendly Huí who is pleased to welcome foreigners. *Jiǎozi* are sold by the *liǎng*, one-tenth of a *jīn*, at ¥10 ($1.25) per *jīn*. Four *liǎng*, roughly 24 dumplings, is about as much as most people can manage. A related restaurant also called Dàbǎo in Fùníng Jiē specializes in *guōtiē*—the fried version, for the same price. ¥1 per *liǎng*. *Làmiàn* is also available from neighbouring restaurants for ¥2.50 for a big bowl.

Yùhuáng Gé Nánjiē has two interesting attempts at fast food, defined by the plasticized and brightly lit interior decor characteristic of Western chains. The **Xīkēdēng Kuàicāntīng** has a concrete statue of a boy carrying a burger outside, but their main business is mainstream Huí foods. Their hot, crisp vegetables, spicy chicken with peanuts, etc., are different from most fast-food restaurants insofar as the food is rather good. The walls are bizarrely decorated with posters from Japanese *manga* comics and *anime* cartoons. The **Lùlù Kuàicāntīng** (waitresses wear hats saying 'Lulu Quicklunch') has a weakness for playing 'Blame it on the Bossanova' and other pseudo-Latin classics. Downstairs it's similar to the Xīkēdēng, but without televisions blaring away. Upstairs it has 'Western' foods: fried eggs, omelettes, frankfurters, pastries, ice cream and excellent apple pie (¥4).

Two bright and clean Huí restaurants (but selling every traditional Chinese dish except those involving pork) can be found at 78 Zhōng Shān Nánjiē, on the west side north of the Nán Mén Lóu. The right tends to take the overspill from the left, which is very popular with local people, full of bustle, and ruled over by a lady with a voice of iron. Beef is around ¥10 ($1.25) per dish, chicken ¥15 ($2), vegetables ¥6 to ¥8. Everything is hot and tasty and in good-sized portions.

At night Xīnhuá Dōngjiē between Zhōng Shān Nánjiē and Yùhuáng Gé Nánjiē becomes a food street with stalls selling Huí specialities: *shashlyk* (kebabs, *kǎoròuchuàn*), snails, *làmiàn*, black rice soup, *bā bǎo*, and 'Eight Treasures'—a concoction of sticky sweet rice and jujubes (a small kind of date).

Gāo Miào, Zhōngwèi

Zhōngwèi to Xī'ān

Níngxià Backroads

The land northwest of Xī'ān was crossed by several alternative routes so that most towns and villages there claim to have seen Silk Route trade. Most of these routes are long forgotten in favour of what was sometimes called the 'Imperial Highway', the main route more directly west from the ancient capital. The towns remain mostly sleepy backwaters that few foreigners visit.

The route from Zhōngwèi to Xī'ān (or vice versa) is less travelled than others in this book (except the southern Taklamakan route east of Khotan), but has a great deal to see, including some of China's most important Daoist mountains and Buddhist caves, other superb temples and mosques, and a variety of desert and mountain scenery. Unlike on other back roads, accommodation, while not luxurious, is of reasonable standard, and prices are mostly lower than on main routes. Other facilities are limited: take full supplies of everything you may need, and do not expect to be able to cash traveller's cheques or to extend your visa.

A new railway line opened for passengers in mid-1996, with stations at all the small towns on this route. However, with only two slow trains a day on the single track, bus remains the most convenient way to travel. For most of the interior of Níngxià both road and railway follow the Qīngshuǐ Hé, a less murky tributary of the Yellow River. When the road turns more to the southeast to head towards Xī'ān, the railway heads further south to join the main Lánzhōu to Xī'ān line. While buses are far from comfortable, the road, though not classed as a major highway, is adequately surfaced, and winds through the lusher south of Níngxià across a mountainous neck of Gānsù dropping down to the Shǎnxī plain.

For those who do not wish to continue all the way to Xī'ān there are various ways to cut across to Tiānshuǐ.

Zhōngwèi

中卫 Zhōngwèi is a small, unappealing market town consisting of a few streets around a central crossroads, marked by a compact drum tower. Despite its much smaller size, Zhōngwèi seems more aggressive than Yínchuān, and the menus with missing prices, the extra *yuán* added to the bill and other tricks are back in force. However, there are a number of very cheap and reasonably friendly hotels where the prices for foreigners and Chinese are the same, and a stop at Zhōngwèi is convenient, whether you are passing through between Yínchuān and Lánzhōu or between Tóngxīn and one of these. The town's main attraction is a collection of remarkable temples, the Gāo Miào, although it is also famous regionally for its stocky little goats.

Further north the Hèlán Shān protect the road and rail routes which follow the Yellow River from one of the Gobi's southernmost fingers, the Tengger Desert (Ténggélǐ Shāmò), but by Zhōngwèi these have petered out. To make the railway line possible, in 1958 a 65km stretch of desert was quilted with grasses, lined with woven windbreak, and planted with a now flourishing belt of trees, using techniques pioneered by the local desert research institute, and which can be seen in operation on the southern Taklamakan route, too. The large, menacing dunes are not far off, however, and it is overstating it to say, as local authorities do, that the 'Yellow Dragon has been tamed'.

Getting to and from Zhōngwèi

The railway station is less than 10 minutes' walk north of the Drum Tower in the centre, and the bus station less than 10 minutes east. The easiest way to and from Yínchuān is by bus, and to and from Lánzhōu by train.

by train

Trains to Lánzhōu include the 531 at 11.48, arr 22.01, the 201 at 02.27 arr 10.43, and the 43 at 14.07 arr 21.18. Trains via Yínchuān towards Běijīng include the 44 at 16.76, arr Yínchuān 19.28, Bāotóu East 3.58, Hohhot 7.13, Dàtóng 11.58, and Běijīng 19.50. The 202 at 03.28 arrives in Yínchuān at 6.43, in Bāotóu East at 17.28, and terminates at Hohhot at 20.15. The 532 at 18.16 goes to Yínchuān arriving at 22.55. Your best chance for good seats to Lánzhōu is on train 43 and to Běijīng the 44, for which the station has a handful of numbered hard seats and sleepers. Also try the new Lǚyóu (check times at the station).

There is a slow connection to Wǔwēi along a separate line avoiding Lánzhōu, but it is hugely inconvenient. Take a train to the next stop south, Gāntáng, about 1½hrs and 72km away, and change to train no.517, which leaves at 05.48, arriving at 10.53, taking more than 5 hours to travel 158km. Don't get off at Wǔwēi Nán (south) station half an hour before the terminus.

There are also connections to Xī'ān via Tóngxīn, Gùyuán, and Píngliáng—two slow trains daily.

by bus

There are buses to Yínchuān departing between 6.40am and 4pm (167km, ¥13), Gùyuán at 7.30am (244km, ¥18.50/$2.50), passing through Tóngxīn (2½hrs, 123km, ¥9.50). The sleeper bus directly to Xī'ān at 2pm (644km, ¥96) is the only option direct to Píngliáng (330km, ¥50), and can also be used to reach Tóngxīn and Gùyuán, for around double the prices quoted above. These buses often have two rows of double beds, and there may be some resistance to selling you a single berth if you are taking the bus beyond Tóngxīn or Gùyuán and through the night by yourself.

Getting Around

Everything is within 10 minutes' walk of the drum tower, of the same period as its larger Xī'ān counterpart and in good condition, but not open for climbing. The four streets radiating out from this point, the unsurprisingly named Dōng, Nán, Xī, and Běi (East, South, West, and North) Dàjiē, contain everything that you might need.

Zhōngwèi Ⓟ (0953)   ## Tourist Information

CITS is hidden away in the Huáng Hé Bīnguǎn used for tour groups out to the west, and there's another travel operator in the Zhōngwèi Bīnguǎn, but there is little need for them. Other private operators may track you down in your hotel (*see* 'Around Zhōngwèi', below). There is a **post office** almost opposite the bus station, but all other administration including money changing and visa extensions are best dealt with before coming to Zhōngwèi, and there are few facilities on the route directly from here to Xī'ān, either. There is a small **bookshop** on the west side of Běi Dàjiē with some English novels, but there are no maps available.

Gāo Miào and Dìyù

Open 8–5.30; adm ¥10,
plus a further ¥10 for Hell.

高庙，地狱

Originally built in the Míng dynasty during the reign of the Emperor Yǒnglè (1403–24), this tightly knit group of temple buildings has been through the usual exhausting cycles of destruction and repair, being damaged by earthquake in 1710, expanded again in in the 19th and early 20th centuries, damaged by fire in 1942, repaired between then and 1947, damaged again in the Cultural Revolution (1966–76) and repaired again. Nevertheless, this is a larger and more impressive version of the Yùhuáng Gé in Pínglúo, and is Buddhist architecture at its most flamboyant and gothic. Each separate building has multi-pinnacled roofs, their ridges carved into sequences of flowers, with each ridge and pinnacle topped with perforated brick carved dragons. The buildings are connected by aerial walkways and stand compactly close together so that the shapes of the roofs merge into one vast, feathery mass. Almost every square inch of every building has been carved or painted. Doors and screens have beautifully carved wood, walls have panels of stone relief, and even the roof tiles are very elaborate.

As you enter there is a plan of the temples' layout to your left. Behind the first hall (Bǎo'ān Sì) steep stairs lead through a fine decorated brick archway to a towering gate with a superb relief of a tiger that seems to spring from the wall. Beyond is a magnificent triple level hall connected to the gate through which you have just walked, and on to further pavilions by aerial walkways, reached by climbing stairs at the rear. Further stairs on either side lead to the top floor, where you may see a chanting monk in full lotus position, and you can look down on the intricate roofscape.

The temples have a history of being multi-purpose, and although now dominated by Buddhist statues, there are elements of Daoism and Confucianism here, too.

To the right of the first hall, stairs lead down to Hell. Imagine a pre-animatronics Disneyland show called *Danteworld*, and you have an idea of this garish, grotesque, tawdry, and bizarre display. Underground passages contain a series of tableaux with inept *son-et-lumière*, and show the ten halls of hell and its 18 jails. Much of the imagery will also be familiar to those brought up in Western traditions of punishment after death for wrongs committed when alive. Jails in which people are sawed in half, have their eyes cut out or their tongues extracted, have a familiar Edgar Allen Poe quality, although according to Amnesty International accounts in China it's not always necessary to die before having similar experiences.

Around Zhōngwèi

Within a few hours of arriving at your hotel you may receive a visit from private operators offering you tours to the desert. A typical touristy two-day tour, particularly popular with groups from Hong Kong, would include yet another set of 'singing sands' (*see* 'Dūnhuáng', p.212), camel riding, floating on animal skin rafts on the Yellow River, seeing the large and intricate waterwheels (used for lifting water from the river for irrigation rather than for motive power), and a visit to the Shāpōtóu Desert Research Institute. The first asking price is a negotiable ¥600 ($72) to ¥700 ($84) per person; ¥250 ($30) would be more reasonable.

Shíkōng Shíkū

石空石窟

Heading in the direction of Yínchuān (¥3.50 from the bus station), get off at the 16km marker a little less than one hour outside Zhōngwèi and before Shíkōng itself (which is where the bus turns off for Zhōngníng and Tóngxīn). There's a path leading off towards the cliff with caves and temples visible in the distance. This is a pleasant 20-minute walk through a small village of mud and brick, past sleeping sows, scampering piglets, massed choirs of frogs like an ancient telephone exchange, and peasants hard at work in the rice and wheat fields.

At the site, the temples, occupied by nuns, are in good condition, but the caves are completely neglected. The main cave behind the left-hand buildings had rows of the miniature 'thousand Buddhas' but in relief rather than as murals. These have mostly been smashed off. Multiple statues of various sizes remain sitting in rows, all severely damaged, and there is no invigilation, so it's perfectly possible for visitors to pick up further pieces to take away, and no doubt some do. A double cave to the left has a larger statue and walls which were originally lined with plaster, now mostly smashed off. Further to the right are lesser caves with clay statuary mostly smashed back to its wooden armatures, an altogether dismal sight. But the scenery is pleasant, and the caves are instructive—a response to critics of the foreign archaeologists who removed murals and statuary earlier in the century.

It's possible to walk to another site along the watercourse you cross just before reaching the temples, although this is locked up and unmanned, and then further along to turn right to get back to the road near the 11km marker.

Where to Stay

Hotels in Zhōngwèi mostly have in common evening hot water and dubious bathrooms.

The most comfortable hotel in the centre is the **Zhōngwèi Bīnguǎn**, ✆ 701 2690 ext 8000, ✉ 701 2350, west of the tower on the north side, with doubles for ¥110 ($13.50), suites for ¥280 ($34), and a/c singles for ¥168 ($21), all foreigner prices. There's nothing remarkable about this hotel, but it is set back from the road somewhat, making it quieter than most of the rest. The reception is in the building immediately on your left as you enter the compound.

If you are looking for cheaper accommodation and arrive by or plan to depart by train, the **Tiělù Bīnguǎn** (Railway Hotel), opposite the station, ✆ 701 1441, has decent singles for ¥60 ($7.50), doubles for ¥30 ($4) per bed and triples for ¥20 ($2.50) per bed, all with bathroom. Walking into town down Běi Dàjiē, the **Zhōngwèi Fàndiàn** just before the drum tower, ✆ 701 1572, has a vast range of choice: doubles ¥30 ($4) per bed, triples ¥28 ($3.50) with bath. Singles ¥30 ($4), doubles ¥18 ($2.50) and ¥16 ($2), triples ¥12 ($1.50) and ¥10, and quads ¥8.50 (the latter with the iron-framed beds more common in *zhāodàisuǒ* (hostels) than *fàndiàn*). Staff may be surprised at your interest in these last two, because 'there's only black and white television'.

Arriving at the bus station and walking towards the tower along Dōng Dàjiē, the friendly **Míngzhū Bīnguǎn** on the left, ✆ 701 6812 ext 6811, has bright rooms with tiled floors, and has doubles for ¥30 ($4, with telephone) and ¥24 ($3), triples for ¥26 ($3.50) and ¥21 ($2.50) all with bath, and for ¥17.50 ($2) without. All prices are per bed. There's a reasonable buffet-style hotpot restaurant on the second floor. Further in on the right there's the **Zhōngwèi Dàshà** with similar prices and carpets if you prefer, but with somewhat reluctant staff.

Eating Out

Nothing special here. There are plentiful hotpot restaurants, and a lot more pig on the menus if you've come through Yínchuān and have been missing it. There are cheap dumpling restaurants on the west side of Běi Dàjiē (north of the drum tower), but cheating with the bill is widespread.

Tóngxīn

同心 The road from Zhōngwèi returns in the direction of Yínchuān for about 50 minutes, before turning off and crossing the Yellow River to Zhōngníng. After Zhōngníng the landscape becomes intermittently more desolate, with rivers having cut deep ravines for themselves in the soft soil. In general the scenery is similar to that of parts of the southern Taklamakan route, although not as desiccated. The greenery that lines the route swells intermittently into larger villages, almost all with new mosques.

In recent years this area has suffered from repeated crop failure and the threat of starvation, warded off by supplies of central government grain. Peasants scour the hills for a wiry wild vegetable called *fà cài*, 'hair vegetable', which is beloved of Chinese gourmets not for its bland flavour, but for its similarity in sound to *fācái*, meaning 'to get rich'. This must have an ironic sound to the peasants who gather it and bring it to market, impoverished as they are by poor land and poor weather alike. The average annual per capita income of the area is said to be just ¥400 ($48), compared to an average urban annual salary for China of ¥3249 ($391). Backward as Tóngxīn seems, with its many mud-walled dwellings, it is the height of sophistication and luxury in comparison to villages less than 30 minutes away, which lack even electricity and where many children go without education.

Tóngxīn (whose name—'work in unison'—sounds somewhat manufactured) is a small, dusty town, most of whose residents are fairly surprised to see foreigners. Get the bus to drop you not at the bus station but slightly further on at the traffic island/roundabout in the centre, and turn left (north) to find the **Hóngyàn Bīnguǎn**, ✆ (0953) 802 2147, just past the **post office** (*open 8am–9pm*) on the left, and entered from an alley immediately beyond it. This simple but friendly hotel is the best in town with bed prices of ¥60 ($7.50) in suites, ¥25 ($3) in doubles, ¥20 ($2.50) in triples, and ¥15 ($2) in quads, all with bath. In desperation only try the **Tóngxīn Fàndiàn**, ✆ (0953) 802 2667, almost opposite, a collection of low-rise buildings with beds in decrepit suites for ¥30 ($4), doubles for ¥20 ($2.50) and ¥17 ($2), triples also for ¥17, and very primitive doubles for ¥12 ($1.50). There are bathroomless doubles and triples for ¥7 per bed. There's a 6% construction tax on all bed prices in Tóngxīn. A Xīnhuá Shūdiàn can be found just north of the Tóngxīn Fàndiàn, but don't expect much choice in English books. Nor can you change traveller's cheques or extend your visa.

The main sight is the **mosque**, which is reached by returning to the main junction and turning left. Immediately before the bridge take a track on the right down to the river and cross on stepping stones, turning right. The roofs of the mosque are visible from the bridge, and just before reaching a road you will see steps up leading to a moon gate through which you will find the mosque. Go round it to the right to find the entrance. The high, crenellated, brick plinth is topped by unpainted halls, 4–500 years old, and has a martial look. The attendants are delighted to receive visitors, have no wish to exclude non-Muslims, and will invite you to look inside at no charge. Around the courtyard are panels of finely carved brick, one representing a series of shelves with clock and bowl of fruit. To the east there is a mud-walled Muslim graveyard and a track follows the north side of this to lead you back to the main road. If the river is in spate, or if you wish to avoid the somewhat smelly descent, you can use this route to reach the mosque by crossing the bridge and turning right about five minutes further on where you see the graveyard through a break in the wall at the corner.

Buses leave at 6am for Gùyuán, 6am and 7.30am for Yínchuān, 8am and 8.30am for Zhōngníng (where you can change), and many others pass through town and can be found at the bus station or flagged down elsewhere. The run to Gùyuán takes three hours and costs ¥9. The road is good, and runs through a pretty countryside of well-watered plains and valleys, occasionally breasting low ranges of hills. The remains of beacon towers are clearly visible on many high points, often with footpaths leading up to them which would make good walking. One of these leads from the south side of **Sānyíng** over to the east, about two hours from Tóngxīn and one hour from Gùyuán. Sānyíng also has the turning to the **Xūmí Shān Shíkū** (caves—*see* p.417). Twenty minutes south of Sānyíng, ten minutes before Gùyuán, and immediately before entering a cutting through the hilltop, the low remains of a tower and Qín dynasty Great Wall can be seen on the right. If you are coming from the south look left after passing through the cutting following the toll gate.

Gùyuán

固原　A small uninteresting town, Gùyuán, although still inside Níngxià, is 'within the wall', as the Qín dynasty ruins to the north attest. Genghis Khan is said to have visited, and further ruins on top of the hills to the south are held to be the remains of a fortification built in his day, probably around 1227. Gùyuán also claims to have the largest Huí population in Níngxià, although one might expect that prize to go to Yínchuān. However, it is not Islam but Buddhism which should bring you to the town, in the form of the extensive and little-visited caves at Xūmí Shān.

The **Jiāotōng Fàndiàn**, ✆ (0954) 203 2395 ext 8000, at the bus station, is above average for these transit hotels, being double-glazed to keep the bus station noise down. The staff here are friendly and at least apologize for making you pay for a whole double rather than one bed: ¥46 ($6) double with bath, common bath triples at ¥20 ($2.50) and ¥12 ($1.50) per bed, and quads at ¥9, plus ¥1 insurance one time only, with evening hot water. Turning right out of the bus station, the pink **Yúlèchéng Bīnguǎn** has similar standards and prices to the Jiāotōng but is marginally quieter, while turning left out of the station brings you to the **Gùyuán Fàndiàn**, more downmarket but cheaper. The **Dōngfāng Bīnguǎn** (East Hotel), almost opposite, is problematic, its tiled-floor doubles being slightly overpriced at ¥88 ($11) and then doubled in price *after* you check in, and there are yet more expensive doubles still. The other relatively comfortable hotel is the glum **Gùyuán Bīnguǎn**, ✆ 203 2173, reached by turning right out of the bus station, right into Zhōngshān Lù, and second right into Zhèngfǔ Jiē. The hotel, further up on the left, is old-school unhelpful and incompetent, with doubles between ¥84 ($10.50) and ¥184 ($22), or ¥64 ($8) without bath. Triples with bath are ¥56 ($7), and without ¥20 ($2.50), all plus 8% city construction tax and ¥1 per person insurance. There's a **travel agent** at the gatehouse which can book air tickets between Yínchuān and other Chinese cities, but although theoretically open from 7.30am to 9pm their principal occupation appears to be to hide out of sight, listen to personal stereos and read the newspaper, even while they are asked questions. The reception is straight ahead. The **post office** (*open 8–6 for mail and 7.30–6 for telephone calls*) is reached by turning right out of the bus station; take the first right and it's on the right.

The **Gùyuán Bówùguǎn** (*open 8–12 and 2.30–6.30; closed Sat and Sun; adm*) is a surprisingly large museum, and in fact one of this small town's bigger buildings. There's nothing in English, of course, but despite its slightly chaotic ground floor (half of it has become a furniture store), it is well organized and contains some surprises. To find it continue past the Gùyuán Bīnguǎn to the end of the street, and the museum is straight ahead. The entrance fee of ¥20 ($2.50) gives you three tickets for different sections.

Displays are in the usual chronological order of dynasty, with pottery, tools, and bronzes unearthed from various sites in the city and surrounding areas. Upstairs on the right is a large model of Gùyuán in the Qīng dynasty, demonstrating that it has since lost two complete sets of walls, one inside the other, no less than ten major gate towers, a bell tower and a temple. According to staff this all disappeared in 1972 during the Cultural Revolution (1966–76), but a few cones of earth and the odd longer stretch still poke up behind buildings around town.

Also upstairs is a room devoted to the Silk Routes, with photos of various old sites, followed by an exhibition of small Buddhist finds. Beyond this is a striking set of tomb figurines with movable heads, and a splendid model ox-cart. An attempt has been made to recreate the process of walking down the sloping ramp into a typical tomb chamber, with reproduction murals in place, to find a further small army of brightly painted 8cm-high figures. Unusually these include a large body of female figures preceded by three rows of horsemen of increasing size. There are other beautifully fashioned burial items, too, and the room also contains the museum's star exhibit: a vase, unmistakably Greek, carrying illustrations of the story of the Trojan Horse, eloquent witness of Gùyuán's position on trade routes to the West.

The second ticket gains you entrance to a separate hall to the rear of the main building on the left. This contains skeletons still lying in the earth in which they were found, showing an apparent preference for burying people on a slope with their heads lower than their feet. Four tomb reproductions from different periods have been constructed, demonstrating the changes in style of construction, which involve your walking down ramps into the earth. The first is Northern Wèi (386–535) containing a few more nodding head figurines. The second is Northern Zhōu from AD 569, with reproduction murals in place, and more of the miniature figures. The third is Northern Sòng (960–1127) with more patches of mural, and the fourth is Yuán (1271–1368). Outside at the rear a few tomb guardians and other stones have come to rest. The third ticket admits you to a reproduction stockade-cum-castle, containing a number of stelae.

On the way to the museum you will pass the **Dōnghú Gōngyuán** (park) on your left, which costs ¥0.50 to enter, and contains a rather forlorn small section of city wall with a brick entranceway. The remainder is an earthen embankment with views down to children's rides and the drained lake after which the park is named (East Lake), topped with a small pagoda. The staff will also be keen for you to see their bear. At the time of writing this poor beast, caught near Zhōngníng, had been kept in a cage barely twice its own size for one year, and plans to build larger accommodation appeared to be on hold. Like all Chinese animal exhibits this is to be avoided unless you wish to be disgusted or upset.

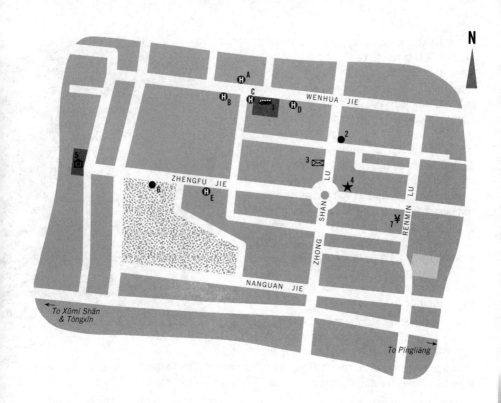

KEY

长途汽车站	1	Long-distance bus station Chángtú qìchēzhàn
新华书店	2	Xīnhuá Bookshop Xīnhuá Shūdiàn
邮电局	3	Post and telephone office Yóudiànjú
公安局	4	PSB Gōng'ānjú
固原博物馆	5	Gùyuán Bówùguǎn
东湖公园	6	Dōnghú Gōngyuán
中国银行	7	Bank of China Zhōngguó Yínháng

HOTELS AND RESTAURANTS

东方宾馆	A	Dōngfāng Bīnguǎn
固原饭店	B	Gùyuán Fàndiàn
交通饭店	C	Jiāotōng Fàndiàn
娱乐城宾馆	D	Yúlèchéng Bīnguǎn
固原宾馆	E	Gùyuán Bīnguǎn

STREET NAMES

南关街	Nánguān Jiē
人民路	Rénmín Lù
文化街	Wénhuà Jiē
政府街	Zhèngfǔ Jiē
中山路	Zhōng Shān Lù

Gùyuán

Xūmí Shān Shíkū

须弥山石窟

Open daylight hours; adm ¥20 ($2.50).

To reach the caves first travel 40km north to Sānyíng. The turning to Xūmí Shān is on the other side of the town, so stay on the bus. Northbound buses for local destinations start outside the front of Gùyuán bus station, and Sānyíng is ¥3. Upon arrival minibus drivers and farm vehicle owners alike become overexcited upon seeing you—always a bad sign. They ask you what you want to pay, refusing to quote a price. ¥1–2 for a seat would be about right for the under 20km, but while the road passes through several villages, the last part of the route is for tourists only. In summer you may be lucky to find minibuses gradually filling up with passengers, and you can simply join them, but in general the best procedure is to make a deal for something to take you there, wait two hours or so, and then bring you back. This leaves you able to spend as much time as you like at the site, come back when you please, and avoid overcharging for the return journey. A farm vehicle should be ¥10, and minibus ¥20 ($2.50). In summer there are sometimes minibuses that run directly from outside the bus station in Gùyuán which should take you all the way there for about ¥5 or 6.

Work on the Xūmí Shān caves probably began in the reign of the Emperor Xiàowéndì (AD 477–99) of the Northern Wèi dynasty, and continued during the Northern Zhōu and Táng periods. Of the more than 130 caves and innumerable niches, only a few still contain statuary.

The caves are cut into red cliffs overlooking a river-carved ravine. Begin by walking around to the left to see the 22m Buddha statue whose protecting building long ago fell down but which is in remarkably good condition nevertheless, and now shelters under a modern but tasteful concrete cover. To the left of this is a 3.7m standing Buddha in niche cave 1, originally lined with murals of which a few details are still visible. You can climb up for a closer look at the big Buddha then proceed round to the right and take a number of steeply climbing routes up to dozens of caves. Most of these have little left intact except some occasional hints of fresco and statuary. There are ledges and paths proceeding in all directions, the steps cut directly into the rock, and at the highest point there's a modern arch. Paths lead off into green valleys with grazing donkeys and views back as far as Sānyíng, or you can take a path round to the right and down to an originally Táng temple covering the most important caves. These include 45 and 46, made between about AD 557 and 581 with many fine statues and reliefs, those in easiest reach having been damaged particularly around the face by Muslims, but others whole and serene. Like many earlier Northern Wèi caves, these caves have substantial central pillars, carved on all four sides, and carved ceilings. The light is poor, so bring a torch if you have one.

Round to the right-hand side of the temple, which can also be reached by taking an earlier right-hand path from the building at the entrance to the site, are innumerable further caves in a pretty, narrow valley. Cave 51 is the largest, containing three imposing and mostly undamaged statues, the largest of which is 6m high. The most intact cave is 62, and being Táng shows a higher level of development of the sculptors' art, although the statues are mostly faceless. Further on still, cave 105 also has substantial amounts of statuary.

To Píngliáng

All the following buses quoted as leaving *before* 7am, leave half an hour later in winter. Buses to Xī'ān depart at 5.30am, 7am, and 9.30am (400km, ¥30.20/$4), to Lánzhōu at 6am (335km, ¥26.50/$3.50), to Píngliáng ten times daily from 6.20am to 4pm (90km, ¥6.80), to Yínchuān six times daily from 9.30am (323km, ¥24.50/$3), and to Tóngxīn at 3.30pm (122km, ¥9). There are also morning buses to Zhōngwèi (233km, ¥17.70/$2), or by a different route through Shíkōng (248km, ¥18.50/$2.50) and directly to Tiānshuǐ.

The road to Píngliáng winds through lush, green, elegantly terraced hills, crossed and recrossed by the new railway line. There are a number of steep climbs to be tackled, and after about one hour, the road passes through a village with substantial remains of old city walls, shortly afterwards passing through its only tunnel.

Píngliáng

平涼 Entering Píngliáng and immediately before arriving at the bus station (a large white building with a clock), you pass the new **Déxū Bīnguǎn**, ✆ (0933) 215014 ext 8119, the best choice in Píngliáng, so get off there if you can. Even larger and whiter than the bus station with acres of blue mirror-glass and capped with ochre tiles, this hotel is hard to miss. Self-consciously Chinese suites (moon gate between rooms) are ¥120 ($15), carpeted singles ¥60 ($7.50), doubles ¥35 ($4.50), and triples ¥28 ($3.50) per bed, tiled triples ¥20 ($2.50), all with bathroom and hot water, 9pm–11pm. There are also common bath quads for ¥16 ($2) per bed, all plus ¥3 per person per day in an assortment of taxes. There's another white tile hotel (with four large red characters on the roof) to the left across the square from the bus station. This is the **Xuánhè Bīnguǎn**, ✆ (0933) 217741, fairly bus-station-like but with carpets, and plain singles for ¥70 ($8.50), doubles ¥35 ($4.50) per bed with bath, ¥26 ($3.50) without. There are common bath triples and quads at ¥23 ($3), ¥20 ($2.50), and ¥13 ($1.50), no taxes. Píngliáng is large enough to warrant a bus to take you to the centre—the no.1 which runs past the front of the Xuánhè Bīnguǎn, but there is no reason to go there.

Kōngtóng Shān
Open daylight hours; adm ¥80.

崆峒山

Eleven kilometres to the west of Píngliáng, the Kōngtóng Shān claim to have received a visit from the first emperor of China, Qín Shǐ Huángdì himself, and to have been the most important Taoist holy mountains ever since. Once the route through Kōngtóng was strategically important as the only option for traders travelling west from Píngliáng. Numerous temples, pagodas and pavilions built during the Táng and almost every subsequent dynasty top various high points, and cliffs are pitted with caves. The buildings are either in an overgrown and dilapidated state, or restored (more or less rebuilt from scratch). To follow the various winding paths is like walking through a classical Chinese landscape painting, its common elements including rocky mountains, long considered the home of immortals, and pines, symbolizing strength and virtue. Paths meander between the sheer-sided peaks and up to higher ground. Optional and somewhat precarious routes include a sheer 378-step staircase cut into the rock, a flimsy plank bridge between peaks, and a set of cliffside footholds with chains to hang on to, resembling something from an early army assault course. From the ticket office near the base of the mountain it's a one-hour stiff walk up the winding track to the main groups of temples, the perfect antidote to too many days spent on buses and trains, although there is transportation available, too. The cool and leafy forests that climb the mountainside are alive with birdsong.

Minibuses start from outside Xuánhè Bīnguǎn up until around midday, but an early start is advisable. It's ¥3.50 to the top of the mountain, which is well beyond the ticket office. Buses return in the afternoon. You can also charter a wide variety of other transport from taxis to farm vehicles. A *miàndī* should cost no more than ¥20–25 ($2.50–3.00) to the ticket office, perhaps ¥30 ($4) on the unmade road to the top, including waiting a few hours for your return. Make it clear what your intentions are. If you take the vehicle to the top of the mountain, you will also have to pay a vehicle entrance fee of ¥6 and buy an entry ticket for the driver, ¥10 (unpleasantly, the foreigners' entrance price is a greedy *eight* times the local price).

To Xī'ān

From Píngliáng there are departures to Gùyuán at 6.40am, 8am, and 9.30am (91km, ¥7.40), and to Xī'ān at 6.40am, 7am, 7.40am, 8.30am (309km, ¥23.40/$3). There are also buses direct to Tiānshuǐ (273km, ¥20.30/$2.50), and to Tóngxīn (215km, ¥16.80/$2). Sleeper buses run to Yínchuān at 6pm (433km, ¥31.90), Lánzhōu at 6pm, and Xī'ān at 7.30pm. The first ticket window on the left is for Yínchuān, Gùyuán, Lánzhōu and Tiānshuǐ. The second on the left is for Xī'ān. A new bus station behind the old one may be completed by the time you read this and the old one probably demolished.

Some of the buses on these route are new, but others are probably Qīng dynasty. The road to Xī'ān is mostly easy and straight, running along the sides of broad river valleys with cliffs riddled with storage caves, some originally residences and some still lived in. Here shelves are cut into hillsides or square courtyards are cut down into the ground, and then entrances cut inwards.

At the 161km marker, there's a set of caves called the Dàfó Sì on the right, with a single large Buddha visible from the road but severely damaged, and no obvious accommodation. Buses usually stop at a group of restaurants between the 159km and 158km stones for 30 minutes, this being almost exactly halfway to Xī'ān, and it may be possible to go back for a quick look by flagging down passing vehicles. The bus will not wait for you. There's a further set of caves between the 155km and 154km markers, in poor condition with some garish modern statuary outside. After the 126km marker an old road to Xī'ān leads off to the left, possibly that taken by the American archaeologist Langdon Warner, and shortly afterwards you enter the town of **Bīnxiàn**, about 3½–4 hours from Xī'ān, and 5–6 from Píngliáng. It would be possible to stop here and return to explore the caves further. You can stay the night at the newish, plain and simple Bīnxiàn Zhāodàisuǒ, ✆ (0910) 492 2380, which is the large white building in the middle of town on the right, coming from Píngliáng. Beds with bathroom are ¥30 ($4) in a double, ¥35 ($4.50) in a triple, and there's evening hot water.

Leaving Bīnxiàn the bus takes ten minutes to climb the 3km up to the highlands again. Farming is increasingly varied as the road goes south. There are fields of corn and small orchards, and in season roadside apiarists in veiled straw hats, looking like escapees from a vicarage tea party. There's a ruined pagoda to the left after the 115km marker, and a gentle descent to the Shǎnxī plain begins at the 110km marker. After that the road is faster for the 2½ hours to Xī'ān, passing some of the sights on the 'west route' (*see* p.133), and at the 62km marker, somewhat unexpectedly, a church with an Orthodox look. The bus stops briefly at Xiányáng, finally trundling into Xī'ān's Yùxiáng Mén Qìchēzhàn in the late afternoon or early evening.

Almaty to Ürümqi

From the Steppes

Glory monument, Almaty

'For sale,' said the scrawl on the base of Lenin's statue. 'President Nazarbayev's constitution will make him a robber-Sultan,' say the leaflets blowing about near its base. The cynicism that sustained ordinary Soviet citizens is alive and well in the new Kazak Republic. The former *nomenklatura* have if anything improved their lot under Nazarbayev, a 'reformed' communist himself. But those such as army officers, who struggled to better themselves by swimming with the tide, now struggle to make ends meet, the system that supported them having disappeared and the value of salary or pension having plummeted with inflation and the fall of the ruble. They think it immoral that 20-year-old 'businessmen' are now driving around in imported cars while they struggle to maintain the obsolete and decrepit Volgas they saved for years to buy. The man on the Prospekt Lenina omnibus shrugs. 'Before we had plenty of money, but there was nothing to buy. Now there is plenty to buy, but we cannot afford anything.' One day in August 1996, nearly five years after Kazak independence, Lenin quietly disappeared, but whether he was indeed sold off to some souvenir-hunter nobody seems to know.

For the visitor Almaty is blossoming, with new pavement cafés and restaurants opening daily, new businesses supplying trekking, climbing, and other tourism services, and the beginnings of a night life. Whatever the West's fears about the new republics of Central Asia, and although it's claimed that nearly 5000 mosques have opened in Kazakstan since 1990, Almaty is no hotbed of Islamic militancy. Alcohol is on sale at almost every shop and kiosk, with alcoholism one of the legacies of Russian rule, and the city's streets are one long fashion parade, with diaphanous dresses, spray-on miniskirts, and high heels more the rule for women than the exception. Russians, Kazaks, Uighurs, Koreans, Kyrgyz and others mix freely, and there are children of every possible combination. The renovation of Zenkov Cathedral continues apace, but the new mosque remains incomplete for lack of funds (another $3 million is needed).

The city slopes gently up from north to south, rising to meet the Tiān Shān peaks that tower so impressively over it. It's just as well that this major navigational aid exists, as the post-independence change to street names have confused everybody. Prospekt Lenina survived until 1996, when it became Dostyk (friendship), but Karl Marx and others lost out to officially sanctioned Kazak heroes some time ago. However, with taxi drivers and most other residents, it's usually useless to use anything except the old Russian names. Russification also survives in the shoddy buildings with their uniquely totalitarian mix of Sputnik-era modernism, malfunction, and decrepitude. Much to the disgust of many rural Kazaks, Russian is the *lingua franca* of Almaty, and few city-dwelling Kazaks can speak their own language, a relative of Turkish.

While there are plentiful ex-pat fat cats looking for pickings from Kazakstan's potentially growing economy and its oil and mineral wealth, there are very few foreigners here simply for pleasure. The result is heavy overcharging at almost all hotels and many restaurants, but a rapid expansion in the number of available beds and menus fuelled by potential profits may help to bring prices down a little in the future. It is the switched-on young entrepreneurs or those working for aid agencies or lower down the pecking order of the multinational companies who have the pulse of the city, know how to live economically, and know the latest places to go.

While a few of the 'taxi' drivers have learned that foreigners on expense accounts will pay whatever they are asked, most visitors in most situations are treated with consideration and charged much the same as locals. Very occasionally a few humourless leftovers from the 'inevitability of history' period will be encountered, in older hotels and at museums. But except at night the city will seem pleasant and relaxed, and for those entering from China it will seem halfway home. Its streets bordered by chuckling streams, Almaty is greener and less polluted than Chinese cities, and there's a refreshing measure of courtesy in day-to-day transactions.

Nothing remains of the ancient Silk Route town that once stood where Almaty stands today. The Russians reached here in 1854, renamed it Verney, and by 1877 it had a substantial population, although ten years later and again in 1911 it was almost flattened by earthquakes. It is only in the days of pre-stressed concrete that Almaty's buildings have dared to creep above one or two storeys, and even in the centre there are many post-earthquake single-storey houses that look more like country cottages than part of a nation's capital. The change of government in 1921, the year the Bolsheviks consolidated their power, brought as big a rash of name changes as those that marked the shrugging off of that authority 70 years later, and Verney became Alma-Ata, or 'Father of Apples'. Like Siberia it was a place of exile; individuals who displeased the regime (Trotsky being the most famous) and sometimes whole ethnic groups were dumped here at one of the empire's remoter edges. Hundreds of thousands of people of both German and Korean descent who found themselves within the Soviet Union's borders during the Second World War were deported en masse to Almaty and neighbouring areas in case their sympathies were with the wrong side. In 1992 Alma-Ata reverted to being Almaty (which refers to the apple trees still found in almost every garden). Those of German descent claimed their right to live in Germany and departed en masse, and the Koreans began importing charismatic Christian preachers, and taking shopping trips to Seoul on chartered jets.

Almaty may soon be radically changed by proposals to move the nation's capital to Akmola (formerly Tselinograd), a small town in the north which has little to recommend it other than its railway junction. Here Nazarbayev plans a new Brasilia by the year 2000, and the jobs that depend on the government and the offices of foreign companies may go too, given the proposed plans for tax incentive schemes. Almaty is to remain a cultural and spiritual centre but, with little indigenous industry to sustain it, it may become a shadow of its current bustling self. 26 ministries were scheduled to move in 1997, but the government was reported to have only 10 per cent of the funds necessary to complete the first stage, and even the building of the presidential palace was behind schedule. Almaty's sleepier sister Bishkek may find itself in receipt of the offices of foreign diplomats and businesses with interests wider than just those of Kazakstan.

Getting to and from Almaty

by air

Tickets for other CIS destinations are about 20% more expensive for foreigners than for local people. Other international flights vary, often being around double price, or triple on Western carriers.

The best connected of the major airlines are **KLM**, with flights to destinations worldwide via Amsterdam on Tuesdays and Saturdays, and **Lufthansa**, via Frankfurt daily except Wednesdays and Sundays. **British Airways** is expected to begin a service between Bangkok and London via Almaty. The cheapest flights are inevitably with local and regional airlines, but often with vastly less comfort and reliability. **Aeroflot** flies into Moscow, with connections to London, Paris, Frankfurt, Hamburg, New

York, and elsewhere worldwide. **Transaero** is connected to British Airways and flies to and from Moscow for the same price as Aeroflot, but uses a new Airbus. Reaching London by a combination of the two costs about $347 one way. Transaero also has connections to Amsterdam, Frankfurt, Madrid, Rome, Zürich, New York, Orlando, and a host of Eastern European and Central Asian destinations. Minsk-based **Belavia** flies to Shannon via London. **Turkish Airlines** flies from Istanbul with connections to Europe and North America, and this is usually the cheapest way to reach Almaty, although under challenge from **Uzbekistan Airways** with connections to Amsterdam, London, New York, and Běijīng through Tashkent. Almaty–Tashkent–London or Amsterdam costs around $781 one way. **Austrian Airlines** flies to Vienna on Wednesdays and Saturdays, **Swissair** via Vienna to Geneva and Zürich, and **PIA** flies to Islamabad weekly on Mondays for $265 one way (book well in advance, preferably before leaving home). Reciprocally, **Kazak Airlines**, if it's flying at all, goes to Vienna, Hannover, Frankfurt, Běijīng, Moscow (cheaper than Aeroflot or Transaero) and Istanbul, as well as Tel-Aviv, Delhi, Ürümqi ($140), and elsewhere. **China Xīnjiāng Airlines** flies to Ürümqi on Mondays and Fridays ($192). **Miat Mongolian Airlines** flies to Ulan Batar for $210. There are flights to most major Central Asian cities both inside and outside Kazakstan.

The *aerovoksal* or **City Air Terminal** is on Zhibek Zholu, corner of Zheltoksan, and sells tickets for a wide variety of local and smaller foreign airlines, including Belavia, Aerosweet, Asia Service, Transaero, Azamat, and Vogelman, China Xīnjiāng Airlines and Kazair. Ticket windows for the local airlines are mostly open 9–1 and 2–6 or 7. Locals can check in here and board a direct bus, but foreign residents and visitors must check in at the airport itself.

To get to the airport take bus 592 from Prospekt Abai, the City Air Terminal, and elsewhere, or take a 'taxi' (400t/$6—*see* 'Getting Around', below). From Almaty I station take bus 42.

by rail

There are two railway stations: Almaty I, ✆ 36 33 91, and Almaty II, ✆ 60 55 44. For non-CIS destinations, call ✆ 60 50 86. The closest to the centre is Almaty II which is at the north end of Prospekt Ablai Khan. Trolleybuses 5 and 6 run along Abai and down Ablai Khan to Almaty II, and this is where to catch the international 'express' to Ürümqi (though you can also board at Almaty I if you wish). *See* 'To China by rail and road', below. There are daily trains from Almaty II to Moscow taking three days. Most other trains also stop at Almaty II, but some trains between the southern CIS republics do not. Tickets for *all* trains are on sale at Almaty II so always check which station you need. Almaty I is considerably further north at the top of Ulitsa Seifulina (200t by taxi).

by bus

The long-distance bus station, ✆ 26 26 44, is west of the city centre on Ulitsa Komsomolskaya (now Tole Bi), corner of Mate Zalka, and can be reached by trolleybus 19, which runs up Prospekt Lenina, along Abai, and down Mate Zalka. Quicker are buses 126 and 43, which go along Komsomolskaya and can be caught from near the Hotels Otrar and Zhetisu. There are several departures to **Bishkek** every day and tickets cost 300t ($5), purchasable on the day or one day in advance. The journey takes about four hours. Central Asian Travel also runs a bus (with a/c, catering, and telephone, no less) from the airport to Bishkek for the somewhat absurd price of $60 one way, $100 return. There are also buses to Tashkent and other CIS destinations. *See also* 'To China by Rail and Road' p.444.

Getting Around

There are few official **taxis** in Almaty, because almost every privately owned car is an informal one. Simply step into the road and hold your arm out and in a few moments a car will pull up. This is most likely to be a decaying Lada, but might be anything from a Datsun to a dented BMW. Avoid brand-new Mercedes full of *mafiosi* heavies. Open the door and tell the driver the two streets which intersect nearest to your destination. If he nods, show him what you want to pay. If he nods again, get in. If he doesn't, just wave him away. The next vehicle will take you for sure. Your 'cab' may often have two people in already, one of whom may be a passenger to a similar destination, or a friend of the driver. All trips within the city centre should cost no more than 60–70t, or about 25t per km. The long-distance bus station will be a little more, perhaps 175t. The airport is another matter. Some incoming foreign residents on your plane will tell you airily, 'Don't pay more than $20.' There is actually no need to pay more than 400t ($6), either there or back. When you leave the international terminal walk round to the front of the airport and along it to a small roundabout (traffic circle) at the other end. Walk round to the left, step in the road, and put out your hand. Arriving or leaving by Lufthansa or KLM in the small hours of the morning, there are still usually more 'taxis' than passengers. It's up to you to decide whether you want to wait it out or pay over the odds to get away. Paying in dollars helps.

An alternative is to stay at the Hotel Aksunkar next to the terminal building, ✆ 57 69 76, with rooms from 1400t ($20) to 1620t ($24) for foreigners.

To order a real-ish taxi which will charge around 25t per kilometre, dial 058. Drivers have a tendency to increase quoted prices when they see the passenger is a foreigner—resist. You will be called back with an arrival time and the car registration number. Some people consider this increased security worth the extra cost.

Car hire is available from Hertz at the airport, ✆ 34 40 70 (*open 6.30am–10.30pm*), or from their office inside the business centre opposite and slightly south of the Hotel Kazakstan (entrance across a car park on the north side), ✆ 63 18 32 (*open 8.30–6*). They have Western vehicles at Western prices.

The city centre can be **walked**, although some blocks are unexpectedly long, which may mean taking an occasional taxi back to the hotel at the end of a long day. The traffic moves erratically, but without much passion, and is reasonably courteous. For maximum safety cross at junctions. Traffic turning into the street you are crossing will usually wait for you to pass. Keep your eye on the lights, however. A flashing green light means that they are about to change, and the moment when one direction's lights hit red is the same when the other direction's hit green.

The buses, trolley-buses, and trams that make up the **public transport** system are a collection of cast-offs and museum pieces from around the world, with the occasional

airlines

Intourist Southern has now been replaced by **Yassawi**, the Kazak state travel agency, which will buy air (and bus and train) tickets for you for a commission of $10 per ticket or $5 per person in a group. They can be found in an office behind the reception of the Hotel Otrar, ℡ 33 00 75, 33 00 45, ✆ 33 20 13, 33 20 56, telex 251223 HOTEL KZ or 251609 PION. A good call to make for comparative pricing is to the **ACS Travel Agency** at 27 Dostyk (formerly Lenina), ℡ 62 22 44/62 12 07, ✆ 62 26 68, which has particularly helpful English speakers, and handles reservations for Lufthansa, Transaero, Finnair, Uzbekistan Airways, Aeroflot, KLM, Austrian Airlines, and some smaller local airlines, and accepts major credit cards. **Central Asian Tourism Corporation**, 52 Amangeldi corner Kazibek Bi, ℡ 50 10 71, ✆ 63 90 20, satellite ℡ 2–581 2451, catfvk@sovam.com, is an agent for Austrian and Swissair, and buys all other tickets for a $10 commission.

Aeroflot, 48 Baytursina, ℡ 39 49 81, and at the airport, ℡ 34 04 61.

Austrian Airlines and **Swissair** can also be found at the airport in the Hotel Aksunkar, room 114, ℡ 34 42 30.

China Xīnjiāng Airlines, Timiryazeva at Auezova opposite the exhibition centre, ℡ 50 94 85, but this 'office' is in fact an unmarked apartment and only Mandarin is spoken. Instead book between 9am and 12 noon at the *aerovoksal* or City Air Terminal.

Kazak Airlines (Kazair) is at 88 Aiteke Bi, cnr Naurizbay Batyr, ℡ 63 95 06, ✆ 69 55 72.

KLM has now taken over the old Intourist Southern office at the front of the Hotel Otrar, ℡ 33 00 07, ✆ 33 12 34.

Lufthansa ℡ 34 04 04/34 47 05, ✆ 34 40 49, is at 152 Morissa Toresa, and in the Hotel Aksunkar on the right of the terminal buildings as you face them.

PIA, ℡ 34 42 97, is also in the Hotel Aksunkar at the airport.

Transaero, 88 Aiteke Bi, ℡ 63 95 08.

Turkish Airlines, 81 Kazibek Bi at Zheltoksan, ℡ 50 62 20.

Uzbekistan Airways, Rm 113, 531 Seyfulina, ℡ 63 50 85.

embassies

Onward visas: it is more reliable to get all the following visas before you leave home. **China**: 137 Ulitsa Furmanova (corner Vinogradova), ℡ 63-49-66 (*open Mon, Wed, Fri, 9–12*). Chinese visas can be purchased here, but only leave it until Kazakstan to purchase your visa if you have no other option. Visas usually take 5 days, sometimes 7, and the cost varies according to your nationality. UK citizens are charged $60, payable in dollars or tenge. An extra $20 might speed up the process. Once you have entered, fight your way to the left-hand window to get your application form, and again to hand it in. One photograph is needed. The right window is where you pay and collect your visa. As at other Chinese embassies, US citizens are given slightly more hassle, usually a longer wait. There is often a queuing system at the gate. A piece of paper hangs from a nail on the guard hut. Write your name in the left column if you want to get a visa application form, and in the right if you have come to collect a visa. Keep your eye on where the guard has his thumb when he begins to call out names, as he is unlikely to be able to pronounce yours.

Kyrgyzstan: 68a Amangeldy, ✆ 63-33-05 (*open Mon–Fri, 10–6, but mornings are more reliable*). This embassy occasionally requests visa support but usually not, and charges $30 for 7 days. Agencies such as Yassawi can arrange Kyrgyz visa support if necessary, but may require you to purchase accommodation or at least try to persuade you. Also try Central Asian Travel in Almaty, Dostuck Trekking or Kyrghyzintourist in Bishkek.

Pakistan: 25 Tulebaeva just north of Makataeva, ✆ 33 15 02 (*open for applications Mon–Fri, 9–1*). The consular office is the last door at the rear of the building. Prices in rupees are posted up and vary according to citizenship and visa type. Hope to get your visa the next day. One photo, payment in dollars.

Russia: 4 Dzhandosova just south of Satpaeva, ✆ 44 23 27 (*open Mon, Wed, Fri, 10–1 and 3–5*). A 1-month tourist visa takes 10 days to process and costs $60. Transit visas are available the same day, valid for 3 days, but if you plan to travel to Moscow by train, these are extended to allow you 2 days in Moscow from the time you arrive. It's probably best to take your ticket to show them. All types of visa require four photos.

Uzbekistan: 36 Baribaeva at Gogola, ✆ 61 83 16 (*open Mon–Fri, 3–5*). A 30-day tourist visa takes 7 working days to process and costs $60; 14 days cost $50, and 7 days $40. Transit visas and multiple-entry visas are also available. Until recently no invitation was needed, but sometimes travellers have been asked for them, and they can be purchased from Central Asian Travel for about $20. Accommodation packages including an invitation can be bought from Yassawi. It is no longer necessary to list the cities you wish to visit on the visa, which can be made valid for the whole of Uzbekistan, *but check to make sure it has been when you get it.* It is not necessary to leave your passport. Only one person at a time is allowed to enter the consular section, so wait at the main gate until invited to continue.

If you need **passport photos**, polaroid prints are available from various photo shops, including the service next to the Shěnyáng Restaurant on Kazibek Bi for 240t for four.

Emergencies:

Australia: 20A Kazbek Bi, corner of 8-go Marta, ✆ 63 94 18.
Canada: 157 Prospekt Abai, corner Rozybakieva, ✆ 50 93 82.
France: 173 Ulitsa Furmanova, ✆ 50 62 36, ✆ 50 61 59.
Germany: 173 Ulitsa Furmanova, ✆ 50 61 56, ✆ 50 62 76.
Italy: 69 Samal 2, 6th floor, ✆ 54 17 99, ✆ 54 19 98.
Japan: 36 Samal 1, ✆ 53 32 05, ✆ 53 31 94.
UK: 173 Ulitsa Furmanova, ✆ 50 61 55, ✆ 50 62 60.
USA: 99 Ulitsa Furmanova, ✆ 63 24 26, ✆ 63 38 83.

maps and books

Maps of Almaty and Kazakstan are only available in the foyers of the larger hotels, are vague, and cost around 200t ($3). A better but Russian-only map can occasionally be found in some bookstores for 75t ($1.10). A reasonable local **guide book** is the red and blue covered **Almaty Guide** by Jane Olsen, whose English is rather whimsical and who has an almost Soviet obsession with statistics, but who is good on background material such as the histories of the Kazak heroes whose names now so confusingly adorn the streets.

Unfortunately this guide is hard to find, and the Hotel Kazakstan reception (not the foyer bookstore) charges $10 a copy. Various ex-pat and diplomatic organizations produce their own lists of hotels, restaurants, foreign businesses, etc., the one produced by Price Waterhouse being most commonly seen. This is theoretically for internal consumption only, but circulates widely. The reception at the Rachat Palace Hotel may let you look at their copy, for instance, and some other hotels have a copy in each room.

money

Money is much less of a problem than it used to be, but for maximum convenience bring US dollars in cash. The notes must be in very good condition and, except for the $1 notes, must be dated 1990 or later, the time when a security strip was introduced to the paper. There are money-changing facilities on every street—always ask for a receipt, which you will certainly get if you exchange in the foyer of one of the more expensive hotels. Cashing traveller's cheques is now possible at the **Texaka Bank** (Bank of Texas and Kazakstan), 4 Zenkova, two floors up in the building to the right of the Museum of Kazak National Musical Instruments (*open Mon–Fri, 9–1 and 2–4*). There is no commission payable, but the rate is not marvellous and only US dollar cheques are accepted. Payment is in tenge. Visa and Mastercard cash advances in dollars are possible at a commission of 5.5%. A better deal is available at the **Alem Bank** (*open Mon–Fri, 9–12*) at 39 Prospekt Lenina (at Jambul), which cashes cheques in all major currencies. Go up one floor to room 201, and to the right-hand-most computer terminal. The rate is not too bad, there is no service charge, and the process is reasonably efficient. Mastercard and Visa advances are also available at a commission of 5%. Sub-branches of Alem in hotel foyers and elsewhere may not offer exactly the same facilities, such as the one on Bocembai Batyr at Mira which only accepts Visa and Mastercard traveller's cheques, and charges 2%. The branch in the Rachat Palace Hotel is open **24 hours**, charges 2% on traveller's cheques, but gives as much as 30% less than the proper rate for currencies other than Deutschmarks, dollars, or pounds.

photographic

Film and developing are now widely available, with several locations on Zhibek Zhoulu between Karla Marxa (now Kunaeva) and Ablai Khan. There's Kodak developing on the corner of Tole Bi and Ablai Khan, and Konica on Gogola, one block west of the Hotel Otrar. There's a two-hour service on Kazibek Bi next to the Shěnyáng Restaurant (*open 9–7*). A 36-shot roll of ASA400 Konica film is 330t ($5), 36-shot developing and prints 960t ($15). There are similar prices at the Konica shop just north of the US embassy on Furmanova. Not surprisingly at these prices there are few cameras to be seen around Almaty, and any decent SLR is likely to attract attention.

post office and telephones

Postcards are not widely available and are usually found for silly prices in the foyers of expensive hotels. The best place to buy them is at the **post office** (*open Mon–Fri 8–7 Sat and Sun, 9–5*) on Ablai Khan at Kirova. Walk along Kirova from Ablai Khan and turn right to enter from the rear. Postcards cost around 5t, plus a 30t stamp for overseas. Stamps for letters to overseas destinations begin at 42t. Several top hotels have their own post offices, but often charge well over the odds for both stamps and cards. **_Poste restante_** services are also available (**посте рестанте**) but it would certainly be inadvisable to send anything important. Incoming mail is kept for two months, and there is no charge for collection.

Residents of any of the major hotels can make **international phone calls** from their rooms, and there are usually fax machines and foyer facilities for non-residents. If you are renting an apartment, some ordinary domestic phones can be used by arrangement with your hosts. The cost for three minutes to the USA, for example, is about $5.50, about one-third of the price in China. There is an international telephone office on Ulitsa Panfilova, just behind the Hotel Almaty (*open Mon–Thurs 8–8, Fri and Sat 8–3*) and another on the south side of Zhibek Zhoulu opposite no.81, east of the TsUM department store. Satellite pay-phones can be found in various locations, including outside the Cosmos Café on the 26th floor of the Hotel Kazakstan, the foyer of the British-French-German Embassy at 173 Furmanova, the ground floor of the business centre opposite the Hotel Kazakstan, and from both the national and international departure areas of the airport. Satellite phone cards can be bought from hotel foyers, from the Galaxy Shop on Kazibek Bi, corner of Kunaeva (now Karla Marxa), and from the telephone office upstairs at the airport's domestic departures terminal. **Local phone calls** only cost a few tenge, but you will be charged much more by the big hotels. Pay-phones are plentiful but often broken, and require the use of a token purchasable from many street kiosks (15t). At Almaty II railway station there is a lady with a phone on a desk in the main booking hall (15t). Otherwise ask at any café you happen to be in, and be prepared to pay 15t. You can send and receive **facsimiles** from the office to the left of the rear main entrance of the post office, ✆ 63 89 30. It costs 40t to receive one page, and 687t to send one page to the UK. A commercial outfit with a slicker approach is **International Net** at 74 Panfilova (enter round corner in the alley, then first door on right). They charge 119t per minute to the US, 124t per minute to the UK, and 8t per page to receive. They have four fax lines, and international calls can be made, too (*open 8–12 and 1–9*). For those obsessed with staying in touch it is also possible to send and receive **e-mail** by prior arrangement with a company called Relcom, ✆ 42 55 54/42 58 18, postmaster@ricc.almaty.kz, for about 28t (40¢) per Kb.

travel agents

New travel agencies are springing up all the time, and if you want climbing, trekking, skiing (including heli-skiing), mountain-biking, bird-watching, rafting, hunting, fishing, ballooning, paragliding, horse-riding, or botanic trips, you will need their help. These agencies are also usually able to arrange the visa support that will allow you to get a proper visa on arrival at Almaty, or even before you leave home, and should be contacted well in advance. One of the most highly recommended is **Kan Tengri Mountain Service**, ✆ 67 78 66, ✆ 50 93 23, @ kazbek@kantengri.almaty.kz, which provides services both to overseas travel companies and directly to individuals and groups. They maintain base camps in the Tiānshān, and have led major mountaineering expeditions there and in the Himalayas. They also arrange Silk Route tours entering China from Almaty, performing a loop, and returning through Kashgar and Bishkek, and a 'Best of Central Asia' tour that includes key sites in the Central Asian republics. Visa support can be purchased without further services. Their office is inside the sports stadium at 48 Prospekt Abai. Walk around the stadium to the left, until you find three doors together on the east side. Take the middle door, and walk along the corridor to your left to the last two doors on the left. There is a fascinating display of dusty sports trophies in the lobby, many looking as though Fabergé had a hand in their design. It's a shame the same inspiration never touched Soviet architecture.

Karlygash Makatova is an experienced trekker with a full-time job making the travel arrangements for USAID, who spends her spare time organizing trips for much of Almaty's ex-pat community, from helicopter day-trips to Issyk-Kul, to weekend rafting, trekking, and climbing trips around the Tiānshān. Her prices are the cheapest, and she is happy to have visitors to make up the numbers. Call ✆ 32 27 67 evenings after 10pm and before 8am, or fax ✆ 32 27 67. Failing that, try ✆ 36 58 88.

luxurious modern import. The flat fare is 10 tenge (15¢), payable on the bus. Most buses are not very crowded for most of the day, and if you've just arrived from China may induce agoraphobia. Particularly useful routes for seeing Almaty's sights are trolley bus 19 from the south side of the Zelyony Bazaar, which goes up Lenina, around the east side of Panfilov Park, and then up Lenina again, and right along Abai, eventually reaching the long-distance bus station. Bus 5 runs along Abai and down Ablai Kahn to Almaty II station. Bus 61 passes the Central Museum, runs down Furmanova and then crosses to Kunaeva (Karla Marxa) to pass the Arasan Baths. Buses 4 and 2 follow circular routes and will give you a tour of Almaty.

The 592 bus is the one to the airport (20t/30¢), and the 6 goes from just south of the Hotel Kazakstan to Medeo, also 20 tenge. Smaller, private buses also run to Medeo, and can charge 40–50 tenge ($1), so check the price before boarding—if there are two or three of you, a taxi may be cheaper. The Medeo route is one of the few that gets really busy as local people escape the town's fumes.

Buses stop at around 10pm, and the street lights go out at around midnight, leaving large patches of pitch darkness. While foreigners have experienced few problems in Almaty, precautions should be taken. If you approach an expensive hotel for foreigners after dark, walk in a group, or drive to the door in a taxi. Avoid parks and their edges. If you take a taxi, make sure that you choose the taxi and not the other way round. If there are two people in the taxi, wave it on and wait for another. This behaviour will puzzle innocent locals, but it reduces your chances of meeting unpleasantness. If you live in a big city in the West you are probably safer in Almaty than you are at home.

Street name changes continue, but the only ones that can be guaranteed to be known by most local people are the Russian originals, although the signs have been replaced. The Russian language has six cases, one of which, the genitive, is used for street names and takes an -a ending. Lenin Street thus becomes Ulitsa Lenina—Lenin's

Other agencies which have been recommended include the somewhat expensive Central Asia Travel Corporation at 52 Armangeldy, corner Tole Bi, © 63 90 17, @ 63 90 20; Zhetisu Travel, 89/27 Kabanbai Batyr, © 62 42 18, @ 63 12 07; and Alpha Omega, a British joint-venture on the 6th floor of 155 Abai at Rozybakieva, © 50 99 44, @ 50 95 73. Fuller details of trips outside Almaty are given in Cadogan's *Central Asia* guide.

visa extensions

If you have a proper tourist or business visa an extension *may* be available from OVIR at Ulitsas Vinogradova and Masanchi, or from the Ministry for Foreign Affairs on the north side of Komsomolskaya between Dzerzhinskaya (now Nauryzbai Batyr) and Mira, but do not count on it. Beware erratic starting and finishing times, and long lunch hours between about 12 and 2pm. Don't arrive with only the visa of another CIS country and expect to buy a tourist visa for Kazakstan unless you have a proper letter of visa support. Seriously consider paying one of the travel agencies to do all this for you.

street. Alternatively, the feminine adjectival form is used which ends in 'aya' and precedes the word for 'street'. Thus Communist Street becomes Kommunisticheskaya Ulitsa.

Dzerzhinskaya	Nauryzbai Batyr	Komsomolskaya	Tole Bi
Gorkova	Zhibek Zholu	Lenina	Dostuk
Kalinina	Kabanbai Batyr	Oktyabrskaya	Aiteke Bi
Karla Marxa	Kunaeva	Pastera	Makataeva
Kirova	Boganbai Batyr	Pravda	Altynsarin
Kommunisticheskaya	Ablai Khan	Sovietskaya	Kazibek Bi

Kazakstan © +7, Almaty © (3272)   **Tourist Information**

Kazakstan has now adopted similar **registration** regulations to those of Kyrgyzstan. If you intend to stay in the country more than three days you must register with OVIR. Unlike in Bishkek, this is far from a smooth procedure—the office is large and full of troubled people, and fanciful sums of money are requested, especially if your visa is not a tourist one. If you have obtained visa support from travel agents Yassawi (Intourist as was) or Kan Tengri, then you can register for free at the Yassawi office behind the reception at the Hotel Otrar. If your visa support has come from another agency try to get them to take on this task, although there will be a fee. If you must do it yourself, OVIR is on Ulitsas Vinogradova and Masanchi, © 62 44 36, with erratic opening hours.

There is no tourist information office in Almaty. You will see few tourists here, and your best source of information will be any ex-pat you might happen to run into, or an English-speaking Kazak. The café in the US embassy is a good place to look (*see* 'Eating Out', p.442), or the library at the British Council (*open Mon–Fri, 9–5.30, except Wed 9–2*) where you can also find British newspapers and magazines. From the British embassy carry on walking south on Furmanova, and through the second large gate on your right you will see the British Council sign. The entrance is round to

KEY

1 Aerovoksal (City Air Terminal)
   Аэровокзал
2 Almaty II railway station
   Железнодорожный Вокзал II
3 US Embassy and Café
   Американское Посольство и Кафе
4 Texaka Bank
   Банк Тексака
5 Alem Bank
   Банк Алем
6 Post Office
   Почта
7 International Telephone
   Интернациональный Телефон
8 OVIR
   ОВИР
9 Ministry of Foreign Affairs
   Министерство Инностранных Дел
10 Chinese Embassy
   Китайское Посольство
11 Kyrgyz Embassy
   Кыргызкое Посольство
12 Pakistani Embassy
   Пакистанское Посольство
13 Russian Embassy
   Русское Посольство
14 Uzbek Embassy
   Узбекское Посольство
15 British, French and
   German Embassies
   Британское, Франсузкое
   и Немецкое
   Посольства
16 Zenkov Cathedral
   Зенковский Собор
17 Glory Monument
   Памятник Славу
18 Museum of Kazakh
   Musical Instruments
   Музей Казахских
   Инструментов
19 Arasan baths
   Бани Арасан
20 Zelyony Bazaar
   Зелёный Базар
21 Central State Museum
   Центральный Музей
22 State Art Museum
   Государстьенный Музей Искусств
23 Circus
   Цирк
24 Archaeology
   Museum
   Музей
   Археологии

25 Klub Kimep
   Клуб Кимеп
26 Club Manhattan
   Клуб Мангаттан
27 LA Club
   Клуб ЛА
28 International Business Club
   Интернациональный Клуб
   Бизнесса
29 Philharmonic Hall
   Зал Филармонии
30 Opera and Ballet Theatre
   Театр Оперы и Балета
31 TsUM
   Цум
32 Butya Store
   Бутя
33 Samal Store
   Самал
34 Galaxy Store
   Галакси

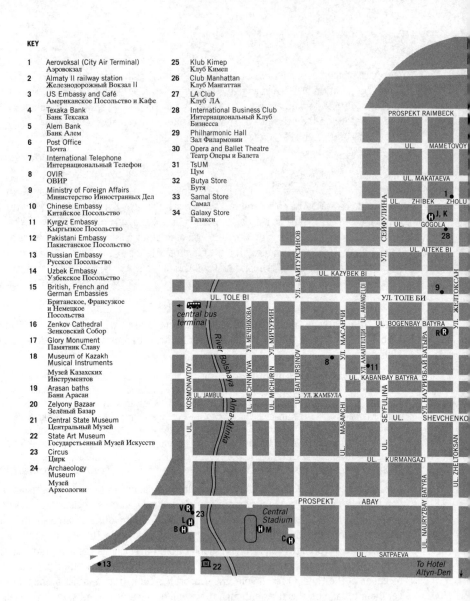

HOTELS & RESTAURANTS

A Otrar (Yassawi, KLM)
   Гостиница Отрар
B Marco Polo Rachat Palace
   Гостиница Марко Поло
   Палата Рачат
C Astana
   Гостиница Астана
D Dostuk
   Гостиница Достук
E Peking
   Гостиница Пекинг
F Almaty
   Гостиница Алматы

G Kazakhstan (Tulbo
   Restaurants, Café Cosmos)
   Гостиница Казахстан (Рестораны
   Тулбо, Кафе, Космос)
H Zhetisu
   Гостиница Жетысу
I Kazpotrepsoyuza/Daulet
   Гостиница Казпотрепсоюза/
   Даулет
J Uyut
   Гостиница Ают
K Kaz Zhol
   Каз Жол

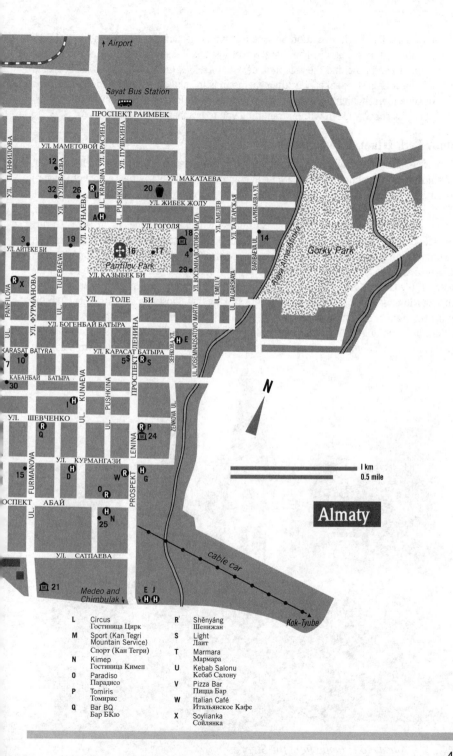

↑ Airport

Sayat Bus Station

ПРОСПЕКТ РАИМБЕК

УЛ. МАМЕТОВОЙ

12

32 26 R 20

A H

3 19 ✝ 16 17 18 4 29

УЛ. АЙТЕКЕ БИ М 14

R X Panfilov Park Gorky Park

УЛ. КАЗЫБЕК БИ

УЛ. ТОЛЕ БИ

УЛ. БОГЕНБАЙ БАТЫРА

KARASAT BATYRA УЛ. КАРАСАТ БАТЫРА H E

7 10 5 $ R S

КАБАНБАЙ БАТЫРА

30

I H

УЛ. ШЕВЧЕНКО

R R P

Q M 24

УЛ. КУРМАНГАЗИ

15 H W R H

D O G

ОСПЕКТ АБАЙ R

H

25 N

УЛ. САТПАЕВА

М 21 Medeo and E J

Chimbulak ↓ H H

cable car

Kok-Tyube

N

1 km
0.5 mile

Almaty

L	Circus Гостиница Цирк	R	Shēnyáng Шенижан
M	Sport (Kan Tegri Mountain Service) Спорт (Кан Тегри)	S	Light Лайт
N	Kimep Гостиница Кимеп	T	Marmara Мармара
O	Paradiso Парадисо	U	Kebab Salonu Кебаб Салону
P	Tomiris Томирис	V	Pizza Bar Пицца Бар
Q	Bar BQ Бар БКю	W	Italian Café Итальянское Кафе
		X	Soylianka Сойлянка

the right. The US Information Service has similar facilities on the sixth floor of 531 Seifulina at Kazibek Bi. The state travel agency **Yassawi** has replaced Intourist Southern and is behind the reception desk at the Hotel Otrar, ✆ 33 00 07. They have a helpful English speaker, but their main job is to sell you their city tours, and trips outside town, which you can arrange more cheaply for yourself. They do, however, offer visa support ($10) without requiring you to purchase other services.

Panfilov Park (Парк Панфилова)

Panfilov is green and leafy and like the many other green spaces in the city kept well sprinkled. The **Zenkov Cathedral** here has something in common with Tiāntán (the Temple of Heaven) at the far end of China in Běijīng, as both are built entirely of wood and without the assistance of nails. Put up in 1904, the cathedral is a giant pink, white, and gold birthday cake of a place, and one of the few buildings to survive the earthquake which levelled the city in 1911. During the Soviet period it was used for cultural events, but following extensive renovation, much of it by volunteers, including the removal of an interior balcony, a growing congregation of mostly middle-aged women gathers daily to worship beneath giant brass candelabra. Due east of the cathedral is the **Glory Monument**, celebrating the role of a group of Almaty men in the 1941 defence of Moscow from the Nazis. Rather more striking than most monuments of its kind, the giant figures seem like escapees from the pages of super-hero comics, all square jaws and determination. In a tradition that has endured throughout the former Soviet Union, newly married couples come to be photographed here, just as they do at the Tomb of the Unknown Soldier in

Zenkov Cathedral

Moscow's Red Square. A little further east at 24 Zenkova is the **Museum of Kazak National Musical Instruments** (*open 10–6; closed Mon*), looking like the Gingerbread House from 'Hansel and Gretel'. Here relatively modern versions of Kazak instruments are placed near their ancient counterparts, and many can be brought to life by pressing a switch beneath their cabinets. In theory, this should only be done by the attendant, but he is more interested in playing a kind of two-string lute (*dombra*) and singing songs to you himself. Pleasant as this is, it leads to a suggestion (in Russian, Kazak, and Mandarin, but not English) that you might like to buy a tape he has made of 32 songs, including some by local bard Abai (of Prospekt fame), and some by himself. Operate the switches yourself when he transfers his attentions to someone else. Tickets are 40t (60¢). On the far west side of the park and across Prospekt Karla Marxa (now Kunaeva), the concrete domed and pepper-potted building is the **Arasan Baths** (*open 8am–10pm, in two-hour sessions*), entered from the south side, with tickets available from below the main entrance. Here are three storeys of steam, massage, and mortification in the style of your choice: Finnish, Russian, or Turkish (which, oddly, they call 'Eastern'). Peddlers on Karla Marxa sell bunches of oak twigs to aid in the process. A two-hour Russian or Finnish session costs 120t ($2) up to the noon session, 240t ($4) from 2pm, 100t/200t ($1.50/$3) for the Turkish, but once you enter you can in fact visit any section you choose; or you can hire a private room for 400t ($6) per hour, in which case enter from the east. Mud baths and massages are also available from 300t ($4.50). The sexes are segregated unless you order a private room, and even then, rather quaintly, proof of marriage is required.

Zelyony Bazaar (Зелённый Базар)

Just north of Panfilov Park up Karla Marxa on the right is Almaty's main bazaar. Everything is available, from Chinese electronics and Pink Floyd tapes to home-made sausages, fruit, horse meat, and kitchenware. This is also the cheapest place to pick up toiletries. It's worth visiting to see a wide range of Kazak society; city people buy and country people sell. Amongst the professionals are others who are simply selling the produce of their cottage gardens to supplement their meagre incomes. On the southwest side there are people standing selling their possessions, perhaps desperate to add to now valueless pensions. If you're interested in taking portraits then this is probably the best place to come in the early morning or late afternoon.

Central State Museum (Центральный музей)

Open Mon–Fri, 10–6, Sat and Sun, 10–5; closed Tues; adm 60t ($1).

This yurt-inspired marble-encrusted building is on Furmanova south of Satpaeva, and is solid and impressive despite its self-consciously Central Asian motifs and leaky roof. Well worth an hour or so, its collections are generally well presented, and the wave of museum revisionism in the southern republics has not yet swept away all the Soviet material. Soviet-style over-manning means you are constantly pointed in the right chronological direction. Beginning with fossils and bones, you move on to maps of migrations, early weaponry and utensils, early books, pastoral life, costume, textiles, Second World War material, and Soviet political posters. The top floor has the plans of Nazarbayev's vanity metro project, and a motley collection of souvenirs from his overseas travels. It's worth paying the extra 30t (50¢) more to see a room full of rather fine jewellery. The copy of the golden suit of armour from the Archaeology Museum is also sometimes found here. Foyer shops offer Kazak and imported carpets.

State Art Museum (Музей искусств)

Open 10–1 and 2–6; closed Mon; adm 60t ($1).

The museum is at 30 Satpaeva, but is best approached from Abai by walking up beside the circus and past the front of the Rachat Palace. It's across Satpaeva on the left. It's a sizeable collection, containing some excellent Russian portraits and landscapes, plenty of naive pictures of idealized Kazak bucolic scenes, the occasional heroic 'Our Kazak Comrades Welcome the Arrival of the Turk-Sib Train' or similar, and local attempts at every style imaginable. Most work is 18th, 19th, or 20th century, but there are some older works with mythical subjects, and a few icons. There are also contemporary sculpture and applied arts products, and occasional visiting exhibitions. Some works are for sale.

Circus

Nowadays politically incorrect in the West, the circus was an approved entertainment for the masses in the Soviet Union, and struggles on in difficult economic circumstances. Shows are mostly at weekends, with dancing bears (and cub), high wire, clowns (who haven't varied their routines for years), trapeze, juggling, acrobats, a live band, and more. The best act is the Kazak horsemen, whose presence in the small building is very large as they thunder round the ring spending a large part of the time anywhere on their mounts except the saddle. The 'tent' is a round concrete building with fountains and a statue of a clown just west of the football stadium on the south side of Abai. A certain modernization and Kazakification has taken place with the introduction of a tableau of a Kazak sage, who is intermittently illuminated to one side of the ring, and a Kazak pop singer. The show lasts about two hours and costs 180t ($3).

Other Museums

Like much else in Almaty, many of the remaining museums are undergoing *remont*—renovation or reconstruction, which may or may not be over by the time you read this. These include the **Book Museum** at 94 Kabanbai Batyr, formerly Kunaeva (*open Mon–Fri, 10–5*), and the **Geology Museum**, 65 Kabanbay Batyr at Lenina (*open Mon–Fri, 10–5*). The **Archaeology Museum of the Academy of Sciences**, 44 Lenina at Shevchenko, ✆ 61 86 32, uphill from the Magazin Russiya next to Magazin Azimut, is above the cinema in a building recessed behind a large fountain (*open Mon–Fri, 10–5*). The director, Rosa Bektureeva, speaks English well. There are various pottery and architectural finds, but the star of the show is the Golden Man: a glittering suit made from overlapping fish scales of gold, of unconfirmed date. The one on show is a copy and the real one is in the vault, but there are many types of ceramic objects and carved wooden beams, as well as models and photographs of excavated sites with Silk Route credentials. The museum was supposed to reopen in early 1997, but call ahead.

Post-*remont* entrance fees are unknown but are unlikely to be more than the equivalent of $1.

Medeo (Медео)

A 30-minute bus journey (no.6 from just south of the Hotel Kazakstan) brings you into the foothills of the Tiān Shān and to the world's biggest skating ring (frozen by nature only—open late autumn to early spring). From here you can look down the valley to smog-shrouded Almaty, and walk up to the ski-lifts to Chimbaluk. For details of this and other trips out of Almaty see Cadogan's *Central Asia* guide.

Shopping

There's not a great deal to buy in Almaty that you can't buy elsewhere. The department stores on the pedestrian section of Zhibek Zhoulu around Ablai Khan are good for Western toiletries if you need to restock (as is the Zelyony Bazaar). The big shop on the corner is TsUM (ЦУМ), the original Soviet store. The carpets on sale on the ground floor are appetizingly priced until you discover that they are 100% acrylic and made in Belgium. Sable, mink, marmot, rabbit (the cheapest) and other fur hats are a bargain, especially in summer. The locals who live with −20°C in winter have little sympathy for animal rights, and regard fur as an essential to be acquired if it can possibly be afforded.

There are increasing numbers of shops selling semi-precious jewellery in elaborately mounted Russian styles, and plainer more modern forms. One of the best is Samotsvyety on the corner of Kabanbai Batyr and Lenina, and a store at the corner of Furmanova and Karla Marxa is also good. The Aksent store on the corner of Furmanova and Shevchenko has a small but fine selection at its southern end, as well as well-made but slightly pricey traditional local dress and hats. There's another branch opposite the Hotel Dostuk. An interesting bazaar in Gorky Park on Sundays has old Soviet memorabilia, such as military and political badges and equipment.

Where to Stay

The numbers of foreign experts and businessmen flooding into Central Asia, and the secondary wave of foreigners providing services to the first lot, have driven up prices to levels which are higher than those in many Western European cities. The expense-account mentality leads to prices being paid for goods and services in these places out of all proportion to value given, or the real cost of providing them. At any level of budget, there are few hotels in Almaty which represent value for money. Single occupancy usually costs the same price as double occupancy, or not more than 15% cheaper, except in some of the older Soviet-era hotels which have purpose-built single rooms at around half-price. Of course, there are lower prices for citizens of other CIS countries and lower ones still for Kazaks, and sometimes foreigners may only be allowed to stay in the most expensive rooms.

In August the centrally supplied hot water may be turned off for the weekend or for several weeks, some say for maintenance before the winter, others to reduce the Kazak national debt; possibly only the Rachat Palace and the newer hotels will have continuous supplies from their own systems.

expensive

The no.1 hotel is the **Marco Polo Rachat Palace**, at the west end of Satpaeva and behind the circus as you come along Abai, © 81 16 20, © 81 16 35, or © toll-free 0800 960501 in the UK, 1-800 735 5740 in the USA and Canada. This Austrian-run hotel opened in May 1995, was the first one to offer if not world-class then good Western standards, and looks the part with glass-fronted elevators sliding up the inside of the atrium. It has hot and cold running everything and accepts all major credit cards. Prices range from $325 a night for a double to $1500 for the two-bedroom

Presidential Suite, plus 20% VAT (sales tax). These rates include access to the health club and massages, the swimming pool, and the business centre. Prices are likely to drop as competition from the Astana (*see* below) bites, and when another five-star hotel, the Ankara, opens in the near future (on Satpaeva near the Presidential Palace).

The brand new **Astana International Hotel** is on Baitursynova just south of Satpaeva, ✆ and ✉ 50 70 50, a smallish (114 rooms) Turkish–French joint venture of standard international quality, with central a/c, satellite television, and private safes in each room. Doubles are $160 and suites $210, both including a sauna or massage, and taxes. Amex, Visa, and Diners' Club cards are accepted.

The **Hotel Dostuk** on Kurmangazy and Kunaeva (Karla Marxa), ✆ 63 65 55, ✉ 63 68 04 or 63 66 12, has a solid old-world charm, having once been the guest house for senior Party officials. The hotel has plentiful restaurants and bars, a sauna, and a business centre. There is a branch of Alem Bank in the foyer which will cash traveller's cheques and exchange dollars for tenge at a not too unreasonable rate. However, $135 is the cost of a single with breakfast but *without* air-conditioning. Doubles begin at $160, rising to $215 for a two-room suite. You can also book in the USA: ✆ (602) 748 1280, or ✉ (602) 748 1347. Credit cards (not Amex) accepted.

The **Hotel Otrar** at 73 Gogola, corner of Karla Marxa, ✆ 33 00 76, ✉ 332013, on the north side of Panfilov Park, is a much better bet despite being a much less appealing building. Rooms have air-conditioning and bathroom, and many have a view over the park to Zenkov Cathedral. Room service is prompt and courteous. Double rooms are from $90 including breakfast, which is served in your room at no extra charge. Amex, Visa, and Mastercard are accepted.

Better still is the **Peking Hotel**, a smaller and more comfortable place tucked away at 52 Zenkova (Vosmoco Martyr), ✆ 54 31 10, ✉ 54 31 18. Go east from Ulitsa Dostyk (Lenina) along Bocembai Batyr (Kirova), and take the first right. There are hints of Chinese ownership in the long-case clock in the hall, and the thermos of boiled water in every room; doubles are $100.

The monolithic, Soviet-atmosphere, and not particularly welcoming **Hotel Almaty** opposite the Opera and Ballet Theatre at 85 Kabanbai Batyr (Kalinina), corner of Panfilova, ✆ 63 09 43, ✉ 63 02 02 offers doubles from $80.

moderate

The **Hotel Kazakstan** is a 26-storey Korean-run tower at 52 Prospekt Lenina just north of the junction with Abai, ✆ 61 99 06/50 61 09, ✉ 61 96 00/50 61 11. Rooms have good views over the city or towards the mountains, but little else to recommend them. A grubby double is $60 with bathroom. The 14th and 15th floors have been refurbished by a German company to higher standards, and doubles cost $120. Visa, Mastercard and Amex accepted.

inexpensive

The **Zhetisu** is directly south of Almaty II railway station on Ablai Khan between Zhibek Zhoulu and Makataeva, ✆ 39 22 22. The reception thinks that the Soviet era is still with us, will not serve you until good and ready, and is closed at meal times. There is a restaurant on the second floor. A face-lift is in progress which will undoubtedly lead to higher prices. For now there is a range of beds from 350t, but foreigners are likely to be bundled into the 1200t ($20) rooms, which have private baths. There are rooms taking six people for 900t ($15), and you may be able to talk your way into one of these if you arrive in a group.

Private rooms are available from people who sit outside the Zhetisu, and sometimes the Dostuk and other hotels, waiting for foreigners. Typically, a room and a bathroom with three meals a day will cost $20, with little room for haggling (but try). Sometimes whole apartments can be rented for the same sum, and you cook for yourself. Given the cost of eating out, this is a bargain, although you may find yourself a little way out from the centre. Karlygash Makatova and some other agents (*see* p.430) can arrange home stays for $10–15 per person depending on the location.

The **Kazpotrepsoyuza**, ✆ 62 04 09, now also calls itself the **Daulet** and has reopened its main entrance on the southwest corner of Karla Marxa (Kunaeva) and Jambul, north of Shevchenko. It costs 3700t ($55) for a comfortable sitting room, double bedroom, and bathroom, with fridge and TV; 1400t ($21) for the same but without the sitting room; 700t ($10.50) for a single room. There is no restaurant. This is probably the best value hotel for the middle-budget traveller.

Also recommended are two hotels close to the *aerovoksal* on the corner of Gogolya and Nauryzbai Batyr (Dzerzhinskaya). The **Uyut**, ✆ 32 32 80, is clean, each room has its own toilet, and there are communal showers in the basement. Rooms are from 1200t ($17.50) to 3000t ($45). The neighbouring **Kaz Zhol**, ✆ 32 40 00, is reportedly both friendly and cheap, although undergoing a partial renovation which may put prices up. A bed in a basic room is just 450t ($7). Rooms with private shower are 800t ($12), and 'luxury' rooms are identical except for the addition of a television, telephone, and fridge, and are 1200t ($17.50) to 2000t ($30)

cheap

The **Circus Hotel** is directly behind the circus on Abai, and has recently been repainted to clash with the Rachat Palace, to which it stands at right angles on the right-hand side and at a lower level, looking like something from a Gerry Anderson TV series (possibly 'Stingray'). Primitive rooms without bath are 700t ($10) to 1000t ($15), but are not available if there is a visiting company in town. A gorgon sits at reception.

The **Altyn-Den** is at 42 Timiryazeva, corner of Auezova, ✆ 44 78 30, reachable by trolleybus 11 from Lenina or Abai. The reception is reached via small and grubby lifts to the fourth floor of the building to the right of the exhibition hall main gates. Single 850t ($13) with bath, double 1350t ($19) with bath. If you stay here you are more interested in economy than comfort. The only foreigners they get are Pakistani traders, who know a good cheap deal when they see one.

The **Hotel Sport** is in the football stadium at the same entrance as the offices of Kan Tengri (*see* 'travel agents', p.429), ✆ 67 40 33. It charges 160t ($2.60) for a single bed in a three-bed, 140t ($2.30) per bed in a quad, 320t ($5.20) in a double. Do not leave valuables here.

Kimep (the management college) has its own guesthouses on campus, Gostinitsa Nos.1 and 2, ✆ 64 37 39. No.1 is cheap, 420t ($7) per bed for the first night and 300t ($4.50) for subsequent ones in a double with bath. Other beds in No.2 are between 700t ($10) and 890t ($13).

The Hotels Medeo (in Medeo) and Ala-Tau on Prospekt Lenina are undergoing reconstruction by an American-Turkish consortium. These both provided good, cheap accommodation in the past, will almost certainly be more expensive when they reopen, but may be worth considering.

Eating Out

Restaurants come in three varieties: those catering for foreign residents with main courses at $15–$30, those catering for Almaty's mostly younger *nouveaux riches* at 400–500t ($7–8), and those for the rest at around 150t ($2.50). Neither professionals on only 3000t per month, nor retired people on now worthless pensions, can afford to eat out at all. In summer street cafés abound, and any cluster of umbrellas with seated locals will provide at least ice-creams and cold drinks at reasonable prices. These are also available from kiosks which occur at least every 100m, together with all your favourite brands of chocolate bar. *Shashlyk* (kebab) vendors can be found in the neighbourhood of markets and at other busy points, with spicy pieces of lamb on knitting-needle-like skewers (35t/50¢ each). Hygiene standards are not bad, and will only bother you if you have just flown in from the West.

Note that as with other services in Almaty, prices may be in dollars but payment is always in tenge. English is rarely spoken, but pointing at dishes and waving a number of fingers usually produces the right results. Some restaurants have photo albums of their dishes. Opening hours are like those of shops with a break in mid-afternoon except that restaurants stay open later.

New restaurants are opening all the time, and word goes round the small foreigner community very quickly if a new place is managing to serve something resembling good quality Western food. Typically things start well, then after six months either the foreign chef leaves and is not replaced, or the place simply closes at the height of its popularity for hidden political or *mafiosi* reasons. Others, such as the restaurant at the Ala-Tau, the Peking (Chinese) Restaurant, and the Tulbo Korean restaurant have begun to adopt strippers and even more explicit floor shows, which tend to bring a slightly threatening atmosphere along with the new clientele.

The brand new **Paradiso** on Abai opposite Kimep has the best Italian food in town, due to its genuine Italian chef. The overly bright interior is worth braving for a menu that can't be matched for thousands of miles in any direction. Dinner for two including imported wine is likely to come to $70, however.

The **Tomiris** is a favourite, at 48 Prospekt Lenina (corner of Shevchenko), one block north of the Kazakstan Hotel. Main courses from an ambitious Western menu are around $15, but with drinks and hard-to-resist desserts the final result will be around $25 per person. The cakes are excellent.

Standards in all the restaurants attached to the Kazakstan Hotel have fallen, or perhaps now that there is more competition the food simply seems poor by comparison. The Korean food at the **Tulbo Restaurant** is not worth the $20 upwards it costs. A standard cold drink here will cost $3, or six times what it costs at a pavement café, so expect your final bill to be substantially more. Eat before 9.30pm if you wish to avoid the floor show. There are also Western chicken and steak dishes from $15.

The once-popular Shaggie's Burger Bar, also attached to the hotel, is to be avoided. This is about as far from McDonald's as Almaty is from New York. Far superior and very substantial real beef burgers can be found at **Bar B Q** on the south side of Shevchenko just east of Furmanova. A cheeseburger with french fries and a small salad, plus a beer will be around 500t, plus 10% service ($9). For sheer volume this may be the best value in town.

The **Café Cosmos** on the 26th floor of the Kazakstan Hotel offers a limited menu of smallish meaty Russian dishes at around 200t, but is almost deserted in the summer in favour of the newer pavement restaurants. The staff speak some English and are friendly. A restaurant called **Light** has a similar menu one block further north of the Tomiris at 36 Prospekt Lenina. One waitress roughly translates the menu into English. There is more choice at night than at lunchtime. The beef stroganoff is recommended. All side dishes are extra, so the bill will be around 300t ($4.50) including a cold drink or beer.

The **Hotel Otrar** has a restaurant like a giant yurt, with a domed, painted ceiling, carpeted walls, and a variety of Western and local dishes for about $15. Not surprisingly given the distance from Almaty to any ocean, the so-called sushi bar in the basement has no sushi. But it does attempt some basic **Japanese** dishes, such as *tsoba*, *ramen*, and *kariraisu*, at $10–12.

The **Dostuk Hotel** has two restaurants with everything from veal *saltimbocca* to pork chops calvados, at around $16 for a main course, side dishes $3. For those craving the comforts of home there is a hot and cold breakfast buffet for $10. In the competition to produce Western food, no-one can compete with the **Rachat Palace Hotel**, but then no-one can compete with the prices either: $25 for a main course, $3 for a cup of tea.

Both the **Peking Restaurant**, next to the Peking Hotel, and the **Shěnyáng**, 136 Bocembai Batyr, have **Chinese** management, but the latter has a much more pleasant atmosphere and a very full and convincing Chinese menu, although if you are about to enter China there's little point in eating in either. About 400t ($6) per dish, 120t ($2) for rice. There's a new Chinese restaurant with a good reputation at the Kazpotrepsoyuza Hotel.

Basic doner kebabs, shish kebabs, *shashlyk* and stuffed peppers are available from **Turkish** restaurants such as the **Marmara Café** on Ablai Kahn at Makataeva for around 200t ($3). They also serve cold beer in large mugs for 140t ($2). The best Turkish food is at the **Kebab Salonu** on Kunaeva just south of Zhibek Zhoulu, with excellent lentil soup and kebabs for around 500t ($7.50) per person, but no alcohol. Microwaved pizza (250t), fried chicken, and kebabs are available at the tiny underground **Café Bistro** where the pedestrianized Zhibek Zhoulu passes under

Furmanova. Better pizza is available at the slightly gloomy restaurant at 169 Furmanova (at Satpaeva). Here a 10-inch one liberally sprinkled with truffles costs 148t ($2) plus 15% service charge. The **Pizza Bar** at the front of the circus on Abai just to the west offers a slice of very mushroomy pizza for 150t ($2.25), cold drinks for 38t, and very good cappuccino-like coffee for 95t. Other simple Italian-style dishes are available at the **Italian Café** in the business centre opposite the Hotel Kazakstan, from 150t ($2.25).

To eat like the locals, simply follow the people leaving their offices at lunchtime and see where they disappear to. Baked pastries stuffed with lamb and vegetables, *mante* dumplings stuffed with lamb, and deep-fried samosa-like items (stuffed with lamb) are sold from tables covered with plastic for about 20t (30¢) each. These are not particularly appetizing but are at least filling. You may also discover soup-kitchen-like restaurants such as the one on the corner of Komsomolskaya and Ablai Khan. Here you will find noodle and other meaty Russian soups, *mante*, and rice dishes served **canteen-style** and piping hot, for around 100t ($150). Tea is a realistic 4t, with hot water refills free. Pay at the cash register and then queue up to hand your receipt in at the counter.

Another similar canteen, slightly more upmarket, is the **Café Soylianka** on the corner of Panfilov and Kazibek Bi Streets. The interior is air-conditioned, non-smoking, fly-free, and spotless. One or two of the staff speak a little English. Queue for yoghurt, meat, noodles, *mante*, chicken, fish, and even crayfish, and pay at the end. The food is hot and tasty, and an enjoyable meal should cost no more than 300–500t. Probably the best value for money in this price range (closes early at 7pm).

For similar prices the café inside the **US embassy** (*open Mon–Fri, 8–8*), run by a friendly and helpful Scot, Jim Oliver, welcomes foreign visitors as well as a lively mixture of embassy staff and other ex-pats, particularly at lunch time. Ask to see one of Almaty's more unlikely sights: the kitchen is said to be part of that given by Elvis Presley to his unit during his military service. The remainder of a vast set of equipment has gone to the German Theatre.

Eating In

For the ultimate budget traveller, street-corner *shashlyk* near markets and especially at night (30t per skewer) and the **Zelyony Bazaar** itself will provide a varied diet. Bread in a variety of shapes and sizes, butter and cheese sold by weight, and tomatoes provide the basis of chunky, filling sandwiches, requiring only a penknife for completion, and can be followed up with a wide choice of fruit. Peaches, for instance, look a bit rough compared to the picture-perfect varieties at home, but taste far better than many, are raised without chemical assistance because no-one can afford it, and are no more than 45t per kilo for the very best. For those in an apartment with access to cooking equipment, there's also a wide variety of vegetables and meats, and some canned foods.

Shops with imported food and drink such as the **Butya** stores are springing up every-where, but prices can be double or triple those at home. Items such as bacon or yoghurt can be found in food shops such as the one on the paved section of Zhibek

Zhoulu, at Tulebaeva. Imported UHT milk can be bought for 150t per litre at the **Samal Supermarket** (*open 10–10*) on Ablai Khan between Vinogradova and Kalinina, along with good meat, imported cheese, tinned, and other preserved goods (Marmite, Nutella, Western breakfast cereals, etc.). There is a similar store, but without the milk, on the north side of Gogola one block west of the Hotel Otrar, and another, the **Galaxy**, with a wide range of Western goods at 45 Kazbek Bi at Ablai Khan. Hungarian fruit juices, Western, Indian, and Russian soft drinks, and a wide variety of alcoholic ones can be bought from kiosks, or more cheaply from state-run food shops (*culinaria*) easily identifiable from images of wheat, milk bottles, etc., in bright colours on their windows. Try Seifulina at Gogolya, Shevchenko at Kosmonovtov, Panfilov at Tole Bi, and Kazibek Bi at Zheltoksan. Interesting dark and light local **beer** can occasionally be found in the market but not in restaurants, where it's mostly gaseous American stuff, and other imports. Beware of buying vodka or mineral water in the market. All that's labelled is not the real thing. Kiosks are more reliable, but check bottle seals carefully. On almost every street corner, they are also reliable suppliers of chocolate, biscuits and cold drinks.

Entertainment and Nightlife

As the fashionable young offspring of those who are making money look for something other than European fashions on which to spend it, an entertainment industry is rising to meet the demand.

The main outlet is discos, but as in other countries the entertainment industry is attractive to underworld elements, and it is not wise just to wander into some place that you happen to notice. An exception is **Klub Kimep**, originally started by ex-pats for ex-pats, but also popular with their Kazak girlfriends, their girlfriends' girlfriends, and so on. This has an undergraduate feel except in the way that the local girls dress, which is interestingly flashy. Friday and Saturday nights are for dancing, with darts and jazz on other evenings. It's theoretically a private club, but any more or less presentable foreigner who doesn't happen to displease the very large Kazak bouncers will be allowed in for 400t ($6). Beers are around 120t ($2) each. The club's continued existence depends upon there being ex-pats around who want to continue to run it. Reaching the club is not straightforward. Walk along Prospekt Abai from the junction with Lenina on the left-hand (south) side of the road, and take the first left. About 200m up turn left through some big black gates, and turn left again. Follow the path round to the right, then in a curve around the outside of a building and you'll find the club down some stairs in the far left-hand corner of where you emerge. When inside, if you look out of the windows you'll find yourself looking down on Abai and Lenina, having doubled back on yourself. The club closes at about 2am.

There is increasingly harder-edged nightlife available at clubs such as **Manhatten**, corner of Kunaeva and Zhibek Zhoulu, admission 1200t ($18), and **LA Club**, Ablai Khan just north of Abai, adm 800t ($12), which take their dancing and posing seri-ously until about 3am. Both feature extortionate drink prices, a clientele made up 75 per cent of Kazak girls who look 15 (but also as if they flew to Europe to buy their clothes), and reasonable light and video shows with an excess of strobe, tuneless throbbing music perfect for dancing. Both will have been superseded by something trendier by the time you arrive. Only obsessive clubbers from big cities will find these places inferior.

Early evening on Friday at the **International Business Club** is where foreign residents meet before disappearing off to parties and other entertainment. It's on the south side of Gogola between Dzerzhinskaya and Mira. There's also food and occasional live music here.

The state-sponsored **orchestra, ballet, opera, and theatre** have been struggling since independence. The **Philharmonic** plays in a hall at the east end of Panfilov Park, and there are performances of opera and ballet at the theatre at the south end of Panfilova, almost opposite the Hotel Almaty. Go to the ticket offices in the halls themselves, or ask an English speaker at the desk of one of the bigger hotels to look in the newspaper for you. The Russian **Lermentov Theatre** is on Abai, corner of Ablai Khan. **Freitag**, the German theatre and theatre academy, is at 64 Satpaeva, © 63 66 52, freitag@frei.almaty.kz, and in between productions shows imported films on Thursday nights (not only German ones). There are Kazak productions at the **Auezov Theatre** at 103 Abai, and Chinese, Uighur, and Korean ones at venues on Nauryzbai Batyr.

To China by Rail and Road

Full Chinese transit or tourist visas must be held and are not available at border crossings.

By Train

The train to Ürümqi trundles a considerable distance northeast up the old Turk Sib line to get round a spur of the Ala-Too before turning southeast to pass the sizeable Ala-Kul and take a broad and shallow pass long favoured by invading armies moving in either direction. Druzhba, the Kazak side of the crossing point, has now been remaned Dostyk, both meaning 'friendship'. Given the Kazak border officials' behaviour, this is clearly meant as irony. The newest section of line, only opened in 1992, then runs from Ālāshānkŏu on the Chinese side along the north side of the Borohoro Mountains to Ürümqi.

The ticket window for international trains is no.1 at the far left-hand end of Almaty II as you enter (*open 9–1 and 2–4*). The Saturday train is Kazak, and the Monday train is Chinese. There are two classes; one with two beds to a compartment (*liux* in Russian), and one with four (*kupe*), costing 5976t ($95) and 3902t ($60) respectively on the Kazak train, and 8336t ($130) and 4488t ($70) on the Chinese one—there is usually no need to book in advance. On the Chinese train the cars with hard sleeper (*yìngwòchē*) on the side are actually the usual soft sleepers, and the ones with soft sleeper (*ruǎnwòchē*) are ultra-soft, with two beds and a comfy chair per compartment. The provision of a dining car is erratic, so take plenty of food and drink to see you through the double overnight, 35-hour journey, which includes an 8- or 9-hour wait at the border for bogie changing, Kazak customs thievery (*see* warnings below), military searches of the train, and other absurdities. Photography is unwise in the border area. The Kazak dining car on the Chinese train only has drinks.

The Chinese restaurant car joins the train at the Chinese side of the border at Ālāshānkŏu and opens at about 11pm Běijīng time, where Russians rowdily celebrate their successful passage through Kazak customs with liquid dinners. The Chinese train has a thermos of boiled water in each compartment (as do all trains in China) which is topped up from time to time by the attendant (or do it yourself from the boiler at the end of each carriage), so take a mug, tea, and coffee. All the timings given at the station are in Moscow time, so although train no.13 to Ürümqi is shown as leaving at 6.10pm, it actually leaves at 9.10pm Almaty time (8.10 in winter), stopping 30–35 minutes later at Almaty I. The arrival time in Ürümqi is 10am Běijīng time, which is 8am in the opinion of local Xīnjiāng people and the sun. For details of the journey from Ürümqi to Almaty, see 'To Kazakstan by Rail and Road', p.259.

The **Kazak customs** operation at the border is simply organized thievery. Tour groups rarely face problems, but independent travellers need a little strength of mind to avoid being victims. Various individuals in military and civilian uniform will demand your passport, until one finally hands you fresh declaration forms to complete. The customs officer who finally sits down with you will want to see your passport again, the form you completed when entering the CIS and the one you have completed for departure, and may want to see receipts for hard currency exchange. You should use the first as a model for completing the second, only altering the monetary information to show the hard currency that you have spent.

The officer's aim is to find a discrepancy in your documents, or to convince you that he has done so, and then to 'fine' you. One method is to suggest that you cannot demonstrate that you have changed hard currency legally, because you do not have receipts. In fact you are legal as long as you are exporting less hard currency than you originally imported. To avoid debate, however, it's better to balance your books by making sure that you get a receipt when you cash traveller's cheques or cash. If for some reason you have had to pay out cash for which you do not have a receipt, you can cheat by drawing extra cash on a credit card and destroying the receipt. The officer will certainly want to see your money, and reach for it to count it. Do not give it to him or you may not get it back, but count it in front of him, taking your time. He will not be interested in traveller's cheques, and one simple way to thwart him is not to be carrying any cash, making you impervious to his greed. Even these people don't have the nerve to try to take valuables from you, although they will from local people, and can be seen laughingly carrying off bundles of goods belonging to Uzbek and Chinese traders. Be aware, though, that a very thorough search may be made of both your bags and person, so do not underdeclare what cash you have. Neither declare nor carry any tenge with you, as exporting tenge is illegal, and this will immediately be confiscated and an additional 'fine' will be levied.

Failing success with the declaration forms, other reasons to cause you trouble may be looked for. At all times be both polite and firm. The aim is to intimidate, and if you simply refuse be intimidated then there are many Kazaks and Chinese on the train who can be terrified with greater ease. Remember that any threat to take you off the train for an imaginary offence will lead to reports to superiors, and by law must lead to your embassy being contacted. If such a threat is issued, gather your things together and comply. There will be a sudden change of heart. It helps if you cannot or do not speak Kazak or Russian, and so cannot understand the 'reasons' being given as to why you should pay up. If unsure of yourself, make friends with other foreigners, Kazaks and Chinese in your compartment for a bit of group solidarity. Taking a little extra food for offering round helps to overcome the language barriers. In the end you will not part with any money, although you will see others do so. Do not *offer* money under any circumstances.

Prepare for all this by using the lavatory before the train arrives at the border—it will be locked for much of the day—and by locking away portable valuables, such as personal stereos, pens, and packets of cigarettes. The search of your compartment done by military personnel tends to happen with the door closed, and smaller items can unexpectedly develop legs.

The trip between border posts is brief, and may be broken up by one final search involving sniffer dogs, and armed guards on the roof of the train. The Chinese officials take away your passport for a short time, but are comparatively welcoming, courteous, efficient, and keen to get it over with, although still a little surprised to see individual travellers.

By Bus

There is a bus from the long-distance bus station daily except Sunday to Ürümqi via Khorgos (Huòěrgásì in Mandarin) which leaves at 7am and takes at least 24 hours. It is considerably quicker if less comfortable than the train, stopping only for the border and brief meal breaks. Tickets are $50. The Khorgos crossing (*open 8.30–4; closed from midday on Saturday and all day Sunday*) is south of the Druzhba route taken by the train, and thus considerably shorter. The road has to go over the Borohoro Mountains after entering China, and then parallels the railway line. In late 1996 the road on the Chinese side had been turned into a mud-bath by rebuilding, and buses were often held stationary for a few hours to allow coal trucks to wade through the mush ahead of them, lengthening the total journey time to nearer 40 hours.

Problems with Kazak officials are growing here, but are not yet so great as those at Druzhba. Khorgos has been set up as a free trade zone, but business has been disappointing and development funds have run out on the Chinese side. Kazakstan sends fertilizer, wool, and ores to China and receives low-quality manufactured goods in return, but most of these go by train.

Look out for charges for entering the free trade zone. As a tourist you shouldn't have to pay these, but probably will have to if you want to cross the border.

There is also a bus from Almaty to **Gulja** (Yíníng) just over the border on Mon, Wed, Thur, and Sat, 12 hours, $30 (the buses to Ürümqi do not pass through here). Gulja is not of great interest, but provides a break in the journey, and also the opportunity for those on their way to Kashgar to avoid Ürümqi, by changing to buses over reportedly stunning mountain scenery direct to Kuqa, and on to Kashgar. Sleeper bus tickets are about ¥120 ($15.50, although some are asked to pay double), and there are ordinary buses departing at 8.30am, which take two days, breaking the journey for the night at the fairly high and thus chilly town of Bayanbulak (Bāyīnbùlùkè) halfway to Kuqa, ¥72 or ¥144 ($9 or $18).

It is also possible to do the whole trip by local transport, with a little difficulty. First get to Zharkant (formerly Panfilov), about 340km from Almaty by bus. There are five departures daily from 8am, and tickets are 425t ($6.25). Then negotiate a bus or taxi ride the remaining 40km or so to Khorgos from there. There is a single cheap hotel, if you need it. Buses shuttle between the two border posts, and once on the Chinese side you're at the mercy of your own negotiating skills with the private transport there. The nearest town is Qīngshuǐhé, where the roads to Yíníng and Ürümqi part company. It's probably best to go only as far as here and then take a proper bus (although if you are leaving China it's better not to stop here but to continue in a loop to Yíníng, where there is more choice of transport and accommodation).

Bishkek to Kashgar

The Torugart Pass

Bishkek (Бишкек)

'We are a small Switzerland' was one of the slogans of the early days of Kyrgyz independence, and in terms of mountain scenery this was perhaps an understatement. A Swiss standard of living is however likely to remain a pipe dream. If anything Kyrgyzstan, a country of merely 4.5 million people, seems more like Andorra, with little chance of development except through tourism. Of the new republics' visas, Kyrgyz ones are the easiest to obtain.

Bishkek sits a mere 40km from the base of the snowy Kyrgyz Ala-Too range, which towers at the end of every north–south artery. The road to the border at Torugart winds over 3000m passes and alongside the Tiān Shān's sharpest peaks before leaping into China. The city is a smaller, more relaxed and even greener version of Almaty.

There's also less of an overt *mafiosi* presence, less traffic, and less pollution, although the partial collapse of industry is one of the reasons for this. Local people estimate that growing Kyrgyz nationalism has led to 25 per cent of the Russian population leaving for Russia, and almost all Germans leaving for Germany, but unfortunately these were the people with the necessary technical and administrative skills. Emigration has slowed, but GDP is still in decline and, whilst remaining Russians may sneer at Kyrgyz management skills, they have been treated with considerably more liberality than in some of the other new republics. Unlike in Kazakstan, there have been moves to make Russian an official language, and dual nationality with the Russian Federation is acceptable. Most renamed streets have kept their old signs next to the new, and Lenin still stands in the former Ploshchad Lenina. Some people say that the Kyrgyz can't quite believe the truth of their independence and, fearful that things may return to 'normal' at short notice, are hedging their bets.

Now free to move around as they please, many rural Kyrgyz have come to Bishkek, but most remain jobless. Privatization and administrative reforms have been more thorough and widespread than elsewhere, making President Akayev the international financial community's favourite Central Asian leader, although not quite the pure democrat they had hoped. Backed by a $74 million IMF loan, and despite inflation of more than 30 per cent, the Kyrgyz som is the most stable currency in Central Asia, rarely moving from around 12 to the US dollar. Kyrgyzstan looks towards China for trade, although the results are far from romantic Silk Route revivalism. The Kyrgyz complain that China tends to dump on them shoddy goods that cannot be sold in more sophisticated markets, and the Osh Bazaar in Bishkek is awash with the results. Bartering is back on a large scale however, as Kyrgyzstan trades electricity from Tiān Shān hydroelectric plants for Xīnjiāng gas.

Like Almaty, Bishkek is thoroughly Russified in clothing, drinking and general attitudes, although religious problems may lurk a little nearer the surface. In 1996 the State Mufti declared the willingness of Kyrgyz Muslims to carry out the Khomeini *fatwa* against the writer Salman Rushdie.

Bishkek began life under the name of Pishpek as a fortress built in 1852 by the Khan of Khokhand, before being overrun by the Russians in their southward expansion 10 years later. Miles from anywhere, its promotion to the status of town in 1878 made little difference until following the Bolshevik Revolution it was further promoted to the status of capital of the Kyrgyz Soviet Republic under the new name of Frunze (*see* p.456) in 1926. Following independence it reverted to the Kyrgyz version of its earlier name. Its centre sports a number of substantial, cubic, marble-encrusted office buildings which are not out of keeping with the Russified neo-classicism of earlier ones. Yet this grandeur seems surprising in what otherwise is an altogether sleepier town than Almaty, most of its streets and even the showcase centrepiece of Ala-Too (formerly Lenin) Square being largely empty of people. Part of Bishkek's charm is that just one block away from Lenin himself are cottages with gardens full of chickens.

Getting to and from Bishkek

by air

Bishkek's Manas Airport, 20km north of the city, and a minibus ride from the long-distance (west) bus station, has been opening and closing according to fuel availability, but has recently become more reliable. Both Almaty and Tashkent have far better international connections, and Almaty is a comfortable 4hr bus journey from Bishkek. **Kyrgyzstan Airlines** (Kyrgyzstan Aba Joldoru), originally the only one operating out of Manas, has now been joined by Turkish Airlines, a private Pakistani company called Aero Asia, Aeroflot, British Mediterranean, and a handful of regional airlines. Much of Kyrgyzstan Airlines' business is charters—so-called 'shopping trips' to Seoul, Běijīng, Delhi, Karachi, Aleppo, Warsaw and Bangkok. The Běijīng charter usually but not necessarily departs on Monday and returns on Friday, and is run by Mariam, 32 Prospect Chu, ✆ 28 53 78. There are also scheduled flights to Istanbul (Mon, Thurs, $385), Frankfurt (weekly, $623), Moscow (daily except Tues, 2270 som/$190), and St Petersburg (Thurs, 3083 som/$257), all prices one-way. There is now also a weekly flight to Ürümqi and back on Tuesdays (probably soon to be joined by a parallel China Xīnjiāng Airways service). The dollar prices must be paid in dollars, and the som prices are recalculated every Friday to take account of the movement of the ruble. The office has a helpful English speaker, and is at 105 Ulitsa Sovietskaya, corner of Bokonbaeva, ✆ 28 08 86, ● 42 29 22 (*open daily 8–12 and 1–7*). They also sell tickets for Transaero's flights from Almaty to London, Berlin, Frankfurt, and Eilat via Moscow, tickets for many other companies flying out of Almaty (not Lufthansa or Austrian Airlines), and Turkish Airlines flights from Bishkek to Istanbul (Wed, Sat), with onward connections via British Airways and other carriers. Transaero tickets to Moscow are around $300, and a further $1065 to continue to London, plus $16 Moscow departure tax. **Turkish Airlines** tickets are up to 20% cheaper if bought from Turkish's own agent in the new Ak-Keme Hotel: ✆ 48 38 53.

British Mediterranean flies fortnightly to London Heathrow, bookable through the nearest British Airways office or agent, and there's not one here. Try Almaty, or a long-distance phone call.

The private Pakistani airline **Aero Asia** flies between Bishkek and Karachi every Sunday. They have an office at 57 Ulitsa Pravda, Apartment 1/2, ✆ 28 48 26.

Neufeld GmbH, 199/81 Ulitsa Bokonbaeva, ✆ and ● 24 83 04, operates Kyrgyzstan Airlines charters to Hannover two to five times a month for DM750 plus 250 som ($21). There are also flights to Frankfurt every Sunday, and to Stuttgart and Köln two to five times a month in summer. In Germany call ✆ (052) 612271.

Glavtours at 93 Toktogula at Krasnooktyabrskaya, ✆ 22 12 53, ● 22 02 55, sells tickets for flights from Tashkent, Moscow, and Almaty with Aeroflot, Russian Airlines, *embassies*

Onward visas:

China: 196 Toktogula, ✆ 22 24 23 (*open Mon, Wed, Fri, 9–11.00am only*). Get your visa before leaving home, if possible. Visas issued here are usually valid for 30 days, but stamped as *not* good for the Torugart Pass, unless you can wave an invitation fax or telex from a state travel agency such as CITS. If you arrive at the embassy without such documentation you may be told that the pass is closed for other than Chinese and Kyrgyz nationals. Visas take five working days for $30 rising to $60 for speedier processing. One photograph is needed.

Kazakstan: 10 Tokolok Moldo, between Toktogul and Moskva, ✆ 22 32 20 (*open 9–1 and 2–6*). You will not be able to purchase a tourist visa without visa support, but with it you can usually get it the same day. A one-week visa costs $30, two weeks $60. One photograph is needed.

Russia: 17 Razzakova, ✆ 22 16 91, 22 17 75 (*open only Mon and Thurs, 4–5*). This embassy is less co-operative than that in Almaty. Acquisition of a tourist visa requires buying expensive accommodation or other services.

Pakistan: Hotel Dostuck have moved to 347A Panfilova, ✆ 27 27 60/22 72 09.

India: 164A Prospekt Chu, third floor, ✆ 21 08 75 (*open Mon–Fri, 2–4 for applications and 4–5 for collection of visas*).

There are also Iranian and Turkish embassies in Bishkek.

Emergencies:

Germany: 28 Ulitsa Razzakova (Pervomayskaya), ✆ 22 48 11.
USA: 66 Bulvar Erkindik, ✆ 22 27 77/22 32 10. After hours call ✆ 22 53 58.

There are far more embassies in Almaty, which can be called from Bishkek using ordinary phones. Dial 8 then the city code. *See* p.426.

maps and books

Maps of Bishkek and Kyrgyzstan and **guides** are available from hotel foyers, and from the Akademkniga bookshop at the corner of Kievskaya and Erkindik. Although in need of an update, American resident Daniel Prior's *Bishkek Handbook* is a well-researched guide with a detailed history section, and costs 90–100 som ($8). Detailed maps suitable for trekking and more general maps can be found at the State Geodetic and Cartographic Agency, 107 Kievskaya between Ivanova and Tokulok Moldo (*open Mon–Fri, 7.30–12 and 1–4.30*). Enter from the building's left-hand side and go to the fifth floor, room 510. Locals pay an assortment of prices, but foreigners seem to pay 42 som ($3.50) for any map, from cheap souvenir maps to those with detailed relief.

money

Bring plenty of dollars in cash to Bishkek because **foreign exchange** from traveller's cheques is more difficult to arrange than in Almaty, and there is no bank currently accepting credit cards. There are exchange bureaux everywhere, but particularly up Sovietskaya, doing cash transactions between dollars, Deutschmarks, rubles, tenge, and som. The rates tend to start low and improve during the day until around 7–8pm when most close. Not all give receipts, but if you're going to leave the CIS by any route except flight you would be wise to find places that do (for instance inside the Fortuna store on the south side of Chu west of Sovietskaya). Buy all the som you need before leaving Bishkek for the Chinese border. **Traveller's cheques** can be cashed into dollars at **Bank Bishkek**, corner Toktogul and Turusbekova (*open Mon–Fri, 8 –12 and 1–5)*, with a commission of 5%. Only US$, DM and sterling cheques are accepted. Enter from Turusbekova. A more expensive alternative is **Bank Maksat** on Frunze just east of Isanova, (*open Mon–Fri, 8–12 and 1–3)*. Go to room 102 in the corridor straight ahead as you enter. Here US$ and DM cheques are cashed at a commission of 7%. The lobby cash counter exchanges a wider variety of cash than most, accepting French and Swiss francs, as well as pounds, US dollars and Deutschmarks.

photographic

Film and developing can be obtained in the Central Department Store (TsUM) on the north side of Prospekt Chu just east of Sovietskaya. A roll of 36 shot Kodak print film costs around 75 som ($6), and C41 developing is 11 som (92¢) plus 6 som (50¢) per print, plus 5% VAT. There's also a film and developing specialist with a wide variety of Kodak materials on the northeast corner of Sovietskaya and Moscovskaya.

post office and telephones

The **post office** at the junction of Sovietskaya and Chuisky (Prospekt Chu) is open seven days a week, and has a wide selection of cheap but uninteresting postcards, but no *poste restante* facility. The post box is just inside the door, and you should use the rear slot. Stamps for overseas letters cost 7 som (60¢), and 3 som (25¢) for postcards. At times you will be directed to a separate international section. Bishkek's **telephone** system is in a sorry state, with only one or two modern exchanges. Expect to get frequent engaged signals from any business you call as there is a shortage of lines. International calls have to be booked even by businesses, and take about 45 minutes to come through. Queues for calls from the **telephone office** next to the post office can be long, and you are better off going to the Hotel Dostuk, which has a business centre with a satellite uplink where you can also send and receive **facsimiles** for around $5 in som per minute. Otherwise telex is a more reliable method of communication. **Local phone calls** from public phones require a 1 som (8¢) token purchasable from kiosks, or you can pay to make your call from a restaurant or at the railway station. You can send and receive **email** at Dostuck Trekking and some other agencies for a small sum, but the dial-up connection takes a while to establish. Unless you are going to Dostuck anyway a better choice would be **El Cat** at 54 Razzakova (formerly Pervomayskaya) near Toktogula, ✆ 22 75 85, which is connected to the Internet via the Ministry of Communication. Send mail to root@cct.bishkek.su. You can also use telnet to download mail from your own site.

travel agents

City tours and excursions are on offer through **Kyrghyzintourist** (*see* 'Tourist Information' p.456), but they still much prefer to deal with groups, and prices for individuals can be punitive compared to the cost of doing it yourself. A half-day city tour is $10 per person in a group, and $15 for individuals. A five-hour trip to the Burana Tower is $15 per person in a group, and a trip to Issyk-kul $50. The company also sells invitations (also known as visa support) without requiring you to buy other services—$20 per individual, or $10 for group members. **Dostuck Trekking**, © 42 74 71/41 91 29, © 41 91 29, 22 39 42, nikolai@dostuk.bishkek.su, telex c/o Kyrghyzintourist, is a fairly reliable agency which, although now a Kyrgyz-British joint stock company, retains a family-run feel. Dostuck arranges almost anything from simple tours and horseback treks to top-level climbing and heli-skiing trips. They produce a brochure of sample tours but will produce a quote for the trip of your choice with a little advance warning. Prices are in dollars but reasonable, and a high level of service is provided. The office, at 42–1, 18th Linea St (pronounced *Vossimnadsataya Linea*) is a little difficult to find. From the railway station cross the footbridge just to the east, and go through the fence to the main road. Turn right, and first left up Ulitsa Fatianova. Pass one small lane that forks right, and take the second one. Keep straight on across two junctions bearing slightly left and down the narrower lane if in doubt. The office is on the right, less than 10 minutes' walk from the station altogether. Another company rooted in government geology and geography and from which Dostuck is a splinter is **Tian Shan Travel**, the privatized adventure sports section of Intourist, at 1/2 Ulitsa Malybaeva, © 42 99 20, ✆ 42 99 22. Other recommended companies are **Genrih Cruise** of 70a Tolstoyeva, © 22 23 68, ✆ 22 55 18, who have been

Transaero, Uzbekistan Airlines, and Kazair (although the latter seems on the brink of collapse). Uzbek's Wednesday Tashkent to Manchester flight costs $676 one way. Almaty to Moscow $400 with Transaero, $200 with Kazair. Uzbek also have their own agent, © 22 18 42, may have cheaper tickets from Tashkent, including the Manchester flight.

by train

There are trains to and from Moscow, Tashkent and Almaty every day, but it is easier to reach Almaty by bus. Security on trains can be a problem but less so than in Russia.

Kyrgyzstan's only internal line is to Balikchi (formerly Rybach'ye) at the west end of Lake Issyk-Kul. There are theoretically but not necessarily three trains a day in summer. From here you can take a private bus to Naryn or beyond to At-Bashi.

The railway station is linked to the west bus station by trolley bus 48.

by bus

There are regular and comfortable Hungarian buses to Almaty from Bishkek's west bus station. The journey takes around four hours and costs 52 som ($4.30), with 3.50 som known to arrange for private vehicles to enter China and for Chinese visas at short notice, and **Kyrghyz Concept**, more expensive and more geared to ex-pats, at 100 Razzakova, ℭ 26 58 22/21 00 02, ℗ 62 00 20, kyrghyz@infotel.bishkek.su.

visas

Upon arrival in Bishkek, if you intend to stay more than three days you must report to OVIR (**ОВИР**) to have a further **validation stamp** put in your passport. *This must be done within three working days of your arrival or you will be fined.* If there is any danger of ambiguity, bring hotel receipts or tickets to prove that you were not in the the country any earlier, as OVIR officials have been known to decide quite arbitrarily that you were, and to 'fine' you accordingly. Usually, however, the process is fairly smooth. OVIR (Office of Visa and Registration) is in the Interior Ministry building on the south side of Ulitsa Kievskaya, half a block east of Sovietskaya (*open de facto Mon–Fri, 9.30 to 12 and 2 to 5.30 although the hours are officially longer*). Unless you are expecting any complications, first pay the registration fee. Go through the door furthest to the left, marked only by a sign on the wall saying photo (**фото**), go up to the second floor (three half-flights of stairs), through the door ahead of you and turn left. The cash office is the last door on your right. Show your passport and pay a total of 39.50 som (about $3.50). Return to the ground floor (down two half-flights), go through the door ahead, turn left and immediately left into an office. Knock on the door on your right and go in, and present your receipt and passport. If you have obtained visa support through a travel agency, expect them to take care of this procedure for you, for a small fee. If you fail to get the stamp both you and they face large fines. OVIR is also the place to try to obtain **visa extensions**. In case of difficulty, purchase visa support for $10–15 from companies like Kyrghyzintourist or Dostuck Trekking.

(30¢) extra if you wish to stow your baggage underneath the bus. There are also buses to Tashkent. Buy your ticket from the main hall at the top of the stairs (the window is on the near left-hand side as you go in) or from a kiosk at the bottom of the stairs on the other side of the hall. Seats are numbered and no standing is allowed.

State-run buses to Naryn have now ceased, and you must go to the west bus station and take a private bus, which will leave only when it is full.

The long-distance (west) bus station is reached by the meandering bus 48 from the Railway Station and Hotel Ala-Too, which also passes Osh Bazaar; bus 35 from Sovietskaya and Frunze, and bus 7 from Prospekt Chu.

For information on getting to China, *see* 'To China via the Torugart Pass', p.460.

by jeep

This is the only really reliable way to get around the interesting side roads to places such as Son-Kul and Tash-Rabat, and to the Chinese border. You might try negotiating directly with a jeep owner if you happen to meet one, but in general the situation with petrol, 'entrance fees', repairs, equipment, and fluctuating currencies is so complicated that you are better off dealing with one of the established travel companies.

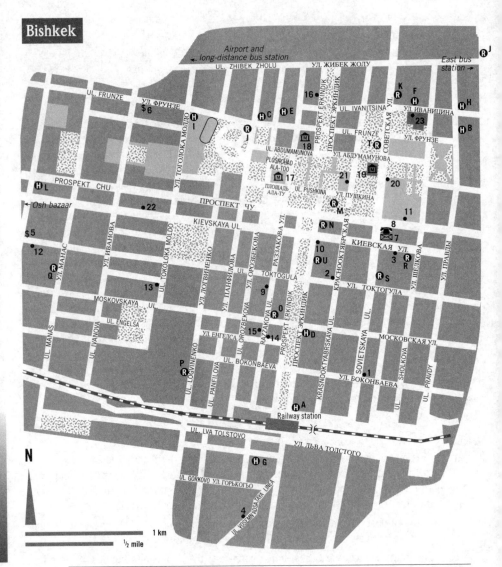

Getting Around

Bishkek is laid out on a fairly regular grid, with the leafy Prospekt (or Bulvar) Erkindik running north–south like a long, thin public park. Parallel, two blocks to the west, is Sovietskaya Ulitsa, which has much of the shopping, and is the only street in the city that ever looks busy. Prospekt Chu is the major east–west route, crossing the south side of the city's central plaza, Ala-Too Sq. Name changes to streets have not been as widespread as those in Almaty, but those that have stuck include Razzakova for Pervomayskaya, Manas for Belinsky, and Chuisky for Lenina. Otherwise the older Russian names are more widely recognized and are used here.

1	Kyrgyzstan Airlines Кыргызстанские	13	Kazak Embassy Казахское Посольство
2	Glavtours Главтур	14	Russian Embassy Русское Посольство
3	OVIR ОВИР	15	German Embassy Немецкое Посольство
4	Dostuk Trekking Достук Треккинг	16	American Embassy Американское Посольство
5	Bank Bishkek Банк Бишкек	17	History Museum Музей Истории
6	Bank Maksat Банк Максат	18	Frunze's House and Museum Дом-музей Фрунзе
7	Post Office Почта	19	State Fine Art Museum Музей Изобразительных Искусств
8	Telephone Office Телефон	20	Opera and Ballet Theatre Театр Опери и Балета
9	El Cat Ел Кат	21	Russian Drama Theatre Русский Художественный Театр
10	Akademkniga Академкнига	22	State Geodetic and Cartographic Agency Агенство Картографии
11	TsUM ЦУМ	23	Circus Цирк
12	Chinese Embassy Китайское Посольство		

HOTELS

A	Hotel Ala-Too and Kyrghyzintourist Гостиница Ала-Ту
B	Hotel Dostuk Гостиница Достук
C	Bishkek Business Centre and Hotel of the International School of Business and Management Гостиница Колледжа Бизнеса
D	Hotel Bishkek Гостиница Бишкек
E	Hotel Sary-Celek Гостиница Сары-Челек
F	Hotel Ak-Sai Гостиница Ак-Сай
G	Rahat Guesthouse Гостиница Рачата
H	Ilbirs Complex Гостиница Илбирс Комплекс
I	Hotel Spartak Гостиница Спартак

RESTAURANTS

J	Restaurant Ak-Örgo Ресторан Ак-Орго
K	U Mazaya Restaurant Ресторан У Мазая
L	Doka Pizza Дока Пизза
M	Restaurant Ak-Sakal Ресторан Ак-Сакал
N	Restaurant Son-Kul Ресторан Сон-Куль
O	Nooruz Ресторан Нооруз
P	Yuza Ресторан Юза
Q	Primevara Ресторан Примевара
R	Slavic University Café Славский Университетский Кафе
S	Café Altyn-Kush Кафе Алтын-Куш
T	Café Feniks Кафе Фунукс
U	East-West Restaurant Ресторан Васток-Запад

City transport is by **bus** and trolleybus. Buses tend to follow circuitous routes, and as most of what you will want to see is central, you're better off on foot. There is less private motoring in Bishkek than in Almaty and the buses are fuller, but still much less so than in China. Enter the bus by the middle and rear doors, and pay as you leave by the front: 1 som (8¢). Bus 35 runs up Sovietskaya from the railway station and along Frunze to the long-distance bus station, and bus 7 gets there along Prospekt Chu. *Marshrutnoe* taxis look like ancient US school buses, and run the same routes for double the price.

Taxis are fairly commonplace, without meters. Negotiate the fare before you travel; 15 som ($1.25) is the fare for most journeys within the city, but try opening the bargaining at 10 (80¢). 20 som ($1.60) will get you to the west bus station. You can also flag down private cars, or ask anyone who seems to be parked and doing nothing.

Tackling the city on foot at night requires the same level of caution as in Almaty. Avoid poorly lit areas and the edges of parks (although frequent green spaces and inter-mittent street lights make this almost impossible to do). There is safety in numbers. Approach upmarket hotels like the Dostuk in groups if on foot, or by car.

Kyrgyzstan ℡ +996, Bishkek ℡ (3312)   ***Tourist Information***

Tourist information is readily available through **Kyrghyzintourist**, on the ground floor of the Hotel Ala-Too, ℡ 22 63 42, ℡ 22 39 42, telex 245144 INTUR KH, although they hope that you will buy a tour. English and German are spoken (*see* 'Bishkek Directory', p.452).

Museums

The **History Museum (музей Истории)** (*open 10–1 and 2–6; closed Mon; adm 2 som/ 16¢*), formerly the Lenin Museum, is on the south side of Ala-Too Square, formerly Ploshchad Lenina and still dominated by his statue. It has not yet shaken off all its Soviet past. The ground floor now has a display devoted to *Manas*, the thousand-year-old epic poem consisting of a hit parade of Central Asian myths with one central character as the star of all of them. In addition to early copies of the poem in various languages, there are items of traditional weaponry, costume, and jewellery. The unbelievably sumptuous first floor has as yet been left untouched and is full of larger than life-size tableaux of scenes from the revolution, copies of Lenin's letters to local soviets, and other grotesque but now historic minutiae of the Soviet period, which should be allowed to remain as an awful warning. On the top floor the same elaborate presentation cases have been stripped and local artefacts put in them, ranging from prehistoric finds to samples of handicrafts.

On the corner of Ulitsas Frunze and Razzakova, the **Frunze's House and Museum** (*open 10–6; closed Mon; adm free*) is going through the same kind of transformation. You are directed to the top floor first, where on the right there is a series of displays devoted to the traditions of all the minorities that make up Kyrgyz society, and a yurt which is pointed out by the attendant with particular pride, and who will escort you round the whole display talking in Russian, regardless of whether you understand or not. The rest of the floor covers a Soviet version of local history, the next floor down is shut for revision, and the ground floor has what may be the cottage in which Mikhail Frunze may have lived. Frunze was a local boy and a student of Lenin's, who was sent during the revolution to prevent the secession of the south. Local cynics say the wrong cottage was preserved, but its period interior is nonetheless charming, as is the thatched roof, now vanished elsewhere in Bishkek.

The **State Fine Art Museum (музей изобразительных искусств)** (*open 10–6; closed Mon; adm 1 som/8¢*) is at 196 Ulitsa Sovietskaya, near Kirova, and contains a mixture of Soviet and Kyrgyz nationalist politics expressed in art: paintings of heroic labourers, factories, combine harvesters; rural idylls, yurts, mountains. There are also local modern paintings in various styles, carpets, and the inevitable yurt.

Osh Bazaar

A long way west on Ulitsa Kievskaya, this is Bishkek's biggest market, combining local food-stuffs with shoddy Chinese imported goods. Soviet products, although far from wonderful, were generally longer lasting, but sources have now dried up. There's also a flea market, where local handicrafts are sold. Stallholders have the skills of magicians when it comes to adding hidden pressure to the scales to give you short weight, and in slipping you inferior goods under the cover of better ones. It's colourful, but keep a hand on your wallet, and shop elsewhere.

Where to Stay

Until recently much cheaper than Almaty, Bishkek seems to be showing signs of trying to catch up, with single rooms disappearing and prices jumping by up to 40% in hard currency terms. Hot water is centrally supplied, and may disappear during parts of the summer, although the upmarket hotels have back-up systems.

expensive

The **Hotel Dostuk**, 429 Ulitsa Frunze, ✆ 28 42 42/28 42 78, @ 28 44 66, is the best hotel in central Bishkek. Apparently modern on the outside, it's slightly decrepit inside, but has all the facilities you expect from a serious hotel, and the business centre is particularly helpful. Rooms have BBC and CNN, and the satellite link also circumvents Bishkek's ailing telephone system. Bucking the trend, prices have recently fallen slightly: single rooms are $77 and doubles $94, including breakfast and VAT. Major credit cards except Amex accepted.

The **Bishkek Business Centre**, a Canadian joint-venture, is a small and efficient hotel occupying the fourth floor of the Hotel of the International School of Business and Management, at 237 Panfilova, corner of Frunze. The exterior is dull but the fourth floor is bright and spruce, and the double rooms are actually small suites, with fridge and kitchenette, and TV with CNN. Doubles are $95 (inc. VAT), but prices go down the longer you stay, and include a substantial breakfast served in your room; ✆ 22 28 43, 22 25 85, @ 62 00 38.

Almost as far out to the south as the old airport at 93 Prospekt Mira, ✆ 48 38 53, ✆ and @ 62 02 78, is the brand new **Ak Keme Hotel**, a Turkish joint-venture, close to the mountains, with beautiful views. Single rooms are $95, doubles $125, and suites $200 to $280.

moderate

The **Hotel Ala-Too**, conveniently opposite the station, ✆ 22 60 41, @ 22 39 42 (at Kyrghyzintourist on ground floor), has an attractive, solid, old-world charm, and a reasonable restaurant, although with ominous amplifiers and microphones on a stage at one end. Some rooms have balconies, and there is hot water in the evenings on occasions when the city's system shuts down. Double rooms are $50 and singles $25 plus 5% VAT and including breakfast. The mooted restoration by a German company has not yet materialized, but will probably bring an increase in prices.

The charmless Soviet-style **Hotel Bishkek** at 21 Prospekt Erkindik, ✆ 22 02 20, has doubles for $70 and singles for $65. Too far out for convenience, the **Issyk-kul**, 103 Prospekt Mira, ✆ 44 81 68, several kilometres south, has rooms from $47, with several floors being Korean-run as a rather more spruce but also more expensive operation, ✆ 44 88 55, @ 44 88 58, with rooms from $55.

Gloomy, and still recovering from broken water-pipe damage, the **Sary-Chelek**, on Orozbekova just north of Frunze, ✆ 22 14 67, at least has sizeable rooms and is relatively cheap at $20 for single or double with bath.

The **Hotel of the International School of Business and Management** is a better choice (address as Bishkek Business Centre above), ✆ 22 04 14, although it has now perhaps over-priced itself with simple, slightly grubby doubles at 195 som ($16). Pairs of rooms share a bathroom with fairly constant hot water, and there are more expensive and more luxurious rooms with TV and fridge, and also suites.

The **Hotel Ak-Sai** at 117 Ulitsa Ivanitsyna, ✆ 26 14 65, behind the circus, is like a Chinese transport hotel with all facilities shared, but the small rooms are bright and clean. A double is 174 som ($14.50) and a single 90 som ($7.50).

Staying in a **private apartment** is not so easy to arrange as in Almaty, but try looking for contacts outside the TsUM Department Store on Prospekt Chu (Chuisky). Dostuck, Intourist, and other agencies can also arrange private apartments in central locations from $7 to $10 per person. Almost anyone who has a decent apartment and some relatives who can take them in for a while will be willing to rent out their place. Apartments often show signs of having been thoroughly scrubbed and tidied, and have a certain *Marie Celeste* quality—a radio is playing, the kettle is still warm. Clean linen and towels are put out, and sometimes flowers. Altogether this is the best deal for you, and a very significant benefit for local people living through hard times.

cheap

The friendly Uighur-owned **Rahat Guesthouse**, ✆ 42 08 08, has clean and simple rooms, and primitive but adequate washing facilities. Double rooms are 70 som ($6), and a single bed 35 som ($3). From the railway station cross the tracks using the footbridge to the east, turn right, take the second major left turn, and walk one block south to Ulitsa Kulatova Pereulok. Turn left and look for a café sign on your right a short distance down the street. More basic still, the **Ilbirs Complex Gostinitsa**, immediately north of the Dostuck on the other side of Ivanitsyna, ✆ 26 13 04, has grim common bath doubles for 26 som ($2) per bed, and the **Hotel Spartak** (Spartacus) in the sports stadium, entered from the corner of Frunze and Tokolok Moldo, is much the same.

Eating Out

Shashlyk, kebabs, Russian soups, *mante* dumplings, beef stroganoff, pilaf, and noodle soups constitute the sum total of most menus, including most of those attached to the hotels listed above, with main courses at 15–20 som ($1.25–1.70). New cafés are opening all the time featuring these dishes in clean, pleasant surroundings and, as in Almaty, many of the older restaurants are introducing strippers in order to attract customers, although not those listed below. In almost all cases, the purchase of a beer or two will almost double the cost of your meal, whatever price range you're in.

The same dishes plus some Korean food and excellent small salads can be found reasonably at the restaurant **Ak-Örgö**, with a roof shaped like an umbrella, diagonally opposite the Business Centre Hotel on the corner of Ulitsas Panfilova and Frunze, although this has begun a *remont* (renovation/reconstruction); main courses around 10 som (90¢). For a change in diet and character, the **U Mazaya Restaurant** specializes in succulent **rabbit** dishes for around 17 som ($1.50) and is located in a slightly gothic dungeon below 199 Sovietskaya, just north of Ivanitsyna, and round the corner from the Hotal Ak-Sai. Walk along the right-hand side of the building, and you'll see steps leading down. **Doka Pizza**, in the foyer of an old theatre on the corner of Chu and Turusbekova, does a reasonable impression of that Italian basic for about 40 som ($3.30), with live middle-of-the-road jazz from around 9pm. Reasonably good if slightly Turkish **pizza** is also available at **Flash Pizza and Hamburger**, 36 Prospekt Chu, six blocks east of Sovietskaya, from 26 som ($2.30) upwards. Beware the overpriced drinks. There is a small Uighur-run restaurant next to the Hotel Ak-Sai with main courses from 7 to 12 som (up to $1), and the **Restaurant Ak-Sakal** with a choice of two or three main courses only for around 7 som (60¢) each, in the circular building in the park to the right of Erkindik and north of Prospekt Chu. The restaurant **Son-Kul** on the corner of Chu and Erkindik is overpriced, and has remarkably small portions, but the café next door with a barbecue in the street does good *shashlyk*, *mante* and tea, very cheaply.

Turkish food with good service in a near-Western atmosphere is available at **Nooruz**, 73 Moskva, known to resident foreigners as 'Hoopys' because that's what the Cyrillic characters look like. A salad and main course cost around 85 som ($7). Similar, and with tables outside, is **Yusa**, on Logvinenko just south of Bokonbayeva. Good if not large Russian dishes are available in a pleasant atmosphere at what everyone calls **Primavera** (although the restaurant insists on calling itself 'Primevara') on Manas just south of Toktugul, at the same mid-range prices. Reportedly better and a little cheaper is the brand-new **Way In** at 92 Kievskaya just east of Erkindik. In the same price range, the Indian food at the **East-West** restaurant on Erkindik between Kievskaya and Toktogula is best avoided, but the Russian dishes are reasonable. The tables and booths are set round a large dance floor, but the music levels are kept reasonable.

Hearty canteen-style Russian food is available at the café in the basement of the **Slavic University** on Kievskaya immediately east of OVIR, open all day until around 5pm, with, for instance, stroganoff, potatoes, shredded vegetable salad, a glass of compôte, and a cup of instant coffee totalling only slightly more than a US dollar. A large piece of chicken with a side salad, cup of *bouillon*, bread and a soft drink, will come to about 50 som ($4) at the **Café Altyn-Kush** on Sovietskaya between Kiev and Toktogul. There are similar prices and cuisine with slightly better food at the **Café Feniks** (Phoenix) further north near the junction of Frunze.

eating in

Osh Bazaar is too far away to be practical for regular shopping, but there's a market on Moscovskaya just west of Sovietskaya with bread, fruit, vegetables, and meat. There's a food store set back from the road on the east of Sovietskaya two blocks south of the post office, and others dotted around town. The further they are from the centre the cheaper they tend to be, such as the one on the same side of Sovietskaya south of the railway line. Kiosks and vendors all over town sell local and imported ice creams, biscuits, and chocolate. Fruit and vegetable sellers are now taking up corner locations.

The **Opera and Ballet Theatre**, ✆ 26 48 63, is the most elegant building on Sovietskaya, opposite the State Fine Art Museum, and has Russian and Kyrgyz performances from time to time, well worth the 15 som ($1.25) ticket price. The red, gold, and cream interior would put many a London theatre to shame. The concrete **circus** building on the north side of Frunze just east of Sovietskaya, ✆ 27 35 67, seems to have remained more popular with local people than its equivalent in Almaty and has more performances. Tickets are 15 som ($1.25).

Nightclubs, discos, and restaurants with floor shows (often strippers) are increasing in number but random wandering into one of these is not always safe for your person, and certainly not for your wallet. On the north and west sides of the **Russian Drama Theatre**, in Dubovy Park on the west side of Krasnooktyabrskaya north of Pushkina, live bands entertain seated and dancing people at night who drink beer and eat ice-cream. There's a safe nightly open-air disco until 11.30pm in Panfilov Park just east of the sports stadium close to the Business Centre Hotel. Adm 5 som (40¢).

For shopping, **ЦУМ** (TsUM, pronounced Tsoom), the **Central Department Store** on Prospekt Chu east of Sovietskaya, is the place to find most of your practical needs, plus a better selection of carpets than in Almaty. Here you can also buy traditional Kyrgyz costume, and especially the white embroidered felt hats you see many men wearing. Well-made jewellery from semi-precious local stones is available at Samosvety, 35 Erkindik.

To China via the Torugart Pass

You are more likely to be entering Kyrgyzstan by this route than leaving it, due to the difficulties imposed by the Chinese. The situation is similar to that of the early days of the Karakoram Highway from Pakistan, as there are still no regular through buses in either direction, and entry into China depends on the acquisition of permits and expensive CITS or other state travel company assistance. Chinese visas valid for the Torugart Pass will not be issued in Bishkek without confirmation of a booked tour. The pass is open all year round for those vehicles that can tackle it, but it is always closed at weekends, and on all Kyrgyz and Chinese public holidays (*see* p.27 for a list), including 1 August, the anniversary of the founding of the People's Liberation Army, which is ignored by almost everyone else in China. The Kyrgyz border post is open Monday–Friday, 9–12 and 2–3.30.

For independent and organized travellers this crossing can be tricky, depending on a combination of somewhat bloody-minded border authorities, both of whom regard this border as sensitive, despite recent exchanges of presidential visits and talk of demilitarization. Having the right paperwork and the right amount of patience helps. The Kyrgyz have become more tolerant of the significant numbers of disconsolate returnees from the Chinese side, and now allow re-admission to Kyrgyzstan without too much fuss (athough this may depend on who is on duty).

If you are on an unaccompanied organized tour *absolutely insist* that your travel company issues you with a copy of a fax, letter, or telex clearly naming the *Chinese* travel company responsible for collecting you, their contact phone number in Kashgar, the date you will cross the border, and the number of people in your party, preferably with a list of their names and nationalities. Chinese travel companies are universally unreliable, and if your transport does not appear you will be turned back to Kyrgyzstan. If you have the document described above, there is a slight possibility that further investigation will be made, and you might possibly be allowed to proceed on buses returning to the Chinese post, but probably not. Without this document you are certainly lost. Kyrgyz travel company vehicles will now usually wait while you complete Kyrgyz border formalities and then take you on the 20-minute drive between the main Kyrgyz post and the first Chinese one, about 12km in all. If your Chinese transportation is not there, try to make the vehicle that brought you wait until it arrives. If it won't, and you are sent back, your options are set out under 'To Kyrgyzstan via the Torugart Pass', *see* p.289.

Cyclists are usually allowed to cross no-man's land under their own steam, and pedestrians sometimes walk it. There's a bus which shuttles between the two borders for $5, ¥40, or 50 som. Tenge and Deutschmark equivalents are probably also acceptable. Under no circumstances will you be allowed to board the minibuses down to the main border post 104km inside China, or to cycle there: you *must* have pre-booked transport waiting for you, and a fax or telex to prove it. (You can cycle again once in Kashgar.) Various travel agencies in Bishkek have direct contact with Kashgar ones, or you can fax or telex directly yourself (*see* 'Kashgar', p.282).

In a good four-wheel drive or minibus the trip to the main border post takes about two hours. Put your watches forwards three hours in winter and two in summer to **Běijīng time** which is used for all official notices of starting and opening times, and all times in this book. Xīnjiāng time, used only in speech, is the same as Kyrgyz summer time, one hour later in winter. The Chinese border post is *open Mon–Fri, 10–1 and 4.30–6*. Here is where the major border formalities are completed. You may be asked to complete a health questionnaire and declaration form. Neither is important, but keep the declaration form in case you are asked for it when you leave. There are unreliable money-changing facilities, but since your transport will be taking you directly to Kashgar you can change money there.

Kyrghyzintourist in Bishkek has contact with CITS via telex to Kashgar, but despite being from the same school of high prices and surliness, even they despair of successfully despatching people there. They obtain confirmation telexes, but the Chinese vehicle often fails to turn up on the other side, and permission to enter China is refused. They will take you to their yurt camp at Naryn for an overnight stay, and then up to the old Chinese border post the next morning, and sometimes on to the new one. A car taking up to four people costs $400. An overnight stay in the yurt camp costs $45 per person full board (not recommended—but they can arrange home stays instead for around $10 per person per night including meals). CITS' fee for collecting you at the old Chinese post will be a further ¥1200 ($145) per vehicle, and probably the same if they only come as far as the new post, 104km nearer Kashgar.

Companies such as **Dostuck Trekking** offer short tours: overnight accommodation in Bishkek (private apartment); drive by jeep to Son-Kul (a superb track, *see* below) and camp; drive to Tash-Rabat and do some walking, camp; drive to Torugart the next day. 'Full service' including first night's accommodation and food, sleeping bags, tents and all necessary equipment, English-speaking guide, all meals (better food than most restaurants), transport, fuel, entrance fees, etc. would cost around $650 for two, but telex, fax, or email for an up-to-date quote. The more of you there are, the more equipment of your own you bring, and the more you do for yourselves, the less it costs per person.

From Bishkek's west bus station you can take a **private bus** to Naryn, and further buses may take you a little further, such as to At-Bashi, but there are no buses to the border, and you will be reduced to chartering a taxi or private car, or hitching. **Private cars** willing to undertake the trip all the way from Bishkek to the border may be found at the bus station, railway station, and Osh Bazaar. Be clear about how many people will be in the vehicle, when you will leave, and whether you will spend the night on the way (usual, and it's helpful to get an early start at the border next day). You'll get the best deal by going to the bus station and negotiating with a Bishkek car to leave the next day (in which case you can be collected from your hotel) or by being prepared to leave immediately with someone on their way back to At-Bashi or Naryn. Don't be surprised if you are handed over to another friend or family member part-way, say at Naryn, in which case making a partial payment is fine.

If you stand by the side of the road and hitch, expect to pay at least as much as a bus fare, and probably the same as if you'd haggled with a vehicle directly in the first place. Don't use your thumb, but simply hold out your arm and wave the vehicles down. It is pointless to proceed to the border intending to cross unless you have an invitation and transport meeting you on the Chinese side; but it is worth going almost as far as the border simply for the sake of the scenery.

The Road to the Torugart Pass

The road to China is first of all the road to the Issyk-Kul, the nearest thing to a holiday resort in Kyrgyzstan, where the *nomenklatura* dallied during the Soviet period, and Kyrgyz who can afford it still do. The road runs east parallel to the Kygyz Ala-Too, turning south through the gorge of the River Chu, before carrying on eastwards until 20km short of the lake where it forks southwards again. Those continuing straight on towards Balikchi instead, for a view of the lake, will find themselves paying money to the police at a road barrier; about 50 som ($4.20) per vehicle. There is another turning to the south side of Issyk-Kul further on at Sary-Bulak, where there are also a few places to eat.

The road south deteriorates as it crosses the 3300m pass at Dolon, but improves again afterwards. There is a road maintenance depot here, but the state of the Kyrgyz economy means that there is likely to be little work done in the foreseeable future. Beyond Naryn the road is likely to deteriorate further. If you are in a jeep, the best route is via Son-Kul (*see* p.464).

There's an aerial view of **Naryn (Нарын)**, which seems more attractive before the road drops steeply down to it. Seven hours from Bishkek, it is small and unappealing, and in winter is the coldest city in Kyrgyzstan. Camping at Son-Kul or Tash-Rabat (*see* p.464) or even on the moon would be preferable to staying at Naryn's only hotel, **Hotel Ala-Too**, which is filthy and basic with an appalling café, and costs 15 som ($1.25) for a single or 30 som ($2.50) for a double, both with bath. It would be better to talk to local people about taking you in, and better to eat on the street. Another alternative is the clean and friendly **Gostinitsa Tilek**, on Prospekt Lenina. As you enter Naryn turn left along Lenina, and the guest house is a little way down set back from the road on the right, 20 som ($1.70) per bed.

The road descends slightly and crosses a fertile plain, running southwest parallel to the At-Bashi range, and reaching the turning to the town of At-Bashi after about 30km. There are occasional yurts with friendly Kyrgyz serving simple meals, Russian tea from wood-fired and ornate samovars, and vodka—keep an eye on your driver. With steaming chunks of lamb and hunks of bread, this makes the perfect introduction to Kyrgystan if you are entering from China.

The turning to At-Bashi is as far as buses are likely to take you, about 145km from the pass, unless you carry on into the town itself, where there is a rudimentary hotel. After a further

48km or so the surfaced road is reduced to gravel, stones and holes. The main border post is about two hours away. Despite the obvious attractions of trekking around here, do not stray from the road unless you have the triple permissions required, and a reliable guide. There are long sections of electrified fence—probably powerless but discouraging.

At the 74km marker (counting down towards the border) there is a small settlement, with tiny boys atop large horses, and 15 minutes later the outer checkpoint where you must show your passport. There is an ugly military encampment and shooting ranges where troops practise, but the guards are friendly to foreigners. The road having looped around the end of the At-Bashi range, now doubles back on itself to run northeast between the massive Tiān Shān and the cool, smooth sweep of Chatyr-Kul. A few yurts are dotted about the lush grazing, and mounted nomads tend herds of sheep, cows, and hobbled horses. The road turns sharply south and climbs to the main border post, before disintegrating completely as it crosses the 3752m Torugart Pass to China. Your driver will be unable to take you past the main border post unless he has a special permit. Taxis (haggle)

Grave stone, Burana Tower

and buses (50 som or $5) will offer instead, or you can attempt to hitch with a tanker.

There is simple accommodation at the main border post on the Kyrgyz side, either in wooden caravans with no sanitary facilities, or in a beaten-up hotel that's little better (20–25 som/$2). There is no accommodation on the Chinese side until Kashgar, and you must cross in time to reach the new border post, a further 104km away, before it closes at 6pm Běijīng time.

This section of the road has interesting Great Game credentials. In 1905 George Macartney, on a reconnaissance trip from the British consulate at Kashgar, discovered that the Russians had built a cart road 27ft wide from At-Bashi to the top of the Torugart Pass, and about half a mile into Chinese territory. He reported to his superiors that the remainder of the route to Kashgar could easily be made good, and that should the Russians decide to annex all or part of Xīnjiāng this was the way that troops would come. In 1906 the Chinese capitulated to Russian pressure to complete the road on the Chinese side using a loan from a Russian bank (the 'Russo-China Bank') with the intention that the value of the loan should be recouped from tolls. The Russians were granted a monopoly of control over the trade, enhancing still further the advantages they had over traders from British India. The Chinese craftily then set the tolls at such a high rate that few used the route, and the road fell into disrepair.

The Burana Tower (Бурана)

50km east of Bishkek and about 12km south of Tokmok, the Burana Tower can be reached by taking a bus from Bishkek's east bus station to Tokmok and then chartering a local taxi. It can be done as a day trip or as a slight diversion on the way to the Torugart Pass.

The tower dates from the first half of the 11th century and is thought to be one of Central Asia's earliest minarets, standing at the heart of the Silk Route town of Balasagun, which thrived from the 10th to the 12th centuries during the existence of a Kharakhanid state stretching from Ili to the Amu Darya river. Restored in the '20s and again in the '70s, it is thought to have been 45m high but lost its top 19m in a 15th-century earthquake. From the top, reached by a short but slightly eerie climb up a very narrow, steep and dark internal staircase, something of the original layout of the city can be seen. A central fortress was surrounded by two rings of walls enclosing around 20 to 30 square kilometres of land. Close to the tower are reconstructions of the layouts of three mausoleums, and a large number of gravestones which take the form of distinctly individual squat statues of the dead, dating from the 6th to the 10th centuries, and brought from various sites around Kyrgyzstan. A two-room museum contains a variety of items excavated from the ruins including coins and ceramics clearly indicative of Silk Route trade. The museum entrance fee of 10 som (80¢) includes a guided tour in Russian, and also gains you entrance to the tower.

Son-Kul

4km beyond Sary-Bulak is the right turn onto a jeep track to Son-Kul. Ladas do take this road but it's really four-wheel-drive territory as it features steep climbs and drops. Most people are on horseback herding sheep, goats, yak and more horses, which are brought up to the area of the lake for summer grazing. Occasionally a supercilious camel can be seen. Wildlife includes marmots, rabbits, eagles, and smaller hawks. There is almost no traffic, and almost no permanent habitation, so renting a jeep is the only option. The lake itself is at 3020m, has a vast bird population and is surrounded by beautiful peaks, and there are encampments of yurts in the summer. Here you may be invited in to sample mutton and *kumis*, the famous mildly alcoholic fermented mare's milk. At least taste a little of everything you are offered. Times are also hard for these apparently self-sufficent semi-nomads, so expect to be asked for a little something in return: medicine, or fuel for the family Lada. From the lake an even more beautiful jeep track leads back down to join the main road 44km before Naryn.

Tash-Rabat Caravanserai

About 88km and 1½ hours short of the border, 17km after the end of the surfaced road, and 1½ hours from Naryn, there is a side turning to the east. Shortly after the turning a bridge is down, making the route only accessible by car between May and September (four-wheel drive preferred). At a gate in the road, 6km further on, a charge of 5 som (40¢) per person is levied. The justification for this is, 'What else am I going to live on?' and there is no apparent connection with the site itself. There, a further 3 som (25¢) per person is payable to the watchman in the white house opposite in order to gain entrance (although a small gift such as a polaroid photograph will also do the job). From Bishkek to Tash-Rabat via Son-Kul is approximately 520km altogether, or 420km on the main road.

Tash-Rabat is a carefully and unobtrusively restored stone building of unknown date on a 10th-century site, set into the hillside in an exquisite valley in the foothills of the Tiān Shān. A place of rest and worship, it also served to protect caravans on a route to and from China much earlier than the Torugart way. A central domed space with small traces of the original and probably painted plaster is surrounded by individual domed cells and a kitchen. This is probably the most intact Silk Route building you will see and no other retains as much of its original atmosphere, with the loudest noises the sound of the river, the calls of birds, and the occasional hoofbeats of passing Kyrgyz. You can rent horses and a guide from the watchman or the yurts for an 8km ride over the 3968m Tash-Rabat Pass to the chilly waters of Chatyr-Kul; as authentic a form of travel as you will find on one of the oldest Silk Routes.

The Khunjerab Pass

Islamabad to Kashgar

The Karakoram Highway

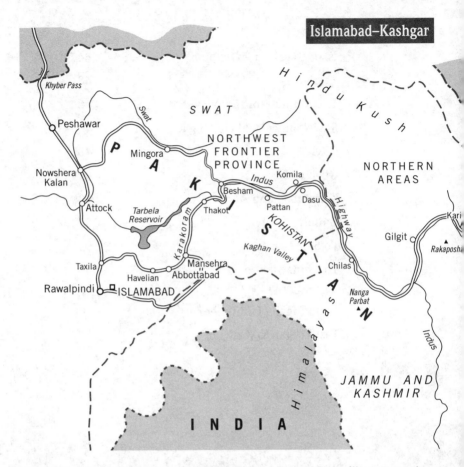

The Karakoram Highway is the longest roller-coaster ride you'll ever experience, and the only one with overtaking: its 1500 kilometres of writhing tarmac are often cut from sheer cliffs, with dizzying drops of up to 500 metres to rocky river beds, and not a crash barrier in sight. Passing several 7–8000m permanently snow-capped peaks (and the 8125m Nanga Parbat), it switchbacks across rivers on bridges incongruously decorated with Chinese lions and 'double-happiness' characters. Pieces of it have a habit of disappearing into the void, necessitating off-road diversions by non off-road vehicles. On the other hand pieces of mountain have a habit of appearing on the road, pulverizing the surface and causing tail-backs while bulldozers and engineers with explosives clear away the rubble. They are permanently on alert.

Chinese explorers may have come this way via the Karakoram route as early as the Western Hàn dynasty of 206 BC–AD 9, and from 1958 about 30,000 of them came to join 15,000 Pakistanis in carving one of the world's less likely roads. Twenty years in the construction, it cost nearly 900 lives. It follows the Indus,

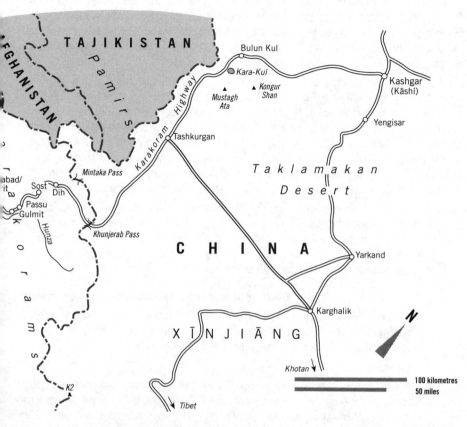

Hunza and Khunjerab rivers, cuts through the spiny Karakorams, and crosses to China at the 4934m Khunjerab Pass, the highest metalled border crossing in the world on one of its highest surfaced roads. The highway then slides down the somewhat gentler Pamirs along lush well-watered valleys to Kashgar.

Islamabad and Rawalpindi

Wham! Step out of the airport and the heat, noise and smell of the Indian sub-continent hit you like a series of blows. The Siamese twins of ordered, spacious, administrative Islamabad and seething, fretful, commercial Rawalpindi are both infested with honking buses, vans, taxis and horse-drawn tongas. Islamabad has broad streets, air-conditioned concrete towers, and carefully planned shopping centres. Rawalpindi has alleys of peeling antiquity, with sagging fretwork balconies overhanging the teeming bazaars of merchants and craftsmen.

An umbilical of 5km connects dull but green Islamabad with dusty, chaotic Rawalpindi. Eventually 'Pindi will be absorbed by the carefully planned progress of Islamabad, and the bureaucrats will surround the merchants. There is little reason to stay long in either.

Islamabad is an interesting experiment in planning, with towers and mosques of already crumbling Islamicized concrete, but feels remarkably provincial despite its capital city status. It is the home of diplomats, government departments, and those who serve or prey on them. However, if onward visas or registration are required, staying in Islamabad is better than making multiple journeys from Rawalpindi in a lumbering pyschedelic bus or sardine-tin Suzuki pick-up.

All Rawalpindi has to offer is its bazaars, which merge into each other in a tangle of sunbleached streets, and cooler, awning-hung alleys. With hundreds of small hotels, this is the territory of the budget traveller, of street food, and exchanged information about new visa regulations and hernias in the Karakoram Highway. For all this, even Rawalpindi is restrained by the standards of the Indian sub-continent, and is home to some of the most charming people that you will meet anywhere on the Silk Routes. Shopkeepers' pleas are muted, and often phrased in the most polite English imaginable. Casual meetings in the street lead to offers of a handshake, and then to further offers of hospitality, with nothing required in exchange.

Rawalpindi was of no importance until the 1840s when the British decided to build their biggest military base there, the Cantonment. It had a brief spell as temporary capital of Pakistan following independence and before Islamabad was ready for occupation. Islamabad, built from scratch and still under construction, was declared the official seat of government in 1962, replacing steamier and less healthy Karachi.

Getting to and from Islamabad and Rawalpindi

The major international gateway for Pakistan is not Islamabad but Karachi, although a few airlines fly on to Islamabad afterwards, or have connections with local shuttle airlines, and all major international airlines maintain offices there.

by air

Pakistan International Airways or PIA (*Perhaps I Arrive, Please Inform Allah, Passengers In Agony*, etc.) entirely deserves its bad press. It flies to **Běijīng** twice a week, and to **Almaty** once a week on Mondays. This flight is often heavily booked, so plan ahead. Economy class is around $250 one way. Even more heavily booked is the spectacular flight to **Gilgit**, with a variable schedule of two and sometimes three flights daily, and last-minute changes of schedule and cancellations almost guaranteed. Try to book this with PIA before leaving home. The offices of the PTDC (Pakistan Tourism Development Corporation) have two seats reserved for tourists and can give you a letter to give to PIA if the flight is otherwise fully booked. Unfortunately everyone knows this so these seats are often booked, too. Flexibility as to departure date is important. PIA also serves other major Pakistani cities, with two small domestic airlines as competition. Departure tax of Rs700 ($22) may not be included in your ticket—check when getting quotes from agents. **China Xīnjiāng Airlines** flies to Ürümqi on Wednesdays and Sundays. **British Airways** flies direct to Manchester and London Gatwick three times a week, with connections worldwide.

A taxi to or from the airport to Islamabad may be as much as Rs100. 'Pindi should be no more than Rs40–50 ($1.50).

by train

There are several trains a day between Taxila and Rawalpindi. The most useful ones from 'Pindi are at 7.15am, 8.15am, 2.10pm, and 4.40pm, with second class at Rs7, and 'lower a/c' (air-conditioned) at Rs65 ($2). The 30km distance is quicker by bus, but if you are heading up the KKH the trip to Taxila (and on to Havelian) is the only part of your journey that you can do by train, with the added advantage that the station is very close to the Taxila site. Trains also leave Rawalpindi for other major cities, such as Lahore, Quetta and Peshawar, although at times some of these routes are unsafe, and flying is recommended. It is sometimes possible to travel to India by train from Lahore, and sometimes not, but if you ask at Rawalpindi you will be told to proceed to Lahore and ask for further information. The crossing to Amritsar from there is more easily accomplished by wagon and bus.

by bus

Buses to Taxila leave from Haider Road in Saddar Bazaar, Rs5, but the train is a better choice. Natco (Northern Areas Transport Company) runs buses to Gilgit and points between (Abbottabad, Mansehra, Besham, Chilas, etc.) from the Pir Wadhai bus terminal, as does the private company Mashabrum Tours. Another private operation, Sargin Travels, runs buses from Kashmiri Bazaar. Natco has the most departures, but the private companies are sometimes slightly quicker—15 hours versus 17. Prices range from Rs180 to Rs250 ($6–8) depending on the vehicle, some of which are described as 'de luxe', but your opinion may differ. Loud music is played throughout the journey, interior lights are not always turned off, sleep is unlikely, and will anyway be broken by the need to descend three times from the bus to put your passport details in ledgers at check points. Much of the enjoyment of the Karakoram Highway and its scenery will be lost. Begin your journey at Taxila, and take it in easy steps from there (*see* p.481). Other major Pakistani cities are also served by bus from Pir Wadhai, and by private companies such as Flying Coach on Murree Road between Tipu Road and Liaquat Chowk.

Getting Around

Rawalpindi is a ramshackle cluster of busy junctions called chowks, connected by bazaars, *bazaar* being used to name both streets and market areas. The cantonment on its southeastern side bordered by The Mall has a comparatively abstract military orderliness, but little going on. Except for the upmarket locations, all the restaurants, hotels and other services you might need are clustered in the various bazaars, and in particular Saddar Bazaar, Liaquat Chowk (also known as Liaquat Bagh) and Rajah Bazaar.

Islamabad is still in its infancy, and consists primarily of three rows of large blocks, each row having a letter designation F, G, or H going south, and each column a number increasing from west to east. To confuse matters, each block has a name, too, and is divided into four quarters around a central shopping area, the quarters being numbered one to four, beginning at the bottom left and going clockwise. The key areas for the visitor are the Diplomatic Enclave G5, where most embassies are found, and the Blue Area—a section of highway with useful banks and other offices which runs along the boundary of F6 (Super Market) and G6 (Melody Market). Super Market

and Jinnah Super Market (F7) are both good for shopping and eating, and Aabpara Market (on the south side of G6) for transport connections.

Transport is easy. Frequent and garish **buses, wagons** (minibuses), and **Suzukis** (small pick-ups with bench seats along the sides) link the main bazaars of 'Pindi with each other and with Aabpara in Islamabad, which is the central point for most routes crossing the city. While there are some obvious starting, finishing, and stopping points where vehicles gather, in general you can wave down a vehicle anywhere and before you can even ask the conductor he will have told you several times where he's going. Before that a passer-by will very likely have asked you where you want to go, and

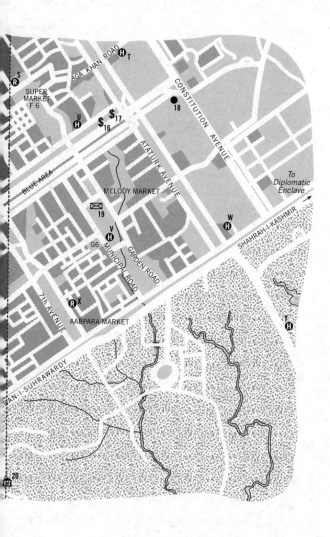

KEY

15	Faisal Mosque
16	Bank of America
17	American Express
18	Awami Markaz building
19	Post office
20	Lok Virsa Museum
21	Senior Superintendent of Police

HOTELS AND RESTAURANTS

S	Heaven and Munchies
T	Marriott Hotel
U	President Hotel
V	Holiday Inn
W	Youth Hostel Islamabad
X	Food stalls
Y	Tourist Campsite

airlines

PIA's main booking office is on The Mall in Rawalpindi, ☎ 567011, but the men on the international counters are lazy and obstructive, and seem to believe that their job is to prevent ticket sales if at all possible. They will only sell the Almaty tickets if you have a vaccination certificate (although they are not specific as to which vaccinations you must have and do not understand the certificates anyway) and a Kazak visa (no other CIS visa is acceptable, whatever CIS governments might say). Reconfirm frequently, and expect to be told that you have been bumped even when you haven't. No-one knows what's going on.

China Xīnjiāng Airlines: No 1 building, F8/3 No.10 Avenue, Islamabad, ☎ 851816, ✉ 282725.

British Airways: Pearl Continental Hotel, The Mall, Rawalpindi, ☎ 566791/ 565413.

embassies

All the embassies are in Islamabad, mostly concentrated in the Diplomatic Enclave in the southeast corner of the city, but with newer embassies, including those of some CIS countries, scattered around the northwest.

Onward visas:

China: Shahrah-I-Kashmir, G-4, ☎ 821114, (*open Sun–Thurs, 9–12*). Tourist visas are usually valid for one month, sometimes longer, beginning any time in the next 30 days, and can be extended in China. Prices vary according to nationality and phases of the moon: Canada Rs1550 ($48), UK Rs1600 ($50), and US Rs300 ($9.50). US nationals must also pay an 'examination fee' of Rs600 ($19), which is not refundable if a visa is refused. Visas usually take four working days (so not including Fri or Sat), but three days for an extra Rs300, and Rs900 ($28) for same or next day. One photo is needed. If possible, get your Chinese visa before leaving home. Occasionally visas are stamped as *only* good for overland travel via the Khunjerab Pass, so make your intentions clear if you want to fly in, or enter by another route.

India: Near 1st Ave and 1st Street in the Diplomatic Enclave, ☎ 814371. The length of time taken to get an Indian visa varies according to the state of tension between India and Pakistan from 24 hours to several weeks, although four days is fairly usual. You will probably need a letter of introduction from your own embassy, to be handed in when you *collect* the visa, which shows what a farce this is.

The **Kazakstan** embassy is in F8/3, Street 4, House 66, ☎ 262920 (*open for drop-off Sun, Tues, Thurs, 9–10.30; pick-up 12–1 daily*). Visas are often obtainable the same day. Tourist visas will not be given without visa support (*see* pp.8 and 429–31) and are always for two weeks. One official's explanation: 'Our country is not very interesting. Two weeks is enough.' You should be able to get a transit visa without problems if you have any other CIS visa or an air ticket out of Almaty. With another CIS visa you are allowed to enter Kazakstan for 72 hours without a transit visa, but Chinese officials may refuse to let you out of China, and Kazak officials may attempt to extort money from you if you do not have one. PIA will not let you take the Islamabad to Almaty flight without a visa or a visa support fax or telex. A transit visa is $15, a tourist one $30, payable in dollars or rupees. You will be sent to the Bank of America in the Blue Area to pay and get a receipt. One photograph is needed.

Kyrgyz visas must still be obtained from the **Russian** embassy, in G4 next to the Chinese embassy; enter from the rear, ℭ 214604 (*open Mon, Wed, 9–12*). These limited opening hours mean long queues, so go early. However easy Kyrgyz visas may be to get in the West, the Russians require you to have visa support for Kyrgyz tourist visas (*see* pp.8 and 452–3 on how to acquire this). Transit visas should not be a problem if you have another CIS visa, or an onward air ticket. Prices vary according to nationality; UK Rs1900 ($60). Three photographs are needed.

Polaroid **passport photos** are widely available at photo shops in Islamabad and Rawalpindi at Rs8 for four.

Emergencies:

Most Western nations have embassies or high commissions in the Diplomatic Enclave G5, including:

Canada: Bari Amam Road, G5, ℭ 211101.
France: Corner Constitution Avenue and Shahrah-I-Kashmir, G5/4, ℭ 823981.
Germany: Bari Amam Road, G5, ℭ 212412.
USA: University Road, G5, ℭ 826161.
UK: G5, ℭ 822131.

With the exception of the newer CIS embassies, the taxi drivers generally know where the embassies are, and although some Suzukis from Aapbara pass by the Chinese and Russian embassies, a taxi at probably only Rs20 from Aapbara is the best option. Most embassies take Friday and Saturday off.

maps and books

Maps, guides, and books in English can be found in several bookshops in Super Market, Islamabad, such as **Mr Books** (motto: 'Reading cures brain damage'), and at **Book Centre** on Saddar Road, Rawalpindi (and two other locations nearby), along with foreign-language newspapers and magazines. For those planning further travel in Pakistan, Isobel Shaw's *Pakistan Handbook* is far and away the best available. There are also second-hand books on everything from Management Economics to Microwave Cookery from **Old Book Fair** and **Old Book Centre** in Super Market, and from pavement stalls in Kashmir Road as part of the bazaar which takes over Saddar pavements on Fridays.

money

Most branches of the **National Bank of Pakistan** handle foreign exchange, such as the one on Bank Road just west of Kashmir Road in Rawalpindi (*open Sun–Thurs, 9–1.30*), as do some branches of **Habib Bank**, such as the safety deposit branch on The Mall, open the same hours, which handles cash and cheques in most major currencies. **American Express** (*open Sun–Thurs, 9–1 and 2.15–4.45; Sat, 9–12.45*) has offices in Islamabad at 1E Ali Plaza in the Blue Area, and in Rawalpindi at Rahim Plaza, Murree Road, and will change cheques in all major currencies to rupees, dollars and other money. Cardholders can also cash cheques drawn on their personal bank accounts. The **Bank of America** (*open Sun–Thurs, 9–4*), 1st Floor, Awan Arcade, 1B Blue Area, just west of Amex in Islamabad, ℭ 828801, will give Mastercard and Visa **credit card** advances in rupees (1%)

or dollars (3.5%). **Money changers**, who give much better rates than the bank for cash, and also work with US dollar cheques, can be found clumped near the junction of Kashmir Road and The Mall in Rawalpindi.

photographic

Photographic supplies are also widely available from shops well decorated with Fuji, Agfa and Kodak logos. Try to buy from one with a relatively cool, dark interior, and check expiry dates carefully. Islamabad and Rawalpindi are the only places on the route to China where you will find slide film, usually Fuji Sensia. It is also the only place where you will get slide film developed, probably only Fuji. Foto Plaza in Super Market, Islamabad, quotes around Rs95 ($3) for 36-shot print film, and Rs235 ($7.50) for slides. C41 processing takes 1hr and costs Rs20 plus Rs4 or 5 per print depending on size. Slide developing costs a flat Rs60 ($2). In Rawalpindi **Asiatic Optical Co** at 73 Kashmir Road near Bank Road can supply slide film for about Rs190 ($6).

post office and telephones

The main **post office** in Rawalpindi is on Kashmir Road between Bank Road and Haider Road and in Islamabad in the northern part of Melody Market, and on the inter-city bus and wagon route. Both accept **poste restante** addressed to GPO Rawalpindi or GPO Islamabad. Pak Telecom has **international telephone and facsimile** facilities. In Rawalpindi this is on Kashmir Road just south of The Mall (*open 7 days, 24 hours*). The charges are in whole minutes and some staff delight in overcharging, so make sure they put the stopwatch where you can see it, or put yours where they can. It's cheaper to call at night. You can also receive faxes for Rs10 per page, but beware a mysterious Rs250 'registration fee' requested by some staff but not others. In Islamabad the most useful building for communication is the **Awami Markaz** centre, on Constitution Avenue just north of the Blue Area, almost opposite the Presidency. Here in air-con chilliness you will find a post office and a Pak Telecom office for international telephone and fax, together with PIA and Pakistan Railways offices. You can also receive and send faxes at the main GPO in Islamabad. **Postcards** are widely available from bookshops and hotel foyers in 'Pindi and Islamabad. Stamps for cards are Rs12 to North America, and Rs11 to most of the rest of the world. Letters are Rs15.

pointed you in the right direction. Major points to pick up transport are Aabpara Market in Islamabad, Haider Road in Saddar Bazaar, and on Murree Road just south of Liaquat Chowk. Between points in Rawalpindi the fare is Rs1–2, and between Islamabad and Rawalpindi, Rs5. **Taxis** are yellow and black and ubiquitous. Any meter is purely decorative (see the pretty flashing lights!), so negotiate a price before you start. You will always pay more than local people, but short trips around town are an affordable Rs20–30. If you are planning to go to an embassy to pick up a visa for instance, the taxi will usually be happy to wait, so negotiate a round-trip fare. Between

Even Pakistanis are sceptical of their **travel agencies**, and you should go straight to the bus operators, airlines, or other companies to buy your tickets, or use a recognized agency such as American Express (*see* 'money', p.473) if in a hurry. Exceptions are larger, more reputable agencies such as **Travel Walji's** in Aabpara, ✆ 812151, and **Javed Travels** in Pothowar Plaza, Blue Area, ✆ 814484, ✉ 220039, both of which also tailor itineraries using their own vehicles. If you do decide to book tickets through other agents, remember to check that all charges, taxes, departure taxes, and so on are included in the quoted price, and make it clear that you will not accept any change in price between when you book and when you receive the ticket. Get a receipt for any deposit, and pay as little in advance as possible.

visa extensions

Islamabad is the only place to arrange **visa extensions**. To get to the National Passport and Immigration Office (*open Sun–Thurs, 9–1 for drop-off and 4–6 for pick-up*) from Aapbara, take a wagon no.105 (Rs4) which terminates outside Peshawar Mall, and the office is diagonally opposite. Fill out a form there, go across the street and make one copy, and two copies of your passport's information and Pakistani visa pages. You will also need two photographs. Extensions can usually be collected in the afternoon of the next working day, valid for two months. Fees for extensions vary by nationality as they do for visas. Occasionally you may be asked to get a letter of recommendation from your embassy, which can usually be run off from a computer very quickly (the Iranian and Indian Embassies often ask visa applicants for such a letter, too).

If your stay is going to take you beyond 30 days in Pakistan, you are required to **register** before the 30th day, and if your visa extension will bring your potential stay to 30 days or more, you may also be sent to register before your extension is granted. If you are staying in Rawalpindi you must go back and register with the Office of Inspector General of Police, Foreigner Registration Branch, known more commonly as the SSP (Senior Superintendent of Police), past Kecheri Chowk on the airport Suzuki route (*open Sun to Thurs, 9–5*). Tell them 'Rawalpindi SSP'. If you are staying in Islamabad, register at the SSP office in Ayu Market (F8). Two passport photographs are required.

Islamabad and Rawalpindi the fare will be Rs70–80 ($2.50). To hire a taxi for half a day to go from Rawalpindi to Islamabad or vice versa, run around several places, and come back, should cost around Rs400, but to avoid argument make your intentions very clear. **Car hire** is available from many hotels, or more cheaply directly from local companies, such as Abbasi Tours just off The Mall on Masood Akhtar Road, next to the Pearl-Continental Hotel. Trips outside the local area (Taxila counts as local) involve compulsory use of a chauffeur, and a one-week hire of a Toyota Corolla, for instance, would cost Rs600 ($19) per day plus Rs6 per kilometre including fuel and all

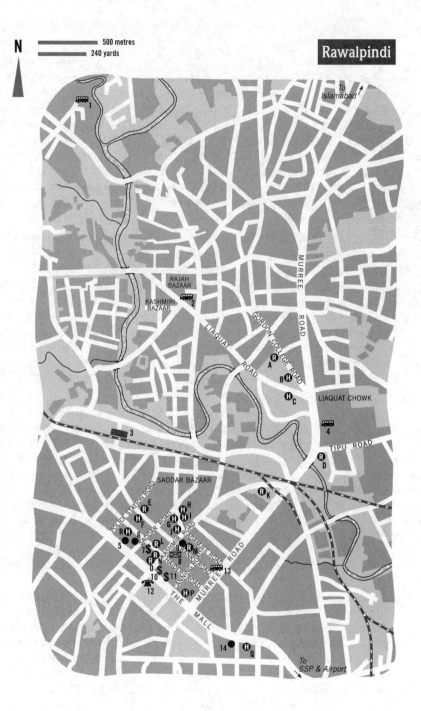

N

500 metres
240 yards

Rawalpindi

To Islamabad

MURREE ROAD

RAJAH BAZAAR

KASHMIRI BAZAAR

GORDON COLLEGE ROAD

LIAQUAT ROAD

R A
B H
H C

LIAQUAT CHOWK

4

TIPU ROAD

3

R D

SADDAR BAZAAR

R K

POLICE STATION ROAD

R E
H F
R 6
R H
5
7 $
R L
R N
D
10
12

H H
6 H I
J
9 R
8 M
13

KASHMIR ROAD
ADAMJEE ROAD
BANK ROAD
HAIDER ROAD
CANTT ROAD

$ 11

H P

THE MALL

MURREE ROAD

14 H Q

To SSP & Airport

RAWALPINDI

1	Pir Wadhai general bus stand
2	Buses to Taxila
3	Railway station
4	Flying Coach office
5	PIA office
6	Rahat Bakery
7	National Bank of Pakistan
8	Post office
9	Unique Bakery
10	Money changers
11	Habib Bank
12	International telephone office
13	Suzukis to the airport
14	Abbasi Tours

HOTELS AND RESTAURANTS

A	Savour Foods
B	Rawalpindi Popular Inn
C	Adil Hotel
D	Excellency Table
E	Chung Po Restaurant
F	Pakland International
G	Venus Hotel
H	Shah Taj Hotel
I	Lalazar Hotel
J	Hotel Avanti
K	Pizzeria Pizza House
L	Data Kabana
M	Kamran Café
N	Meher Ali Restaurant
O	Shezan Restaurant
P	Flashman's Hotel and PTDC office
Q	Pearl-Continental Hotel
R	Taj Mahal Hotel

costs except Rs125 ($4) per day for the chauffeur's food and accommodation. A beaten-up small Suzuki car for driving yourself around town costs Rs800 ($25) per day with unlimited mileage, but you buy the fuel. Any major Western driving licence seems to be acceptable, but take an international driving permit to be sure.

Pakistan ℂ +92, Islamabad and Rawalpindi ℂ (051) **Tourist Information**

The **Pakistan Tourism Development Authority** has information offices in the airport, Flashman's Hotel, and F-7/2 College Rd in Islamabad, operated with varying levels of enthusiasm. The staff of many of the smaller hotels listed below are an excellent source of practical information on current prices, where to buy tickets, etc.

Lok Virsa Museum

Open 9–1 and 2–5; closed Mon and Fri.

The museum is on Shakarparian Hill, which is passed by buses from Rawalpindi. Get off after the bus reaches Islamabad's outskirts and before it turns right along Khyaban-I-Suhrwardy at a junction known as Zero Point. From there cross over and take a small footpath leading uphill south of a bridge over the road to 'Pindi, and near a slip road. It takes about 20 minutes; it's simpler to take a taxi.

This small museum has a good collection of art and handicrafts from all over Pakistan, as well as a library and research facilities. Opening times tend to be a little unpredictable, so enquire before departing on ℂ 812675.

Faisal Mosque

One of Asia's largest mosques, this marble and concrete extravaganza is impressive because of its scale. The angled planes of the roof of the central hall make it look as though it was designed for skateboarding, while the four minarets look as if they might be launched in an attack on India. Acres of marble ablution areas and forecourt lead to an interior that's much less imposing. Despite its spaciousness the atmosphere and look are similar to that of the lobby of a multinational's office block, rather than a place of worship. Restrained behaviour and sober dress are requested, and admission is not allowed during periods of prayer, so especially avoid Fridays. Admission is free, but there is a cloakroom charge of Rs1 when you collect your shoes, which you must leave at the entrance.

Around Islamabad and Rawalpindi

Taxila

Taxila can be visited as a day trip from Rawalpindi, and indeed is the main point of interest in the area. But if you are heading north it would be better to take a train to Taxila and spend one or two nights. The museum is excellent and the site is vast, seeming even bigger on days when the sun is hot. *See* below, p.481.

Where to Stay

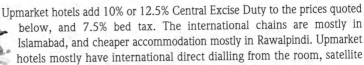

Upmarket hotels add 10% or 12.5% Central Excise Duty to the prices quoted below, and 7.5% bed tax. The international chains are mostly in Islamabad, and cheaper accommodation mostly in Rawalpindi. Upmarket hotels mostly have international direct dialling from the room, satellite television including BBC and CNN, air-conditioning throughout, and 24-hour hot water. Mid-price rooms usually have individual air-conditioning, local phone calls from the room, international calls through an operator, satellite TV, carpets, and hot water most of the time. Cheaper hotels have fans, and hot water only for a few months a year. Hot water in buckets can be ordered if needed. Only in the upmarket hotels does a double mean a double bed; almost everywhere else it means twin beds. At all levels an extra bed can be added for a moderate increase in price. Most moderate and cheaper hotels have squat toilets, not Western bowls. Cheaper hotels may have a little more wildlife than you would like.

Cheap and moderately priced hotels are legion around the main bazaars, and many will be similar to those mentioned below, so don't be afraid to try neighbouring places.

expensive

In Islamabad, the 140-room **Holiday Inn** at G6 Civic Centre, Melody Market, ✆ 827311, ✉ 224263, operates a free collection and delivery service to the airport, and lives up to the usual standards. A single room is Rs3200 ($100), a double Rs3800 ($120). The 290-room **Marriott** at Aga Khan Road, Shalimar-5, ✆ 223344, ✉ 820648, has a tinkling foyer piano, glacial air-conditioning, and is thoroughly comfortable. Singles are from Rs5500 ($172), and doubles from Rs6500 ($205). There is also a Sheraton.

In Rawalpindi the best choice is the **Pearl-Continental** on The Mall, © 566011, ✉ 563927, owned by the same people as the Marriott, but with more of a local flavour. The upgraded Executive Floor has its own lounge and free café facilities. Singles are from Rs4000 ($125), doubles from Rs4500 ($141). Also on The Mall, the PTDC-run **Flashman's Hotel**, © 581480, ✉ 566760, is more than 100 years old, but surprisingly lacking in character. The large VIP suites in the dated sixties block, which have a private garden and give onto a secluded swimming pool, might be worth considering, especially if you are travelling as a family; Rs3000 ($94).

moderate

In Rawalpindi's Saddar Bazaar, the bright and clean **Hotel Avanti** on Adamjee Road at Massy Gate, © 566905, has carpeted singles for Rs300 ($9.50), and large comfortable doubles for Rs350 ($11) with spotless white bathrooms, some with Western toilets. The old-fashioned **Pakland International** on Bank Road has air-conditioned rooms with satellite TV for Rs430 ($14) single and Rs 484 ($15) double, or for less without TV. In Islamabad the **President Hotel** at 1B Nazimuddin Road in the Blue Area, close to American Express, © 217142, ✉ 220995, is more upmarket, with singles at Rs1400 ($44) and doubles from Rs1600 ($50). The **Taj Mahal** on Haider Rd, one block north of PIA on the south side, has been recommended as particularly friendly with non-a/c but cool doubles with bath for Rs240 ($7.50).

inexpensive

In Rawalpindi, one of Pakistan's friendliest hotels is the family-run **Rawalpindi Popular Inn**, Gordon College Road, Liaquat Chowk, © 531884, with a variety of scruffy doubles from Rs120 ($4) with common bath to Rs180 with bath, and dorms at Rs60 ($2). There are bright front rooms with balcony and traffic noise, and cooler rear ones. The staff are extremely helpful, and Liaquat Bagh is generally a quieter place to stay than the bazaars, and conveniently on the Liaquat Road route between Saddar Bazaar and Islamabad. Also on Liaquat Road close to the Chowk is the clean **Adil Hotel**, © 70730, with singles for Rs80 ($2.50) and doubles for Rs130 ($4), both with bath. This is better value for money than most backpacker hotels, but little English is spoken. In Saddar, the somewhat dingy **Venus Hotel** on Hathi Chowk, Adamjee Road, © 566501, is the most popular with backpackers, with singles for Rs60 ($2), doubles Rs90 ($3) and triples Rs140. There are two almost identical places, the **Shah Taj** and the **Lalazar**, opposite.

cheap

In Islamabad the **Youth Hostel Islamabad** behind the Aabpara PBS petrol pumps on Shaheed Millel Road, © 826899, is a bright, modern building with beds for only Rs40 ($1.25), or Rs23 if you are a student. Membership of the IYHF is required. You can pitch a tent on a platform at the **Tourist Campsite**, just south of Aabpara for Rs15, or on the ground for Rs8. You can also lie down on the concrete floor of a room for Rs15, or in the open air for Rs3. The site is cool, green and leafy, and you can park vehicles of all kinds here for only a few rupees.

Eating Out

Menus in Islamabad and 'Pindi are not as long as you might expect, and interesting food is not that easy to find. Most people eat in their hotels, where menu prices correspond fairly accurately to room prices; the higher the one, the higher the other. There are hundreds of restaurants, but few offer more than a hotel at the same price level. Bony mutton dishes are cheap, and equally bony chicken is much more expensive. Familiar items such as *biriyani* and *korma* dishes don't seem familiar when delivered, and chicken *tikka*, for instance, often means a leg of chicken, not chicken in small, boneless pieces. The best Western food is to be had in the big hotels, and most of what is produced as Western or Chinese food outside of them bears little resemblance to the real thing. The best food is the simplest: *dal* and *chappatis*. Sweet or sour *lassies* (yoghurt drinks) make filling and nutritious snacks, but be careful of hygiene.

expensive

The big hotels all have good restaurants with large local and Western menus and attentive service. The **Chung Po** on Bank Rd in Rawalpindi has a convincing **Chinese** restaurant atmosphere (as seen in the West), but less convincing food, since the cook is Baltistani. Prices are similar to Western ones, and Mastercard and Visa are accepted.

moderate

The **Excellency Table** on the corner of Murree Rd and Tipu Rd, closer to Liaquat Chowk, has excellent and substantial set menus from Rs60 ($2), and an all-you-can-eat buffet from Rs140 ($4.50), including delicious sweets. Individidual main courses are from Rs45 ($1.50). The **Pizzeria Pizza House**, at 313 Gul-e-Akra Plaza on Murree Road, has good pizza in a fast-food atmosphere for around Rs150 ($5), and neighbouring fried chicken and lasagne restaurants. In Saddar Bazaar, the **Shezan** restaurant, next to the Meher Ali (*see* below), has reasonable Pakistani food for around Rs80 ($2.50), and Western dishes from Rs100 ($3).

inexpensive

In Rawalpindi the **Meher Ali** on the corner of Haider Road and Kashmir Road has good basic rice and meat dishes for around Rs40 ($1.25) per dish. The **Kamran Café** on Bank Road near Kashmir Road serves good *lassies* and a variety of local and Western snacks. In Islamabad's Super Market, **Heaven** fast food is not so fast, but has tolerable burgers, sandwiches, and fish and chips for around Rs50 ($1.50). Nearby **Munchies** has cheap kebabs, fruit *chats*, *pooris*, and other snacks from Rs10. Street restaurants around Aabpara have excellent chicken *karahi* and other cheap Balti dishes. **Savour Foods** in Liaquat Bagh on Gordon College Road has chicken *pulao* in four varieties from Rs25. **Data Kabana**, opposite Ciros Theatre in an alley off Haider Road to the north, has good traditional Pakistani kebabs, chicken *karahi*, and so on; Rs40 ($3) for a full-size meal.

Eating In

There are some excellent bakeries in Rawalpindi, including the **Unique Bakery** on the corner of Bank and Kashmir Rds (lemon sponge cake, chocolate éclairs, and pistachio *barfi*), and the **Rahat Bakery** on Saddar Road, which also has refrigerated chocolate, cheese, instant coffee and tinned foods. Fresh fruit and vegetables can be bought at the roadside and at many small shops. Take away sweets such as *gulab jamun* and *barfi* are widely available; better from less fly-blown shops than street stalls.

Shopping and Entertainment

The sprawl of Rawalpindi's multiple bazaars offer entertaining browsing as well as shopping. As throughout Asia, shops and stalls with similar products tend to huddle together, which makes for lively bargaining, which should always be done hard, but with a smile and never in haste. The best prices will always be obtained by researching one day and shopping the next. Confusingly the word 'bazaar' is used for areas, street names, and markets in or off those streets. In the labyrinthine **Rajah Bazaar** area one market flows into another. The Ladies (Moti) Bazaar on the north side of Iqbal Road is gaudy with bangles, beads, and iridescent fabrics, both on the stalls and on the women who shop there. Bara Bazaar has electronics (as you will be able to hear from a distance) and pottery. There is further competitive noise from cassette shops on Liaquat Road. The Karan Bazaar on Sarafa Bazaar between Urdu Bazaar and Rajah Bazaar (got that?) has blockprinted and other fabrics, scarves, hats and bedspreads. A little further east on Sarafa Bazaar are many jewellery shops and an ancient British post box. In **Saddar Bazaar** the Haider Rd between Saddar and Kashmir Rds has shops with excellent cashmere shawls. The north side of Bank Rd has shops with fine linen, including Nalik Fabrics, the Bombay Cloth Store and Hyatts. The east side of Canning Rd between Haider and Bank Rds is good for shopping for brassware, carpets, and antiques.

The **Australian Embassy** has become famous amongst budget travellers for its Thursday night open house, which although theoretically for Australians and their guests, in fact often has few Australians in sight. Entrance is Rs300 ($9.50) but this gives you a book of vouchers to exchange for beer and barbecued food, strictly for consumption on the premises only.

Taxila

Taxila is mentioned in the Indian classical epics the *Ramayana* and the *Mahabarata*, and in the Buddhist *Jataka* stories. Alexander the Great passed through here in 326 BC. Herodotus knew of the province of which Taxila was a part, and apocryphal stories of the acts of St Thomas have him performing and witnessing miracles here in around AD 30. The Buddhist pilgrims from China, Făxiăn and Xuánzàng, both passed through here in AD 403 and 630 respectively.

From being part of the Persian empire of Darius I, the region was reconquered by Alexander, and under Greek rule until his death soon afterwards in 323 BC. After a brief hiatus, Taxila was incorporated into the Mauryan empire of the Punjab, eventually becoming a regional capital and usually the seat of the emperor's heir. The area covered, called Gandhara, included parts of modern India, Pakistan, and Afghanistan. The dynasty's most famous member, Ashoka (272–236 BC), ruled here before becoming king himself. Ashoka's conversion to Buddhism in about 262 BC was to have an impact well beyond the borders of his territory, as for the next 25 years until his death he was to devote himself to promoting his new faith. Acquiring the remains of the Sakyamuni Buddha, Ashoka caused them to be distributed to various important Buddhist communities, which built stupas to house them. These included a large stupa at Dharmarajika in Taxila and the one at Fămén Sì near Xī'ān (along with reportedly 18 others in China). Despite further changes of ruler, including the Greeks again, Parthians and Kushans, Buddhism grew rapidly in popularity, and Xuánzàng was able to report the existence of 1000 monasteries or so when he passed by 800 years later, although much was by then in ruins.

Gandhara was the site of the adaptation of Hellenic artistic ideas for the expression of Buddhism, particularly during its high point under the Kushans in AD 60–455, and from here these ideas travelled into the oases of the Taklamakan and beyond. Taxila never recovered from the destruction wrought by the White Huns who swept through the area in around AD 460.

There are altogether more than 50 sites scattered over a large area, but many have little enough left above ground to be of interest only to the archaeologist. Taxila can be visited as a day trip from Rawalpindi, but it's better to make it the first stop on your journey up the KKH, and to spend one or two nights here. The 1.25pm train from Rawalpindi gets you to Taxila in plenty of time to check in to a hotel, and to see the museum and Bhir Mound. The next day in the early morning, taking plenty of water and sunscreen, you can walk or ride to Dharmarajika (seeing Bhir Mound on the way if you didn't see it the previous day), continuing on foot cross-country or going back to the road and up to Sirkap, then retiring out of the heat. In the mid-afternoon you can catch a Suzuki or bus to the turning to Jaulian, walk there and on to Mohra Moradu, returning by the same route.

Getting to and from Taxila

From Rawalpindi the quickest route is by road, but the train is the gentler option, and the station is within walking distance of the museum and hotels. For a day trip take the 9.45am train and then return by Suzuki, wagon or bus from Taxila town.

by rail

There are three trains a day from Rawalpindi, at 9.45am, 1.25pm and 5pm, taking between 30 and 45 mins to get to Taxila Cantt. Railway Station, and costing Rs5 to Rs7 for third class, or Rs65 ($2) for lower a/c (on some trains only). The 1.25pm train arrives at Taxila at approximately 2.10pm, and a walk of less than 10 minutes, or a Suzuki for Rs2, or a tonga for Rs5 gets you to the museum in plenty of time to browse in its relative coolness. Trains to Rawalpindi leave at approximately 9am, 11am, 5pm and 6pm.

by bus

Buses to Taxila go from Saddar Bazaar, Rajah Bazaar, and the Pir Wadhai bus terminal. Private companies on Murree Road south of Liaquat Bagh have a/c minibuses for Rs65 ($2). These drop you in the town itself, from where you'll have to take a wagon or Suzuki to the museum, sites and accommodation.

Getting Around

Buses and Suzukis run past the museum and turn down to the railway station and on into Taxila town, Rs2. In the other direction they take you past the well-marked turnings to the principal sites mentioned here, all on the right-hand side.

Tourist Information

The sites, the museum and the hotels are all out of town. From Taxila station cross the footbridge and walk straight ahead away from the town, turning left at the T-junction. The Bhir Mound is visible on your right with the road to Dharmarajika; the Youth Hostel, the PTDC Motel, and the Taxila Hotel appear one after the other on your left, and the museum is opposite the Motel. It's less than 10 minutes' walk, or you can hire one of the waiting tongas for Rs5. Continuing up the same road by bus or Suzuki brings you successively to the turnings for Sirkap (Rs1) and Jaulian (Rs2), both on the right-hand side, as well as those for other sites.

The **PTDC** information office is based at the PTDC Motel. A little English is spoken but they have no maps, and their main purpose is to sell you guided tours for up to Rs500 ($16) a time. The same kiosk which sells you an entrance ticket to the museum also has a number of books and pamphlets about Taxila, but these can be bought more cheaply in Rawalpindi, Islamabad or Gilgit. The best **maps** of the Taxila sites can be found in Sir John Marshall's book *Guide to Taxila*, but the text is perhaps too technical for the casual visitor.

There is a **post office** on the right as you go into town from the railway station. Carry on past the post office and turn left at the T-junction, crossing the railway tracks to find the international **PCO** (Phone Call Office), on the left, opposite the hospital.

Taxila Museum

Open 1 April–30 Sept, 8.30–12.30 and 2.30–5.30; 1 Oct–31 Mar, 9–4; adm Rs4. Admission tickets are available from a kiosk on your left as you enter the gate.

The Taxila Museum is a cool and pleasant brick building set in formal gardens with topiary vaguely reminiscent of Surrey, were it not for the exotic species. Inside is one of the most important collections of Gandharan art and artefacts. Well-displayed and labelled, the museum gives a perfect introduction to the Buddhist culture that eventually spread to the oases of the Taklamakan desert and on into China proper, and is best seen before tackling the Taxila sites themselves.

Half of the museum's collection is domestic: cooking utensils; hairpins and jewellery of ivory, bone and shell; children's toys and whistles, as well as cult objects, and weapons. Seeing these items helps you to imagine the bustle of thriving communities when you visit the somewhat desolate sites. The remainder of the collection is items taken from the sites themselves for preservation; statuary in stucco, phyllite, clay and terracotta, including the missing heads from many of the decapitated Buddhas. A separate small room houses a collection of silver artefacts and a display of coins showing the rulers of Taxila in chronological order from Azes I, King of Taxila, 90–40 BC, to Hermaios, the Greek King of Kabul, AD 45–50.

There is a useful relief map showing the layout of the entire area and the relationship of the sites to each other. A contribution to dating the sites was the different methods of construction

A Pakistani bus

used in creating walls, many of which are astonishingly straight and accurate. At the rear of the museum are sample sections with dates which give you the opportunity for some amateur archaeology as you tour the sites. A reproduction of the miniature stupa at Mohra Moradu shows you the design of the spire and layers of 'umbrellas' which originally topped the stupas whose bases you will see.

Bhir Mound

Just south of the museum a clearly marked road leads to Dharmarajika, and about 200 metres' walk south of this is the Bhir Mound. This is the site of the first Taxila (6th–2nd centuries BC), and although there is little to see above ground, the partially excavated site is just a few minutes' walk from the road close to the museum, an easy diversion through cricket-playing children and grazing sheep, and worth seeing. The layout of the visible foundations give a clear idea of tightly interlocking streets around houses with central courtyards, and occasional open spaces for markets.

Dharmarajika

Returning to the road from the Bhir Mound, it's a further 20 minutes' walk to Dharmarajika, ending with two stream crossings, the first on slightly wobbly stones, and the second on solid concrete blocks. A short climb up then brings you to the southeast corner of Dhamarajika, where you will be met by the *chowkidar* (watchman) who will sell you an entry ticket for Rs4, which admits you to most of the major sites.

Here are the substantial remains of a large stupa, surrounding votive stupas, and an attached monastery with various bathing and other facilities for the monks. The bases of the stupas are all that remain of most, but the base of the main one is about 50m in diameter, and about 15m high. The visible outer shell is the last of a series of layers around an original built by Ashoka to house some of the ashes of the Buddha. The remains of decorative stonework on the east side give some idea of what the whole might have looked like originally, and there's more on the base of a large votive stupa to the east.

Sirkap

Either walk back to the main road and catch a Suzuki up past the museum to the turning to Sirkap, or proceed across country. There are multiple paths, so get the *chowkidar* to point you in the right direction. The most easy to follow is that along the valley, but which ends in a steep climb over a hill. Sticking to the ridge is better, but more difficult to navigate. It's about 30 minutes' walk.

The Bactrian Greeks moved Taxila to the Sirkap site at the beginning of the 2nd century BC, which was continually occupied for three centuries, despite several changes of rulers. The original Greek town plan (complete with *acropolis*) was overlaid with the constructions of those who followed, and sections of the original 3 miles of city wall, stupa bases, remains of the palace and other buildings are extensive. Enter from the north.

Jaulian

Jaulian is the best preserved of all the sites, and if you only have time for one, this is the one to see, taking a bus or Suzuki to the turning. There's a simple street restaurant here with the usual *dal*, vegetables, *chappatis*, tea, etc., and after a 20-minute walk down the lane you find two stalls with shady seating and fans selling very cold drinks for Rs8. Here you will be asked to show your ticket or pay Rs4 if you don't have one. A short climb up some steps brings you to the site, where the *chowkidar* will escort you round.

There are three main sections: the lower stupa court, the main stupa court, and the monastery, complete with cells. The particular attraction is the amount of intact statuary, although much of it is beheaded, of Buddhas and Bodhisattvas. The buildings were originally constructed in the time of Kushan rule in the 2nd century AD, and were destroyed by the White Huns towards the end of the 5th century.

Mohra Moradu

Returning down to the drink stalls, walk to the aqueduct and take the path to the right which follows it. When you get up to its level you can either walk along the concrete 'bank', or stay on the path. Ignore the persistent 'Hello pen' children and their wilful misdirections and continue to the end of the channel, where you will see the site slightly above you and to the left.

The site consists of the remains of a large monastery and stupa side by side on a raised terrace. The buildings here were fairly well preserved from having been buried in material slipped down from the surrounding hills, although as part of the stupa remained protruding, like the one at Dharmarajika it had been cut open by treasure-hunters. Both the main and a subsidiary stupa were entirely covered in stucco reliefs, many of which remain, although of the same date as those of Jaulian, they are considered to be livelier and of finer quality. The monastery contains fine statuary, as well as a finely carved miniature stupa preserved in a cell on the left side.

There are three places to stay almost directly opposite the museum. The most comfortable and the most expensive is the **PTDC Motel**, which has seven doubles, three with a/c at Rs480 ($15), and four without at Rs370 ($12), but bargainable to at least Rs100 less. A notch down is the **Taxila Hotel** with clean, carpeted doubles for Rs180 ($6), Rs150 ($5) single, and friendly management. At the bottom is the spartan **Youth Hostel**. There are two double rooms with bath, and a dormitory. Members are charged Rs55 ($1.75), and non-members Rs85 ($3) for the doubles, Rs40/25 for the dormitory. For a non-member couple, the Taxila Hotel represents better value.

Basic street food is available in Taxila Town. The PTDC Motel has a good menu but is seriously overpriced—watch out for the Rs17 cold drink. The Youth Hostel food is primitive but cheap, being the same as that eaten by the manager's family, and the best option is the restaurant at the Taxila Hotel. The owner lived 25 years in Europe, understands that Westerners like meat not bone or fat, and has trained his staff to make one of the best mutton dishes that you will have in Pakistan.

The Karakoram Highway

To understand the difficulties needs a little look at plate tectonics. The traveller along the KKH is a microbe travelling across the crumple zones of two vehicles during a slow-motion head-on collision. The plate on which India sits arrived from the south around 70 million years ago, and is busy burying itself under the Asian plate, buckling Tibet, the Tarim Basin and much of the rest of Central Asia, and producing the ranges of mountains in between, which are still growing. Vast layers have been folded and upended, and on the way up through Gilgit to Hunza, most of them are revealed in date order—a geologist's playground. The contortions of the folding rock and the consequent frequent tremors and rockfalls make even keeping the road open hard work. But it does make for breathtaking scenery, and even more breathtaking driving. As the Pakistanis put it, 'Our drivers are not drivers: they are pilots—fighter pilots!'

Rawalpindi/Taxila to Gilgit

From Taxila (or from 'Pindi if you visited Taxila as a day trip) to Gilgit the road, rather than the places through which it passes, is the star. If you take the 17-hour direct bus, much of your trip will be in darkness, and much of your body will be in pain. It is better to break the journey up into sensible parts. The best stops of any size are Abbottabad, Mansehra, Besham and Chilas. **Abbottabad** is a fairly unexciting town divided into a quiet and neatly laid out cantonment area and a more typically rowdy Pakistani bazaar. More than anywhere else on this route you get a clear picture of how the Raj isolated itself from its subjects by creating the Home Counties in miniature; lawn sprinklers, the club, and the Book of Common Prayer. At 1220m above sea level, Abbottabad is pleasantly cool, reached by a steady climb from the plain. It takes 2 to 2½ hours by bus from Taxila (Rs15), a little more from Rawalpindi. Equally cool and a better choice of first stop after Taxila is **Mansehra**, 20 minutes by wagon beyond Abbottabad (Rs5). Mansehra can be reached directly from 'Pindi, but from Taxila you take a wagon from the bus station which drops you on the KKH below Mansehra, and a Rs1 Suzuki takes you up into town and past the Errum and Zam Zam Hotels successively—all the drivers know these places. Near where you get off the KKH are the **Ashoka Rocks**, one of several places where the emperor set out his ideas of good behaviour and good government following his discovery of Buddhism. Unfortunately the script is now almost illegible. Of a digestible size, Mansehra almost feels more like a village. The **Errum Hotel** has comfortable carpeted hot-water doubles for Rs300, and singles for Rs150. It also has mid-priced but good food. The fairly friendly and clean **Zam Zam** is the backpacker's choice. There are hot-water doubles with bucket-style bathing for Rs90 ($3), and singles with shared bath for Rs35 ($1).

The next morning, refreshed, you can catch a Suzuki back down to the bus stand on the KKH, walk 100 metres further up and cross over to find the NATCO office and departure point. Buses leave for Gilgit and places in between at 7am, 2pm, 4pm, 8pm and 11pm approximately. To go all the way to Gilgit will cost Rs137 ($4.50) and take 12 to 13 hours—it's better to take another break. The obvious choice is **Besham**, which is more or less the halfway point between Gilgit and Rawalpindi, taking around 3 hours to reach for Rs35 ($1). Unfortunately it has nothing else to recommend it at all, being noisy and somewhat aggressive. There are far too many guns in evidence, and if you take a bus going north that passes through the area at night, you will probably pick up an armed guard at this point. A better stop is **Chilas**, reached from Mansehra by bus in 8 to 9 hours for Rs96 ($3). An alternative is to take a wagon for 2 hours (Rs16) from the Mansehra bus stand to Batgram (various alternative spellings), and another to Besham (Rs16, 1½ hours). From where you are dropped you can catch another wagon to Chilas. Book a seat with the driver and get a ticket, then have lunch. By the time you have eaten the wagon may be full enough to depart. Chilas is 5 hours away; Rs110 ($3.50).

From Mansehra the road winds sinuously through terraced agricultural land and pretty conifered valleys, but as you approach Besham the mountains close in, and the Indus and the road are squeezed tightly together, the one high above the other. At Thakot the road drops to meet the river and switches sides. The Chinese-built bridge is incongruously decorated with lions which, in an eerie echo of the damage done by Muslims to murals at ancient Silk Route sites, have all had their faces vandalized. At Besham a narrow winding road leads over the Mingora Pass to the Swat valley, but the KKH sticks to the Indus, sometimes tens, sometimes hundreds of metres above it. Long detours are made up the valleys of tributaries until a place to cross is found. The murky Indus looks as if it has been ejected from a washing machine doing a load of particularly dirty non-fast coloureds, while the tributaries are a chilly blue, and briefly add a splash of colour as they join the main river.

Chilas is slightly above the KKH to the right but, unless you require rock-bottom accommodation in the bazaar, the best places to stay are on the highway itself, about half a kilometre beyond the police check point on the right, going north. The **Mountain Echo** (formerly the Kashmir Inn), ✆ 315, is the best of the cheaper hotels with doubles for Rs350 ($11) and singles for Rs250 ($8). Mid-range options are the comfortable and friendly **Panorama Hotel**, ✆ 340; doubles Rs710 ($22), single occupancy Rs525 ($17); and the neighbouring **Chilas**

Inn, ✆ (0572) 2225, doubles Rs500 ($16), singles Rs450 ($14), both with cooled air and hot water. Below the highway at the police checkpoint, a 10-minute walk down a stony jeep track towards the river leads to the Silk Route equivalent of 'Kilroy was here', a series of inscriptions or petroglyphs by travellers dating from the 1st century onwards. This site is signposted as **Chilas II** and there is a second site, **Chilas I**, 4 kilometres further up the highway, also signposted. Both can be a little difficult to find; get clear directions from your hotel, rent a jeep for a short tour, or get someone to show you on foot. There is no shade, so go early in the morning.

You can flag down passing vehicles on the highway in the morning, but to be sure of a seat take a Suzuki up to the village and catch a wagon from the bazaar. Gilgit is 135km, 3 hours, and Rs50 ($1.50) away. From Chilas the highway is not quite so constricted, but the scenery is increasingly barren and moonscape-like, with only occasional cultivated areas. The lower peaks obscure the great masses behind them, but eventually you catch sight of the snow-capped 8125m Nanga Parbat ('Killer Mountain'), helpfully signposted to the right. Just before the road recrosses the Indus on the Raikot bridge there's a road up to the expensive camping grounds of Fairy Meadows, and further on after Jaglot there's a track to Skardu. Passing the confluence of the Indus and Gilgit rivers, the highway follows the latter. Finally the mountains step back for the green oasis of Gilgit itself, with gossamer suspension bridges across the Gilgit River. The wagons terminate at the stand on Domial Link Road, close to the Mir's Lodge hotel, passing the Hunza Inn, the PTDC Chinar Inn, and the Mountain Refuge on the way. NATCO buses terminate at the stand opposite the Madina Hotel.

Gilgit

Slightly schizophrenic, Gilgit is the meeting point for smiling Ismailis (who, luckily for travellers, run most of the hotels), other Shias, and Sunnis from neighbouring valleys who vary from aloof and dignified to somewhat hostile. There is a strong, armed, military presence on the street to keep discord between these groups to a minimum. This sounds alarming, but isn't. Nevertheless, the town quietens down soon after dark.

Gilgitis are used to changing their religion at sword-point. Early pilgrims from China found a thriving Buddhist culture, the remnants of which can be seen in a cliff-face carved Buddha not far outside town. Hinduism took over in the 10th century, followed by Shia Islam in the 11th. Ismailism, their current faith, is a branch of Shia, which they adopted from the 14th century.

Gilgit's position at the meeting point between two major rivers made it also the meeting point of trade routes that followed the valleys down from eight or nine different Central Asian passes in the Hindu Kush and Karakorams. Today heavily-loaded Chinese trucks can still be seen conducting complicated manoeuvres in warehouse yards, and the lock-up shops of Gilgit streets are full of Chinese silk, thermos flasks, and tea sets.

The first documented modern European visitor was **Dr G. W. Leitner**, an arrogant German ethnologist and linguist, who arrived semi-disguised as a Mohammedan mullah in 1866. At that time ownership of Gilgit was somewhat ambiguous, but a Kashmiri garrison was defending itself against attacks by the various local tribes, collectively named 'Dards' by Leitner. Following his visit he claimed expert status, although he spent less than two whole days in Gilgit. He did bring back two locals from whom he set about eliciting the vocabulary and grammar of their language, and subsequently collected natives from other valleys at his bungalow in Lahore. On visits to London he took the first Yarkandi (1868), Kafir (1873), and Hunzakut (1887) to be seen in Europe. Later he built Western Europe's first mosque in Woking, England.

The British dithered over Gilgit for some time, finally establishing a permanent political mission here in 1889. The territory did not seem promising for Pax Britannica. In the previous fifty years, control of Gilgit had changed hands twice, and the neighbouring valleys were hostile to each other let alone to alien rulers, indulging themselves in the plunder of caravans and slave trading and seeming to like nothing more than a good fight. Scarcely any two valleys spoke the same language, and even today their fierce independence means that Pakistan central government control over many of them is little more than theoretical.

Following the British subjugation of Hunza and Nagar in 1891–2, the route through Gilgit to Yarkand became more favoured than that from Leh, although passing explorers, adventurers and archaeologists such as Aurel Stein (who first passed through in 1900) complained that the road built by British engineers was little more than a narrow bridle path over dizzying heights.

Gilgit's appearance as part of Pakistan is the result of a last-minute coup that wrested control from a Kashmiri garrison in 1947, as India and Pakistan both gained independence from the British Empire.

Getting to and from Gilgit

by air

There are two or three flights a day to and from Islamabad with PIA on twin propeller Fokker Friendships, which are usually heavily booked. If possible it is better to book before leaving home as the local booking system is in complete chaos. The flights are sometimes cancelled due to bad weather, which leads to considerable bumping—those on yesterday's cancelled flight may take priority today and push you back to tomorrow or the next day. To confirm your flight, leave your ticket at the office on the morning of the day before you fly, collecting it in the afternoon. If the flight is cancelled you must reconfirm for the next one. Gilgit's PIA office, which has no computer and only deals with flights to Islamabad and Skardu, is in JSR Plaza on the south side of Airport Road just west of Domial Link Road. Tickets to and from Islamabad are Rs850 ($27) one way, Rs1700 ($54) return. Two seats on every flight are under the control of the PTDC office in the Chinar Hotel and reserved for tourists, but as everybody knows this these are often booked up, too. A long-mooted runway extension has yet to appear, but if it does will allow jets with larger capacity to land.

by bus

NATCO at NLI Chowk runs buses to Rawalpindi at 11am for Rs180, at 4am, 2pm, 5pm, 8pm and 9pm for Rs220 ($7), and 'luxury' buses at 9am for Rs250 ($8). The trip takes approximately 17 hours. Private competition includes Masherbrum Tours in Cinema Bazaar, at 4pm for Rs180 ($6), and at 1pm and 7pm for Rs220 ($7, 'de luxe' bus), and Sargin Travel in JSR Plaza at 2pm and 4pm for Rs250 ($8). These companies are slightly quicker, taking around 15 hours. The buses have in common a lack of leg room or comfort and night-long high-volume music. You can of course get off at points in between, too. The road down is spectacular, and it is better done in daylight sections, with stops in Chilas, Mansehra and Taxila, for instance (see p.486). Wagons

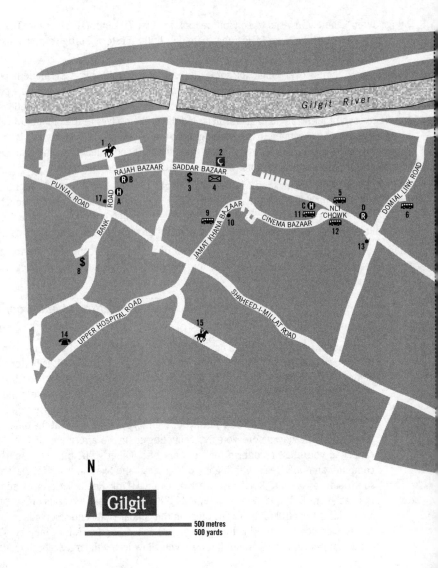

N

Gilgit

500 metres
500 yards

HOTELS AND RESTAURANTS

A New Golden Peak Inn
B Haidry Tea Shop
C Madina Hotel
D Pathan Hotel
E Mountain Refuge Hotel
F PTDC Chinar Inn and tourist information
G Hunza Inn
H Hunza Tourist House
I Gilgit Serena Hotel

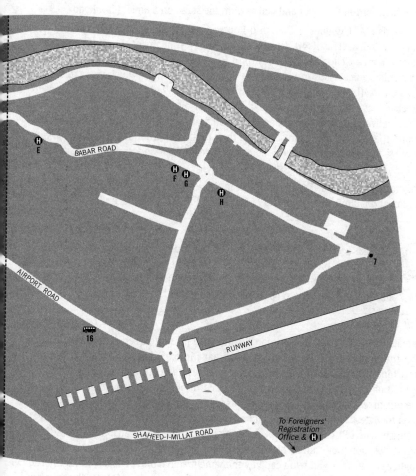

KEY

1 Polo ground
2 Mosque
3 Allied Bank
4 Post office
5 NATCO bus station
6 Wagons to Chilas
7 Airport terminal
8 National Bank
9 Wagons to Hunza
10 G. M. Beg Son's Bookshop
11 Jeeps to Hunza
12 Masherbrum Tours
13 JSR Plaza, Alam Money Changer, PIA ticket office, Sargin Travel
14 Phone Call Office
15 Old polo ground
16 Northern Hunza Coach Service
17 Cemetery, George Hayward's grave

leave whenever full to Jiaglot and Chilas from the stand on Domial Link Road.

Northwards NATCO goes to Sost in 6 hours at 8am for Rs70 ($2.25). Ganesh (for Karimabad and Altit) is Rs40, and Passu Rs58; buy your ticket the day before. The Northern Hunza Coach Service on Airport Road east of Domial Link Road, © 3553, has a smaller, quicker bus to Sost daily at 10am for Rs100 ($3) which you can take to Ganesh for Rs40, and Passu for Rs60; buy your ticket at 9am. Northbound wagons to Karimabad leave from near the Madina Hotel intermittently. Jeeps which have come south to deliver people or goods and are returning to points north can also sometimes be found there, and having already made their profit are sometimes available for very reasonable prices. Cargo jeeps you see being loaded outside shops may also have room for passengers in the front. Just ask.

Going north, stopping at Karimabad/Altit in the exquisitely beautiful Hunza valley is essential, and Gulmit (the one north of Ganesh) and Passu also make pleasant stops.

Getting Around

Suzukis scurry up and down Airport Road and through the bazaars for Rs1–3 depending on distance travelled. The more remote hotels, such as the Serena Lodge, offer free drop-off and pick-up from the city centre as well as collection and delivery to NATCO or the airport.

Gilgit © (0572)   Tourist Information

The main axis is the east–west Airport Road, which runs into a series of bazaars consti-tuting the town centre. **PTDC** is in the Chinar Inn on Babar Road (called on some maps Chinar Garden Road after the chinar trees planted opposite), and has a remark-able fund of information and anecdote in the form of Riaz Ahmad Khan. This active office organizes cultural festivals, as well as guides and transportation. It has informa-tion on the latest state of the road, and has been known to arrange for a military flight for tourists when PIA was overbooked. **Books and maps** are available at G. M. Beg's famous bookshop (now run by his son) in Jamat Khana Bazaar. Unfortunately fame has brought a rise in prices and you can buy the same material more cheaply in Karimabad or Islamabad. The **National Bank** just off Bank Road south of Punial Road (*open Sun–Thurs, 9–1.30*) changes cash and traveller's cheques in US dollars, pounds and Deutschmarks, but at poor rates. The exchange desk is in the far right-hand corner behind the counter. The **Allied Bank** in Saddar Bazaar (*open Sun–Thurs, 9am–1.30pm*) has slightly better rates but only deals with US$ cheques, and dollars and pounds in cash. The best bet, and with similar rates, is the **Alam Money Changer** in JSR Plaza (*open 8–6*), which changes cash and cheques in most major currencies. The main **post office** is in Saddar Bazaar (*open Sat–Wed, 8am–4pm; half day Thurs*). The stamp window is to the left of the main entrance, and not inside the building. For franking the international office is the first door on the right down an alley to the right of the main building. If this is closed go right round to the back. The **telephone** is a problem if you use the official PCO on Upper Hospital Road. This is run by the military with appalling attitudes and connections: their main purpose is to subsidize the army by fleecing you. It's better to use one of the private offices such as one in JSR Plaza. Calls to most overseas destinations are Rs80 ($2.50) per minute, minimum charge

3 minutes. **Facsimile** machines are few and far between, especially ones with international connections. You will be directed to Pamir Tours where the extremely complacent owner will quote you prices that suggest you want to buy his fax machine rather than simply use it. It's better to do all this kind of thing in Islamabad or Rawalpindi, but you might also try G. M. Beg's bookshop. Agfa, Kodak and Fuji film is widely available, and there are a number of standard C41 developing machines around. Try **Rahim Photo Studio** or **Gilgit Colour Lab**, both in Cinema Bazaar past NLI Chowk. Developing is Rs25, plus Rs5 or 6 per print, depending on size. There is a small local guide book called **Let's Go Gilgit**, which is updated annually. It's mainly an advertising medium for local businesses but many of these are useful to the visitor, and it also has a small map. It refers to Gilgit as 'the big apricot', and is given away free by some hotels; Rs15 in shops. Visa extensions can only be obtained in Islamabad, but if you are coming up to 30 days in Pakistan you can (and must) obtain a **certificate of registration** from the Foreigners' Registration Office (*open Sat–Thurs, 9–12*), 2km beyond the airport going east and just beyond the North Hotel, Rs3 by Suzuki. The process is swift and free, but two passport photos are required, and can be obtained from a Polaroid photo shop opposite the Jama mosque.

George Hayward's Grave

Not much to look at, but a must for Great Game enthusiasts. Hayward was an enthusiastic player of the Game and a winner of the coveted Royal Geographical Society Gold Medal for his pioneering travels. His headline-grabbing death at the hands of men of the Maharaja of Kashmir led to him being portrayed as a martyr, and eulogized in an apalling piece of doggerel by Sir Henry Newbolt (a schoolfellow of Sir Francis Younghusband), *He Fell Amongst Thieves*. Some of those who met him had different views, seeing him as unreliable and scarcely able to take care of himself. Robert Shaw, the tea planter turned Game player who in 1869 was the first Briton to visit Kashgar and to meet the rebel leader Yakub Beg, found his carefully planned expedition compromised by Hayward's insistence on taking the same route, and by his breaking of an agreement to give Shaw time to make the delicate negotiations needed to pave the way. Hayward later exposed appalling butchery by the Maharaja of Kashmir, who then controlled Gilgit, by publishing his findings in a newspaper. He then foolhardily returned to the area and camped solo in a remote spot, with deadly results. The headstone was put up by the Royal Geographical Society following Hayward's murder in July 1870.

Polo

A thrilling spectacle, polo is essential viewing if you happen to be in Gilgit at the right time. Pounding hooves throw up clouds of dust that almost obsure the colourful uniforms of the riders and the sweating horses. A noisy band encourages the players, and strikes up the theme tune of the team in possession. The game is played full tilt with riders often barely pulling up their horses before crashing into the excited crowd. The backdrop is the steep cliffs of the valley's sides and the snowy heights behind.

The main tournaments are in April and at the beginning of November (the time when Gilgit celebrates its independence), but there are frequent practice sessions in the weeks leading up to them. Gilgit sports two polo grounds, the main one at the west end of town in Rajah Bazaar opposite Bank Rd, which is where tournaments take place. Practice sessions are held there, at another older polo ground off Hospital Rd near the junction with Shaheed-i-Millat Rd, and in nearby villages. Even detailed cross-questioning of PTDC and your hotel manager is likely to lead to some confusion as to where polo will be taking place on any particular day.

Polo, said to have been a sport even before the time of Alexander the Great's visit to the region, was in decline when 'discovered' by British cavalry officers in the 1850s, who then did much to re-promote it to popularity. As then played in Hunza, it was an egalitarian game in which kings, ministers and anyone who had a horse could and did join in, jostling together in what amounted to little more than a mounted riot. With the arrival of the internal combustion engine, not to mention the decline of local rulers, horses are far fewer, and most games feature military and police teams.

Polo crossed the Pamirs to be played at the British consulate in Kashgar until a fatal accident put an end to the games. In 1940, during the time of consul Eric Shipton, it was revived only for a man to be thrown from his horse and killed two minutes after play began. The polo field was given over to melons and fruit trees.

Around Gilgit

From the Serena Lodge, reachable by Suzuki from Airport Road, a road and paths lead uphill to a water channel which runs right across the valley high above Gilgit. The town can clearly be seen as an oasis surrounded by sheer and barren rock faces, and an hour's walk along the channel brings you to paths leading down to Upper Hospital Road.

A 6km drive up a jeep track in the direction of the Kaghar Valley, followed by a short climb, leads to views of a large **Buddha** with a severe expression, carved in shallow relief in a cliff face with a curious natural overhang functioning as a canopy. Local legends say either that a shaman used magical powers to carve it at the request of a princess as a rebuke to her brutal father; that the Emperor Ashoka, heavily influenced by Buddhism, had it carved as a boundary marker; or that it was made by two Tibetan generals who had come searching for missing traders. It is estimated to be 700 years old, which rather rules out the Ashoka theory. Following the now dry water channel below the Buddha to the left leads you after about 15 minutes to the area's earliest ruins, those of a small monastery. Following the same channel to the right gives a pleasant 40-minute walk above the fields to trout hatcheries and a small, Chinese-built hydroelectric plant. A jeep from your hotel should be no more than Rs100, or the whole trip can be done or foot, or partly by flagging down passing transport. Head out of Gilgit on the Punial Road, fork left after about 2km, and ask for directions. The local name for the Buddha is *girat gachani.*

Where to Stay

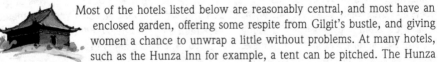 Most of the hotels listed below are reasonably central, and most have an enclosed garden, offering some respite from Gilgit's bustle, and giving women a chance to unwrap a little without problems. At many hotels, such as the Hunza Inn for example, a tent can be pitched. The Hunza Tourist House, Hunza Inn and Chinar Inn can be reached in a few minutes' walk along Babar Road from the airport terminal. The Madina is opposite the NATCO bus stand, and the Mir's Lodge near the stand for wagons from and to the south. All but the cheapest offer free pick-up and drop-off from the airport and the NATCO bus station.

Nothing in the centre quite matches comfortable **Gilgit Serena Hotel,** well out of town in the Jutial area, ✆ 2330, ✉ 2525, which is pleasantly decorated in a local style, has good views and a pleasant garden. It also has international telephone connections, satellite television, fridges, and an excellent restaurant. Free drop-offs and pick-ups in Gilgit, about 10 minutes away, are provided, and Suzukis from Airport Road and the bazaars pass nearby. Single rooms are Rs1700 ($53) single, and Rs2150 ($67) double. Major credit cards and traveller's cheques are accepted.

moderate

The **Mir's Lodge** in Domial Link Road, ✆ 2875, has 'VIP' doubles for Rs950 ($30), standard doubles for Rs650 ($21), and singles for Rs450 ($14). 'VIP' means with satellite television, fridge, etc. Those on a budget but wanting comfortable surroundings might take advantage of a few basic rooms for Rs300 ($9.50) with up to four beds. The quieter PTDC motel **Chinar Inn** on Babar Road, ✆ 2560, ✉ 2562, has doubles for Rs700 ($22), singles for Rs600 ($19).

inexpensive

The budget travellers' current favourite is the **Madina Hotel** in NLI Chowk with rooms at a variety of prices from Rs80 to Rs200, and dorm beds for Rs30–40 with shared hot showers. The management is full of information, the evening set meal is excellent, and there's a billiard table. The hotel may change location in the next two years, but if so will be worth tracking down. The **Hunza Inn** in Babar Rd has basic cold-water doubles for Rs150, and larger, carpeted suites with hot water for Rs400 ($12.50), Rs300 ($9.50) single. Occupants of the cheaper rooms have use of a hot-water bathroom if one is free. The enclosed courtyard and garden is perfect for those needing security for vehicles or bicycles. The **Hunza Tourist House**, also on Babar Road nearer the airport, ✆ 2388, has doubles for Rs470 ($15) and singles Rs350 ($11), with discounts for groups. At the other end of the town, close to the polo ground and George Hayward's grave, the **New Golden Peak Inn** in Bank Road, ✆ 3890, run by the very friendly and helpful Saddiq Ali, the new manager, has doubles with bath and plentiful hot water for Rs200 ($7) and common bath Rs150 ($5), including an enormous dinner. There are also cheaper rooms. The **Mountain Refuge Hotel**, west of the Chinar Inn in Chinar Garden Rd (a continuation of Babar Rd), has triples for Rs50 ($1.50) per person with hot common shower at no extra charge. This is very quiet, has a friendly management, and another operation in Sost.

Eating Out

Almost all hotels have restaurants of sorts, with prices on a scale similar to their room charges.

expensive

The **Serena Hotel** has possibly the best food in Gilgit, with an all-you-can-eat buffet in the evening for around Rs200 ($7) per person. One night is Italian, one Chinese, one a barbecue, and the remainder local food.

Local restaurants abound serving spicy vegetables, and beef, chicken and mutton cooked and served local style in a small metal wok. The cooking area is usually at the front, with seating behind. A good example is the **Pathan Hotel** on Airport Road just west of Domial Link Road. A meal of excellent boneless beef *masala*, vegetables, and *chappatis* will cost around Rs45 ($1.50). The **Madina Hotel** has a popular and strongly Western-influenced set dinner in the evenings for Rs50.

Featured in several travel articles, the **Haidry Tea Shop**'s eponymous owner sits on the platform in Wellingtons ladling large quantities of boiled water into tea pots with a mixture of tea, cardamoms and other spices to make a justifiably famous and highly addictive brew. A contender for the title of best tea you'll ever drink.

Central Asian Borders

The shadowy conflict between Russia and China over the borders in this remote region saw much ducking, weaving and feinting, but rarely a blow thrown. The British called it the 'Great Game', and the Russians the 'Tournament of Shadows'. For the British the Hunza valley was the cockpit of Great Gaming.

Russian advances in Central Asia and British ones in what is now Pakistan had left the two superpowers facing each other across unknown territory, neither quite sure of the other's ability to progress further. In Britain there were those who expected a Russian attack on the honey-pot of India almost daily. Their suggested response, known as 'forward policy', was to move ever further into the Karakorams and Pamirs to secure British positions. Others thought there to be no danger, suspecting that the immense mountain ranges were impenetrable to a Russian force of any size due both to the height of the passes and the probable lack of supplies. Their response, known as the doctrine of 'masterly inactivity', was to do nothing that would stretch military resources any further, or expand the borders of the empire with consequent responsibilities and liabilities.

A certain amount of political bartering went on, the British recognizing Russian influence in one area in return for Russian recognition of their own in another. It became clear, however, that some formal boundary was needed between the two empires in order to avoid conflict, and in the 1870s the two powers sent out joint survey parties to decide where that boundary should be. Inept British line drawing on maps of other peoples' territory has caused much bloodshed this century, and some of the resulting disputes continue long after British influence has withered away. Russian line drawing in Central Asia was mostly on the principle of divide and rule, and is responsible for much of the unrest in the newly independent republics. The joint efforts of the two empires to arrange Afghan and Chinese territory to preserve the modesty of each other's political ambitions was never likely to be a great success.

The natural frontier was the Oxus (Syr Darya), but that river inconveniently described an enormous Z, and in some places had people from the same tribe living on both banks. At the last minute the British agreed to a Russian proposal to draw a straight line from the eastern end of Lake Victoria to the junction of the Kochka River with the Oxus, resulting in the Granville-Gortchakov Agreement of 1873, named after the two foreign secretaries concerned. This somewhat dubious arrangement not only led to further land grabs by the Russians, but also left a gap of 60 miles between Afghanistan and Chinese territory, thereby preventing it from forming an effective buffer zone at all. The Russians gained nearly 1000 sq miles to which they had neither historic nor ethnic right, which angered the Afghans, who also claimed them. In 1877 the Chinese retook Kashgar from the rebel Yakub Beg, leaving the three powers once again confronting each other across mountainous territory of undefined ownership.

In 1880 Colonel Kostenko, a member of the Tashkent General Staff, drew the Pamir no-man's-land with its non-existent boundaries to the attention of his colleagues. By 1883 three explorers had covered most of it as far east as the approaches to Roshan and Shignan, and there was evidence of Russian intrigues with the Indian state of Chitral.

Of the five remaining tiny Muslim border states, crushed between the opposing sides, most were intractable to alliances of any kind, and one, Hunza, actually paid tribute to the emperor of China. Hunza and Nagar both supplemented meagre arable land by plundering caravans on the Leh–Yarkand route, and by slave trading. Having formed an independent Kashgaria, Yakub Beg stopped the plundering, and so the two states turned to the Maharajah of Kashmir for support and for an annual subsidy, in return pledging to stop raids on Kashmiri territory. The Kashmiris took control of a fort at the entrance to the Hunza-Nagar gorge.

To the British this seemed like progress, until one of the Mir of Hunza's sons, Safdar Ali Khan, decided to gain access to the throne early by murdering his father, and then conspired with a cousin in Nagar to eject the the Kashmiri troops from the fort they had occupied. The two valleys turned back to China for support, with the result that a diplomatic note was presented to the British Minister in Běijīng, complaining that the Kashmiris had attacked Chinese territory.

In 1888 the Viceroy of India concluded that although Hunza was small it was important, being directly adjacent to the gap between Afghanistan and China. If Chinese rights were acknowledged, and if the Russians then became the successors of the Chinese in Kashgar, they would take over those rights, bringing the two superpowers into direct contact with each other, and on the wrong side of the mountains. The badly run Kashmir state was unable to take control of the situation. Safdar Ali Khan returned to attacking Leh–Yarkand traffic, now re-established followed the death of Yakub Beg. More worrying still, in 1888 he received a party of Russians led by one Captain Gromchevsky.

The British finally took action, removing the Maharaja of Kashmir and replacing him with a state council. They reorganized and trained the Kashmiri army, establishing a British agency at Gilgit, and beginning a road up from Srinagar. In 1889 they appointed Younghusband to explore the Hindu Kush passes and their suitability for military passage. He found two possibilities, including a place where a small military force might stay all year round, and then bumped into Gromchevsky, camping two nights with him, and exchanging dinner invitations. Their parting was one of mutual respect and friendship, but Younghusband admitted privately that he had deliberately pointed Gromchevsky and his party of Cossacks in the wrong direction, which led to the loss of their horses on the high passes and the temporary crippling of Gromchevsky himself. So much for British fair play.

Ney Elias, another British spy who visited Yarkand in 1885, recommended that the gap in the border be closed up, and in 1890 the British decided to try to persuade the Afghans and Chinese to come to an agreement. Younghusband was to survey the Chinese claims to the Pamirs and to try to persuade them to make those claims effective. George Macartney, eventually to become British Consul-General in Kashgar, was Younghusband's interpreter.

At the request of the authorities in Kashgar, they travelled to Somatash in Afghanistan, to see a border marker placed there by the Chinese 150 years before. On the basis of this Younghusband extended China's land area to meet Afghanistan at that point, one which the Chinese were incapable of defending, but promising them British military assistance. This was beyond his brief, and following complaints from the Amir of Afghanistan, Younghusband's superiors made it plain they would not support him. In late 1890 the Afghans expelled the Chinese from Somatash by force, and what little credibility Younghusband had with the Chinese administration in Kashgar was lost. There was further fighting also involving the Russians over the next three years. Younghusband's intervention was a complete failure and the border issue remained unsettled. In 1891 Younghusband left Kashgar for India intending to return via the Pamirs, but bumped into a Russian colonel called Yanoff and a force of Cossacks, who were busy claiming almost all of the mountains for Russia, and expelling the Chinese from Somatash, using the Granville-Gortchakov agreement as their main justification. Humiliatingly, Younghusband was summarily expelled, too.

In 1891 Safdar Ali of Hunza appealed to the Dàotāi of Kashgar for help against the British who had finally decided to quell the caravan thieves once and for all, and were extending their road to Gilgit on into the Hunza valley. Younghusband's news of Russian military activity in the Pamirs had been alarming, and there was also much concern that Safdar Ali was in contact with the Russian Governor-General of Turkestan via the Russian Consulate in Kashgar. The British moved a force of 200 Gurkhas to Gilgit.

On 29 November 1891 the British sent an ultimatum to Safdar Ali. Deciding on defiance, he forced the Nagaris into co-operation, obviously hoping for help from Russia and China. On 2 December the British successfully stormed the fortress of Chalt in the Nagar valley. The Russian consul, Petrovsky, threatened the Chinese that unless they stood up for their authority in Hunza, the Russians would take the Tashkurgan area for themselves. Macartney encouraged the Chinese to stand firm against the Russians, and the British captured Nilt on 20 December before either party could take further action. By the end of the month the whole valley was in British hands. Safdar Ali fled to China.

In January 1892 large Russian forces were gathered at Osh, and it seemed that an invasion of Hunza was imminent. Two hundred Chinese troops returned to Somatash to rebuild the small fort there, which the Afghans were claiming to be part of their own territory, and which the Russians claimed was theirs under the terms of an earlier Russia-China agreement, the 1881 Treaty of St Petersburg. To complicate matters further, Macartney forecast that if fighting broke out between the Russians and Chinese there would be an uprising of Xīnjiāng's Kyrgyz.

In 1893 Russian forces roamed the Pamirs, justifying their presence on the grounds that the mountains had once belonged to Kokand, and now Kokand belonged to them, and re-expelled the Chinese from Somatash. They threatened to take over the entire Sarikol area near Tashkurgan, and local Kyrgyz began to flee. The Afghans suddenly abandoned all claims to the Pamirs in order to avoid bloodshed, exposing several passes to potential Russian occupation. The long-expected Russian takeover of Kashgar seemed imminent when a mob handed the Russians a pretext by manhandling Petrovsky and an aide, but no invasion appeared.

In November 1893, a British mission to the Amir of Afghanistan succeeded in persuading him to relinquish his trans-Oxus territories, and to take control of the territory of Wakhan resulting in the narrow tongue of Afghan territory stretching towards China that still today separates

Pakistan from Tajikistan. This prepared the way for an agreement between the British and the Russians over the remainder of the border, and Russian activity began to decrease.

On 11 March 1895 the Pamir Agreement was confirmed, drawing a line east from Lake Victoria to the Chinese boundary and giving the territory between there and the Hindu Kush to the Afghans to be held as neutral territory. The Afghans had to evacuate their territories north of this line, and the Russians and British appointed a boundary commission to decide exactly where the Chinese border was, hoping subsequently to get agreement from the Chinese. Even then the border between British India and China remained uncertain, including the issue of China's control of the Hunza Valley, and of certain lands on the Chinese side of the Pamirs the Hunzakuts had traditionally cultivated. The agreement did not mark the end of Russian moves in the region. Petrovsky, much more aggressive in his attitudes than his own government, constantly intrigued to find excuses to bring a sizeable armed force to Kashgar, but only succeeded in getting a few Cossacks based at Tashkurgan, ostensibly to protect the mail service.

From the end of the Manchu Qīng dynasty in 1911, authority in Xīnjiāng was confused, with local uprisings producing sudden death for government officials in some areas. Others chose voluntarily to remove the pigtails they had been forced to wear as a sign of allegiance to the Manchus. Except for the Dungan uprising in Ili, the majority of disturbances were contrived by members of a secret anti-Manchu society, who stirred up the unsavoury local Chinese and half-Chinese, half-Turki vagabonds and shiftless demobbed soldiers, known collectively as the 'gamblers', to actions more bloody than were taking place in the east.

In 1912 Sokov, a successor to Petrovsky, finally succeeded in bringing the first European-trained troops onto Chinese territory: a force half made up of Cossacks and half infantry, with 28 officers and 700 other ranks. In theory these troops were brought in to protect the Europeans from the marauding 'gamblers', but the Chinese had only ever fought amongst themselves and neither the local Turkis nor any foreign interests had been threatened. By now the 'gamblers' had almost all taken up the offer of joining a new regiment for pay, and had thus been organized into relative quiescence, but the Russian cavalry stayed until the First World War took them elsewhere.

Borders remain uncertain today. China and India are in dispute over the Aksai Chin area, and Kashmir has been divided into two since the partition of India. The successes of the largely Pathan Taliban movement in Afghanistan have led to fears that Pathan provinces of Pakistan will secede to an enlarged Afghanistan. The Chinese are also still in dispute with the Tajiks about the border between their territories, and it is feared by some that parts of Tajikistan may also disappear to Afghan control.

Gilgit to Sost

> The track was narrow, along the edge of steep cliffs, and one of the ponies, having lost its footing, fell to the rocks below, where it must have met instantaneous death.
>
> Captain H. H. P. Deasy, *In Tibet and Chinese Turkestan*, 1901

Even the so-called road built by the invading British forces in 1891 was little more than a narrow bridle path, and most people preferred to ride and leave the sure-footed local ponies to find their own way along it.

Twenty kilometres after leaving Gilgit the mountains close in again and overhang the road from time to time, trapping it in a narrow, sunless cleft. There are frequent slide areas with the cheerful 'Relax' signs once you pass them, which only serve to make you wonder how worried you should be when you enter the next. Traces of the footpath which originally provided the only line of communication up the Hunza Valley, the most beautiful on the KKH, can be seen on the opposite side, clinging to near-vertical slopes. There are occasional steeply terraced areas of cultivation, with slender poplars and bushy apricot trees lining the road. There are glimpses of the 7788m snowy bulk of Rakaposhi, until finally the road swings right, and it comes into full view straight ahead. But soon it is hidden again by lower peaks until helpfully signposted at the unimaginatively named Rakaposhi View Hotel, when almost its full vertical height becomes spectacularly visible. The road crosses back to the left-hand side of the river on a Chinese bridge with lions intact this time, and in doing so takes you from the Nagar to the Hunza side of the river.

The Hunzakuts are Ismailis and followers both of their Mir, who can trace his ancestors back for 900 years, and of their spiritual leader, the Geneva-based Aga Khan. Relatively progressive and tolerant, they make a refreshing change from the gun-toting Pathans below Gilgit. Their level of education is higher than the average for Pakistan, and almost every village, however small, boasts at least one government or Aga Khan-funded school. They seem to have absorbed long ago the idea that educated women produce better educated children, and priority is given to educating girls. The women are not veiled, are more generally visible, and do not always cover their hair (although photography is still not usually welcome). Taking a jeep trip for glacier walking in the Nagar valley, you can still feel the difference in atmosphere as you enter orthodox Shia territory.

Other than the difficulty of the terrain itself, the first problem of the British force sent to unseat Safdar Ali from Hunza was to get past the fort at Nilt, which proved impervious to the seven-pounder guns supposed to destroy it. Instead what amounted to almost a suicide party made their way to the gates of the fort to blow them up. Algernon Durand, the commanding officer, standing up to observe, was promptly shot in the groin, although he lived to fret about the campaign from convalescence in Gilgit. A confusion in the commanding officer's orders meant that instead of pursuing the fleeing Hunza forces, the British forces allowed them to take yet more impregnable and gun-proof fortifications further up the valley. After three weeks of failure to find any method of turning the position, another suidical attack was made, this time by a team who had climbed down to the bottom of the chasm in the dark, and taken a morning to scale the sheer cliff directly beneath defended breastworks under fire and falling rock. A chain reaction of fleeing defenders was set off once their target was finally reached. Safdar Ali and wives fled to China and the British occupied Baltit Fort.

Karimabad and Altit

If you plan to stay in this area, get off the bus at Aliabad or Ganesh, and proceed up the hill by jeep or Suzuki to Karimabad, Hunza's capital. You can also walk up from Ganesh in 30 to 45 minutes. Altit is a further 15 to 20 minutes on foot, or 5 minutes by jeep. This is the most beautiful, comfortable and friendly area of the entire Hunza Valley, and perhaps of the whole of the Pakistani side of the Karakoram Highway. The village of Karimabad is a single street, perched on the hillside above the highway, which despite the sprouting of multiple hotels and tourist gifts shops, still offers marvellous views of major peaks, and access to everything from casual strolls to major treks. Quieter Altit can also be used as a base for glacier walks. Every handkerchief-sized plot that can be wrested from the sheer-sided mountains is carefully cultivated. Long water channels form contour lines around the slopes, carrying water from sources sometimes many kilometres away, and providing useful paths. Apricot orchards are everywhere, and of dazzling beauty when in blossom.

Getting to and from Ganesh and Aliabad

Aliabad and Ganesh are close together, about 2½ hours from Gilgit, and 2 hours from Sost, 1 hour from Gulmit. Roads leading up from each join and proceed up to Karimabad. The NATCO northbound bus passes Ganesh at 11.30am and 12.30pm, and southbound at between 7.30am and 9am. A minibus leaves Karimabad at about 5.30am each morning for Gilgit. Minibuses begin to pass Ganesh in both directions from about 8am. The fare to Gilgit is Rs40 ($1.25), to Gulmit Rs20.

Getting up to Karimabad and Altit

Some hotels such as the Kisar Inn often have jeeps waiting to take you up from Ganesh to Karimabad or Altit, and if you stay in the hotel in question this service is free. Otherwise expect to be asked for perhaps Rs25 to go up in a jeep, or Rs10 for a seat in the back of a Suzuki. Altit is a 20-minute walk from Karimabad on a jeep track that disappears through an aqueduct arch halfway up the village, and is clearly sign-posted by various inns.

It's a steep but enjoyable walk up, taking 30 to 45 minutes depending on your luggage and stamina, by either the original old, rough jeep track, a newer metalled one, or the newest one direct to Altit. Any local will point you in the right direction.

A jeep from Karimabad directly down to Gilgit or up to Sost will cost Rs1000–1300 ($31–40).

Tourist Information

All hotels double as **travel agents**, and there are a number of independent operators, too, offering jeep tours, ticket booking and trekking guides. Most are reliable, but prices vary greatly. In general you are better going through your hotel, which has more to lose if it fails to provide a good service. There is a small **library** in Altit, past the polo ground, which has books in English about the area. The **post office** in Karimabad (*open Sat–Wed, 9–4; half-day Thurs*) is on the right just above the track to Altit and up some stairs. There is also a post office on the left just beyond the polo ground in Altit, which is in a shop. The **National Bank** at the lower end of Karimabad on the old jeep track (*open Sun–Thurs, 9–1.30*) only cashes US dollar traveller's cheques. The **Alam Money Changer**, halfway up on the right, is open all day seven days a week, and cashes traveller's cheques in most major currencies. **Film** is available from the Karim General Store and other shops in the village. **Maps** and **guidebooks** to Pakistan and elsewhere (including Cadogan guides) are available from Hoor Shah's bookshop between the Altit turning and the post office.

The Forts

Baltit Fort,

considerably larger than Altit, with Tibetan architectural influences and in its current version 400–600 years old, has spent more than five years under scaffolding, and is continuously predicted to be about to reopen as a museum. If it is closed, still take the winding path from the upper end of Karimabad to view the exterior and to see its commanding views across the valley. It

Altit Fort

was here that the British came looking for Safdar Ali, who had long disappeared with most of his booty. **Altit Fort** (*open 7 days, 7–6.30, adm Rs10*) is thought to be considerably older, reached by taking the jeep track through an arch on the right halfway up Karimabad. It's a pleasant 2km walk to Altit where you cross the now disused polo ground to the fort. This ramshackle mud-built warren of small, dark rooms perches on top of a 300m cliff, with commanding views of the valley and the vast bulk of Rakaposhi. The upper rooms can be reached via the roof of one section, and the top of the tower by a scramble involving a near-rungless ladder and a few poles. Below are the roofs of the village, used for drying apricots, dung and clothes.

Around Karimabad and Altit

Tracks and water channels are so numerous that there are a near-infinite number of possible walks and treks, and your hotel or the many travel agents will be delighted to make suggestions. Day trips by jeep from here are also legion, one of the most popular being the trip back down to the river and across it, followed by a sharp right turn that takes you on a jeep track up into Nagar for walking on the Hopar glacier. It takes 1½ hours to reach the glacier, and the jeep waits for 3 hours or so while you slip and slide your way over its grimy, groaning surface. About Rs800 ($25) for the vehicle.

Shopping

Many shops in Karimabad sell traditional hats and waistcoats of Hunza wool, and carpets and other handicrafts. There are also a number selling cut and uncut gems, but you would be unwise to make a purchase unless you are fully familiar with the stones of your choice, their value at home, and such delicate matters as cut, clarity, carat-weight and colour. Well-made necklaces of semi-precious materials such as lapis lazuli, amber and coral can be acquired more safely, but shop around for quality, compare like with like and bargain hard. If you are continuing to Almaty in Kazakstan there are better-made items to be found there at reasonable fixed prices.

If you are southbound, Karimabad and Altit both have tailors who can make you a *shalwar kamiz* or baggy clothing of your choice to prepare you for the more rigorous Muslims in and beyond Gilgit.

Where to Stay

Karimabad

Explosive growth fuelled by government loans at rather un-Islamic interest rates has turned Karimabad into a bustling single street mini-metropolis, with hotels and guest houses springing up like weeds, and new metalled roads to link them to the valley below. Just below where the old jeep track meets the newer metalled one at the lower end of the village is the grumpy but relatively plush **Mountain View Hotel**, ✆ 7053, with singles for Rs400 ($12.50), doubles Rs500 ($16), and triples Rs550 ($17); the original rock-bottom Hunza Inn slightly above it has been renamed the **Haider Inn** with dorm beds for Rs15, doubles Rs50. Further up, the **Karakurum Hotel** has a pleasant garden and doubles at Rs200 ($7). At the top of the village on the left just after the fork, the quieter **Garden Lodge** (formerly Garden Hotel) has a terraced garden and apricot orchard with triples for Rs200 ($7), doubles Rs150 ($5), dorm beds Rs40. The prestige address, if ever completed, will be the **Rakaposhi View Hotel** with multiple stars and a swimming pool.

Altit

The friendly and helpful **Kisar Inn**, ✆ 47041, 20 mins' walk from the centre of Karimabad, is a better place to stay, with frequent and free jeep pick-ups and drop-offs at Ganesh on the KKH, and plentiful good food. Dormitory beds are Rs35, doubles Rs100 ($3) and 200 ($7). The same management has the lofty **Eagle's Nest** higher up at nearly 3000m, visitable just for spectacular dawn views, or an overnight stay in dorm or double, and well worth the stiff climb. A jeep can also be used.

Eating Out

All hotels have restaurants, but in general standards are not high. Quite a few offer 'Chinese' food, particularly rice and noodle dishes, but while these make a change they only vaguely resemble Chinese food as we know it, or as the Chinese do. The same goes for 'Western' dishes, and for the sake of your stomach you would be better to stick with the simple local dishes with which the cooks are more familiar.

Gulmit

Continuing up the KKH, the Hunza runs in a broader, siltier basin, splitting into multiple streams and rejoining itself. The road recrosses it about halfway to Gulmit and the valley becomes steeper and narrower. Gulmit, 35km from Ganesh, is an excellent last stop before crossing the border to China and would be a better place than Sost to spend your last night. However, you will need to get to Sost earlier than public transport begins going north, so unless you are in a group and can share the cost of a jeep (about Rs5–600) this will be expensive. Gulmit is also the perfect place to recover from the two-day journey from Kashgar, and to adjust to Pakistan.

Gulmit is a small area of relatively flat, irrigated and fertile land, straddling the road. The centre of the village is the polo ground, a short walk uphill on a variety of tracks leading from the highway. If in doubt ask anyone, or follow signs to the Village Inn or Marco Polo hotels. The village is laced with small paths and jeep tracks, often following water channels, and any number of walks can be improvised, giving views of several major glaciers and peaks.

The people here and on up to Sost are mostly of the same stock as the Tajiks you will meet in Tashkurgan, and the inhabitants of Afghanistan's Wakhan Corridor to the north, and speak Wakhi, a relative of Persian.

Getting to and from Gulmit
by road

Gulmit is about 1 hour and 58km from Sost, 40mins and 35km from Karimabad, and 3 hours and 144km from Gilgit. Between Ganesh (the arrival and departure point for Karimabad) and Gulmit, and from Gulmit to Sost the minibus fares should be Rs20, or Rs15 for the NATCO bus, which passes Gulmit southbound before 7am. The first minibus passes anytime from 6.30am. There is a second burst of southbound traffic in the late afternoon after the bus from China has arrived at Sost. The first northbound minibus passes at about 11am, and the NATCO bus between 12 noon and 1pm. A jeep to Karimabad is about Rs5–600 ($16–19).

If you don't plan to proceed to China you could use Gulmit as a base to see the Khunjerab Pass as a day trip by jeep, costing Rs1800–2000 ($57–63).

Tourist Information

The owner of the Tourist Cottage, Mohammed Jaffar, speaks good English and is an excellent source of **historical and practical information**. His father has copies of National Geographic magazines featuring the Hunza Valley dating from the '50s, '70s, and '90s, one of which contributed to the popular myth of Hunza longevity, actually more due to optimism and an inability to count. The **Aga Khan Study Centre** (*open Sat–Thurs, 2–5*) has a good selection of books in English about the area, many long out of print, including the memoirs of the hapless Algernon Durand. From the polo ground take the path uphill to the right of the Gulmit General Store for a few metres. The branch of the National Bank next to the Tourist Cottage **does not do foreign exchange**, so change enough money at Tashkurgan, Sost or Karimabad to keep you going. If desperate, you may be able to persuade the Silk Route Lodge to cash a cheque. The **post office** is across the road (*open Sat–Wed, 9–4; half-day Thurs*) and the sleepy **telephone office** from which you can phone elsewhere in Pakistan but not internationally is round the back of the same building (*open 24 hours, 7 days*). Postcards (including ones of Singapore) can be bought at the Gojal Gifts store just up from the bank, and from various other small stores and hotels.

Gulmit Village

The centre of town is the **polo ground**, which can be reached by following almost any path uphill. Following the arrival of the highway, the jeep gradually replaced the horse, and polo is no longer played. At the top end is a mansion still occasionally occupied by the Mir of Hunza, and to the left of it the rapidly decaying remains of a traditional two-storey balconied house. The main attraction is **Gulmit Museum**, slightly downhill on the path leading to the Marco Polo Inn. The one-room museum was the first in the Northern Areas and the collection has been put together by Raja Hussain Khan, a cousin of the Mir, who also runs the Marco Polo, and who will show you around. The dim and dusty atmosphere could not be less museum-like, and the remarkable assortment of local bric-a-brac—tea pots, musical instruments, the horns of Marco Polo sheep, gifts from various dignitaries—is all touchable. Also remarkable is the stuffed snow leopard which looks as though it died from electrocution. There is also a matchlock gun, perhaps the one which was used to shoot Algernon Durnad with a garnet encased in lead (once removed, this bullet ended up with his sister).This is one of the few museums which genuinely and unpretentiously captures the spirit of the place it represents. If your knock does not produce a response, enquire at the Inn just below. Adm Rs10.

Around Gulmit

Andra Fort is a 1½-hour stiff climb from Gulmit, or a more gentle 2–3-hour one via the village of Kamaris. Ask your hotel for directions. Only a few walls remain of the 200-year-old building, which was used as a place of refuge and defence by Gulmit people when under attack.

Just south of Gulmit a **cable bridge** across the Hunza River offers a little adventure. Walk out of the village with the river on your left. Just round the right-hand bend and on your left is a dry-stone wall ending in a boulder, and 30 paces further on is a well-trodden sandy gap through trees. Follow the path steeply down towards the river, and then to the left by which point the way to the bridge is obvious—altogether not more than 10 minutes. The bridge is made from six cables; four have pieces of wood woven between them (which only someone in advertising could call planks), spaced 2 to 3 feet apart, and the other two function as handrails. The rewards are spectacular views in both directions, and photographs with which to frighten any elderly relatives. You can continue to the village of Upper Shishkot (Nazimabad), across a small wooden bridge to Lower Shishkot, and then back to Gulmit via the highway, taking 4 hours or so.

Where to Stay

moderate

The most hotel-like hotel in Gulmit is the 20-room **Silk Route Hotel**, on the right-hand side of the highway going north, ✆ 18. All rooms are comfortable doubles with hot-water bathrooms and balconies with good views up and down the valley for Rs720 ($23). This hotel is often heavily booked by tour groups in peak season. Traveller's cheques in major currencies are accepted but not at a particularly favourable rate. Beware the souvenir shop with over-priced gems, brassware and other goods.

The friendly **Marco Polo Inn**, well signposted from the highway, ☎ 07, has a garden and 24-hour hot water. A well-appointed double with large bathroom is Rs650 ($20).

The newest hotel in Gulmit is the **Shatubar Inn**, clearly signposted from the highway and 2 minutes on foot from it. The comfortable fitted-carpet doubles with spotless white-tiled bathrooms and all-day hot water are fairly priced at Rs550 ($17).

inexpensive

The best place to stay is the **Gulmit Tourist Cottage**, conveniently just off the highway on the left going north shortly after entering the village. The staff are friendly and eager to please. Clean doubles with bathroom and occasional hot water are Rs280 ($9). There are also dormitories in traditional Gojal style, with mattresses placed on raised, rug-covered platforms around a central fireplace; Rs60 ($2). If there is room here, look no further. You can also bring a tent and camp with access to a bathroom for Rs40 ($1.25). The other cheap option is the **Village Inn**, ☎ 12, a short walk up the footpath behind the Tourist Cottages to the polo ground. Doubles cost Rs300 ($9.50).

Eating Out

Eat in at your hotel, or out at one of the others. As elsewhere, food prices tend to match the room prices. An economical dinner of meat, *dal*, rice, and chappatis will cost around Rs45 ($1.50) at the Tourist Cottages, Rs100 ($3) at the Village Inn, Rs145 at the Silk Route, and Rs150 ($4.50) at the Shatubar or Marco Polo, for more or less the same meal.

Entertainment

There is sometimes local music and dancing at the Marco Polo or Silk Route if a tour group is in town, and you may be able to watch on payment of a small entrance fee.

To Sost

On the way to Passu glaciers are visible to the left, two of them, the Ghulkin and the Passu, coming right down to the road. Beyond them you may catch glimpses of several of the Batura peaks, three of them over 7700m. The nearby mountains have become distinctly spinier and have closed right in on the road, and the river has become an icy blue torrent and lost its siltiness. **Passu**, only 14km from Gulmit, has several places to stay, of which the **Passu Village Guest House** is the best choice, a signposted short walk into the village. In a traditional wooden house, it has comfortable hot-water doubles for Rs400 ($12.50) and dorm beds for Rs40 ($1.25). The dormitory is Gojal-style: raised platforms for sleeping surround a central fireplace, above which the roof, supported by slender pillars, is the same set of overlapping squares and diamonds with a central skylight that you may have seen at the museum in Gulmit and in some of the rooms in Altit fort. There are innumerable casual walks and serious treks in the area, although few of the latter should be undertaken without a proper guide.

Local people sometimes like to persuade foreigners that for any walking in the area a guide is compulsory, upon pain of a large fine. There are fairly easy walks to the Passu and Batura glaciers.

Sost

After winding up through a few small villages for 34km, the road finally reaches Sost. Aim to reach here by mid-afternoon in order to buy your bus ticket and prepare for the trip to China. There's nothing to see except a few small hot springs a little way beyond the customs post.

Getting to and from Sost
by road

Northbound NATCO buses from Gilgit stop at Sost and take about 5 hours to get there. Onward NATCO and PTDC buses to China leave Sost each morning through the summer at about 8am, usually coming to your hotel to collect you, and then almost immediately stopping at Pakistani customs where there are sometimes tiresome searches of your entire possessions; be patient. A one-way ticket to Tashkurgan (where you spend the night) on either bus is Rs850 ($27). (A Chinese bus from Tashkurgan to Kashgar is ¥77/$9.25.) The PTDC bus is for foreigners only, can sometimes be a comfortable minibus, and is amenable to stops for photographs. Tickets can be bought the previous day from the PTDC office on the right as you approach the customs building.

Arriving from China at mid-afternoon local time, customs and immigration procedures tend to be rather smoother. Citizens of most developed countries can usually arrive without a visa, and whereas they once were given a mere three days of what would probably be nonstop travel to make it to Islamabad for conversion to a tourist visa, increasingly more reasonable periods are granted. Going south, buses, minibuses, Suzukis and jeeps all wait for the bus from China to arrive mid-afternoon. As with any international border crossing, first asking prices are sky high, but if you've been talking to any Pakistanis on the two-day trip from Kashgar, they will often help you to get the right price. At least you can now bargain in English. Rs30 should be plenty to get you to Gulmit in a wagon, less for Passu. Don't forget that in Pakistan women are usually seated either at the very front or the very rear, and screened from Pakistani men by their foreign companions.

Tourist Information

The helpful **tourist information** office of the PTDC where you can book your bus ticket is on the right in the village beyond the Mountain Refuge. There is little to know about Sost, but they can answer all your questions about the border crossing, customs formalities and the road to China. There is a small branch of the **National Bank** here opposite the customs post by the barrier in the road, with slightly erratic opening hours. If coming from China, buy rupees in Tashkurgan to smooth your move on to Passu, Gulmit or beyond the same afternoon. There's a tiny **post office** next to the Mountain Refuge Hotel, and a number of small shops in the village have biscuits and other dried snacks for the trip to China, although at somewhat inflated prices.

Few people stay more than one night in Sost, and this has given the several hotels lining the road up to the customs post a truckstop atmosphere. No one tries too hard to please. An exception is the Sost Mountain Refuge, with the same friendly owners as the Mountain Refuge in Gilgit. Plain and simple hot-water doubles are Rs300 ($9.50), cold-water Rs100 ($3) and dorms Rs35-40. The hotel does a good set evening meal, and has a reasonable snack and breakfast menu.

To China via the Khunjerab Pass

The Chinese used to call the Karakorams and Pamirs the Greater and Lesser Headache Mountains, attributing the discomfort they experienced to the wild onions growing here, rather than to the altitude of the passes. Sost is only at 2760m, so there's still nearly 2200m to climb to the top of the Khunjerab Pass.

The bus usually leaves customs at around 9.15am, depending on the number of passengers. Don't put your passport away, as there are further checks and further registers to be filled in during the 83km run to the pass, and before you even reach China.

The road soon becomes squeezed together with the Khunjerab River in a narrow valley, and after 5km passes the hot springs which lie close to a petrol station where the bus may stop to refuel. Opposite there's a high path more like the original track, which leads to the 4827m Kilik pass to Afghanistan's Wakhan Corridor, and the 4726m Mintaka pass to an adjoining tongue of Chinese land. The Mintaka was once the most popular way to reach Tashkurgan, but both are now closed to foreigners. There are herds of grazing yak and dzos. The Scrabble-player's favourite animal, the dzo (also spelt dzho, zho and zo) is a cross between a yak and a domestic cow.

The road continues up narrow, winding and gloomy valleys that see little sun, and the river becomes increasingly boulder-strewn. Rockslides are particularly frequent here, and the river occasionally takes bites from the road. Crossing the river again, the road enters the Khunjerab National Park, with a stop at Dih, 50km before the pass, for a passport check.

Fourteen kilometres futher on the road passes the turning to the Boroghil Valley on the left, and then the Kuksal Valley on the right with views of the Kuksal I and II peaks, then begins a steep winding climb of about 1000m in 17km. If you are going to see any larger wildlife such as the Marco Polo sheep or snow leopard it will be here, but the Pakistani bus drivers who come this way several times a month claim never to have seen the one and only twice the other in several years of crossings. Unfortunately, despite conservation efforts, you will be able to see many snow leopard skins on sale in shops near Kashgar's Idkah Square.

The pass itself is flat, and from here on there's a recognizable change to the smoother, rounded shapes of the Pamirs. The Karakorams may be the northwestern extension of the world's mightiest mountain range (Nanga Parbat and Rakaposhi are Asia's 6th and 11th highest mountains respectively), but the gentler Pamirs, which divide the Tarim and Oxus (Syr Darya) basins, close the gap between the Karakorams and the Tiān Shān, completing the bottling up of the Tarim Basin's western end. There's a final Pakistani check, photographs by the border marker, and then the bus trundles past the signs helpfully reminding drivers to switch sides of the road, and past the guard tower into China, about 2½ hours after leaving

Sost. The Karakoram Highway has now become the Zhōng Bā Gōnglù—the 'Chi-Pak Highway'. There are 125km to Tashkurgan, and 414km to Kashgar. After 2km there is the first Chinese passport check, which takes place on the bus. When they are in the mood, the border guards, who usually look as if their mothers have bought oversized uniforms for them to grow into, line up and salute the bus. One of them lowers a red flag and flaps a green one smartly to indicate that the bus may move off.

The road winds down much more gently then it came up, and the bus performs for an audience of marmots, who sit and watch it go past, occasionally giving a shrill whistle, or scampering for the safety of their burrows, where they hibernate in winter.

After about 45 minutes the bus arrives at Pirali, in a broad, flat and fairly barren valley, although not without its occasional yak or goat and horseback border guard. Pirali was once the Chinese-side immigration and customs post, but this has now been moved to Tashkurgan, and there's a simple passport check instead. From here it's 1849km to Ürümqi, and another 2500km to the Chinese heartlands.

Shortly afterwards the Mintaka Valley leads off towards Afghanistan and the Mintaka and Kilik passes, with turnings at the 1834 and 1821km markers. It may now be said that you are travelling 'in the footsteps of' **Marco Polo**, who, if he came to China at all, came this way in the 1270s. The Pamirs were also crossed by the Jesuit **Benedict de Goës** late in the autumn of 1603, and he wrote of the great cold and desolation, and the difficulty of breathing (something he was to give up altogether in Jiǔquán, Gānsù Province, before he could complete his journey to his colleagues in Běijīng).

The road follows the Tashkurgan River, passing the oddly isolated 6261m Taghdumbash Pamir to the west and entering the Sarikol Valley. The lush Sarikol was the only one of the Pamir glacial valleys to be able to support grazing beyond the summer season, and was thus claimed by tribes as far away as the Hunza Valley, as well as attracting the attention of the three empires at whose borders it stood. Tajikistan lies just beyond the peaks to the west, but there are no border crossings open to foreigners, not least because it's still not entirely agreed exactly where that border is.

The bus arrives at Tashkurgan in mid-afternoon. Běijīng time is 3 hours later than Pakistan time, but Tashkurgan is so far west that Xīnjiāng time, 2 hours earlier than Běijīng and 1 later than Pakistan, is often used. As opening, closing, and departure times are published in Běijīng time, those are used in this book unless otherwise stated. Have a pen ready—in your first contact with Chinese officialdom, you must fill out a health declaration, an arrival card, and even possibly a customs declaration, although those have died out almost everywhere else. Foreigners are sometimes asked for cholera certificates, but the matter is only pressed if you are Pakistani, and most enquiries are merely a formality. Officers rarely search bags, and have even learned to say 'Welcome to China' in English.

Tashkurgan (Tǎshíkùěrgān)

塔什库尔干 Welcome to China—a China where many people are Tajik-speaking Indo-Europeans. Tashkurgan is the capital of a Tajik 'autonomous' county, and while as usual the Hàn run most things of any importance, the Tajiks are plentifully in evidence, too, with the buzz and chirrup of their dialect of Persian. The men wear sheepskin coats tied at the waist with the wool outwards, and the women wear similar colourful dresses and thick stockings to the Uighur women, but with a pillbox hat covered in a shawl. There are also Uighurs and Kyrgyz in town. Even if you arrive from Pakistan it still feels more like the end of China rather than the beginning, and you are conscious of entering through a back door.

Tashkurgan's position has always made it something of a crossroads. Roads lead to Kashgar, Yarkand, to Pakistan, Afghanistan and Tajikistan, although the Kashgar to Sost road is the only one you can take. British diplomat Eric Teichman described it as 'a storm centre of Asian politics'. Younghusband and Macartney arrived here on 25 September 1890 on their way to inspect the Chinese border marker at Somatash (now in Afghanistan), and it was to here that in 1891 the deposed Safdar Ali fled from the British forces entering Karimabad. The Russians occupied the fort with a party of Cossacks prior to the First World War, and later Soviet Russia manipulated events from what had become the Tajik SSR, interrupting the mail service to India run by the British with a station in Tashkurgan.

The mud and brick lanes behind the main street have probably not altered much since those days, although there are now several large tiled buildings including the customs complex and hotels, and the main street, which runs at right angles to the highway, has become artificially broad. Reboarding the bus after customs clearance, you are taken down it, and probably dropped at the most expensive hotel, the Pamir.

Getting to and from Tashkurgan

The bus station is near the junction of the main street and the highway, behind the Transportation Hotel. Buses leave every morning at about 10.30am for Kashgar, ¥77 ($9.50). There are cheaper local buses on certain days, but you will be prevented from boarding these. After some argument it is possible to buy cheaper tickets for intermediate points such as Karakul (lake—Kǎlākùlì Hú in Mandarin) for ¥40 ($5). Leaving there involves flagging down passing buses and haggling, but should only cost a futher ¥37 ($4.50). There are also often jeeps for hire, and you can continue straight on to Kashgar the same day you arrive, with a little luck. Pakistani traders who cross frequently are often keen to do this and share costs.

If you've arrived in Tashkurgan by local transport it's also possible to board the international bus to Sost here, for ¥202 ($24). The trip begins with a visit to the Chinese customs post on the main highway.

With the truck traffic from the border it's also possible to hitch to Karakul for as little as ¥15 ($2) and not more than ¥30, although the first asking price will be higher.

Tourist Information

There are branches of the **Bank of China** and the **National Bank of Pakistan** at the customs and immigration post, which open to meet buses going in both directions, and which cash cheques and convert between Pakistani rupees and Chinese RMB.

Tashkurgan Fort

Xuánzàng, returning this way from India, remarked that there may have been a settlement here as early as the 4th century. Wandering around town you may stumble upon a small mosque, and old graveyards decorated with the horns of Marco Polo sheep, but the only real sight in Tashkurgan is the fortress. Possibly 14th-century and impressively bulky, it is reached up an alley just beyond the Pamir Hotel, and by climbing over two garden walls. The substantial mud walls can be climbed to get a view over the town.

Where to Stay

Tashkurgan is at more than 3000m, and nights tend to be cool even in summer; downright miserable at any other time. Neither heating nor hot water are guaranteed, and electricity cuts are quite common. Remember that if you are coming from Kashgar on the Sost bus you will not have access to your baggage, so be prepared.

The bus may stop at the **Pamir Hotel**, Tashkurgan's smartest, at the end of the main street on the left. Doubles in the newer hot-water wing are ¥180 ($22); triples in the older cold-water one are ¥100 ($12). The Tajik-run restaurant serves set dinners for ¥25 ($3). The remaining hotels are fairly primitive. Common bath doubles (¥30/$4 per bed) and four-bed rooms (¥25 per bed) are available in the new **Khunjerab Hotel** next to the customs department on the highway. The basic **Ice Mountain** on the main street just before the Pamir is Pakistani-run and cheaper at ¥25 per bed in a carpeted four-bed room, or ¥15 without carpet, all with common bath; ¥50 ($6) per bed in a double with bath. Pakistani food is available cheaply from the restaurant. The **Transportation Hotel**, next to the bus station just off the highway, is the same price as the Ice Mountain but considerably grimmer.

Eating Out

In addition to the hotel restaurants there are numerous small Hàn places catering to the international trade, several of which have shown themselves more than ready to exploit the inexperience of travellers arriving from Pakistan. Take care to fix all prices and calculate the total before you eat, even if they are written on a menu.

Tashkurgan to Kashgar

There is an alternative route to Kashgar via Yarkand, at times a more important trading town than Kashgar itself, and originally more important than the route north, but it is not open to foreigners as yet. This is still tightly controlled border territory, and even on the road directly to Kashgar there are two more passport checks where you must get out of the bus.

When Eric and Diana Shipton, the last occupants of the British consulate, came this way in the 1940s it was still seven days by pony from Kashgar to Tashkurgan, 285km. Men had to dismount and wade waist deep in cold, fast rivers to prevent their donkeys from being swept away. Diana Shipton made these crossings on yak-back: 'as comfortable as an armchair and about as rapid', she remarked.

The road is in considerably better condition than on the Pakistani side, but has to cope with gentler gradients and a great deal less falling rock, although climbing again to a 4100m pass. Roadside *mazary* with conical and yurt-shaped tombs, and others like miniature mosques, are the same as those seen elsewhere throughout Central Asia (there's a particularly fine set after the 1751km marker). The road bends round the pointy mass of 7500m Mustagh Ata on the right, and reaches the icily blue **Karakul** (Kălākùlì Hú). You will be dropped near two yurt camps of which one is much newer and cleaner than the other. It's only ¥15 per night to stay, but food is very expensive. Local people have rapidly learned to generate income from tourists, becoming a little too pushy at times, but you can ride their camels and horses—¥10 ($1.25) per hour for a fairly good horse, slightly more for a camel.

The road continues past a smaller lake to the left, and then passes the 7707m Kongur to the right. It tumbles off the high-altitude plateau to a marshy silty basin, and the worst and the best are over. Usually the bus rumbles into Kashgar in the early evening, stopping at the Chini Bagh Hotel, and then the Sèmăn.

The emperors once forbade their subjects to teach foreigners Chinese on pain of death. Never shy of considering their jurisdiction to be global, they also forbade foreigners to learn it. James Flint, sent by the East India Company in 1759 to present complaints to the Qīng court about corruption in Canton and restrictions on trade, was subsequently imprisoned for three years, partly for having learned the language. Today the Chinese tourist industry still makes a great deal of its money from foreigners' unwillingness to tackle even Mandarin rudiments by charging them high prices for services that they would be able to negotiate directly for themselves at a fraction of the cost.

Although learning English is back in fashion, and many cities have 'English corners', usually in public parks, where enthusiasts gather to practise, visitors will encounter few English speakers away from the travel agents and the police stations of larger cities. In larger international hotels most of the staff speak some English, but in others that accept foreigners there is perhaps one designated English speaker whose reputation amongst her colleagues may last only until she actually has to deal with a foreigner. Most foreigners spend their entire time in China without being able to speak a word, but those who at least master the ability to order food, ask prices, and ask for directions have an easier time. While Chinese do sometimes take lost foreigners in hand and try to solve their problems, many consider the gulf of understanding too vast even to try, and most are anyway getting on with sorting out their own problems. Having just a few words can rapidly break these barriers down and greatly add to the enjoyment of the trip.

> *I have picked up a lot of Toorkee (there is no master of languages like the absence of interpreters), and we talk about peace and war, geography and history; what could the most skilful linguists do more?*

> Robert Shaw, *Visits to High Tartary, Yarkand and Kashgar*, 1871

Kazak, Kyrgyz and Uighur are closely related variations of an old form of Turkish, spoken in Kazakstan, Kyrgyzstan and China's Xīnjiāng Autonomous Region. However, almost everyone in Xīnjiāng can speak at least some Mandarin, and almost all positions of authority from post-office clerk upwards are held by Hàn. In urban Kazakstan and Kyrgyzstan the *lingua franca* is still Russian, and many Kazaks and Kyrgyz cannot speak their own language. Independent Kazakstan has moved swiftly to remove Russian from its signs,

Language

schools and place names, and has decreed that all Kazaks and Russians resident in Kazakstan must learn Kazak in the next few years. Kyrgyzstan, recognizing that having a common language with its biggest trade partner is quite helpful, has been considerably more tolerant. In both countries the Cyrillic alphabet, formerly used to spell both Russian and local words, is being replaced by the

Roman alphabet. Uighurs, Kazaks and Kyrgyz will all appreciate any efforts you make to utter a word or two of their languages. Russian will still be spoken more in Bishkek and Almaty. English is of more use there than in China, but not widely known. A few words of German can also help.

In Pakistan, heading up the Karakoram Highway, the languages change from valley to valley, but English is widely understood, and taught in many schools from primary level upwards.

Learning Mandarin

Younghusband, crossing the Gobi by camel, bemoaned the difficulties of Chinese. Wanting assistance in remounting his beast, he met with a blank refusal from his guides.

> It then struck me that 'chi' also means 'to eat,' and he had thought I meant I wanted some of his bread, and had pointed to my saddle-bags, where I had my own. I ought to have said 'Yau chi' in a surprised tone, whereas (not being in my usual amiable state of mind) I had said it in an angry tone, and the meaning was immediately altered from 'I want to ride' to 'I want to eat.' Such are some of the intricacies of the Chinese language.
>
> Captain Frank E. Younghusband, *The Heart of a Continent*, 1896

Younghusband's account is confused, but indicates some of the traps into which foreigners can easily fall. *Chī*, pronounced something like 'chir', to rhyme with 'sir', is said in a high, level tone, and means 'to eat'. *Qí*, pronouced 'tchee', and said with a rising tone, means 'to ride'. An account of tones and their use in Mandarin is given with an introduction to Chinese characters and a few basic grammar points in 'How Chinese Works', *see* p.105.

No-one needs to be able to assemble perfectly grammatical sentences in Mandarin to get what they want, any more than they do in any other language. Learning to pronounce the sounds or near approximations is vital, and to get a grip on the tones is important, although context will often help you out of difficulties. A lot more will be covered in a full phrase book than can be put here. Berlitz *Chinese for Travellers* is sensibly organized, although it sometimes seems to imagine a more orderly China than really exists. The pocket-size *Concise English–Chinese Chinese–English Dictionary* from Oxford University Press can be of major assistance, with *pīnyīn* pronunciation (*see* below) throughout, and you can give it to others to find the characters they mean and show you the English. This dictionary can sometimes be found in branches of the state book shop Xīnhuá Shūdiàn in China itself.

Pronunciation

Pīnyīn, the official Romanization of Mandarin, uses the familiar alphabet and leaves the letters with values that most English speakers expect. Differences are:

c   *ts*, as in *bits*

q   *ch*, as in *chin*, but more aggressive

r   no true English equivalent; the *r* in *reed* is close (and you will be understood), but the tip of the tongue should be near the top of the mouth and the teeth together

x   between the s in *seep* and the *sh* in *sheep*

zh   like the *dge* in *judge*

Vowels sounds are simple and consistent:

a   as in *father*

e   as in *err; lěng* ('cold') is exactly like *lung* in English

i   after most consonants is pronounced *ee*, but after c, ch, r, s, sh, z, and zh, sounds a little like the *u* in *upon* (and will be understood), but the teeth are together and the noise is more a buzz at the front of the mouth

o   as in *song*

u   as in *too*

ū   as the purer French *tu* and German *ū*; a more forward *oo*, with the lips pursed. After j, x, q and y, *ū* (annoyingly) is written without the ¯. Since *l* and *n* can be followed by either *u* or *ū*, the ¯ is used when necessary.

Two vowels together retain their individual sounds, (e.g. *ai* like 'eye', *ei* as the *ey* in 'hey'), with the exception of *ian*, where the *an* sounds like the *en* in 'engine', and the whole like 'yen'. This is very common: *qián* ('tchee-en') is 'money'. Also watch out for the difference between *ou* as in 'toe', and *uo*, which sounds a little like 'or'; *ui* sounds like 'way'; *i* by itself is written *yi*, and *ian* by itself is *yan*.

To learn these sounds, and in particular to master the tones, there is no substitute for listening to a tape or a native speaker. To get the purest sounds try to find a northern Chinese, and particularly someone from Běijīng. Cantonese speakers who know Mandarin as a second language rarely seem able to shed their southern accent. The student should begin with a sing-song approach, overstressing the tones to get them right. In relaxed everyday speech, Chinese only actually stress the tones of the words necessary to make the meaning of the sentence clear. Note that when two or more third (dipping) tone sounds follow each other, only the final one is clearly sounded, the others becoming second (rising) tones.

The Běijīng dialect has influenced Mandarin, and tends to contract some sounds and add an *r* to them. This is done more frequently the more colloquially it is spoken, but some are now enshrined in official Mandarin. *Nǎli* (where) becomes *nǎr*, which rhymes with 'far', with a little more stress on the *r*. *Yìdiǎn*, 'a little', is written *yìdiǎnr*, but the *n* is not pronouced so that the final sound is also –ar. The final *r* sound is indicated phonetically with a Chinese character which by itself is pronounced *ér*.

Names

It helps if you can arrange a Mandarin name for yourself, otherwise you will be addressed throughout any conversation as *Lǎo Wài*, 'Foreigner'. Ideally get an English speaker to make a name that suits you and sounds genuinely Chinese, rather than a phoneticized version. 'Peter', for instance, is often rendered as *Bǐdé*, but this is obviously foreign whereas its translation as Yán ('ee-en', remember, not 'yang' without the *g*) meaning 'rock', as 'Peter' does, is more Chinese. Surnames are not sur- at all—they come first. For foreigners the trick is often to take the first sound of the family name, and look for a similar Mandarin sound which is part of the very limited list of Chinese family name possibilities.

The Chinese often refer to common people, the 'masses', as *lǎobǎixìng*, 'old hundred names'. There are only 3100 family names, of which all but 150 are single character names. The number of people called Wáng in China is greater than the total population of many other countries, and the masses show precious little imagination in their choice of given names, either. In the port city of Tiānjīn east of Běijīng, more than 2300 people are called Zhāng Lì, while Shěnyáng in the northeast has 4800 residents all called Liáng Shūzhēn, and several other names have more than 3000 takers. Notoriously police round up dozens of people who share the name of a suspect they are looking for and then sort out who's who, but even Chinese newspapers have told stories of people crushed in political campaigns and imprisoned for years before it was discovered that the real culprit was walking free. As in other parts of the world, names come and go in fashion, and it's a fairly safe bet that if someone's given name means 'Love Máo' or 'Build Socialism', then they were born between 1966 and 1976 during the now deeply unfashionable Cultural Revolution (and are sometimes embarrassed by their names).

People are usually called by their entire name, rather than by the given name alone, but friends drop the given name and prefix the family name with *Lǎo* ('old') if the friend is older, and *Xiǎo* ('little'), if not.

A Few Structural Notes

Basic Chinese sentences are like English ones: subject, verb, object. 'I want' + noun, or 'I want' + verb (to go, do, buy, etc.) + noun will get you a long way. Note, though, that if you are specific as to quantity, instead of the noun you must use number + measure word + noun. Read 'How Chinese Works', p.105, for an introduction to measure words and a few other important points. Where you are likely to be specific about quantity ('I want to buy three tickets' as opposed to 'I want to see temples') and the multi-purpose measure word *ge* won't do, the correct measure word is given below.

Some basic conversational items are dealt with first, followed by a practical travel vocabulary, and then a list of verbs to try out.

Basic Courtesies

I	wǒ	我
you (singular)	nǐ	你
he	tā	他
she	tā	她
it (rarely used)	tā	它

To make any of the above into the plural add *mén:*

We	wǒmén	我们
You plural	nǐmén	你们
They, etc.	tāmén	他们
Hello	Nǐ hǎo?	你好？
How are you?	Nǐ hǎo ma?	你好吗？
Goodbye	Zài jiàn	再见

Excuse me, I'm sorry	Duìbuqǐ	对不起
Please...	Qǐng...	请
Excuse me (I want to ask you a question)	Qǐng wèn,...	请问
Thank you	Xièxie nǐ	谢谢你
Sorry to bother you, thanks for your trouble	Máfan nǐ	麻烦你
You may hear:		
Bú yòng xiè	No need to say 'thanks'	不用谢

Basic Questions and Requests (begin with 'Qǐng wèn' if appropriate)

Where is X?	X zài nǎr? (X is where?)	X 在哪儿？
Where is the station?	Huǒchēzhàn zài nǎr?	火车站在那儿？
Where's the nearest X?	Zuìjìn de X zài nǎr?	最近的 X 在哪儿？
Who is X?	X shì shéi (X is who?)	X 是谁？
Who are you?	Nǐ shì shéi?	你是谁？
What is X?	X shì shénme? (X is what?)	X 是什么？
What is this/that?	Zhè/nà shì shénme? (This/that is what?)	这、那是什么？
Why?	Wèishénme?	为什么？
Why is there no bus today?	Wèishénme jīntiān méiyǒu chē? (Why today not have bus?)	为什么今天没有车？
When?	Shénme shíhou?	什么时候？
When will the bus leave?	Chē shénme shíhou kāi? (Bus what time start?)	车什么时候开？
What time is it?	Xiànzài jǐ diǎn le? (Now how many hours?)	现在几点了？
How much is X? (price)	X duōshǎo qián?	X 多少钱？
How much and how many? (quantity), expecting a small answer/large answer	Jǐ ge/duōshǎo ge?	几个、多少个？
May I?/Is this OK?	Xíng bu xíng?	行不行？
Do you speak English?	Nǐ huì shuō Yīngyǔ ma?	你会说英语吗？
Please help me	Qǐng bāng wǒ	请帮我
I want...	Wǒ xiǎngyào...	我想要
I'd like...	Wǒ xǐhuān...	我喜欢
Please give me...	Qǐng gěi wǒ...	请给我

Basic Answers (yours and theirs)

To say yes or no in Chinese, identify the main verb in the question, and repeat it to agree, or negate it (put *bù* in front unless it's *yǒu*, to have, in which case use *méi*). The closest statements to 'yes' are:

Correct	Duì	对
Good (OK, let's do that)	Hǎo	好

There are more approximations of 'no':

Not correct	bú duì	不对
Is not	bú shì	不是
Not have	méi yǒu	没有
Not acceptable, forbidden	bù xíng	不行
Bad (I can't go along with that)	Bù hǎo	不好

Other general answers:

I'm sorry, I don't understand	Duìbuqǐ, wǒ tīng bù dǒng	我听不懂
I don't speak Mandarin	Wǒ bú huì shuō pǔtōnghuà	我不会说普通话
I don't know	Wǒ bù zhīdào	我不知道
I'm not sure/not clear	Wǒ bù míngbai	我不明白

General Curiosity

There is a small set of questions which very many Chinese will ask you, given the chance. Some are dealt with below.

What nationality are you?	Nǐ shì nǎ guó rén?	你是哪国人？

The answer is *Wǒ shì* (I am) or *Wǒmen shì* (We are) + country + *rén* (person). Copying the characters for destination countries on to your mail may help to speed it up.

'I am Britain person'	Wǒ shì Yīngguó rén	我是英国人
Australia	Àodàlìyǎ	澳大利亚
Belgium	Bǐlìshí	比利时
Canada	Jiānádà	加拿大
Denmark	Dānmài	丹麦
France	Fǎguó	法国
Germany	Déguó	德国
Holland	Hélán	荷兰
New Zealand	Xīnxīlán	新西兰
Norway	Nuówēi	挪威
Sweden	Ruìdiǎn	瑞典
USA	Měiguó	美国
What is your name? (very polite)	Nín guì xìng?	您贵姓？
My family name is X, and my first name is Y	Wǒ xìng X, míngzi jiào Y	我姓X，名字叫Y
How old are you?	Nǐ jīnnián duōdà suìshu le?	你今年多大岁数了？
I'm X years old	Wǒ X suì le	我X岁了

Practical Needs and Administration

Where's the lavatory/toilet?	Cèsuǒ zài nǎr?	厕所在哪儿?
Signs: men's toilet	nán (man/men)	男
women's toilet	nǚ (woman/women)	女
travel agent	lǚxíngshè	旅行社
Bank of China	Zhōngguó Yínháng	中国银行
post office	yóujú	邮局
poste restante	cún jú hòu lǐng	存局候领
telephone office	diànxīn lóu	电信楼
facsimile (fax)	chuánzhēn	传真
email	diànzǐ yóujiàn	电字邮件
Xīnhuá Book Shop	Xīnhuá Shūdiàn	新华书店
Foreign Languages Book Shop	Wàiwén Shūdiàn	外文书店
city map	chéngshì dìtú	城市地图
English books	Yīngwén shū	英文书
police (Public Security Bureau)	gōng'ān jú	公安局
Foreign Affairs Office	Wàibàn	外办
visa extension	yánshēn qiānzhèng	延伸签证

Numbers

Note that *yī* ('one') changes its tone according to what follows it, and is only pronounced *yī* when said by itself or at the end of a word (*shíyī*, eleven). Otherwise it's a fourth (falling) tone, but second (rising) tone before other fourth tones. The numbers on banknotes, and sometimes on receipts, tickets and even on entrance fee signs are written in a fuller form to reduce fraud, and are given in brackets after the everyday forms below. In speech be careful to differentiate between *sì* (four) and *shí* (ten).

zero	líng	0 （零）
one	yī	一 （壹）
two	èr	二 （贰）
three	sān	三 （叁）
four	sì	四 （肆）
five	wǔ	五 （伍）
six	liù	六 （陆）
seven	qī	七 （柒）
eight	bā	八 （捌）
nine	jiǔ	九 （玖）
ten	shí	十 （拾）
eleven	shí yī	十一
twelve	shí èr	十二
thirteen	shí sān	十三
twenty	èr shí	二十
thirty	sān shí	三十

thirty-one	sān shí yī	三十一
thirty-two	sān shí èr	三十二
one hundred	yì bǎi	一百
two hundred	èr bǎi	二百
three hundred	sān bǎi	三百
one thousand	yì qiān	一千
ten thousand	yí wàn	一万
one million	yì bǎi wàn ('a hundred ten-thousands')	一百万
3.75	sān diǎn qī wǔ ('three point seven five')	三点七五
no.3 (*not* for buses, trains, etc. —*see* 'Getting Around', p.522)	sān hào	三号

To make cardinals into ordinals, use *dì* + number + measure word:

the third one	dìsān ge	第三个

Money

money	qián	钱
yuán (written)	yuán	元
(spoken form)	kuài	块

Kuài is a *measure word* (*see* 'How Chinese Works', pp.105–10, for an explanation), *Yí kuài* means 'a piece of', and the full expression is *yí kuài qián*. Before measure words *èr* (two) becomes *liǎng* (but this is the only number that changes).

jiǎo (one-tenth of a yuán)	jiǎo	角
(spoken form)	máo	毛
fēn (100th of a yuán)	fēn	分

Mandarin assumes any figure given after the units quoted is for the next size unit down, unless otherwise specified.

¥2.40	liǎng kuài sì	两块四

No need to say *liǎng kuài sì máo qián*. But note:

¥2.04	liǎng kuài líng sì	两块零四
¥20.04	èrshí kuài líng sì fēn	二十块零四分

Similarly in daily speech what's in the brackets is optional:

¥0.24	liǎng máo sì (fēn qián)	两毛四（分钱）
¥240	liǎng bǎi sì (shí kuài qián)	两百四（十块钱）
¥2400	liǎng qiān sì (bǎi kuài qián)	两千四（百块钱）

But again, drop more than one size of unit and you must make it clear:

¥2040	liǎng qiān líng sìshí (kuài qián)	两千零四十（块钱）
I want to change money	Wǒ yào huàn qián	我要换钱
a traveller's cheque	yì zhāng lǚxíng zhīpiào	一张旅行支票

a credit card	yì zhāng xìnyòngkǎ	一张信用卡
to give change (also 'to look for')	zhǎo	找
small change	língqián	零钱

Time

one o'clock	yī diǎn zhōng	一点钟
five o'clock in the morning	zǎoshang wǔ diǎn	早上五点
ten o'clock in the morning	shàngwǔ shí diǎn	上午十点
four o'clock in the afternoon	xiàwǔ sì diǎn	下午四点
eight o'clock at night	wǎnshang bā diǎn	晚上八点

Fēn are small units of many different kinds of quantities, in this case minutes.

9.23pm	wǎnshang jiǔ diǎn èrshí sān (fēn zhōng)	晚上九点二十三
a quarter past eleven	shíyī diǎn yí kè	十一点一刻
early morning (before work)	zǎoshang	早上
morning	shàngwǔ	上午
noon	zhōngwǔ	中午
afternoon	xiàwǔ	下午
evening	wǎnshang	晚上
night	yè	夜
day	báitiān	白天
three hours	sān ge xiǎoshí	三个小时

Days of the week are numbered, Monday being the first. Only Sunday is different.

Monday	Xīngqī yī	星期一
Wednesday	Xīngqī sān	星期三
Sunday	Xīngqī tiān	星期天
the day before yesterday	qiántiān	前天
yesterday	zuótiān	昨天
today	jīntiān	今天
tomorrow	míngtiān	明天
the day after tomorrow	huòtiān	后天
three days	sān tiān	三天

Months are also numbered, beginning with January

January	Yí yuè	一月
February	Èr yuè	二月
March	Sān yuè	三月
December	Shíèr yuè	十二月
23rd August	bā yuè èrshí yī hào	八月二十一号
17th May	wǔ yuè shíqī hào	五月十七号
last month	shàng ge yuè	上个月
this month	zhèi ge yuè	这个月

next month	xià ge yuè	下个月
spring	chūntiān	春天
summer	xiàtiān	夏天
autumn	qiūtiān	秋天
winter	dōngtiān	冬天
1997	yī jiǔ jiǔ qī nián	一九九七年
1998	yī jiǔ jiǔ bā nián	一九九八年
1999	yī jiǔ jiǔ jiǔ nián	一九九九年
2000	èr líng líng líng nián	二零零零年
last year	qùnián	去年
this year	jīnnián	今年
next year	míngnián	明年

Getting Around and Directions

East	Dōng	东
South	Nán	南
West	Xī	西
North	Běi	北
to/on the left	dào/zài zoǔmiàn	到、在左面
to/on the right	dào/zài yòumiàn	到、在右面
go straight on	yìzhí qù	一直去
alley, lane	hútòng	胡同
alley, lane	xiàng	巷
street, road	jiē	街
road, street	lù	路
avenue, larger street	dàjiē	大街

The above are used in street names. A road in general is:

a road	yì tiáo lú	一条路
crossroads	shízì lù	十字路
end of the road, corner	lù kǒu	路口
aeroplane	fēijī	飞机
train	huǒchē	火车
metro	dìtiě	地铁
public bus	gōnggòngqìchē	公共汽车
direct line, limited stop	zhuānxiàn	专线
minibus	miànbāochē	面包车
trolleybus	diànchē	电车
taxi	chūzū qìchē	出租汽车
brand of little red taxi	xiàlì	夏利
minivan	miàndī	面的
bicycle	zìxíngchē	自行车
boat/ferry	chuán	船

airport	fēijīchǎng	飞机场
ticket office	shòupiàochù	售票处
air ticket office	mínháng shòupiàochù	民航售票处
railway station	huǒchēzhàn	火车站
(long distance) bus station	chángtú qìchēzhàn	长途汽车站
bus stop/station	qìchēzhàn	汽车站
I want to get off	Wǒ yào xià chē	我要下车
customs	hǎiguān	海关
left-luggage office	xíngli jìcúnchù	行李寄存处
a ticket	yì zhāng piào	一张票
baggage	xíngli	行李
soft sleeper	ruǎn wò	软卧
soft seat	ruǎn zuò	软坐
hard sleeper	yìng wò	硬卧
hard seat	yìng zuò	硬坐
dining car	cān chē	餐车
a seat (e.g on a bus)	yí ge wèizi	一个位子
Are there any seats?	Yǒu méi yǒu wèizi?	有没有位子？
carriage attendant	fúwùyuán	服务员
Is there a plane/train/bus to X?	Yǒu méi yǒu qù X de fēijī/huǒchē/qìchē?	有没有去X的飞机、火车、汽车？
What time does the plane/train/ bus to X depart?	Qù X de fēijī/huǒchē/ qìchē jǐ diàn kāi?	去X的飞机、火车、汽车几点开？
What time does it reach X?	Shénme shíhou dào X?	什么时候到X？
Two tickets to X, please	Duìbuqǐ, wǒ xiǎng mǎi liǎng zhāng qù X de piào.	对不起，我想买两张去X的票
insurance	bǎoxiǎn	保险
Is there a bus to the airport/ to the town?	Yǒu méi yǒu qù fēijīzháng/ zhōngxīn de gōnggòngqìchē?	有没有去飞机场、中心的公共汽车？
How far is it to X?	X dūoyuǎn?	X多远？
Chinese 'mile' (0.5km)	lǐ	里
kilometre	gōnglǐ	公里
metre	mǐ	米

Bus and train numbers are often like telephone numbers, spoken as individual digits. Additionally note that *yī* (one) becomes *yāo*, and that there are a variety of ways to describe the services of each. Bus no.113 is *yāo yāo sān lù*.

Which number bus goes to X?	Jǐ lù chē qù X?	几路车去X？
no.97 (train)	jiǔ qī cì	九七次
service no.636 (for long distance buses and for flights)	liù sān liù bān	六三六班

You'll see *cì* and *bān* heading the columns of bus and train numbers on station timetables. Many bus and railway stations display each other's timetables, although it's usually clear which is which.

You'll frequently hear the following on buses and trains:

Kuài yìdiănr (repeated)	Hurry up	快一点儿
Măi piào (repeated)	Buy a ticket	买票
Dào năr?	Where to?	到哪儿？
Jĭ ge?	How many (people need tickets)?	几个？

Sights

Chinese saying about tourism: '*Bái tiān kàn miào. Wănshang shuìjiào.*' During the day see temples [because that's all there is], in the evening go to sleep [because there's nothing else to do]. Now far from true.

caves, grottoes	shíkū	石窟
museum	bówùguăn	博物馆
screen	bì	壁
temple	sì	寺
temple	miào	庙
temple (lamasery)	zhào	召
mosque	qīngzhēnsì	清真寺
tomb	mù	墓
tomb	líng	陵
public park	gōngyuán	公园
What time does it open?	Jĭ diăn kāi mén?	几点开门？
What time does it close?	Jĭ diăn guān mén?	几点关门？
How much is a ticket?	Yì zhāng piào duōshăo qián?	一张票多少钱？
I'll buy two (of them)	Wŏ măi liăng zhāng	我买两张
'outside guest' (higher foreigner price)	wài bīn	外宾
'inside guest' (Chinese)	nèi bīn	内宾

Hotels

Terms for hotels are given in very rough order of likely comfort.

hotel	bīnguăn	宾馆
hotel	dàjiŭdiàn	大酒店
hotel	fàndiàn	饭店
hotel	lŭshè	旅社
hotel	lŭguăn	旅馆
hotel	zhāodàisuŏ	招待所

Use the above to identify what's a hotel from the signs, but if asking for one, say:

Excuse me, where's a hotel?	Qĭng wèn, bīnguăn zài năr?	请问，宾馆在哪儿？
a room	yí ge fángjiān	一个房间

bathroom	wèishēng jiān	卫生间
reception	zǒngtái	总台
attendant (floor lady)	fúwùyuán	服务员
Do you have any rooms?	Yǒu méi yǒu fángjiān	有没有房间？
I would like...	Wǒ xǐhuan...	我喜欢
...a single room	...dān rén jiān	单人间
...a double room	...shuāng rén jiān	双人间
...a triple room	...sān rén jiān	三人间
...a dorm bed	...duō rén jiān	多人间
...a suite	...tào jiān	套间
I only want to pay for one bed	Wǒ zhǐ xiǎng mǎi yí ge chuángwèi	我只想买一个床位
What time is there hot water (for washing)?	Xǐzǎoshuǐ shénme shíhou lái?	洗澡水什么时候来？
I don't have any boiled water (for drinking)	Wǒ méi yǒu kāishuǐ	我没有开水
My sheets aren't clean	Wǒ de chuángdān bù gānjìng	我的床单不干净
The X doesn't work (point at X)	X huài le	X坏了
I'm checking out	Wǒ tuìfáng	我退房
Please return my deposit	Qǐng tuìgěi wǒ yājīn	请退给我押金
Please give me a receipt	Qǐng gěi wǒ fāpiào	请给我发票

You'll hear:

Jǐ ge rén?	How many people?	几个人？
Hùzhào!	Passport! (needed for check-in)	护照
Méi yǒu	We don't have any	没有

Restaurants

See 'Food and Drink', p.29.

restaurant	fànguǎn	饭馆
restaurant	jiǔjiā	酒家
restaurant	cāntīng	餐厅
bazaar/market	shìchǎng	市场
café	kāfēiguǎn	咖啡馆
tea house	chá guǎn	茶馆
bar	jiǔbā	酒巴
breakfast	zǎofàn	早饭
lunch	wǔfàn	午饭
dinner	wǎnfàn	晚饭
chopsticks	kuàizi	筷子
knife and fork	dāochā	刀叉
spoon	chí	匙

You'll be asked:

Jǐ wèi?	How many people? (polite)	几位？
Chī shénme?	What'll you eat?	吃什么？
Hē shénme?	What'll you drink?	喝什么

You'll say:

Waiter/waitress!	Fúwùyuán!	服务员
Please bring a menu	Qǐng gěi wǒ càidān	请给我菜单
Do you have...	Yǒu méi yǒu...	有没有
Please bring a portion of...	Qǐng lái yí fènr...	请来一份儿
I'd like to pay	Wǒ yào jiézhàng	我要结帐

Single dish meals, snacks, and street food:

snack	xiǎochī	小吃
bread	miànbāo	面包
cake, biscuit (cookie), roll, pitta, etc.	bǐng	饼
noodles	miàntiáo	面条
noodle soup	tāngmiàn	汤面
fried noodles	chǎomiàn	炒面

There seems to be some confusion about the classic spicy dish of noodles with meat and peppers which appears on signs in one version that reflects how the noodles are made, and another similar-sounding version which reflects the spiciness.

'pulled' noodles	lāmiàn	拉面
'peppery' noodles	làmiàn	辣面
rice	mǐfàn, báifàn	米饭。白饭
fried rice	chǎofàn	炒饭
steamed/boiled dumplings (ravioli)	jiǎozi	饺子
steamed dumplings (more bread-like)	bāozi	包子
a steamer of (dumplings)	yì lóng (jiǎozi)	一笼（饺子）
fried dumplings, 'potstickers'	guōtiē	锅贴
kebabs (*shashlyk*)	kǎoròuchuàn	烤肉串
steamed bread roll	mántou	馒头
yoghurt	suānnǎi	酸奶
soup	tāng	汤

Menus usually begin with cold dishes, which it's usually wiser to avoid on hygiene grounds, unless you are in a very upmarket location, and especially if you are on a short trip. The remainder of the dishes usually have four and five character names which in many cases simply describe the contents and the cooking method. What follows are the main cooking verbs, flavour expressions, and some ingredients, followed by some popular dishes you'll find on almost every menu, and the characters versions of local specialities discussed in detail in the main text.

to steam	zhēng	蒸
to boil	zhǔ	煮
to bake, cook, braise	shāo	烧
to stir-fry	chǎo	炒
to quick-fry, sauté	bào	爆
to deep-fry	zhá	炸
to roast (broil)	kǎo	烤
to be hot (spicy)	là	辣
to be sweet	tián	甜
to be sour, vinegary	suān	酸
to be salty	xián	咸
pork	zhū ròu	猪肉

Ròu by itself also means pork, as does:

'big meat'	dà ròu	大肉
chicken	jī	鸡
fish	yú	鱼
beef	niú ròu	牛肉
lamb	yáng ròu	羊肉

Lamb is rarely found outside Muslim areas, Mongolia, Tibet, and big city areas.

Chinese cuisine leaves the bone in unless specified. If you want boneless meat look for the following in the name of the dish:

diced, small pieces	dīng	丁
slices, flat thin pieces	piàn	片
shreds, tiny strips	sī	丝

Other ingredients:

aubergine (eggplant)	qiézi	茄子
bean curd/tofu	dòufu	豆腐
bean sprouts	dòuyá	豆芽
bamboo shoots	sǔn	笋
beans	biǎndòu	扁豆
bell pepper, capsicum	làjiāo	辣椒
cabbage	báicài	白菜
carrots	húluóbo	葫萝卜
cucumber	huángguā	黄瓜
eggs	jīdàn	鸡蛋
garlic	suàn	蒜
ginger	jiāng	姜
(green) vegetables	qǐngcài, shūcài	青菜, 疏菜
mushrooms	mógu	蘑菇
onions	cōng	葱
peanuts	huāshēng	花生
peas	wāndòu	豌豆

| potatoes | tǔdòu | 土豆 |
| tomatoes | xīhóngshì, fānqié | 西红柿，蕃茄 |

A few popular dishes (some of which have special names not derived from the terms above):

Spicy diced chicken with peanuts	gōng bǎo jī dīng	宫保鸡丁
spicy *dòufu* ('pock-marked old woman's *dòufu*')	mápó dòufu	麻婆豆腐
sweet and sour pork tenderloin	tángcù lǐji	糖醋里脊
dried cabbage with fatty pork	měi cài kòu ròu	梅菜扣肉
pork shreds in garlic sauce ('fish fragrance pork')	yúxiāng ròusī	鱼香肉丝
'return to pot' pork	huí guō ròu	回锅肉
quick-fried beef and onions	cōng bào niǔ ròu	葱爆牛肉
beef with tomatoes	xīhóngshì chǎo niǔ ròu	西红柿炒牛肉
braised fish in red sauce	hóng shāo yú	红烧肉

Not only fish (above) but most meats can be 'red-cooked' in this way.

| sweet and sour fish | tángcù yú | 糖醋鱼 |

Vegetarians: dishes are mostly cooked in vegetable oil (although Uighur streetside dishes in Xīnjiāng may be cooked in mutton fat). You can ask for any of the vegetables above (or others) cooked together (although you'll be breaking some rules of Chinese cuisine) in the method of your choice. Sometimes you need to make it really clear that you're a vegetarian. The following speech should achieve that (or just show them the characters):

I'm a vegetarian. I don't eat meat.	Wǒ chī sù. Wǒ bù chī ròu.	
I don't eat chicken. I don't eat fish.	Wǒ bù chī jī. Wǒ bù chī yú.	
	我吃素。我不吃肉。我不吃鸡。我不吃鱼。	

I'd like some noodle soup	Wǒ yào chī méi yǒu ròu	我要吃没有肉的汤面
without meat in it	de tāngmiàn	
Don't put any meat in	Bié fàng ròu	别放肉
What vegetables do you have?	Yǒu shénme sùcài?	有什么素菜？

If shown to the kitchen, point at what you want:

| I'd like this one, this one, and this one all stir-fried together | Wǒ yào zhèi ge, zhèi ge, gēn zhèi ge yìqǐ chǎo | 我要这个，这个，跟这个一起炒 |

Dishes mentioned in the text:

Běijīng roast duck	Běijīng kǎo yā	北京考鸭
hot pot	huǒ guō	火锅
pork casserole	shāguō báiròu	砂锅白肉
Shāndōng dumplings	shāomài	烧麦
camphor tea whole duck	zhāng chá quán yā	樟茶全鸭
rice crust pork slices	guō bā ròu piàn	锅巴肉片

Eight Treasures (sweet rice with jujubes)	bā bǎo fàn	八宝饭
bread and lamb stew	yángròu pàomó	羊肉泡馍
special Xi'ān dumpling	guàntāng bāozi	灌汤包子

Dessert (best stick to fruit you can buy in the market and peel for yourself):

| ice cream | bīngqílín | 冰淇淋 |
| fruit | shuǐguǒ | 水果 |

Drinks:

boiled water	kāi shuǐ	开水
mineral water	kuàngquán shuǐ	矿泉水
tea	chá	茶
coffee	kāfēi	咖啡
milk	niǔ nǎi	牛奶
fruit juice	shuǐguǒ zhī	水果汁
cola	kělè	可乐
beer	pí jiǔ	啤酒
wine (not recommended)	pútao jiǔ	葡萄酒
spirits	bái jiǔ	白酒
Bottoms up, cheers, etc. ('dry cup')	Gān bēi!	干杯！

Shopping

Quantities:

I want to buy...	wǒ xiǎng mǎi...	我想买
Please let me have a look at...	Qǐng gěi wǒ kànyíkàn...	请给我看一看
this one	zhèi ge	这个
that one	nèi ge	那个
a 'catty' or jin (0.5 kilos)	jīn	斤
a kilo	gōngjīn	公斤
one tenth of a jin	liǎng	两
metre	mǐ	米
centimetre	gōngfēn	公分
a bottle of...	yì píng...	一瓶
a can/jar/tin of...	yí guàn...	一罐

Goods:

a book	yì běn shū	一本书
a Chinese chess set	yí fù xiàngqí	一副象棋
a go set	yí fù wéiqí	一副围棋
a mahjong set	yí fù májiàng	一副麻将
a painting	yì fú huà	一幅画
a pair of chopsticks	yì shuāng kuàizi	一双筷子
a writing brush	yì zhī máobǐ	一支毛笔

carpet	dìtǎn	地毯
cloisonné	jǐngtàilán	景泰蓝
jade	yù	玉
seal (chop)	yìnzhāng	印章
silk cloth	sī chóu	丝绸

Description:

big	dà	大
small	xiǎo	小
old	jiù	旧
new	xīn	新
excellent	fēicháng hǎo	非常好
beautiful	měilì	美丽

Some Verbs

to speak	shuō	说
to think	xiǎng	想
to eat	chī	吃
to sleep	shuìjiào	睡觉
to drink	hē	喝
to know	zhīdào	知道
to understand	dǒng	懂
to look/see/read	kàn	看
to like/love	ài	爱
to work	gōngzuò	工作
to want	yào	要
to go	qù	去
to come	lái	来

Oxford University Press (OUP), Dover, and more recently Kodansha have reprinted many of the best accounts of travel across China on the Silk Routes, but even some of these have had time to go out of print again. However, even those not reprinted were often best-sellers in their day, and they remain widely available in larger libraries.

Travel and Memoirs

Early Travellers

Fa-Hien (Faxian), *A Record of Buddhistic Kingdoms* (Lok Virsa, date unknown). This translation by James Legge was originally published in 1886, and is still available in Pakistani bookshops.

Polo, Marco *The Travels of Marco Polo*. The complete Yule-Cordier Edition is a splendid read. Originally published by Yule in 1903, revised and updated by Cordier a little later, it was reprinted as two volumes by Dover, 1993. The pleasure lies as much in the illustrations and footnotes as in the original text whose length they exceed. They include contributions by Aurel Stein and many another pioneer, attempting to make sense of Polo's remarks, identify his place names with real ones, and excuse his mistakes. There's also a translation by Ronald Latham, Penguin, 1958. Either version should be followed up with **Frances Wood**'s thoroughly enjoyable *Did Marco Polo Go To China?* (Secker and Warburg, 1995).

William of Rubruck, *The Mission of Friar William of Rubruck* (trans Peter Jackson, The Hakluyt Society, London, 1990). The most easily available of the early overland accounts.

Adventurers, Military Men

Deasy, Captain H. H. P. *In Tibet and Chinese Turkestan* (T Fisher Unwin, London, 1901). A Great Gamer wannabe, Deasy writes entertainingly of travel up the KKH and on the southern Taklamakan route.

Lattimore, Owen *The Desert Road to Turkestan* (Kodansha America, 1995, first published 1929). Few writers bring China to life as well as Lattimore in this account of a crossing of the Gobi with a camel caravan, a contender with Fleming's book (*see* below) for the title of best travel book ever written about China. See also the companion account of the second half of this trip, *High Tartary*, covering northern Xīnjiāng and the Karakorams.

Shaw, Robert *Visits to High Tartary, Yarkand and Kashgar* (OUP, 1984, first published 1871). Shaw was one of the first to visit Kashgar, and the first Westerner to give an account of the rebel Yakub Beg.

Further Reading

Younghusband, Captain Frank E. *The Heart of a Continent* (Charles Scribner's Sons, 1896). A self-satisfied account of a crossing of China by a man never as competent or as influential as he thought himself to be. Also see **Patrick French**'s lively biography, *The Last Great Imperial Adventurer* (HarperCollins, 1994).

Diplomats, Journalists, and 'Spies'

Bailey, F. M. *Mission to Tashkent* (OUP, 1992, first published 1946). Unbelievable if written as fiction, this is a British officer's modest account of his escape from Central Asia during intense searches for him by Bolshevik revolutionaries, in which he ended up taking part while in disguise.

Fleming, Peter *News from Tartary* (Abacus, 1994, first published 1936). Often imitated but never equalled, Fleming's professed amateurism is belied by his instinct for journalism in a drily funny account of a dangerous trip from China to India through Gānsù, Qīnghǎi, and the southern Taklamakan. One of the most entertaining travel books ever written, and never out of print. Compare with his travelling companion **Ella Maillart**'s account of the same trip, *Forbidden Journey* (Holt, 1937).

Knight, E. F. *Where Three Empires Meet* (Indus Publications, 1890). A Pakistani reprint of an account of the Hunza campaign, in which Knight, a *Times* correspondent, played a small part.

Macartney, Lady *An English Lady in Chinese Turkestan* (Earnest Benn, OUP, 1985, first published 1931), and **Diana Shipton**, *The Antique Land* (OUP 1987, first published 1950). Two accounts of life at the British Consulate in Kashgar, with dinner party disasters and complaints about the servants punctuated with moments of real danger. For a more detailed history *see* **C. P. Skrine and Pamela Nightingale**, *Macartney at Kashgar* (Methuen & Co, 1973).

Nazaroff, Paul *Hunted Through Central Asia* (OUP, 1993, first published 1932). Nazaroff was forced to flee Tashkent following a failed anti-Bolshevik insurrection, and eventually escaped over the Torugart Pass to Kashgar. Full of detailed observations of Central Asia peoples and customs, wildlife, natural resources and physical features, from a man with a frightening breadth of education, seething with anger at the waste and destruction he sees around him.

Sykes, Miss Ella and Brigadier-General Sir Percy *Through Deserts and Oases of Central Asia* (1920). A commentary by a brother and sister team filling in for Macartney during a period of leave.

Teichman, Eric *Journey to Turkistan* (OUP, 1988, first published 1937). An account of a laborious journey across the Gobi and all the way to Kashgar by lorry.

Wu, Aitchen K. *Turkistan Tumult* (OUP, 1984, first published 1940). One of the few easily accessible Chinese accounts of the region from a man who lived through the sieges of Ürümqi, and acted as an emissary to the rebel 'Big Horse'.

Missionaries

Cable, Mildred with French, Francesca, *The Gobi Desert* (Virago, 1984, first published 1942). Detailed accounts of daily life and minority peoples garnered from 12 years of travel beyond Jiāyùguān by the first Western women to go there.

Huc and Gabet, *Travels in Tartary, Thibet and China* (Dover, 1987, first published in English 1851, French 1850). The Lazarists' account (principally Huc's) of their travels in Inner Mongolia, Níngxià, Gānsù and Qīnghǎi are good for their observations of daily life, although a penetrating introduction by Paul Pelliot casts doubt on the honesty of much of the narrative.

Archaeologists and Geographers

Hedin, Sven *Central Asia and Tibet* (Hurst and Blackett Ltd, 1903), *The Silk Road* (Book Faith India, 1994, first published 1938). These are two of several books that Hedin churned out concerning his often reckless journeying in Chinese Central Asia, which included boating down the Tarim River, and driving across the Gobi in the thick of civil war.

von Le Coq, Albert *Buried Treasures of Chinese Turkestan* (trans. Anna Barwell, OUP, 1985, first published 1928). Openly contemptuous of his colleagues and patronizing towards the local people, Le Coq's book does not make pretty reading, but his accomplishments were remarkable.

Stein, M. Aurel *Ancient Central Asia Tracks* (Pantheon Books, 1964, first published 1941). This is an account of several expeditions aimed at the general reader. More detailed and technical accounts are in individual tomes such as *Sand-Buried Ruins of Khotan* (T. Fisher Unwin, 1903).

Warner, Langdon *The Long Old Road in China* (Doubleday Page & Co, 1926). A lacklustre account of a relatively unsuccessful archaeological expedition.

History

Benson, Linda *The Ili Rebellion* (New York, 1990). A scrupulously detailed account of the circumstances of one uprising against Chinese rule in Xīnjiāng which throws light on the contemporary independence movement.

Black, George and Munro, Robin *Black Hands of Beijing* (John Wiley, 1993). The most clear-headed, balanced and accurate book on the Tiān'ān Mén protests of 1989, putting them in the context of other movements for Chinese *glasnost.*

Boulnois, Luce *La Route de la Soie* (Editions Olizane, updated edition 1992, also available in English translation). A little florid, but a good read.

Franck, Irene M. and Brownstone, David M. *The Silk Road: A History* (Facts on File Publications, 1986).

Gousset, René *The Empire of the Steppes* (trans. Naomi Walford, Rutgers University Press, 1970, originally published in 1939). The definitive guide to mounted pillage and plunder from Gānsù to the Black Sea. A battle on every page.

Hopkirk, Peter *Foreign Devils on the Silk Road* (John Murray, 1980), *The Great Game* (John Murray, 1990), and *Setting the East Ablaze* (John Murray, 1984). Hopkirk has taken the best parts of contemporary narratives and backed them with his own research to produce histories that are fast-paced and entertaining. *Foreign Devils* deals with the race amongst foreign archaeologists to extract the treasures of the Taklamakan. *The Great Game* is an account of political and military skulduggery on the KKH and throughout Central Asia up to the establishment of more-or-less firm borders. *Setting the East Ablaze* is an account of the revival of espionage and derring-do in the area following the Russian Revolution. Essential reading.

Keay, John *The Gilgit Game* (John Murray, 1979). An enjoyable account of the British Empire's encounters with the fiercely independent tribes occupying the land between the Indian, Russian, and Chinese borders.

Spence, Jonathan D. *In Search of Modern China* (Hutchinson, 1990). The best introduction to the forces that have shaped modern China, beginning in the late Ming. Spence also writes excellent books on individual figures in Chinese history.

Other Guides

Shaw, Isobel *Pakistan Handbook* (The Guidebook Company, Hong Kong, 1996). Far and away the best guide book to the country from someone who lived there and loves it, but not uncritically.

Whittell, Giles *Central Asia, The Practical Handbook* (Cadogan Books, 1996). Whittell's book, now in its second edition, was the first guide to the then newly independent Central Asian republics, and takes over where this one leaves off.

General Introductions to Chinese Culture and Art

Hook, Brian (ed.), *The Cambridge Encyclopaedia of China* (2nd edition, 1991). An inexhaustible single-volume companion to everything you might want to know about Chinese history, culture, economics, geography, thought and art.

Rawson, Jessica (ed.), *The British Museum Book of Chinese Art* (British Museum Press, 1992). A thorough single-volume introduction to Chinese arts and crafts, illustrated with pieces from the museum's collection.

Note: Page references to chapter titles and main entries are in **bold**
Page references to maps are in *italic*

Index

KLM ROYAL DUTCH AIRLINES TO THE WORLD

KLM Royal Dutch Airlines has one of the most extensive worldwide route networks of any carrier, stretching to more than 150 cities, across six continents.

Based at Amsterdam's ultra-modern Schiphol Airport, KLM fulfils its role as a global airline by attracting passengers from neighbouring countries to fly to their final destination via its Amsterdam hub. Similarly, passengers arriving at Schiphol on long-haul flights can travel on to a wide choice of European cities by transferring to a second KLM flight.

This policy is extended in countries such as the UK, where KLM works with its partner airlines to offer the widest possible range of departure airports from which to fly to Amsterdam.

Changing aircraft at one-terminal Schiphol Airport couldn't be easier. Passengers are issued with two boarding cards when they check-in – one for the flight to Amsterdam and a second for the connecting service. On arrival at Schiphol they simply walk straight to the departure gate of their onward flight, while luggage is automatically transferred.

The longest established commercial airline, KLM has a regal history stretching back more than 75 years. Today KLM is renowned worldwide for its reliable and high quality service.

KLM Reservations, Amsterdam:
☎ (20) 4747 747.

IF YOU'RE FLYING WITH UNITED, THAI, SAS, OR AIR CANADA, YOU'LL STILL BE CLOCKING UP THE MILES WITH LUFTHANSA.